Pattern Languages of
Program Design 3

The Software Patterns Series

John Vlissides, Consulting Editor

The Software Patterns Series (SPS) comprises pattern literature of lasting significance to software developers. Software patterns document general solutions to recurring problems in all software-related spheres, from the technology itself, to the organizations that develop and distribute it, to the people who use it. Books in the series distill experience from one or more of these areas into a form that software professionals can apply immediately. *Relevance* and *impact* are the tenets of the SPS. Relevance means each book presents patterns that solve real problems. Patterns worthy of the name are intrinsically relevant; they are borne of practitioners' experiences, not theory or speculation. Patterns have impact when they change how people work for the better. A book becomes a part of the series not because it embraces these tenets but because it has demonstrated that it fulfills them for its audience.

The Design Patterns Smalltalk Companion, Albert/Brown/Woolf

Pattern Languages of Program Design 3, edited by Martin/Riehle/Buschmann

Pattern Languages of Program Design 3

Edited by

Robert C. Martin

Dirk Riehle

Frank Buschmann

ADDISON-WESLEY

An imprint of Addison Wesley Longman, Inc.

Reading, Massachusetts • Harlow, England • Menlo Park, California
Berkeley, California • Don Mills, Ontario • Sydney
Bonn • Amsterdam • Tokyo • Mexico City

The publisher offers discounts on this book when ordered in quantity for special sales. For more information, please contact:

Corporate & Professional Publishing Group
Addison Wesley Longman, Inc.
One Jacob Way
Reading, Massachusetts 01867

Library of Congress Cataloging-in-Publication Data

Pattern languages of program design 3 / edited by Robert C. Martin, Dirk Riehle,
    Frank Buschmann.
    p.   cm. -- (The software patterns series)
    Includes bibliographical references and index.
    ISBN 0-201-31011-2
1. Computer software--Development. 2. Object-oriented programming
(Computer science) I. Martin, Robert C. II. Riehle, Dirk. III. Buschmann, Frank.
IV. Series.
QA76.76.D47P3753   1998
005.1'2--dc21   97-24997
                                                                            CIP

Production and project management: Editorial Services of New England, Inc.

ISBN 0-201-31011-2
Text printed on recycled and acid-free paper.
1 2 3 4 5 6 7 8 9 10—MA—0100999897
First printing, October 1997

For Helen Vlissides and Steven Newkirk . . .
. . . A child is a joy whose blinding brilliance never fades.

Contents

Introduction

Hybrid Vigor and Footprints in the Snow

> We hope, of course, that many of the people who read, and use this language, will try to improve these patterns—will put their energy to work, in the task of finding more true, more profound invariants—and we hope that gradually these more true patterns, which are slowly discovered, as time goes on, will enter a common language, which all of us can share.
>
> Christopher Alexander et al., *A Pattern Language, xv.*
> [Alexander+77]

What's new here is that there's nothing new here.   Patterns are about what works. Patterns give us a way to talk about what works. Stewart Brand, in his book *How Buildings Learn* [Brand94], recounts an oft-told (and perhaps apocryphal) tale of a brilliant but lazy college planner who built a new campus with no sidewalks at all. She waited for the first winter and photographed where people made paths in the snow between the buildings. The next spring, she put the pavement there. Patterns have this quality. Instead of making brash, premature, and probably erroneous conjectures about what might work, pattern writers look for footprints in the snow, and describe what has already worked.

Talking about what works seems so obvious. Why hasn't this happened before? Why is it happening now? In the academic world, there is a relentless focus on the new. Academics are veritable novelty vampires who consume new ideas rapaciously. This phenomenon is particularly acute in computer science, where four-month-old technology can be deemed "traditional." Patterns, on the other hand, are dispatches from the trenches about what works. They are about recurring solutions, and if a lot of people have been doing something for a long time, it can't be considered new, can it?

Because patterns are drawn from experience, they are not about invention or creation per se. Pattern writers don't play God and create the universe in their image, but they do play Adam and Eve, by choosing names for the denizens of their garden. This is a responsibility that is not to be taken lightly.

Ralph Johnson has pointed out that it is common in other academic disciplines to study subject matter that the researchers did not themselves create. Entomologists collect and categorize butterflies, talk about these categories, and wonder why they exist. However, biologists do not create new forms of life (at least, not yet). Still, they can gather specimens, make observations, and discover categories without worrying about being accused of plagiarizing nature. Similarly, pattern writers can play not only Adam and Eve, but Carolus Linnaeus as well.

Computer science is a young discipline that for too long has seen itself as a stepchild of mathematics and electrical engineering. While computer scientists spent their first generation trying to behave like mathematicians and physicists, they too often ignored the rich vein of *indigenous* subject matter that ran directly under their feet: the experience that can be gleaned from real programmers and real systems. It is a sign of new maturity and self-reliance that they can now borrow from architecture, biology, literature, communications, and, finally, even themselves.

The patterns movement is in tune with a distinctly '90s cultural Zeitgeist. It is a second-generation phenomenon, like Java. It's about innovation in an age of sampling. Sampling has become a way of life on the World Wide Web. Some popular musicians in the '90s borrow shamelessly from their predecessors, not by merely quoting phrases, but by using digital samplers to directly embed snippets of other people's actual performances into their own work. But their artistic predecessors broke every rule of harmony and composition as they strove unrelentingly for originality. Now, this exploration of increasingly inhospitable new frontiers is over. Musicians in the '90s are solving their originality problem by ignoring it. Instead, they build on the past by combining existing elements of their artistic heritage in new ways.

From the beginning, one thing that has distinguished the patterns community has been its aggressive disregard for originality. When people say that new music, poetry, or art *isn't* really music, poetry, or art at all, it is a good sign that something new is happening. People argue about whether patterns are really computer science, or even research. If what we are doing isn't computer science, it ought to be.

While academia may be addicted to change, on the other hand, industry certainly has no problem with things that are tested and proven. However, it does have a problem with talking about them. Why indeed should people in industry give their architectural insights away to their competitors? Why give away the store? What is gained by paying people to write patterns instead of programs? These are legitimate concerns. We certainly don't expect PLoP to become a trade secrets show-and-tell conference.

PLoP USA is held at Allerton House, a turn-of-the-century manor surrounded by statues and formal gardens, set on a wooded estate on the banks of the Sangamon River in rural Illinois. Pattern pilgrims travel through forty miles of corn and soybeans to reach Robert Allerton's monument to architectural eccentricity. In making this journey through some of the richest farmland in the world, the term "hybrid vigor" somehow comes to mind.

Nature invented cross-pollination to propagate successful innovations throughout a population rapidly. Farmers and horticulturists later learned that they could manipulate this process to create hybrids to counteract inbreeding and to enhance characteristics they found desirable. The introduction of new genetic material from distant relatives frequently produced exceptionally productive and robust new varieties, hence the term "hybrid vigor."

PLoP draws people and patterns from what must seem, on the surface, like an unworkably diverse pool. It draws academics and practitioners, managers and programmers, consultants and students, and even the odd building contractor. Why is the patterns community so eclectic? Maybe it's because there really are underlying architectural principles beneath seemingly disparate areas. Maybe there really *are* good ideas that scale, generalize, and travel well.

Perhaps that six months from now, when I am writing a program, I will need to use a caching scheme I heard about in a pattern taken from an application that looks nothing like the ones I write. This potential for hybridization is one reason for industry to be interested in patterns. The cross-pollination among the unique cross-section of industry and academia at PLoP allows best practices to be dis-seminated quickly and widely, thereby bringing a healthy touch of hybrid vigor to all involved. So patterns people can play not only Adam and Eve, and Carolus Linnaeus, but Luther Burbank as well. Industry has more to gain than to fear from a real engineering handbook for software architecture.

That which a culture glorifies will flourish. Unfortunately, software architecture is often hidden. The patterns community provides software architects with some-thing they have never had before: an audience. Software architecture is often an afterthought. We reward results, even if they come from slash-and-burn engineer-ing and produce sprawling, shantytown architectures. For too long, software architects have toiled like the medieval artisans who carefully carved the backs of their gargoyles, knowing that high above the ground, their artistry could be seen only by God. Now that we have a forum where practitioners, theorists, program-mers, and professors can get together to laud that which has worked. The archi-tectural and aesthetic achievements of anonymous software designers can begin to receive some belated and well-deserved recognition.

Languages, libraries, and frameworks are the media in which software archi-tecture is ultimately expressed. Patterns tell us how other architects have success-fully put these pieces together. By drawing attention to recurring problems, patterns can drive the evolution of our tools, processes, languages, and frame-works, thus enabling reusable artifacts to address these problems directly. We can then use these artifacts off the shelf, and focus our design energy on ever loftier architectural concerns.

A system might have good or bad architecture, but it must have *some* architecture. Software architecture is just now emerging as a discipline. Whether by encouraging the infrastructure for wide-scale reuse, or by helping the components that underlie the latest rapid prototyping environment to emerge, architecture is the key to the division of labor that characterizes mature engineering disciplines.

Reuse is an act of trust. The pioneer who blazes a trail knows if he or she turned left to avoid a two-hundred-mile detour or simply to avoid a fallen branch. Those who follow do not have the benefit of this insight. They know only that the trail turns left. Architecture needs to be about ideas that can stand on their own. Designers need a vocabulary that conveys meaning without requiring an encyclopedic, white-box knowledge of every abstraction of everyone who uses it.

Thomas Malthus was a nineteenth-century clergyman and economist who grimly hypothesized that successful communities grow until their needs exceed the resources available to sustain them. In 1996 PLoP received over 70 submissions and nearly 110 registrations—Dr. Malthus had come to Allerton Park. Our infrastructure was bursting at the seams and our submissions were more eclectic than ever. It seems inevitable that these forces will cleave our diamond in the rough along its natural fissures. Indeed, these facets are already emerging. EuroPLoP, TelePLoP, ChiliPLoP, and UP have joined good ol' PLoP Classic USA. New books about patterns are sprouting like high-yield hybrids in the hot summer sun. The success of patterns has even turned them into a lightning rod for new academic research.

Powerful forces have been set into motion, and have set us into motion. It's fascinating to contrast a design conversation today with one we might have had a few years ago. For instance, the architectural notions presented in the Gang-of-Four book [Gamma+95], once considered abstruse, are now common knowledge, and they can be proposed, compared, and dismissed with one simple name. They are becoming part of a design lexicon that may well be with us for generations. The power and conciseness that this new vocabulary gives its speakers is striking. But we are still a long way from having a pattern language for software architecture similar to the one Alexander attempted for building. Still, three years ago, few of us really had any idea where all of this might be headed. Now we know we are witnessing something important and enduring.

Just under a century ago, two brothers could build an airplane in a bicycle shop. Just a generation later, no single person could master all the engineering expertise that went into a pre-World War II warplane. The pioneers had been supplanted by teams of superbly skilled, highly specialized collaborators who together defined the architectural lexicon and division of labor that allowed them to partition their work and then reintegrate it into a working whole. They were able to divide up their work because they could discern the distinct, emerging architectural elements in their engineering domain, as well as the boundaries between them. Small groups of skilled designers can still juggle the pieces, but these pieces are cast at a much higher level.

In many ways, software architecture is just leaving its bicycle-shop era. Brad Cox [Cox95] has observed, for instance, that "unlike the hardware industry, which has organized itself into a fully elaborated rainforest of mutually interdependent structures of production trees, the software industry remains stuck in the unicellular, bacterial stage of the primordial ooze."

Today, interstate highways run over the tracks left by the wheels where westbound wagon trains once rolled. The pioneers could never have conceived of the engineering effort necessary to build the spectacular bridges and tunnels we have built, nor of the machinery used to move veritable mountains of stone, concrete, and asphalt that now dwarf the pyramids. In just a few hours, we can make the journey that took them months. Yet, we did this not by blazing new trails of our own, but by looking for footprints in the snow and putting the pavement there.

Brian Foote, Urbana, Illinois

REFERENCES

[Alexander+77] C. Alexander, S. Ishikawa, and M. Silverstein. *A Pattern Language*. Oxford: Oxford University Press, 1977.

[Brand94] S. Brand. *How Buildings Learn: What Happens After They're Built.* New York: Viking Press, 1994.

[Cox95] B. Cox. "No Silver Bullet Revisited." *American Programmer Journal.* November, 1995.

[Gamma+95] E. Gamma, R. Helm, R. Johnson, and J. Vlissides. *Design Patterns: Elements of Reusable Object-Oriented Software.* Reading, MA: Addison-Wesley, 1995.

Preface

This is the third in the series of PLoPD books, and it represents something of a departure from the previous two. This is the first book in the PLoPD series in which fewer than half of the papers submitted at the corresponding PLoP conferences are being published. In addition, this is the first PLoPD book in which papers from more than one conference are being published. More than 80 papers were submitted to PLoP '96 and EuroPLoP '96, so we could not publish them all. Therefore, we had the unhappy task of deciding which of those papers *not* to publish. Because all the papers submitted were of very high quality—something we have come to expect from the PLoP conferences—this task was not easy. Fortunately, our burden was lightened by all the folks who helped out with the review and selection process.

The process of creating this book.　We recruited a veritable army of reviewers, and three reviewers read each of the more than 80 papers. The reviewers' recommendations were then passed on to the three editors (Robert Martin, Dirk Riehle, and Frank Buschmann). Then we began a rather long and heated exchange. None of us had any problem being choosy; indeed, the three of us settled on a large core of papers to be published. Still, there were a few papers we did not agree upon. And thereupon lay the long and arduous process of defining the final contents of this book. None of us thinks that this book is perfect, but all of us think it is a top-notch collection of superb papers.

What were our selection criteria? The choice of papers was constrained by our target audience: software engineers. First and foremost, the papers had to be of interest to this audience. Although patterns about music are interesting to musicians, we did not think they should be included here. Second, the papers had to be of practical value to our audience. Although papers of abstract theory are certainly interesting, we gave preference to papers that provide techniques or tools that would be of immediate use to our audience. Finally, the papers should include patterns. There were lots of good papers written about software engineering, but we gave preference to those that described patterns related to software engineering.

To be sure, these criteria were not clearly stated up front. Like all high-quality projects, the requirements evolved during development. It was during this process that we learned about each other's expectations and visions for the book, and our own expectations and visions changed through discussion and argument. All in all, it was a very rewarding, if somewhat exhausting, experience.

In the spirit of Ralph Johnson's suggestion to catalog patterns as design specimens, just like biology catalogs and classifies its animal and non-animal specimens, we organized the book by topic. It comprises general design patterns as well as patterns for specific technical or business domains. It also contains patterns for designing user interfaces and for helping with software processes; it even contains a chapter on patterns for writing patterns. We did not distinguish between patterns and pattern languages, but focused on putting together patterns by topic so you can take a look and see whether these patterns are of interest to your needs and application domains.

Design Patterns, a 1997 perspective.   It has been two years since the publication of the GoF book. During that time, interest in design patterns has increased at a phenomenal rate. Today it is very unlikely that any serious software engineer is unfamiliar with the concept of design patterns. Some major magazines run regular columns about design patterns. *The C++ Report* runs a monthly section about design patterns. Several other books by major authors have been published. All this indicates that the concept of design patterns is significant in the evolution of software engineering, and that its significance will continue to grow for years to come.

With this growth in awareness and significance comes a danger. It would be easy to switch our enthusiasm from the patterns themselves to the concept of patterns in general. In our opinion, this would be a mistake. The use of well-worn design patterns in a given project can be of great benefit. But force-fitting lots of different patterns into the same project would be worse than useless. Just because a pattern exists does not mean it should be used. A particular pattern fits into a project when there is a problem to be solved and that pattern offers useful strategies for solutions. One cannot justify the use of a particular pattern just because it is a pattern. For example, an engineer cannot justify using the Visitor pattern simply because it is included in the GoF book. Design patterns are tools to be used by engineers who understand where and when those tools are best applied.

Where are your weapons?   *Dr. Who* is an old British science fiction television series. In one episode, the doctor escorts a silicon-based life-form into his space ship. The life-form looks around and exclaims: "Impressive! But where are its weapons?" The doctor stares the life-form right in the eyes, points at his temple, and says: "Here!"

Recently, one of us (Robert) spoke at a conference in Chicago to a rather large audience regarding design patterns. He asked who had purchased the GoF book. About 80 percent raised their hands. Then he asked everyone who had not actually read the book to put their hands down. About half the hands went down. Then he asked who could explain the Visitor pattern. Nearly all the hands went down.

The patterns in this book, or in any of the excellent patterns books that have been published since 1995, do you no good if you do not read and understand them. Some folks like to think that they can use the various patterns books as a catalog in which to look up solutions when they have problems, but this is probably not an effective practice. Instead, you must study the patterns and integrate them into your mental model of software design. Then when you are designing software, the patterns will present themselves before you even know you have a design problem.

So read the patterns. Read them carefully. Make sure your weapons for attacking software design problems are firmly ensconced within your brain.

ACKNOWLEDGMENTS

First of all, a very special thanks to the Hillside group for sponsoring the PLoP conferences, and for providing the motivating force for these books. Without their effort and dedication there might not be any PLoPD books at all.

Then, we thank our friends at Addison-Wesley for helping us get going. We especially thank Anne Starr and her colleagues at Editorial Services of New England who emerged victorious in the face of a complex book production process. Finally, we thank Rosemary Simpson of Brown University for building such an excellent index.

Thanks to Doug Schmidt whose sanity is contagious. Thanks to Jim Coplien (Cope) who reminded us that our work has a moral, as well as technological, imperative. Thanks to John Vlissides, the series editor, for keeping his hand on the tiller while the storm raged. Thanks to Walter Tichy for keeping us humble. Finally, a personal thanks from Bob to Dirk and Frank for keeping him from bouncing too far off the wall.

We would also like to thank all the authors who submitted papers to PLoP '96 and EuroPLoP '96, the shepherds who helped guide those papers to the conference, and the reviewers who helped the editors make the hard choices. Their names follow: Alan O'Callaghan, Alejandra Garrido, Alistair Cockburn, Amiram Yehudai, Amnon H. Eden, Amund Aarsten, Andreas Rüping, António Rito Silva, Becky Fletcher, Benoît Garbinato, Bernd-Uwe Pagel, Bindu Rama Rao, Björn Eiderbäck, Bobby Woolf, Bran Selic, Brian Foote, Bruce Anderson, Bruce Lombardi, Charles D. Knutson, Charles Weir, Chris Cleeland, Chrystalla C. Alexandrou, Clazien Wezeman, Curtis R. Cook, D. Janaki Ram, D. Schwabe, Daniel A.

Rawsthorne, Daniel Megert, David E. DeLano, Davide Brugali, Dirk Bäumer, Don Roberts, Douglas C. Schmidt, Edward J. Posnak, Elizabeth A. Kendall, Erich Gamma, Eugene Wallingford, Eyun Eli Jacobsen, Fernando das Neves, G. Rossi, George A. Papadopoulos, Gerard Meszaros, Giuseppe Menga, Hans Rohnert, Harrick M. Vin, Heinz Züllighoven, Ilir Kondo, Irfan Pyarali, James Noble, Jan Newmarch, Jean Tessier, Jean-Lin Pacherie, Jean-Marc Jézéquel, Jens Coldewey, Jim Doble, Jim Lee, João Pereira, John Brant, John Vlissides, John W. Gilbert, José Alves Marques, Joseph Gil, Joseph Yoder, K. N. Anantha Raman, K. N. Guruprasad, Ken Auer, Kent Beck, Kyle Brown, Lennart Ohlsson, Leonor Barroca, Linda Rising, Liping Zhao, Lizette Velázquez, Lorraine L. Boyd, Margaret T. Malkoun, Mario Winter, Mark Bradac, Martin E. Nordberg III, Martin Fowler, Michel de Champlain, Neil B. Harrison, Omer Karacan, Palle Nowack, Pascal Felber, Paul Dyson, Pedro Henriques, Peter H. Feiler, Peter Molin, Peter Sommerlad, Prashant Jain, R. Greg Lavender, R. J. A. Buhr, Rachid Guerraoui, Ralph Johnson, Reinhard Müller, Robert Engel, Robert Hirschfeld, Robert S. Hanmer, Rudolph K. Keller, Serge Demeyer, Steve Berczuk, Suchitra Raman, Suzanne Robertson, Ted Foster, Theo Dirk Meijler, Thomas Kühne, Tim Harrison, Timothy A. Budd, Todd Coram, Walter F. Tichy, Wolf Siberski, and Wolfgang Keller.

Robert C. Martin
Dirk Riehle
Frank Buschmann

PART 1

General Purpose Design Patterns

All six patterns in this part follow the style that is most familiar to mainstream software developers, that of *Design Patterns* [Gamma+95]. These patterns would feel right at home in that collection. If you're doing object-oriented development, you will likely apply—or else reinvent—one or more of these patterns.

Chapter 1: Null Object, by Bobby Woolf. If you program in an object-oriented language long enough, you'll find yourself needing an object to plug an implementation hole. Or you'll be forced to initialize an instance variable even though it will never be used in your application. Or you'll want to avoid cluttering your code with conditionals that check for a null value. A solution to all these difficulties lies in the Null Object pattern. A Null Object implements an interface entirely with null operations; hence it does nothing—exactly what conditional tests for null often do. But a Null Object does nothing wherever a fully functional object *wouldn't* do something, thereby obviating a test for null. Null Object is yet another example of how polymorphism can simplify and regularize your code—a hallmark of good object-oriented design.

Chapter 2: Manager, by Peter Sommerlad. Most programmers agree that class methods and variables should be used sparingly, since they have many of the same drawbacks that global functions and variables have in procedural languages: They are difficult or impossible to extend uninvasively, and they may have far-reaching side-effects that complicate maintenance and admit subtle bugs. But class methods and variables become attractive when there is a need to control instances of a class en masse. The Manager pattern addresses this need without incurring the drawbacks.

A Manager encapsulates the objects in question and implements the erstwhile class methods as normal methods. This approach is not without pitfalls; in particular, you may be tempted to apply the pattern in a way that compromises the encapsulation of the managed objects. But applied with Peter's caveats in mind, Manager can yield a marked improvement over ubiquitous class methods and variables.

Chapter 3: Product Trader, by Dirk Bäumer and Dirk Riehle.

Originally entitled "Late Creation" [Riehle96], this pattern tells you how to create objects without naming names—especially concrete class names. Why would you want to do this? To delay binding class names to runtime. A classic example of late-bound instantiation is creating objects from a stream; it's also useful in dual-inheritance hierarchies [Martin97], where objects from one hierarchy are instantiated using objects from the other.

Yet another application uses the pattern to choose the best implementation for an interface based on desired runtime results. In fact, Product Trader is key to partitioning object-oriented systems along architectural, organizational, and developmental boundaries because it ensures that software systems really do depend on interfaces and not implementations [Gamma+95]. The pattern discusses not only the concept of product trading, but also how to implement it efficiently, on the order of a table look-up—it is fast enough for all but the innermost of inner loops.

Chapter 4: Type Object, by Ralph Johnson and Bobby Woolf.

This pattern describes how to replace an entire class hierarchy with just two classes, Type and Instance. An instance of the Type class replaces each class in the original hierarchy, while an instance of Instance takes the place of each instance of the original classes. Thus the Type Object pattern generates an object metamodel, complete with class objects, instances, and attributes. The goal here is to introduce new object types at runtime. That means you won't need to develop a new application with every change in type requirements—a new product category, for example, or an extension of an old one. What's more, you're likely to need this pattern whenever the space of classes you manage is large, and most of the classes vary often but not substantially.

Chapter 5: Sponsor-Selector, by Eugene Wallingford.

The Strategy pattern [Gamma+95] lets you switch algorithms easily, even at runtime. But it says little about the ramifications of switching or the criteria on which to base the switch. That's where Sponsor-Selector comes in. This pattern ensures that clients receive the service that's right for them at the time of their request. Clients do not need to know very much about the range of services or the selection criteria; a client simply makes its wishes known, and the Sponsor-Selector does the rest. If you question the need for such prescient behavior, the pattern's Known Uses section may well surprise you.

Chapter 6: Extension Object, by Erich Gamma. A nagging problem in object-oriented design is the difficulty in adding operations to existing interfaces. The traditional solution involves modifying the root class to add new operations, perhaps with default implementations, and then reimplementing the operations in each subclass that cannot make do with the default. The traditional problem with this solution is the massive recompiles the changes induce. The most sophisticated programming environment cannot avoid a lot of processing when faced with pervasive change. Even if you are prepared to absorb these costs, repeated interface extension will lead to bloated, incoherent, and nearly incomprehensible interfaces.

Design Patterns includes two patterns that address this problem: Visitor and Decorator. Extension Object is another pattern in this vein, written by one of the same authors. In this pattern, extended operations are placed in separate classes that are mixed into the original using either inheritance or composition. This is perhaps the most extensible alternative to date, in the sense that it is the pattern of choice in highly dynamic environments like COM and OpenDoc. But it's a complex alternative, too. So while understanding *how* to use Extension Objects is essential, knowing *when* to use them—or not—is equally so. The Applicability, Consequences, and Implementation sections in this chapter are crucial to that understanding.

REFERENCES

[Gamma+95] E. Gamma, R. Helm, R. Johnson, and J. Vlissides. *Design Patterns: Elements of Reusable Object-Oriented Software.* Reading, MA: Addison-Wesley, 1995.

[Martin97] R. C. Martin. "Design Patterns for Dealing with Dual Inheritance Hierarchies in C++." *C++ Report* 9(4), April 1997, pp. 42–48.

[Riehle96] D. Riehle. "Patterns for Encapsulating Class Hierarchies." In J. M. Vlissides, J. O. Coplien, and N. L. Kerth (eds.). *Pattern Languages of Program Design 2.* Reading, MA: Addison-Wesley, 1996, pp. 87–104.

Chapter 1

Null Object

Bobby Woolf

Intent

A Null Object provides a surrogate for another object that shares the same interface but does nothing. Thus, the Null Object encapsulates the implementation decisions of how to do nothing and hides those details from its collaborators.

Also Known As

Active Nothing [Anderson95]

Motivation

Sometimes an object that requires a collaborator does not need the collaborator to do anything. However, the object wishes to treat a collaborator that does nothing the same way it treats one that actually provides behavior. Consider for example the Model-View-Controller framework in Smalltalk-80 and VisualWorks Smalltalk. A view uses its controller to gather input from the user. This is a Strategy, since the controller is the view's strategy for how it will gather input [Gamma+95, p. 315].

A view can be read-only. Since the view does not gather input from the user, it does not require a controller. Yet View and its subclasses are implemented to expect a controller, and they use their controller extensively.

If no instances of the View class ever needed a controller, then the class would not need to be a subclass of View. It could be implemented as a visual class similar to View that did not require a controller. However, this would not work for a class that has some instances that require a controller and some that do not. In that case, the class would need to be a subclass of View, and all of its instances would require a controller. Thus the View class requires a controller, but a particular instance does not.

A common way to solve this problem would be to set the instance's controller to nil. This would not work very well though, because the view constantly sends messages to its controller that only Controller understands (like isControl-Wanted, isControlActive, and startUp). Since UndefinedObject (nil's class) does not understand these Controller messages, the view would have to check its controller before sending such messages. If the controller were nil, the view would have to decide what to do. All of this conditional code would clutter the view's implementation. If more than one View class could have nil as its controller, the conditional code for handling nil would be difficult to reuse. Thus, using nil as a controller does not work very well.

For example, this is how VisualPart (the topmost class in the View hierarchy) would have to implement objectWantingControl, one of its key messages

```
VisualPart>>objectWantingControl
    ...
    ^ctrl isNil ifFalse:
        [ctrl isControlWanted
            ifTrue: [self]
            ifFalse: [nil]]
```

Note the check that ctrl is not false before sending it a controller message like isControlWanted. This simple check causes a number of problems. First, not only does this check clutter the code, it obscures its behavior. What does this implementation return when the controller is nil? (The method returns nil, which works, but is it what the author intended?) Second, there are several views and controllers that send isControlWanted to an unknown controller. They would all have to check for nil and handle that case not only appropriately but also consistently. Third, if a developer implements new code that sends isControlWanted to a controller, he will need to add this check. If he forgets, his code may have a very subtle failure built into it. Finally, not only would most senders of isControlWanted have to be protected, but so would most senders of other key controller messages, like isControlActive and startUp.

Another way to solve this problem would be to use a read-only controller. Some controllers can be set in read-only mode so that they ignore input. Such a controller still gathers input, but when in read-only mode, it processes the input by doing nothing. If it were in edit mode, it would process that same input by changing the model's state. This is overkill for a controller which is always going to be read-only. Such a controller does not need to do any processing depending on its current mode. Its mode is always read-only, so no processing is necessary. Thus a controller which is always read-only should be coded to perform no processing.

Instead, what we need is a controller that is specifically coded to be read-only. This special subclass of Controller is called NoController (see Figure 1-1). It

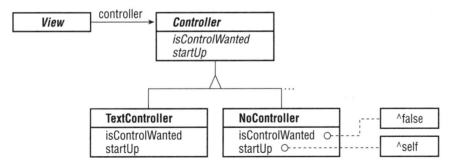

Figure 1-1 *A null controller*

implements all of `Controller`'s interface, but does nothing. When asked `isCon-trolWanted`, it automatically answers `false`. When told to `startUp`, it automatically does nothing and returns `self`. It does everything a controller does, but it does so by doing nothing.

This diagram illustrates how a view requires a controller and how that controller may be a `NoController`. The `NoController` implements all of the behavior that any controller does, but it does so by doing nothing.

For example, this is how `VisualPart>>objectWantingControl`, shown in Figure 1-1, is really implemented.

```
VisualPart>>objectWantingControl
    ...
    ^ctrl isControlWanted ifTrue: [self] ifFalse: [nil]
```

If the controller is a real `Controller`, such as a `TextController`, then `isCon-trolWanted` works normally. But if the controller is a `NoController`, `isControl-Wanted` automatically returns `false`; `objectWantingControl` works correctly without having to know whether its controller is a real `controller` or a null one. Any other sender of `isControlWanted`, or `isControlActive`, or `startUp` can also send these messages without knowing whether the controller is real or null. Whenever the controller is a `NoController`, all senders will behave consistently because `NoController` encapsulates the do-nothing behavior.

`NoController` is an example of the Null Object pattern. The Null Object pattern describes how to develop a class that encapsulates how a type of object should do nothing. Because the do-nothing code is encapsulated, its complexity is hidden from the collaborator and can be easily reused by any collaborator that wants it.

The key to the Null Object pattern is an abstract class that defines the interface for all objects of this type. The Null Object is implemented as a subclass of this abstract class. Because it conforms to the interface of the abstract class, it can be used any place this type of object is needed.

Keys

A framework that incorporates the Null Object pattern has the following features.

- A type whose classes provide the desired behavior
- An object of the same type that fulfills its interface by doing nothing
- A client class that collaborates with this type and can use any of its instances

Usually, such a framework also has the following features.

- A separate class that implements the null object
- An abstract superclass that defines the interface for the regular classes and the null one
- The null class typically has no state and may only have a single instance

Applicability

Use the Null Object pattern

- When an object requires a collaborator. This collaboration already exists before the Null Object pattern is applied.
- When some collaborator instances should do nothing.
- When you want clients to be able to ignore the difference between a collaborator that provides real behavior and one that does nothing. This way, the client does not have to explicitly check for nil or some other special value.
- When you want to be able to reuse the do-nothing behavior so that various clients that need this behavior will consistently work the same way.
- When all of the behavior that might need to be do-nothing behavior is encapsulated within the collaborator class. If some of the behavior in that class is do-nothing behavior, most or all of the behavior of the class will be do-nothing [Coplien96].

The primary alternative to the Null Object pattern is to use nil. Use a variable set to nil in these instances.

- When very little code actually uses the variable directly.
- When the code that does use the variable is well encapsulated—at least within one class—so that it will hide the nil variable. Because the code using the variable is all encapsulated in one place, it is easily consistent with itself, does not have to be consistent with any other code, and will not need to be reused.
- When the code that uses the variable can easily decide how to handle the nil case and will always handle it the same way.

Structure

An example of the Null Object pattern typically has the structure shown in Figure 1-2.

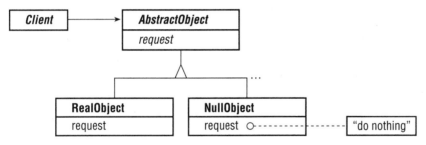

Figure 1-2 *Structure of the Null Object pattern*

Participants

- **Client (View):**
  - requires a collaborator with a specific interface.
- **AbstractObject (Controller):**
  - defines a type and declares the interface for Client's collaborator.
  - implements default behavior for the interface common to all classes, as appropriate.
- **RealObject (TextController):**
  - defines a concrete subclass of AbstractObject whose instances provide useful behavior that Client expects.
- **NullObject (NoController):**
  - provides an interface identical to AbstractObject's, so that a NullObject can be polymorphically substituted for a RealObject.
  - implements its interface to do nothing. Exactly what "do nothing" means is subjective and depends on the sort of behavior the Client is expecting. Some requests may be fulfilled by doing something which gives a null result.
  - when there is more than one way to do nothing, more than one NullObject class may be required.

Collaborations

Clients use the AbstractObject class interface to interact with their collaborators. If the receiver is a RealObject, then the request is handled to provide real behavior. If the receiver is a NullObject, the request is handled by doing nothing or at least providing a null result.

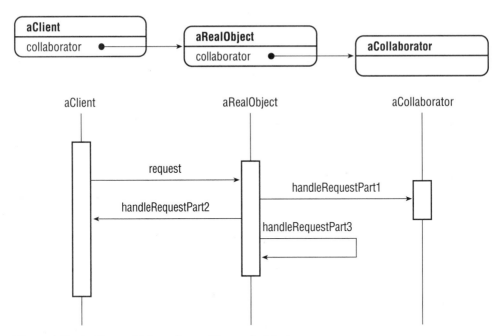

Figure 1-3 *A client collaborating with a real object*

Figure 1-3 shows how `aRealObject` handles a request. When `aClient`'s collaborator is `aRealObject` and it sends the collaborator a message such as `request`, the real object implements the message with real behavior by sending more messages to other collaborators, even back to the client and to itself. This is a routine collaboration between objects.

On the other hand, as shown in Figure 1-4, when the same client's collaborator is `aNullObject`, not much happens. In this case, when `aClient` sends the collaborator a `request` message, the null object implements the message by doing nothing. This is an unusual collaboration because the null object never does much of anything.

Consequences

The advantages of the Null Object pattern are that it

- *Uses polymorphic classes.*   The pattern defines class hierarchies consisting of real objects and null objects. Null objects can be used in place of real objects when the object is expected to do nothing. Whenever client code expects a real object, it can also take a null object.
- *Simplifies client code.*   Clients can treat real collaborators and null collaborators uniformly. Clients normally don't know (and shouldn't care) whether they're

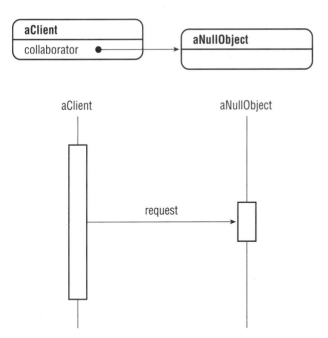

Figure 1-4 *A client collaborating with a null object*

dealing with a real or a null collaborator. This simplifies client code, because it avoids having to write special testing code to handle the null collaborator.

- *Encapsulates do nothing behavior.* The do-nothing code is easy to find. Its variation from the `AbstractObject` and `RealObject` classes is readily apparent. It can be efficiently coded to do nothing, rather than having to go through the motions of doing something, but ultimately doing nothing. It does not require variables that contain null values because those values can be hard-coded as constants, or the do-nothing code can avoid using those values altogether.

- *Makes do-nothing behavior reusable.* Multiple clients which all need their collaborators to do nothing can reuse the `NullObject` class so that they all do nothing the same way. If the do-nothing behavior needs to be modified, the code can be changed in one place, and the various clients will still behave consistently.

The disadvantages of the Null Object pattern are that it

- *Forces encapsulation.* The pattern makes the do-nothing behavior difficult to distribute or mix into the real behavior of several collaborating objects. The same do-nothing behavior cannot easily be added to several classes unless those classes all delegate the behavior to a collaborator that can be a null object class.

- *May cause class explosion.* The pattern can necessitate creating a new `Null-Object` class for each new `AbstractObject` class.

- *Forces uniformity.* The pattern can be difficult to implement if various clients do not agree on how the null object should do nothing.
- *Is non-mutable.* A NullObject always acts as a do-nothing object. It does not transform into a RealObject.

Implementation

There are several issues to consider when implementing the Null Object pattern. One is the special null instance of RealObject. As mentioned in the Consequences, the Null Object pattern can cause a single RealObject class to explode into three classes: AbstractObject, RealObject, and NullObject. Thus, even if the entire abstract object hierarchy can be implemented with one RealObject class (and no subclasses), at least one subclass is required to implement the NullObject class. One way to avoid this class explosion is to implement the null object as a special instance of RealObject rather than as a subclass of AbstractObject. The variables in this null instance would have null values. This may be sufficient to cause the null instance to do nothing. For example, see NullTimeZone in the Known Uses section.

Second, clients don't agree on null behavior. If some clients expect the null object to do nothing one way and some another, multiple NullObject classes are required. If the do-nothing behavior must, then, be customized at run time, the NullObject class will require pluggable variables so that the client can specify how the null object should do nothing (see the discussion of pluggable adaptors in the Adapter pattern [Gamma+95, p. 142]). Again, a way to avoid this explosion of NullObject subclasses of a single AbstractObject class is to make the null objects special instances of RealObject or a single NullObject subclass. If a single NullObject class is used, its implementation can also be a Flyweight [Gamma+95, p. 195]. The behavior that all clients expect of a particular null object becomes the Flyweight's intrinsic behavior, and that which each client customizes is the Flyweight's extrinsic behavior.

A third issue is transformation to RealObject. A NullObject cannot be transformed to become a RealObject. If the object may decide to stop providing do-nothing behavior and start providing real behavior, it is not a null object. It may be a real object with a do-nothing mode, such as a controller which can switch in and out of read-only mode. If it is a single object which must mutate from a do-nothing object to a real one, it should be implemented with the Proxy pattern [Gamma+95, p. 207]. Perhaps the proxy will start off using a null object, then switch to using a real object, or perhaps the do-nothing behavior is implemented in the proxy for when it doesn't have a subject. The proxy is not required if the client is aware that it may be using a null collaborator. In this case, the client can take responsibility for swapping the null object for a real one when necessary.

Finally, the NullObject class is not a mixin. NullObject is a concrete collaborator class that acts as the collaborator for a client which needs one. The null behavior is not designed to be mixed into an object that needs some do-nothing behavior. It is designed for a class which delegates to a collaborator all of the behavior that may or may not be do-nothing behavior [Coplien96].

Sample Code

For an example implementation of the Null Object pattern, look at the implementation of the NoController class in VisualWorks Smalltalk (described in the Motivation section). NoController is a special class in the Controller hierarchy. A Controller, part of the Model-View-Controller architecture in Smalltalk-80 and VisualWorks Smalltalk, handles input for a View. Container visuals can pass control to their component visuals' controllers, which in turn can pass control to their component visuals' controllers. This passing of control from a controller to a subcontroller is an example of Chain of Responsibility [Gamma+95, p. 223].

Visuals (Views) form a tree. Since most visuals have controllers, controllers form a tree indirectly via the visual tree. One responsibility of this tree of controllers is to determine which one should have control. VisualPart>>objectWantingControl looks for a visual whose controller wants control. Then the system gives control to the controller in VisualPart>>startUp. Finally, in Controller>>controlLoop, the controller keeps control until it no longer wants control.

```
Object ()
  Controller (model view ...)
  VisualPart (container)

VisualPart>>objectWantingControl
      ...
      ^ctrl isControlWanted ifTrue: [self] ifFalse: [nil]

VisualPart>>startUp
      | ctrl |
      ctrl := self getController.
      ^ctrl notNil
            ifTrue: [ctrl startUp]
            ifFalse: [nil]

Controller>>controlLoop
      [...
      self isControlActive]
            whileTrue:
                  [...]
```

So when a controller wants control, isControlWanted returns true. To give control to a controller, its view sends it startUp. Finally, when a controller has control and wants to keep it, isControlActive returns true.

How does a controller decide when it wants to get and keep control? Essentially, if a controller's view contains the mouse cursor, the controller wants control. Once it has control, it runs its controlLoop until it doesn't want control anymore.

These main controller methods—isControlWanted, startUp, and isControlActive—are implemented in Controller. Some subclasses enhance these implementations, but few override them completely.

```
Controller>>isControlActive
        ^self viewHasCursor and: [...]

Controller>>startUp
        self controlInitialize.
        self controlLoop.
        self controlTerminate

Controller>>isControlWanted
        ^self viewHasCursor
```

A NoController is a controller that never wants control. When asked if it wants control (isControlWanted), it responds with false. When offered control (startUp), it does nothing. And when asked if it wants to keep control (isControlActive), it responds with false again.

```
Object ()
  Controller (model view ...)
    NoController ()
  VisualPart (container)

NoController>>isControlWanted
        ^false

NoController>>startUp
        ^self

NoController>>isControlActive
        ^false
```

By overriding just these three methods, NoController can inherit the two dozen messages in Controller and implement them to do nothing. Meanwhile, NoController has the interface that a View expects, so the View does not have to check for a special case like nil. Instead, the visual can ask questions like isControlWanted and be assured that the controller will respond successfully. Because the do-nothing code is encapsulated in NoController, all views with null controllers will behave the same.

Known Uses

The Null Object pattern is very commonly used, so there are many examples of it.

Null Strategies.   NoController, the Null Object class in the motivating example, is a class in the Controller hierarchy in VisualWorks Smalltalk [VW95].

NullDragMode is a class in the DragMode hierarchy in VisualWorks Smalltalk. A DragMode implements the dragging of widgets in the window painter. Subclasses represent different ways that the dragging can be done. CornerDragMode lets the user resize the visual, and SelectionDragMode lets him move it. A NullDragMode represents an attempt to resize a visual that cannot be resized. It responds to the mouse's drag motions by doing nothing [VW95].

Null Adapters.   NullInputManager is a class in the InputManager hierarchy in VisualWorks Smalltalk. An InputManager provides a platform-neutral object interface to platform events that affect internationalized input. Subclasses such as X11InputManager represent specific platforms. NullInputManager represents platforms that don't support internationalization. Its methods do little if anything, whereas their counterparts in X11InputManager do real work [VW95].

Null States.   Null_Mutex is a mutual exclusion mechanism in the ASX (ADAPTIVE Service eXecutive) framework for C++. The framework provides several mechanisms for concurrency control. Mutex defines a nonrecursive lock for a thread that will not call itself. A RW_Mutex lock allows multiple threads to read but only one to write. Null_Mutex defines a lock for a service that is always run in a single thread and does not contend with other threads. Since locking is not really necessary, Null_Mutex doesn't lock anything; its acquire and release methods do nothing. This avoids the overhead of acquiring locks when they're not really needed [Schmidt94].

Null Lock is a type of lock mode in the VERSANT Object Database Management System. The database locks objects so that they can be read and written. A read lock allows other read locks, but blocks write locks. A write lock blocks all other read and write locks. Null Lock does not block other locks and cannot be blocked by other locks. This guarantees the user immediate access to the object, even if another process has already locked it, but it does not guarantee that the object is in a consistent state. Null Lock is not really a lock because it doesn't perform any locking, but it acts like a lock for operations that require one [Versant95].

Null Proxies.   The Decoupled Reference pattern shows how to access objects via Handlers so that their true location is hidden from the client. When a client requests an object that is no longer available, rather than let the program crash, the framework returns a Null Handler. This Handler acts like other Handlers, but fulfills requests by raising exceptions or otherwise causing error conditions [Weibel96].

Null Iterator.   The Iterator pattern documents a special case called `NullIterator` [Gamma+95, pp. 67–68, 262]. Each node in a tree might have an iterator for its children. Composite nodes would return a concrete iterator, but leaf nodes would return an instance of `NullIterator`. A `NullIterator` is always finished with traversal; when asked `isDone`, it always returns `true`. In this way, a client can always use an `iterator` to iterate over the nodes in a structure even when there are no more nodes. See z-node under Procedural Nulls below.

Null Instances.   `NullTimeZone` is a special instance of the `TimeZone` class in Visual-Works Smalltalk. A `TimeZone` converts clock times between Greenwich Mean Time (GMT) and local time and accounts for daylight savings time (DST). This is useful for UNIX machines whose clocks are set to GMT, but unnecessary in Windows and Macintosh machines because their clocks are already set to local time. On these machines, VisualWorks uses `NullTimeZone`, a special instance (not subclass) of `TimeZone` that converts the clock by doing no conversion. All of its variables are set to zero so that all of the offsets it adds to the local clock don't actually change the clock value. This is simpler than checking for a `TimeZone` which is `nil` or testing the platform to determine if it needs a `TimeZone` [VW95].

Reusable Nulls.   `NullScope` is a class in the `NameScope` hierarchy in VisualWorks Smalltalk. A `NameScope` represents the scope of a particular set of variables. `StaticScopes` hold global and class variables whereas `LocalScopes` hold instance and temporary variables. Every scope has an outer scope. They form a tree that defines all variables in a system. Even the global scope has an outer scope, a `NullScope` that never contains any variables. When the lookup for a variable reaches a `NullScope`, it automatically answers that the variable is not defined within the code's scope. This could be handled as a special case in the `StaticScope` that holds global variables, but `NullScope` handles it more cleanly. This allows `NullScope` to be reused by clean and copy blocks, simple blocks that have no outer scope. `NullScope` is also a Singleton [Gamma+95, p. 127] as well as a Null Object [VW95].

Procedural Nulls.   Procedural languages have null data types that are like null objects. Sedgewick's z-node is a dummy node that is used as the last node in a linked list. When a tree node requires a fixed number of child nodes but does not have enough children, Sedgewick uses z-nodes as substitutes for the missing children. In a list, the z-node protects the delete procedure from needing a special test for deleting from an empty list. In a binary tree, a node without two children would need one or two null links, but the null z-node is used instead. This way, a search algorithm can simply skip z-node branches; when it has run out of non-z-node branches, it knows the search did not find the item. (This is similar to a null iterator, discussed above.) In this way, z-nodes are used to avoid special tests the way null objects are [Sedge88].

Null Object Anti-Example. The LayoutManager hierarchy in the Java AWT toolkit does *not* have a null object class but could use a class such as NullLayoutManager. A Container can be assigned a LayoutManager (a Strategy [Gamma+95, p. 315]). If a particular Container does not require a LayoutManager, the variable can be set to nil. Unfortunately, this means that Container's code is cluttered with lots of checks for a nil LayoutManager. Container's code would be simpler if it used a null object like NullLayoutManager instead of nil [Gamma96].

Related Patterns

When a null object does not require any internal state, the NullObject class can be implemented as a Singleton [Gamma+95, p. 127], since multiple instances would act exactly the same and their state cannot change.

When multiple null objects are implemented as instances of a single NullObject class, they can be implemented as Flyweights [Gamma+95, p. 195].

NullObject is often used as one class in a hierarchy of Strategy classes [Gamma+95, p. 315]. It represents the strategy to do nothing. It is also often used as one class in a hierarchy of State classes [Gamma+95, p. 305]. There, it represents the state in which the client should do nothing, such as when the state is unknown. NullObject can also be a special kind of Iterator [Gamma+95, p. 257], which doesn't iterate over anything.

NullObject may be a special class in a hierarchy of Adapters [Gamma+95, p. 142]. Whereas an adapter normally wraps another object and converts its interface, a null adapter would pretend to wrap another object without actually wrapping anything.

Null Object can be similar to Proxy [Gamma+95, p. 207], but the two patterns have different purposes. A proxy provides a level of indirection when accessing a real subject, thus controlling access to the subject. A null collaborator does not hide a real object and control access to it, it replaces the real object. A proxy may eventually mutate and begin acting like a real subject. A null object will not mutate to provide real behavior, it will always provide do-nothing behavior. However, a Proxy hierarchy can contain a Null Proxy subclass that pretends to be a proxy but will never have a subject. Bruce Anderson has written about the Null Object pattern, which he also refers to as "Active Nothing" [Anderson95].

Null Object is a special case of the Exceptional Value pattern in The CHECKS Pattern Language. An Exceptional Value is a special Whole Value (another pattern) used to represent exceptional circumstances. It will either absorb all messages or produce Meaningless Behavior (another pattern). A Null Object is one such Exceptional Value [Cunningham95].

ACKNOWLEDGMENTS

I would like to thank my coworkers at KSC for their help in developing this pattern, Ward Cunningham for his shepherding help, and everyone at PLoP '96 who made suggestions for improving this paper.

REFERENCES

[Anderson95] B. Anderson. "Null Object." UIUC patterns discussion mailing list (patterns@cs.uiuc.edu), January 1995.

[Coplien96] J. Coplien. E-mail correspondence.

[Cunningham95] Ward Cunningham, "The CHECKS Pattern Language of Information Integrity" in J. O. Coplien and D. C. Schmidt (eds.), *Pattern Languages of Program Design*. Reading, MA: Addison-Wesley, 1995, pp. 145–155.

[Gamma+95] E. Gamma, R. Helm, R. Johnson, and J. Vlissides. *Design Patterns: Elements of Reusable Object-Oriented Software*. Reading, MA: Addison-Wesley, (URL: http://www.aw.com/cp/Gamma.html), 1995.

[Gamma96] E. Gamma. E-mail correspondence.

[PLoPD95] J. Coplien and D. Schmidt (editors). *Pattern Languages of Program Design*. Reading, MA: Addison-Wesley (URL: http://hegschool.aw.com/cseng/authors/coplien/pattern-lang/patternlang.html), 1995.

[Schmidt94] D. Schmidt. "Transparently Parameterizing Synchronization Mechanisms into a Concurrent Distributed Application." *C++ Report*. SIGS Publications, Vol. 6, No. 3, July 1994.

[Sedge88] R. Sedgewick. *Algorithms*. Reading, MA: Addison-Wesley, 1988.

[Versant95] *VERSANT Concepts and Usage Manual*. Menlo Park, CA: Versant Object Technology (URL: http://www.versant.com), 1995.

[Wallingford96] E. Wallingford. E-mail correspondence.

[Weibel96] P. Weibel. "The Decoupled Reference Pattern." Submitted to EuroPLoP '96.

[VW95] VisualWorks Release 2.5. Sunnyvale, CA: ParcPlace-Digitalk, Inc. (URL: http://www.parcplace.com), 1995.

Bobby Woolf can be reached at bwoolf@ksccary.com.

Chapter 2

Manager

Peter Sommerlad

The Manager design pattern encapsulates management of the instances of a class into a separate manager object. This allows for variation of management functionality independent of the class and for reuse of the manager for different object classes.

Example

Suppose you are developing an object-oriented application, such as a library information system. This system deals with its domain objects, such as books and library users. All books in the library should be represented as instances of a Book class. Each domain object is identified and accessed by a unique key attribute, such as a book by its ISBN. In C++ these requirements could be accomplished by introducing static class members.

```
class Book {
    // ... many things left out
    static Map<String,Book*> allBooks;
public:
    Book(String ISBN, String Authors, String Title);
    String getAuthors() const;
    String getISBN() const;
    String getTitle() const;
    String getPublisher() const;
    const JpegImage *getCover() const;
    HTMLpage *getTableOfContents() const;
// static members for retrieving books
    static Book *search(String isbn);
    static List<Book*> findBooksOfAuthor(String author);
};
```

To substitute the collection holding all books by another type, it will be necessary to recompile all client code using the Book class. To implement other search functions, for example, a search for books by publisher or by title, we need to extend and modify the Book class again, forcing recompilation of all client components, even if they do not use the new functionality. A class representing the library users will copy a lot of the managing code to provide access to user objects by their identification.

Context

Object handling

Problem

When designing a class of business or domain objects, we often face the challenge of dealing with all instances of this class in a homogeneous way. For example, a search of instances with a specific property requires access to a collection of all instances. Using class variables and class methods for this purpose may restrict flexibility too much. It is not easy to vary the way the objects are managed without changing the class itself. In C++ we have to recompile all files depending on the class, even if they are not affected by the management change itself.

Another problem is objects we want to create on demand, but later share among client components, for example, font description objects in a GUI framework. Creating such a font object is typically an expensive operation; because of the large number of fonts it is not possible to create all font objects up front.

A similar situation arises when we have to deal with persistent objects that reside in a database. To delegate work to such objects, we have to create an in-memory representative. This requires additional work with several points of possible failure, especially when using a relational database instead of an object-oriented database.

To summarize, we often want to control the life cycle of all objects of a class in a homogenous way. When we want to get rid of in-memory copies of persistent objects, however, we need to keep track of objects used.

Often several classes of an application share such requirements. It would be helpful if code managing these objects is also shared and not copied. In particular, it is necessary to address the following forces:

- All objects of a class should be accessible as a whole.
- Variation of the objects' implementation should not affect the way they are managed.
- Additional services related to handling domain objects, like storing them in a database, should be easy to add.
- Several classes require almost identical control of their objects.

Solution

Introduce a separate component, the manager, that treats the collection of managed objects as a whole. The manager component deals with issues related to accessing, creating, or destroying the managed objects.

Clients requiring a specific managed object retrieve a reference to it from the manager. Thereafter, the client component carries out all interaction directly with the domain object. When it is no longer needed, the client component may return the domain object to the manager. The managed objects perform their tasks on behalf of the client. We refer to them as subjects in this pattern.

Structure

The client component is coded against the subject's interface. However, to obtain an object of this class, the client needs to exploit the manager object.

The manager is the only object that creates and destroys subjects. It keeps track of managed subjects in a collection of references to the subjects. Typical managing functionality includes searching subjects for a specific key. Since the manager object is not directly included within the subject class, it is possible to modify or create a subclass and extend the manager independently.

The subject class implements the domain objects in this pattern. It provides the domain services required by clients. The participants and their relationships are shown in Figure 2-1.

Dynamics

The following scenario depicted in Figure 2-2 shows the library example implemented with the Manager pattern. The scenario demonstrates how a subject is requested, used, and retired by the client.

- First, the client asks the single manager object for a subject identified by its key (the ISBN in the book example).
- The manager searches its registry of all subject objects to determine whether the one required is already available. In this scenario it is not.
- The new subject (a book) is created.

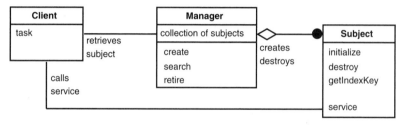

Figure 2-1 *The participants of the manager pattern*

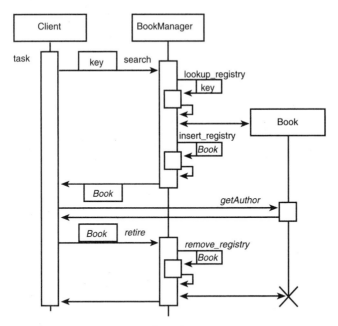

Figure 2-2 *Interaction within the Manager pattern*

- Before the manager returns the newly created subject, it inserts the subject into the registry for later reference.
- At this point, the client is ready to perform the required functionality with the subject (`book->getAuthor()`).
- After using the subject, the client returns responsibility to the manager, which in this case decides to delete the subject.

Implementation

To implement the Manager pattern, perform the following steps.

1. *Identify the management services required for your subjects.* The kind of services you need depends on the nature of your application. One common service is to provide functions for retrieving a subject, for example, by searching on a key attribute. Other sevices might include creating a new subject, iteration [Gamma+95] over all available subjects, or subject retirement that may result in the deletion of subjects.

Example

In our library information system we need access for searching for particular books. Since books are stored in a database, some initialization code is also needed. So the following functions might be needed.

```
void initialize(Database *db);
Book *search(String ISBN);
List<Book*> findBooksOfAuthor(String author);
Iterator<Book*> makeBookIterator();
```

2. *Define the interface of the manager component.* From the first step, take the required functionality and put that into the manager class. Typically the manager acts as a Factory [Gamma+95] for subject objects. If you want to manage instances of a subject class hierarchy, the factory function of the manager needs to acquire information about which subclass to instantiate. This information can either be given by a client as a parameter or calculated upon creation, for example, by reading the type information from a database.
3. *Design the access mechanism of the manager component.* To ensure that only one Manager object exists, you can apply the Singleton pattern [Gamma+95].

Example

To obtain access to the iterator over all books, the Factory Method [Gamma+95] makeBookIterator() is included. The resulting code looks like

```
class BookManager {
    Map<String,Book*> loadedBooks;
    BookManager();
    friend class Book; // for accessing constructor only
    static BookManager *theManager; // singleton
public:
    // implement singleton:
    static BookManager *getInstance() ;

    Book *search(String ISBN);
    List<Book*> findBooksOfAuthor(String author);
    Iterator<Book*> makeBookIterator();
    void retire(Book *oldBookObject);
};
BookManager *BookManager::theManager = 0; // singleton
```

4. *Design and implement the subject class.* This step depends on your concrete application. However, if it is necessary to consult an external medium like a database to create a subject instance, you have to decide where to put this code. It can be in either the subject's constructor or in the manager class. If the manager is responsible for accessing external media, you may be able to implement the subject class independent of where and how the instance information is stored.

Example

For our library information system, we get the class definition for books.

```
class Book {
    // ... some things left out
    String isbn,authors,title,description,publisher;
    // books are added by the manager only
    Book(String ISBN, String Authors, String Title);
    virtual ~Book();
    friend class BookManager;
public:
    String getAuthors() const;
    String getISBN() const;
    String getTitle() const;
    String getPublisher() const;
    const JpegImage *getCover() const;
    HTMLpage *getTableOfContents() const;
};
```

5. *Implement the manager component.* After the subject class is finished, you can implement the manager's functionality. For this step, decide what kind of collection to use for holding the subject references. You will eventually need several dictionaries if you want to search subjects for different aspects.

If subject references are shared, the manager may not arbitrarily delete objects that are retired by one client; another client might still use the reference. In C++, this problem can be resolved by using the Counted Pointer idiom [Buschmann+96] and returning handles instead of pointers to the clients.

If the manager is responsible for accessing external information, like a database on subject creation, it becomes feasible to exchange that information source at will. Thus you are able to implement reading instances from a file and test the system before investing in a full-fledged database management system. However, using a database raises more issues, such as transaction control, than can be discussed here.

6. *Design and implement client components using the manager and subject.* The client obtains a subject reference via the manager and thereafter uses the subject reference directly. This situation corresponds to the Client-Dispatcher-Server design pattern [Buschmann+96] in which the dispatcher establishes a communication channel between client and server that is then used without accessing the dispatcher.

Example

In our example, the client component might contain code like the following:

```
Book *aBook = BookManager::getInstance()->search("0471958697");
if (aBook)
    cout << "You should read" << aBook->getTitle()
         << " it was written by " << aBook->getAuthors() ;
```

VARIANTS

Manager Template

If a system contains multiple classes that may take the subject role in the Manager pattern, it can be a good idea to extract all common manager code into a single template manager class. This is possible if all subject classes implement a common interface required by the managers. An example for such a method is getIndex-Value() to obtain the search key for a subject. Individual management behavior can be added by subclassing the instantiated manager template class.

Example

A Manager Template class with the parameters subject type T and index type INDEXTYPE can be used in our example to manage not only the books in the library but also information about the user class. The code might appear as follows.

```
template <class T, class INDEXTYPE>
class TManager
{
    // this class requires
    //             T::T(istream&)
    // INDEXTYPE   T::getCode()
    // void        T::finalize(ostream&)
    // and a destructor for T
    friend class T; // for T::getManager()
    // TManager<T,INDEXTYPE> created by T::getManager()
protected:
    TManager ();
    virtual ~TManager (); // needed if subclassed
    virtual T* add(T *m);
    virtual T* remove(INDEXTYPE code);
    virtual T* remove(T *m);
public:
// read T object from stream, as text representation
    virtual T* createNew(istream &in=cin);
// read initial data from file:
    virtual void initialize(istream & in ) ;
// for testing store data to file:
    virtual void finalize(ostream & out);
```

```
// TManager is for indexed access:
    virtual T* search(INDEXTYPE code);// look up a T
    virtual void retire(T *t);
protected:
    Map<INDEXTYPE,T*> code2Index ;   // contains all Ts
};
```

To relieve clients from having to specify template syntax for an individual manager in many places and to give only a single point of reference for the Singleton, the example code uses a slightly different implementation technique for Singleton. It provides the subject class with a function getMgr() for accessing its manager object.

Our Book class from the ongoing example can be modified in the following ways.

```
class Book {
    // ... some things left out
    String isbn,authors,title,description,publisher;
    // books are added by the manager only
    Book(String ISBN, String Authors, String Title);
    virtual ~Book();
    friend class TManager<Book,String>;
public:
    String getCode() const { return getISBN(); }
    String getAuthors() const;
    String getISBN() const;
    String getTitle() const;
    String getPublisher() const;
    const JpegImage *getCover() const;
    HTMLpage *getTableOfContents() const;
// manager access:
    static TManager<Book,String>* getMgr();
};

TManager<Book,String>* Book::getMgr(){
    static TManager<Book,String>* theMgr = 0;
    if (! theMgr) {
        theMgr = new TManager<Book,String>;
        theMgr->initialize("allbooks");
    }
    return theMgr;
}

// adapt createNew to parse book information
Book *TManager<Book,String>::createNew(istream &in){
    String isbn,authors,title;
    in >> isbn >> authors >> title;
```

```
    // details omitted ! ...
    return new Book(isbn, authors, title);
```

The client code using books now might read

```
Book *aBook = Book::getMgr()->search("0201895277");
if (aBook)
    cout << "Also a nice book about patterns:"
        << aBook->getTitle();
```

Class Methods

In languages with separate class objects, or languages that are not typed statically (like Smalltalk), it can be sufficient to implement the manager functionality with class methods and class variables. In such instances, a change of the manager functionality does not imply a recompilation of all the subject's subclasses. However, the principle of separation of concerns might be applied to get to a solution according to the Manager pattern.

Known Uses

Flyweight [Gamma+95], Command Processor, and View Handler [Buschmann+96] are well-known patterns that use the Manager pattern as a part of their solution. Each proposes a central component like flyweight manager, command processor, or the view handler that keeps track of existing subjects that are flyweight instances, command objects, or view objects respectively.

Consequences

The Manager pattern implies the following *benefits*.

- *Iteration over managed objects.* This can be used to obtain summary information, calculate statistics, and update the database rows with information from the transient objects when closing an application.
- *Independent variation of management functionality.* For example, it is possible to modify the access layer to the database within the manager class without changing the subject class at all.
- *Substitution of management functionality on demand.* By subclassing a manager's class and exchanging the singleton instance access method, it is easy to substitute manager functionality with minimal impact on existing code.
- *Reuse of management code for different subjects.* The Manager Template variant allows the reuse of management code for different, even unrelated, subject classes.

However, the Manager pattern also has its *liabilities*.

- *Misuse.*   It is easy to misuse the Manager pattern to break encapsulation of the subject classes.
- *Splitting functionality between manager and subject classes.*   It may be hard to decide how to divide functionality between manager and subject classes, for example, in which class to deal with database access and error handling.
- *Meta-information required.*   If a single manager object controls a hierarchy of subject classes, you usually need some kind of meta-information for the managed objects to associate an object's class when instantiating objects. See the Reflection pattern [Buschmann+96] for detailed discussion.

See Also

The distribution patterns Broker and Client-Dispatcher-Server [Buschmann+96] share some attributes with the Manager pattern because they provide access to a collection of server objects on behalf of clients. But instead of being responsible for the complete life-cycle of the servers, Broker and Dispatcher are only responsible for registered and thus already existing servers.

ACKNOWLEDGMENTS

Many thanks to the shepherd Robert Martin and to Erich Gamma and the participants of the writers workshops at PLoP '96 and the Componentware Users Conference 1996 in Munich.

REFERENCES

[Gamma+95] E. Gamma, R. Helm, R. Johnson, J. Vlissides. *Design Patterns: Elements of Reusable Object-Oriented Software.* Reading, MA: Addison-Wesley, 1995.

[Buschmann+96] F. Buschmann, R. Meunier, H. Rohnert, P. Sommerlad, M. Stal. *Pattern-Oriented Software Architecture: A System of Patterns.* New York: J. Wiley & Sons, 1996.

[Brown+96] K. Brown, B. G. Whitenack. "Crossing Chasms: A Pattern Language for Object-RDBMS Integration." In J. M. Vlissides, J. O. Coplien, and N. L. Kerth (eds.), *Pattern Languages of Program Design 2.* Reading, MA: Addison-Wesley, 1996, pp. 227–238.

Peter Sommerlad can be reached at sommerlad@ifa.ch.

Chapter 3

Product Trader

Dirk Bäumer and Dirk Riehle

Intent

The Product Trader design pattern allows clients to create objects by naming an interface and by providing a specification. A Product Trader decouples the client from the product and thereby eases the adaptation, configuration, and evolution of class hierarchies, frameworks, and applications.

Also Known As

Virtual Constructor, Late Creation

Motivation

Suppose you have designed a class hierarchy of domain value types like Account-Number, Amount, InterestRate, or SocialSecurityNumber. These value types will be used in several applications. For example, one such application will present a form on the screen and let users edit its fields. The value types of the fields correspond to the domain value types. Since each value type has its own semantics and editing constraints, you might want to provide specialized widgets for each of these value types as shown in Figures 3-1 and 3-2.

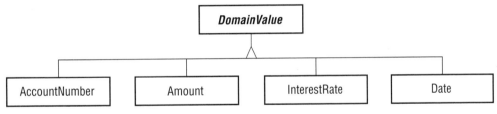

Figure 3-1 *DomainValue class hierarchy*

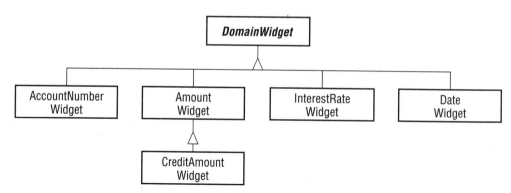

Figure 3-2 `DomainWidget` *class hierarchy with specialized* `AmountWidget` *class*

Given a Form object with all the fields and associated value types, how do you create the widgets corresponding to the value types? You might be tempted to write an all-inclusive case statement for all value types that creates a widget for a given value type, but this is cumbersome and might require frequent changes and enhancements. You might use a Factory Method for the value types so that each value type can return a default widget for it. But then you will only be able to provide a single widget type for a value type. Moreover, if the value types are used in a noninteractive environment, like nightly batch runs, the batch application will have to link the window system even though it isn't needed. You might also consider using an Abstract Factory. While this hides the creation process from the client, it doesn't clarify what happens behind the factory interface. You might still have to write an extensive case statement to distinguish between the different value types.

It is much better to go to some object and ask it to return an instance of a `DomainWidget` subclass that fits a given value type best. This object might be the abstract `DomainWidget` class itself, or a factory object or trader object. We call this pattern Product Trader, and its purpose is to do this flexibly and efficiently.

Suppose `DomainWidget` offers a class operation that lets you do this. In C++, it looks like

```
static DomainWidget* DomainWidget::createFor(DomainValue*);
```

and in Smalltalk, it looks like

```
DomainWidget class>>createFor: aDomainValue.
```

Internally, the widget class might maintain a dictionary of all its subclasses, which it indexes with the class representing a given value type. Then `createFor` can be easily implemented: The `DomainWidget` class takes the value type's class as a key for the dictionary, which returns the widget subclass specifically designed for the value type. The `DomainWidget` then creates an instance of the widget subclass that it returns to the client. This process is fast and requires only constant time.

The actual class that is to be instantiated is determined only at run time, and it is accessed using abstract classes only. Thus, the concrete subclasses are hidden from the client. Moreover, the dictionary can be changed and reconfigured at run-time. This lets you easily configure and evolve class hierarchies, frameworks, and applications.

Applicability

Use a Product Trader if

- You want to make clients fully independent from concrete implementations of the abstract Product class (decoupling argument); or
- You want to dynamically select a product class according to selection criteria available only at run time (dynamic selection argument); or
- You want to configure the kinds of product classes instantiated for a given selection criterion, either statically or at run time (flexible configuration argument); or
- You want to change and evolve the product class hierarchy without affecting clients (evolution argument).

Do not use a Product Trader as a replacement for Factory Methods or direct object creation.

Structure

The structure diagram is shown in Figure 3-3.

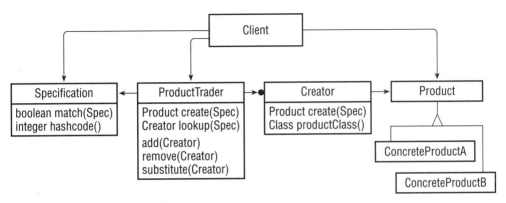

Figure 3-3 *Structure diagram of the Product Trader pattern*

Participants

- **Client (Form):**
  - creates a `Specification` for a `ConcreteProduct` class.
  - initiates the creation process by providing the `ProductTrader` with a `Specification`.

- **Product (DomainWidget):**
  - defines the interface to a class hierarchy of which objects are to be instantiated.

- **ConcreteProduct (DateWidget, AmountWidget):**
  - represents a concrete `Product` class.
  - provides enough information to decide whether it matches a `Specification`.

- **ProductTrader (DomainWidget class object):**
  - provides operations that let a client supply a `Specification` for a `ConcreteProduct` class.
  - maps a `Specification` onto a `Creator` for a `ConcreteProduct` class.
  - provides operations to configure the mapping by some configuration mechanism.
  - `ProductTrader` can be as simple as a hashtable and as complex as a trader object.

- **Creator (ConcreteProduct class objects):**
  - defines the interface to create instances of a `ConcreteProduct`.
  - knows how to instantiate exactly one `ConcreteProduct`.

- **Specification (DomainValue subclasses):**
  - represents a specification of a `ConcreteProduct` class.
  - is used as the lookup argument for a `Creator` instance.
  - can be as lightweight as a string and as heavyweight as a propositional calculus formula.

Collaborations

Figure 3-4 shows an interaction diagram of a `Product` selection and creation process. The following collaborations are involved.

1. The `Client` asks the `ProductTrader` for a `Product` instance matching a `Specification`.
2. The `ProductTrader` maintains a dictionary of `Creator` instances.
3. The `ProductTrader` looks up a `Creator` for a given `Specification`.
4. The `ProductTrader` delegates the creation process to a `Creator`.
5. A `Creator` creates a `ConcreteProduct` instance.

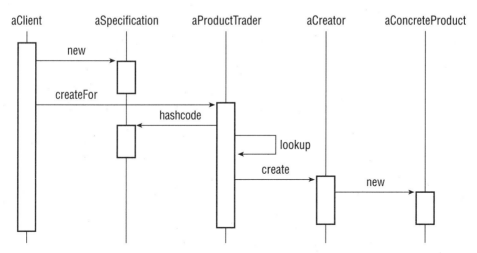

Figure 3-4 *Interaction diagram of* `ProductTrader`

Consequences

The Product Trader pattern has the following advantages and consequences.

- **`Clients` *become independent of* `ConcreteProduct` *classes.*** `Clients` are fully decoupled from the internal structure of the `Product` class hierarchy. Once you have written the code that creates the `Specification` instance and calls the `createFor` operation of the `ProductTrader` class, you are done with the client code.
- *Product classes are determined at run time.* Sometimes, the criteria that best define the class fitting a task are not known until run time. Product Trader lets you turn these criteria into a `Specification` at run time and use it for `Concrete-Product` class lookup. Thus, you get the maximum flexibility for selecting `ConcreteProduct` classes.
- *Products can be configured for specific domains.* Product Trader lets you configure the available `ConcreteProduct` classes created via the abstract `Product` class by adding, substituting, and removing `Creators` for `ConcreteProduct` classes. This lets you easily configure frameworks and applications for specific domains.
- *Product class hierarchies can be evolved easily.* Since clients are fully decoupled from the internals of the `Product`, class hierarchy, class names, hierarchy structure, and implementation strategies of `ConcreteProduct` classes can be changed without affecting them (as long as the `ConcreteProduct` classes preserve the semantics of the abstract `Product` class).

- *New product classes can be introduced easily.* It is very easy to add new `ConcreteProduct` classes to an existing framework—it does not require any changes to the framework. New `ConcreteProduct` classes can be written without having to change existing code. Only configuration code or makefiles have to be changed.
- *Products need not be single classes; they can be any complex component.* The `Creator` might hide potentially complex creation processes, for example, by cloning complex Prototype structures.

The Product Trader pattern has some disadvantages and liabilities.

- *Increased control and dependency complexity.* The pattern turns compile-time dependencies of product creation into run-time dependencies. This makes the resulting system harder to understand, because the dependencies are not explicitly written down as code.
- *Need for advanced configuration mechanisms.* When applying Product Trader, objects of classes can and will be created that are not statically referenced, starting with some root class. Thus, a linker might consider those classes superfluous and decide not to link them. See the Implementation section for techniques for dealing with this problem.
- *Ambiguous specifications.* Depending on the type and implementation of a specification, several classes may match it. They constitute the set of equivalent classes with respect to the `Specification`. This does not pose problems, since any class matching the requirements will do the job. However, ambiguities might indicate that the specification itself was either imprecise or inadequately determined.
- *Special constructor parameters require overhead.* If a `ConcreteProduct` class requires special constructor parameters during the early object-building process, you must supply them in advance. It requires some overhead to do so. You could broaden the creation interface or put the constructor parameters into a generic parameter carrier object. You should be careful, however, not to make any implicit assumptions about specific subclasses being selected by your specification.

Implementation

The implementation of the Product Trader pattern requires consideration of four main dimensions: implementation of the mapping from `Specification` to `Creator`, implementation of the `Creator` itself, implementation of `Specifications`, and, finally, configuration of frameworks and applications.

- *Implementing the mapping from* Specification *to* Creator. The mapping can be realized by a simple dictionary in the abstract Product class, by delegating the task to a product-specific ProductTrader object, or by delegating the task to a global ProductTrader object.

  – *Using a simple dictionary* puts the management of the mapping into the abstract Product class. This is advisable only if the Product Trader pattern is applied solely to the Product hierarchy and if the handling of specifications is very specialized for this particular class hierarchy. Otherwise, consider using a ProductTrader object.
  – *Using a* ProductTrader takes the burden of managing Specifications, Creators, and mapping from Specifications to Creators from the Product class. Each class hierarchy can have its own ProductTrader object which handles specifications for this class hierarchy. This solution is both flexible and offers good code reuse.
  – *Using a single global* ProductTrader *object* centralizes all specifications and all class semantics in one single place. This goes beyond the class hierarchy-specific ProductTrader and should be applied if complex class retrieval and run-time configuration issues must be considered.

- *Implementing* Creators. Creators can be implemented as prototypes, class objects, or specific dedicated Creator objects, generated, for example, by C++ templates. You will want to avoid manually introducing a Creator class for every Product class, so consider using one of these variants.

  – *Using prototypes or class objects* amounts to about the same. These objects are included with any major system and usually provide a clone or a create operation that can carry out the actual creation of the Product instance. The clone operation must be robust with respect to copying.
  – *Using dedicated* Creator *objects.* In C++, you can use macros or templates to generate the Creator objects. We present a C++ template-based version as a type-safe solution. An analysis of the Creator's responsibilities leads to a definition of a Creator and ConcreteCreator template

```
template<class ProductType, class SpecType>
class Creator
{
public:
  Creator(SpecType aSpec) : _aSpecification(aSpec) {}
  SpecType getSpecification() { return _aSpecification; }
  ProductType* create() =0;

private:
  SpecType _aSpecification;
};
```

```
template<class ProductType, class ConcreteProductType, class SpecType>
class ConcreteCreator : public Creator<ProductType, SpecType>
{
public:
  ConcreteCreator(SpecType aSpec)
   : Creator<ProductType, SpecType>  (aSpec) {}
  ProductType* create() { return new ConcreteProductType; }
}
```

The `Creator` template requires two formal arguments, the `ProductType` and the `SpecType` (specification type). Usually, the `Specification` itself is not maintained by the `Creator`; rather it is the argument for the mapping which leads to the `Creator`. However, for management purposes in `ProductTrader` it is convenient to store a specification with the `Creator`, given that there is only a single specification which leads to the specific `Creator`. Eventually, the `ConcreteCreator` template adds the code for actually creating an instance of a `ConcreteProduct` class.

A closer look at the templates reveals that they are fairly simple, essentially only defining interfaces and the create operation for concrete product classes. These templates can only be used for product classes in which the constructor doesn't need any parameters. In case parameters must be passed to the `Product` class constructor, additional templates are needed. A replication of the above two template classes is the result.

- *Implementing* **Specifications.** Specifications can be realized either directly in the parameters of the creation operation by some primitive value types or by encapsulating them as classes of their own. This issue affects the implementation of the mapping.

  - *Using built-in value types* like integers and character strings often requires additional support, like free floating operations to compute hash-codes. Essentially, you must define operations which make the value types usable as lookup arguments for the mapping.
  - *Using explicit* `Specification` *objects* allows you to define the proper interface for `Specifications` once and reuse it for every new `Specification`. Moreover, `ProductTraders` can be written based on this explicit interface and reused. Such a `Specification` interface might look like

```
class Specification
{
public:
    // returns Product class, that is the root class of classes
    // addressed by this type of specification
  virtual Class* getProductClass() =0;
```

```
    // initialize specification to match semantics
    // of a given Product class
  virtual void initForProduct(Class* pc) { this->adaptTo(pc); }

    // initialize specification to match
    // semantics of a given Product class
  virtual void adaptTo(Class*);

    // match two specifications for equivalence
  virtual bool matches(Specification*) =0;
};
```

- *Configuring frameworks and applications.* The Product Trader pattern creates objects only indirectly by interpreting specifications. Thus, `ConcreteProduct` classes are not directly referenced by framework or application code, but only by abstract interfaces like the `Product` class. As a consequence, you must specify explicitly which classes are to be linked to an application, because linkers might not link classes that are not directly referenced by code reachable from some root object (or main).

  - *Using makefiles* is a straightforward approach. For every application, you explicitly specify the set of `ConcreteProduct` classes that are to be linked. You can do so by issuing commands to the linker. Since dependencies might exist between `ConcreteProduct` classes from different class hierarchies (covariant redefinition), do not forget dependent classes.
  - *Using source code to configure systems* is straightforward. You might simply write a configuration operation in the system's root class, the main application class, or close to the main operation that references the classes required to be linked. The linker will then take care that the right classes are linked to the final executable.
  - *Using register objects.* If you want to support the Product Trader pattern for all classes linked to the system you should consider using a register class that is responsible for adding a `ConcreteCreator` object with a `Specification` to the `Product` class.
  - *Using configuration scripts.* In large projects, where a lot of applications are developed, it is important to easily understand the configuration of the system. When using Product Trader in C++, this can be accomplished by using configuration scripts. The goals of configuration scripts are to be one place that describes the configuration of the system, and to reference all needed `ConcreteProduct` classes, so that the linker includes them in the application.

    An easy way to satisfy these goals is to create the `ConcreteCreator` and `Specification` objects inside a configuration script and add these objects to the `Product` class, depending on the configuration of the system. The Sample Code section presents some examples.

- *Providing convenience operations.* You can use the abstract `Product` class to hide the implementation of a specification as an instance of a dedicated `Specification` class. The client simply calls the `createFor` operation with parameters that are native to the specification, and the implementation of `createFor` in the `Product` class converts these parameters into a `Specification` object.
- *Providing initialization parameters.* Sometimes objects require elaborate initialization parameters which must be available during the early object-building process. These parameters can be packaged into the `Specification` objects, or they can be passed along a chain of operation calls that then must provide matching parameter lists (which requires code generation as discussed above).
- *Consider dynamic link libraries explicitly.* Classes from dynamically linked libraries are not directly accessible, simply because they are not contained in the run time image. However, the `Creator` objects are usually very lightweight. They can therefore represent not yet loaded classes. The creation procedure of a `Creator` for a class in a dynamically linked library might have to load that class first, but this might be exactly what you want. `Creators` and the `ProductTrader` can be effectively used to hide the factoring of large applications into DLLs or the expense of having to deal with complex configuration issues.

Sample Code

We will discuss three examples: one for instantiating objects from a stream, one for mapping widget types on value types, and one which uses a general `Product-Trader` object.

Instantiating Objects from a Stream. As a first example, we will present a simple implementation using prototypes as `Creators` and a dictionary as the mapping from `Specification` to `ConcreteCreator`. The dictionary is maintained by the `Product` class.

Assume you are reading objects from a stream. A leading string indicates the class of the object to be read. Thus, the class name represents the specification for the class to be instantiated.

`Serializable` is the abstract `Product` class for all objects that can be read from a stream. `String` is the specification type, and we assume that every subclass of `Serializable` can provide a prototype. The `Serializable` class might then implement `createFor`

```
Serializable* Serializable::createFor(String& className) {
  Serializable* prototype = lookup(className);
  return prototype->clone();
}
```

Lookup simply retrieves the prototype for a given class name from a dictionary maintained by the Product class (a static member variable in C++ or a class variable in Smalltalk)

```
Serializable* Serializable::lookup(String& className) {
  return mapping[className];
}
```

A simple configuration scheme might be to make the prototypes register themselves in the Serializable class at system startup (when the prototypes are created), thus

```
Customer::Customer(CustomerPrototypeConstructorIndicator* dummy) {
  Serializable::addCreator(this);
}
```

Serializable implements addCreator by using the class name to put the prototype into the dictionary

```
Serializable::addCreator(Serializable* prototype) {
  mapping[prototype->getClassName()] = prototype;
}
```

This implementation uses prototypes as Creators, a simple built-in value-type specification, and a static registering and configuration scheme. It is a lightweight approach which works well if the Product Trader pattern is to be applied to single class hierarchies with only simple specification requirements.

Configuring Widgets for Value Types.   As a second example, we use C++ templates to illustrate implementation of the introducing domain widget and value problem. In this example, specifications are realized by C++ typeids denoting the class of the DomainValue. The configuration scheme of the system is realized by configuration scripts. The mapping from the Specification to the Creator is realized by a simple dictionary. The code uses the templates from the Implementation section.

```
DomainWidget* DomainWidget::createFor(DomainValue* aValue) {
  Creator<DomainWidget, type_info&>* aCreator = mapping[typeid(aValue)];
  return aCreator->create();
}

DomainWidget::addCreator(Creator<DomainWidget, type_info&>* aCreator)
{
  mapping[aCreator->getSpecification()] = aCreator;
}
```

We use the templates from the implementation section to configure the `DomainWidget` class. This class maps the `typeid` of the `DomainValues` to the `Creator` object for the `DomainWidgets`:

```
StandardDomainWidgetConfiguration() {
  ...
    // map Amount on AmountWidget
  DomainWidget::addCreator(
    new ConcreteCreator<DomainWidget, AmountWidget, type_info&>(
      typeid(Amount)));
    // map Currency on CurrencyWidget
  DomainWidget::addCreator(
    new ConcreteCreator<DomainWidget, CurrencyWidget, type_info&>(
      typeid(Currency)));
  ...
}
```

If we want to offer a new configuration for an application, we only have to write a new configuration script to make the required changes. As an example, consider a credit application which uses a special domain widget for the domain value `Amount`. To add the new widget to the application, you have to implement the new domain widget and then use a configuration script to register it. The new configuration script might be

```
CreditConfiguration() {
  ...
    // use the specific CreditAmountWidget for the domain value Amount
  DomainWidget::substituteCreator(
    new ConcreteCreator<DomainWidget, CreditAmountWidget, type_info&>(
      typeid(Amount)));
  ...
}
```

The system's root object, or the main operation, must call the `DomainWidgetConfiguration` and the `CreditConfiguration` operation to install the necessary `Creator` objects. Only these calls are needed, no further code changes are required.

Using a General `ProductTrader`. As a final example, we will use Smalltalk to implement a full `ProductTrader` that can be reused by every class hierarchy to provide the Product Trader pattern at its root for any number of different specifications. This example is derived from [Riehle+96] where a more detailed discussion can be found. This implementation uses a general `ProductTrader` object which maintains a picture of the semantics of all classes in the system by means of specifications. The `ProductTrader` organizes these specifications so that it can easily look up the classes matching a given specification.

Every `Product` class can provide convenience operations which are implemented in terms of the system-wide `ProductTrader`, a Singleton. Classes take over the role of creators, specifications are implemented as subclasses of a general `Specification` class, and the Product Trader role is realized by the `Product-Trader` object just introduced.

The `ProductTrader` provides a mapping from a specification to a class object for every specification type. Specification types are represented by the classes in a `Specification` class hierarchy. The mapping is implemented as a dictionary which takes a `Specification` instance as a key and returns a collection of all classes that match the `Specification`. Since the specification type is represented as a class, it can be used in a further dictionary to retrieve the dictionary containing the specification to classes mapping.

The `ProductTrader` has two main lookup methods.

```
ProductTrader>>getSpecificationDictionary: aClass
  "returns dictionary representing a specification to classes mapping"
  ( self specTypeDict includesKey: aClass )
    ifTrue: [ ^self specTypeDict at: aClass ]
    ifFalse: [ ^nil ]

ProductTrader>>getClassCollection: aSpecification
  "returns collection of classes matching aSpecification"
  | specDict |
  specDict := self getSpecificationDictionary: aSpecification class.
  ( specDict includesKey: aSpecification )
    ifTrue: [ ^self specDict at: aSpecification ]
    ifFalse: [ ^nil ]
```

The first method returns the mapping dictionary for a given specification type, and the second method returns a collection of all classes matching the given specification. The implementation of `createFor` becomes a simple two-stage retrieval process now. A product class, for example `DomainWidget`, simply does the following.

```
DomainWidget>>createFor: aDomainValue
  "create Specification instance and delegate to ProductTrader"
  | aSpecification |
  aSpecification := DomainWidgetSpecification new: aDomainValue class.
  ^self ProductTrader createFor: aSpecification

ProductTrader>>createFor: aSpecification
  "create object for given specification"
  | classCol |
  classCol := getClassCollection: aSpecification.
```

```
( classCol notNil )
  ifTrue: [ ^classCol first new ]
  ifFalse: [ ^nil ]
```

The actual problem is how to set up the dictionaries so that the retrieval and creation process can be carried out easily. This is a two-step process. In the first step, the `ProductTrader` collects all classes from the `Specification` class hierarchy. In the second step, it calculates the mapping for every `Specification` class; this is done by traversing the product class hierarchy as indicated by the `Specification` class and by creating a `Specification` instance for every `Product` class. This process is based on information which has to be provided by the specification classes themselves. Thus, `Specification` declares the class and instance methods

```
Specification class>>getProductClass
  "returns Product class"
  self subclassResponsibility

Specification class>>newFromClient: anObject
  "used by clients which supply the specification information"
  self subclassResponsibility

Specification class>>newFromManager: aClass
  "used by ProductTrader to instantiate spec for a
  ConcreteProduct class"
  ^super new adaptTo: aClass

Specification>>adaptTo: aClass
  "adapts spec instance to given product class"
  self subclassResponsibility

Specification>>matches: aSpecification
  "matches with another specification"
  ^( self class = aSpecification class )
```

These methods must be overwritten by subclasses in order to fit a certain specification's semantics. For `DomainWidgetSpecification`, this leads to the following code.

```
DomainWidgetSpecification class>>getProductClass
  ^DomainWidget

DomainWidgetSpecification class>>newFromClient: aDomainValueClass
  self domainValueClass: aDomainValueClass

DomainWidgetSpecification>>adaptTo: aDomainWidgetClass
  self domainValueClass: aDomainWidgetClass getDomainValueClass
```

```
DomainWidgetSpecification>>matches: aSpecification
  ( super matches: aSpecification ) ifFalse: [ ^false ].
  ^( self domainValueClass = aSpecification domainValueClass )

DomainWidgetSpecification>>hash
  ^domainValueClass symbol
```

When created by a client or a convenience operation of DomainWidget, the DomainWidgetSpecification instance receives the DomainValue class that the new DomainWidget instance will have to fit. When created by the ProductTrader, the DomainWidgetSpecification instance is created for a specific DomainWidget class, which it requests for the specific DomainValue class for which it has been written. The last method is used to build the mapping of domain values to domain widgets. The ProductTrader traverses the DomainWidget class hierarchy, creates a DomainWidgetSpecification instance for each class, and puts the class into the mapping dictionary with the Specification instance as the key. The hash method then maps a client-created DomainWidgetSpecification instance on a collection of DomainWidget classes.

This approach is based on the assumption that the Specification instance is able to retrieve enough information from the Product class to serve as a key in the mapping. In our example, the DomainWidget class provides a getDomainValueClass method, which returns the domain value class. If this is not an option, the class semantics of Product classes must be specified externally to that class, for example in a database.

This approach lets us introduce new specifications simply by introducing a new specification subclass. Implementing ProductTrader for object streaming, as shown in the first example, can be done by creating a ClassSymbolSpecification which looks like this

```
ClassSymbolSpecification class>>getProductClass
  ^Object

ClassSymbolSpecification class>>newFromClient: aSymbol
  self classSymbol: aSymbol

ClassSymbolSpecification>>adaptTo: aClass
  self classSymbol: aClass symbol

ClassSymbolSpecification>>matches: aSpecification
  ( super matches: aSpecification ) ifFalse: [ ^false ].
  ^( self classSymbol = aSpecification classSymbol )

ClassSymbolSpecification>>hash
  ^classSymbol
```

The general `ProductTrader` is a mighty approach for avoiding the hard-coding of creation dependencies in the class implementations themselves. It has served us well in making our frameworks more easily adaptable and configurable.

Known Uses

The first example in the Sample Code section, creating objects from a stream, can be found in almost every application framework which provides streaming support. It requires the mapping from some class identifier, for example the class name, to an object which is capable of instantiating this class. You can implement the specification as a string representing the class name, the creator objects by some class object or prototype, and the mapping as a dictionary which maps the class name on the object representing the class. For example, the `ClassManager` of ET++ [Weinand+94] implements Product Trader by maintaining class objects in a dictionary, and so do the Tools and Materials Metaphor Frameworks [Riehle+95, Riehle+96].

Next to this very frequent but specialized application, Product Trader is often used to select a subclass as a specific implementation of the abstract `Product` class which fulfills certain criteria, for example one which performs very fast or uses only a limited amount of memory resources. Lortz and Shin [Lortz+94] implement Product Trader according to Coplien's generic autonomous exemplar idiom [Coplien92]. The `Product` class maintains a list of prototypes for each of its subclasses, it uses strings as a specification mechanism, and it traverses the list matching each prototype with the specification. Lortz and Shin use Product Trader to select container classes based on performance requirements in the context of a real-time database system.

The most interesting application of Product Trader, however, is the creation of objects from one hierarchy depending on objects from another hierarchy, as demonstrated by the introductory example. In the Tools and Materials Metaphor frameworks [Bäumer+97, Riehle+96, Riehle+95], we have made extensive use of the pattern to map hierarchies onto each other. We instantiate widgets depending on value types, we instantiate user-interface parts depending on domain models, we instantiate tools depending on the materials they have to work on, and we instantiate domain components depending on other domain components.

All these tasks are carried out on the level of abstract classes. This helped us achieve a degree of decoupling that significantly eased system evolution and configuration. Product Trader is an important asset in making the frameworks consisting of more than 2,000 classes adaptable, configurable, and, eventually, manageable.

Related Patterns

The global `ProductTrader` is a Singleton [Gamma+95]; Product Trader is used to create objects from a stream in the Atomizer pattern [Riehle+97]; Convenience operations (used to encapsulate complex `Specification` objects) are an example of the Convenience Method pattern [Hirschfeld96]; and Product Trader is used to create `ConcreteExtension` objects for `ConcreteSubject` objects in the Extension Object pattern [Gamma97].

Product Trader serves as a companion to Factory Method [Gamma+95] and works well where Factory Method works poorly and vice versa. Factory Methods often introduce cyclic dependencies between the `Product` and the `Creator`, in particular if the `Product` is going to work on the `Creator` later on. This is the case with applying Factory Method in the introductory example where a value object would create a widget object. This is also the case with a container creating its iterators. It is additionally the case with a model object creating its views. If a different product is required, the creator has to be changed. The widget class, the container class, and the model class would have to be changed. Furthermore, no two different products can coexist and be selected due to some dynamic selection criteria. We think of Product Trader as a third fundamental creational pattern next to Factory Method and Prototype.

ACKNOWLEDGMENTS

We wish to thank our shepherd, Erich Gamma, and the participants of the writer's workshop at PLoP '96 for their helpful comments.

REFERENCES

[Bäumer+97] D. Bäumer, G. Gryczan, R. Knoll, C. Lilienthal, C. Riehle, and H. Züllighoven. "The Tools and Materials Metaphor Series of Frameworks." *Submitted for publication.*

[Coplien92] J. O. Coplien. *Advanced C++: Programming Styles and Idioms.* Reading, MA: Addison-Wesley, 1992.

[Gamma97] E. Gamma. "Extension Object." Chapter 6, this volume.

[Gamma+95] E. Gamma, R. Helm, R. Johnson, and J. Vlissides. *Design Patterns: Elements of Reusable Design.* Reading, MA: Addison-Wesley, 1995.

[Hirschfeld96] R. Hirschfeld. "Convenience Method." In *Preliminary Conference Proceedings of EuroPLoP '96.* Washington University, Department of Computer Science, Technical Report WUCS-97-07, 1997.

[Lortz+94] V. B. Lortz and K. G. Shin. "Combining Contracts and Exemplar-Based Programming for Class Hiding and Customization." In *Proceedings of OOPSLA '94, ACM SIGPLAN Notices* 29, 10 (October 1994), pp. 453–467.

[Riehle+95] D. Riehle and H. Züllighoven. "A Pattern Language for Tool Construction and Integration Based on the Tools and Materials Metaphor." In J. O. Coplien and D. C. Schmidt (eds.), *Pattern Languages of Program Design.* Reading, MA: Addison-Wesley, 1995, pp. 9–42.

[Riehle+96] D. Riehle, B. Schäffer, and M. Schnyder. "Design of a Smalltalk Framework for the Tools and Material Metaphor." *Informatik/Informatique* (February 1996), pp. 20–22.

[Riehle+97] D. Riehle, W. Siberski, D. Bäumer, D. Megert, and H. Züllighoven. "Serializer." Chapter 17, this volume.

[Weinand+94] A. Weinand and E. Gamma. "ET++—a Portable, Homogenous Class Library and Application Framework." In W. R. Bischofberger and H.-P. Frei (eds.), *Proceedings of the Ubilab Conference '94, Zürich*. Konstanz: Universitätsverlag Konstanz, 1994, pp. 66–92.

Dirk Bäumer can be reached at Dirk.Baeumer@TakeFive.co.at.
Dirk Riehle can be reached at Dirk.Riehle@ubs.com **or** riehle@acm.org.

Chapter 4

Type Object

Ralph Johnson and Bobby Woolf

Intent

A Type Object decouples instances from their classes so that those classes can be implemented as instances of a class. Type Object allows new classes to be created dynamically at runtime, lets a system provide its own type-checking rules, and can lead to simpler and smaller systems.

Also Known As

Power Type [Martin+], Item Descriptor [Coad93], Metaobject [Kiczales+91], Data Normalization.

Motivation

Sometimes a class requires not only an unknown number of instances, but an unknown number of subclasses as well. Although an object system can create new instances on demand, it usually cannot create new classes without recompilation. A design in which a class has an unknown number of subclasses can be converted to one in which the class has an unknown number of instances.

Consider a system for tracking the videotapes in a video rental store's inventory. The system will obviously require a class called `Videotape`. Each instance of `Videotape` will represent one of the videotapes in the store's inventory. However, since many of the `videotapes` are very similar, the `Videotape` instances will contain a lot of redundant information. For example, all copies of *Star Wars* will have the same title, rental price, MPAA[1] rating, and so forth. This information is different

---

[1] The Motion Picture Association of America, the industry group that rates movies in the United States as G, PG, R, and so on.

for *The Terminator*, but multiple copies of *The Terminator* also have identical data. Repeating this information for all copies of *Star Wars* or all copies of *The Terminator* would be redundant.

One way to solve this problem is to create a subclass of `Videotape` for each movie. Thus, two of the subclasses would be `StarWarsTape` and `Terminator-Tape`. The class itself would keep the information for that movie. So the information common to all copies of *Star Wars* would be stored only once. It might be hardcoded on the instance side of `StarWarsTape` or stored in variables on the class side or in an object assigned to the class for this purpose. Now `Videotape` would be an abstract class; the system would not create instances of it. Instead, when the store bought a new copy of *The Terminator* videotape and started renting it, the system would create an instance of the class for that movie, an instance of `TerminatorTape`.

This solution works, but not very well. One problem is that if the store stocks lots of different movies, `Videotape` could require a huge number of subclasses. Another problem is what would happen when, with the system deployed, the store starts stocking a new movie—perhaps *Independence Day*. There is no `Inde-pendenceDayTape` class in the system. If the developer had not predicted this situation, he would have had to modify the code to add a new `Independence-DayTape` class, recompile the system, and redeploy it. If the developer had predicted this situation, he could provide a special subclass of `Videotape`—such as `UnknownTape`—and the system would create an instance of it for all videotapes of the new movie. The problem with `UnknownTape` is that it has the same lack of flexibility that `Videotape` had. Just as `Videotape` required subclasses, so will `Unknown-Tape`, so `UnknownTape` is not a very good solution.

Instead, since the number of types of videotapes is unknown, each type of videotape needs to be an instance of a class. However, each videotape needs to be an instance of a type of videotape. Class-based object languages give support for instances of classes, but they do not give support for instances of instances of classes. So to implement this solution in a typical class-based language, you need to implement two classes: one to represent a type of videotape (`Movie`) and one to represent a videotape (`Videotape`). Each instance of `Videotape` would have a pointer to its corresponding instance of `Movie`.

The class diagram in Figure 4-1 illustrates how each instance of `Videotape` has a corresponding instance of `Movie`. It shows how properties defined by the type of videotape are separated from those which differ for each particular videotape.

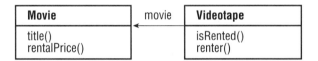

Figure 4-1 *Classes in the video store system*

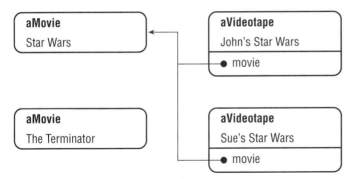

Figure 4-2 *Instances in the video store system*

In this case, the movie's title and how much it costs to rent are separated from whether the tape is rented and who is currently renting it.

The instance diagram (Figure 4-2) shows how there is an instance of `Movie` to represent each type of `videotape` and an instance of `Videotape` to represent each video the store stocks. *Star Wars* and *The Terminator* are movies; videotapes are the copy of *Star Wars* that John is renting versus the one that Sue is renting. It also shows how each `Videotape` knows what type it is because of its relationship to a particular instance of `Movie`.

If a new movie, such as *Independence Day*, were to be rented to Jack, the system would create a new `Movie` and a new `Videotape` that points to the `Movie`. The movie is Independence Day and the tape is the copy of *Independence Day* that Jack ends up renting.

`Videotape`, `Movie`, and the is-instance-of relationship between them (a `Videotape` is an instance of a `Movie`) is an example of the Type Object pattern. It is used to create instances of a set of classes when the number of classes is unknown. It allows an application to create new "classes" at runtime because the classes are really instances of a class. The application must then maintain the relationship between the real instances and their class-like instances.

The key to the Type Object pattern is two concrete classes, one whose instances represent the application's instances and another whose instances represent types of application instances. Each application instance has a pointer to its corresponding type.

Keys

A framework that incorporates the Type Object pattern has three features.

- Two classes, a type class and an instance class.
- The instance class has an instance variable whose type is the type class.
- The instance class delegates its type behavior to the type class via the instance variable.

The framework may also include these variations on the pattern.

- The system may maintain a list of its type class instances.
- The type class instances may maintain a list of their instances.

Applicability

Use the Type Object pattern when

- Instances of a class need to be grouped together according to their common attributes and/or behavior.
- The class needs a subclass for each group to implement that group's common attributes and behavior.
- The class requires a large number of subclasses and/or the total variety of subclasses that may be required is unknown.
- You want to be able to create new groupings at runtime that were not predicted during design.
- You want to be able to change an object's subclass after it has been instantiated without having to mutate it to a new class.
- You want to be able to nest groupings recursively so that a group is itself an item in another group.

Structure

As Figure 4-3 shows, the Type Object pattern has two concrete classes, one that represents objects and another that represents their types. Each object has a pointer to its corresponding type.

For example, Figure 4-4 shows how the system uses a `TypeObject` to represent each type in the system and an `Object` to represent each of the instances of those `TypeObjects`. Each `Object` has a pointer to its `TypeObject`.

Participants

- **TypeClass (Movie):**
  - is the class of `TypeObject`.
  - has a separate instance for each type of `Object`.

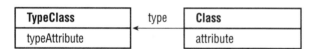

Figure 4-3 *Structure of the Type Object pattern*

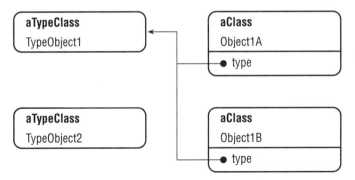

Figure 4-4 *Instances in the Type Object pattern*

- **TypeObject** (*Star Wars, The Terminator, Independence Day*):
  - is an instance of `TypeClass`.
  - represents a type of `Object`. It establishes all properties of an `Object` that are the same for all `Objects` of the same type.

- **Class (Videotape):**
  - is the class of `Object`.
  - represents instances of `TypeClass`.

- **Object (John's** *Star Wars*, **Sue's** *Star Wars*):
  - is an instance of `Class`.
  - represents a unique item that has a unique context. It establishes all properties of that item that can differ between items of the same type.
  - It has an associated `TypeObject` that describes its type. Delegates properties defined by its type to its `TypeObject`.

`TypeClass` and `Class` are classes. `TypeObject` and `Object` are instances of their respective classes. As with any instance, a `TypeObject` or `Object` knows what its class is. In addition, an `Object` has a pointer to its `TypeObject` so that it knows what its `TypeObject` is. The `Object` uses its `TypeObject` to define its type behavior. When the `Object` receives requests that are type specific but not instance specific, it delegates those requests to its `TypeObject`. A `TypeObject` can also have pointers to all of its `Objects`.

Thus `Movie` is a `TypeClass` and `Videotape` is a `Class`. Instances of `Movie`, like *Star Wars, The Terminator,* and *Independence Day* are `TypeObjects`. Instances of `Videotape` like John's *Star Wars* and Sue's *Star Wars* are `Objects`. Since an `Object` has a pointer to its `TypeObject`, John's videotape and Sue's videotape have pointers to their corresponding `Movie`, which in this case is *Star Wars* for both `Videotapes`. That is how the `Videotapes` know that they contain *Star Wars* and not some other movie.

Collaborations

- An `Object` gets two categories of requests: those defined by its instance and those defined by its type. It handles the instance requests itself and delegates the type requests to its `TypeObject`.
- Some clients may want to interact with the `TypeObjects` directly. For example, rather than iterate through all of the `Videotapes` the store has in stock, a renter might want to browse all of the `Movies` that the store offers.
- If necessary, the `TypeObject` can have a set of pointers to its `Objects`. This way the system can easily retrieve an `Object` that fits a `TypeObject`'s description. This would be similar to the `allInstances` message that Smalltalk classes implement. For example, once a renter finds an appealing `Movie`, he would then want to know which videotapes the store has that fit the description.

Consequences

The advantages of the Type Object pattern are

- *Runtime class creation.*   The pattern allows new "classes" to be created at runtime. These new classes are not actually classes, they are instances called `TypeObjects`, that are created by the `TypeClass`, just like any instance is created by its class.
- *Avoids subclass explosion.*   The system no longer needs numerous subclasses to represent different types of `Objects`. Instead of numerous subclasses, the system can use one `TypeClass` and numerous `TypeObjects`.
- *Hides separation of instance and type.*   An `Object`'s clients do not need to be aware of the separation between `Object` and `TypeObject`. The client makes requests of the `Object`, and the `Object`, in turn, decides which requests to forward to the `TypeObject`. Clients that are aware of the `TypeObjects` may collaborate with them directly without going through the `Objects`.
- *Dynamic type change.*   The pattern allows the `Object` to dynamically change its `TypeObject`, which has the effect of changing its class. This is simpler than mutating an object to a new class [DeKezel96].
- *Independent subclassing.*   `TypeClass` and `Class` can be subclassed independently.
- *Multiple Type Objects.*   The pattern allows an `Object` to have multiple `TypeObjects` where each defines some part of the `Object`'s type. The `Object` must then decide which type behavior to delegate to which `TypeObject`.

The disadvantages of the Type Object pattern are

- *Design complexity.*   The pattern factors one logical object into two classes. Their relationship, a thing and its type, is difficult to understand and confusing for modelers and programmers alike. It is difficult to recognize or explain the relationship between a `TypeObject` and an `Object`. This confusion hurts simplicity and maintainability. The solution in a nutshell: "Use inheritance; it's easier."

- *Implementation complexity.* The pattern moves implementation differences out of the subclasses and into the state of the `TypeObject` instances. Whereas each subclass could implement a method differently, now the `TypeClass` can only implement the method one way and each `TypeObject`'s state must make the instance behave differently.
- *Reference management.* Each `Object` must keep a reference to its `TypeObject`. Just as an object knows what its class is, an `Object` knows what its `TypeObject` is. But whereas the object system or language automatically establishes and maintains the class-instance relationship, the application must itself establish and maintain the `TypeObject-Object` relationship.

Implementation

There are several issues that you must always address when implementing the Type Object pattern.

1. **`Object` *references* `TypeObject`.** Each `Object` has a reference to its `TypeObject` and delegates some of its responsibility to the `TypeObject`. An `Object`'s `TypeObject` must be specified when the `Object` is created.
2. **`Object` *behavior vs.* `TypeObject` *behavior*.** An `Object`'s behavior can either be implemented in its class or can be delegated to its `TypeObject`. The `TypeObject` implements behavior common to the type, while the `Object` implements behavior that differs for each instance of a type. When the `Object` delegates behavior to its `TypeObject`, it can pass a reference to itself so that the `TypeObject` can access its data or behavior. The `Object` may decide to perform additional operations before and after forwarding the request, similar to the way a Decorator can enhance the requests it forwards to its Component [Gamma+95, p. 175].
3. **`TypeObject` *is not multiple inheritance*.** The `Class`—not the `TypeObject`— is the template for the new `Object`. The messages that `Object` understands are defined by its `Class`, not by its `TypeObject`. The `Class`'s implementation decides which messages to forward to the `TypeObject`; the `Object` does not inherit the `TypeObject`'s messages. Whenever you add behavior to `TypeClass`, you must also add a delegating method to `Class` before the behavior is available to the `Object`s.

Several other issues also may need to be considered when implementing the Type Object pattern.

1. **`Object` *creation using a* `TypeObject`.** Often, a new `Object` is created by sending a request to the appropriate `TypeObject`. This is notable because the `TypeObject` is an instance, and instance creation requests are usually sent to a class, not an instance. But the `TypeObject` is like a class to the `Object`, so it often has the responsibility of creating new `Object`s.
2. **Multiple `TypeObject`s.** An `Object` can have more than one `TypeObject`, but this is unusual. In this case, the `Class` would have to decide which `TypeObject` to delegate each request to.

3. *Changing* `TypeObject`. The Type Object pattern lets an object dynamically change its class, the type object. It is simpler for an object to change its pointer to a different type object (a different instance of the same class) than to mutate to a new class. For example, suppose that a shipment to the video store is supposed to contain three copies of *The Terminator* and two copies of *Star Wars*, so those objects are entered into the system. When the shipment arrives, it really contains *two* copies of *The Terminator* and *three* copies of *Star Wars*. So one of the three new copies of *The Terminator* in the system needs to be changed to a copy of *Star Wars*. This can easily be done by changing the `Videotape`'s `Movie` pointer from *The Terminator* to *Star Wars*.

4. *Subclassing* `Class` *and* `TypeClass`. It is possible to subclass either `Class` or `TypeClass`. The video store could support videodisks by making another `Class` called `Videodisk`. A new `Videodisk` instance would point to its `Movie` instance just like a `Videotape` would. If the store carried three tapes and two disks of the same movie, three `Videotapes` and two `Videodisks` would all share the same `Movie`.

The hard part of Type Object occurs after it has been used. There is an almost irresistible urge to make the `TypeObjects` more composable and to build tools that let nonprogrammers specify new `TypeObjects`. These tools can get quite complex, and the structure of the `TypeObjects` can get quite complex. Avoid any complexity unless it brings a big payoff.

SAMPLE CODE

Sample code is provided for the example of the video store and for a factory manufacturing example.

Video Store.   Start with two classes, `Movie` and `Videotape`.

```
Object ()
  Movie (title rentalPrice rating)
  Videotape (movie isRented renter)
```

Notice how the attributes are factored between the two classes. If there are several videotapes of the same movie, some might be rented while others are still in stock. Various copies can certainly be rented to different people. Thus the attributes `isRented` and `renter` are assigned at the `Videotape` level. On the other hand, if all of the videotapes in the group contain the same movie, they will all have the same name, will rent for the same price, and will have the same rating. Thus the attributes `title`, `rentalPrice`, and `rating` are assigned at the `Movie` level. This is the general technique for factoring the `TypeObject` out of the `Object`: Divide the attributes that vary for each instance from those that are the same for a given type.

You create a new `Movie` by specifying its title. In turn, a `Movie` knows how to create a new `Videotape`.

```
Movie class>>title: aString
        ^self new initTitle: aString

Movie>>initTitle: aString
        title := aString

Movie>>newVideotape
        ^Videotape movie: self

Videotape class>>movie: aMovie
        ^self new initMovie: aMovie

Videotape>>initMovie: aMovie
        movie := aMovie
```

Since `Movie` is `Videotape`'s `TypeClass`, `Videotape` has a movie attribute that contains a pointer to its corresponding `Movie` instance. This is how a `Videotape` knows what its `Movie` is. The movie attribute is set when the `Videotape` instance is created by `Videotape class>>movie:`.

A `Videotape` knows how to be rented. It also knows whether it is already rented. Although it does not know its price directly, it knows how to determine its price.

```
Videotape>>rentTo: aCustomer
        self checkNotRented.
        aCustomer addRental: self.
        self makeRentedTo: aCustomer

Videotape>>checkNotRented
        isRented ifTrue: [^self error]

Customer>>addRental: aVideotape
        rentals add: aVideotape.
        self chargeForRental: aVideotape rentalPrice

Videotape>>rentalPrice
        ^self movie rentalPrice

Videotape>>movie
        ^movie

Movie>>rentalPrice
        ^rentalPrice
```

```
Videotape>>makeRentedTo: aCustomer
     isRented := true.
     renter := aCustomer
```

Thus it chooses to implement its `isRented` behavior itself, but delegates its `rentalPrice` behavior to its Type Object.

When *Independence Day* is released on home video, the system creates a `Movie` for it. It gathers the appropriate information about the new movie (title, rental price, rating) via a GUI and executes the necessary code. The system then creates the new `Videotapes` using the new `Movie`.

Nested Type Objects. The Type Object pattern can be nested recursively. For example, many video stores have categories of movies—such as New Releases (high price), General Releases (standard price), Classics (low price), and Children's (very low price). If the store wanted to raise the price on all New Release rentals from $3.00 to $3.50, it would have to iterate through all of the New Release movies and raise their rental price. It would be easier to store the rental price for a New Release in one place and have all of the New Release movies reference that one place.

Thus, the system needs a `MovieCategory` class that has four instances. The `MovieCategory` would store its rental price and each `Movie` would delegate to its corresponding `MovieCategory` to determine its price. Thus a `MovieCategory` is the Type Object for a `Movie`, and a `Movie` is the Type `Object` for a `Videotape`.

A `MovieCategory` class requires refactoring `Movie`'s behavior.

```
Object ()
  MovieCategory (name rentalPrice)
  Movie (category title rating)
  Videotape (movie isRented renter)
```

In previous examples, `rentalPrice` was an attribute of `Movie` because all videotapes of the same movie had the same price. Now all movies in the same category will have the same price, so `rentalPrice` becomes an attribute of `Movie-Category`. Since `Movie` now has a Type Object, it has an attribute—`category`—to point to its Type Object. Thus, behavior like `rentalPrice` gets delegated in two stages and implemented by the third.

```
Videotape>>rentalPrice
     ^self movie rentalPrice

Movie>>rentalPrice
     ^self category rentalPrice

MovieCategory>>rentalPrice
     ^rentalPrice
```

This example nests the Type Object pattern recursively where each `MovieCategory` has `Movie` instances and each `Movie` has `Videotape` instances. The system still works primarily with `Videotape`s, but they delegate their type behavior to `Movie`s, which in turn delegate their type behavior to `MovieCategory`s. `Videotape` hides from the rest of the system where each set of behavior is implemented. Each piece of information about a tape is stored in just one place, not duplicated by various tapes. The system can easily add new `MovieCategory`s, `Movie`s, and `Videotape`s when necessary by creating new instances.

Dynamic Type Change.   Once *Independence Day* is no longer a New Release, its category can easily be changed to a General Release because its category is a Type Object and not its class.

```
Movie>>changeCategoryTo: aMovieCategory
      self category removeMovie: self.
      self category: aMovieCategory.
      self category addMovie: self.
```

With the Type Object pattern, an `Object` can easily change its `TypeObject` when desired.

Independent Subclassing.   The system could also support videodisks. The commonalities of videotapes and videodisks are captured in the abstract superclass `RentableItem`, where `Videotape` and `Videodisk` are subclasses. Both concrete classes delegate their type behavior to `Movie`, so `Movie` does not need to be subclassed.

```
Object ()
  MovieCategory (name rentalPrice)
  Movie (category title rating)
  RentableItem (movie isRented renter)
    Videotape (isRewound)
    Videodisk (numberOfDisks)
```

Most of `Videotape`'s behavior and implementation is moved to `RentableItem`. Thus `Videodisk` inherits this code for free.

`Movie` may turn out to be a specific example of a more general `Title` class. `Title` might have subclasses like `Movie`, `Documentary`, and `HowTo`. `Movies` have ratings, whereas `Documentary` and `HowTo` videos often do not. `HowTo` videos often come in a series or collection that is rented all at once, whereas `Movies` and `Documentary`s do not. Thus `Title` might also need a Composite subclass such as `HowToSeries` [Gamma+95, p. 163]. `Movie` itself might also have subclasses like `RatedMovie` for those movies that have MPAA ratings and `UnratedMovie` for movies that do not.

```
Object ()
  MovieCategory (name rentalPrice)
  Title (category title)
    Documentary ()
    HowTo ()
    Movie ()
      RatedMovie (rating)
      UnratedMovie ()
    TitleComposite (titles)
      HowToSeries ()
  RentableItem (title isRented renter)
    Videotape (isRewound)
    Videodisk (numberOfDisks)
```

The code above and Figure 4-5 below show the final set of classes in this framework.

`Movie` and `Title` can be subclassed without affecting the way `RentableItem` and `Videotape` are subclassed. This ability to independently subclass `Title` and `RentableItem` would be impossible to achieve if the `Videotape` object had not first been divided into `Movie` and `Videotape` components. Obviously, all of this nesting and subclassing can get complex, but it shows the flexibility the Type Object pattern can achieve—flexibility that would be impossible without the pattern.

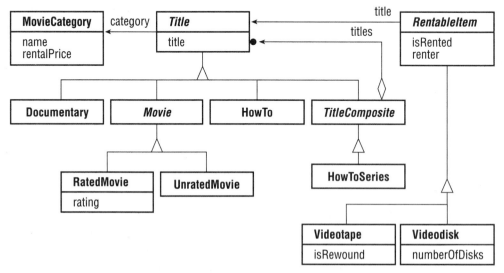

Figure 4-5 *Expanded set of classes in the video store system*

Manufacturing. Consider a factory with many different machines manufacturing many different products. Every order has to specify the kinds of products it requires. Each kind of product has a list of parts and a list of the kinds of machines needed to make it. One approach is to make a class hierarchy for the kinds of machines and the kinds of products. But this means that adding a new kind of machine or product requires programming, since you have to define a new class. Moreover, the main difference between different products is how they are made. You can probably specify a new kind of product just by specifying its parts and the sequence of machine tools that is needed to make it.

It is better to designate objects that represent "kind of product" and "kind of machine." They are both examples of Type Objects. Thus, there will be classes such as `Machine`, `Product`, `MachineType`, and `ProductType`. A `ProductType` has a "manufacturing plan" which knows the `MachineTypes` that make it. But a particular instance of `Product` was made on a particular set of `Machines`. This lets you identify which machine is at fault when a product is defective.

Suppose we want to schedule orders for the factory. When an order comes in, the system will figure out the earliest that it can fill the order. Each order knows what kind of product it is going to produce. For simplicity, assume each order consists of one kind of product. We'll also assume that each kind of product is made on one kind of machine. But that product is probably made up of other products, which will probably require many other machines. Thus, `Product` is an example of the Composite pattern [Gamma+95, p. 163]. For example, consider a hammer that consists of a handle and a head, which are combined at an assembly station. The wooden handle is carved at one machine, and the head is cast at another. `ProductType` and `Order` are also composites, but are not shown. Figure 4-6 shows the classes in the manufacturing system.

There are six main classes:

```
Object ()
  MachineType (name machines)
  Machine (type location age schedule)
  ProductType (manufacturingMachine duration parts)
  Product (type creationDate manufacturedOn parts)
  Order (productType dueDate requestor parts item)
  Factory (machines orders)
```

We will omit all the accessing methods, since they are similar to those in the video store example. Instead, we will focus on how a factory schedules an order.

A factory acts as a Facade, creating the order and then scheduling it [Gamma+95, p. 185].

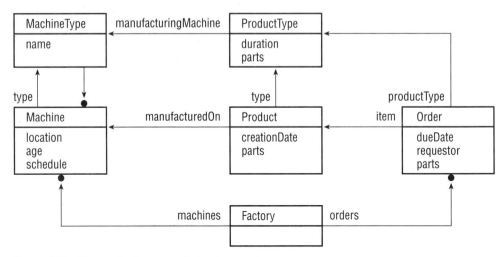

Figure 4-6 *Classes in the manufacturing system*

```
Factory>>orderProduct: aType by: aDate for: aCustomer
        | order |
        order := Order product: aType by: aDate for: aCustomer.
        order scheduleFor: self.
        ^order

Order>>scheduleFor: aFactory
        | partDate earliestDate |
        partDate := dueDate minusDays: productType duration.
        parts := productType parts collect: [:eachType |
              aFactory
                    orderProduct: eachType
                    by: partDate
                    for: order]
        productType
              schedule: self
              between: self datePartsAreReady
              and: dueDate

ProductType>>schedule: anOrder between: startDate and: dueDate
        (startDate plusDays: duration) > dueDate
              ifTrue: [anOrder fixSchedule].
        manufacturingMachine
              schedule: anOrder
              between: startDate
              and: dueDate
```

There are at least two different subclasses of ProductType, one for machines that can only be used to make one product at a time, and one for assembly lines and other machines that can be pipelined and so make several products at a time. A nonpipelined machine type is scheduled by finding a machine with a schedule with enough free time open between the startDate and the dueDate.

```
NonpipelinedMachineType>>schedule: anOrder between:
startDate and: dueDate
    machines do: [:each | | theDate |
        theDate := each schedule
                    slotOfSize: anOrder duration
                    freeBetween: startDate
                    and: dueDate.
            theDate notNil ifTrue:
                    [^each schedule: anOrder at: theDate]].
    anOrder fixSchedule
```

A pipelined machine type is scheduled by finding a machine with an open slot between the startDate and the dueDate.

```
PipelinedMachineType>>schedule: anOrder between:
startDate and: dueDate
    machines do: [:each | | theDate |
        theDate := each schedule
                    slotOfSize: 1
                    freeBetween: startDate
                    and: dueDate.
            theDate notNil ifTrue:
                [^each schedule: anOrder at: theDate]].
    anOrder fixSchedule
```

This design lets you define new ProductTypes without programming. It allows product managers, who usually aren't programmers, to specify a new product type. It will be possible to design a tool that product managers can use to define a new product type by specifying the manufacturing plan, defining the labor and raw materials needed, determining the price of the final product, and so on. As long as a new kind of product can be defined without subclassing Product, it will be possible for product managers to do their work without depending on programmers.

There are constraints between types. For example, the sequence of actual MachineTools that manufactured a Product must match the MachineToolTypes in the manufacturing plan of its ProductType. This is a form of type checking, but it can be done only at run time. It might not be necessary to check that the types match when the sequence of MachineTools is assigned to a Product, because this sequence will be built by iterating over a manufacturing plan to find the available MachineTools. However, scheduling can be complex and errors are likely, so it is probably a good idea to double-check that a Product's sequence of MachineTools matches what its ProductType says it should be.

Known Uses

Coad. Coad's Item Description pattern is the Type Object pattern except that he only emphasized the fact that a Type holds values that all its Instances have in common. He used an aircraft description object as an example [Coad92].

Hay. Hay uses Type Object in many of his data modeling patterns, and discusses it as a modeling principle, but doesn't call it a separate pattern. He uses it to define types for activities, products, assets (a supertype of product), incidents, accounts, tests, documents, and sections of a Material Safety Data Sheet [Hay96].

Fowler. Fowler talks about the separate Object Type and Object worlds, and calls these the knowledge level and the operational level. He uses Type Object to define types for organizational units, accountability relationships, parties involved in relationships, contracts, the terms for contracts, and measurements, as well as many of the things that Hay discussed [Fowler97].

Odell. Odell's Power Type pattern is the Type Object pattern plus the ability for subtypes (implemented as subclasses) to have different behavior. He illustrates it with the example of tree species and tree. A tree species describes a type of tree such as American elm, sugar maple, apricot, or saguaro. A tree represents a particular tree in my front yard or the one in your backyard. Each tree has a corresponding tree species that describes what kind of tree it is [Martin+95].

Sample Types and Samples. The Type Object pattern has been used in the medical field to model medical samples. A sample has four independent properties

- The system it is taken from (e.g., John Doe);
- The subsystem (e.g., blood, urine, sputum);
- The collection procedure (aspiration, drainage, scraping); and
- The preservation additive (heparin, EDTA).

This is easily modeled as a `Sample` object with four attributes: `system`, `subsystem`, `collectionProcedure`, and `additive`. Although the `system` (the person who gave the sample) is different for almost all samples, the triplet (`subsystem`, `collectionProcedure`, and `additive`) is shared by a lot of `Samples`. For example, medical technicians refer to a "blood" sample, meaning a blood/aspiration/EDTA sample. Thus the triplet attributes can be gathered into a single `SampleType` object.

A `SampleType` is responsible for creating new `Sample` objects. There are about 5,000 different triplet combinations possible, but most of them don't make any sense, so the system just provides the most common `SampleTypes`. If another `SampleType` is needed, the users can create a new one by specifying its subsystem, collection procedure, and additive. While the system tracks tens of thousands of `Samples`, it only needs to track about 100 `SampleTypes`. So the `SampleTypes` are `TypeObjects` and the `Samples` are their `Objects` [DeKezel96].

Signals and Exceptions. The Type Object pattern is more common in domain frameworks than vendor frameworks, but one vendor example is the `Signal/Exception` framework in VisualWorks Smalltalk. When Smalltalk code encounters an error, it can raise an `Exception`. The `Exception` records the context of where the error occurred for debugging purposes. Yet the `Exception` itself doesn't know *what* went wrong, just *where*. It delegates the *what* information to a `Signal`. Each `Signal` describes a potential type of problem such as user-interrupt, message-not-understood, and subscript-out-of-bounds. Thus two message-not-understood errors create two separate `Exception` instances that point to the same `Signal` instance. `Signal` is the `TypeClass`, and `Exception` is the `Class` [VW95].

Reflection. Type Object is present in most reflective systems, where a type object is often called a metaobject. The class/instance separation in Smalltalk is an example of the Type Object pattern. Programmers can manipulate classes directly, adding methods, changing the class hierarchy, and creating new classes. By far the most common use of a class is to make instances, but the other uses are part of the culture and often discussed, even if not often used [Kiczales91].

Reflection has a well-deserved reputation for being hard to understand. Type Object pattern shows that it does not have to be difficult, and can be an easy entrance into the more complex world of reflective programming.

Related Patterns

The Type Object pattern is related to several other established patterns.

Type Object vs. Strategy and State. The Type Object pattern is similar to the Strategy and State patterns [Gamma+95, p. 305, 315]. All three patterns break an object into pieces and the "real object" delegates to the new object—either the Type Object, the Strategy, or the State. Strategy and State are usually pure behavior, while a Type Object often holds a lot of shared state. States change frequently, while Type Objects rarely change. State solves the problem of an object needing to change class, whereas Type Object responds to the need for an unlimited number of classes. A Strategy usually has one main responsibility, while a Type Object usually has many responsibilities. So, the patterns are not exactly the same, even though their object diagrams are similar.

Type Object and Reflective Architecture. Any system with a Type Object is well on its way to having a Reflective Architecture [Buschmann+96]. Often a Type Object holds Strategies for its instances. This is a good way to define behavior in a type.

Type Object vs. Bridge. A Type Object implementation can become complex enough that there are Class and Type Class hierarchies. These hierarchies look a lot like the Abstraction and Implementor hierarchies in the Bridge pattern [Gamma+95, p. 151], where Class is the abstraction and Type Class is the implementation. However, clients can collaborate directly with the Type Objects, an interaction that usually doesn't occur with Concrete Implementors.

Type Object vs. Decorator.   An Object can seem to be a Decorator for its Type Object [Gamma+95, p. 175]. An Object and its Type Object have similar interfaces and the Object chooses which messages to forward to its Type Object and which ones to enhance. However, a Decorator does not behave like an instance of its Component.

Type Object vs. Flyweight.   The Type Objects can seem like Flyweights to their Objects [Gamma+95, p. 195]. However, Type Object does not involve a Flyweight Factory that provides access to a Flyweight Pool. Nevertheless, two Objects using the same Type Object might think that they each have their own copy, but instead are sharing the same one. Thus it is important that neither Object change the intrinsic state of the Type Object.

Type Object and Prototype.   Another way to make one object act like the type of another is with the Prototype pattern, when each object keeps track of its prototype and delegates any requests that it does not know how to handle [Gamma+95, p. 117].

ACKNOWLEDGMENTS

We would like to thank our coworkers at KSC and UIUC for their help in developing this pattern, Frank Buschmann and Dirk Riehle for their shepherding help, and everyone at PLoP '96 and EuroPLoP '96 who made suggestions for improving this paper.

REFERENCES

[Buschmann+96] F. Buschmann, R. Meunier, H. Rohnert, P. Sommerlad, and M. Stal. *Pattern-Oriented Software Architecture —A System of Patterns.* New York: Wiley and Sons Ltd., 1996.

[Coad92] P. Coad. "Object-Oriented Patterns." *Communications of the ACM.* 35(9):152–159, September 1992.

[DeKezel96] Raoul De Kezel. E-mail correspondence.

[Fowler97] M. Fowler. *Analysis Patterns: Reusable Object Models.* Reading, MA: Addison-Wesley, 1997.

[Gamma+95] E. Gamma, R. Helm, R. Johnson, and J. Vlissides. *Design Patterns: Elements of Reusable Object-Oriented Software.* Reading, MA: Addison-Wesley (URL: http://www.aw.com/cp/Gamma.html), 1995.

[Hay96] D. Hay. *Data Modeling Patterns.* Dorsett House Publishing, 1996.

[Kiczales91] G. Kiczales, J. des Rivieres, and D. Bobrow. *The Art of the Metaobject Protocol.* Cambridge, MA: The MIT Press, 1991.

[Martin+95] J. Martin and J. Odell. *Object Oriented Methods: A Foundation.* Englewood Cliffs, NJ: Prentice Hall, 1995.

[VW95] VisualWorks Release 2.5, Sunnyvale, CA: ParcPlace-Digitalk, Inc., (URL: http://www.parcplace.com), 1995.

Ralph Johnson can be reached at johnson@cs.uiuc.edu.
Bobby Woolf can be reached at bwoolf@ksccary.com.

Chapter 5

Sponsor-Selector

Eugene Wallingford

Also Known As

Brokered Resources

Intent

The Sponsor-Selector pattern provides a mechanism for selecting the best resource for a task from a set of resources that changes dynamically. It allows a software system to integrate new resources, and new knowledge about resources, at run time in a way that is transparent to users of the resources. This pattern is based on the idea of separating three kinds of responsibilities: knowing when a resource is useful, selecting among resources, and using a resource.

Example

Consider a software system engaged in the task of medical diagnosis. The system has at its disposal a set of subsystems capable of performing particular diagnostic subtasks. The task/subtask structure may look something like Figure 5-1.

At each point during a diagnostic session, the system faces the question: Which subtask should be performed next? This is the question of problem-solving control. Early systems of this kind performed their subtasks sequentially or in some

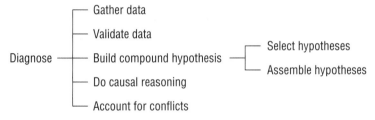

Figure 5-1 *A task structure for diagnosis*

other prescribed order, but such hard-coded control produced unsatisfactory results. Often, the data provided by previous actions indicated the need to break out of the prescribed sequence—say to gather more specific data while doing causal reasoning about a hypothesis—in order to arrive at the best diagnosis in a timely manner.

Ideally, one would think of the diagnostic system as having an agent responsible for performing each task in this hierarchy. At run time, the system would like to select the most appropriate subtask agent to invoke, based on the context information available at that point. This involves determining which of the sub-systems is likely to make the most progress toward the goal of arriving at a useful diagnosis.

Situations like this arise in many domains: An operating system may want to select the best process-scheduling algorithm based on the current state of the system. A central Web server may want to balance access load across a family of Web servers based on their current performance capabilities. A communication network may want to select the best route for a message based on the current state of the network and its components. In all of these examples, a system needs the ability to select a resource dynamically from a set of resources whose attributes may be changing at run time.

Context

You are building a system in which the set of resources used to perform some task, or the system's knowledge about those resources, can change, either statically or dynamically.

Problem

Sometimes a class has a number of other classes (resources) with which it can collaborate, but it cannot know until run time which of these resources it will need in a specific situation. Furthermore, the set of potential collaborators may change over time, either statically by programmer modification or dynamically during system execution. At run time, the class would like to select the best collaborator based on the context information available at that point.

However, designing a control mechanism for such selection introduces new difficulties. One solution, to encode a resource selection mechanism directly into the system, leads to two kinds of difficulties. If the programmer adds a new resource to the system, the system's control knowledge must be modified to make it accessible. And if a new resource is added to the system dynamically at run time—say, through some form of machine learning—the system is unable to use the resource because its control knowledge makes no reference to the new resource.

A second solution is to separate the selection mechanism into a distinct class that specializes in control decision-making, using the Blackboard pattern [Buschmann+96]. This solution makes the system immune to modification in the face of new resources, but still confounds knowledge about resource applicability with knowledge about resource preference, making the new "selection" class prone to the same difficulties when new resources are added to the system.

Any solution to the problem should bring the following forces into equilibrium.

- The system should be able to access resources whenever appropriate.
- It should be possible to add, change, or remove resources, either statically or dynamically, without making extensive modifications to the system.
- The utility of some resources cannot or should not be determined until run time.

Solution

Introduce sponsor and selector components to achieve a higher degree of decoupling between the system and the resources it uses. Each resource has a sponsor whose responsibility is to recommend when the resource can be used. The selector takes these recommendations as input and decides which resource should be used.

In the course of execution, whenever the system needs a resource to proceed, it sends a request to the selector in charge of the corresponding resource set. The selector then broadcasts the request to all of the sponsors in the set. Each sponsor evaluates the applicability of its resource and sends a rating back as its answer. The selector then uses these ratings, along with other preference knowledge and context information, to select the best resource for the client in the current context.

A new resource can be added to the system either statically or dynamically by building a sponsor for it and registering the new sponsor with the appropriate selector. In many situations, the creator of the resource will also need to register specific preferences that relate to the new resource with the selector.

The key to the Sponsor-Selector pattern is the separation of three fundamentally different responsibilities: recommending a resource, selecting among resources, and using a resource.

Structure

The Sponsor-Selector pattern comprises three kinds of components: a selector, a set of sponsors, and a set of resources. Together these components provide a set of services to a client as shown in Figure 5-2.

A `resource` is any one of a set of objects that has specific functionality in some larger context.

Each `sponsor` contains knowledge of when its `resource` is appropriate for use. This knowledge makes reference only to local features of the environments in which the `resource` is useful. If possible, a `sponsor` should make no reference to any `resource` other than its own.

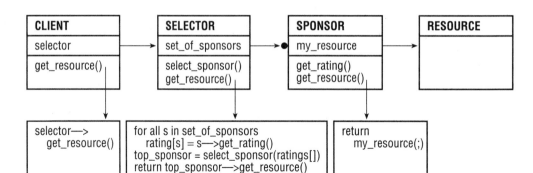

Figure 5-2 *The structure of the Sponsor-Selector pattern*

The selector embodies knowledge of which resource to prefer in particular kinds of situations. This knowledge can express preferences among groups of resources and can make reference to global features of the context, such as issues of run-time efficiency and correctness. The selector sends requests to the set of sponsors and receives a set of ratings in return. It then uses these ratings to select a resource for use in the current context.

The client is a system that uses the resources to perform some part of its task. It sends requests to the selector when it needs a resource and invokes the resource that is returned by the selector.

In our example, the client is the diagnostic system (see Figure 5-3). The resources are the subsystems that perform parts of the diagnostic system's task, for example, the hypothesis builder and the causal reasoner. Each subsystem has an associated sponsor that indicates whether or not the diagnostic system should invoke the subsystem in a given situation. The task selector uses its knowledge to select the subsystem to invoke next, based on the ratings returned by the sponsors and information about the diagnostic system's current context.

Dynamics

A Sponsor-Selector system operates in the manner shown in Figure 5-4. The client reaches a point in its activity at which it needs a resource in order to proceed, so it asks the selector for a resource. The selector broadcasts a request to all sponsors, each of which rates its resource and returns a rating for the resource. The selector uses these ratings to select the most appropriate resource and then asks the corresponding sponsor for its resource. When the selector returns this resource to the client, the client uses the selected resource in the desired way.

In our example, the diagnostic system completes some activity and must begin working on a new subtask. It asks the task selector to select the next subtask to work on. The task selector broadcasts a request to all subtask sponsors, which

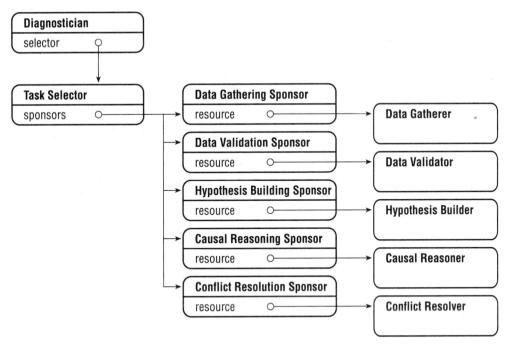

Figure 5-3 *The Sponsor-Selector pattern applied to the diagnostic example*

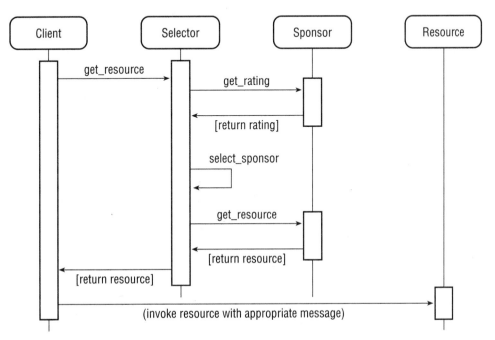

Figure 5-4 *Dynamic behavior of the Sponsor-Selector pattern*

rate their subtasks for applicability in the current context. The task `selector` then uses these ratings to select the next subtask and asks the corresponding `sponsor` for its `resource`. The `selector` returns this subtask to the diagnostic system, which begins working on the subtask.

Implementation

Several common patterns can be used to implement the components of the Sponsor-Selector pattern. `sponsors` may be implemented using the Proxy pattern [Buschmann+96], since they stand in the place of `resources` during the selection process. The `selector` may be implemented using the Broker pattern [Buschmann+96], which coordinates communication between the `client` and its decoupled `resources`. Finally, if the resources themselves are methods to be invoked, they can be implemented using the Strategy pattern [Gamma+95].

Regardless of how the components of the pattern are built, three main implementation decisions must be made.

- *How does each **sponsor** rate the appropriateness of its **resource?*** Each sponsor should be coded with only local considerations in mind: Is my `resource` appropriate in the current context? It should not make reference to any other `resources` or any other global questions (such as client-specific timing issues), if at all possible. Otherwise, modifiability of the structure is impaired. The Memento pattern can be used to transport relevant state information from the `client` to the sponsors [Gamma+95].

- *What constitutes a rating?* In some domains, `sponsors` may be able to rate their resources quantitatively on a continuous scale, such as a real number between 0 and 1, which the `selector` then combines using a continuous function. However, experience in many domains has shown that qualitative ratings of applicability are often more appropriate. One common approach is to have sponsors rate their `resources` on a scale from "highly applicable" through "neutral" to "highly inapplicable." Using qualitative ratings makes it easier to build `selectors` that more nearly correspond to the judgments made by human experts in the domain.

- *How does the `selector` combine the ratings to select a particular **resource?*** The `selector` ordinarily uses the ratings returned by its sponsors as its primary criterion for selection. A `selector` may just select the highest-rated resource, breaking ties using either a default preference on `resources` or a random choice from among the `resources` with the highest ratings. But it may also need to apply more global knowledge that goes beyond the scope of any single `sponsor` (for example, comparisons among specific `resources`). In such cases, it may have to use state information from the `client` that is outside the scope of the individual `sponsor`'s decision.

Four other implementation issues should be considered.

- *Does the* `selector` *directly invoke the selected* `resource` *or return the* `resource` *to the* `client`? Direct invocation by the `selector` makes more sense when the resources are methods to be invoked, since the client may be willing to pass control to the selected method. One advantage of direct invocation is that `resources` no longer need to share a common interface; only the `resource`'s sponsor needs to know the `resource`'s interface. In this case, the `sponsors` serve as Adaptors between the `client` and the `resources` [Gamma+95]. Returning the `resource` to the `client` is more appropriate when the `resource` plays both a static role (as data store) and a dynamic role (as behavior) for the `client`, since the `client` may then need more prolonged interaction—and thus a common interface—with the `resource`.
- *Can the sponsor objects be assimilated directly into the resources?* If sponsorship decisions are trivial, the structure of Sponsor-Selector can be simplified by adding a rating behavior to the `resource` objects. This can be useful when the rating behavior can be implemented in a superclass and inherited by all of the `resource` classes. Such an implementation resembles that of the Blackboard pattern, where the `selector` plays the role of the control object and the `resource` plays the role of the knowledge source [Buschmann+96].
- *How costly is the rating process?* As the cost of rating resources becomes higher, the `client` will pay a run-time penalty for its flexibility. The implementor of a Sponsor-Selector pattern must be sensitive to potential performance issues. One way to use Sponsor-Selector in the face of high rating costs is to use the parallel resource selection variant described below.
- *Must* `resources` *be able to share knowledge?* One of the costs that can be associated with a high degree of modularity is a difficulty in sharing domain knowledge among the `resources`, which can lead to replicated implementations. One way to address this problem is to use Singletons and Flyweights to encode knowledge that must be shared [Gamma+95].

Example Resolved

The use of the Sponsor-Selector pattern resolves the forces at play in our diagnostic system example. By creating `sponsors` for each subtask and encoding the selection mechanism in the task `selector`, changes to the task structure of the system are localized.

Suppose that we wished to add a new subtask, say hypothesis identification, to the system. This subtask might involve selecting a new hypothesis to consider while building the system's diagnosis. A programmer could make this addition to the system by

- Encoding the subtask as a new `resource`;
- Encoding local knowledge of when to identify a new hypothesis or not in a `sponsor` for the `resource`; and
- Registering the new `sponsor` with the task `selector`.

No other changes to the `selector` or to the `client` would be necessary.

However, since all change is localized around the new subtask, the addition could also be done both by the system itself at runtime. During execution, the system could use some form of machine learning to discover and encode new diagnostic knowledge. When a new subtask is discovered, all information that is needed to add the resource to the system (what it is and when it is useful) is created as a part of the learning process. The final step of registering the new sponsor with the `selector` involves little or no change to the structure of the `selector` itself.

Variants

Many of the consequences that follow from using Strategy also follow from using Sponsor-Selector. Sponsor-Selector has the following benefits and drawbacks.

- *Parallel resource selection.* Each `sponsor` is an independent agent charged with the rating of an individual resource's applicability and utility. As such, they can be executed in parallel on separate processors, or in the background on the same processor, while other processes are active. The `selector` can then be implemented as an "anytime algorithm," processing `sponsor` ratings as they become available and providing a `resource` selection to the client on demand.
- *Hierarchies of Sponsor-Selector modules.* Suppose that one `resource` that is available to the client is itself essentially a set of `resources`. For example, the data validation subtask in our diagnostic system may have several different methods by which it can perform its task. In such a situation, multiple Sponsor-Selector patterns can be composed to form a hierarchy.

A hierarchy of Sponsor-Selector patterns (see Figure 5-5) provides a means for organizing complex `resource` sets, such as the many tasks, subtasks, and methods of a large system, in a way that promotes system modifiability in the face of change.

Known Uses

The first documented use of Sponsor-Selector was in DSPL, which used the pattern in a mechanism for selecting design plans in a system that designed air cylinders for aircraft [Brown+86]. The mechanism was incorporated into a shell for building knowledge-based systems that do "routine design," in which much or all of the design task is accomplished through the use of preenumerated design and redesign plans.

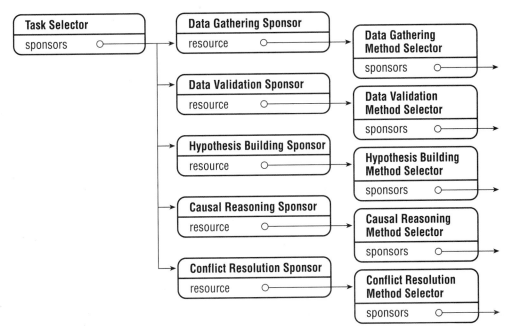

Figure 5-5 *A hierarchy of Sponsor-Selector modules*

TIPS generalizes Sponsor-Selector into a mechanism for making dynamic control decisions about subtasks. Punch has applied TIPS in the construction of a medical diagnostic expert system [Punch+93].

FAULTY-II goes further by using a Sponsor-Selector pattern as the basis of an application framework for dynamically selecting a method for performing each subtask in explicitly represented task structures [Benjamins+93].

IPCA uses Sponsor-Selector as the basis for control plan selection and execution in a system that controls microwave composite material processing in a soft real-time environment [Decker+94].

Goel and his colleagues have used Sponsor-Selector for dynamic method selection in navigational planning for mobile robots [Goel+94]. Experiments in this domain confirm that Sponsor-Selector is a good design solution in situations where the client application is learning new control knowledge. As the planner acquires domain knowledge, Sponsor-Selector enables the agent to incorporate the new knowledge dynamically into its problem solving and to select the method that is indicated by that knowledge. The planner has been embodied in a physical robot that demonstrates the effectiveness of its plans.

Landauer and Bellman have proposed a new technique for developing, integrating, and managing complex software systems based on an idea very similar to that of the Sponsor-Selector pattern [Landauer+95]. Their technique uses two types of component, wrappings and managers. Wrappings are qualitative information about a system component: how to use the component, when and why to use it, and in what combinations it can be used. Managers are algorithms that select and combine components based on the information in their wrappings. This technique extends Sponsor-Selector to apply to all components of a system at all times.

Consequences

Many of the consequences that follow from using Strategy [Gamma+96] also follow from using Sponsor-Selector. Sponsor-Selector offers the following benefits.

- *High degree of modularity.* Resources can be added, modified, or reimplemented with no effect on other resources or on client code. Only the resource's sponsor must be modified. In the case of a new resource, the selector is modified only in that the new sponsor must be registered with it.
- *Decision control is made explicit and independent from other components of the system.* Sponsor-Selector further improves on the Strategy pattern's separation of method and client by further decoupling selection of the ConcreteStrategy from the Context. Strategy leaves the client with the job of selecting the appropriate ConcreteStrategy to instantiate. This can clutter the client with extra data examination code, knowledge that is not part of the client's primary task (thus blurring the explicitness of its representation), and unwieldy control statements.

Sponsor-Selector also imposes some drawbacks.

- *Potentially tight coupling between the Client and the Selector.* Pulling all of the selection knowledge out of the client may be unwise. Selection knowledge may be so context-specific as to be (1) not reusable as a separate object and/or (2) easier to express directly in the client, since large amounts of information may need to be passed from client to selector.
- *Potentially tight coupling between the Selector and the Sponsors.* The Sponsor-Selector pattern may be inappropriate if sponsors need to take into account knowledge about the relative quality of their methods' solutions in a particular context or global constraints to be placed on the resource. For instance, if there are global bounds placed on the time of computation of the resource, it may be difficult to build a local sponsor capable of taking such knowledge into account. One way to address these potential couplings is to use the Observer pattern as a mechanism for allowing selectors and sponsors to view external context information without encoding context into these components.
- *Cost of indirection in hard real-time environments.* Decker [Decker+94] has argued that deadlines associated with hard real-time processing can pose problems for a Sponsor-Selector architecture. In cases where the costs of indirection and rating exceed the resources available to a system, Sponsor-Selector may be an inappropriate pattern.

See Also

As described above, Sponsor-Selector may incorporate many of the features of the Broker, Proxy [Buschmann+96], and Strategy [Gamma+95] patterns. Mementos, Observers, Singletons, and Flyweights [Gamma+95] may be used to address some of the issues that arise when implementing Sponsor-Selector.

Sponsor-Selector is similar to the Blackboard pattern in its decoupling of control from the resources that comprise a system [Buschmann+96]. But Sponsor-Selector also adds an extra degree of flexibility by further decoupling knowledge of when a knowledge source is useful (the sponsor) from the knowledge source itself (resource). This flexibility can be realized by adding an extra layer to the system's architecture.

Client-Dispatcher-Server also resembles Sponsor-Selector in its decoupling of the client from the resources that serve it [Buschmann+96]. But Sponsor-Selector further prescribes that knowledge of when a knowledge source is useful be decoupled from the knowledge of which resource to use at any point in time. The Client-Dispatcher-Server pattern makes no commitment in this respect. Both Sponsor-Selector and Client-Dispatcher-Server can be viewed as architectural forms of implicit invocation, an idea that can be applied even at the level of general-purpose programming languages [Notkin+93].

When taken to the level of wrappings [Landauer+95], Sponsor-Selector can be viewed as a mechanism for implementing the Reflection pattern [Buschmann+96]. Sponsor-Selector provides a means by which a system can reflect about its own subtasks and methods and select resources when they are most useful for achieving the system's goals. Furthermore, Sponsor-Selector allows the system to fully integrate new resources at run time while retaining its ability to reflect about them.

ACKNOWLEDGMENTS

An earlier version of this pattern appeared at PLoP '96. Shepherd Chris Landauer first suggested the relationship between Sponsor-Selector and the ideas of wrapping and implicit invocation. I thank the members of PLoP '96 Working Group 4 for their valuable criticisms and suggestions for improvement. Frank Buschmann, Eric Hughes, and Peter Sommerlad were especially helpful, providing thorough written comments on my paper. Finally, I thank Bobby Woolf, whose thoughtful comments helped me to think about how readers outside the domain of knowledge-based systems might interpret my pattern.

REFERENCES

[Benjamins+93] R. Benjamins. "Problem Solving Methods for Diagnosis." Ph.D. Thesis, University of Amsterdam, 1993.

[Brown+86] D. Brown and B. Chandrasekaran. "Knowledge and Control for a Mechanical Design Expert System." *IEEE Computer*, 19:92–101, July 1986.

[Buschmann+96] F. Buschmann, R. Meunier, H. Rohnert, P. Sommerlad, and M. Stal. *Pattern-Oriented Software Architecture.* New York: John Wiley and Sons, 1996.

[Decker+94] D. Decker, B. Punch, J. McDowell, and J. Sticklen. "An Intelligent Control Architecture for the Microwave Fabrication of Composite Materials Based on the Generic Task Approach to Knowledge-Based Systems." In Proceedings of the AAAI Fall Symposium on Intelligent Systems, New Orleans, November 1994.

[Gamma+95] E. Gamma, R. Helm, R. Johnson, and J. Vlissides. *Design Patterns: Elements of Reusable Object-Oriented Software.* Reading, MA: Addison-Wesley, 1995.

[Goel+94] A. Goel, K. Ali, M. Donnellan, A. Gomez, and T. Callantine. "Multistrategy Adaptive Navigational Path Planning." *IEEE Expert*, 9(6):57–65, December 1994.

[Landauer+95] C. Landauer, and K. Bellman. "Knowledge-Based Integration Infrastructure for Complex Systems." *TAC Technical Report*, 1995.

[Notkin+93] D. Notkin, D. Garlan, W. G. Griswold, and K. Sullivan. "Adding Implicit Invocation to Languages: Three Approaches." In Proceedings of the Object Technologies for Advanced Software Conference, Springer-Verlag, Berlin, 1993.

[Punch+93] B. Punch, and B. Chandrasekaran. "An Investigation of the Roles of Problem-Solving Methods in Diagnosis." In J. M. David, J. P. Krivine, and R. Simmons (eds.), *Second Generation Expert Systems.* Berlin: Springer Verlag, 1993, pp. 673–688.

Eugene Wallingford can be reached at wallingf@cs.uni.edu.

Chapter 6

Extension Object

Erich Gamma

Intent

Anticipate extensions to an object's interface. Extension Object lets you add interfaces to a class, and it lets clients choose and access the interfaces they need.

Also Known As

Facet

Motivation

For some objects it is difficult to foresee how clients will want to use it. Different clients can have different needs, and it can be difficult to meet those needs through a single interface. Combining all the operations and states that different clients need into a single object can result in a bloated interface. Such interfaces are difficult to maintain and understand, since a change can affect the other clients that depend on the interface.

Consider a framework for compound documents. A compound document is made up of components like text, graphics, spreadsheets, or movies. Therefore, the fundamental abstraction of a compound document is the component. To assemble components in various interesting ways, there is a need for a common interface. Let's assume that this interface is defined by a Component abstract class. This interface provides operations to manage and arrange components in a document.

Now think about a spelling checker for a compound document. How can a spelling checker work with an open-ended set of components? We could add operations to Component that allow it to enumerate the words of a component. Textless components like images would implement these operations with do-nothing behavior. However, having a word enumeration interface in Component

contributes to a bloated interface. Moreover, adding these operations to Component requires having access to its source code—which might not be available.

It would be better if new or unforeseen interfaces could be added separately to
just those components that require them. Ideally, each component that can be
spell-checked would furnish its own interface for the spelling checker. In short,
we want to add new interfaces to Component without changing its declaration.

To solve this problem, we define the spelling checking interface in a separate
abstract class TextAccessor. We don't want to incorporate it into the Component
class directly. Now we can add spelling-checking support to a class TextComponent in one of two ways: (1) by inheriting from Component *and* from TextAccessor and (2) by implementing the spelling-checker interface in a separate object.

In the first approach, the spelling checker must first verify that a given component is in fact a TextAccessor before it attempts to spell-check its text. Since multiple inheritance is visible in the interface, adding an interface requires changing a
class declaration so that it inherits from an additional class. The second approach
avoids this drawback through object composition. The object defining the spelling-
checking interface is called an *extension object* of a component. Clients that want to
operate on a component using this interface ask the component for the extension
object. The component defines an operation GetExtension for that purpose. The
diagram in Figure 6-1 shows the involved classes and their relationships.

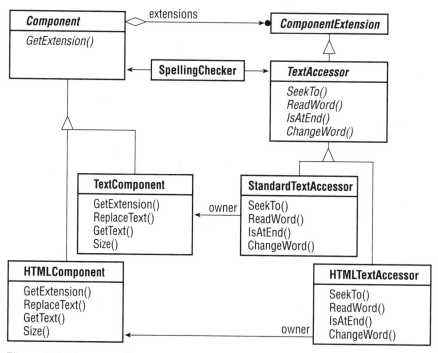

Figure 6-1 *Compound-component extension relationship*

ComponentExtension is the common base class for extensions in this example. Its interface is minimal; it exists merely to define the return type for GetExtension. Subclasses extend it with extension-specific operations. For example, the ComponentExtension subclass TextAccessor defines the interface for accessing text. It includes operations like SeekTo, ReadWord, IsAtEnd for enumerating the words and ChangeWord to correct a misspelled word. TextAccessor is an abstract class used to enable different implementations of this interface for different kinds of components. An HTMLTextComponent, for example, can return a corresponding HTMLTextAccessor that takes care of filtering HTML tags.

Clients need a way to find out whether a component supports a specific extension they are interested in. To enable an open-ended set of extensions, we declare GetExtension so that clients can specify one of arbitrarily many extensions. For the purpose of this example, let's assume that we name an extension with a simple string. To avoid conflicts, there should be a registry for such extensions. The spelling checker can query whether a component provides a certain interface by calling GetExtension(extensionName). If the component provides an extension with the given name, it returns the extension object; otherwise, it returns nil.

TextComponent overrides GetExtension to return a TextAccessor object when it is asked for an extension with the name "TextAccessor." Based on this a spelling checker for a compound document is implemented as follows.

1. Traverse the components in the document.
2. Ask each component for its TextAccessor extension.
3. If a component returns a TextAccessor extension object, then use it to spell check the component (downcasting it to a TextAccessor if necessary); otherwise, skip the component.

Applicability

Use the Extension Object pattern when

- You want to add new or unforeseen interfaces to existing classes and you don't want to impact clients that don't need this new interface. Extension Object lets you keep related operations together by defining them in a separate class.
- Clients perceive different roles for the same abstraction, and the number of such roles is open-ended.
- A class should be extensible without being subclassed directly.

Structure

See Figure 6-2.

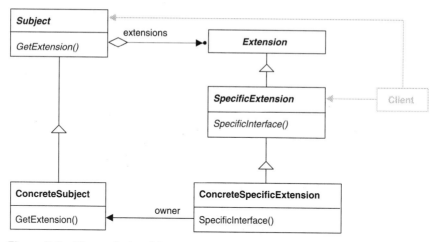

Figure 6-2 *Class relationship*

Participants

- **Subject (Component):**
  - declares an operation to return a particular extension given a specification. A simple example of a specification is a string that identifies an extension.
  - defines how a specification is mapped to an extension.

- **Extension (ComponentExtension):**
  - the base class for all extensions of a subject.

- **ConcreteSubject (StandardTextComponent, HTMLTextComponent):**
  - implements GetExtension to return a corresponding extension object.

- **SpecificExtension (TextAccessor):**
  - declares the interface for a specific extension.

- **ConcreteSpecificExtension (StandardTextAccessor, HTMLTextAccessor):**
  - implements an extension for a particular ConcreteSubject.
  - stores implementation- and extension-specific state.
  - knows its owning subject.

Collaborations

1. A client asks a Subject for an extension.
2. When the extension exists, the ConcreteSubject returns a corresponding extension object. The client subsequently uses the extension object to access additional functionality.

3. If the `Subject` doesn't support an extension, it returns `nil` to signal that it doesn't support it.

Consequences

The Extension Object pattern has several advantages.

- *It facilitates adding interfaces.* New extensions can be added to `Subject` without changes to the `Subject` interface. Multiple inheritance offers an alternative in this regard. With multiple inheritance, you add an additional interface by inheriting from a mix-in class. The diagram in Figure 6-3 illustrates this for the spelling-checker example.

    `TextAccessor` becomes a mix-in class for `TextComponent`. A client uses run-time type identification to discover whether an object supports a specific mix-in interface. In C++ you'd use `dynamic_cast`; in Java the `instanceof` operator. For example, to access the `TextAccessor` extension in Java, we write

```
Component component;

if (component instanceof TextAccessor) {
    checkSpelling((TextAccessor) component);
}
```

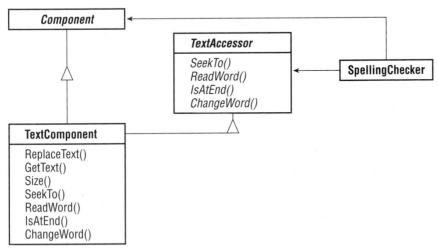

Figure 6-3 *TextAccessor of a mix-in class*

Multiple inheritance can have some drawbacks. In some situations it can lead to a combinatorial explosion of classes. Each combination of mix-ins produces a new class. In addition, in the multiple inheritance case, it is not possible to add an extension to Subject without having to change its interface. Extension Object avoids these drawbacks. Clients can attach one or more extensions at run time.

- *It can prevent bloated interfaces.* An abstraction needn't get polluted with client-specific operations. As an alternative, you could define a minimal base class interface that is extended in subclasses. However, this can result in a class hierarchy that is difficult to manage. It is often difficult to combine different extensions that were implemented in different subclasses.
- *Clients can perceive an abstraction differently.* When an abstraction is used across subsystems it often plays different roles, each having its own state and behavior. Extension Object lets you model a role with an extension object. By keeping the roles separate, one subsystem doesn't have to know the roles used in other subsystems.

The pattern has two main disadvantages.

- *Clients become more complex.* An interface using Extension Object is more complicated to use than a conventional interface. Clients have to ask for the extension explicitly and check whether it is supported. This introduces additional tests and control paths in your program.
- *The Subject interface doesn't express all of its behavior.* Extension Object shifts part of the Subject's interface to SpecificExtension classes. This makes it difficult to understand the Subject's behavior from its interface alone.

Implementation

Here are some issues to keep in mind when implementing Extension Object.

- *Static vs. Dynamic extension objects.* A key issue is how the extensions are created and managed. A ConcreteSubject could simply store its extensions in instance variables. This assumes that the ConcreteSubject knows its extensions statically; we call these static extensions. The disadvantage is that you can't attach new extensions without modifying ConcreteSubject. This implementation adds very little overhead to the Subject, only a GetExtension accessor operation is required.

  Figure 6-4 illustrates a variation that lets clients attach extensions without having to modify ConcreteSubject. The Subject maintains a dictionary that maps extension names to its extension objects. Clients can register an extension in Subject by calling AddExtension(name, extension). Using a dictionary enables clients to add new extensions and doesn't require that the ConcreteSubject knows all its extensions beforehand. A Subject adopts different extensions as needed. Since clients can add new extensions, we call them dynamic extensions.

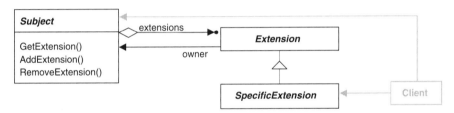

Figure 6-4 *Dynamic extension objects*

- *Specifying extensions.*   Clients have to specify extensions uniquely. A simple specification is to name an extension with a string. An alternative to enforce uniqueness in C++ is to use RTTI and the `typeid` operator. With this kind of specification, `GetExtension` takes a `type_info` as a parameter. To ask for a particular extension, the client passes the `type_info` of the `SpecificExtension` class. The `typeid` operator is used to retrieve a corresponding `type_info`. The sample code describes this in more detail.

  The corresponding solution in Java uses `Class` objects and so-called class literal expressions, for example, `TextAccessor.class`. A class literal expression evaluates the corresponding object of type .

- *Demand loading of extensions.*   Subject defines a clear access point to an extension. As a consequence, it is possible to dynamically load the implementation of an extension when it is needed. The same is true for loading persistent state associated with an extension. It can be activated on demand once a client requests it.

- *Defining SpecificExtensions interfaces.*   In C++, all members of `SpecificExtension` are declared pure virtual. In Java, a `SpecificExtension` is an `interface`.

- *Freeing Extensions.*   In nongarbage collected environments, you must decide who is responsible for reclaiming extension objects. Because the `Subject` hands out a reference to an extension object, it cannot in general control its lifetime. One solution is to use reference counting so that a `Subject` is only deleted when there are no more references to any of its extensions. Counted Pointer [Buschmann+96] is an idiom that can be applied to hide the reference counting from clients.

- *Extending classes in Smalltalk.*   Smalltalk makes it easy to add additional methods to a class. The ENVY/Developer environment simplifies the management of such extensions. ENVY provides the notion of an application that lets a developer manage the added methods of existing classes. However, a class extension can define only new methods, not new state. To associate state with an extension, it can still be useful to use Extension Object.

Sample Code

Here is a C++ implementation of the Motivation example, beginning with the Component class.

```
class Component {
public:
    //...

    virtual Extension* GetExtension(const type_info& type);
};
```

GetExtension takes an extension's typeid as a parameter. In this case, Component::GetExtension doesn't support any extensions by default, so it returns 0.

```
Extension* Component::GetExtension(const type_info&) {
    return 0;
}
```

TextAccessor is defined as a class with pure virtual member functions only.

```
class TextAccessor: public Extension {
public:
    virtual void SeekTo(long position) = 0;
    virtual void ReadWord(char* buffer) = 0;
    virtual bool IsAtEnd() = 0;
    virtual void ChangeWord(const char*) = 0;
};
```

TextComponent implements a StandardTextAccessor that inherits from TextAccessor, and it overrides GetExtension to make it accessible to clients. In this implementation, a new extension object is allocated and returned to the client; the client is responsible for deleting it.

```
class TextComponent: public Component {
public:
    //...
    virtual Extension* GetExtension(const type_info& type);
};
```

Note that TextComponent::GetExtension supports only the TextAccessor extension. Requests for unsupported extensions are passed on to the GetExtension operation of the base class.

```
Extension*
TextComponent::GetExtension(const type_info& type) {
    if (typeid(TextAccessor) == type) {
        return new StandardTextAccessor(this);
    }
    return Component::GetExtension(type);
}
```

Finally, here is how a spelling checker would access the component's `Text-Accessor`.

```
TextComponent* comp;

Extension* extension = comp->GetExtension(typeid(TextAccessor));
if (extension) {
    TextAccessor* accessor = dynamic_cast<TextAccessor*>(extension);
    if (accessor) {
        // use the TextAccessor
    }
}
```

Before the extension can be used, it has to be narrowed to be more specific by using the `dynamic_cast` operator.

Known Uses

- *ODExtension in OpenDoc.* In OpenDoc [Feiler+96], any object can be extended with extensions. The common base class `ODObject` provides the interface for accessing extensions. Extensions descend from the class `ODExtension` and `ODObject` provides a `HasExtension` operation. Extensions are reference counted; clients must call `AcquireExtension` and `ReleaseExtension` to maintain the reference count.
- *QueryInterface in COM.* Interfaces in the Component Object Model (COM) [Brockschmidt93] behave as extensions. Clients use a `QueryInterface` operation to determine whether an object supports a given COM interface. When the client asks for a COM interface, it either receives an error and a `NULL` pointer or a valid pointer to access the interface. `QueryInterface` is part of the `IUnknown` interface, which defines the operations that all COM objects support.
- *View Attributes in CommonPoint.* The user interface framework of Taligent's CommonPoint [Cotter+95] defines a class `TView` that manages a visible portion of the screen. `TView` uses `Attribute` objects to let programmers add interfaces and behavior without subclassing. An `Attribute` can be attached to a view and a client can ask a view for a specific `Attribute`. To add behavior to a view, a client defines an `Attribute` subclass and registers an instance thereof with a view. `TView` supports dynamic extension objects, which it implements using a dictionary.

Related Patterns

Like the Visitor and Decorator patterns, Extension Object addresses the problem of extending class functionality.

Visitor[Gamma+95] centralizes behavior and enables the programmer to add new behavior to a class hierarchy without having to change it. Visitor has similar benefits as Extension Object. In contrast to Visitor, Extension Object doesn't require a stable class hierarchy and doesn't introduce a dependency cycle.

Decorator [Gamma+95] is another pattern to extend the behavior of an object. For the client, the use of decorated objects is more transparent than extension objects. But transparency is compromised when clients of the (decorated) component rely on object identity in any way. That's because the decorator replaces the component and hence changes its identity. Decorators work best in situations when existing operations should be augmented or filtered.

Adaptor [Gamma+95] lets you adapt an existing interface to work like another. Extension Object provides support to add interfaces, sometimes dynamically.

ACKNOWLEDGMENTS

This pattern appeared initially in a column that I authored together with Richard Helm [Gamma+95b]. I would like to thank Michael Stal for providing the insights related to OLE 2 and COM, my shepherd Dirk Riehle, John Vlissides for his extensive help in revising this chapter, and all PLoP '96 writer's workshop attendees who made suggestions for improving the description of this pattern.

REFERENCES

[Buschmann+96] F. Buschmann, R. Meunier, H. Rohnert, P. Sommerlad, and M. Stal. *Pattern-Oriented Software Architecture: A System of Patterns*. New York: John Wiley & Sons, 1996.

[Brockschmidt+93] K. Brockschmidt. *Inside OLE 2*. Redmond, WA: Microsoft Press, 1996.

[Cotter+95] S. Cotter and M. Potel. *Inside Taligent Technology*. Reading, MA: Addison-Wesley, 1995.

[Feiler+96] J. Feiler and A. Meadow. *Essential OpenDoc*. Reading, MA: Addison-Wesley Developers Press, 1996.

[Gamma+95] E. Gamma, R. Helm, R. Johnson, and J. Vlissides. *Design Patterns: Elements* of *Reusable Object-Oriented Software*. Reading, MA: Addison-Wesley, 1995.

[Gamma+95b] E. Gamma and R. Helm. "Designing Objects for Extension." In *Dr. Dobbs Sourcebook* #236, pp. 56–59, May/June 1995.

Erich Gamma can be reached at erich_gamma@oti.com.

PART 2

Variations on Design Patterns

At OOPSLA '94, the seminal work on patterns, the Gang of Four book (GoF), was presented. Although the idea of patterns was no longer novel, the GoF book presented the first catalog of well-described design patterns. Since then, the GoF patterns have spread all over the world, and many software developers are now familiar with them. In more and more systems, the GoF patterns are being explicitly applied.

Over the past three years, people have learned how to use the GoF patterns and discovered the book is not a complete catalog for solving all software design problems. There are issues that the GoF book either does not describe or that it touches just briefly. Because of this, it has become common for people to publish variations of GoF patterns. In *Programming Languages of Program Design 2* [PLoPD2], we see the first representative of this category: Hans Rohnert's "The Proxy Design Pattern Revisited," a precursor to the final pattern description found in Buschmann et al. [Buschmann+96]. In this year's PLoPD volume, we have a whole part devoted to variations on GoF design patterns.

Chapter 7: Acyclic Visitor, by Robert C. Martin. In this chapter, the author presents a pattern that has some of the same effects as the GoF Visitor pattern. Acyclic Visitor allows you to add new functions to an existing class hierarchy. It avoids introducing the dependency cycles that are inherent to the GoF version. The pattern requires runtime type information facilities to be present in the programming language you use.

Chapter 8: Default and Extrinsic Visitor, by Martin E. Nordberg III. This chapter presents two variants of the original GoF Visitor. Default Visitor provides a class with default implementations for all "visit" methods. From this class, you derive the concrete visitor classes you need in the application under construction. They inherit the default implementations and can override them, if necessary. Extrinsic Visitor specifies how to implement the double dispatch of a Visitor structure with help from runtime type information facilities. This allows for a reduced coupling between visitors and the visited objects compared to the GoF Visitor, but at the cost of some performance overhead due to the use of runtime type information.

Chapter 9: State Patterns, by Paul Dyson and Bruce Anderson. This chapter presents a pattern language regarding how to apply and implement the GoF State pattern effectively and correctly. For example, the patterns address whether a data member should belong to the context class or to a state class. They also discuss when it is appropriate for the context class to initiate state transitions, and when it is more appropriate for the state classes to perform that task. Other patterns help to determine how the correct initial state can be ensured. A total of seven patterns are described.

This chapter presents a true pattern language; all its constituent patterns depend on each other. You start with the initial pattern and are directed to the patterns that apply thereafter. Step-by-step, the language leads you to all aspects to be considered when implementing State.

Summary. As you can see, all three chapters in this part address important aspects of implementing well-known design patterns in a specific context. If you follow the Gang of Four mailing list,[1] you will also notice that the patterns in this part answer some of the frequently asked questions about the GoF patterns and resolve some of the problems that arise when implementing them. For this reason, variations are very important to further detail and complete the existing patterns, whether or not they are variations of the GoF patterns. Also, the patterns in this part show nicely how the pattern community works. By publishing a pattern, you share your expertise in building software systems with every software developer worldwide—as the Gang of Four did. Some colleagues will then pick up your pattern, apply it, and start publishing variations on it. This not only completes your work and helps to spread it, but gives credit to you as the publisher of the original pattern.

This discussion reveals that variations on existing patterns are an important pattern category. We hope to see more of them in the future, and not only for GoF patterns.

---

[1] See http://st-www.cs.uiuc.edu/users/patterns/Lists.html if you would like to subscribe to this or any other patterns mailing list.

REFERENCES

[Buschmann+96] F. Buschmann, R. Meunier, H. Rohnert, P. Sommerlad, and M. Stal. *Pattern-Oriented Software Architecture: A System of Patterns*. New York: John Wiley and Sons, 1996.

[PLoPD2] J. M. Vlissides, J. O. Coplien, N. L. Kerth (eds.). *Pattern Languages of Program Design 2*. Reading, MA: Addison-Wesley, 1996.

Chapter 7

Acyclic Visitor

Robert C. Martin

Intent

The intent of the Acyclic Visitor pattern is to allow new functions to be added to existing class hierarchies without affecting those hierarchies, and without creating the troublesome dependency cycles that are inherent to the GoF Visitor pattern [Gamma+95].

Motivation

Procedural software can be written in such a way that new functions can be added to existing data structures without affecting those data structures. Object-oriented software can be written such that new data structures can be used by existing functions without affecting those functions. In this regard, they are the inverse of each other. Adding new data types without affecting existing functions is at the heart of many of the benefits of OO. Yet there are times when we really want to add a new function to an existing set of classes without changing those classes. The Visitor pattern provides a means to accomplish this goal [Gamma+95, p. 331].

However, the Visitor pattern, when used in static languages like C++, Java, or Eiffel, causes a cycle in the source code dependency structure. (See Figure 7-1 and the legend in Figure 7-2.) A source code dependency means that the source code of one module must refer to (via #include, or import, or some other mechanism) the source code of another module.

The dependency cycle in this case is as follows.

- The base class of the visited hierarchy (`Element`) depends upon the base class of the corresponding visitor hierarchy (`Visitor`).

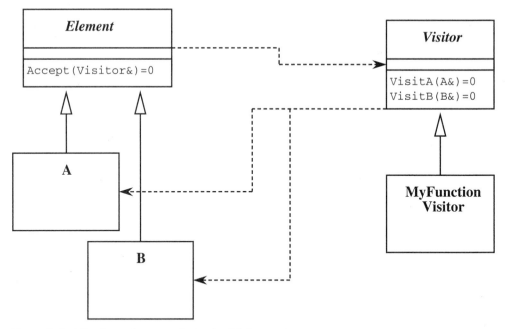

Figure 7-1 *The dependency cycle in the Visitor pattern*

- The `Visitor` base class has member functions for each of the derivatives of the `Element` base class. Thus the `Visitor` class depends upon each derivative of `Element`.
- Of course, each derivative of `Element` depends upon `Element`.

Thus we have a cycle of dependencies that causes `Element` to transitively depend upon all its derivatives.

This knot of dependencies can cause significant troubles for the programmer who must maintain the code which contains them. Any time a new derivative of `Element` is created, the `Visitor` class must also be changed. Since `Element` depends upon `Visitor`, every module that depends upon `Element` must be recompiled. This means that every derivative of `Element`, and possibly every *user* of every derivative of `Element`, must also be recompiled.

Where possible, this dependency cycle should be mitigated by using forward declarations. That is, in many cases the `Element` base class can forward declare the `Visitor` base class, and the `Visitor` base class can forward declare the derivatives of `Element`. This creates a much weaker source code dependency that Lakos refers to as a name only dependency [Lakos96, p. 249]. Although weaker, this is still a dependency cycle and still causes the problems mentioned in the last paragraph. Specifically, even when name only dependencies are used as much as

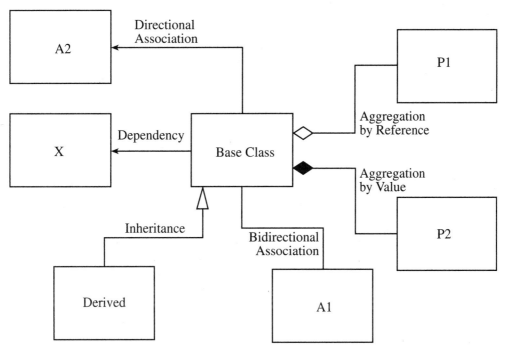

Figure 7-2 *Legend for the 0.91 UML notation*

possible, every time a new derivative of `Element` is created, all the existing derivatives of `Element` must be recompiled.

Partial Visitation.   Another disadvantage to the dependency cycle created by the Visitor pattern is the need to address every derivative of `Element` in every derivative of `Visitor`. Often, there are hierarchies for which visitation is only required for certain derivatives of `Element`. For example, consider a modem hierarchy like that shown in Figure 7-3.

In Figure 7-3 we see a very compelling use for Visitor. We have a typical hierarchy of Modem classes with one derivative for each modem manufacturer. We also see a hierarchy of visitors for the Modem hierarchy. In this example, there is one visitor that adds the ability to configure a modem for UNIX and another that adds the ability to configure a modem for DOS. Clearly, we do not want to add these functions directly to the Modem hierarchy. There is no end to such functions. The last thing we want is for every user of `Modem` to be recompiled every time a new operating system is released. Indeed, we don't want `Modem` to recognize any variation in operating systems. Thus, we use Visitor to add the configuration function to the `Modem` hierarchy without affecting that hierarchy.

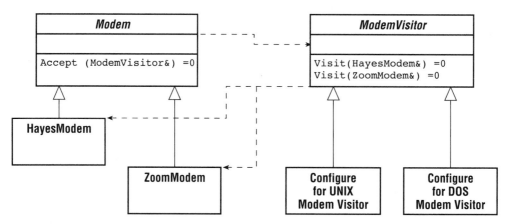

Figure 7-3 *Modem Configuration Visitors*

However, Visitor forces us to write a function for the cross product of all Modem derivatives and all ModemVisitor derivatives. That is, we need to write the functions that configure every type of modem to every type of operating system. Even if we never use Hayes modems with UNIX, Visitor will still force us to write a function to do it. We could, of course, print an error from the function in the Visitor base class, and then allow that function to be inherited, but we would still have to write that function.

Now consider a much larger hierarchy, one in which the cross product of Element derivatives and Visitor derivatives is sparsely populated. The Visitor pattern may become inconvenient in such a hierarchy because every visitor depends upon every derivative of Element. Any time a new derivative of Element is added all derivatives, even derivatives which do not require visitor functions, must be recompiled. We would prefer to write only the functions that need writing and keep them independent from all the other derivatives of Element.

Solution

These problems can be solved by using multiple inheritance and dynamic_cast (see Figure 7-4). The diagram shows how the dependency cycle can be broken. Rather than put pure virtual functions into the ModemVisitor class, we make it completely degenerate; that is, it has no member functions other than a virtual destructor. We also create one abstract class for each derivative of Modem. These classes, HayesVisitor and ZoomVisitor, provide a pure virtual Visit function for HayesModem and ZoomModem, respectively. Finally, we inherit all three of these classes into the ConfigureDOSModemVisitor. Note that this class has exactly the same functions that it had in Figure 7-3. Moreover, they are implemented in exactly the same way.

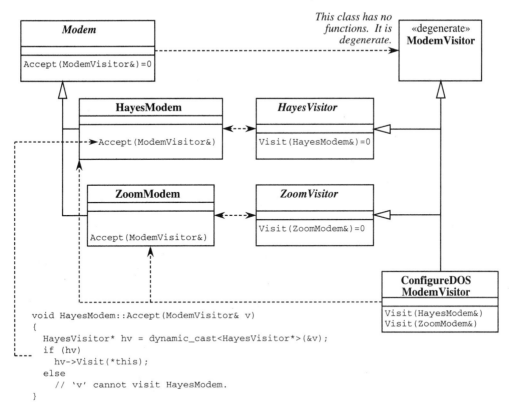

Figure 7-4 *Acyclic Modem Visitor*

The `Accept` function in the derivatives of `Modem` use `dynamic_cast` to cast across the visitor hierarchy from `ModemVisitor` to the appropriate abstract visitor class. Note that this is not a downcast—it is a cross cast. It is one of the great benefits of `dynamic_cast` that it can safely cast to any class anywhere in the inheritance structure of the object it operates on.

Now what happens if we never use Hayes modems with UNIX? The `ConfigureUnixModemVisitor` class will simply not inherit from `HayesVisitor`. Any attempt to use a Hayes modem with UNIX will cause the `dynamic_cast` in `HayesModem::Accept` function to fail, thus detecting the error at that point.

There are no dependency cycles anywhere in this structure. New `Modem` derivatives have no effect on existing modem visitors unless those visitors must implement their functions for those derivatives. New `Modem` derivatives can be added at any time without affecting the users of `Modem`, the derivatives of `Modem`, or the users of the derivatives of `Modem`. The need for massive recompilation is completely eliminated.

Applicability

This pattern can be used anywhere the Visitor pattern can be used.

- When you need to add a new function to an existing hierarchy without the need to alter or affect that hierarchy.
- When there are functions that operate upon a hierarchy, but which do not belong in the hierarchy itself. For example, the `ConfigureForDOS`/`Configure-ForUnix`/`ConfigureForX` issue.
- When you need to perform very different operations on an object depending upon its type.

This pattern should be preferred over Visitor under the following circumstances.

- When the visited class hierarchy will be frequently extended with new derivatives of the `Element` class.
- When the recompilation, relinking, retesting, or redistribution of the derivatives of `Element` is very expensive.

Structure

(See Figure 7-5.)

Participants

- *Element.* The base class of the hierarchy which needs to be visited. Visitors will operate upon the classes within this structure. If you are using Visitor to add functions to a hierarchy, this is the base class of that hierarchy
- *E1, E2, . . .* The concrete derivatives of `Element` that require visiting. If you are using Visitor to add functions to a hierarchy, you will write one function for each of these concrete derivatives.
- *Visitor.* A degenerate base class. This class has no member functions at all. Its sole purpose is as a place holder in the type structure. It is the type of the argument that is taken by the `Accept` method of `Element`. Since the derivatives of `Element` use this argument in a `dynamic_cast` expression, `Visitor` must have at least one virtual function—typically the destructor.
- *E1Visitor, E2Visitor, . . .* The abstract visitors that correspond to each of the concrete derivatives of `Element`. There is a one-to-one relationship between these classes. Each concrete derivative of `Element` will have a corresponding abstract Visitor. The abstract Visitor class will have one pure virtual `Visit` method that takes a reference to the concrete `Element` derivative.
- *VisitForF.* This is the actual Visitor class. It derives from `Visitor` so that it can be passed to the `Accept` function of `Element`. It also derives from each of the abstract visitors that correspond to the concrete classes that this visitor will visit. There is no need for the Visitor to derive from all the abstract Visitor classes; it only needs to derive from the ones for which it will implement `Visit` functions.

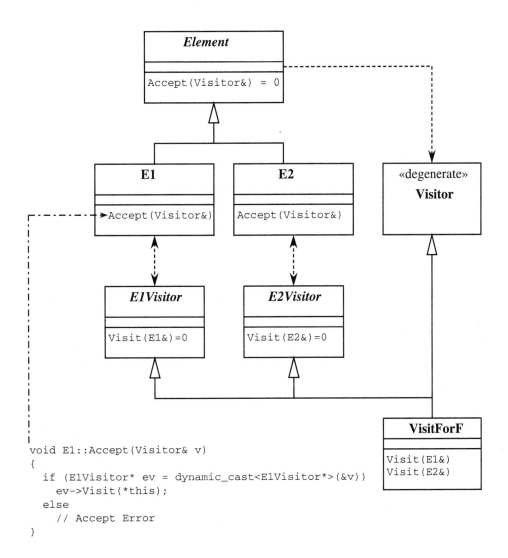

```
void E1::Accept(Visitor& v)
{
  if (E1Visitor* ev = dynamic_cast<E1Visitor*>(&v))
    ev->Visit(*this);
  else
    // Accept Error
}
```

Figure 7-5 *Acyclic Modem Visitor*

Collaborations

1. The process begins when a user wishes to apply one of the visitors to an object in the `Element` hierarchy. The user does not know which of the concrete derivatives of `Element` it actually has; instead it simply has a reference (or a pointer) to an `Element`.

2. The user creates the Visitor object (for example, `VisitForF` in Figure 7-5). The Visitor object represents the function that the user would like to invoke upon the `Element`.

3. The user sends the `Accept` message to the `Element` and passes the Visitor object as a reference to a `Visitor`.

4. The `Accept` method of the concrete derivative of `Element` uses `dynamic_cast` to cast the `Visitor` object to the appropriate abstract visitor class (such as `ElVisitor` from Figure 7-5).

5. If the `dynamic_cast` succeeds, then the `visit` message is sent to the Visitor object using the interface of the abstract Visitor class. The concrete derivative of `Element` is passed along with the `visit` message.

6. The actual Visitor object executes the `visit` method.

Consequences

The consequences of this pattern are the same as those for Visitor with several additions. Additional advantages include the elimination of all dependency cycles. Derivatives of `Element` do not depend upon each other. Recompilation is minimized. Further, partial visitation is natural and does not require additional code or overhead.

On the other hand, `dynamic_cast` can be expensive in terms of runtime efficiency. Moreover, its efficiency may vary as the class hierarchy changes. Thus, Acyclic Visitor may be inappropriate in very tight real-time applications where runtime performance must be predictable.

Some compilers don't support `dynamic_cast`, and some languages don't support dynamic type resolution, and/or multiple inheritance.

Also in C++, the Visitor class must have at least one virtual function. Since the class is also degenerate, we typically make the destructor virtual.

Finally, use of this pattern implies that there will be an abstract visitor class for each derivative of `Element`. Thus, classes tend to proliferate rapidly.

Sample Code

The following is the code for the Modem example used in Figure 7-4.

```
// Visitor is a degenerate base class for all visitors.
class Visitor
{
  public:
    virtual~Visitor() = 0;
    // The destructor is virtual, as all destructors ought to be.
    // it is also pure to prevent anyone from creating an
    // instance of Visitor.  Since this class is going to be
    // used in a dynamic_cast expression, it must have at least
    // one virtual function.
};

class Modem
```

```
{
  public:
    virtual void Accept(Visitor&) const = 0;
};

class HayesModem;
class HayesModemVisitor
{
  public:
    virtual void Visit(HayesModem&) const = 0;
};

class HayesModem : public Modem
{
  public:
    virtual void Accept(Visitor& v) const;
};

void HayesModem::Accept(Visitor& v) const
{
  if (HayesModemVisitor* hv = dynamic_cast<HayesModemVisitor*>(&v))
    hv->Visit(*this);
  else
    // AcceptError
}

class ZoomModem;
class ZoomModemVisitor
{
  public:
    virtual void Visit(ZoomModem&) const = 0;
};

class ZoomModem : public Modem
{
  public:
    virtual void Accept(Visitor& v) const;
};

void ZoomModem::Accept(Visitor& v) const
{
  if (ZoomModemVisitor* zv = dynamic_cast<ZoomModemVisitor*>(&v))
    zv->Visit(*this);
  else
    // AcceptError
}
```

```
//-------------------------
// ConfigureForDOSVisitor
//
// This visitor configures both Hayes and Zoom modems
// for DOS.
//
class ConfigureForDosVisitor : public Visitor
                             , public HayesModemVisitor
                             , public ZoomModemVisitor
{
  public:
    virtual void Visit(HayesModem&); // configure Hayes for DOS
    virtual void Visit(ZoomModem&);  // configure Zoom for DOS
};


//-------------------------
// ConfigureForUnixVisitor
//
// This visitor configures only Zoom modems for Unix
//

class ConfigureForUnixVisitor : public Visitor
                              , public ZoomModemVisitor
{
  public:
    virtual void Visit(ZoomModem&); // configure Zoom for Unix
};
```

Known Uses

We have used this pattern in several of the projects we have consulted for. It has been used in the design of the Mark Facility Controller created by the Toolkit Working Group at Xerox. It has also been used in the ETS/NCARB project which can be accessed through Publications at http://www.oma.com.

Notes

This pattern solves a particularly nasty problem of tangled dependencies. I find this interesting in light of the fact that it depends on two such controversial features. The pattern would not be possible were it not for multiple inheritance and run-time type information, both of which have been attacked as being "non-OO."

What's wrong with recompiling?   Recompiles can be very expensive for a number of reasons. First of all, they take time. When recompiles take too much time, developers begin to take shortcuts. They may hack a change in the wrong place, rather than engineer a change in the right place; simply because the right place will force a huge recompilation. Secondly, a recompilation means a new object module. In this day and age of dynamically linked libraries and incremental load-ers, generating more object modules than necessary can be a significant disadvan-tage. The more DLLs that are affected by a change, the greater the problem of distributing and managing the change. Finally, a recompile means a new release of every module which needed recompiling. New releases require documentation and testing, the investment of potentially huge amounts of manpower.

ACKNOWLEDGMENTS

I'd like to thank, in particular, Erich Gamma and Bobby Woolf for their insights. I'd also like to thank Paul Jukubic for showing me the error of my ways. And, of course, thanks to all the organizers and participants of PLoP '96.

REFERENCES

[Gamma+95] E. Gamma, R. Helm, R. Johnson, and J. Vlissides. *Design Patterns: Elements of Object-Oriented Software.* Reading, MA: Addison-Wesley, 1995.

[Lakos96] J. Lakos. *Large-Scale C++ Software Design.* Reading, MA: Addison-Wesley, 1996.

Robert Martin can be reached at rmartin@oma.com. http://www.oma.com.

Chapter 8

Default and Extrinsic Visitor

Martin E. Nordberg III

The Visitor pattern is an increasingly widely used design pattern for the traversal of relatively fixed class hierarchies described in the book *Design Patterns* [Gamma+95]. A number of variations on the Visitor pattern have proved useful for improving the traversal of a structure of "visitable" objects under certain circumstances. These are either specializations of the Visitor pattern or additions to it.

Two variations on the Visitor pattern are presented in this chapter. A Default Visitor provides default handlers for cases where the polymorphism of the hierarchy of elements can reduce the cost of code maintenance. An Extrinsic Visitor implements double dispatch with runtime type information instead of Accept() methods. With the same machinery, it is possible to test the feasibility of a particular visit before performing its operation. The Extrinsic Visitor pattern has several benefits that can ease software development in trade for poorer runtime performance. Interesting design tradeoffs between efficiency and maintainability determine the choice of the Standard, Default, or Extrinsic Visitor pattern in an application.

DEFAULT VISITOR

Intent

Default Visitor adds another level of inheritance to the Visitor pattern and thus provides a default implementation that takes advantage of the inheritance relationships in a polymorphic hierarchy of elements.

Motivation

One difficulty in applying the Visitor pattern is modifying every concrete visitor whenever a new concrete element is added. In this instance, writing each `visitXxxx()` method may be tedious if much of the behavior is the same for different classes derived from a common base class. If `visitXxxx()` is often an exact copy of VisitYyyy(), it is too time consuming to rely on only the most primitive code reuse mechanism (cut and paste). To overcome this difficulty, the Default Visitor pattern provides default VisitXxxx() methods that move the tedious work to a single central location. Then only those VisitXxxx() methods with unique behavior for a given concrete element must be written.

Consider, as a hypothetical example, classes with names like Motor, Sensor, Conveyor, SodaBottleConveyor, ConveyorMotor, and TemperatureSensor in a framework for factory automation—real-time control and management of a small factory. However, our management has recently decided to seek ISO9000 certification and wants to add functionality to this system, that is, to add record keeping and reporting for service histories, quality problems, and the like. Because the new record keeping is secondary to, and separate from, the original (and still primary) purpose of the code, we have decided to implement the new functionality with the Visitor pattern. We will add a small number of new attributes to the existing classes and a small number of new classes in the inheritance graph, and then write concrete visitors for the new functions.

While the choice of the Visitor pattern is well justified by the desire to separate new functionality from existing functionality, we find that we have difficulty taking advantage of polymorphism in the framework hierarchy. For example, all motors are to be inspected every 90 days except machine tool motors that require 60-day inspection intervals. It would be time consuming to design a class called BuildInspectionListVisitor that has a dozen repetitions of the following code for each different kind of motor.[1]

```
void BuildInspectionListVisitor::VisitConveyorMotor(
        ConveyorMotor& conveyorMotor )
{
  If ( Now() - conveyorMotor.LastInspection() >= 90 )
    AddToList( conveyorMotor );
}
. . .
```

If this were the only visitor needed, we might take our lumps and get on with it, but there are many different visitors with different specializations, so we can write the twelve repetitions once

```
/*virtual*/ void DefaultVisitor::VisitMotor
  ( Motor& motor )
{}

Void DefaultVisitor::VisitConveyorMotor
  ( ConveyorMotor& conveyorMotor )
```

---

[1] The code is oversimplified, but the issues are not.

```
{
   VisitMotor ( conveyorMotor ) ;
}
. . .
```

and each common (default) case once

```
class BuildInspectionListVisitor : public DefaultVisitor
{
   . . .
} ;

void BuildInspectionListVisitor::VisitMotor( Motor& motor )
{
   if ( Now() - motor.LastInspection() >= 90 )
     AddToList( motor ) ;
}
```

The new class, `DefaultVisitor`, from which the pattern derives its name, adds `VisitXxxx()` methods for the abstract elements as well as the concrete elements and provides default implementations that traverse the inheritance graph as shown in Figure 8-1.

If we add a new class, `WizBangRobotMotor`, we still must modify `Default-Visitor`, but need to modify only a small subset of our concrete visitor classes.

Applicability

Apply the Default Visitor pattern when: (a) You would consider applying the Visitor pattern; (b) Elements to be visited come from a small set of polymorphic class hierarchies; and (c) Several concrete visitors can employ default handlers for a small set of abstract elements rather than requiring a specific implementation for every distinct concrete element.

Structure

Figure 8-2 shows the typical structure found in the Default Visitor pattern.

Participants

The classes that participate in the Default Visitor pattern are the same as for the standard Visitor pattern, except for the addition of class DefaultVisitor.

Visitor. The Visitor class defines a `VisitXxxx()` method for each concrete class in the inheritance hierarchy of elements. As in the normal visitor class, the signa-

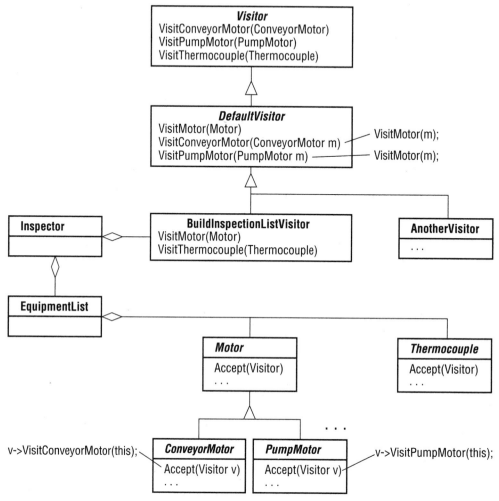

Figure 8-1 *Structure of part of a factory automation framework after addition of a DefaultVisitor class*

ture and name of each `VisitXxxx()` method identify the concrete class of the element (Xxxx) being visited.[2]

---

[2] If function overloading is used to name each method "`Visit`," there is no need to add a new method to `Visitor` and `DefaultVisitor` when a new concrete element class is added that needs no special treatment in any of the concrete visitors. However, this only delays (and probably magnifies) the maintenance headaches until later when a new concrete visitor appears or a concrete element's behavior changes. The advice of the Gang of Four book [Gamma+95, p. 337] still holds: include the element name in each `Visit` method name for best results in the long run.

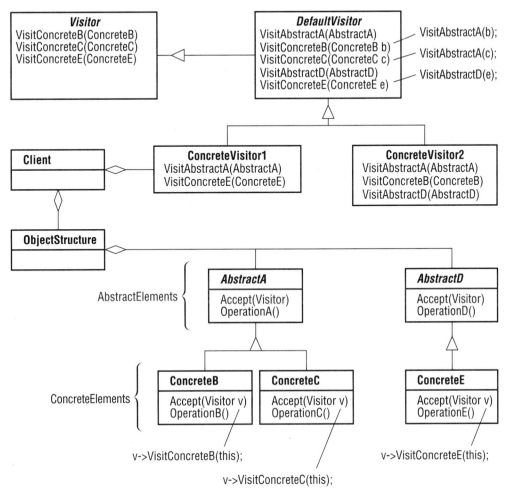

Figure 8-2 *General structure of the Default Visitor pattern*

DefaultVisitor. Derived from Visitor, a `DefaultVisitor` overrides each of the `VisitXxxx()` methods in Visitor and defines similar `VisitXxxx()` methods for each of the abstract classes in the inheritance hierarchy (or hierarchies) of elements. Each `VisitXxxx()` method, instead of being a do-nothing function, calls (with dynamic binding) the `VisitXxxx()` method for each base class of its argument.

ConcreteVisitor. `ConcreteVisitor` implements a meaningful version of those `VisitXxxx()` methods that are relevant to the application. It may implement a combination of `VisitXxxx()` methods for concrete and abstract elements, taking advantage of the polymorphism in the element class hierarchy.

AbstractElement. `AbstractElement` defines an `Accept()` method that receives a visitor as its argument. The `Accept()` method is the starting point for a client to cause a traversal of a structure of elements. Note that multiple abstract elements may exist in an inheritance hierarchy of elements.

ConcreteElement. A concrete element implements a specific `Accept()` operation that calls the appropriate `VisitXxxx()` method of its visitor. For reduced complexity in this pattern (among other reasons [Meyers94]) each concrete element is preferably a leaf node of the inheritance hierarchy.

ObjectStructure. The object structure is some collection of elements. An ObjectStructure provides the mechanism to traverse the collection, or that mechanism is provided by either the elements themselves or helper functions in the base Visitor class.

Collaborations

With very little variation from the Standard Visitor pattern a client creates a `ConcreteVisitor` object and then traverses the object structure. All that changes is that some of the `VisitXxxx()` implementations may simply be the default ones. As an example, Figure 8-3 is the behavior of `ConcreteVisitor1` from the previous structure diagram.

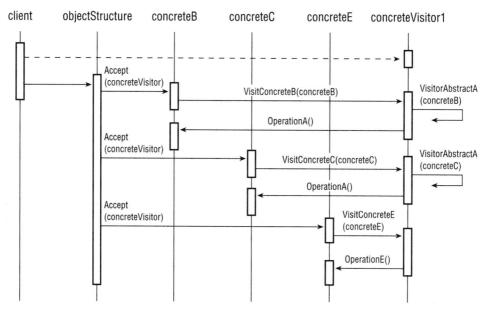

Figure 8-3 *Interactions for a typical call through the methods of the Default Visitor pattern*

The contribution of the object structure and the location for structure traversal may vary from one design to another. The client, the elements, or the visitor could optionally play some of the roles played by the object structure above.

Consequences

The consequent advantages and disadvantages of Default Visitor may determine whether it is applicable in a specific instance.

- A default visitor makes it easier to add new ConcreteElement classes (compared to an ordinary visitor). As with the Visitor pattern, each new concrete element requires a new `VisitXxxx()` method in classes Visitor and `Default-Visitor`. However, in cases where polymorphism is used to advantage (that is, in cases where the Default Visitor pattern is used to advantage), the default implementation of the new `VisitXxxx()` method in `DefaultVisitor` will often be adequate for many of the different concrete visitor classes. Some of the concrete visitors may require no modification at all.
- Even if the default visitor does not provide a perfectly reusable `VisitXxxx()` implementation, it may provide a base implementation that can be augmented by a derived visitor in the same way that virtual members of derived classes often call their base class equivalents.
- Though it is easy to add new leaf nodes to the element inheritance hierarchy, it is more difficult to change the inheritance hierarchy of abstract classes. Each such change must be carefully accounted for in the `VisitXxxx()` methods of class `DefaultVisitor`. Each concrete visitor must also be checked to make sure reliance on default implementations still makes sense.
- The default visitor pattern requires more work in writing and maintaining class `DefaultVisitor` in return for less work in writing and maintaining each `ConcreteVisitor` class.
- All of the remaining advantages and disadvantages of the Default Visitor pattern are much the same as described by Gamma et al. for the Visitor pattern.

Implementation

Implementation of the Default Visitor pattern is much the same as for the Standard Visitor pattern except for the `VisitXxxx()` members of the `DefaultVisitor` class. These methods should simply call the `VisitXxxx()` methods for the base classes of their argument. Figure 8-2 showing the pattern's structure includes notes suggesting implementations for the example `VisitXxxx()` methods of `DefaultVisitor`.

With care, even multiple and virtual inheritance can be handled. Each `Visit-ConcreteXxxx()` method should call the `VisitXxxx()` methods for its virtual base classes before calling the `VisitXxxx()` methods for its immediate, nonvirtual base classes. The order of `VisitXxxx()` calls can in this way be made parallel to the order of constructor calls.

If all visitors in a system benefit from default handlers, then the Visitor class may be collapsed into the `DefaultVisitor` class. If not all visitors are properly polymorphic, it is desirable to leave the Visitor class separate in order to avoid errors in a standard concrete visitor when a concrete element is added to the hierarchy. Another reason to leave the Visitor class separate is to reduce recompiling when a new abstract element is added.

Known Uses

Default visitors appear widely in the C++ MetaCode Framework now under development by the author. For example, in this framework describing C++ code, it is often sufficient to visit an Identifier, rather than to visit Classes and Functions and Enumerators and all the other types of identifiers in the framework hierarchy.

Related Patterns

Default Visitor is a straightforward specialization of the Visitor pattern.

EXTRINSIC VISITOR

Intent

The Extrinsic Visitor pattern trades the performance overhead of a small number of runtime type tests for reduced complexity and coupling in the visitor and element classes of the pattern. The pattern also provides (in a single body of code) the ability to easily test the feasibility of a visit operation before actually performing it.

Motivation

Consider a graphics system that incorporates widespread use of drag and drop operations. Imagine that in this system many different items can be dragged and dropped on one another, but only specific combinations of items are meaningful, and that meaning varies with each different combination. The drop operation is thus a perfect candidate for double dispatch: the operation of dropping is likely to be outside the appropriate encapsulation for the items being dropped, and the dynamic binding of the drop operation depends on the types of two items. A modern user interface provides greater feedback to the user during the drag operation by highlighting the item dropped on and changing the cursor style according to the potential drop operation. We need our visitor to provide not only `visit()` operations (for the drop) but `canVisit()` operations (for the drag).

The standard Visitor pattern does not directly provide a mechanism for determining whether a particular combination of concrete visitor and concrete element is meaningful. Such a capability could be included by adding a parameter to the `Accept()` and `VisitXxxx()` methods to tell whether to perform the operation or merely test for its feasibility. Those two methods would then need to return a Boolean value indicating the feasibility. This approach is straightforward, but it adds to the maintenance difficulties when adding new concrete element classes. Another approach, which has at least equal maintenance difficulties, is to provide a separate, parallel visitor class to accomplish the test.

The Extrinsic Visitor pattern performs its dynamic dispatch with, in essence, a lookup table by runtime type of the visited element. The dispatch mechanism centralizes the distinction between performing an operation and testing for the feasibility of performing an operation. This approach thus trades runtime performance for easier code maintenance.

The Extrinsic Visitor pattern may also be appropriate, completely independent of the above arguments, to add an operation to a hierarchy of classes that do not accept visitors and cannot be modified to do so. The extrinsic visitor does not require `Accept()` methods in its elements; it requires only a common base class and runtime type information. Even if `Accept()` methods are feasible, the nonintrusiveness is another significant benefit for code development since it eliminates the cyclic dependency between class `Visitor` and each of the concrete elements.

Applicability

Apply the Extrinsic Visitor pattern when: (a) You would consider the Visitor pattern for reasons of separation of dissimilar operations or easy addition of new operations; (b) Elements to be visited all derive from a single (or a small number) of base classes; (c) The number of distinct concrete elements visited by the typical concrete visitor is small; and (d) It is preferable to trade runtime performance for reduced intrusiveness of the Visitor pattern into the element hierarchy (no `Accept()` methods) and reduced complexity of the visitors themselves. Or, when it is desirable to easily test whether a particular concrete visitor handles a particular concrete element without actually performing the operation on that element.

Structure

Figure 8-4 shows the structure typically found in the Extrinsic Visitor pattern.

Participants

The participants in the Extrinsic Visitor pattern differ from standard Visitor only in the renaming of class `Visitor` to `ExtrinsicVisitor`. However, the mechanism to accomplish a visit is more complex.

ExtrinsicVisitor. This class is the root of the Extrinsic Visitor structure and provides two public functions to its clients: `Visit(AbstractElement)` and Boolean `CanVisit(AbstractElement)`. Each of these depends on a single abstract method called `Dispatch()` which tests for the feasibility of operating upon a particular concrete element and optionally performs the appropriate operation.

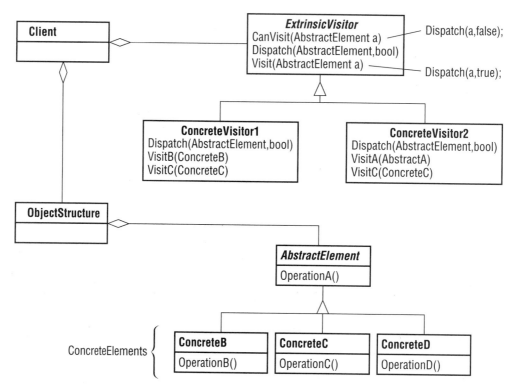

Figure 8-4 *General structure of the Extrinsic Visitor pattern*

ConcreteVisitor.   Each concrete visitor class provides `VisitXxxx()` methods for relevant concrete element types and implements a corresponding version of `Dispatch()`, which translates `Visit()` calls into `VisitXxxx()` calls or tests the feasibility for `CanVisit()` calls.

AbstractElement.   `AbstractElement` is the base class of the element structure. It participates in the Extrinsic Visitor pattern only to the extent that it provides runtime type information. Concrete elements could be derived from a small set of abstract base elements, but `ExtrinsicVisitor` would need separate `CanVisit()`, `Visit()`, and `Dispatch()` methods for each abstract element.

ConcreteElement.   Concrete elements (such as `ConcreteB` and `ConcreteC`) are the items to be visited. They provide runtime type information.

ObjectStructure.   As in the Standard Visitor pattern, the Object Structure is some container of items to be visited. In typical applications of the Extrinsic Visitor pattern it is common to visit only one item out of this structure rather than traversing the entire structure.

Collaborations

Because the Extrinsic Visitor pattern includes no `Accept()` methods, a visit starts with a direct call to the visitor. The visitor then dispatches the generic `Visit()` call to a `VisitXxxx()` call as shown in Figure 8-5.

Because of the call graph, the object structure must have knowledge of the `ExtrinsicVisitor`, or the object structure may be bypassed altogether, with the initial call to `Visit()` coming from the client. In appropriate applications of the Extrinsic Visitor pattern, it is much more common for single elements to be visited rather than entire structures.

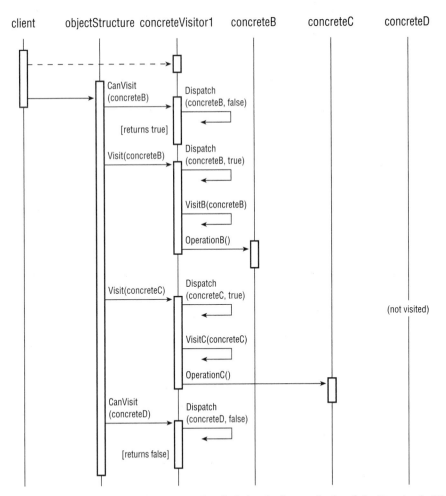

Figure 8-5 *Interactions for a typical call through the methods of the Extrinsic Visitor pattern*

Consequences

The consequences of employing the Extrinsic Visitor pattern instead of the Standard Visitor pattern are as follows.

- It is much easier to add new concrete classes to the Extrinsic Visitor pattern because only those concrete visitors that operate on objects of the new class need to be changed. The ExtrinsicVisitor base class needs modification only if a new base abstract element class is added.
- The Extrinsic Visitor pattern also eliminates the need to recompile every concrete element when a new concrete element is added to the hierarchy. The Standard Visitor pattern has a cyclic dependency between each element and the abstract visitor. With Accept() methods gone, the dependency is one way (visitors depend on elements) and the need for recompilation is reduced. In fact, not all concrete visitors need to be recompiled, only those that are modified to operate on objects of the new class.
- None of the elements needs an Accept() method, but they all need to provide runtime type information. In up-to-date C++, this is redundant because of the single base class requirement (the abstract base class presumably has a virtual destructor). The requirement may be more difficult to satisfy in other environments.
- The Extrinsic Visitor pattern implements dynamic binding through a relatively brute-force lookup table that depends on the runtime type of concrete elements. Depending on the implementation (see below) this approach may be considerably slower at runtime than the use of two virtual function tables in the Standard Visitor pattern. (The difference may, nonetheless, be small compared to the work done during the visit.)
- The Extrinsic Visitor pattern requires a single abstract base class for its elements (or at least a small set of base classes). This may be undesirable for other design reasons (and has been a subject of much debate).

Implementation

Most of the implementation details center around how to implement the Dispatch() methods in each concrete visitor. One straightforward implementation is to provide a table of method pointers indexed by the type ID of each concrete element. If implemented as an array, the table emulates the virtual function table normally built by a compiler except that many entries will be null.

If implemented as a map, the table provides a space-efficient representation of the dynamic binding needed, but with a small performance overhead. Both of these methods require extra code (and more difficult code maintenance) to build and maintain the dispatch table. In C++, neither method readily allows for the advantages of the Default Visitor pattern without careful hand coding of the table or extra runtime type information providing an IsDerivedFrom() mechanism. For multiple or virtual inheritance in the element hierarchy, the task may be impossible. The author has had success with an implementation that trades even slower performance for relatively easy code creation and maintenance with the runtime type information provided directly by the C++ language. For example, the following code performs the dynamic dispatch needed by ConcreteVisitor1 in Figure 8-4 in the Structure section.

```cpp
// perform the dispatch operations needed by
// ConcreteVisitor2 from the example earlier
bool ConcreteVisitor1::Dispatch
  ( AbstractElement& visitee ,
    bool do_the_call            )
{
  ConcreteB* concreteB =
    dynamic_cast<ConcreteB*>(&visitee);
  if ( concreteB != 0 )
  {
    if ( do_the_call )
      VisitB( *concreteB );
    return true;
  }

  ConcreteC* concreteC =
    dynamic_cast<ConcreteC*>( &visitee );
  if ( concreteC != 0 )
  {
    // . . similar to above . .
  }

  return false;
}
```

It is more convenient to extract the repeated structure of the Dispatch function into a separate helper function. Each concrete visitor implements its dispatch mechanism by a series of calls to this global template function.

```cpp
// perform the dispatch operations needed by
// ConcreteVisitor2 from the example earlier
bool ConcreteVisitor2::Dispatch
  ( AbstractA& visitee ,
    bool do_the_call      )
{
  // below is the "dispatch table"
  return
  AbstractDblDispatch( this , &ConcreteVisitor2::VisitC ,
    visitee , do_the_call ) ||
```

```
    AbstractDblDispatch( this , &ConcreteVisitor2::VisitA ,
      visitee , do_the_call );
}
```

It may not be apparent from this example, but the order of the calls to Abstract-DblDispatch is significant both for correctness and for efficiency. For example, if they were reversed, VisitC would never be reached. In a larger system the calls could also be subordered for efficiency, with more common cases placed first. The global[3] template function AbstractDblDispatch performs the runtime type test using the built-in dynamic_cast operator.

```
// test for or perform double dispatch
template < class T_Visitor , class T_Visitee >
bool AbstractDblDispatch
   ( T_Visitor* visitor ,
     void (T_Visitor::*visit) ( T_Visitee& ) ,
     AbstractA& abstract_visitee ,
     bool do_the_call                                          )
{
  T_Visitee* visitee =
    dynamic_cast<T_Visitee*>( &abstract_visitee );

  if ( visitee == 0 )
    return false; // quit if can't dispatch

  if ( do_the_call )
    (visitor->*visit) ( *visitee );

  return true;
}
```

This template function is unusual because the class and argument types of a method pointer distinguish instantiations of the template.

If the item to be visited is a fully concrete element rather than an abstract element, a more efficient dispatch mechanism is possible:

```
// test for or perform double dispatch on a
// specific concrete element
template < class T_Visitor , class T_Visitee >
bool ConcreteDblDispatch
   ( T_Visitor* visitor ,
     void (T_Visitor::*visit) ( T_Visitee& ) ,
     AbstractA& abstract_visitee ,
```

---

[3] It could be a member template function of class Extrinsic Visitor given a compiler with that capability.

```
    bool do_the_call ,
    const type_info& visitee_type                )
{
  if ( visitee_type == typeid(T_Visitee) )
  {
    if ( do_the_call )
    {
      // (use static_cast here if no virtual inheritance)
      T_Visitee*  visitee =
        dynamic_cast<Visitee*>( &abstract_visitee );
      (visitor->*visit) ( *visitee );
    }
    return true;
  }
  return false;
}

bool ConcreteVisitor2::Dispatch
  ( AbstractA& visitee ,
    bool do_the_call            )
{
  const type_info& visitee_type = typeid(visitee);

  return
  ConcreteDblDispatch( this , &ConcreteVisitor2::VisitC ,
    visitee , do_the_call , visitee_type ) ||
  AbstractDblDispatch( this , &ConcreteVisitor2::VisitA ,
    visitee , do_the_call                    );
}
```

Though requiring only one `dynamic_cast`, `ConcreteDblDispatch` still requires searching through a list of options. If only concrete elements are to be dispatched, and we are allowed a minor intru sion into the element hierarchy to provide a `ClassID()` method for each element type, then a constant time implementation of the Extrinsic Visitor pattern is possible.

```
bool ConcreteVisitor1::Dispatch
  ( AbstractA& visitee ,
    bool do_the_call            )
{
  switch ( visitee.ClassID() )
  {
  case ConcreteB::TheClassID:
    // (use static_cast if no virtual inheritance)
    if ( do_the_call )
      VisitB( dynamic_cast<ConcreteB&>(visitee) );
    return true;
```

```
case ConcreteC::TheClassID:
  if ( do_the_call )
    VisitC( dynamic_cast<ConcreteC&>(visitee) );
  return true;
default:
  return false;
}
}
```

Note that `ClassID()` does not require the cyclic dependency that `Accept()` does and may be useful for other purposes. Figure 8-6 is a comparison of the three different implementations of Extrinsic Visitor under Windows 95 with two different compilers. These results are for a single-level element hierarchy with a varying number of relevant concrete elements (visited with equal probability). Other compilers, platforms, or hierarchies will, of course, have different relative performance. The performance of the Standard Visitor is also shown for comparison.

Known Uses

The Extrinsic Visitor pattern is used in the C++ Metacode Framework now under development by the author. Design pattern implementations or simpler tool

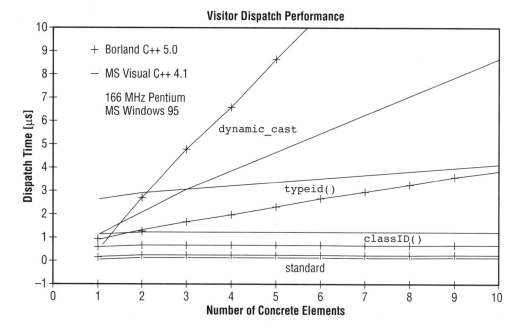

Figure 8-6 *Performance of different Extrinsic Visitor dispatch mechanisms for two compilers*

extensions (extrinsic visitors) may be dragged and dropped on individual classes or functions (elements) in a computer-aided software engineering (CASE) tool. Extrinsic visitors in this CASE application form one basis for users of the tool to add functionality to it.

Related Patterns

Extrinsic Visitor is primarily a different implementation of the Visitor pattern. As a mechanism for implementing double dispatch, the Extrinsic Visitor pattern extends in a straightforward manner to multiple dispatch, wherein the dynamic binding of an operation depends on the concrete type of a visitor and two or more different arguments (visitees). This is not true of the Standard Visitor pattern.

CHOOSING A VISITOR PATTERN VARIATION

The three pattern variations Visitor, Default Visitor, and Extrinsic Visitor are all solutions to the same problem that optimize different aspects of code performance and maintainability. An obvious question is when to choose each variation. Materials scientists studying ceramics often draw triangle-shaped ternary phase diagrams. In such a diagram, each vertex of the triangle represents 100 percent of one of the three components. Points within the triangle represent mixtures of the three materials. The relative nearness of a point to each vertex indicates the relative fraction of each component. For example, the center of the triangle represents a 1 : 1 : 1 mixture of the three components. Labeled regions within a ternary phase diagram represent phases, states of the material that are preferred at equilibrium (after cooling from a liquid). The author proposes the approximate ternary phase diagram in Figure 8-7 for the three Visitor variations based on the relative proportion of `VisitXxxx()` methods that are specific, default, and empty in a typical concrete visitor.

The three phases are EV (Extrinsic Visitor), DV (Default Visitor), and V (Visitor). The vertex labeled S indicates a concrete visitor in which every concrete element must have its own specific implementation of `VisitXxxx()`. Vertex D represents a concrete visitor in which every `VisitXxxx()` implementation can use the default implementation of class Default Visitor. Vertex N represents a concrete visitor in which all `VisitXxxx()` methods are no-ops or nonfeasible. The gray shaded region represents an impossible condition: every concrete visitor must have at least one specialized `VisitXxxx()` in order to be meaningfully called a concrete visitor. The region where the Extrinsic Visitor pattern is applicable is smallest on this diagram because of its runtime overhead. This region would increase given a further requirement for a `CanVisit()` capability.

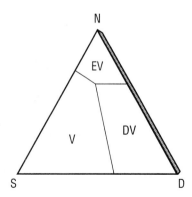

Figure 8-7 *Ternary phase diagram for the appropriateness of the three Visitor pattern variations*

The regions of the graph are meant to be design guidelines under ideal circumstances. In the same way that ceramics can be super-cooled into a state different from their phase diagram, some designs may fall outside these guidelines because of other constraints. For example, an Extrinsic Visitor structure may be chosen because of the nonfeasibility of adding `Accept()` methods to an existing class hierarchy. In such a case, the diagram may be a hint to optimize the implementation of the pattern in a different way. Perhaps the existing classes support a `ClassID()` mechanism and we can choose the more efficient implementation of Extrinsic Visitor.

The following table shows, in a general way, some of the tradeoffs that a designer makes when choosing from the three alternatives. Some of these tradeoffs are common to many areas of software engineering.

Pattern	Coupling Between Visitors and Elements	Runtime Efficiency	Ease of Maintenance
Standard Visitor	Very High	High	Low
Default Visitor	High	High	Medium
Extrinsic Visitor	Low	Low	High

CONCLUDING THOUGHTS

Having completed this small catalog of variations on the Visitor design pattern, I raise the question whether "variation on a pattern" is the right name for them. Are these really separate design patterns, merely implementation details, or something in between? As evidence of the relevance of the question, neither of the patterns of this article stands on its own. Each assumes that the reader has already considered the Visitor pattern and is looking to solve some problem of fit between that pattern and his or her application. The motivation and applicability sections, in particular, have been written this way. A better name for these patterns might be subpatterns or pattern implementations.

The question is a general one in the development of software design patterns: how specific can they be and still be patterns? Do we need different names for patterns as they slide along a continuum of implementation detail from "write-readable programs" to `module->Accept(codeGenerationVisitor):` programs? Researchers have developed metrics to measure object-oriented software interdependency, abstraction, reusability, domain independence, and so forth. Perhaps similar (though less formal) metrics will one day be applied to software design patterns.

The variations on the Visitor pattern presented in this chapter have proved very useful to the author in the context of developing a CASE tool and are general enough to prove useful to developers in other application areas.

ACKNOWLEDGMENTS

The author acknowledges the constructive suggestions offered by primary reviewer Robert C. Martin, particularly concerning the performance comparison and coupling issues in the Extrinsic Visitor pattern. He also offered the current names for both pattern variations. The work also benefited from constructive criticism received during its review at the PLoP '96 conference.

REFERENCES

[Gamma+95] E. Gamma, R. Helm, R. Johnson, and J. Vlissides, *Design Patterns—Elements of Reusable Object-Oriented Software.* Reading, MA: Addison-Wesley, 1995.

[Gautier96] P. Gautier. "Visitor Revisited." *C++ Report* 8(8) (September 1996).

[Martin96] R. C. Martin. "Acyclic Visitor." Chapter 7, this volume.

[Meyers94] S. Meyers, "Code Reuse, Concrete Classes, and Inheritance," *C++ Report* 6(6) (July–August, 1994).

[Nguyen96] M. Nguyen. "Extending the Visitor Design Pattern." *Dr. Dobb's Journal* 252 (October 1996).

Martin Nordberg can be reached at http://www.quintessoft.com;mn@quintessoft.com.

Chapter 9

State Patterns

Paul Dyson and Bruce Anderson

As our understanding of how we build software grows, we document recurrent design decisions in the form of patterns. As our understanding of each pattern grows, we extend and refine these patterns so that the advice they give is more concrete and comprehensive. Here, we present seven patterns that refine and extend the State pattern found in Gamma, et al. (also referred to as the Gang of four, or GoF, book). The refinements are concrete advice for some of the decisions mentioned, but not dealt with in detail, in the original pattern. The extensions are new advice for making decisions that we have repeatedly had to make while implementing the State pattern.

The first pattern, State Object, represents what we see as the core of the GoF pattern: the delegation of state-dependent behavior to an object that encapsulates state. If, in a given set of circumstances, the reader decides that State Object is not a suitable pattern for his needs, then none of the other patterns will be of much use. If, however, the reader decides that he should use State Object, the other patterns give concrete advice on how to implement its key concepts. By splitting up what could be a very large single pattern, and presenting it in the form of a pattern language, the reader can decide on the suitability of the pattern based on the prime motivation for using it, and then gradually proceed through the language to obtain more detail about the decisions required to implement such a solution.

PATTERNS SUMMARY

The patterns are presented in the form of a pattern language; they don't stand alone but rather have dependencies on the other patterns in the language. These dependencies are shown in Figure 9-1, with the single-headed arrows pointing to preceding patterns and the double-headed arrow indicating two patterns in ten-

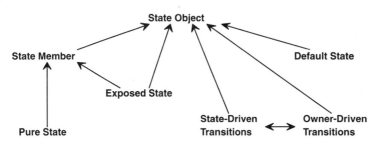

Figure 9-1 *State pattern dependencies*

sion with each other. State Object represents the core of the State pattern as presented in Gamma, et al.: the encapsulation of state as an object to which state-dependent actions are delegated.

The State Member pattern deals with whether data members should be placed in the owning object or in the State Object. This is an extension of the GoF State pattern.

The absence of any State Members leads to a State Object with Pure State: Pure State is a special case of State Member. This pattern shows how to share such State Objects among a number of owning objects. Pure State is a refinement of the GoF pattern's section on shareability.

Usually, the use of State Object to implement the state-dependent behavior of an owning object will be encapsulated within the owning object's class. However, sometimes it is necessary to allow external objects direct access to the owning object's State Object. Exposed State details when such an implementation is appropriate. This is an extension to the GoF pattern.

State-Driven Transitions and Owner-Driven Transitions are in tension with each other. State-Driven Transitions deals with the State Object responsible for the transition from one state to another. Owner-Driven Transitions deals with the alternative approach, which is for the owning object to implement the finite state machine. These two patterns are refinements of the GoF pattern, which deals mainly with the benefits and consequences of having the State Objects drive the state machine and only briefly mentions making the owning object responsible.

The final pattern, Default State, deals with the creation of the correct initial State Object when creating a new owning object. This is an extension of the GoF pattern.

A summary of the problems addressed by the patterns, and their solutions, is presented in Table 9-1.

Table 9-1 *State Pattern Problems and Recommended Solutions*

Pattern Name	Problem	Solution
State Object	How do you get different behavior from an object depending on its current state?	Encapsulate the state of the object in another, separate, object. Delegate all state-dependent behavior to this State Object.
State Member	How do you decide whether a data member belongs in the owning class or in the State Object class?	If a data member is only required for a single state, then place it in the corresponding State Object class. If the data member is required for some, but not all, states, then it should be placed in a common superclass. If the data member is state-independent, place it in the owning class and pass it to the State Object if necessary.
Pure State	You have a lot of State Objects. Is it possible to cut down on the number required?	When a State Object has no State Members, it can be said to represent Pure State—nothing but state-specific behavior. A single Pure State object can be shared among any number of owning objects, drastically reducing the number of objects required.
Exposed State	How do you prevent the owning class from having an excessive number of state-specific, state-dependent methods?	Expose the State Object by defining a method in the owning class that returns a reference to it. Make state-specific enquiries directly to the State Object.
State-Driven Transitions	How do you get the State Object to change when the owning object's state changes?	Have the State Object initiate the transition from itself (the current state) to the new State Object. This ensures transitions are atomic and removes state-dependent code.

Table 9-1 *State Pattern Problems and Recommended Solutions (Continued)*

Pattern Name	Problem	Solution
Owner-Driven Transitions	How do you reuse State Object classes among owning classes with different state-transition profiles?	If State Object classes are to be used by more than one owning class, and those owning classes have different FSMs, have the owning class initiate the transition between states.
Default State	When creating a new owning object, how do I ensure that it has the correct initial State Object?	Use a method, called by the `#initialize` method, that returns the default State Object. Redefine this method in a subclass if a different default state is required.

STATE OBJECT

Problem

How do you get a different behavior from an object depending on its current state?

Forces

We often want an object to behave differently depending on its current state. For example, if we have a `LibraryBook` object and we wish to borrow it, we want it to react differently to the `#checkOutBy:` message (the `LibraryBook` should be able to check itself out to a `LibraryUser`) depending on its current loan state: if it is available for loan, then it can be checked out, if it is already checked out, then an error has occurred. We could set a flag in the `LibraryBook` object that indicates whether it is currently being borrowed or not. If we took this approach, the `#checkOutBy:` method would look like

```
checkOutBy: aUser
"Check self out to aUser"

(currentlyBorrowed = 1)
    ifTrue: [^self error: 'The book is currently out on loan.'].

"Check the book out"
```

There are two problems with this approach (as described in Choosing Method [Beck96]). One is that adding new states for the `LibraryBook` requires more flags and more conditional tests. The other is that this kind of logic will have to be repeated in other methods. This means that several methods have to be maintained.

Solution

Encapsulate the state of the object in another, separate, object. Delegate all state-dependent behavior to this State Object as shown in Figure 9-2.

We create an abstract class: `LibraryBookState`, which represents the state of the `LibraryBook` object and declares a `#checkOut:by:` method. We then inherit from this class to create two new concrete classes: `Available` and `OnLoan`. These classes define `#checkOut:by:` to perform in a manner appropriate to the state they represent. `LibraryBook` now delegates checking itself out to its State Object.

```
LibraryBook>>checkOutBy: aUser
    state checkOut: self by: aUser
```

`LibraryBookState` defines `#checkOut:by:` to be implemented by its subclasses. The concrete state classes: `Available` and `OnLoan`, define the method according to the state they represent.

```
LibraryBookState>>checkOut: aBook by: aUser
    ^self implementedBySubclass

Available>>checkOut: aBook by: aUser
    "Check out aBook to aUser"
```

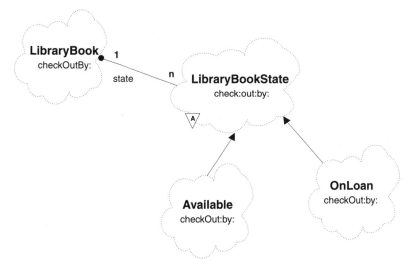

Figure 9-2 *Encapsulating state as a separate object*

```
OnLoan>>checkOut: aBook by: aUser
    ^self error: 'Book is already out on loan'
```

With a hierarchy of states, adding a new state is now a matter of inheriting from `LibraryBookState` and redefining `#checkOut:by:` to perform an action appropriate to that new state. Suppose we want to allow a book to be reserved, where reservation is equivalent to a copy of the book being placed on a reserved shelf in the library until the reserving user comes to pick it up. This is a new state because it is mutually exclusive of the existing states: the book is neither available for loan nor currently out on loan. To represent this new state we create a new subclass of `LibraryBookState` (`Reserved`) and redefine `#checkOut:by:`

```
Reserved>>checkOut: aBook by: aUser
    (aUser = reservingUser)
        ifTrue: ["Check out aBook to aUser"]
        ifFalse: [^self error: 'The book is currently reserved']
```

The main drawback to using this pattern is the increased complexity caused by the introduction of another level of indirection and as many extra classes as there are states. State Object may not be appropriate where it is necessary to adhere to strict performance and memory-usage requirements (e.g., small embedded application). State Object is the central pattern to this language, all the other patterns are subsequent to this one.

STATE MEMBER

You are using State Object.

Problem

How do you decide whether a data member belongs in the owning class or in the State Object class?

Forces

Data members are part of an object's state, but not all of them belong in the State Object class and, for those that do, it is sometimes difficult to determine which State Object class they should be placed in. How do we choose whether to place a data member in the State Object class or in the owning class, passing it as a parameter in a message when required?

Returning to the previous example of the `LibraryBook` object, we wish to reference the `LibraryUser` who has checked out the book. Does this reference go in the `LibraryBook` class, or one of the `LibraryBookState` classes? We also wish to introduce a more sophisticated implementation of reservations, where the book can be reserved like a hotel room. The reservation is made for a period of time from a particular date and the book can still be borrowed outside of the reservation period. Multiple reservations can be placed for a single book as long as they don't overlap.

Solution

If a data member is only required for a single state, then place it in the corresponding State Object class. If the data member is required for some, but not all, states, then it should be placed in a common superclass. If the data member is state-independent, place it in the owning class and pass it to the State Object if necessary.

We only wish to have a reference to the user borrowing the book if it is actually out on loan; having a reference to a borrowing user is unnecessary if the state is anything but `OnLoan`. Hence, we make `currentBorrower` a State Member of the `OnLoan` State Object class (see Figure 9-3).

Unlike `currentBorrower`, a list of reservations is state-independent: the reservations remain valid whether the `LibraryBook` is `Available` or `OnLoan`. Because of this, we make the list of reservations a member of `LibraryBook`. When it has been decided not to make a data member a State Member, we must further decide whether it is necessary to pass the data as a parameter to the State Object. In this example, checking out the `LibraryBook` is affected by the reservations made on it. The state of the book may be `Available`, but it cannot be checked out for a period which overlaps an existing reservation, so we pass `currentReservations` to the State Object as a parameter (see Figure 9-4).

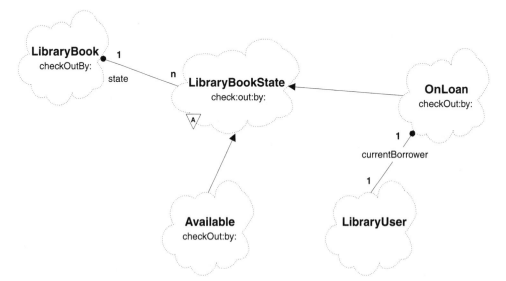

Figure 9-3 *Placing the data member in the State Object class*

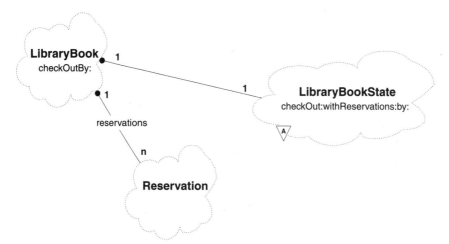

Figure 9-4 *Passing the data member to the State Object as a parameter*

The new methods for checking out a book now look like

```
LibraryBook>>checkOutBy: aUser
    state checkOut: self withReservations: reservations by: aUser

LibraryBookState>>checkOut: aBook withReservations: someReservations by: aUser
    ^self implementedBySubclass

Available>>checkOut: aBook withReservations: someReservations by: aUser
    "If checking out aBook doesn't invalidate any of the reservations,
    check out aBook to aUser"

OnLoan>> checkOut: aBook withReservations: someReservations by aUser
    ^self error: 'Book is already out on loan'
```

The use of State Member means that the State Object is very closely coupled to its owning object, and these two separate objects represent two parts of the whole. In the example above, the `currentBorrower` is held in the `OnLoan` object but is part of the `LibraryBook`'s state. This relationship is complicated if the State Member is placed in a common superclass because a number of different State Objects will have the same attribute, which has to be kept synchronized as transitions between states occur.

A State Object that has no State Members is an example of Pure State. Introducing State Members may require the use of Exposed State.

PURE STATE

You are using State Object but not State Member.

Problem

You have a lot of State Objects; is it possible to cut down on the number required?

Forces

The State Object pattern requires two objects (owning and State Object), where one had been sufficient. This increases complexity and can be inefficient in terms of memory usage.

Solution

When a State Object has no State Members, it can be said to represent Pure State, nothing but state-specific behavior. A single Pure State object can be shared among any number of owning objects, drastically reducing the number of objects required.

The Available State Object is Pure State; it simply implements the state-specific behavior for checking out a `LibraryBook`. Because of this, any number of `LibraryBook` objects can share a single `Available` object (see Figure 9-5). They only need separate `OnLoan` objects because each `OnLoan` object records some state-specific data (which `LibraryUser` is borrowing the book). A Pure State object is an example of a Flyweight and is also often a Singleton [Gamma+95].

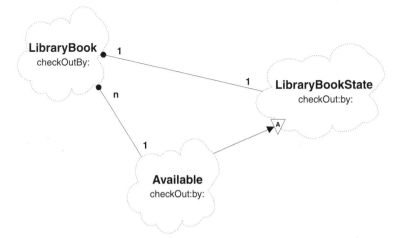

Figure 9-5 *A shared Pure State object*

EXPOSED STATE

You have a State Object encapsulated within an owning object.

Problem

How do you prevent the owning class from having an excessive number of state-specific, state-dependent methods?

Forces

State Object is an implementation pattern; it describes how we might implement state-specific behavior in a separate object. Following the principle of encapsulation, the owning object's class provides all the state-dependent methods in its interface; we don't see that these messages are actually delegated to another object. This can cause a problem when a lot of the state-dependent messages are also state-specific (see Figure 9-6).

LibraryBook declares two methods, #borrower and #returnDate, that return the user currently borrowing the book and the date it is due to be returned, respectively. These are state-specific enquiries, they have no meaning when the book is available for loan.

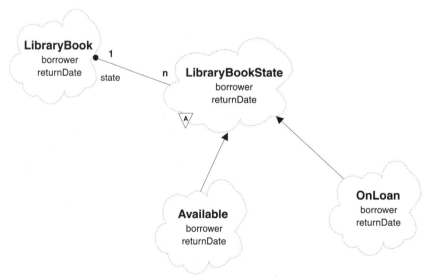

Figure 9-6 *Delegation of state-specific messages*

```
LibraryBook>>borrower
    ^state borrower

LibraryBook>>returnDate
    ^state returnDate

LibraryBookState>>borrower
    ^self implementedBySubclass

LibraryBookState>>returnDate
    ^self implementedBySubclass
Available>>borrower
    ^self error: 'Book not out on loan'

Available>>returnDate
    ^self error: 'Book not out on loan'

OnLoan>>borrower
    ^currentBorrower

OnLoan>>returnDate
    ^dueDateOfReturn
```

Another problem arises when we add a new state to the hierarchy. If we wish to add a `Reserved` state, which has a `reservingUser` State Member, we need to update the interfaces of `LibraryBook`, `LibraryBookState`, `Available`, and `OnLoan` to accept the `#reserver` message, with `Available`'s and `OnLoan`'s versions generating an exception.

Solution

Expose the State Object by defining a method in the owning class that returns a reference to it. Make state-specific enquiries directly to the State Object. This would change the example above to look like Figure 9-7. `LibraryBook`'s `#state` method simply answers the State Object

```
LibraryBook>>state
    ^state
```

and state-specific inquiries are made directly to it. Using this pattern, `Reserved` could be added and inquiries made about the user making the reservation without needing to update the interfaces of the other State Object classes.

The major drawback of using Exposed State to help control interface complexity is that we need to be sure that the owning object is in the required state to make state-specific inquiries. In Smalltalk this problem is partially alleviated by the exception-handling mechanism; if the state method returned an `Available`

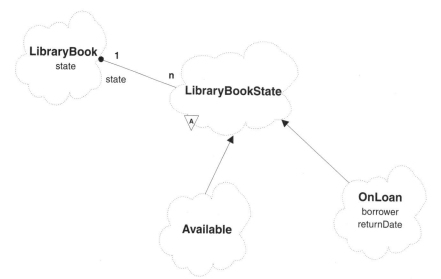

Figure 9-7 *Exposing the State Object*

object, a doesNotUnderstand exception would be generated in response to the #borrower message. C++, however, performs static type checking, and downcasting from the abstract LibraryBookState to the concrete OnLoan class (to force the compiler to allow the borrower message to be passed) would be required to make Exposed State work. In the absence of runtime type identification, Exposed State can be a very dangerous pattern in C++ if used carelessly. Exposed State is usually required when we have a large number of State Members, and so a large number of methods in the State Object classes.

STATE-DRIVEN TRANSITIONS

You are using a number of State Objects to implement a state machine.

Problem

How do you get the State Object to change when the owning object's state changes?

When we can express the behavior of an object in terms of the states it can be in, and the actions which affect transitions between those states, we can use State Object to implement a "finite state machine." The (simplified) state diagram for LibraryBook looks like Figure 9-8.

LibraryBook's interface is extended to allow its state to be changed, which the State Object does when a transition is required.

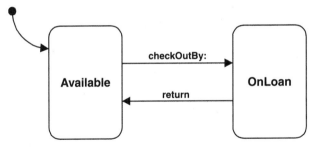

Figure 9-8 *State diagram for* `LibraryBook`

Solution

Have the State Object initiate the transition from itself (the current state) to the new State Object. This ensures transitions are atomic and removes state-dependent code (see Figure 9-9).

```
LibraryBook>>checkOutBy: aUser
    state checkOut: self by: aUser

LibraryBook>>return
    state return: self

LibraryBook>>setState: aBookState
    state := aBookState
```

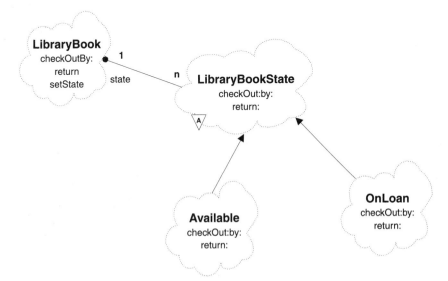

Figure 9-9 *State transitions initiated by State Object*

```
Available>>checkOut: aBook by: aUser
    "Check out aBook to aUser"
    aBook setState: (OnLoan to: aUser) "a new OnLoan State Object"

OnLoan>>return: aBook
    "Register aBook as being returned"
    aBook setState: (Available new)
```

State-Driven Transitions is in tension with Owner-Driven Transitions.

OWNER-DRIVEN TRANSITIONS

You are using a number of State Objects to implement a state machine. You are considering using State-Driven Transitions.

Problem

How do you reuse State Object classes among owning classes with different state-transition profiles?

Forces

State-Driven Transitions describes how to implement a finite state machine using State Objects and have those objects manage the transitions between states. If you wish to use those State Objects for another owning object, the new owning object must follow the same state machine, otherwise you need a new set of State Objects.

Let's widen the example of the Library system to include other things available for loan, such as audio/visual equipment for teaching purposes. We can create an abstract superclass, `LoanableItem`, and inherit `Book` and `VideoRecorder` from it as shown in Figure 9-10.

When a `VideoRecorder` is returned after being checked out, it is sent for maintenance to see that it hasn't been damaged while out on loan. Once the check and any required work have been carried out, maintenance has finished and the `VideoRecorder` is available for loan again (see Figure 9-11).

The FSMs for these two subclasses of `LoanableItems` are different. In this example, the code for checking out and returning the `VideoRecorder` is the same as that for the book. If, because we were using State-Driven Transitions, we created a new set of State Objects for `VideoRecorder`, we would be repeating a lot of what is already in `Available` and `OnLoan`, even though the only difference between `VideoRecorderOnLoan` and `BookOnLoan` would be the state transition in `#return`.

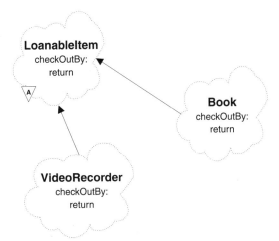

Figure 9-10 *Adding* VideoRecorder*s to the library system*

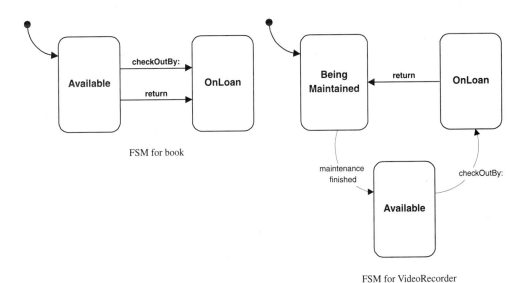

Figure 9-11 *State diagrams for the* LibraryBook *and* VideoRecorder

```
BookOnLoan>>return: aLoanableItem
    "Return aLoanableItem"
    aLoanableItem setState: (Available new)

VideoRecorderOnLoan>>return: aLoanableItem
    "Return aLoanableItem"
    aLoanableItem setState: (BeingMaintained new)
```

In addition to the missed reuse, the design has become more confused because of the extra classes, and we have introduced coupling between owning and state classes at the concrete rather than the abstract level.

Solution

If State Object classes are to be used by more than one owning class, and those owning classes have different FSMs, have the owning class initiate the transition between states.

Rather than have the state transitions encoded into `Available`, `OnLoan`, and `BeingMaintained`, `Book` and `VideoRecorder` take responsibility for changing their own state.

```
Book>>checkOutBy: aUser
    state checkOut: self by: aUser.
    "if no exceptions have been raised: the book has been checked out..."
    self setState: (OnLoan to: aUser)

Book>>return
    state return: self.
    self setState: (Available new)

VideoRecorder>>checkOutBy: aUser
    state checkOut: self by: aUser.
    self setState: (OnLoan to: aUser)

VideoRecorder>>return
    state return: self.
    self setState: (BeingMaintained new)
```

This pattern is in tension with State-Driven Transitions which should be used as a default unless it is anticipated that State Objects will be used in different state machines. Even if some of the State Objects are to be used across different FSMs, it may still be possible to use State-Driven Transitions by using a Template Method [Gamma+95] to avoid redundancies between different implementations of the State Objects. This should be considered only when there are only slight changes in transition or when there are only a few occurrences of reusing the State Objects.

The owning object in Owner-Driven Transitions is taking on the role of a Mediator [Gamma+95]. Transition Methods [Ran95] also address this problem.

DEFAULT STATE

You are creating a new object that is implemented with State Object.

Problem

When creating a new owning object, how do I ensure that it has the correct initial State Object?

Forces

Creating a new instance of an owning object requires that its state is initialized. The default state could be written into the `#initialize` method.

```
LoanableItem>>initialize

    state := Available new
```

But, what happens if we need to change the default state? We could subclass and rewrite initialize, but the state would still be initialized to `Available`, only to be reinitialized to the new default state. With a nontrivial State Object, this could be very expensive. Another approach would be to pass the initial state as a parameter to the constructing method, but this would require the explicit creation of a State Object every time an owning object is created.

Solution

Use a method, called the `#initialize` method, that returns the default State Object (see Figure 9-12). Redefine this method in a subclass if a different default state is required.

The initial state for `Book` is `Available`, but for `VideoRecorder` it is `Being-Maintained` (we can assume that new books are okay, but we have to check that

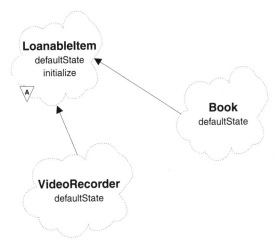

Figure 9-12 *Different default states for* `LibraryBook` *and* `VideoRecorder`

new video recorders work correctly). Having the `#initialize` method as a Template Method [Gamma+95] ensures that each new class must define what its Default State is but doesn't dictate what that should be.

```
LoanableItem>>initialize
    "Some initialization"
    state := self defaultState

LoanableItem>>defaultState
    ^self implementedBySubclass

Book>>defaultState
    ^Available new

VideoRecorder>>defaultState
    ^BeingMaintained new
```

This implementation of Default State works in Smalltalk but not in C++ where constructors are not polymorphic (see Coplien [Coplien92] for C++ virtual constructors). Default State is an example of Modifying Super [Beck96].

ACKNOWLEDGMENTS

Many thanks to Walter Zimmer who was the EuroPLoP shepherd for this chapter and gave some excellent and concrete advice on how it might be improved. Thanks also to the members of the EuroPLoP Pattern Languages writer's workshop and Alexander Ran, for their reviews and comments.

REFERENCES

[Beck96] K. Beck. *Smalltalk Best Practice Patterns Volume 1: Coding.* Englewood Cliffs, N.J.: Prentice Hall, 1996.

[Coplien92] J. O. Coplien, *Advanced C++ Programming Styles and Idioms.* Reading, MA: Addison-Wesley, 1992.

[Gamma+95] E. Gamma, R. Helm, R. Johnson, and J. Vlissides. *Design Patterns: Elements of Object-Oriented Software.* Reading, MA: Addison-Wesley, 1995.

[Ran95] A. Ran. "MOODS: Models for Object-Oriented Design of State." In J. Vlissides, J. O. Coplien, and N. Kerth (eds.), *Pattern Languages of Program Design 2,* Reading, MA: Addison-Wesley, 1996, pp. 119–142.

Paul Dyson can be contacted at pdyson@essex.ac.uk.
Bruce Anderson can be contacted at bruce_anderson@uk.ibm.com.

PART 3

Architectural Patterns

Architectural patterns help you to specify the fundamental structure of a software system, or important parts of it. For example, Regine Meunier's Pipes and Filters pattern [PLoPD1] specifies basic structural principles for an application. Or they define specific subsystems together with their collaboration, such as Mary Shaw's Repository pattern [PLoPD2]. Yet other architectural patterns specify complete infrastructures for software systems, such as the Broker pattern [Buch96] for distributed applications. Consequently, architectural patterns have an important impact on the appearance of concrete software architectures. They define a system's global properties, such as how distributed components cooperate and exchange data. Furthermore, the selection of an architectural pattern is a fundamental design decision; it governs every development activity that follows. In this volume of the PLoPD series, we present two architectural patterns.

Chapter 10: Recursive Control, by Bran Selic. This chapter presents a pattern that applies to structuring large-scale real-time systems. It separates real-time control aspects from application functionality and also real-time control interfaces from control mechanisms. Thus, a real-time system consists of a control interface for real-time functions, an internal control component that handles these functions, and components that implement the application functionality. Each of these functional parts can be recursively structured again into the three parts—the reason why the pattern is called Recursive Control.

As a result, the same two structuring principles for integrating real-time aspects apply in every part of the system, from the largest to the smallest part. Independent of how global or local a real-time aspect is, they are all handled homogeneously. This helps with understanding the structure of a real-time application and supports maintaining and extending the system.

Chapter 11: Bureaucracy, by Dirk Riehle. The Bureaucracy pattern helps with building self-contained hierarchical structures of objects or components. Clients can interact with every element of the structure in the same way, independent of its level in the hierarchy. Furthermore, the structure itself maintains its inner consistency, such as state dependencies between its elements. The pattern works best if there is no need for external control.

The Bureaucracy pattern is composed of four well-known patterns from the Gang of Four: Composite, Mediator, Chain of Responsibility, and Observer [Gamma+95]. Yet the Bureaucracy pattern is more than just a combination of these four patterns. It addresses aspects of handling and maintaining object or component hierarchies that cannot be resolved by any of its constituent patterns alone. For example, it suggests how to propagate an event to all elements of the hierarchy, whether the elements are at higher or lower levels of the hierarchy or in different subhierarchies. Bureaucracy describes how these four patterns cooperate as a team to define hierarchical structures that are stable and self-contained on the one hand, but still extensible and adaptable on the other hand.

Summary. As you can see from these brief characterizations, architectural patterns let you think in terms of a whole system. Software architectures should be easy to understand, change, extend, adapt, and maintain so that architects, designers, and programmers feel habituated to it [Gabriel96]. To achieve this, you need an architectural vision; the software architecture must be structured according to some common design principles, in every part and at every level of abstraction. A nice example for such a principle is the way Recursive Control separates application functionality from real-time control. The same principle tends to recur, thus defining the architectural vision for such systems.

Another aspect of architectural patterns, as shown by the Bureaucracy pattern, is that applying design patterns is not a mechanical task. Applying patterns and composing their instances requires experience in order to build large structures in a coherent and meaningful way. We can distinguish between composing applied and composite patterns. The first, composing applied patterns, takes place on a concrete level—whenever you design something of nontrivial size using patterns. The second, composite patterns, are new patterns that capture larger structures than single atomic patterns could do alone. Describing composite patterns through their constituent patterns alone is not feasible: it would distract readers from understanding the essence of the composite. Moreover, every other complex structure in which they play a role must be described. A better approach is to describe structures that are composed of other patterns as patterns of their own. All relevant issues can be discussed in one place and in their correct context. You see, Composite Patterns is a very important pattern category. Bureaucracy is one of its first representatives.

REFERENCES

[Buch96] S. Buch. "Broker." In F. Buschmann, R. Meunier, H. Rohnert, P. Sommerlad, and M. Stal, *Pattern-Oriented Software Architecture*. New York: John Wiley and Sons, 1996, pp. 99–122.

[Gabriel96] R. P. Gabriel. *Patterns of Software*. Cambridge: Oxford University Press, 1996.

[Gamma+95] E. Gamma, R. Johnson, R. Helm, and J. Vlissides. *Design Patterns: Elements of Reusable Object-Oriented Software*. Reading, MA: Addison-Wesley, 1995.

[PLoPD1] J. O. Coplien and D. C. Schmidt (eds.). *Pattern Language of Program Design*. Reading, MA: Addison-Wesley, 1995.

[PLoPD2] J. M. Vlissides, J. O. Coplien, and N. L. Kerth (eds.). *Pattern Languages of Program Design 2*. Reading, MA: Addison-Wesley, 1996.

Chapter 10

Recursive Control

Bran Selic

Before any system can perform the functions that are its primary purpose, it first has to reach some type of "operational" state. For many software systems this is achieved simply by running the necessary initialization code that opens up the required files, sets internal variables to the appropriate initial values, and so on. Real-time software, however, is more complicated, since, to reach an operational state, it first needs to synchronize itself with the state of the external world in which it is embedded. Furthermore, once this state is reached, continual activity may be required to keep it in that state due to various external disruptions, such as equipment failures or interventions by human operators. The physical world surrounding real-time software is inherently unpredictable, dynamic, and generally complex. Consequently, the software that has to contend with these aspects is itself correspondingly complex. In larger real-time systems, it is quite common that the complexity of the code devoted to establishing and maintaining an operational state far exceeds the complexity of the code that handles the primary functionality of the system. That is, in such systems, control is the dominant and most difficult aspect of the software.

Unfortunately, this fact often goes unrecognized since our intuition and training compel us to first focus on the primary system functionality and then, typically much later, to retrofit the control aspects around it. For instance, control functionality is often found in exception handlers—a secondary mechanism whose semantics are defined by the implementation language and not by the designer. This also leads to a haphazard dispersal of control, making it very difficult to define consistent and effective control policies. The resulting software is often unnecessarily complex and uncontrollable.

This effect is exacerbated as new functionality is added in response to new requirements. Since the control aspects have been molded around the structure imposed by the primary functionality, it becomes very difficult to change one without affecting the other.

What is required, then, is a design approach that would enable proper emphasis of control issues during design with the ability to define and evolve them independently of primary system functionality.

THE RECURSIVE CONTROL PATTERN

The Recursive Control pattern introduced here is intended for structuring the control-related components of large real-time systems where complex issues of control dominate. It is a general architectural framework whose structure is independent of the actual functionality of the system. In fact, the architecture, the component interrelationships, of the functional components of the system is not constrained by the Recursive Control pattern and may be entirely driven by the needs of the problem at hand.

Control

We have already defined control to mean the set of mechanisms required to bring and maintain a system into the desired operational state. This includes software-based activities such as system and component activation (start up) and deactivation (shut down), failure detection and recovery, interaction with external control entities such as human operators, various forms of preventive maintenance, performance monitoring, and, in some cases, on-line loading and unloading of software.

In very large software systems issues of control are far more critical than in smaller systems simply because the number and diversity of components and states that must be controlled are large. In such systems, particularly if they are distributed, it is very difficult to ensure a consistency of control policies that would yield controllability. A case in point is the well-known failure of a large part of the North American long-distance telephone network caused by unforeseen conflicts between node-level and network-level recovery policies that resulted in enormous damage [Meyers90].

Design Principles

The Recursive Control pattern is a consequence of two fundamental design principles that reflect the controllability requirement: first, the separation of control from function and second, the separation of control policies from control mechanisms.

Separating Control from Function

Components responsible for control should be decoupled as much as possible from components responsible for functional aspects. This allows each to be defined, implemented, and evolved independently. Furthermore, by virtue of this separation, the likelihood is increased that crucial control issues, traditionally viewed as second-level concerns, will actually receive the consideration they deserve.

Separating Control Policies and Control Mechanisms

Control strategies in many systems are prone to change. For example, a traffic light controller may start as a stand-alone system but might eventually be integrated into a greater traffic control network. This means that its internal control system would have to evolve from being autonomous to being an executive agent of a higher control authority. To simplify and standardize the handling of such situations, we require that control policies be kept as distinct as possible from control mechanisms. Control policies are realized by software that makes decisions based on state feedback and that issues control commands to secure those decisions. Control mechanisms, on the other hand, are the components that either provide state feedback or that respond to commands.

For example, in a communications system, a component that detects the failure of a transmission link is part of the control mechanisms. However, a component that dictates the fault recovery procedure is part of the control policies. By separating the two, it becomes possible to change the recovery procedure without affecting the failure detection software and vice versa.

The Recursive Control Pattern

The Recursive Control pattern is illustrated by the structure in Figure 10-1. The purpose of the functional components in the canonical model is to provide the required system functionality through one or more functional interfaces of the overall real-time system (RTSystem). The operational state of the functional components is controlled by the internal control component of the system. The control policy for managing the system may either be integrated into the internal control or it may come from an external higher-level control system through the control interface of the system. Note that although internal control is shown as a single monolithic component, it may be realized by a confederation of separate components.

In this model, each functional component also has two sets of interfaces: a control interface to the internal control system and one or more functional interface

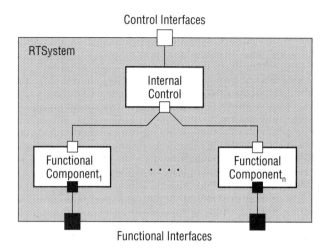

Figure 10-1 *The structure of the Recursive Control pattern[1]*

for the services it provides to its clients.[2] The client interface of each of the n functional components is "exported" to the interface of the system. The net result is a system with one control interface and a number of functional interfaces.

Each functional component, just like the system as a whole, has a control interface and one or more functional interfaces. This suggests that, for more complex functional components, the same base pattern can be applied. That is, these components might be further decomposed in the same way—with their own internal control components and a set of finer-grained functional components (Figure 10-2). This recursion means that, in principle, the same pattern can be used for arbitrarily complex systems.

Collaborations

When a control input, such as reset, is received through the top-level control interface, the internal controller of the overall system translates this into one or more control inputs for a subset of the top-level functional components. If the functional components are decomposed further, these inputs are received by the internal controllers and are, in turn, resolved into yet finer control signals for their own

---

[1] In these object instance diagrams (as opposed to class-based diagrams), we use the convention of explicitly rendering object's interfaces by smaller squares that appear on the border of an object. For clarity, control interfaces are represented by white squares while filled black squares denote functional interfaces. The line segments that connect object interfaces are abstractions of various types of inter-object links such as pointers, sockets, or pipes.

[2] There may be additional interfaces between the functional components, but these are not relevant to our discussion.

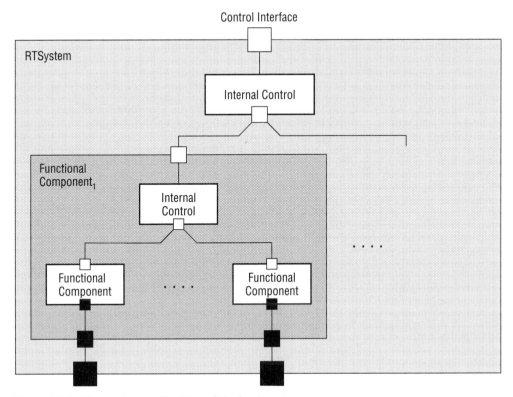

Figure 10-2 *Recursive application of the basic pattern*

functional subcomponents, and so on. In effect, the contained internal controllers provide a set of control mechanisms for realizing the control policies of their higher-level controllers.

In the reverse direction, functional components notify their controllers whenever they detect control situations, such as various types of component failures, that require intervention by their controller. Functional components also collaborate with external clients to provide their respective services.

Applicability

Recursive Control is useful in situations, typical in event-driven real-time applications, where a complex software-based server system needs to be controlled dynamically in some nontrivial manner. It is particularly applicable in situations where there is a high likelihood that control policies may change over time.

Participants

- Internal Control accepts control inputs received from external (higher-level) controllers, through the system's control interface, and, based on its inherent control policies, resolves these into control commands for the functional components directly under its control. It also reacts to internal events that emanate from the controlled functional components. Reaction responses may be purely local, based on the control policies built into the controller, or they may result in control events that are relayed on to a higher-level controller for handling. For completely autonomous systems, there may not be a control interface at the top level.
- Functional Components provide the basic service functions of the system through one or more functional interfaces as well as a set of mechanisms for effecting the control policies of their controllers. They are also responsible for administering internal control policies through, for example, their contained internal controllers for control situations that do not require intervention by their controllers. If they are complex enough, functional components may be further decomposed into an internal control and a set of lower-level functional components.

Consequences

The Recursive Control pattern does the following:

- Increases the likelihood that software control issues will be properly addressed in the design of complex real-time software.
- Simplifies the implementation of complex systems since it is based on a recursive application of a single structural pattern. In essence, it provides basic architectural structure for such systems at all levels of decomposition from top to bottom.
- Simplifies development (and understanding) of both functional and control aspects by decoupling them from each other.
- Allows control policies to be changed without affecting the basic functionality of the system.
- Adds overhead due to its hierarchical nature and the decoupling between control and function.

Relationship to More Basic Patterns

The Recursive Control pattern is a combination of other more fundamental patterns. The principle of separating control from function is an embodiment of the Strategy pattern as defined by Gamma, et al., in which the main idea is to protect a client from having to contend with implementation differences in a strategy (service) that it requires. The Control component of the Recursive Control pattern

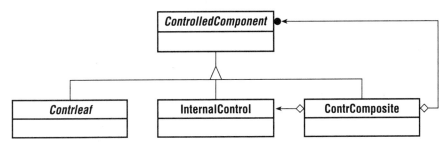

Figure 10-3 *Recursive Control as a variant of the Composite pattern*

plays the role that Context plays in the Strategy pattern. It delegates the realization of its control strategy to the various functional components (the concrete strategies) through a common interface.

Structurally, the Recursive Control pattern is related to the Composite pattern described by [Gamma+95, p. 163]. Composite is a recursive pattern that is used in situations where it is necessary to treat components uniformly, regardless of whether they are primitive or composite objects.

Note that, in structural diagram of Recursive Control shown in Figure 10-3, since all the participants in the pattern have a common control interface, they are all subclasses of a common abstract class `ControlledComponent`. One of those subclasses is `ContrComposite`, which represents the control-function structure. It consists of exactly one `InternalControl` component and a number of functional components that are specific subclasses of `ControlledComponent`.

From a behavior perspective, Recursive Control incorporates the Chain of Responsibility pattern [Gamma+95, p. 223]. That is, external controllers issuing control inputs are unaware of the hierarchy of internal controllers that are actually responsible for executing the corresponding control actions—external controllers simply issue commands to the system through its unique control interface.

Example

To illustrate the relationship between control and function, we consider the example of a communication system that uses the alternating bit protocol [Bartlett+69, p. 260]. The exact details of this protocol are beyond the scope of this chapter, so suffice it to say that it is a flow-controlled protocol that deals partially with the negative effects of an unreliable communications medium, such as message duplication, reordering, and loss. A typical execution sequence of this protocol is depicted in Figure 10-4.

The function of the communication system is to transfer information between two of its users: a `Server` and a `Client` who are presently connected by an unreliable communications network. The system itself consists of a `Sender` component collocated with the `Server` and a `Receiver` collocated with the `Client`. The

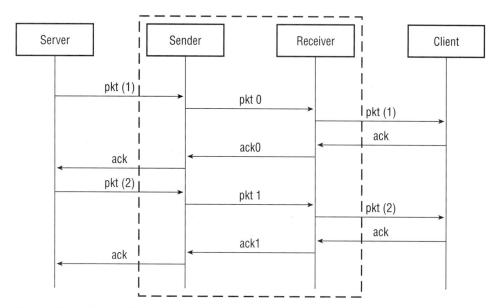

Figure 10-4 *Alternating bit protocol—a typical scenario*

Server periodically formulates an information packet (pkt(x)) which it sends to the Client using the services of the Sender component. When it receives an acknowledgment (ack) from the Client (via the system), the Server transmits the next packet. To protect against reordering, duplication, or loss of messages, the Sender labels each information packet with a sequence number (0 or 1) and refrains from sending the next packet until the previous one has been acknowledged. To avoid confusion about which packet is being acknowledged, the Receiver includes the sequence number of the last successfully delivered packet in its acknowledgment. Thus, if a packet with a sequence number of zero is sent, an acknowledgment with a sequence number of zero is expected. If the expected acknowledgment does not arrive within some predefined maximum time interval, the previous information packet is resent by the Sender. For simplicity, we assume that the Server never sends a packet until the previous one has been acknowledged by the Client.

This is a simple case of a two-level communication protocol in which a high-level protocol (Client-Server) is overlaid on a lower-level protocol (Sender-Receiver). The lower-level protocol hides some of the complexity of dealing with an unreliable communications medium, thereby simplifying implementation of the higher-level protocol. A common way of specifying the lower-level alternating bit protocol is through a pair of simple cooperating finite-state machines as shown in Figure 10-5.

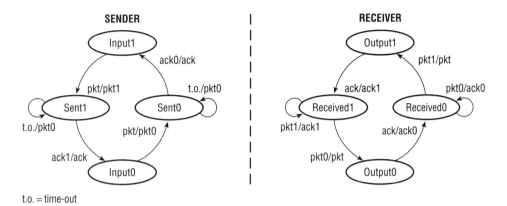

Figure 10-5 *Alternating bit protocol—formal specification*

In this form, the specification does not take into account a variety of practical control-related concerns that must be addressed. Let us assume that the following basic capabilities are also required of this system.

- Both the Sender and the Receiver need to be initialized with configuration data, such as address data, that uniquely identifies each station. Let us assume that this data comes from a message sent by an external control entity.
- For maintenance reasons, it is necessary to be able to *restart*, that is, start the protocol from the beginning, without reloading the data for the two entities. The restart command comes in the form of a message sent by an external control entity.
- In some cases, it is necessary to fully reset the entire Sender/Receiver complex. A full reset does require that the configuration data be reloaded. The reset is also initiated by a message from an external entity.
- To ensure proper synchronization of the two ends in case of resets and restarts, we will assume that neither the Sender nor the Receiver will commence with the protocol until it is explicitly directed to do so by an external start message.
- If the Sender does not receive the expected acknowledgment from the Receiver after several retries (retries are initiated by time-outs), it should enter an error state from which it can be either restarted or reset. In this state, it no longer responds to the Receiver. Similarly, we could define an error state in the Receiver which is triggered if it receives too many wrong signals in succession from the Sender. The purpose of the error state is to identify that the two ends of the protocol are hopelessly out of sync and that something needs to be done to resolve the deadlock.

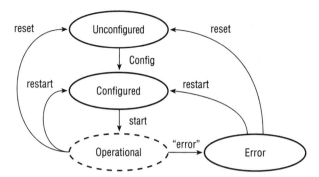

Figure 10-6 *The control state machine for the* Sender *and* Receiver

The additional messages added to the specification are control signals that serve to properly synchronize the operation of the two ends in a realistic environment.[3] In effect, they represent a second protocol, the protocol between the Sender (or Receiver) and its immediate controller. If we abstract out the details of the alternating bit protocol defined in Figure 10-5, then the process of controlling each of the two ends can be described by another state machine (Figure 10-6).

The Operational state in the above diagram does not really exist; it is a shorthand notation for the two finite state machines detailed in Figure 10-5. The actual complete diagram, for the Sender, is shown in Figure 10-7 (to reduce visual clutter, transition labels are not shown).

The most obvious difference between the specification of the Sender in Figure 10-5 and in Figure 10-7 is that the latter is much more complex. In general, the synthetic quality of a graphical rendering is lost in such cases because of excessive detail. Some of that complexity can be removed by various graphical shorthand tricks, including the use of constructs such as "any" state. Nevertheless, there still remains the issue that, in Figure 10-7, the alternating-bit protocol and the control protocol have become hopelessly intertwined, even though they are defined independently. Neither protocol is depicted in its pure form but in the context of the other protocol. This not only hinders comprehension, but complicates maintenance. Someone who is not fully aware of the separate nature of the two protocols may, during maintenance activity, inadvertently couple them further or violate one while trying to fix the other.

There is one other serious problem here. We have already noted that the control protocol for the Sender and the Receiver are practically the same. This is a common feature of well-designed control systems since it decouples the control system from the specifics of what is being controlled. The major disadvantage is that

---

[3]In fact, only a limited set of failure modes are considered in this example; a real implementation would likely have to contend with additional ones.

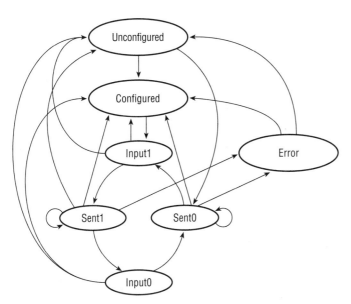

Figure 10-7 *The complete state machine diagram of the* `Sender`

by merging the two protocols into a single superprotocol, the common control protocol needs to be reimplemented separately ("cloned") for each controlled element. Furthermore, if the control protocol needs to be changed, the same modifications have to be made manually to each separate instance. This increases the amount of effort and the probability of coding errors.

Implementation

In looking at how the Recursive Control pattern can be implemented, we show how hierarchical state-machine formalisms, such as statecharts [Harel87, p. 231] or ROOMcharts [Selic+94], which are commonly used for modeling complex event-driven systems, can be used to great advantage for this purpose, especially when they are combined with the inheritance mechanism.

Hierarchical finite-state machine formalisms allow an entire state machine to be abstracted into a single state at the next higher level of abstraction. This allows very complex event-driven behavior to be modeled by a graduated series of hierarchically related state machines. For example, either of the state machines in Figure 10-5 (`Sender` or `Receiver`) can be subsumed into the `Operational` state of the control state machine in Figure 10-6. The resulting top-level state machine for both objects is depicted in Figure 10-8 using the ROOMchart notation. (The two transitions, `reset` and `restart`, emanating from the border containing the state machine are a shorthand way of saying that these transitions can originate in any state.)

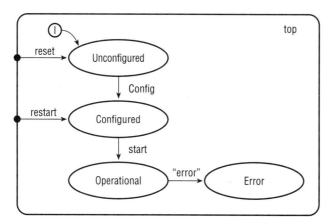

Figure 10-8 *The top-level state machine for the* `Sender` *and* `Receiver`

For a controlled component to perform its function, it must first be in the appropriate operational state. In our alternating-bit protocol example, both the `Sender` and the `Receiver` first had to pass through the `Configured` state (where they received their configuration data) and be explicitly activated (for synchronization reasons) before they could perform their primary function. This means that in specifying behavior, control predicates function. That is, the dominant, or upper-level, behavior is the control framework; it subsumes (encapsulates) the functional behavior.

Note that the `Sender` and the `Receiver` have the same top-level behavioral specification. However, they have different functional state machines represented by the left and right sides of the specification in Figure 10-5. It appears as though the two objects would require two separate state machines that have the same top-level state machine, but that differ in the way that the `Operational` state is decomposed. (The hierarchical nature of the `Operational` state is indicated graphically by its thicker border.)

At this point, we can take advantage of inheritance and define a class hierarchy such that the two have a common abstract class that captures the top-level behavior and two distinct subclasses for the `Sender` and `Receiver` (Figure 10-9). In the abstract superclass (`ContrLeaf`, which inherits from `ControlledComponent`, as shown in Figure 10-3), the `Operational` state is a simple leaf state, but in the subclasses, it is refined into submachines. For the `Sender` subclass, the submachine will correspond to the left-hand side of Figure 10-5 while in the `Receiver` subclass, the submachine matches the right-hand side of Figure 10-5. In effect, the `Operational` state is an abstract state analogous to a C++ virtual function. (The use of virtual functions or their equivalents for this purpose would be the most natural technique for applications that are not directly implemented as state machines.)

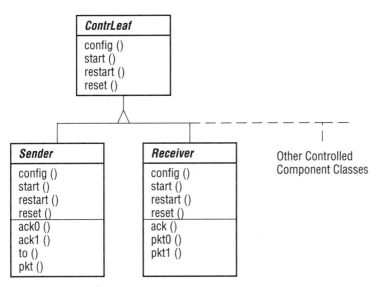

Figure 10-9 *The inheritance hierarchy for the alternating bit protocol*

In fact, as shown in Figure 10-9, the same abstract class can serve as a parent for any components, regardless of their place in the system hierarchy, that conform to the same control protocol. This not only saves development time and simplifies maintenance, but also encourages uniform control strategies ultimately leading to systems that are easily controlled. The net result is a more reliable system that can be produced with significantly less effort than through conventional development techniques. Note that this use of inheritance is actually a form of the Template Method pattern as defined in .

Consider next the case of a more complete system that is distributed across two processing nodes as shown in Figure 10-10. The ServerNode contains the Sender as well as the Server application that uses the Sender (see Figure 10-4), while the ClientNode contains the Client and the Receiver. To ensure proper operation of the functional components in each node, we introduce an internal Node-Controller component. Among other things, this component ensures that the Sender (Receiver) is activated *before* the Server (Client). Using the same rationale, we also introduce a supercontroller component, the SystemController, which synchronizes the operation of the two nodes. For example, if the Server-Node fails for some reason, the SystemController would notify the clientNode so that proper recovery action, perhaps switching to another server, can be undertaken.

The structure shown in Figure 10-10 is, in fact, an application of the Recursive Control pattern. In this case, the SystemController and the NodeControllers are both examples of internal controllers, although they occur at different levels of

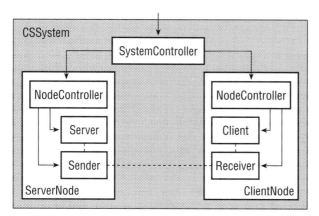

Figure 10-10 *The Client-Server system example*

decomposition. Both can be subclasses of the same abstract class, `Internal-Control` (Figure 10-9). The `Sender`, `Receiver`, `Server`, and `Client` components are all different subclasses of the `ContrLeaf` abstract class while the two aggregate node components, `ServerNode` and `ClientNode`, as well as the overall `CSSystem` are different subclasses of the abstract class, `ContrComposite`.

The operation of the control hierarchy can be illustrated using the boot scenario sequence. At start-up time, all components automatically come up in the `Unconfigured` state as shown in Figure 10-8. Once the `CSSystem` controller is fully activated (since this is the "top" level of the system, activation could either be driven by a higher-level external control system or it could be automatic), it proceeds to activate the two `NodeControllers` in the proper sequence (for example, activating first the `ServerNode` and then the `ClientNode` `NodeControllers`). When a `NodeController` is activated, it can in turn activate its corresponding functional components in order. Analogous activities occur in other control situations such as component failures and controlled shutdown.

S U M M A R Y

In the design of real-time software it is standard practice to treat control functions as second-level concerns despite the fact that such aspects often represent the greater portion of the overall software. This often leads to unnecessary complexity with diverse and inconsistent control policies at different levels of the system and with control and functional aspects of the system inextricably coupled so that they cannot be understood or modified independently. This has negative impacts on system reliability and maintainability.

In this chapter, we have introduced a design pattern, the Recursive Control pattern, that helps avoid these problems for practically any real-time system where there is a need for dynamic control. One of the characteristics of the pattern is that system service functionality is encapsulated within its control functionality. The rationality of this characteristic takes into account that a system must first reach an "operational" state before it can properly perform its service function. Thus, the Recursive Control pattern reverses traditional design practice and places control *before* function.

An important feature of the pattern is its applicability at any level of decomposition including the top level, thus making it an "architectural" pattern. If the pattern is applied recursively and uniformly, the result is a system that is both simple and highly controllable. The Recursive Control pattern can be expressed particularly concisely and effectively if inheritance is used to capture common control behavior in an abstract class.

ACKNOWLEDGMENTS

I would like to thank the anonymous referees for their extensive help in revising this paper and also Rod Iversen of ObjecTime Limited who helped in presenting this paper at PLoP '96.

REFERENCES

[Bartlett+69] K. Bartlett, R. Scantelbury, and P. Wilkinson. A note on reliable full-duplex transmission over half-duplex lines. *Communications of the ACM*, 12(5): 260–265, May 1969.

[Gamma+95] E. Gamma, R. Helm, R. Johnson, and J. Vlissides. *Design Patterns: Elements of Reusable Object-Oriented Software.* Reading, MA: Addison-Wesley, 1995.

[Harel87] D. Harel. "Statecharts: A visual formalism for complex systems." *Science of Computer Programming* 8: 231–274, July 1987.

[Meyers90] M. Meyers. "The AT&T Telephone Network Outage of January 15, 1990." Invited presentation at the 20th IEEE International Symposium on Fault-Tolerant Computing, Newcastle upon Tyne, England, June 26–28, 1990.

[Selic+94] B. Selic, G. Gullekson, and P. T. Ward. *Real-Time Object-Oriented Modeling.* New York: John Wiley & Sons, 1994.

Bran Selic can be reached at bran@objectime.com.

Chapter 11

Bureaucracy

Dirk Riehle

The Bureaucracy pattern is a recurring design theme used to implement hierarchical object or component structures which allow interaction with every level of the hierarchy and maintain their inner consistency themselves. It is a composite pattern that is based on the Composite, Mediator, Chain of Responsibility, and Observer patterns. Composite patterns require new presentation and modeling techniques because their complexity makes them more difficult to approach than noncomposite patterns. In this chapter, role diagrams are used to present the Bureaucracy pattern and to explore its design and implementation space. Role diagrams have proved useful to get a grip on this complex pattern, and they should work well for design patterns in general.

The Bureaucracy pattern is a composite pattern that helps developers build self-contained hierarchical structures that can interact with clients on every level, but need no external control and maintain their inner consistency themselves. This pattern scales well to structure large parts of an application or a framework. It is based on the idea of modern bureaucracy [Weber47] which seems to work well for software systems.

A composite pattern is first of all a *pattern*. It represents a design theme that keeps recurring in specific contexts. I call it a *composite* pattern, because it can best be explained as the composition of some other patterns. However, a composite pattern goes beyond a mere composition to capture the synergy arising from the various *roles* an object plays in the overall composition structure. As such, composite patterns are more than just the sum of their constituting patterns.

The presentation of the Bureaucracy pattern is based on the notion of roles rather than the notion of "participants" employed in the design pattern template of the Gang of Four [Gamma+95]. The notion of role is crucial to understanding the idea of composite patterns. An object in an instantiation of a composite pattern can play several roles and thus participate in different overlapping pattern instantiations. A composition of patterns turns into a composite pattern, if and only if (1) a relevant synergy arises between the roles an object plays and (2) this synergy can be observed as a recurring design theme.

In its second section, the chapter presents the pattern without referring to the process and means of digging it out. However, there are many other composite patterns worthy of being documented, so the third section presents the concepts and techniques used for eliciting the Bureaucracy pattern in the hope they will be helpful to other pattern writers. This includes the role diagram notation for design patterns, the role relationship matrix as a means for analyzing prototypical pattern applications, and ways of interpreting the matrix.

THE BUREAUCRACY PATTERN

The general presentation form for the Bureaucracy pattern is based on the design pattern template of the Gang of Four [Gamma+95], with some enhancements. In particular, the Structure and Collaboration sections are based on roles rather than on participants. This enhancement lets us discuss the pattern's structure and implementation issues on a broader scale.

The pattern requires prior understanding of the Composite, Mediator, Chain of Responsibility, and Observer patterns on which it is based (see Gamma, et al., for their documentation). To avoid possible confusion, when "composite" is written with a small "c" as in "a composite pattern," it denotes a pattern composed from further patterns. When written with a capital "C," it refers to the Composite pattern, either to the pattern itself or to its Composite participant as described in Gamma, et al.

Intent

Define a self-contained hierarchical structure which maintains its inner consistency, accepts interaction with clients on any level of the hierarchy, and scales for application design. This pattern combines the Observer, Chain of Responsibility, Mediator, and Composite patterns to form a composite pattern.

Motivation

Suppose you are developing a small tool for managing the compilation of shell scripts and other utilities of a much bigger project. This tool lets you work on a new version of the compilation support separate from the one currently in use. Such a tool will have at its heart a browser which will let you select and edit text files. It might also offer a shell window for syntax checking and testing scripts, as well as compiling C utilities. Finally, the tool will need some configuration data of its own, for example, the working and the target directories.

The utility manager is a single application with an overall tool structure likely to follow the Composite pattern depicted in Figure 11-1. It is built from tools, with

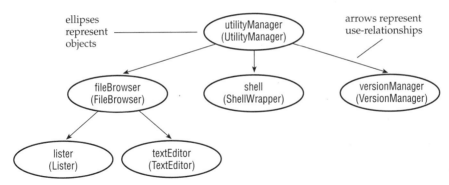

Figure 11-1 *A hierarchy of tool components forming a utility manager tool*

the utility manager tool at the top; then a file browser, shell, and version manager tool in the middle; and a lister and text editor tool at the bottom.

A tool structure like this makes it challenging to correctly distribute functionality and responsibility among the participating tools. Without following a coherent pattern, spreading responsibilities over the hierarchy is likely to lead to confusion where it is unclear which tool component is allowed to carry out which request at what point in time. Uncontrolled behavior and unmaintainable code are the consequences.

The Bureaucracy pattern shows how to coherently distribute responsibilities in such a hierarchy. Objects or components in a Bureaucracy hierarchy play two or three out of four roles. The four roles are the Clerk, Manager, Subordinate, and Director. Every object plays the Clerk role. A bottom-level object plays both the Clerk and Subordinate roles. An intermediate-level object plays the Clerk, the Manager (for its Subordinates), and the Subordinate roles (for its Manager). A top-level object, that is, the hierarchy's root object, plays the Clerk, Manager, and Director roles.

An object playing the Manager role coordinates and manages objects playing the Subordinate role. The resulting responsibility assignments are defined by the Mediator pattern. The hierarchical structure is defined by the Composite pattern, with every object being a Clerk and either a Manager or Subordinate, or both. The hierarchy's boundary conditions are the Manager, which is a Director and therefore represents the root of the hierarchy, and the Subordinates that are not Managers and thus manage no further Subordinates.

The communication protocol between a Subordinate and its Manager is defined by the Chain of Responsibility and the Observer patterns. If a Subordinate is asked to carry out a request which it cannot fully handle itself, it forwards the request up the hierarchy to its Manager, expecting the Manager to possess more context knowledge to carry out the request. This process is defined by the Chain of Responsibility pattern. If a Subordinate fully handles a request, it

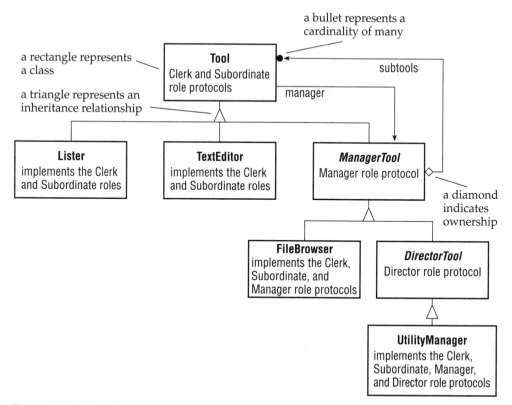

Figure 11-2 *Class diagram for implementing the utility manager tool*

informs its Manager about relevant state changes which might have occurred. The Manager interprets the state changes and might initiate further action. This communication protocol is defined by the Observer pattern.

Figure 11-2 illustrates a class hierarchy frequently used for implementing the Bureaucracy pattern. The class hierarchy shows how the roles from the constituting patterns are assigned to class interfaces. The Composite pattern defines the Node, Child, Parent, and Root roles, and the Mediator pattern defines the Colleague and Mediator roles. The Chain of Responsibility pattern defines the Handler, Successor, Predecessor, and Tail roles and the Observer pattern defines the Subject and Observer roles. Combining the Composite with the Mediator, Chain of Responsibility, and Observer patterns helps build complex object hierarchies while staying in control of how functionality and responsibility is distributed among the participating objects.

Applicability

Use the Bureaucracy pattern to structure a large object-oriented body of state and behavior that can be expressed well in the form of a hierarchy, where

- clients are free to interact with any part of the hierarchy at any time, and
- the integrity of the overall hierarchy has to be maintained by the hierarchy itself.

Do not use the Bureaucracy pattern, if everything above seems to hold, but

- the hierarchy is not self-sufficient, has to be controlled in detail by some external clients, and the requirements of this external control are hard to anticipate in advance.

If the hierarchy is subject to fine-grained manipulation by clients, it will have to go through inconsistent states until the client commits its interaction. This is not appropriate for the Bureaucracy pattern.

Structure

Figure 11-3 shows the structure of the Bureaucracy pattern. It is presented as a role diagram, a notation which focuses on roles rather than on classes. A role diagram supports all relationships between roles that are also possible between objects, including association and aggregation. In addition, it defines the notion of composition constraint, which lets you specify whether or not two roles are always played together. A composition constraint is depicted by a gray arrow; it is a binary relationship between two roles. In Figure 11-3, an object playing the

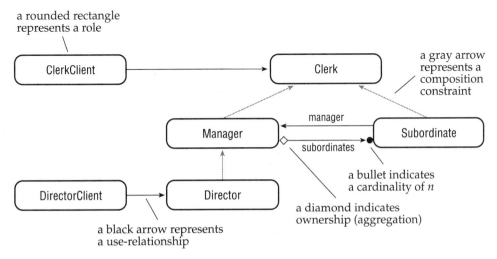

Figure 11-3 *Role diagram of the Bureaucracy pattern*

Manager role also always plays the Clerk role, and so on. It maps nicely on class inheritance on an implementation level.

A role defines the responsibilities of an object within a collaboration of objects. It is expressed as a role protocol. An object can participate in several collaborations and, therefore, can play several roles at once. A class implementing an object has to implement all those roles the object is playing in the different collaborations. The class interface will then be composed from the different role protocols.

A role can be composed from further roles. For example, the Mediator role from the Mediator pattern is an atomic role, while the Subordinate role from the Bureaucracy pattern is a composite role comprising the Child, Colleague, Predecessor, and Subject roles from the Composite, Mediator, Chain of Responsibility, and Observer patterns.

Figure 11-4 shows the most commonly found class diagram used for implementing the Bureaucracy pattern. The static structure of the class diagram is governed by the Composite pattern, with the `Subordinate` class representing the Component class [Gamma+95], the `Manager` class representing the Composite class, and the `Director` class representing the Root class.

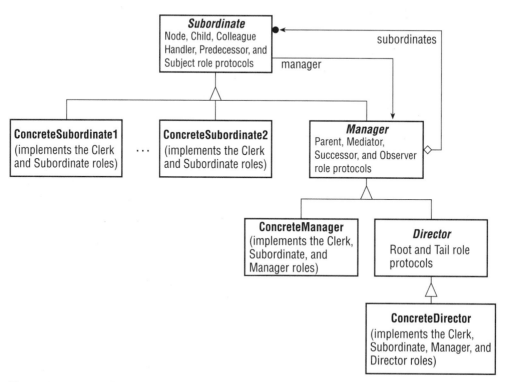

Figure 11-4 *Most frequently found class diagram of the Bureaucracy pattern*

The dynamic behavior of the pattern is governed by the Mediator, Chain of Responsibility, and Observer patterns. The Manager acts as a Mediator to its Subordinates which act as Colleagues. The communication protocol from Subordinates to their Managers is described by the Chain of Responsibility and Observer patterns. Each pattern follows its own dynamics as described by the interaction diagrams referenced in Gamma, et al. The integration of the different roles from the constituting patterns in a single object delivers the synergy which drives the Bureaucracy pattern.

Figure 11-4 is not the only class diagram that can be used to implement the Bureaucracy pattern. In principle, every role protocol can be represented as an interface class of its own, and concrete classes of objects participating in a Bureaucracy hierarchy can selectively inherit from those interface classes according to the roles they play in the various collaborations.

Roles

The roles of the Bureaucracy pattern from Figure 11-3 build on the roles from the constituent patterns.

- The Manager role combines the Parent, Mediator, Handler, Successor, and Observer roles. A Manager coordinates objects playing the Subordinate role. It receives requests from them and observes their state changes.

  - Playing the Mediator role from the Mediator pattern, it manages, coordinates, and delegates to its Subordinate objects. It does whatever it needs to do to keep the hierarchy in a consistent state.
  - Playing the Successor role from the Chain of Responsibility pattern, it receives requests from its Subordinate objects. It can either handle these requests or forward them to its own Manager.
  - Playing the Observer role from the Observer pattern, it receives state change notifications from its Subordinate objects. It can react to these notifications, for example, by manipulating its Subordinate objects or by generating requests.

- The Subordinate role combines the Child, Colleague, Predecessor, and Subject roles. A Subordinate is managed and coordinated with other Subordinates by a Manager. It receives requests from clients and decides whether to execute them or to forward them to its Manager. It notifies its Manager about state changes, for example, when it has finished executing a client request.

  - Playing the Colleague role from the Mediator pattern, the subordinate is subject to management by its Manager.
  - Playing the Predecessor role from the Chain of Responsibility pattern, it forwards client requests to its Manager.
  - Playing the Subject role from the Observer pattern, a Subordinate object is subject to observation by its Manager.

- The Director role holds the ultimate responsibility for the hierarchy and manages it according to its needs and purposes. An object playing the Director role also always plays the Manager, extending the Manager role with the Root and Tail roles.

  - Playing the Root role from the Composite pattern, it holds full responsibility for the whole object hierarchy, which it manages according to its needs and purposes.
  - Playing the Tail role from the Chain of Responsibility pattern, it has the final decisive power in handling client requests. It might decide to handle them, ignore them, or to raise an exception.
  - The Clerk role defines the standard behavior of an object in the hierarchy as its responsibility to external clients. It combines the *Node* and *Handler* roles from the Composite and Chain of Responsibility patterns. Every object in the hierarchy always plays the role of Clerk.

Collaborations

The single roles have the responsibilities of the participants as described by the constituting patterns Composite, Mediator, Chain of Responsibility, and Observer. Of interest to a composite pattern, however, is the synergy which arises from the integration of several roles in a composite role played by a single object.

Playing roles in different pattern instantiations requires switching contexts during execution. An action in one context can cause an object to act in another context. The interface to each context, that is, a pattern instance, is the object's role in that context.

- *Mediator and Successor (Manager).* If an object playing both the Mediator and Successor roles receives a request from a `Subordinate` object, it reacts to this request in terms of the whole object (sub-)hierarchy it stands for. If it chooses to handle the request, it might have to coordinate changes in subtrees different from the one from which the request emerged.
- *Mediator and Observer (Manager).* If an object playing both the Mediator and Observer roles receives a change notification from a `Subordinate` object, it has to react to changes in one of its subtrees. This might include coordinating all needed changes to other subtrees, including the one from which the change notification emerged.
- *Observer and Handler (Manager).* If a `Manager` observing a `Subordinate` receives a state change notification from it, it might choose to create a request which it forwards to its own `Manager`. Thus, the interpretation of a `Subordinate`'s state change causes a request to be created and forwarded up the hierarchy.
- *Handler and Subject (Subordinate).* An object might change its own and other object's state in reaction to an external request. This state change has to be announced and its `Manager` notified.

- *Root and Tail (Director).*   The Director of the whole tree has the final power to decide what will happen with a client request. If every subordinate object has given up on handling a request, the Director has the last word, either to handle the request, to raise a system error, or to ignore the client's request altogether.

These role/role relationships to be integrated in a single object embody the synergy between the constituting patterns, which turns the Bureaucracy pattern from an arbitrary composition of some patterns into a composite pattern.

Consequences

On the positive side, the Bureaucracy pattern

- defines a Composite hierarchy consisting of Managers and Subordinates. It can be assembled easily and is based on recursive decomposition. This hierarchy is self-stabilizing and follows inner rules of consistency which cannot be changed by clients (unless a Legislature protocol is introduced to the Director role).
- helps you build complex hierarchical structures which might define large parts of an application or framework. A Bureaucracy has its own rules which it enforces. This turns instantiations of the pattern into autonomous entities. They are either at the forefront of an interaction with the client, or they interact as agents with other system components.
- makes it easy to introduce new Managers and Subordinates. Due to predefined protocols, new objects can be embedded and reused easily. Viewed the other way around, a Bureaucracy instantiation can be easily assembled, since the involved patterns define a simple plug-and-play structure.
- shows how you can distribute complex functionality over a large object structure in a coherent way. By applying the principle of divide-and-conquer, you can get a better grip on the system's complexity.

As for its disadvantages, the Bureaucracy pattern

- restricts client interactions to a rather coarse-grained level. A client request is carried out according to the Bureaucracy's inner rules, usually allowing for no client interference. Client requests might cause complex hierarchy internal control and data flow, and might include hierarchy restructuring.
- might cause communication overhead, because Subordinates cannot communicate directly with each other. Instead, communication flow is always mediated by the Manager.

Implementation

Issues relevant to the implementation of the constituting patterns can be found in Gamma, et al. Additional issues arise from the pattern interaction synergy. When implementing the Bureaucracy pattern, consider the following aspects.

- *Who's in charge?* The basic question to be answered when implementing a Bureaucracy is which responsibilities to assign to the various levels in the hierarchy. Generally speaking, the higher a Manager in the hierarchy, the more power and the more context knowledge it has to control the other objects.

  The ideal bureaucracy is built on the idea that the higher a clerk is positioned, the more knowledge and qualification he or she possesses [Weber47]. Here the analogy breaks down. There is no need to provide Managers high in the hierarchy with more specialized and elaborate implementations. In fact, objects high up in the hierarchy might be provided rather general implementations, while objects further down the hierarchy do much of the detailed work.

- *Separation of Observer and Chain of Responsibility protocol.* You might consider reusing the Observer protocol to implement the Chain of Responsibility. However, this can make control flow hard to understand. Therefore, the protocols should be kept separate. It should be clear at any time whether an object is notifying its observer about a state change or whether it is forwarding a request it cannot handle alone.

- *Sharing of implementation state.* In the Bureaucracy pattern, the Parent of a Child, the Mediator of a Colleague, the Successor of a Handler, and the Observer of a Subject is always the same object so that it can be handled by a single object reference.

- *Interaction on all levels versus interaction via the Director object.* The type of interaction with clients determines whether these clients might be allowed to interface with any object within the hierarchy or may be restricted to communicate only with the Director.

  In graphical user interfaces, a user playing the role of a client can usually interact with any object in the hierarchy, thereby directly manipulating it. This is an important aspect of the Bureaucracy pattern, since this interaction is the reason for composing the four patterns. Such client interaction can bring the hierarchy into an inconsistent state at any level. The combination of Mediator, Chain of Responsibility, and Observer is used to stabilize the hierarchy.

  In some situations, it is desirable to allow interaction only via the Director. In such situations, each Manager is allowed an opportunity to intervene and possibly interrupt the intended interaction of a client with its target object in the hierarchy. Furthermore, each Manager has the power to decide which way the interaction should go, thus selecting the Subordinate to which a request is delegated.

- *Short communication paths.* Some systems, for example HotDraw [Johnson92], allow Subordinates to observe other Subordinates in order to facilitate short communication paths. This may defeat the purpose of the Mediator role played by the Subordinate's Manager and should be applied only if it is clear that the Manager will never have to interfere with this communication.

- *Initialization of the hierarchy.* Usually the hierarchy is built once. Sometimes it is desirable to exchange whole subtrees, as is the case in user interfaces where some flags determine which variant of a user interface is to be shown and which is to be hidden. These subtrees can be created in advance and exchanged at runtime, for example, by mapping and unmapping them.

  If clients frequently change the hierarchy, the Bureaucracy pattern might not be applicable. The more detailed a client's manipulation of the hierarchy, the more likely it will conflict with the hierarchy's inner consistency rules. If a parent/child relationship is all you can define, there is no need to introduce the Observer and Chain of Responsibility patterns, and hence no Bureaucracy pattern.

There are some general issues related to implementing patterns based on role modeling. When implementing composite patterns, you have to face a number of difficult problems.

- *Class interface construction.* Role protocols can be defined as Protocol classes. Using multiple inheritance, a class implementing a role from the Bureaucracy pattern can simply inherit from all role protocols those it needs to support. If multiple inheritance is not available, the role protocols might be maintained on paper and copied by hand into the class interfaces. In single inheritance systems, tool support for protocol mix-in is likely to be very helpful [Reenskaug96, Riehle+96].
- *State integration.* If you use a single class to implement a Manager or a Subordinate, you can make sure that the abstract state defined in the different role protocols maps well on a single implementation state. In complex role modeling situations, however, you will probably use Decorators [Gamma+95] to adapt a core object to a specific collaboration. Riehle shows how to look up context adaptation objects for a given specification [Riehle95].

State integration of the abstract state defined by different interfaces in a single component is a difficult research problem, addressed by different researchers now. This includes the work of Reenskaug, et al., Harrison and Ossher, Kiczales, et al., and the work of our group.

Sample Code

This section illustrates a possible implementation of the class diagram presented in Figure 11-2. To simplify the discussion, each tool component is represented as a simple object. Class `Tool` comprises the role protocols of Child, Mediator, Handler, and Observer as composed by the Subordinate role. This leads to the following interface.

```
class Tool
{
public:
    // Child role
  virtual ManagerTool* getManager();
  virtual void setManager(ManagerTool* newManager);
  virtual ManagerTool* asManagerTool();

    // Handler role
  virtual void forwardRequest(Request* request);

    // Subject role
  virtual void notify(Event* event);

protected:
  ManagerTool* manager;
};
```

A `Tool` object uses the Handler and Subject protocol to communicate with its Mediator when playing the Colleague role. Thus, there is no need to define an additional Colleague protocol which could be introduced only on a derived class level.

ManagerTool enhances the `Tool` interface with the role protocols of Manager, Successor, and Observer.

```
class ManagerTool : public Tool
{
public:
    // Parent role
  virtual ManagerTool* asManagerTool();

    // Successor role
  virtual void handleRequest(Request* request);

    // Observer role
  virtual void update(Tool* tool, Event* event);
};
```

A Mediator role protocol can be specified only on the level of a concrete Manager, like the `FileBrowser` class discussed below. Thus, there is no explicit Mediator role protocol in the `ManagerTool` class interface.

In general, the various role protocols are implemented according to the different patterns from which they are derived. Of interest is the interaction between the different roles in a single object, which might be illustrated by two scenarios described in the Motivation section.

In the first scenario, the user double-clicks on an item in the list box of the lister. After catching and dispatching the selected callback from the user interface, the following operation of `Lister` is called.

```
void Lister::selectItemRequested(int index) {
  DirItem* item = directory->at(index);
  Request* request = new SelectItemRequest(item, index);
  forwardRequest(request);
}
```

This operation interprets the user interaction as a request to select an item. By definition, the `Lister` cannot fully handle this itself, but forwards it to its Manager, the `FileBrowser`. The browser dispatches the request to its implementation of `handleSelectItem`, an operation of its Mediator role protocol.

```
void FileBrowser::handleSelectItem(SelectItemRequest* request) {
  String itemName = request->item->getName();

  if (editor->hasDocChanged()) {
    // warning dialog
  }
  else
  if (!FileSystem::Instance()->isAvailable(itemName)) {
    forwardRequest(request);
  }
  else {
    selectItem(request);
  }
}
```

Once everything has been properly prepared, `selectItem` of `FileBrowser` is called. This might be done either from the superordinate utility manager tool or from the operation just listed. Thus, `selectItem` might look like

```
void FileBrowser::selectItem(SelectItemRequest* request) {
  lister->selectItem(request);
  String itemName = request->item->getName();
  Document* doc = FileSystem::Instance()->LoadDocument(itemName);
  editor->setDocument(doc);
}
```

This scenario demonstrates how a client request travels up the hierarchy and is handled based on the tools' responsibility assignments. Handling such a request often means coordinating subordinate tools such as the lister and the text editor.

A second scenario illustrates the interaction between Observer and Chain of Responsibility. Assume that the user has edited a file and just pushed the Save button. The activate callback of the push button is caught and dispatched to the following operation.

```
void TextEditor::saveRequested() {
    // transfer changes from working copy to original
    ...
    // notify Manager about save
  Event event = new OriginalUpdatedEvent;
  notify(&event);
}
```

The editor has been designed in such a way that it lets users manipulate a working copy of a document and upon the Save command transfers the changes to the original Document object. No client request has to be created since the editor fully handles the user interaction. However, an important state change of the editor (and the document) has occurred, and the superior tool has to be informed about this.

Thus, notify(&event) is dispatched to

```
void FileBrowser::checkOriginalUpdated() {
  Document* doc = editor->getDocument();
  FileSystem::Instance->SaveDocument(doc);
  Request* request = new CheckDocumentRequest(doc);
  forwardRequest(request);
}
```

The state change notification of the TextEditor is interpreted and handled by the FileBrowser. It creates and forwards a request to the utility manager to handle the situation of a new document version. The utility manager has to react to the changed set of utility and configuration files. If the document is a C file, it might start up a C compiler, or it might check the file into the version control system. However, this is irrelevant to the FileBrowser. It has been defined in such a way that it can handle a changed file to some extent, but eventually has to forward the request to a superior tool.

These two scenarios illustrate the interaction of Observer and Chain of Responsibility patterns and their use as communication mechanisms between Subordinates and their Managers as required by the Mediator pattern. Both patterns are used to make tools more easily so that they can fit into a self-stabilizing hierarchy.

The Observer pattern is used if a Subordinate has carried out a request to its own satisfaction. The Manager is notified upon request completion. It then interprets and reacts to the Subordinate's state change according to its context, possibly creating a request. However, it faces a situation in which the original request has already been fully handled, so that no detailed control is possible or needed.

The Chain of Responsibility pattern is used if components know that they can only partially handle a request. Thus, they are designed in such a way that they can do their part of the work, but also allow Managers to apply their broader context knowledge. The request is passed up the hierarchy until a Manager fully handles it.

Observer and Chain of Responsibility interlock: one starts where the other one ends. A change notification using Observer might cause a Manager to create a request using Chain of Responsibility. Handling the request might then lead to a state change which causes another change notification, and so on.

Known Uses

Many frameworks for the design of interactive applications use the Bureaucracy pattern, including ET++, InterViews, HotDraw, PowerPlant, and the Tools and Materials Metaphor frameworks. Class names are adjusted in the following examples to increase readability.

ET++ [Weinand+94] provides a class `EventHandler` that defines the Chain of Responsibility protocol. The Observer protocol is already in place within the framework's root class `Object`. The `Manager` subclass of `EventHandler` defines the composite structure of Managers which can be embedded in Managers. In addition, each Manager acts as a Mediator to its subordinate Managers. As in frameworks such as PowerPlant, ET++ defines a break between nonvisual classes like `Manager` (and its subclasses like `Application` and `Document`) and `VisualObjects` directly accessible in the user interface. `VisualObjects` is at the forefront of interaction with the user and thus far down the Bureaucracy hierarchy. The `VisualObject` hierarchy is also derived from `EventHandler`. Unlike `Manager`, it defines a `CompositeVisualObject` class to make the Composite pattern explicit.

`PowerPlant` [Trudeau96] offers an interesting implementation of the Bureaucracy pattern that separates the various protocols into different superclasses. The Chain of Responsibility protocol is, for example, defined by the `LCommander` class and the Observer protocol is defined by the `LListener` and `LBroadcaster` classes. `LCommander` also defines a protocol for managing subcommmanders so that it represents an application of the Composite pattern. The Mediator protocol is always concrete and therefore not available as a protocol class. This allows users to mix and match the different protocols, which thereby become independent from a predefined single inheritance hierarchy. PowerPlant applies the Bureaucracy pattern in a fashion similar to ET++ by providing `Application`, `DocApplication`, `Document`, `View`, and `Pane` classes, the instances of which form a Bureaucracy.

The Tools and Materials Metaphor frameworks [Riehle+95b, Riehle+96] use the Bureaucracy pattern to structure the functional parts of tools. Thus, the `Func-`

tionalPart class represents the Subordinate role and the class Composite-FunctionalPart represents the Manager role [Riehle+95a]. It implements the Bureaucracy pattern in a rather clean way, as discussed in the Structure section.

The PLOTS pattern language of transport systems [Zhao+96] presents an application of the Bureaucracy pattern in the domain of transport systems. The class RouteComponent is the root class of a Composite pattern application that is several layers deep. The inner consistency of the hierarchy is maintained using the Chain of Responsibility, Observer, and Mediator patterns.

CONCEPTS AND TECHNIQUES

This section details the concepts, notations, and techniques used to dig out the Bureaucracy pattern. The first subsection presents the *role diagram* notation for design patterns and applies them to the Composite, Mediator, Chain of Responsibility, and Observer patterns. The second subsection defines the notion of *prototypical pattern application* and introduces the *role relationship matrix*, an analytical means for eliciting the relationships between roles from overlapping pattern instantiations. The Bureaucracy pattern is used as an example. The third subsection finally discusses the interpretation of the role relationship matrix and shows how it helps to derive the essence of the Bureaucracy pattern.

Role Diagrams

Role diagrams are a means for describing collaborations of objects based on the roles the participating objects play in the collaboration. A role has a role protocol associated with it which represents the interface through which an object is accessed within the described collaboration. The notion of role diagram is based on Reenskaug's role models [Reenskaug96] and enhanced with the idea of composition constraint to indicate constraints between roles, for example, if an object always plays a certain set of roles together.

Role diagrams are more abstract than class diagrams—they are less implementation oriented. Thus, role diagrams and class diagrams complement each other: Role diagrams focus on the essential collaboration and omit implementation details, while class diagrams show how the collaboration can be implemented efficiently. (For a more detailed discussion of the resulting levels of abstraction for patterns and pattern composition, see Riehle96.) Figures 11-5 to 11-8 show the Composite, Mediator, Chain of Responsibility, and Observer patterns using role diagrams.

Figure 11-5 illustrates the Composite pattern in which every object always plays the Node role. The Child role abstracts from the Component participant [Gamma+95], and the Parent role abstracts from the Composite participant.

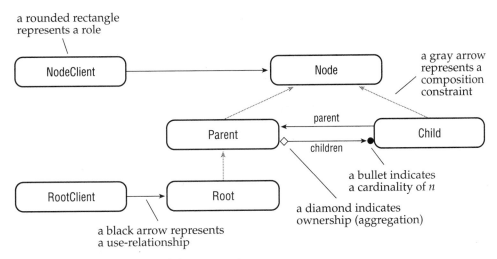

Figure 11-5 *Role diagram of the Composite pattern*

Furthermore, the Root role is introduced as an extension to the Composite pattern. It represents the root of the object hierarchy and thus offers a more elaborate protocol than the basic Parent role protocol. There are three composition constraints. First, an object playing the Root role always also plays the Parent role, which also always plays the Node role. Finally, an object playing the Child role also always plays the Node role.

Figure 11-6 shows the Mediator pattern, which corresponds to the original version. Figure 11-7 describes the Chain of Responsibility pattern. The Handler participant in the original pattern has been split into the three roles: Handler, Predecessor, and Successor, each with distinct protocols. In addition, the Tail role is introduced as a specialization of the Successor role. The Chain of Responsibility pattern also faces three composition constraints. An object playing the Tail role also always plays the Successor role, which in turn also always plays the Handler role. An object playing the Predecessor role also always plays the Handler role. Finally, Figure 11-8 presents the Observer pattern. It corresponds to the original pattern but omits the `ConcreteSubject` and `ConcreteObserver` subclasses. This role diagram is less implementation oriented than the original class diagram and thus allows for wider class design and implementation space [Riehle96].

Figure 11-6 *Role diagram of the Mediator pattern*

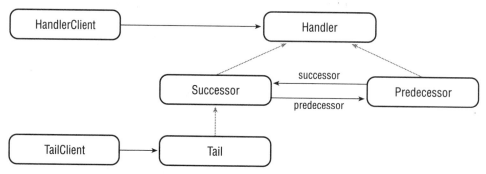

Figure 11-7 *Role diagram of the Chain of Responsibility pattern*

Figure 11-8 *Role diagram of the Observer pattern*

Role Relationship Matrix

Patterns stem from observations, experience, and reflection on existing systems, which then require adequate concepts and techniques for digging out patterns. These include means for describing patterns (previous subsection), means for analyzing existing systems (this subsection), and means for appropriately interpreting analysis results (next subsection). One simple analytical means, the role relationship matrix, determines the composite roles in the Bureaucracy pattern.

A first step is to abstract from the concrete pattern instantiations and devise a *prototypical pattern application* which exhibits all the properties considered important for the proposed pattern, but omits unimportant implementation details. Figure 11-9 shows such a prototypical application of the Bureaucracy pattern, derived from the utility manager example. It uses its object structure, but lists only the roles the objects play in the overall collaboration.

Figure 11-10 is a *role relationship matrix*, which displays the relationships between two roles as they appear in the prototypical pattern application. Thus, the matrix determines which roles may coexist in a single object and which may not. This determination defines the design space of the Bureaucracy pattern.

In the role relationship matrix, each row and column stands for a role, and the matrix entry (A, B) for each intersection describes the relationship between these two roles. A white rectangle designates "an object playing role A which *never* plays role B," a gray rectangle means "sometimes but not always plays," and a black rectangle means "always plays." Role A comprises the roles from the top row, and role B comprises the roles from the left column.

Node, Parent, Root, Mediator, Handler, Tail, Successor, Observer
Node, Child, Parent, Colleague, Mediator, Handler, Observer, Subject, Successor
Node, Child, Colleague, Handler, Predecessor, Subject
Node, Child, Colleague, Handler, Predecessor, Subject
Node, Child, Colleague, Handler, Predecessor, Subject
Node, Child, Colleague, Handler, Predecessor, Subject

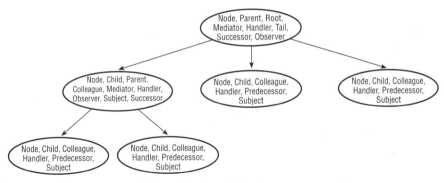

Figure 11-9 *A prototypical application of the Bureaucracy pattern*

RootClient
Root
Parent
Child
NodeClient
Node
Mediator
Colleague
TailClient
Tail
Successor
Predecessor
HandlerClient
Handler
Observer
Subject
RootClient$_{C}$
Root$_{C}$
Parent$_{C}$
Child$_{C}$
NodeClient$_{C}$
Node$_{C}$
Mediator$_{M}$
Colleague$_{M}$
TailClient$_{CoR}$
Tail$_{CoR}$
Successor$_{CoR}$
Predecessor$_{CoR}$
HandlerClient$_{CoR}$
Handler$_{CoR}$
Observer$_{CoR}$
Subject$_{O}$

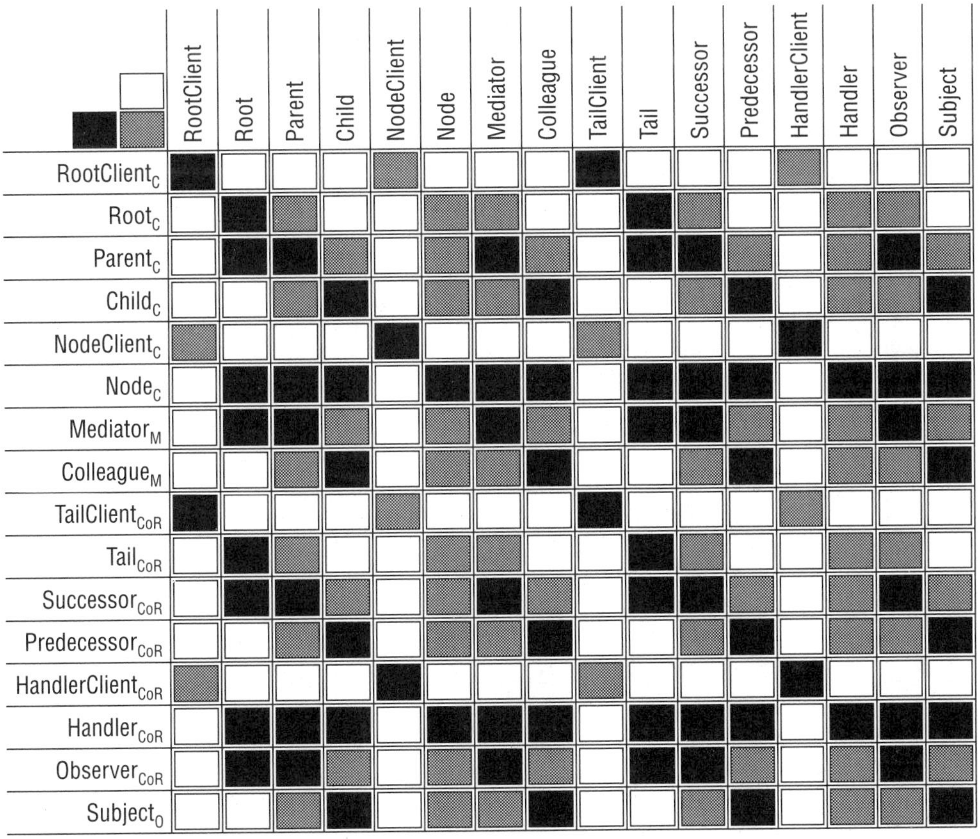

Figure 11-10 *Role relationship matrix of the Bureaucracy pattern*

Matrix Interpretation

The matrix illustrates the role relationships found in the prototypical pattern application, and thus in every concrete pattern instantiation. Analysis of the matrix shows that certain rows and columns always are identical. Each resulting set of equivalent rows and columns can be interpreted to constitute a composite role which comprises all the roles listed in the set. The prototypical application and the role relationship matrix define the following composite roles.

$$
\begin{aligned}
\text{DirectorClient}_B &= \{ \text{RootClient}_C,\ \text{TailClient}_{CoR} \} \\
\text{Director}_B &= \{ \text{Root}_C,\ \text{Tail}_{CoR} \} \\
\text{Manager}_B &= \{ \text{Parent}_C,\ \text{Mediator}_M,\ \text{Successor}_{CoR},\ \text{Observer}_O \} \\
\text{Subordinate}_B &= \{ \text{Child}_C,\ \text{Colleague}_M,\ \text{Predecessor}_{CoR},\ \text{Subject}_O \} \\
\text{ClerkClient}_B &= \{ \text{NodeClient}_C,\ \text{HandlerClient}_{CoR} \} \\
\text{Clerk}_B &= \{ \text{Node}_C,\ \text{Handler}_{CoR} \}
\end{aligned}
$$

Subscripts represent the name of the pattern in which the role is defined. Every composite role comprises the responsibilities of the constituting roles. For example, the Manager composite role comprises the Parent, Mediator, Successor, and Observer roles, and its role protocol comprises the constituting roles' protocols.

Figure 11-11 depicts the role relationship matrix after reducing the roles to composite roles, which shows how the new roles relate to each other. Every object playing Subordinate, Manager, or Director roles, also always plays the Clerk role. In addition, every object playing the Director role also always plays the Manager role. The introduction of composite roles and the evaluation of their specialization relationships resulted in the diagram found in Figure 11-3, the key role diagram of the Bureaucracy pattern.

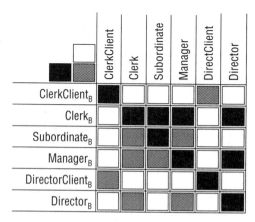

Figure 11-11 *Role relationship matrix for the Bureaucracy pattern based on composite roles*

Evaluation of Approach

The concepts and techniques presented in this section emerged while grappling with the complexity of the pattern and represent some of the means used to clarify the essence and intent of the Bureaucracy pattern. Can they be expected to work well for other patterns? I believe the concepts and techniques will be useful for analyzing and evaluating further composite patterns that are amenable to description by means of role diagrams. These will be mainly behavioral patterns, for the techniques probably will not work well with structural patterns. Application of the techniques to further composite patterns has been successful.

CONCLUSIONS

The Bureaucracy pattern, a pattern frequently found in interactive software systems and beyond, describes how to structure large object or component hierarchies which allow interaction on every level and have to maintain their internal consistency. It helps developers to coherently and concisely assign functionality and responsibility to objects or components in the hierarchy and represents a coherent pattern to control the dynamics of complex hierarchical structures.

The composition of patterns is a nontrivial task and composite pattern presentation might become lengthy and its structure arbitrary. By presenting the Bureaucracy pattern as a composition of four patterns, it is possible to leave out many implementation details that can be found in the constituent patterns' descriptions. The presentation can thus focus on the synergy arising from the composition, thereby demonstrating that the Bureaucracy pattern is more than just the sum of its constituent patterns; it is a true pattern in its own right.

Role diagrams are used to describe patterns for three reasons. First, role diagrams seemed to be an appropriate means for presenting patterns, composite or noncomposite, because of their clear distinctions between the various responsibilities assigned to objects. Secondly, the clear distinction between the different roles allowed the simplified composition of patterns to form larger wholes like the Bureaucracy. Finally, it subjected pattern composition to more rigorous analysis and thereby helped to increase confidence that we had, indeed, ferreted out the heart of the pattern.

Role diagrams have proved to be very useful in this instance and I believe they will prove to be as useful for describing patterns in general.

ACKNOWLEDGMENTS

I wish to thank Neil Harrison, Ralph Johnson, Trygve Reenskaug, and Wolf Siberski for reading and commenting on an earlier version of the pattern. I would also like to thank participants in the writer's workshop at EuroPLoP '96, whose comments helped me to improve the pattern. Special thanks is due to the Swiss PTT Telecom which provided me with first-hand experience of a real-world bureaucracy [Telecom95].

REFERENCES

[Gamma+95] E. Gamma, R. Helm, R. Johnson, and J. Vlissides. *Design Patterns: Elements of Reusable Design*. Reading, MA: Addison-Wesley, 1995.

[Harrison+93] W. Harrison and H. Ossher. "Subject-Oriented Programming (A Critique of Pure Objects)." OOPSLA '93, *Conference Proceedings.* See also: *ACM SIGPLAN Notices* 28, 10 (October 1993): 411–428.

[Johnson92] R. E. Johnson. "Documenting Frameworks using Patterns." OOPSLA '92, *Conference Proceedings.* See also: *ACM SIGPLAN Notices* 27, 10 (October 1992): 63–70.

[Kiczales+96] G. Kiczales, J. Irwin, J. Lamping, J.-M. Loingtier, C. V. Lopes, C. Maeda, and A. Mendhekar. "Aspect-Oriented Programming." http://www.parc.xerox.com/spl/projects/aop/.

[Kristensen+96] B. B. Kristensen and K. Osterbye. "Roles: Conceptual Abstraction Theory and Practical Language Issues." *Theory and Practice of Object Systems* 2, 3 (1996): 143–160.

[Reenskaug96] T. Reenskaug, with P. Wold and O. A. Lehne. *Working with Objects.* Greenwich: Manning, 1996.

[Riehle95] D. Riehle. "How and Why to Encapsulate Class Trees." OOPSLA '95, *Conference Proceedings.* ACM Press, 1995, pp. 251–264.

[Riehle96] D. Riehle. "Describing and Composing Patterns Using Role Diagrams." WOON '96 (1st Int'l Conference on Object-Orientation in Russia), *Conference Proceedings.* St. Petersburg Electrotechnical University, 1996. Reprinted in K.-U. Mätzel and Hans-Peter Frei (eds.), *Proceedings of the Ubilab Conference '96, Zürich.* Germany, Universitätsverlag Konstanz, 1996, pp. 137–152.

[Riehle+96] D. Riehle, B. Schäffer, and Martin Schnyder. "Design of a Smalltalk Framework for the Tools and Materials Metaphor." *Informatik/Informatique* 3 (February 1996), 20–22.

[Riehle+95a] D. Riehle and M. Schnyder. *Design and Implementation of a Smalltalk Framework for the Tools and Materials Metaphor.* Ubilab Technical Report 95.7.1. Zürich, Switzerland: Union Bank of Switzerland, 1995.

[Riehle+95b] D. Riehle and H. Züllighoven. "A Pattern Language for Tool Construction and Integration Based on the Tools and Materials Metaphor." In J. O. Coplien and D. Schmidt (eds.), *Pattern Languages of Program Design.* Reading, MA: Addison-Wesley, 1995, pp. 9–42.

[Telecom95] D. Riehle. "Experiences with the Swiss PTT Telecom." http://swt-www.informatik.uni-hamburg.de/~riehle.

[Trudeau96] J. Trudeau. *Metrowerks Powerplant Book.* Metrowerks, Inc., 1996.

[Weber47] M. Weber. *The Theory of Social and Economic Organization.* New York: Oxford University Press, 1947.

[Weinand+94] A. Weinand and E. Gamma. "ET++ — a Portable, Homogenous Class Library and Application Framework." In W. R. Bischofberger and H.-P. Frei (eds.), *Computer Science Research at UBILAB.* Konstanz: Universitätsverlag Konstanz, 1994, pp. 66–92.

[Zhao+96] L. Zhao and T. Foster. "A Pattern Language of Transport Systems (Point and Route)." Chapter 23, this volume.

Dirk Riehle can be reached at Dirk.Riehle@ubs.com **or** riehle@acm.org.

PART 4

Distribution Patterns

This section presents seven patterns used in the design and implementation of distributed systems. Distributed systems have always received significant attention, but with the recent increase of interest in intranets and the Internet, it has become even more important to build understandable, manageable, adaptable, and reliable distributed systems.

Chapter 12: Acceptor and Connector, by Doug Schmidt. This paper presents two patterns: Acceptor and Connector. These are complementary patterns that work together to establish communication channels between the clients and servers. An Acceptor is an object that waits passively for a client to establish a communication channel. A Connector issues this request. A Connector is an object that actively establishes connections to a service via an Acceptor. A Reactor is used to decouple Acceptor and Connector objects from incoming and outgoing connection requests, respectively. The Reactor, which is described in detail in the first volume of this series [Coplien+95], demultiplexes these requests to the indicated Acceptor or Connector.

These and further distribution patterns have been documented as a family of patterns in the 1996 TAPOS special issue on patterns [Berczuk96, Schmidt96]. In addition to concise descriptions of the Acceptor and Connector patterns, this article features the Reactor, Active Object, and Router patterns, thereby providing developers with an integrated set of widely used infrastructure patterns for distributed system design and implementation.

The Connector pattern motivates the need to create name-spaces for patterns. Pattern name-spaces provide a way to unambiguously identify the patterns we are talking about. For example, the concept of a connector is also used in the software architecture community to denote the link between two or more components [Shaw+96]. Mary Shaw, who has been an author in the first two volumes of this series, and David Garlan use a different notion of connector than is used in this paper. Clearly, we must qualify names of architectures and design patterns to avoid possible confusion. Properly naming patterns will be an important issue in the future, along with classifying and putting them into handbooks or capturing them as parts of pattern languages.

Chapter 13: Bodyguard, by Fernando Das Neves and Alejandra Garrido. This paper describes a pattern used to share objects in distributed environments. The Bodyguard pattern works together with the Proxy pattern [Buschmann+96, Gamma+95]. A Remote Proxy is a placeholder for a remote object and represents it in a process different from the one where the remote object resides. The Proxy offers the same interface to clients as the remote object does, but instead of directly forwarding an operation call, it delegates it to an accompanying Bodyguard object. The Bodyguard checks whether the client issuing the request actually has the permission to do so, and either aborts the operation or forwards it to the remote object. Thereby, the Bodyguard implements a specific access control strategy and encapsulates the marshalling and forwarding algorithm. This helps to make object sharing in distributed systems transparent to the client.

Chapter 14: Asynchronous Completion Token, by Irfan Pyarali, Tim Harrison, and Douglas C. Schmidt. Often, distributed applications must perform long duration operations asynchronously to avoid blocking the processing of other pending events. When these asynchronous operations are complete, applications may need more information than simply the notification itself to handle the event properly. This paper shows how to use the Asynchronous Completion Token pattern to efficiently associate state with the completion of asynchronous operations.

An Asynchronous Completion Token (ACT) is an opaque key that is issued by a client when making a request to a server. This opaque key is a handle to the client's execution context. Once the request is executed, the server replies to the client, passing along the ACT. The client can use the ACT to regain the execution context of the request quickly. A well-known application of the ACT pattern is the use of request ids that remote procedure call (RPC) services return with their replies.

Chapter 15: Object Recovery, by António Rito Silva, João Pereira, and José Alves Marques. This paper deals with the recovery of earlier states of an object due to Undo requests or object state corruption. The latter can result from interference of concurrent activities or, more dramatically, from events like system crashes. This pattern helps to implement a generic object recovery mechanism that can be configured with different policies. It shows how to do so without interfering with the functional aspects of the object. Each object has a recovery interface that hides a specific recovery strategy. This strategy can be exchanged at runtime. The recovery strategy manages several recovery points that represent state snapshots similar to the Memento pattern [Gamma+95]. Working together, these objects let you exchange recovery strategies to adapt the recovery mechanism to an object's needs.

While this pattern is not inherently distributed, the complexity it addresses becomes particularly important in distributed systems. Managing complexity is an important aspect of this pattern, because it separates the recovery mechanism from other object functionality. In [RitoSilva+95] António and his colleagues present further examples of what they call "object concerns" such as concurrency and synchronization, and show how these independent concerns can be composed. This helps to deliver applications that cover all relevant requirements, but which do not tangle them all in one single object implementation.

Chapter 16: Patterns for Logging Diagnostic Messages, by Neil B. Harrison.   This paper addresses an important aspect of complex distributed systems by presenting three patterns for logging and tracking diagnostic messages. Diagnostic messages like warnings, errors, and fatal failures must be reported to a logging service in order to let users or developers track a system's state over time.

The author describes three key patterns: Diagnostic Logger, Diagnostic Context, and Typed Diagnostic Messages. A diagnostic logger is a service that hides all the logging details from its clients. It may dump messages to a file, or it may display them on a console to provide on-line information. A diagnostic message always appears in a specific execution context (a transaction, for example). Since a diagnostic message might happen at any time in the processing, the information in the current processing context cannot be guaranteed to be meaningful. Furthermore, if many messages are logged, it might be cumbersome to keep sending a lot of context information to the diagnostic logger. Therefore, it is best to provide the diagnostic logger with a diagnostic context at the *beginning* of a transaction, and to close it at the end. Finally, diagnostic messages might become very elaborate, providing a large amount of detailed information. Frequently, it is best to treat them as complex objects in their own right. Typed diagnostic messages do exactly this. The different kinds of diagnostic messages are mapped on a message inheritance hierarchy that reflects the complexity of the messages that occur.

Summary.   This section is the second largest part of the book. It is only surpassed by Part 1, which deals with general design patterns. This reflects the importance of distributed systems, and the need to document the many patterns that ease their development. We hope that this section has taken a further step in this direction, and we look forward to learning more about distributed systems patterns in future books of the Software Patterns Series.

REFERENCES

[Berczuk96] Steve Berczuk (ed.). "Special Issue on Patterns." *Theory and Practice of Object Systems* 2 (1), 1996.

[Buschmann+96] F. Buschmann, R. Meunier, H. Rohnert, P. Sommerlad, and M. Stal. *Pattern-Oriented Software Architecture.* New York: John Wiley and Sons, 1996.

[Coplien+95] J. O. Coplien and D. C. Schmidt (eds.). *Pattern Languages of Program Design.* Reading, MA: Addison-Wesley, 1995.

[Gamma+95] E. Gamma, R. Johnson, R. Helm, and J. Vlissides. *Design Patterns: Elements of Reusable Object-Oriented Software.* Reading, MA: Addison-Wesley, 1995.

[RitoSilva+95] A. Rito Silva, P. Sousa, and J. Alves Marques. "Development of Distributed Applications with Separation of Concerns." In *Proceedings of the 1995 Asia-Pacific Software Engineering Conference (APSEC '95).* Los Alamitos, CA: IEEE Computer Society Press, 1995.

[Schmidt96] D. C. Schmidt. "A Family of Design Patterns for Application-Level Gateways." In [Berczuk96], pp. 15–30.

[Shaw+96] M. Shaw and D. Garlan. *Software Architecture: Perspectives on an Emerging Discipline.* Englewood Cliffs, NJ: Prentice Hall, 1996.

Chapter 12

Acceptor and Connector

Douglas C. Schmidt

Chapter 12 describes the Connector and Acceptor patterns. The intent of these patterns is to decouple the active and passive initialization roles, respectively, from the tasks a communication service performs once initialization is complete. Common examples of communication services that utilize these patterns include WWW browsers, WWW servers, object request brokers, and superservers, which provide services like remote login and file transfer to client applications.

This chapter illustrates how the Connector and Acceptor patterns can help decouple service initialization-related processing from service processing, which yields more reusable, extensible, and efficient communication software. When used in conjunction with related patterns like the Reactor [Schmidt95], Active Object[Lavender+96], and Service Configurator [Jain+96], the Acceptor and Connector patterns enable the creation of extensible and efficient communication software frameworks [Schmidt+94] and applications [Pyarali+96].

The next section describes the Acceptor and Connector patterns in detail, followed by a section of concluding remarks, and the Appendix at the back of the chapter outlines background information on networking and communication protocols necessary to understand the patterns in this paper.

THE ACCEPTOR AND CONNECTOR PATTERNS

Intent

The intent of these patterns is to decouple service initialization from the tasks performed once a service is initialized. The Connector pattern is responsible for active service initialization, whereas the Acceptor pattern is responsible for passive service initialization.

Also Known As

The Acceptor pattern is also known as Listener [Rago93].

Motivation

Context. To illustrate the Acceptor and Connector patterns, consider the multi-service, application-level Gateway shown in Figure 12-1. The Gateway routes several types of data (such as status information, bulk data, and commands) that are exchanged between services running on the Peers. The Peers are used to monitor and control a satellite constellation. Peers can be distributed throughout local area networks (LANs) and wide-area networks (WANs).

The Gateway is a Mediator [Gamma+95] that coordinates interactions between its connected Peers. From the Gateway's perspective, these Peer services differ solely by their message-framing formats and payload types. The Gateway uses a connection-oriented interprocess communication (IPC) mechanism (such as TCP) to transmit data between its connected Peers. Using a connection-oriented protocol simplifies application error handling and enhances performance over long-latency WANs.

Each communication service in the Peers sends and receives status information, bulk data, and commands to and from the Gateway using separate TCP connections. Each connection is bound to a unique address (such as an IP address and port number). For example, bulk data sent from a ground station Peer through the Gateway is connected to a different port than status information sent by a tracking station Peer through the Gateway to a ground station Peer. Separating connections in this manner allows more flexible routing strategies and more robust error handling when network connections fail.

Common Traps and Pitfalls

One way to design the Peers and Gateway is to designate the initialization roles *a priori* and hard-code them into the server implementation. For instance, the Gateway could be hard-coded to actively initiate the connections for all its services. To accomplish this, it could iterate through a list of Peers and synchronously connect with each of them. Likewise, Peers could be hard-coded to accept connections and passively initialize the associated services.

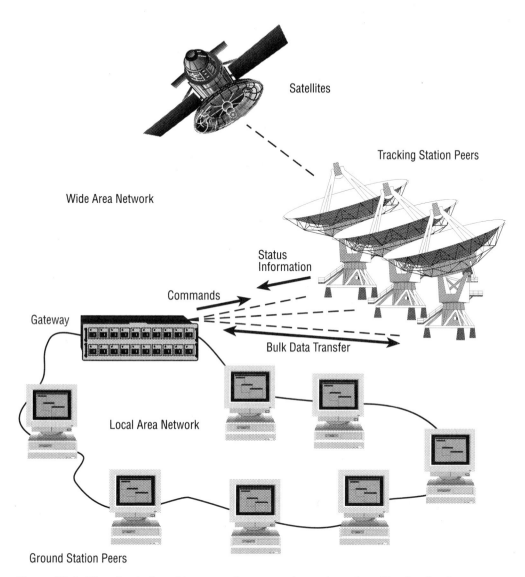

Figure 12-1 *The physical architecture of a connection-oriented application-level gateway*

In addition, the active and passive connection code for the Gateway and Peers, respectively, could be implemented with conventional network programming interfaces (such as sockets or TLI). In this case, a Peer could call socket, bind, listen, and accept to initialize a passive-mode listener socket and the Gateway could call socket and connect to actively initiate a data-mode connection socket. Once the connections were established and the associated service handler objects were initialized, the Gateway could route data for each type of service it provides.

However, this approach has the following drawbacks.

- *Limited extensibility and reuse of the* `Gateway` *and* `Peer` *software.* The type of routing service (for example, status information, bulk data, or commands) performed by the `Gateway` is independent of the mechanisms used to establish connections and initialize services. However, the hard-coded approach described above tightly couples service initialization and service behavior. This makes it hard to reuse existing services or to extend the `Gateway` by adding new routing services and enhancing existing services.
- *Lack of scalability.* If there are a large number of `Peers`, the synchronous connection establishment strategy of the `Gateway` will not take advantage of the parallelism inherent in the network and `Peer` endsystems.
- *Error-prone network programming interfaces.* Conventional network programming interfaces (such as sockets or TLI) do not provide adequate type-checking since they utilize low-level I/O handles [Schmidt+94]. The tight coupling of the hard-coded approach described above makes it easy to accidentally misuse these interfaces and I/O handles in ways that cannot be detected until runtime.

Solution

A more flexible and efficient way to design the `Peers` and `Gateway` is to use the Acceptor and Connector patterns. These two patterns decouple the active and passive initialization roles, respectively, from the communication services performed once services are initialized. These patterns resolve the following forces for communication services that use connection-oriented transport protocols.

- *The need to avoid rewriting initialization code for each new service.* The Connector and Acceptor patterns permit key characteristics of services (such as application-level communication protocols and message formats) to evolve independently of the strategies used to initialize the services. Application-level service characteristics often change more frequently than initialization strategies. Therefore, this separation of concerns helps reduce software coupling and increases code reuse.
- *The need to enable flexible strategies for executing communication services concurrently.* Once a connection is established and the service is initialized using the Acceptor and Connector patterns, peer applications use the connection to exchange data while performing the service. Regardless of how the service was initialized, however, these services may be executed in a single-thread, in multiple threads, or multiple processes.
- *The need to make connection establishment software portable across platforms.* Many operating systems provide network programming interfaces (such as sockets and TLI) and communication protocols (such as TCP/IP and IPX/SPX) whose semantics are only superficially different. Therefore, the syntactic incompatibilities of these interfaces make it hard to write portable pro-

grams, even though the initialization strategies transcend these differences. It is particularly hard to write portable asynchronous connection establishment software since asynchrony is not supported uniformly by standard network programming interfaces like sockets, CORBA, or DCOM.

- *The need to actively establish connections with large number of peers efficiently.* The Connector pattern can employ asynchrony to initiate and complete multiple connections without blocking the caller. By using asynchrony, the Connector pattern enables applications to actively establish connections with a large number of peers efficiently over long-latency WANs.

- *The need to ensure that passive-mode I/O handles are not accidentally used to read or write data.* Strongly decoupling the initialization role of the Acceptor pattern from the communication role of the initialized service ensures that passive-mode listener endpoints are not accidentally used incorrectly. Without this strong decoupling, services may mistakenly read or write data on passive-mode listener endpoints (which should only be used to accept connections).

As outlined above, the Connector and Acceptor patterns address very similar forces. For instance, the first three forces above are resolved by both the Acceptor and Connector pattern—only the passive and active roles are reversed. The remaining forces are only resolved by one pattern each, however, due to the asymmetrical connection roles played by each pattern. For example, the Connector pattern addresses an additional force (connection scalability) by using asynchrony to actively initialize a large number of peers efficiently. This force is not addressed by the Acceptor since it is always the passive target of active initialization requests. Conversely, a Connector does not wait passively for services to initialize it. Unlike the Acceptor pattern, therefore, the Connector pattern need not decouple the listener endpoint from the data endpoint.

The following section describes the Acceptor and Connector patterns using a modified version of the GOF pattern form [Gamma+95].

Applicability

- Use the Acceptor and Connector patterns when tasks performed by a service can be decoupled from the steps required to initialize the service; and
- Use the Connector pattern when an application must establish a large number of connections with peers residing across long-latency networks (such as satellite WANs); or
- Use the Acceptor pattern when connections may arrive concurrently from different peers, but blocking or continuous polling for incoming connections on any individual peer is inefficient.

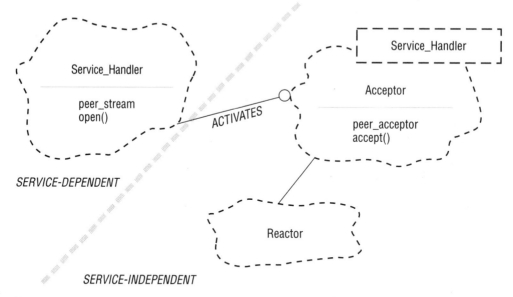

Figure 12-2 *Structure of participants in the Acceptor pattern*

Structure and Participants

The structure of the participants in the Acceptor and Connector patterns is illustrated by the Booch class diagram [Booch93] in Figure 12-2 and Figure 12-3, respectively.[1] The two participants (`Reactor` and `Service_Handler`) common to each pattern are described first, followed by participants that are unique to the Acceptor and Connector patterns:

Reactor. For the Acceptor pattern, the `Reactor` demultiplexes connection requests received on one or more communication endpoints to the appropriate `Acceptor` (described below). The `Reactor` allows multiple `Acceptors` to listen for connections from different peers efficiently within a single thread of control. For the Connector pattern, the `Reactor` handles the completion of connections that were initialized asynchronously. The `Reactor` allows multiple `Service_Handlers` to have their connections initiated and completed asynchronously by a `Connector` configured within a single thread of control.

---

[1] In these diagrams, dashed clouds indicate classes; dashed boxes in the clouds indicate template parameters; a solid undirected edge with a hollow circle at one end indicates a uses relation between two classes.

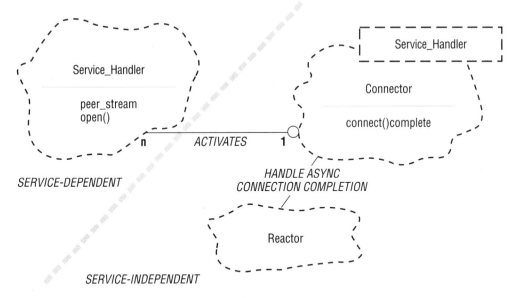

Figure 12-3 *Structure of participants in the Connector pattern*

Service_Handler. This class defines a generic interface for a service. The Service_Handler contains a communication endpoint (peer_stream_) that encapsulates an I/O handle (also known as an I/O descriptor). This endpoint is initialized by the Acceptor and Connector and is subsequently used by the Service_Handler to exchange data with its connected peer. The Acceptor and Connector activate a Service_Handler by calling its open hook when a connection is established. Once a Service_Handler is completely initialized (by either an Acceptor or a Connector), it typically does not interact with its initializer.

The following participant is unique to the Acceptor pattern.

Acceptor. This class implements the strategy for passively initializing a Service_Handler, which communicates with the peer that actively initiated the connection. The Reactor calls back to the Acceptor's accept method when a connection arrives on the passive-mode peer_acceptor_ endpoint. The accept method uses this passive-mode endpoint to accept connections into the Service_Handler's peer_stream_ and then activates a Service_Handler by calling its open hook.

The following participant is unique to the Connector pattern:

Connector. This class connects and activates a Service_Handler . The connect method of a Connector implements the strategy for actively initializing a Service_Handler, which communicates with the peer that passively accepts the connection. The Connector activates a connected Service_Handler by calling its open method when initialization is complete. The complete method finishes activating `Service_Handlers` whose connections were initiated and completed asynchronously. In this case, the `Reactor` calls back the `complete` method automatically when an asynchronous connection is established.

Collaborations

The following section describes the collaborations between participants in the Acceptor and Connector patterns.

Acceptor Collaborations   Figure 12-4 illustrates the collaboration between participants in the Acceptor pattern. These collaborations are divided into three phases.

1. *Endpoint initialization phase,* which creates a passive-mode endpoint that is bound to a network address (such as an IP address and port number). The passive-mode endpoint listens for connection requests from `peers`.

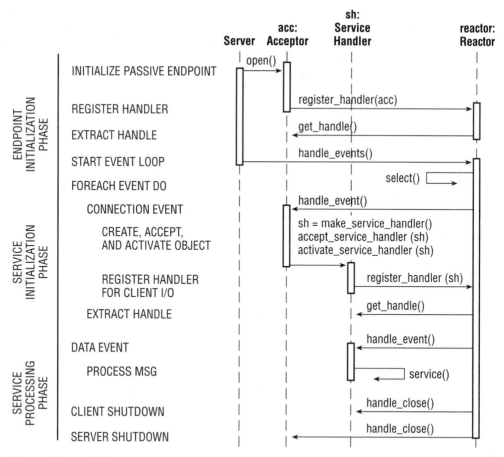

Figure 12-4 *Collaborations among participants in the Acceptor pattern*

2. *Service initialization phase,* which activates the `Service_Handler` associated with the passive-mode endpoint. When a connection arrives, the `Reactor` calls back to the `Acceptor's` `accept` method. This method performs the strategy for initializing a `Service_Handler`. The `Acceptor's` strategy assembles the resources necessary to (1) create a new `Concrete Service_Handler` object, (2) accept the connection into this object, and (3) activate the `Service_Handler` by calling its `open` hook. The `open` hook of the `Service_Handler` then performs service-specific initialization (such as allocating locks, opening log files, etc.).

3. *Service processing phase.* Once the connection has been established passively and the service has been initialized, service processing begins. In this phase, application-specific tasks process the data exchanged between the `Service_Handler` and its connected `Peer`.

Connector Collaborations.   The collaborations among participants in the Connector pattern are also divided into three phases.

1. *Connection initiation phase,* which actively connects one or more `Service_Handlers` with their peers. Connections can be initiated synchronously or asynchronously. The `Connector's` `connect` method implements the strategy for actively establishing connections.

2. *Service initialization phase,* which activates the `Service_Handler` by calling its `open` hook when the connection completes successfully. The `open` hook of the `Service_Handler` then performs service-specific initialization.

3. *Service processing phase.*   Once the `Service_Handler` is activated, it performs the application-specific service processing using the data exchanged with its connected `Peer`.

Figure 12-5 illustrates these three phases of collaboration using asynchronous service initialization. Note how the connection initiation phase is temporally separated from the service initialization phase. This enables multiple connection initiations and completions to proceed in parallel within each thread of control.

The collaboration for synchronous service initialization is shown in Figure 12-6. In this case, the `Connector` combines the connection initiation and service initialization phases into a single blocking operation. Note, however, that only one connection is established per thread for each invocation of `connect`.

In general, synchronous service initialization is useful for the following situations.

• If the latency for establishing a connection is very low (for example, establishing a connection with a server on the same host via the loopback device); or
• If multiple threads of control are available and it is feasible to use a different thread to connect each `Service_Handler` synchronously; or

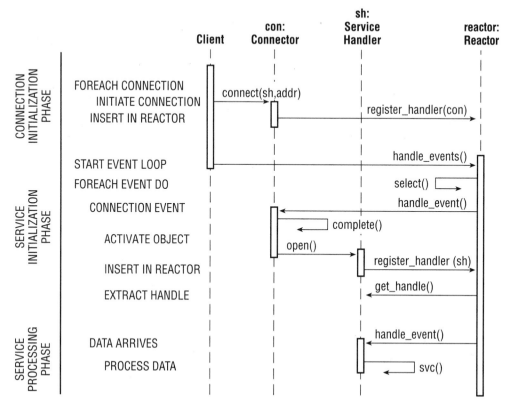

Figure 12-5 *Collaborations among the Connector pattern participants for asynchronous initialization*

- If the services must be initialized in a fixed order and clients cannot perform useful work until a connection is established.

In contrast, asynchronous service initialization is useful in the following situations.

- If the connection latency is high and there are many peers to connect with (for example, establishing a large number of connections over a high-latency WAN); or
- If only a single thread of control is available (such as when the OS platform does not provide application-level threads); or
- If the order in which services are initialized is not important and if the client application must perform additional work (such as refreshing a GUI) while the connection is in the process of being established.

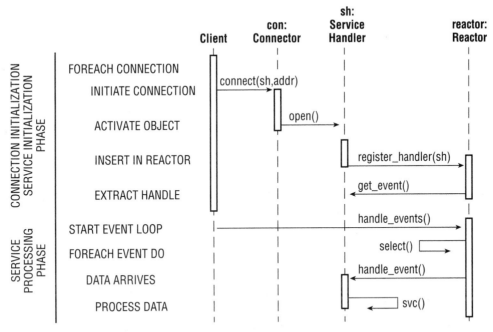

Figure 12-6 *Collaborations among the Connector pattern participants for synchronous initialization*

Consequences

Benefits. The Acceptor and Connector patterns provide the following benefits:

• They enhance the reusability, portability, and extensibility of connection-oriented software by decoupling mechanisms for passively initializing services from the tasks performed by the services. For instance, the application-independent mechanisms in the `Acceptor` and `Connector` are reusable components that know how to (1) establish connections passively and (2) initialize the associated `Service_Handler`. In contrast, the `Service_Handler` knows how to perform the application-specific service processing.

   This separation of concerns is achieved by decoupling the initialization strategy from the service handling strategy. Thus, each strategy can evolve independently. The strategy for active initialization can be written once, placed into a class library or framework, and reused via inheritance, object composition, or template instantiation. Thus, the same passive initialization code need not be rewritten for each application. Services, in contrast, may vary according to different application requirements. By parameterizing the `Acceptor` and `Connector` with a `Service_Handler`, the impact of this variation is localized to a single point in the software.

- They improve application robustness. Application robustness is improved by explicitly decoupling the `Service_Handler` from the `Acceptor`. This decoupling ensures that the passive-mode `peer_acceptor_` cannot accidentally be used to read or write data. This eliminates a common class of errors that can arise when programming with weakly typed network programming interfaces such as sockets or TLI [Schmidt+94].
- Additionally, they efficiently utilize the inherent parallelism in the network and hosts. By using the asynchronous mechanisms shown in Figure 12-7, the Connector pattern can actively establish connections with a large number of peers efficiently over long-latency WANs. This is an important property since a large distributed system may have several hundred `Peers` connected to a single `Gateway`. One way to connect all these `Peers` to the `Gateway` is to use the synchronous mechanisms shown in Figure 12-6. However, the round-trip delay for a three-way TCP connection handshake over a long-latency WAN (such as a geosynchronous satellite or transatlantic fiber cable) may take several seconds per handshake. In this case, synchronous connection mechanisms

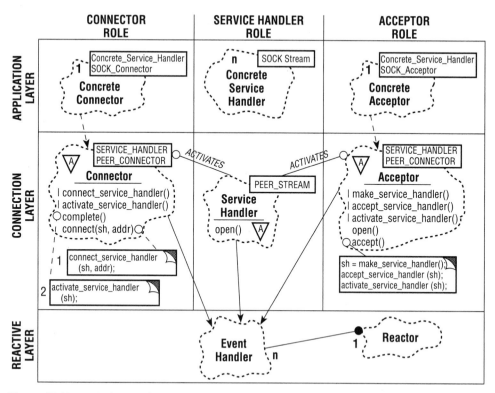

Figure 12-7 *Layering and partitioning of participants in the Acceptor and Connector patterns*

cause unnecessary delays since the inherent parallelism of the network and computers is underutilized.

Drawbacks. The Acceptor and Connector patterns have the following drawbacks.

- Both the Acceptor and Connector patterns may require additional indirection compared with using the underlying network programming interfaces directly. However, languages that support parameterized types (such as C++, Ada, or Eiffel) can often implement these patterns with no significant overhead since compilers can inline the method calls used to implement these patterns.
- These patterns may also add unnecessary complexity for simple client applications that connect with a single server and perform a single service using a single network programming interface.

Implementation

This section describes how to implement the Acceptor and Connector patterns in C++. The implementation described below is based on reusable components provided in the ACE OO network programming toolkit [Schmidt+94].

Figure 12-7 divides participants in the Acceptor and Connector patterns into the Reactive, Connection, and Application layers.[2] The Reactive and Connection layers perform generic, application-independent strategies for handling events and initializing services, respectively. The Application layer instantiates these generic strategies by providing concrete template classes that establish connections and perform service processing. This separation of concerns increases the reusability, portability, and extensibility in this implementation of the Acceptor and Connector patterns.

The implementations of the Acceptor and Connector patterns are structured very similarly. The Reactive layer is identical in both, and the roles of the `Service_Handler` and `Concrete_Service_Handler` are also similar. Moreover, the `Acceptor` and `Concrete_Acceptor` play roles equivalent to the `Connector` and `Concrete_Connector` classes. The primary difference between the two patterns is that in the Acceptor pattern these two classes play a passive role in establishing a connection. In contrast, in the Connector pattern they play an active role.

Reactive Layer. The Reactive layer is responsible for handling events that occur on endpoints of communication represented by I/O handles (also known as descriptors). The two participants in this layer, the `Reactor` and `Event_Handler`, are reused from the Reactor pattern [Schmidt95]. This pattern encapsulates OS

---

[2] This diagram is based on the extended Booch variation: directed edges indicate inheritance relationships between classes; a dashed directed edge indicates template instantiation; and a solid circle illustrates a composition relationship between two classes.

event demultiplexing system calls (such as `select`, `poll` [Stevens90] and `Wait-ForMultipleObjects` [Custer93]) with an extensible and portable callback-driven object-oriented interface. The Reactor pattern enables efficient demultiplexing of multiple types of events from multiple sources within a single thread of control. The implementation of the Reactor pattern is described in [Schmidt95]. The two main roles in the Reactive layer are summarized below.

- *Reactor.* This class defines an interface for registering, removing, and dispatching `Event_Handler` objects (such as the `Acceptor`, `Connector`, and `Service_Handler`). An implementation of the `Reactor` interface provides a set of application-independent mechanisms that perform event demultiplexing and dispatching of application-specific `Event_Handlers` in response to events.
- *Event Handler.* This class specifies an interface that the `Reactor` uses to dispatch callback methods defined by objects that are preregistered to handle events. These events signify conditions such as a new connection request, a completion of a connection request started asynchronously, or the arrival of data from a connected `peer`.

Connection Layer. The Connection layer is responsible for (1) creating a `Service_Handler`, (2) passively or actively connecting it with a `peer`, and (3) activating it once it is connected. Since all behavior in this layer is completely generic, these classes delegate to the concrete IPC mechanism and `Concrete_Service_Handler` instantiated by the Application layer (described below). Likewise, the Connection layer delegates to the `Reactor` to handle initialization-related events (such as establishing connections asynchronously without requiring multithreading). The three primary roles (`Service_Handler`, `Acceptor`, and `Connector`) in the Connection layer are described below.

Service_Handler. This abstract class provides a generic interface for processing services. Applications must customize this class to perform a particular type of service. The middle part of Figure 12-7 illustrates the interface of the `Service_Handler`. The interface of the `Service_Handler` is shown below.

```
// PEER_STREAM is the type of the Concrete IPC mechanism.
template <class PEER_STREAM>
class Service_Handler : public Event_Handler
{
public:
  // Pure virtual method (defined by a subclass).
  virtual int open (void) = 0;

  // Conversion operator needed by Acceptor and Connector.
  operator PEER_STREAM &() { return peer_stream_; }
```

```
protected:
  // Concrete IPC mechanism instance.
  PEER_STREAM peer_stream_;
};
```

The open hook of a ServiceHandler is called by the Acceptor or Connector once a connection is established. The behavior of this pure virtual method must be defined by a subclass, which typically performs any service-specific initializations.

Service_Handler subclasses can also define the service's concurrency strategy. For example, a Service_Handler may inherit from the Event_Handler and employ the Reactor [Schmidt95] pattern to process data from peers in a single-thread of control. Conversely, a Service_Handler might use the Active Object pattern [Lavender+96] to process incoming data in a different thread of control than the one the Acceptor object used to connect it. The Sample Code section illustrates how several different concurrency strategies can be configured flexibly without affecting the structure or behavior of the Acceptor or Connector patterns.

Connector. This abstract class implements the generic strategy for actively initializing communication services. The left part of Figure 12-7 illustrates the interface of the Connector. The key methods and objects in the Connector are shown below.

```
// The SERVICE_HANDLER is the type of service. The PEER_CONNECTOR is
// the type of concrete IPC active connection mechanism.
template <class SERVICE_HANDLER, class PEER_CONNECTOR>
class Connector : public Event_Handler
{
public:
  enum Connect_Mode {
    SYNC, // Initiate connection synchronously.
    ASYNC // Initiate connection asynchronously.
  };

  // Initialization method.
  Connector (void);

  // Actively connect and activate a service.
  int connect (SERVICE_HANDLER *sh,
               const PEER_CONNECTOR::PEER_ADDR &addr,
               Connect_Mode mode);

protected:
  // Defines the active connection strategy.
  virtual int connect_service_handler
    (SERVICE_HANDLER *sh,
     const PEER_CONNECTOR::PEER_ADDR &addr,
     Connect_Mode mode);
```

```
    // Register the SERVICE_HANDLER so that it can
    // be activated when the connection completes.
    int register_handler (SERVICE_HANDLER *sh, Connect_Mode mode);

    // Defines the handler's concurrency strategy.
    virtual int activate_service_handler (SERVICE_HANDLER *sh);

    // Activate a SERVICE_HANDLER whose non-blocking connection completed.
    virtual int complete (HANDLE handle);

private:
    // IPC mechanism that establishes connections actively.
    PEER_CONNECTOR connector_;

    // Collection that maps HANDLEs to SERVICE_HANDLER *s.
    Map_Manager<HANDLE, SERVICE_HANDLER *> handler_map_;

    // Inherited from the Event_Handler -- will be called back by reactor
    // when events complete asynchronously.
    virtual int handle_event (HANDLE, EVENT_TYPE);
};

// Useful "short-hand" macros used below.
#define SH SERVICE_HANDLER
#define PC PEER_CONNECTION
```

The Connector is parameterized by a particular type of PEER_CONNECTOR and SERVICE_HANDLER. The PEER_CONNECTOR provides the transport mechanism used by the Connector to actively establish the connection synchronously or asynchronously. The SERVICE_HANDLER provides the service that processes data exchanged with its connected peer. Parameterized types are used to decouple the connection establishment strategy from the type of service handler, network programming interface, and transport layer connection acceptance protocol.

The use of parameterized types is an implementation decision that improves portability by allowing the wholesale replacement of the mechanisms used by the Connector. This makes the connection establishment code portable across platforms that contain different network programming interfaces (such as sockets but not TLI, or vice versa). For example, the PEER_CONNECTOR template argument can be instantiated with either a SOCKConnector or a TLIConnector, depending on whether the platform supports sockets or TLI.

An even more dynamic type of decoupling could be achieved via inheritance and polymorphism by using the Factory Method and Strategy patterns described in [Gamma+95]. Parameterized types improve runtime efficiency at the expense of additional space and time overhead during program compiling and linking.

The implementation of the `Connector`'s `connect` method is detailed in Figure 12-7.[3] The `connect` method is the public entry point for a `Connector`, as shown below.

```
template <class SH, class PC> int
Connector<SH, PC>::connect (SERVICE_HANDLER *service_handler,
                     const PEER_CONNECTOR::PEER_ADDR &addr,
                     Connect_Mode mode)
{
  connect_service_handler (service_handler, addr, mode);
}
```

This method provides the external entry point into the `Connector` factory. It uses the Bridge pattern[4] to delegate to the `Connector`'s connection strategy, `connect_service_handler`, which initiates a connection.

```
template <class SH, class PC> int
Connector<SH, PC>::connect_service_handler
    (SERVICE_HANDLER *service_handler,
     const PEER_CONNECTOR::PEER_ADDR &remote_addr,
     Connect_Mode mode)
{
  // Delegate to concrete PEER_CONNECTOR
  // to establish the connection.

  if (connector_.connect (*service_handler, remote_addr, mode) == -1) {
    if (mode == ASYNC && errno == EWOULDBLOCK)
    // If the connection hasn't completed and we are using non-
    // blocking semantics then register ourselves with the Reactor
    // Singleton so that it will callback when the connection is
    // complete.
    Reactor::instance ()->register_handler (this, WRITE_MASK);

    // Store the SERVICE_HANDLER in the map of pending connections.
    handler_map_.bind (connector_.get_handle (), service_handler);
  }
  else if (mode == SYNC)
    // Activate if we connect synchronously.
    activate_service_handler (service_handler);
}
```

---

[3] To save space, most of the error handling in this paper has been omitted.
[4] The use of the Bridge pattern allows subclasses of `Connector` to transparently modify the connection strategy without changing the interface.

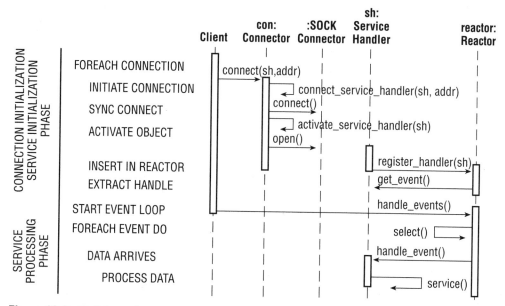

Figure 12-8 *Collaborations among the Connector participants for synchronous initialization*

If the value of the `Connect_Mode` parameter is SYNC, the SERVICE_HANDLER will be activated after the connection completes synchronously, as illustrated in Figure 12-8.

To connect with multiple `Peers` efficiently, the `Connector` must be able to actively establish connections asynchronously, that is, without blocking the caller. Asynchronous behavior is specified by passing the ASYNC connection mode to `Connector::connect`, as illustrated in Figure 12-9.

Once instantiated, the PEER_CONNECTOR class provides the concrete IPC mechanism for initiating connections asynchronously. The implementation of the Connector pattern shown here uses asynchronous I/O mechanisms provided by the operating system and communication protocol stack (for example, by setting sockets into nonblocking mode and using an event demultiplexer like `select` or `WaitForMultipleObjects` to determine when the I/O completes).

The `Connector` maintains a map of `Service_Handlers` whose asynchronous connections are pending completion. Since the `Connector` inherits from `Event_Handler`, the `Reactor` can automatically call back to the `Connector`'s `handle_event` method when a connection completes.

The `handle_event` method is an Adapter that transforms the `Reactor`'s event handling interface to a call to the Connector pattern's `complete` method, which activates by SERVICE_HANDLER invoking its `open` hook. The `open` hook is called

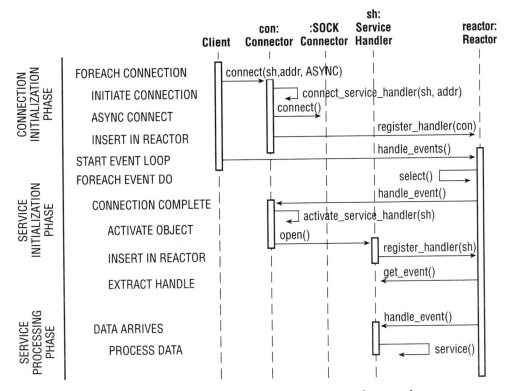

Figure 12-9 *Collaborations among the Connector participants for asynchronous initialization*

when a connection is established successfully, regardless of whether connections are established synchronously or asynchronously. This uniformity of behavior makes it possible to write services whose behavior can be decoupled from the manner in which they are actively connected and initialized.

The Connector's handle_event method is shown below.

```
template <class SH, class PC> int
Connector<SH, PC>::handle_event (HANDLE handle, EVENT_TYPE type)
{
    // Adapt the Reactor's event handling API to the Connector's API.
    complete (handle);
}
```

The complete method then activates a SERVICE_HANDLER whose nonblocking connection just completed successfully.

```
template <class SH, class PC> int
Connector<SH, PC>::complete (HANDLE handle)
```

```
{
  SERVICE_HANDLER *service_handler = 0;

  // Locate the SERVICE_HANDLER corresponding to the HANDLE.
  handler_map_.find (handle, service_handler);

  // Transfer I/O handle to SERVICE_HANDLER *.
  service_handler->set_handle (handle);

  // Remove handle from Reactor.
  Reactor::instance ()->remove_handler (handle, WRITE_MASK);

  // Remove handle from the map.
  handler_map_.unbind (handle);

  // Connection is complete, so activate handler.
  activate_service_handler (service_handler);
}
```

The `complete` method finds and removes the connected SERVICE_HANDLER from its internal map, transfers ownership of the I/O HANDLE to the SERVICE_HANDLER, and initializes the service by calling `activate_service_handler`. This method delegates to the concurrency strategy designated by the SERVICE_HANDLER::open hook, as follows.

```
template <class SH, class PC> int
Connector<SH, PC>::activate_service_handler
  (SERVICE_HANDLER *service_handler)
{
  service_handler->open ();
}
```

Acceptor. This abstract class implements the generic strategy for passively initializing communication services. The right-hand part of Figure 12-7 illustrates the interface of the `Acceptor`. The key methods and objects in the `Acceptor` are shown below.

```
// The SERVICE_HANDLER is the type of service. The PEER_ACCEPTOR is the
// type of concrete IPC passive connection mechanism.
template <class SERVICE_HANDLER, class PEER_ACCEPTOR>
class Acceptor : public Event_Handler
{
public:
// Initialize local_addr listener endpoint and register with Reactor
// Singleton.
  virtual int open (const PEER_ACCEPTOR::PEER_ADDR &local_addr);
```

```
    // Factory that creates, connects, and activates SERVICE_HANDLER's.
    virtual int accept (void);

protected:
    // Defines the handler's creation strategy.
    virtual SERVICE_HANDLER *make_service_handler (void);

    // Defines the handler's connection strategy.
    virtual int accept_service_handler (SERVICE_HANDLER *);

    // Defines the handler's concurrency strategy.
    virtual int activate_service_handler (SERVICE_HANDLER *);

    // Demultiplexing hooks inherited from Event_Handler -- used by
    // Reactor for callbacks.
    virtual HANDLE get_handle (void) const;
    virtual int handle_close (void);

    // Invoked when connection requests arrive.
    virtual int handle_event (HANDLE, EVENT_TYPE);

private:
    // IPC mechanism that establishes connections passively.
    PEER_ACCEPTOR peer_acceptor_;
};

// Useful "short-hand" macros used below.
#define SH SERVICE_HANDLER
#define PA PEER_ACCEPTOR
```

The Acceptor is parameterized by a particular type of PEER_ACCEPTOR and SERVICE_HANDLER. The PEER_ACCEPTOR provides the transport mechanism used by the Acceptor to passively establish the connection. The SERVICE_HANDLER provides the service that processes data exchanged with its connected peer. Parameterized types are used to decouple the connection establishment strategy from the type of service handler, network programming interface, and transport layer connection initiation protocol.

As with the Connector, the use of parameterized types improves portability by allowing the wholesale replacement of the mechanisms used by the Acceptor. This makes the connection establishment code portable across platforms that contain different network programming interfaces (such as sockets but not TLI, or vice versa). For example, the PEER_ACCEPTOR template argument can be instantiated with either a SOCKAcceptor or a TLIAcceptor, depending on whether the platform supports sockets or TLI. The implementation of the Acceptor's methods is presented below.

Applications use the open hook to initialize an Acceptor. This method is implemented as follows.

```
template <class SH, class PA> int
Acceptor<SH, PA>::open (const PEER_ACCEPTOR::PEER_ADDR &local_addr)
{
  // Forward initialization to the PEER_ACCEPTOR.
  peer_acceptor_.open (local_addr);

  // Register with Reactor.
  Reactor::instance ()->register_handler (this, READ_MASK);
}
```

The open hook is passed to the local_addr network address used to listen for connections. It forwards this address to the passive connection acceptance mechanism defined by the PEER_ACCEPTOR. This mechanism initializes the listener endpoint, which advertises its service access point (IP address and port number) to clients interested in connecting with the Acceptor. The behavior of the listener endpoint is determined by the type of PEER_ACCEPTOR instantiated by a user. For instance, it can be a C++ wrapper for sockets [Booch93], TLI [Rago93], STREAM pipes [Presotto+90], Win32 Named Pipes, and so forth.

After the listener endpoint has been initialized, the open method registers itself with the Reactor Singleton. The Reactor performs a double dispatch back to the Acceptor's get_handle method to obtain the underlying HANDLE, as follows.

```
template <class SH, class PA> HANDLE
Acceptor<SH, PA>::get_handle (void)
{
  return peer_acceptor_.get_handle ();
}
```

The Reactor stores this HANDLE internally and uses it to detect and demultiplex incoming connection from clients. Since the Acceptor class inherits from EventHandler, the Reactor can automatically call back to the Acceptor's handle_event method when a connection arrives from a peer. This method is an Adaptor that transforms the Reactor's event handling interface to a call to the Acceptor's accept method, as follows:

```
template <class SH, class PA> int
Acceptor<SH, PA>::handle_event (HANDLE, EVENT_TYPE)
{
  // Adapt the Reactor's event handling API to the Acceptor's API.
  accept ();
}
```

As shown below, the `accept` method is a Template Method [Gamma+95] that implements the Acceptor pattern's passive initialization strategy for creating a new `SERVICE_HANDLER`, accepting a connection into it, and activating the service.

```
template <class SH, class PA> int
Acceptor<SH, PA>::accept (void)
{
  // Create a new SERVICE_HANDLER.
  SH *service_handler = make_service_handler ();

  // Accept connection from client.
  accept_service_handler (service_handler);

  // Activate SERVICE_HANDLER by calling its open() hook.
  activate_service_handler (service_handler);
}
```

This method is very concise since it factors all low-level details into the concrete `SERVICE_HANDLER` and `PEER_ACCEPTOR` instantiated via parameterized types. Moreover, all of its behavior is performed by virtual functions, which allow subclasses to extend any or all of the `Acceptor`'s strategies. This flexibility makes it possible to write services whose behavior can be decoupled from the manner in which they are passively connected and initialized.

The `Acceptor`'s default strategy for creating `SERVICE_HANDLERs` is defined by the `make_service_handler` method.

```
template <class SH, class PA> SH *
Acceptor<SH, PA>::make_service_handler (void)
{
  return new SH;
}
```

The default behavior uses a demand strategy, which creates a new `SERVICE_HANDLER` for every new connection. However, subclasses of `Acceptor` can override this strategy to create `SERVICE_HANDLERs` using other strategies (such as creating an individual Singleton [Gamma+95] or dynamically linking the `SERVICE_HANDLER` from a shared library).

The `SERVICE_HANDLER` connection acceptance strategy used by the `Acceptor` is defined below by the `accept_service_handler` method:

```
template <class SH, class PA> int
Acceptor<SH, PA>::accept_service_handler (SH *handler)
{
  peer_acceptor_->accept_ (*handler);
}
```

The default behavior delegates to the accept method provided by the PEER_ACCEPTOR. Subclasses can override the accept_service_handler method to perform more sophisticated behavior (such as authenticating the identity of the client to determine whether to accept or reject the connection). The Acceptor's SERVICE_HANDLER concurrency strategy is defined by the activate_service_handler method:

```
template <class SH, class PA> int
Acceptor<SH, PA>::activate_service_handler (SH *handler)
{
  handler->open ();
}
```

The default behavior of this method is to activate the SERVICE_HANDLER by calling its open hook. This allows the SERVICE_HANDLER to select its own concurrency strategy. For instance, if the SERVICE_HANDLER inherits from Event_Handler, it can register with the Reactor. This allows the Reactor to dispatch the SERVICE_HANDLER's handle_event method when events occur on its PEER_STREAM endpoint of communication. Subclasses can override this strategy to do more sophisticated concurrency activations (such as making the SERVICE_HANDLER an active object [Lavender+96] that processes data using multithreading or multiprocessing).

When an Acceptor terminates, either due to errors or due to the entire application shutting down, the Reactor calls the Acceptor's handle_close method, which enables it to release any dynamically acquired resources. In this case, the handle_close method simply closes the PEER_ACCEPTOR's listener endpoint.

```
template <class SH, class PA> int
Acceptor<SH, PA>::handle_close (void)
{
  return peer_acceptor_.close ();
}
```

Application Layer. The Application Layer is responsible for supplying a concrete interprocess communication (IPC) mechanism and a concrete Service-Handler. The IPC mechanisms are encapsulated in C++ classes to simplify programming, enhance reuse, and to enable wholesale replacement of IPC mechanisms. For example, the SOCKAcceptor, SOCKConnector, and SOCKStream classes used in the Sample Code section are part of the SOCK_SAP C++ wrapper library for sockets [Schmidt+94]. SOCK_SAP encapsulates the stream-oriented semantics of connection-oriented protocols like TCP and SPX with efficient, portable, and type-safe C++ wrappers.

The three main roles in the Application layer are described below.

- *Concrete Service Handler.* This class implements the concrete application-specific service activated by a `Concrete_Acceptor` or a `Concrete_Connector`. A `Concrete_Service_Handler` is instantiated with a specific type of C++ IPC wrapper that exchanges data with its connected peer. The sample code examples in the Sample Code section use a `SOCKStream` as the underlying data transport delivery mechanism. It is easy to vary the data transfer mechanism, however, by parameterizing the `Concrete_Service_Handler` with a different `PEER_STREAM` (such as an SVR4 `TLIStream` or a Win32 `NamedPipeStream`).
- *Concrete Connector.* This class instantiates the generic `Connector` factory with concrete parameterized type arguments for `SERVICE_HANDLER` and `PEER_CONNECTOR`.
- *Concrete Acceptor.* This class instantiates the generic `Acceptor` factory with concrete parameterized type arguments for `SERVICE_HANDLER` and `PEER_ACCEPTOR`.

In the Sample Code section, `SOCKConnector` and `SOCKAcceptor` are the underlying transport programming interfaces used to establish connections actively and passively, respectively. However, parameterizing the `Connector` and `Acceptor` with different mechanisms (such as a `TLIConnector` or `NamedPipeAcceptor`) is straightforward since the IPC mechanisms are encapsulated in C++ wrapper classes.

The following section illustrates sample code that instantiates a `Concrete_Service_Handler`, `Concrete_Connector`, and `Concrete_Acceptor` to implement the `Peers` and `Gateway` described in the Motivation section. This particular example of the Application layer customizes the generic initialization strategies provided by the `Connector` and `Acceptor` components in the Connection layer. Note how the use of templates and dynamic binding permits specific details (such as the underlying network programming interface or the creation strategy) to change flexibly. For instance, no `Connector` components must change when the concurrency strategy is modified in the Sample Code section.

Sample Code

The sample code below illustrates how the `Peers` and `Gateway` described under Motivation use the Acceptor and Connector patterns to simplify the task of passively initializing services. The `Peers` play the passive role in establishing connections with the `Gateway`, whose connections are initiated actively by using the Connector pattern. Figure 12-10 illustrates how participants in the Acceptor pattern are structured in a `Peer` and Figure 12-11 illustrates how participants in the Connector pattern are structured in the `Gateway`.

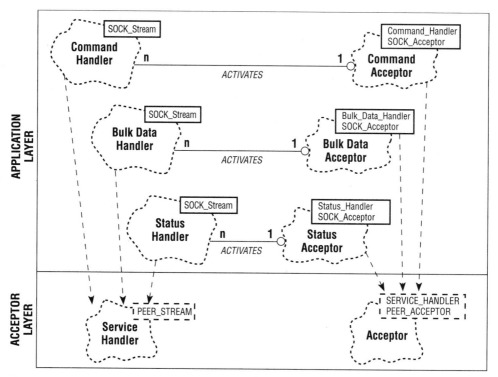

Figure 12-10 *Structure of Acceptor pattern participants for* `Peers`

Peer Components

Service Handlers for Communicating with a Gateway. The classes shown below, `status_Handler`, `Bulk_Data_Handler`, and `Command_Handler`, process routing messages sent and received from a `Gateway`. Since these `Concrete_Service_handler` classes inherit from `Service_Handler` they are capable of being passively initialized by an `Acceptor`.

To illustrate the flexibility of the Acceptor pattern, each `open` routine in the `ServiceHandlers` can implement a different concurrency strategy. In particular, when the `Status_Handler` is activated it runs in a separate thread; the `Bulk_Data_Handler` runs as a separate process; and the `Command_Handler` runs in the same thread as the `Reactor` that demultiplexes connection requests for the `Acceptor` factories. Note how changes to these concurrency strategies do not affect the implementation of the `Acceptor`, which is generic and thus highly flexible and reusable.

We start by defining a `ServiceHandler` that uses `SockStream` for socket-based data transfer.

```
typedef Service_Handler <SOCK_Stream> PEER_HANDLER;
```

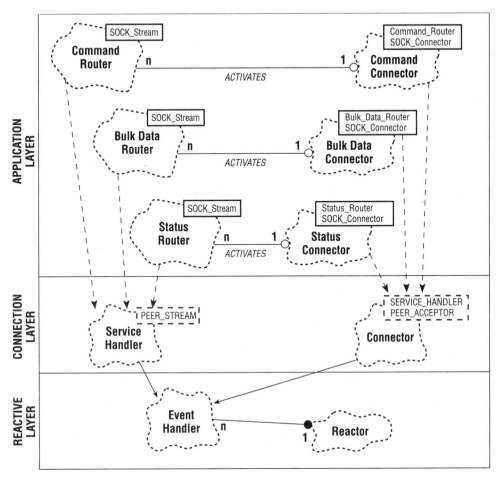

Figure 12-11 *Structure of Connector pattern participants for the* Gateway

The PEER_HANDLER typedef forms the basis for all the subsequent service handlers. For instance, the StatusHandler class processes status data sent to and received from a Gateway.

```
class Status_Handler : public PEER_HANDLER
{
public:
  // Performs handler activation.
  virtual int open (void) {
    // Make handler run in separate thread (note that Thread::spawn
    // requires a pointer to a static method as the thread entry point).
    Thread::spawn (&Status_Handler::service_run, this);
  }
```

```
// Static entry point into thread, which blocks on the handle_event ()
// call in its own thread.
  static void *service_run (Status_Handler *this_) {
    // This method can block since it runs in its own thread.
    while (this_->handle_event () != -1)
      continue;
  }

  // Receive and process status data from Gateway.
  virtual int handle_event (void) {
    char buf[MAX_STATUS_DATA];
    stream_.recv (buf, sizeof buf);
    // ...
  }

  // ...
};
```

The `Bulk_Data_Handler` and `Command_handler` classes can likewise be defined as subclasses of `PEER_HANDLER`. For instance, the following class processes bulk data sent to and received from the `Gateway`.

```
class Bulk_Data_Handler : public PEER_HANDLER
{
public:
  // Performs handler activation.
  virtual int open (void) {
    // Handler runs in separate process.
    if (fork () == 0) // In child process.
      // This method can block since it runs in its own process.
      while (handle_event () != -1)
        continue;
    // ...
  }

  // Receive and process bulk data from Gateway.
  virtual int handle_event (void) {
    char buf[MAX_BULK_DATA];
    stream_.recv (buf, sizeof buf);
    // ...
  }

  // ...
};
```

The following class processes bulk data sent to and received from a `Gateway`.

```
class Command_Handler : public PEER_HANDLER
{
public:
  // Performs handler activation.
  virtual int open (void) {
    // Handler runs in same thread as main Reactor singleton.
    Reactor::instance ()->register_handler (this, READ_MASK);
  }

  // Receive and process command data from Gateway.
  virtual int handle_event (void) {
    char buf[MAX_COMMAND_DATA];
    // This method cannot block since it borrows
    // the thread of control from the Reactor.
    stream_.recv (buf, sizeof buf);
    // ...
  }

  //...
};
```

Acceptors for creating Peer Service Handlers. The s_acceptor, bd_acceptor, and c_acceptor objects shown below are Concrete_Acceptor factories that create and activate Status_Handlers, Bulk_Data_Handlers, and Command_Handlers, respectively.

```
// Accept connection requests from Gateway and activate Status_Handler.
Acceptor<Status_Handler, SOCK_Acceptor> s_acc;

// Accept connection requests from Gateway and activate
// Bulk_Data_Handler.
Acceptor<Bulk_Data_Handler, SOCK_Acceptor> bd_acc;

// Accept connection requests from Gateway and activate
// Command_Handler.
Acceptor<Command_Handler, SOCK_Acceptor> c_acc;
```

The Peer main function. The main program initializes the concrete Acceptor factories by calling their open hooks with the well-known ports for each service. As shown in the Implementation section, the Acceptor::Open method registers itself with an instance of the Reactor. The program then enters an event loop that uses the Reactor to detect connection requests from the Gateway. When connections arrive, the Reactor calls back to the appropriate Acceptor, which creates the appropriate PEER_HANDLER to perform the service, accepts the connection into the handler, and activates the handler.

```
// Main program for the Peer.

int main (void)
{
  // Initialize acceptors with their well-known ports.
  s_acc.open (INET_Addr (STATUS_PORT));
  bd_acc.open (INET_Addr (BULK_DATA_PORT));
  c_acc.open (INET_Addr (COMMAND_PORT));

  // Loop forever handling connection request
  // events and processing data from the Gateway.

  for (;;)
    Reactor::instance ()->handle_events ();
}
```

Figure 12-12 illustrates the relationship between Acceptor pattern objects in the Peer after four connections have been established. While the various Handlers exchange data with the Gateway, the Acceptors continue to listen for new connections.

Gateway Components

Service Handlers for Gateway routing. The classes shown below, Status_ Router, Bulk_Data_Router, and Command_Router, route data they receive from a

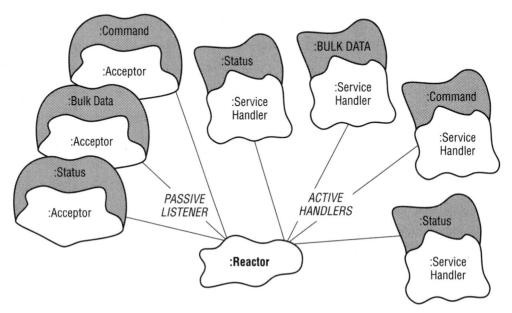

Figure 12-12 *Object diagram for the Acceptor pattern in the* Peer

source `Peer` to one or more destination `Peers`. Since these `Concrete_Service_` `Handler` classes inherit from `Service_Handler` they can be actively connected and initialized by a `Connector`.

To illustrate the flexibility of the Connector pattern, each open routine in a `Service_Handler` implements a different concurrency strategy. In particular, when the `Status_Router` is activated, it runs in a separate thread; the `Bulk_Data_` `Router` runs as a separate process; and the `CommandRouter` runs in the same thread as the `Reactor` that demultiplexes connection completion events for the connector factory. As with the `Acceptor`, note how changes to these concurrency strategies do not affect the implementation of the `Connector`, which is generic and thus highly flexible and reusable.

We'll start by defining a `Service_Handler` that is specialized for socket-based data transfer.

```
typedef Service_Handler <SOCK_Stream> PEER_ROUTER;
```

This class forms the basis for all the subsequent routing services. For instance, the `Status_Router` class routes status data from/to `Peers`:

```
class Status_Router : public PEER_ROUTER
{
public:
  // Activate router in separate thread.
  virtual int open (void) {
    // Thread::spawn requires a pointer to a
    // static method as the thread entry point).
    Thread::spawn (&Status_Router::service_run, this);
  }

  // Static entry point into thread, which blocks
  // on the handle_event() call in its own thread.
  static void *service_run (Status_Router *this_) {
    // This method can block since it runs in its own thread.
    while (this_->handle_event () != -1)
      continue;
  }

  // Receive and route status data from/to Peers.
  virtual int handle_event (void) {
    char buf[MAX_STATUS_DATA];
    peer_stream_.recv (buf, sizeof buf);
    // Routing takes place here...
  }

  // ...
};
```

The `Bulk_Data_Router` and `Command_Router` classes can likewise be defined as subclasses of `PEER_ROUTER`. For instance, the `Bulk_Data_Router` routes bulk data from/to `Peers`.

```
class Bulk_Data_Router : public PEER_ROUTER
{
public:
  // Activates router in separate process.
  virtual int open (void) {
    if (fork () == 0) // In child process.
      // This method can block since it runs in its own process.
      while (handle_event () != -1)
        continue;
    // ...
  }

  // Receive and route bulk data from/to Peers.
  virtual int handle_event (void) {
    char buf[MAX_BULK_DATA];
    peer_stream_.recv (buf, sizeof buf);
    // Routing takes place here...
  }

};
```

The `Command_Router` class routes Command data from/to `Peers`.

```
class Command_Router : public PEER_ROUTER
{
public:
  // Activates router in same thread as Connector.
  virtual int open (void) {
    Reactor::instance ()->register_handler (this, READ_MASK);
  }

  // Receive and route command data from/to Peers.
  virtual int handle_event (void) {
    char buf[MAX_COMMAND_DATA];
    // This method cannot block since it borrows
    // the thread of control from the Reactor.
    peer_stream_.recv (buf, sizeof buf);
    // Routing takes place here...
  }
};
```

A Connector for creating Peer Service Handlers. The following `typedef` defines a `Connector` factory specialized for `PEER_ROUTERS`.

```
typedef Connector<PEER_ROUTERS, SOCK_Connector> PEER_CONNECTOR;
```

The Gateway Main function. The main program for the Gateway is shown below. The get_peer_addrs function creates the Status, Bulk_Data, and Command_ Routers that route messages through the Gateway. This function (whose implementation is not shown) reads a list of Peer addresses from a configuration file. Each Peer address consists of an IP address and a port number. Once the Routers are initialized, the Connector factories defined above initiate all the connections asynchronously (indicated by passing the ASYNC flag to the connect method).

```
// Main program for the Gateway.

// Obtain lists of Status_Routers, Bulk_Data_Routers, and
// Command_Routers from a config file.

void get_peer_addrs (Set<PEER_ROUTERS> &peers);

int main (void)
{
  // Connection factory for PEER_ROUTERS.
  PEER_CONNECTOR peer_connector;

  // A set of PEER_ROUTERs that perform the Gateway's routing services.
  Set<PEER_ROUTER> peers;

  // Get set of Peers to connect with.
  get_peer_addrs (peers);

  // Iterate through Routers and initiate connections asynchronously.
  PEER_ROUTER *peer;

  for (Set_Iter<PEER_ROUTER> set_iter (peers);
       set_iter.next (peer) != 0;
       set_iter++)
    peer_connector.connect (peer,
                            peer->address (),
                            PEER_CONNECTOR::ASYNC);
  // Loop forever handling connection completion events and
  // routing data from Peers.

  for (;;)
    Reactor::instance ()->handle_events ();

  /* NOTREACHED */
}
```

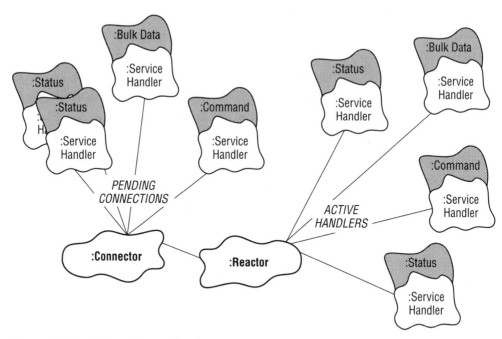

Figure 12-13 *Object diagram for the Connector pattern in the* Gateway

All connections are invoked asynchronously. They complete concurrently via Con-nector::complete method, which is called back within the Reactor's event loop. The Reactor also demultiplexes and dispatches routing events for Command_ Router objects, which run in the Reactor's thread of control. The Status_Routers and Bulk_Data_Routers execute in separate threads and processes, respectively.

Figure 12-13 illustrates the relationship between objects in the Gateway after four connections have been established. Four other connections that have not yet completed are owned by the Connector. When all Peer connections are com-pletely established, the Gateway can route and forward messages sent to it by Peers.

Known Uses

The Acceptor and Connector patterns have been used in a wide range of frame-works, toolkits, and systems.

- *UNIX network superservers* such as inetd [Stevens90], listen [Rago93], and the Service_Configurator daemon from the ACE ASX framework [Schmidt+94]. These superservers utilize a master Acceptor process that listens for connections on a set of communication ports. Each port is associated with a communication-related service (such as the standard Internet services ftp, telnet, daytime, and echo). The Acceptor pattern decouples the functionality in the inetd superserver into two separate parts: one for establishing connections and another for receiving and processing requests from peers. When a service request arrives on a monitored port, the Acceptor process accepts the request and dispatches an appropriate preregistered handler to perform the service.

The listen superserver always executes services in a separate process, the inetd superserver can be configured to allow both single-threaded and separate processes, and the Service_Configurator supports single-threaded, multithreaded, and multiprocess execution of services.

- *CORBA ORBs.* The ORB Core layer in many implementations of CORBA [OMG] (such as VisiBroker and Orbix) use the Acceptor pattern to passively initialize server object implementations when clients request ORB services.

- *WWW Browsers.* The HTML parsing components in WWW browsers like Netscape and Internet Explorer use the asynchronous form of the Connector pattern to establish connections with servers associated with images embedded in HTML pages. This behavior is particularly important so that multiple HTTP connections can be initiated asynchronously to avoid blocking the browsers main event loop.

- *Ericsson EOS Call Center Management System.* This system uses the Acceptor and Connector patterns to allow application-level Call Center Manager Event Servers [Schmidt+94] to actively establish connections with passive Supervisors in a distributed center management system.

- *Project Spectrum.* The high-speed medical image transfer subsystem of project Spectrum [Pyarali+96] uses the Acceptor and Connector patterns to passively establish connections and initialize application services for storing large medical images. Once connections are established, applications then send and receive multimegabyte medical images to and from these image stores.

- *ACE Framework.* Implementations of the Reactor, Service_Handler, Connector, and Acceptor classes described in this chapter are provided as reusable components in the ACE object-oriented network programming framework [Schmidt+94].

Related Patterns

The Acceptor and Connector patterns use the Template Method and Factory Method patterns [Gamma+95]. The Acceptor's accept and the Connector's connect and complete functions are Template Methods that implement a generic service initialization Strategy for connecting with peers and activating a Service_Handler when the connection is established. The use of the Template Method pattern allows subclasses to modify the specific details of creating, connecting, and activating ServiceHandlers. The Factory Method pattern is used to decouple the creation of a ServiceHandler from its subsequent use.

The Connector pattern has an intent similar to the Client-Dispatcher-Server pattern described in [Buschmann+96]. They both are concerned with separating active connection establishment from the subsequent service. The primary difference is that the Connector pattern addresses both synchronous and asynchronous service initialization, whereas the Client-Dispatcher-Server pattern focuses on synchronous connection establishment.

CONCLUDING REMARKS

This chapter describes the Acceptor and Connector patterns and gives a detailed example illustrating how to use them. Implementations of the Acceptor, Connector, and Reactor patterns described in this chapter are freely available via the World Wide Web at URL www.cs.wustl.edu/~schmidt/ACE.html. This distribution contains complete source code, documentation, and example test drivers for the C++ components developed as part of the ACE object-oriented network programming toolkit [Schmidt+94] developed at Washington University, St. Louis. The ACE toolkit is currently being used on communication software at many companies including Bellcore, Siemens, DEC, Motorola, Ericsson, Kodak, and McDonnell Douglas.

ACKNOWLEDGMENTS

Thanks to Hans Rohnert for helpful comments during the shepherding process.

REFERENCES

[Booch93] G. Booch. *Object Oriented Analysis and Design with Applications (Second Edition).* Redwood City, CA: Benjamin/Cummings, 1993.

[Buschmann+96] F. Buschmann, R. Meunier, H. Rohnert, P. Sommerlad, and M. Stal. *Pattern-Oriented Software Architecture: A System of Patterns.* New York: J. Wiley and Sons, 1996.

[Custer93] H. Custer. *Inside Windows NT.* Redmond, WA: Microsoft Press, 1993.

[Gamma+95] E. Gamma, R. Helm, R. Johnson, and J. Vlissides. *Design Patterns: Elements of Reusable Object-Oriented Software.* Reading, MA: Addison-Wesley, 1995.

[Jain+97] P. Jain and D. C. Schmidt. "Service Configurator: A Pattern for Dynamic Configuration of Services." From *The Third USENIX Conference on Object-Oriented Technologies and Systems,* Portland, Oregon, June 1997.

[Lavender+96] R. G. Lavender and D. C. Schmidt. Active Object: An Object Behavioral Pattern for Concurrent Programming, from *Pattern Languages of Program Design.* J. O. Coplien and J. Vlissides and N. Kerth (eds.). Reading, MA: Addison-Wesley, 1996.

[OMG] Object Management Group. *The Common Object Request Broker: Architecture and Specification.* 1995 (May).

[Presotto+90] D. L. Presotto and D. M. Ritchie. "Interprocess Communication in the Ninth Edition UNIX System." *UNIX Research System Papers, Tenth Edition,* 2(8), pp 523–530, 1990.

[Pyarali+96] I. Pyarali and T. H. Harrison and D. C. Schmidt. "Design and Performance of an Object-Oriented Framework for High-Performance Electronic Medical Imaging," *USENIX Computing Systems Journal,* Vol. 9, No. 4, Nov/Dec, 1996.

[Rago93] S. Rago. *UNIX System V Network Programming.* Reading, MA: Addison-Wesley, 1993.

[Schmidt+94] D. C. Schmidt and T. Suda. "An Object-Oriented Framework for Dynamically Configuring Extensible Distributed Communication Systems." *IEE/BCS Distributed Systems Engineering Journal (Special Issue on Configurable Distributed Systems),* Vol 2, pp. 280–293, December 1994.

[Schmidt+95] D. C. Schmidt. "Reactor: An Object Behavioral Pattern for Concurrent Event Demultiplexing and Event Handler Dispatching." From *Pattern Languages of Program Design.* J. O. Coplien and D. C. Schmidt (eds.). Reading, MA: Addison-Wesley, 1995.

[Stevens90] W. R. Stevens. *UNIX Network Programming.* Englewood Cliffs, NJ: Prentice Hall, 1990.

Douglas C. Schmidt can be contacted at schmidt@cs.wustl.edu.

APPENDIX

Connection-oriented protocols (such as TCP [Stevens90]) reliably deliver data between services connected by two or more endpoints of communication. Initializing these service endpoints involves the following two roles.

- *The passive role*—which initializes a service endpoint that is listening at a particular address and waits passively for the other service endpoint(s) to connect with it; and
- *The active role*—which actively initiates a connection to one or more service endpoints that are playing the passive role.

Figure 12-14 illustrates how these initialization roles behave and interact when a client actively connects to a passive server using the socket network programming interface and the TCP transport protocol [Stevens90]. In this figure the server plays the passive initialization role and the client plays the active initialization role. Note that the distinction between "client" and "server" refer to communication roles, not necessarily to initialization roles. Although clients often play the active role when initiating connections with a passive server these initialization roles can be reversed, as described in the Motivation section.

The primary goal of the Acceptor and Connector patterns is to decouple the passive and active initialization roles, respectively, from the tasks performed once the endpoints of a service are initialized. These patterns are motivated by the observation that the tasks performed on messages exchanged between endpoints of a distributed service are largely independent of the following initialization-related issues:

- **Which endpoint initiated the connection.** Connection establishment is inherently asymmetrical since the passive endpoint waits and the active service endpoint initiates the connection. Once the connection is established, however, data may be transferred between endpoints in any manner that obeys the service's communication protocol (such as peer-to-peer, request-response, one-way streaming). Figure 12-14 illustrates (1) the client-side and (2) server-side connection establishment process, and (3) the service processing between two connected service endpoints that exchange messages.

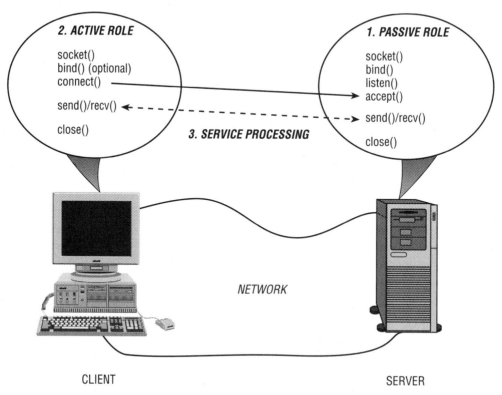

Figure 12-14 *Active and passive initialization roles*

- *The network programming interfaces and underlying protocols used to establish the connection.* Different network programming interfaces (such as sockets [Stevens90] or TLI [Rago93]) provide different library calls to establish connections using various underlying communication protocols (such as the Internet TCP/IP protocol or Novell's IPX/SPX). Regardless of the mechanism used to establish a connection, however, data can be transferred between endpoints using uniform message passing operations (for example, UNIX `send/recv` calls or Win32 `readfile/writefile`).

- *The creation, connection, and concurrency strategies used to initialize and execute the service.* The processing tasks performed by a service are often independent of the strategies used (1) to create an instance of a service, (2) connect the service instance to one or more peers, and (3) execute this service instance in one or more threads or processes. By explicitly decoupling these initialization strategies from the behavior of the service, the Connector and Acceptor patterns increase the potential for reusing and extending service-specific behavior in different environments.

Chapter 13

Bodyguard

Fernando Das Neves and Alejandra Garrido

Intent

The intent of the Bodyguard pattern is to allow objects to be shared and to control access to them in a distributed environment without system-level support for distributed objects. The Bodyguard is an object behavioral pattern that simplifies the management of object sharing over a network. It provides message dispatching validation and assignment of access rights to objects in nonlocal environments to prevent incorrect access to an object in collaborative applications.

Motivation

To illustrate the Bodyguard pattern, consider a distributed environment for building and browsing the common knowledge of a team about World Wide Web pages, like the one depicted in Figure 13-1. Pages are collected by WWW browsers as team members visit WWW nodes. Those browsers capture pages, create

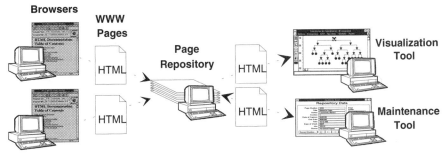

Figure 13-1 *Tools working together, probably on different computers, over a common repository of WWW pages. Some of the tools can add pages to the repository (like browsers), others can inspect them (Visualization tool), and others can perform both activities (Maintenance tool).*

WWW Page objects, and pass these objects to a repository running on a different host, which tentatively classifies the pages.

The repository is simultaneously accessed by many tools. Let us focus on object sharing among the repository and the tools. The respository can be consulted by two kinds of tools: those that are used to analyze and query the repository content and those that are in charge of cleaning and organizing the repository (by deleting irrelevant pages and reclassifying some others that were classified mistakenly by the repository).

The forces that need to be considered in this problem are:

- The need to share objects among a server and many accessing and updating tools, marshaling messages to support the communication.
- The need to control access rights to prevent improper access to any object which is distributed, depending on the context usage. In this example, querying and visualization tools should not be allowed to delete entries in the repository.
- The need to provide support for distributed objects. Sometimes an operating system does not support distributed objects (as CORBA does), or you do not want to pay the price for the flexibility and wide range of services those systems provide when you do not need all of them. Also there are applications with limited needs for object distribution running on platforms (for example, low-end UNIX boxes) where the supposition of CORBA availability conspires against the portability of the application.

A preliminary solution could be achieved by exchanging data with standard operating system mechanisms like RPC and message-passing, but there is an impedance mismatch between applications which benefit from objects throughout their design and the sharing of these objects using these low-level mechanisms.

What we need is to decouple the object sharing from communication and from access control. In the example, the repository would only be in charge of maintaining pages and reply queries for the pages it contains. An object that we call `Transporter` would be in charge of message marshaling and communication between different servers. We can use proxies to maintain surrogate objects in remote sites. A special object, called `Bodyguard`, would be in charge of maintaining and controlling access rights to the objects for different message categories. These objects and their relationships comprise the Bodyguard pattern.

The Bodyguard pattern is an alternative to being impeded by platform-dependent data-transport system calls and the unclear separation of access control from data transport. It allows decoupling of access control from transport mechanisms and dynamic change of access rights and method dispatching.

The following two figures show how the WWW page-sharing scheme looks when it is designed following the Bodyguard pattern. Figure 13-2 shows the scheme from the point of view of the Maintenance Tool asking to delete a page. Figure 13-3 shows how, using the same scheme, the Visualization tool is prohibited from deleting the page.

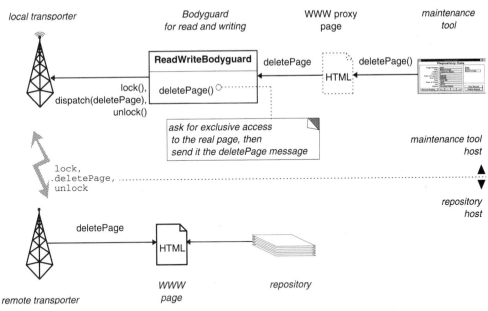

Figure 13-2 *The page-sharing scheme for the Maintenance tool. The tool sends messages to the proxy page, which in turn delegates the message to the* Bodyguard *to check. Since this* Bodyguard *allows writing operations, the message* deletePage() *is sent to the real page. In this example, the repository is not notified of the operations.*

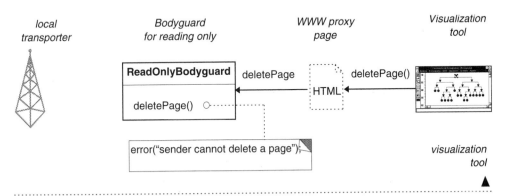

Figure 13-3 *The page-sharing scheme instantiated for the Visualization tool, showing how* ReadOnlyBodyguard *(a kind of* Bodyguard *that does not allow modification messages) denies the request to delete a page. Note that since the* Bodyguard *denies the request, there is no communication with its transporter or between transporters.*

The essential components of the Bodyguard pattern are (1) the object to be shared, (2) the object that controls the access to that object (Bodyguard), and (3) the object that is in charge of the communication among hosts (Transporter). There is one Transporter in every host. Each Transporter may know all objects that can be shared, and so the objects can assure the Transporter exclusive access to them. Proxies redirect messages to their Bodyguards and optionally packs the messages as objects. If the messages are allowed, according to the Bodyguard's access rights, then the local Transporter sends the request to the remote Transporter, which in turn unpacks the request and sends the message to the real object the proxy stands for.

Applicability

Use the Bodyguard pattern when you

- Have control over the construction of applications that access shared objects.
- Need to share objects in a distributed environment with a common object implementation, but the platform lacks system-level support for distributed objects (CORBA or the like), and authentication control is not mandatory.
- Need to synchronize and pool messages passing to shared objects.
- Need fine-grained control of access restrictions, depending on who requests to share the object.
- Need dynamic change in access rights.
- Need identity checking and assignment of access rights to objects in order to prevent incorrect behavior from objects of an application, but not to guard against security violations from those objects.

Do not use the Bodyguard pattern when

- Your application demands strict authentication of object identity in order to grant access rights and to prevent unauthorized access to restricted information.
- You need support for complex distributed object services, like licensing, externalization, and querying (as with CORBAServices).
- You have a very heterogeneous environment, with various object models (like different inheritance and exception propagation models) and different network protocols.

Structure

Structure of the Bodyguard pattern is illustrated in the OMT diagram shown in Figure 13-4. Coming back to the examples and looking at Figures 13-2, 13-3, and the pattern structure, WWWPages correspond to RealSubjects, WWWProxyPages are Proxy instances, and ReadWriteBodyguard and ReadOnlyBodyguard are SpecializedBodyguards. When a tool needs a page, it asks the Repository for the page. If the Repository has the desired page, it answers affirmatively, and a

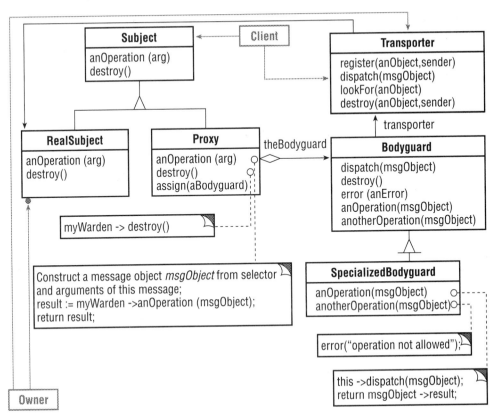

Figure 13-4 *Structure of the Bodyguard pattern*

WWWProxyPage is created by the Transporter at the tool location. Depending on the access rights assigned to the new proxy page by the Repository, an instance of ReadWriteBodyguard or ReadOnlyBodyguard is created and designated as the bodyguard of the new Proxy Page. A ProxyPage class would provide a template for message dispatching. Instances of a Transporter class work as an external interface for communication I/O, marshal messages and their parameters, and register objects that can be shared or their remote images (proxies plus Bodyguards). Classes ReadOnlyBodyguard and ReadWriteBodyguard provide conformance checking for message dispatching, like ReadOnlyBodyguard refusing to delete a page.

Participants

The following delineations define the participants and their roles in the pattern.

- **Real Subject:**

  - defines the object meant to be shared.

- **Transporter:**

  - controls the communication I/O, performing the marshaling that is necessary in order to encode objects and messages to be sent over the communication channel. In fact, we will have a `Transporter` in each remote machine so that marshaling will be encapsulated among the different instances, making it transparent to the rest of the application.
  - registers the associations of shared objects and remote proxies.
  - communicates with other `Transporters` to optionally implement atomic operations over shared objects, such as locking and total reference count of objects.
  - creates proxies of shared objects upon requests to access them.

- **Bodyguard:**

  - works as a mediator between `Proxy` and `Transporter` instances by sending method-dispatching requests, notifying objects of destruction and optionally handling error notifications. `Bodyguard` is an abstract class; `SpecializedBodyguard` is the one that implements concrete `Bodyguards`.
  - controls client's access to the real subject, asking the `Transporter` to carry messages out to the `RealSubject`, when permitted.
  - specifies the protocol that will be implemented by `SpecializedBodyguards`.

- **SpecializedBodyguard:**

  - implements methods to provide conformance checking for message dispatching, both in access rights restrictions and low-level synchronization and exclusion. There will be a subclass of `SpecializedBodyguard` for each kind or group of operations that needs a particular access right.

- **Proxy:**

  - acts as a surrogate to the real subject .
  - provides an interface identical to `RealSubject`.
  - maintains a reference to a `Bodyguard` for the `RealSubject` and delegates every request to it.

Collaborations

- An object that is intended to be shared will be passed as a parameter of the message register sent to the `Transporter` in order to become broadly known (see in Figure 13-5). The `Transporter` then records the object. The sender of the request to register is designated as the owner of the object and is allowed to destroy the object.

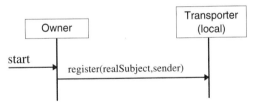

Figure 13-5 *Interaction diagram for Object Registration*

- The first access to a remote object is performed by asking the local `Trans-porter` for it. The `Transporter` will search for the object in the network. If it finds the object, then it will create a local `Bodyguard` and `Proxy` to control access to the remote object (see Figure 13-6).
- In subsequent transactions, when a client needs to send a request to the remote object, the client will interact with the `Proxy` that, in turn, delegates the request to the `Bodyguard`. The `Bodygard` will check the validity of the request and, when appropriate, communicate with its local `Transporter`, which is in charge of sending the request to the `Transporter` in the remote host. The remote `Transporter` will then send the request to the remote object and send back the proper response (see Figure 13-7).

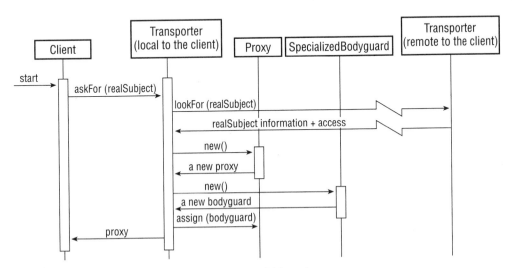

Figure 13-6 *Interaction diagram for Remote Object Access*

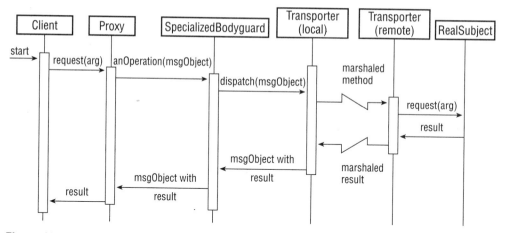

Figure 13-7 *Interaction diagram for Remote Method Dispatching*

Consequences

The Bodyguard pattern decouples access control from transport mechanisms, allowing the dynamic change of access rights. This decoupling allows the separation of data transport from the definition of different types of access rights over the objects meant to be shared, and from synchronization control. It also isolates the access restriction mechanism, because `Bodyguards` are only visible for proxies and not for external objects.

It trades generality for simplicity. In situations with restricted requisites and limited resources, the Bodyguard pattern offers an object-sharing scheme that is easier to understand and implement than a full, system-level object-sharing system. `Bodyguards` may also be used to record debugging or tracing information as completed messages, queued messages, and so forth.

As a drawback, the pattern implies augmenting the levels of indirection to reach an object. If communication speed is more important than access validation, then a scheme in which objects talk directly to each other should be implemented.

Variants

Variations on the Bodyguard pattern as described include the following.

- *Rights Assignment by Class vs. Identity.* At the moment a `Transporter` receives a request to access a shared object and the availability of the object is confirmed, the `Transporter` has to decide which access rights to assign and create the corresponding `Bodyguard`. Access rights can be divided into general categories and one of the categories assigned depending upon the class the client belongs to and the kind of object it is requesting (or upon the class of the object to be shared plus the object identity of the client). Assignment by class is best performed by the `Transporters`; assignment by identity is best performed by collaboration between the `Transporter` and the object owner.

- *General Bodyguards vs. Protocol Bodyguards.* The number of `Bodyguard` subclasses that need to be implemented depends heavily on how specific the control should be and the different access rights combinations. `Bodyguards` implement access control by the definition of a set of operations that express the general categories in which methods can be classified. Every operation stands for a kind of access, like reading, writing, and deleting. `Proxy` instances send requests for method dispatching by calling the proper type of operation in their `Bodyguards` for the category the method belongs to.

Granularity of the set of operations varies depending on the security enforcement needed by the classes whose instances will be shared. It ranges from checking only reading and writing permissions to extreme cases in which every operation in a `Proxy` has the same operation in a `Bodyguard`. In that case, operations in the `Bodyguard` are implemented knowing the semantics of the operations they will control in a particular `Proxy`, at the cost of having to code a particular `Bodyguard` for every protocol to be checked. It should be noted that it is not always necessary to implement a `Bodyguard` subclass for every class whose objects are going to be shared. Instead, a single `Bodyguard` can be used for a whole hierarchy. For example, in Smalltalk a single `CollectionBodyguard` class can be used to control the `Collection` hierarchy for a single access right, as the protocol is completely defined in the abstract class `Collection`.

Implementation

Message marshaling, or the way proxies redirect a message invocation to their `Bodyguards` for checking and dispatching, and the way the `Transporter` expresses that remote invocation, depends heavily on the language.

Languages that keep metainformation about classes make it easier to know what method we are trying to remotely dispatch and to send that knowledge to the remote site. For instance, messages in Smalltalk are objects in themselves. For any message it is possible to obtain a symbol describing the message selector (message header). Conversely, having a selector and a class, it is possible to find the method that matches the selector. This means that an easy path exists from a message to a symbol and back, a path the `Transporter` can use to marshal the message.

On the opposite side, there are languages that discard class and object metainformation at compile time. For those languages, a message object needs to be explicitly created by a `Bodyguard` every time one of its methods is called. The `Bodyguard` then checks access rights, the `Transporter` at the origin marshals the parameter, and the `Transporter` at the destination decodifies the message invocation and calls the real object.

Sometimes a backend operation is implemented to provide the metainformation the language discards and to add accessory information for garbage collection and atomic operations. A language-independent implementation of a backend facility for supporting distributed objects on languages with no metaclass protocol can be found in *Amadeus* [McHugh93+].

Participant Implementation

- *Proxies.* A detailed explanation of implementations of proxies for remote access can be found in Rohnert96 as *Remote Proxies.*
- *Transporter.* They manage the shared objects residing on every host. A Transporter is composed of two concurrent units. One is in charge of marshaling the arguments of a message for a remote message invocation and deciding each argument Whether to pass-by-proxy or pass-by-copy [McCullough87]. Some values cannot be passed by proxy, like numbers on hybrid languages like C++. The second unit manages the communication in the opposite direction, from a remote host to a local object.

  Transporter implementation can vary from a concurrent process to an independent daemon, depending on the complexity and flexibility of the services provided. Nevertheless, the context of the problem that Bodyguard addresses and all of the implementations to date suggest using one process or many collaborative processes. Either can be implemented using the Reactor pattern [Schmidt95]. Reactor manages three different handlers: `RequestAcceptor` is created in every host to receive incoming requests for sharing an object which resides on that host. It checks that the object resides there and sends a message "OK to share" (the object ID on the host and an access right). At that time, a `MessageHandler` is created by the `RequestAcceptor` for receiving marshaled messages from a given host, if no such an acceptor already exists.

  At the host where the request for a remote object began, an `OK_to_share-Acceptor` waits for acknowledgment to create the remote proxy and the associated `Bodyguard`, depending on the rights the originating `Bodyguard` has determined. After the acknowledgment is received, the `OK_to_shareAcceptor` is eliminated from its `Reactor`.

- *Object Creation.* `Transporters` must create `Proxy` instances upon requests to access shared objects. The strategy to create a `Proxy` depends on the implementation. If the `Transporter` can access all instance variables of the object, and if the object has a copy operator, then it can clone a new object from prototype object. If the `Transporter` is able to know all classes and it can metaclass information, as in Distributed Smalltalk [Bennet87], then it can directly create the instances from the class information. In the most general case, it can use a separate hierarchy of Abstract Factories [Gamma+95].

- *Access rights.* If access rights are going to change dynamically, it could be the case that some object which references a shared object needs to know whether that object is local or remote, shared or private, and the remote object's current access rights before performing an operation. This behavior could be achieved even before the object is shared, by implementing a default protocol in the Subject class and redefining it in its Proxy subclass. Methods like isShared() or isRemote() can be implemented in the Subject class to give a default answer when the queried action has not yet been performed (that is, answering false for isShared() and isRemote()). At the local site, messages are answered automatically by the object by being inherited; at the remote site, messages are answered by the Proxy, which asks the Bodyguard when necessary.

- *Object destruction and garbage collection.* Transporters have to be notified of object creation and destruction in order to keep the list of shared objects up to date. This is not a problem in languages with explicit object destruction; the moment the object destructor is called, it is trapped by the Proxy. In those languages with garbage collection, either a hook can be triggered at the moment of object destruction (like the *finalize* method in Smalltalk-80 [ParcPlace94]) or the garbage collector must be modified to check for local and remote references, as is the case in Distributed Smalltalk [Bennett87]. Object destruction is one of the access rights the Bodyguard grants or prohibits.

Related Patterns

Gamma and Rohnert discuss some issues and housekeeping tasks related to remote proxies [Gamma+95, Rohnert96]. It is evident that we need proxies to provide a local representative for an object in a different address space and to count references to the real object. Gamma and Rohnert also discuss "protection proxies," those which also provide access control. Nevertheless, the Proxy pattern is not enough for a distributed environment, because there is no explicit description of how to achieve low-level synchronization mechanisms. The Bodyguard pattern uses the Proxy pattern but enriches the structure with additional control (Bodyguard) and transport-related (Transporter) objects.

The Reactor and Acceptor patterns [Schmidt95] are also related to the Bodyguard pattern in the way in which the Transporter works. Reactor and Acceptor interact in order to receive login requests and create handlers for them. Transporters perform similar functions each time a remote shared request is made, creating proxies and Bodyguards in order to control access. Transporter and Reactor both pull incoming messages and maintain the association between objects and their proxies, or handlers and their callbacks and clients, respectively. Nevertheless, many differences may be found in the intents of these patterns, because although both operate in distributed environments, Reactor is intended for a client/server architecture whereas Bodyguard pattern is designed for a peer-to-peer environment.

The Bodyguard pattern is also strongly related to the Broker pattern [Busch-mann+96]. In one sense, Bodyguard is a specialized Broker structure (a kind of "Indirect Broker System" in the Broker taxonomy). `Transporters` take the place of Brokers and handle the task of message unmarshaling of server-side proxies. The `Proxy` class in the Bodyguard pattern stands for client-side proxies in the Broker. The main difference between the Bodyguard and Broker Patterns is that Broker is a high-level pattern; it describes interactions among subsystems like the transport subsystem (client proxy, broker, bridge) and language-mapping (server-side broker, object interfaces). As such, the typical application of the Broker pattern involves large-scale and possibly heterogeneous networks that have total independence from system-specific details as a mandatory requirement. There is also a great distance between the Broker pattern and a concrete implementation like CORBA; a large amount of detail must be filled in before being able to produce an implementation.

Bodyguard is a midlevel pattern, in that it expresses a design closer to actual implementation than does the Broker. As is apparent in the following section, the environment of a Bodyguard instantiation is more restricted than that of a Broker. It involves cooperative applications, usually developed as a set, that use access control to ensure global stability in shared objects, rather than ensuring their security. In the example related under Motivation, Bodyguards check that read/write protocols are not violated by any tool.

When `Transporters` need to create `Proxies` and `Bodyguards`, Abstract Factories [Gamma+95] is one of the more general schemes to manage this, although as previously described, it is often the case that simpler schemes, although less general, are used for the sake of performance.

Known Uses

Dollimore shows an implementation of shared objects with access restriction in Eiffel [Dollimore+93]. Objects are represented remotely by proxies, which are associated with a Bodyguard known as a "filter." Proxies and filters together build a Private Access Channel, which guards against unauthorized methods. Access rights can be changed by replacing the filter. Proxies manage remote invocation of methods by RPC and do not approach the remote object directly, but through the filter associated with the object.

Another forwarding mechanism for object sharing is implemented in Small-talk-80, which is composed of proxies on the remote side and transporters (known as `TransporterRooms`) on both sides [McCullough87] An associated `Policy-Maker` is used to decide whether to pass message parameters by proxy or by value. Object creation is directly managed by `TransporterRooms` that work together with a distributed garbage collector to manage the list of available share objects. No access control is provided. `TransporterRooms` are implemented as concurrent processes.

The distributed Smalltalk (DS) [Bennett87] melds the Bodyguard role with the Transporter role (collectively known in DS as `RemoteObjectTable`). In DS it is possible to allow or inhibit access to an object, and also to designate an object as an "agent" of another object. Agents can process messages or redirect them to another object in a manner similar to the way Bodyguards filter messages and redirect them. DS has no way of giving different access rights to proxies; access control is allowed only at the host where the original object resides. Local objects are created by the `RemoteObjectTable` and are directly managed by the `messageProcess`, which works in coordination with a distributed garbage collector. `RemoteObjectTable` is implemented by three concurrent processes.

ACKNOWLEDGMENTS

The authors would like to thank the PLoP '96 shepherd and all the people in the winter's workshops at PLoP '96 and OOPSLA '95 for their useful comments for improvement.

REFERENCES

[Bennett87] J. Bennett. "The Design and Implementation of Distributed Smalltalk," in the proceedings of OOPSLA '87: a Conference on Object-Oriented Programming Systems, Languages and Applications. ACM Press, 1987.

[Buschmann96+] F. Buschmann, R. Meunier, H. Rohnert, P. Sommerlad, and M. Stal. *A System of Patterns*. New York: John Wiley & Sons, 1996, pp. 99–122.

[Dollimore+93] J. Dollimore and X. Wang. "The Private Access Channel: A Security Mechanism for Shared Distributed Objects," the proceedings of TOOLS 10: the Technology of Object-Oriented Languages and Systems. Englewood Cliffs, NJ: Prentice Hall, 1993.

[Gamma+95] E. Gamma, R. Helm, R. Johnson, and J. Vlissides. *Design Patterns: Elements of Reusable Object-Oriented Software*. Reading, MA.: Addison-Wesley, 1994.

[McCullough87] P. McCullough. "Transparent Forwarding: First Steps." In the proceedings of OOPSLA '87: a Conference on Object-Oriented Programming Systems, Languages and Applications. ACM Press, 1987.

[McHugh93+] C. McHugh, and V. Cahill. "Eiffel**: An Implementation of Eiffel on Amadeus, a Persistent, Distributed Applications Support Environment," in proceedings of TOOLS 10: Technology of Object-Oriented Languages and Systems. Englewood Cliffs, NJ: Prentice Hall, 1993.

[ParcPlace94] "Visual Works Object Reference." ParcPlace Systems, Inc., 1994.

[Rohnert96] H. Rohnert. "The Proxy Pattern Revisited," in J. M. Vlissides, J. O. Coplien, and N.L. Keith (eds.), *Pattern Languages of Program Design 2*. Reading, MA: Addison-Wesley, 1996, pp. 105–118.

[Schmidt95] D. Schmidt. "Reactor: An Object Behavioral Pattern for Concurrent Event Demultiplexing and Dispatching," in the proceedings of PLoP '94, the First Annual Conference on the Pattern Languages of Programs, 1994.

[Stal95] M. Stal. "The Broker Architectural Framework." A workshop on Concurrent, Parallel and Distributed Patterns of Object-Oriented Programming held at OOPSLA '95.

Fernando Das Neves can be contacted at babel17@sol.info.unlp.edu.ar.
Alejandra Garrido can be contacted at garrido@sol.info.unlp.edu.ar.

Chapter 14

Asynchronous Completion Token

Irfan Pyarali, Tim Harrison,
and Douglas C. Schmidt

The Asynchronous Completion Token (ACT) pattern allows applications to efficiently associate state with the completion of asynchronous operations. Contemporary applications must respond to many types of events, ranging from user interface notifications to network messages. Delay-sensitive applications, such as network management systems, often perform long-running operations asynchronously to avoid blocking while processing other events. When these asynchronous operations complete, applications may need more information than simply the notification itself to handle the event correctly. This describes how such applications can benefit from the use of the Asynchronous Completion Token pattern.

Intent

To efficiently associate state with the completion of asynchronous operations.

Also Known As

Magic Cookie

Motivation

This section examines and motivates the context in which the ACT pattern may be used.

Context.   When providing asynchronous services to clients, it is often necessary to associate state with asynchronous operations. In particular, clients use this state to determine the appropriate action(s) to perform upon completion of the opera-

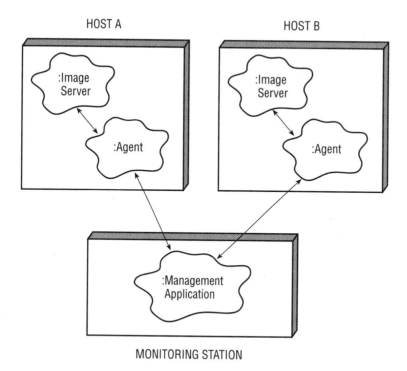

Figure 14-1 *Participants in an EMIS management system*

tions. The key design force resolved by the Asynchronous Completion Token (ACT) pattern is how to efficiently associate application-specific state with completion notifications.

To illustrate the Asynchronous Completion Token pattern, consider the structure of a network Management Application that monitors the performance and status of multiple components in a distributed Electronic Medical Imaging System (EMIS) [Pyarali+96]. Figure 14-1 shows a simplified view of the Management Application and several EMIS components.[1]

The performance and reliability of an EMIS is crucial to physicians, medical staff, and patients using the system. Therefore, it is important to monitor the state of EMIS components carefully. Agents address this need by propagating events from EMIS components (such as Image Servers) back to the Management

---

[1] There are many components in a distributed EMIS, including modalities, clinical and diagnostic workstations that perform imaging processing and display, hierarchical storage management (HSM) systems, and patient record databases. In this chapter, we will consider only Image Servers, which store and retrieve medical images.

REMOTE HOST

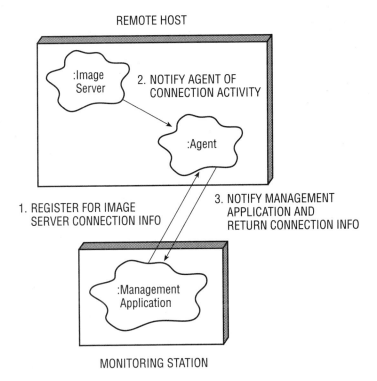

Figure 14-2 *Event registration and callback*

Application at a central Monitoring Station. Administrators use the Management Application to view and control the overall status and performance of the EMIS.

Figure 14-2 shows a typical sequence of events between the `Management-Application`, `Agents`, and EMIS components. The `ManagementApplication` initially registers with an `Agent` for periodic updates. For example, an application may register to receive events every time an `ImageServer` on a particular host accepts a new network connection. When the `Agent` detects a new connection at the `ImageServer`, it sends a `NewConnection` event to the `ManagementApplication`. The `ManagementApplication` can then display the new connection graphically on its console.

Several application-specific actions must be performed when an `Agent` sends an event to a `ManagementApplication`. For instance, the `ManagementApplication` may need to update a graphical display or record the event in a local database. Since the `ManagementApplication` can register for many types of events from any number of `Agents`, it must determine the appropriate action for each event efficiently. More specifically, `Agents` must allow the `ManagementApplication` to associate additional state with an event notification. This associated state must be sufficient for the ManagementApplication to determine the appropriate response (for example, updating a graphical display or logging on to a database) for the event.

Common Traps and Pitfalls

One way to execute multiple long duration operations simultaneously is to utilize threads. For instance, the ManagementApplication could spawn a separate thread for each request to an Agent. Each request would execute synchronously, blocking until its Agent replied. In this approach, the state information required to handle Agent replies could be stored implicitly in the context of each thread's runtime stack.

However, there are several drawbacks with a completely synchronous approach based on threads.

- *Increased complexity.* Threading may require complex concurrency control schemes throughout the application.
- *Poor performance.* Threading may lead to poor performance due to context switching, synchronization, and data movement [Schmidt94].
- *Lack of portability.* Threading may not be available on the OS platform.

Another way to associate state with the completion of an asynchronous operation is to depend on the information returned by the asynchronous service. For example, Agents can store sufficient information in the callback so the ManagementApplication can distinguish between all possible events. However, there are several limitations to this approach.

- *Excessive bandwidth.* Providing sufficient data to the client may require an excessive amount of data exchange. This may be particularly costly for distributed services.
- *Lack of context.* It may be too difficult for the service to know what data is needed by the clients. For instance, EMIS Agents may not know the context in which the ManagementApplication made the request.
- *Performance degradation.* The client may have to perform time-consuming processing (for example, searching a large table) to uniquely identify the completion of an asynchronous event based on the data returned from the service. This extra processing can degrade the performance of the client.

Solution

Often, a more efficient and flexible way to associate state with completion events is to use the Asynchronous Completion Token (ACT) pattern. To illustrate this solution, consider the EMIS example described earlier. When a ManagementApplication registers with an Agent for periodic updates, it creates an ACT and passes it to the Agent. When an EMIS event occurs, the Agent calls the

ManagementApplication and passes back the ACT that was sent to it originally. Since the Agent does not change the value of the ACT, the Management-Application can use the ACT to rapidly regain the state needed to process the event notification.

To make the example more concrete, consider a typical scenario where an EMIS administrator uses the ManagementApplication to log the connections made to a particular Image Server. As usual, the ManagementApplication must register with the Image Server's Agent to be notified of connection events. When these connection events arrive at the ManagementApplication, it must log the data, in addition to performing its normal graphical updates.

The Asynchronous Completion Token pattern addresses this need by allowing the ManagementApplication to pass an opaque value as an ACT. For instance, when registering with the Agent, the ManagementApplication can pass, as the ACT, a reference to a State object. The State object contains references to a user interface (in order to be updated) and a logging object. When connection events arrive, the ManagementApplication can use the State object referenced by the ACT to update the correct user interface and record the event with the appropriate logging object.

Figure 14-3 shows the order of events in our EMIS scenario. Before the Management-Application registers with the Agent, it creates the State object needed to handle the event notifications. Next, the ManagementApplication passes a reference to the State object as an ACT. When a connection is created at the ImageServer, the Agent is notified and subsequently calls back the Management-Application. The ManagementApplication receives the connection information and the ACT, which is used to guide subsequent event-specific actions.

Applicability

Providers of asynchronous services should use the Asynchronous Completion Token Pattern under the following circumstances.

- *The service performs client requests asynchronously.* However, if the operations are synchronous, there may be no need to provide an explicit hook to regain state since the state can be implicit in the activation record where the client thread is blocked.
- *The completion notification does not uniquely identify the operation.* In contrast, if the completion notification uniquely identifies the operation (for example, by providing an explicit return address) the ACT may be unnecessary.
- *The service knows nothing about the client's type system.* ACTs provide a clear separation between application *policy* and service *mechanism*. Since ACTs often can be implemented without regard to type (for example, as void* pointers), services need not know anything about the client's type system.

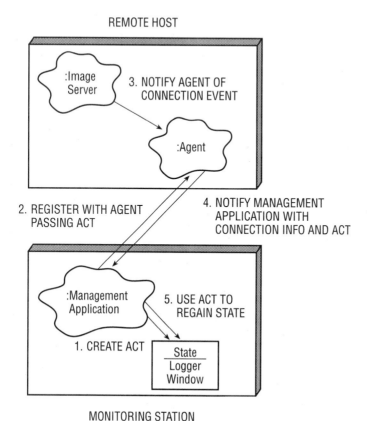

REMOTE HOST

MONITORING STATION

Figure 14-3 *Event registration and callback with ACTs*

Structure and Participants

Figure 14-4 illustrates the following participants in the Asynchronous Completion Token pattern:

- **Asynchronous Completion Token** (`Logger Window State`):

  – Clients pass the Asynchronous Completion Token (ACT) to Services, which then return the ACT on completion of asynchronous operations. ACTs can be indices into tables or direct pointers to memory that hold the state necessary to process the completion of the operation. To the Service, however, the ACT is simply an opaque object that will not be read from or written to. In fact, ACTs are often represented as `void*` pointers to avoid being type intrusive.

- **Service** (`Image Server Agent`):

  – The Service provides some type of asynchronous task to Clients. In the EMIS example, `Agents` asynchronously propagate EMIS events to `Manage-`

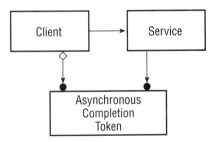

Figure 14-4 *Structure of participants in the Asynchronous Completion Token pattern*

mentApplications. Services may hold a collection of ACTs, the appropriate one of which will be returned to each Client when its asynchronous operation completes.

- **Client** (ManagementApplication):

  - The Client performs requests for asynchronous operations on the Service. To handle asynchronous events correctly, it requires application-specific state, along with the completion notification. In the EMIS example, the ManagementApplication is a Client to the Agent.

Collaborations

As shown in Figure 14-5, the interactions between participants in the ACT pattern can be divided into the following phases.

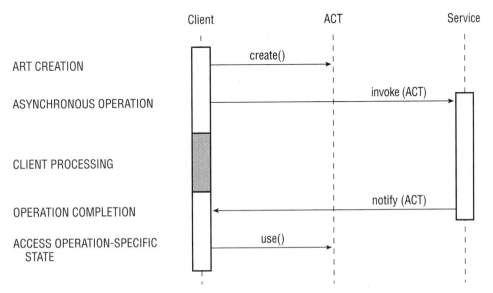

Figure 14-5 *Participant collaborations in the Asynchronous Completion Token pattern*

1. *ACT creation.* Before invoking an asynchronous operation on the Service, the Client creates the state associated with the operation. This state is the ACT passed to the Service.
2. *Asynchronous operation invocation.* When invoking the operation on the Service, the Client passes a reference to the state as an ACT.
3. *Client processing.* The Client continues executing while the Service performs the request from the Client.
4. *Asynchronous operation completion.* When the operation completes, the Service notifies the Client and returns the ACT. The Client uses the ACT to regain the needed state and continue to process the application-specific actions for that operation.

Consequences

There are several advantages to using the Asynchronous Completion Token pattern.

- *Allows efficient state acquisition.* ACTs can be very time efficient because they do not require complex parsing of data returned with the notification. All relevant information about the event can be stored either in the ACT or in an object pointed to by the ACT. Alternatively, ACTs can be used as indices or pointers to operation state for highly efficient access (for example, they eliminates table lookups).
- *Relieves Clients from managing state explicitly.* Clients need not keep complicated records of pending events since the ACT returned on completion provides access to all necessary information.
- *Space efficient.* ACTs need not be large in order to provide applications with hooks for associating state with asynchronous operations. For example, in C and C++, ACTs that are four byte void* pointers can reference larger objects.
- *Flexible.* User-defined ACTs are not forced to inherit from an interface in order to use the Service's ACTs. This allows applications to pass ACTs for which changing the type is undesirable or even impossible. The typeless nature of ACTs can be used to associate an object of any type to an asynchronous operation. When ACTs are implemented in C and C++ as void* pointers, they can be type casted to pointers to any type needed.
- *Separates Client policies from Service mechanisms.* ACTs are typically typeless objects (for example void* pointers). By using typeless objects, the representation of the ACTs remain opaque to the Service and are not type-intrusive to Clients.
- *Does not dictate concurrency policies.* Long-duration operations can be executed asynchronously since the operation state can be recovered efficiently from the ACT. This allows Clients to be single-threaded or multithreaded depending on application requirements. Alternatively, a Service that does not

provide ACTs may force delay-sensitive Clients to perform operations synchronously within threads to handle operation completions properly.

There are also several potential pitfalls to avoid when using the Asynchronous Completion Token pattern.

- *Memory leaks.* If a Client uses ACTs as pointers to dynamically allocated memory and a Service fails to return the ACT (for example, the Service crashes), memory leaks can result. Clients wary of this possibility should maintain separate ACT repositories or tables that can be used for explicit garbage collection in case services fail.
- *Application remapping.* If ACTs are used as direct pointers to memory, errors can occur if part of the application is remapped in virtual memory. This is plausible in persistent applications that may restart after crashes, as well as for objects allocated from a memory-mapped address space. To protect against these errors, indices to a repository can be used as ACTs. This extra level of indirection provides protection against remappings since index values remain valid across remappings whereas pointers to direct memory may not.
- *Authentication.* When an ACT is returned to a Client upon completion of an asynchronous event, the Client may need to authenticate the ACT before using it. This is necessary if the server cannot be trusted to have treated the ACT opaquely and may have changed the value of the ACT.

Implementation

From the viewpoint of the Service, there are four steps to implementing the ACT pattern: defining the ACT representation, accepting the ACT, holding the ACT, and returning the ACT. These steps are described below.

1. *Define the ACT representation.* ACTs can be represented as `void*` pointers or as pointers to abstract base classes. This former approach is frequently chosen when implementing the ACT pattern with low-level languages like C or C++. When a Client initiates an operation on the Service, it creates the ACT and casts it to a `void*` pointer. It is important to consider potential platform differences that might represent `void*` pointers differently. In this case, the developers may choose to use compiler and language constructs (such as, `#defines` and `typedefs`) to ensure uniform representation throughout the system.

   When using a higher-level object-oriented language such as Java or Smalltalk, the developer may represent ACTs as references to abstract base classes. Since the Service typically cannot make assumptions about the use of the ACTs, this class will be (mostly) empty (for example, a Java `Object`). Upon receiving ACTs, clients can use a type-safe `dynamic_cast` to narrow the ACT to a meaningful type.

2. *Accept the ACT.* Typically this step is straightforward. ACTs can be passed as parameters to asynchronous operation invocations. For instance, the sample code shows an example where ACTs are passed as parameters to Service methods.

3. *Hold the ACT.* Depending on the Service, this step can be simple or complex. If the Service operates synchronously, then the ACT can be stored implicitly in the runtime stack of the Service. For instance, if the Service is running in a separate thread or process from the Client, it can perform its operations synchronously while still providing asynchronous services to the Client.

However, Services can internally use asynchronous services and may need to handle multiple requests simultaneously. For instance, consider a `ManagementApplication` that performs requests on an `Agent` that, in turn, performs requests on a timer mechanism. This scenario can be viewed as a Client (that is, the `ManagementApplication`) using a chain of Services. All members in the chain (except the two ends) are both Clients and Services since they receive and initiate requests.

If each member of the chain uses the ACT pattern as Service, there are several choices when performing requests as Clients. If a member need not add state to the operation, it can simply pass along the original ACT received from the previous Client. However, when additional state must be associated with the operation, that state must contain the original ACT and a new ACT must be created. This step is required since the Service cannot normally make any assumptions about the values of received ACTs. If a Service were guaranteed that ACT values were unique, then it could use them as indices into a data structure mapping ACT to operation state. However, if uniqueness cannot be assured, the original ACT cannot be reused to reference new state.

4. *Return the ACT.* In the EMIS example explained above, when the `ManagementApplication` initiated a request on an `Agent`, the ACT was returned once with the response. However, depending on application requirements, ACTs from a single request may be returned multiple times. For instance, if a stream of responses were tagged with the same ACT, the receiving Client could use the ACT to associate additional state with the stream.

In both the single and stream responses, there are several options for how ACTs are returned to Clients when asynchronous operations complete. In other words, you must decide how Clients should be notified when asynchronous operations complete. There are several common approaches.

- *Callbacks.* In the callback approach, Clients specify functions or class methods that are called by the Service when an operation completes [Berczuk95]. Depending on the Service, callback functions can be specified once or on a per-request basis. In the callback approach, the ACT is returned as a parameter to the callback function. The Sample Code shows an example of the callback approach.

- *Queued completion notifications.* This approach queues up completion notifications, which can be retrieved at the Client's discretion. Win32 I/O completion ports use this approach. When Win32 HANDLEs[2] are created, they can be associated with completion ports via the CreateIoCompletionPort function. Completion ports provide a location for completion notifications to be queued by kernel-level Services and dequeued by Clients. When Clients initiate asynchronous reads and writes via ReadFile and WriteFile, they specify OVER-LAPPED structures that will be queued at a completion port when the operations complete. Clients dequeue completion notifications (including the OVERLAPPED structures) via the GetQueuedCompletionStatus function.
- *Asynchronous callbacks.* A variation on the callback approach is used by implementations of POSIX 4.0 Asynchronous I/O [POSIX95]. Clients can specify that completion notifications for asynchronous I/O operations be returned via UNIX signals. This approach is similar to the callback approach, that is, a registered signal handler is called. However, it differs since Clients need not explicitly wait for notifications—for example, they need not block in an event loop.

Consider the chain of Services example explained above. In addition to deciding how ACTs are returned to Clients, a chain of Services must decide which Service calls back the client. If no Service in the Chain created new ACTs to associate additional state with the operation, the last Service in the chain could notify the Client. This would optimize the process since, in this case, unwinding the chain of Services is unnecessary. In the EMIS example, Agents associate additional state with the timer operations, so unwinding is required.

Regardless of how the ACTs are returned to the Clients, once they are returned, the job of the Service is done. Clients are responsible for handling the completed operation and freeing any resources associated with the ACT.

Sample Code

The sample code below uses EMIS ManagementApplications and Agents to illustrate the use of ACTs with asynchronous I/O operations. The code defines an implementation of a ManagementApplication class that handles asynchronous EMIS events received from Agents.

```
// Use a generic C++ pointer.
typedef void *ACT;
```

---

[2] For Win32 overlapped I/O, handles are used to identify network connection endpoints or open files. Win32 handles are similar to UNIX descriptors.

```
class EMIS_Event_Handler : public Receiver
    // Defines the pure virtual recv_event() method.
{
public:
  // References to States will be passed as ACTs when invoking asynch
  // operations.
  struct State
  {
    Window *window_; // Used to display state.
    Logger *logger_; // Used to log state.
    // ...
  };

  // Called back by Agents EMIS when events occur.
  virtual void recv_event (const Event& event, ACT act)
  {
    // Turn the ACT into the needed state.
    State *state = static_cast <State *> (act);

    // Update a graphical window.
    state->window_->update (event);

    // Log the event.
    state->logger_->record (event);

    // ...
  }
};
```

The following code defines the Agent interface that can be invoked by clients to register for EMIS event notifications.

```
class Agent
{
  // Types of events that applications can register for.
  enum Event_Type
  {
    NEW_CONNECTIONS,
    IMAGE_TRANSFERS
    // ...
  };

  // Register for <receiver> to get called back when the <type> of EMIS
  // events occur. The <act> is passed back to <receiver>.
  void register (Receiver *receiver, Event_Type type, ACT act);
  // ...
};
```

The following code shows how a `ManagementApplication` invokes operations on an `Agent` and receives events.

```
int main (void)
{
  // Create application resources for logging and display.  Some events
  // will be logged to a database, while others will be written to a
  // console.
  Logger database_logger (DATABASE);
  Logger console_logger (CONSOLE);

  // Different graphical displays may need to be updated depending on
  // the event type. For instance, the topology window showing an iconic
  // system view must be updated when new connection events arrive.
  Window main_window (200, 200);
  Window topology_window (100, 20);

  // Create an ACT that will be returned when connection events occur.
  EMIS_Event_Handler::State connection_act;
  connection_act.window_ = &topology_window;
  connection_act.logger_ = &database_logger;

  // Create an ACT that will be returned when image transfer events
  // occur.
  EMIS_Event_Handler::State image_transfer_act;
  image_transfer_act.window_ = &main_window;
  image_transfer_act.logger_ = &console_logger;

  // Object which will handle all incoming EMIS events.
  EMIS_Event_Handler handler;

  // Binding to a remote Agent that will call back the
  // EMIS_Event_Handler when EMIS events occur.
  Agent agent = ... // Bind to an Agent proxy.

  // Register with Agent to receive notifications of EMIS connection
  // events.
  agent.register (&handler,
                  Agent::NEW_CONNECTIONS,
                  (ACT) &connection_act);

  // Register with Agent to receive notifications of EMIS image transfer
  // events.
  agent.register (&handler,
                  Agent::IMAGE_TRANSFERS,
                  (ACT) &image_transfer_act);

  run_event_loop ();
}
```

The application starts by creating its resources for logging and display. It then creates `State` objects that identify the completion of connection and image transfer events. The `State` objects contain references to `Window` and `Logger` objects. The address of the `State` objects are used as the ACTs. Next, the application registers the `ManagementApplication` instance with the `Agent` for each type of event. Finally, the application enters its event loop, where all GUI and network processing is driven by callbacks.

When an event is generated by an EMIS component, the `Agent` sends the event to the `ManagementApplication`, where it is delivered via the `recv_event` upcall. The `ManagementApplication` then uses the `ACT` returned to access the state associated with the event. With the `State` object, it updates a graphical window and logs the event. Note that the `ManagementApplication` uses ACTs to decide the appropriate action for each event. Image transfer events are displayed on a main window and logged to the console, whereas new connection events are displayed on a system topology window and logged to a database.

Variations

Non-opaque ACTs.   In some implementations of the ACT pattern, Services do not treat the ACT as a purely opaque object. For instance, Win32 OVERLAPPED structures are nonopaque ACTs since certain fields can be modified by the kernel. One solution to this problem is to pass subclasses of the OVERLAPPED structure that contain the additional state.

Synchronous ACTs.   ACTs can also be used for operations that result in synchronous callbacks. In this case, the ACT is not really an asynchronous completion token, but a synchronous one (that is, a SCT). Using ACTs for synchronous callback operations provides a well-structured means of passing state related to the operation through the Service. It also maintains a decoupling of concurrency policies. Thus, the code which receives the ACT can be used for synchronous or asynchronous operations.

Known Uses

As described below, the Asynchronous Completion Token (ACT) pattern is widely used in many systems software (such as Win32), communication middleware (such as RPC toolkits), as well as in less technical domains (such as Fedex inventory tracking).

- *OS asynchronous I/O mechanisms.* ACTs can be found in Win32 handles, Win32 Overlapped I/O, and Win32 I/O completion ports [Custer93], as well as in the POSIX Asynchronous I/O API [POSIX95]. When an application is performing multiple asynchronous operations (such as network and file I/O), there is typically one location (such as a Win32 I/O completion port) where the operation completion results are queued. For UNIX and POSIX asynchronous I/O read and write operations, results can be dequeued through the `aio_wait` and `aio_suspend` interfaces, respectively.

- *RPC transaction identifiers.* Client-side stubs generated by Sun RPC [Sun95] use ACTs to ensure that requests from a client match up with responses from the server. Every client request carries a unique opaque transaction ID (the ACT), which is represented as a 32-bit integer. This ID is initialized to a random value when the client handle is created and is changed every time a new RPC request is made. The server returns the transaction ID value sent by the client. Client routines test for a matching transaction ID before returning an RPC result to the application. This assures the client that the response corresponds to the request it made. SUN RPC is an example of the nonopaque variation of the ACT pattern. Although the server can test the ACT for equality (for example, to detect duplicates), it is not allowed to interpret the ACT any further.

- *EMIS network management.* The example described throughout this paper is derived from a distributed Electronic Medical Imaging System being developed at Washington University for Project Spectrum [Pyarali+96]. A network Management Application monitors the performance and status of multiple components in an EMIS. Agents provide the asynchronous service of notifying the Management Application of EMIS events (such as connection events and image transfer events). Agents use the ACT pattern so that the Management Application can efficiently associate state with the asynchronous arrival of EMIS events.

- *FedEx inventory tracking.* One of the most intriguing examples of Asynchronous Completion Tokens is implemented by the inventory tracking mechanism used by Federal Express postal services. A FedEx Airbill contains a section labeled: "Your Internal Billing Reference Information (Optional: First 24 characters will appear on invoice)." The sender of a package uses this field as an ACT. This ACT is returned by FedEx (the Service) to you (the Client) with the invoice that notifies the sender that the transaction has completed. FedEx deliberately defines this field very loosely, that is, it is a maximum of 24 characters, which are otherwise untyped. Therefore, senders can use the field in a variety of ways. For instance, a sender can populate this field with the index of a record for an internal database or with a name of a file containing a to-do list to be performed after the acknowledgment of the FedEx package delivery has been received.

Related Patterns

An Asynchronous Completion Token is typically treated as a Memento [Gamma+95] by the underlying framework. In the Memento pattern, Originators give Mementos to Caretakers who treat the Mementos as opaque objects. In the ACT pattern, Clients give ACTs to Services that treat the ACTs as opaque objects. Thus, the ACT and Memento patterns are similar with respect to the participants. However, the patterns differ in motivation and applicability. The Memento pattern takes snapshots of object states, whereas the ACT pattern associates state with the completion of asynchronous operations.

ACKNOWLEDGMENTS

Thanks to Paul McKenney and Richard Toren for their insightful comments and contributions. In addition, thanks to Chris Cleeland for helping to convert this chapter into Microsoft Word format.

REFERENCES

[Berczuk95] S. Berczuk. "A Pattern for Separating Assembly and Processing," from *Pattern Languages of Program Design,* eds. J. O. Coplien and D. C. Schmidt. Reading, MA: Addison-Wesley, 1995.

[Custer93] H. Custer. *Inside Windows NT.* Redmond, WA: Microsoft Press, 1993

[Gamma+95] E. Gamma, R. Helm, R. Johnson, and J. Vlissides. *Design Patterns: Elements of Reusable Object-Oriented Software.* Reading, MA: Addison-Wesley, 1995.

[POSIX95] *Information Technology—POSIX Realtime Extension (C Lanaguage).* Technical report. IEEE, 1995.

[Pyarali+96] I. Pyarali, T. H. Harrison, and D. C. Schmidt. *Design and Performance of an Object-Oriented Framework for High-Performance Electronic Medical Imaging,* Cambridge, MA: MIT Press, 1996. Also, *USENIX Computing Systems Journal 9,* (4), Nov/Dec, 1996.

[Schmidt+94] D. C. Schmidt. "ASX: an Object-Oriented Framework for Developing Distributed Applications," from *Proceedings of the 6th USENIX C++ Technical Conference.* Cambridge, MA: USENIX Association, 1994.

[Sun95] Sun Microsystems. *Open Network Computing: Transport Independent RPC.* Sun Microsystems, 1995.

Irfan Pyarali can be contacted at irfan@cs.wustl.edu.
Tim Harrison can be contacted at harrison@cs.wustl.edu.
Douglas C. Schmidt can be contacted at schmidt@cs.wustl.edu.

Chapter 15

Object Recovery

António Rito Silva, João Dias Pereira,
and José Alves Marques

This chapter describes a design pattern for Object Recovery. The Customizable Object Recovery pattern defines a generic object recovery algorithm and decouples the recovery part from the object's functional part. Different policies can be supported (update-in-place, deferred-update, copy, and compensating). The Customizable Object Recovery pattern isolates recovery from persistence and object synchronization issues, allowing the recovery of transient objects to a previously defined state. Moreover, the recovery pattern can be used to implement user undo and redo models of interaction.

Intent

The Customizable Object Recovery pattern abstracts several object recovery policies. It decouples object recovery policies from object-specific functionality.

Also Known As

Log

Motivation

The following example provides the motivation for the Object Recovery pattern.

Example

Consider the design of a Cooperative Drawing Application allowing cooperative manipulation of graphical documents. Users at different terminals can simultaneously access the same graphical document, and changes made by one user are immediately seen by the other users.

A possible architecture (Figure 15-1) for such an application contains several client applications having their own objects (application space) and sharing a set

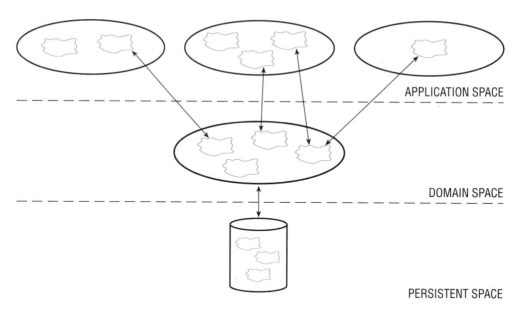

Figure 15-1 *Cooperative Drawing Application*

of domain objects (domain space) which may be kept in a data store (persistent space). The application space has interface objects, such as scrollbars and shapes; the domain space has shared objects, such as the shapes' data; and the persistent space stores documents, such as a graphical document including the data of its shapes.

The architecture uses several design patterns from [Gamma+95]. Users' interactions with the application are encapsulated with the Command pattern. Commands invoke operations on both application and domain space objects. Typical commands are `create`, `delete`, and `update` for a `Shape` object. The Observer pattern is applied to `Shapes` in the application and domain spaces. A domain `Shape` may be shared by several application `Shapes` which are its observers. Domain `Shapes` are proxy objects of persistent `Shapes`: Proxy pattern. Proxies know how to read and write themselves from and to the persistent space. A proxy object caches data read from the persistent space. Invocations are executed on cached data.

Problem

The Cooperative Drawing Application may need to undo operations for three different reasons.

- A user decides to undo a command and thus it is necessary to revert all the involved objects to a previous state; the user, therefore, uses an undo/redo model of interaction.

- Some operations done by client applications invoke methods on shared domain objects. Invocations to domain objects make use of a synchronization policy to avoid data corruption. In some conditions, synchronization policies need to retract effects of operations.
- During a system failure, if shape objects are being written to the persistent space, it is necessary to restore the persistent space to a consistent state.

The Memento pattern is used to externalize an object's state, without violating encapsulation, such that the object can be restored later [Gamma+95]. However, it does not provide a complete solution for the problem, as stated below.

- Several object recovery policies may be needed. For instance, recovery of a shared object requires invocations to proceed in a copy of the object if an optimistic synchronization is used.
- Object-oriented incremental development advocates adding object recovery after the object is coded and tested. The object should not need to be modified. Furthermore, the object can be augmented with undo and redo or concurrency recovery responsibilities. For instance, in the Cooperative Drawing Application, a graphical document can be either shared and recoverable from concurrent accesses or private and undoable by the user.

Forces

An object-oriented solution for the above problem has to resolve the following forces.

- *Encapsulation* requires the object recovery part to be associated with the object itself rather than spread out among its clients. The object is responsible for its own recovery because the recovery policy may need to access the object's internal representation.
- *Modularity* requires separation of recovery from persistency, synchronization, and object functionality. For instance, persistent objects should be recoverable, but sometimes volatile objects also need to be recoverable, for example, the user expects a scrollbar to return to its previous state. This orthogonality enhances reuse and allows for policy switching with no repercussions for other components.
- *Extensibility* requires abstraction of recovery policies. It is not possible to find an optimal policy for all situations; it should be possible to customize the policy for each situation. The most suitable policy depends on the domain object and its operations semantics.

Applicability

Use the Customizable Object Recovery pattern when

- *An operation's effects may need to be rolled back.* Effects of invocations on objects may need to be retracted due to an external decision.
- *It is necessary to recover transient objects.* Recovery should be independent of persistence. The decision to recover is not only due to a crash but also to application semantics, such as a user's undo or synchronization.
- *It is premature to decide on which recovery policy to use.* It may be early to decide on a specific policy at a given stage of the development process. It should be possible to test the performance of several policies before choosing. A predefined default recovery policy can be reused to test the application's functionality with recovery.
- *Different recovery policies may be used by objects of a class.* This allows policy interchange.

Structure and Participants

The Booch class diagram in Figure 15-2 illustrates the Customizable Object Recovery pattern's structure [Booch94]. The main participants in the Customizable Object Recovery pattern are

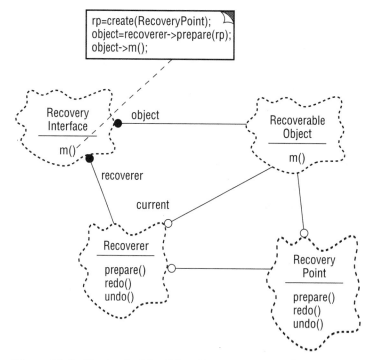

Figure 15-2 *Customizable Object Recovery pattern's structure*

- *Recovery Interface.* It is responsible for intercepting invocations to the `RecoverableObject` encapsulating it. Intercepted invocations are directed to a `RecoverableObject` returned by the `prepare` operation. Effects of invocations done through this interface are recoverable.
- *Recoverer.* Defines the object-independent part of the recovery policy. It refers to the current `RecoverableObject`, which is used as the initial point for redoing and undoing invocation effects. `Recoverer` integrates operations `prepare`, `redo`, and `undo` such that a consistent policy is implemented. Particular policies are implemented by reusable `Recoverer` subclasses.
- *RecoveryPoint.* Defines object-specific semantics which are used by the generic algorithm. It is responsible for preparing, redoing, and undoing `RecoverableObject` invocations. Operations `prepare`, `redo`, and `undo` may have to know the `RecoverableObject`'s internal data.
- *RecoverableObject.* Encapsulates data that is invoked and which may be recovered. It may define an internal interface to be used by `RecoveryPoint` objects. To support recoverability, several copies of the same `Recoverable-Object` may coexist.

Collaborations

The Booch interaction diagram in Figure 15-3 illustrates collaborations between objects in the Customizable Object Recovery pattern. The diagram describes four phases of collaboration.

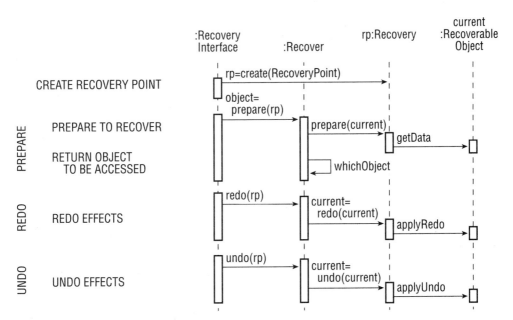

Figure 15-3 *Customizable Object Recovery pattern's collaborations*

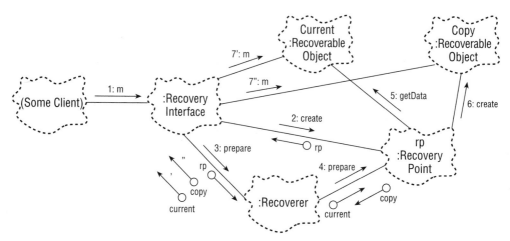

Figure 15-4 *Customizable Object Recovery pattern's collaboration scenario*

1. *Create RecoveryPoint.* This phase creates the `RecoveryPoint` object, which identifies the invocation during the other phases.
2. *Prepare.* The `RecoveryInterface` object sends a `RecoveryPoint` object to `Recoverer` and receives the `RecoverableObject` that should be invoked. During this phase, data needed for recovery actions may be copied. The `Recoverer` object may return to the `RecoveryInterface`, either the current `Recoverable-Object` or a copy of it, depending on the policy being implemented (operation `whichObject`).
3. *Redo.* The redo phase sets `current` to a `RecoverableObject`, which state is the result of the invocation identified by the `RecoveryPoint` object. In some policies, the `RecoverableObject` is already up-to-date because the operation invocation was done on the current `RecoverableObject`, while in others the current `RecoverableObject` needs to be updated because the operation has been executed on a copy.
4. *Undo.* The undo phase sets `current` to a `RecoverableObject` whose state is the same as before it was invoked by the operation identified by the `Recovery-Point` object. In some policies, the current `RecoverableObject`'s state does not reflect the last changes. This happens because the invocation was done on a copy, while in others the current `RecoverableObject` needs to be restored.

The Booch object diagram in Figure 15-4 illustrates a particular collaboration scenario which includes the first two phases. Interactions 7' and 7" represent the alternatives of executing in the `current` or in a `copy` of `RecoverableObject`. Note the two alternative values, `current` and `copy`, returned by the `Recoverer`.

Consequences

This pattern has the following advantages.

- Isolates recovery code from an object's client, such that the recovery policy is the object's responsibility. Recovery is, thus, transparent to clients.
- Separates the recovery code from the object code, allowing separate development, test, and reuse.
- Separates recovery policies from persistence, allowing the recovery of transient objects. This way, the pattern can be used for both persistent and transient objects. The writing of `RecoveryPoint` objects on the persistent space depends on failure recovery policies, such as write-ahead.
- Abstracts several recovery policies, using the same generic interface. It is possible to replace policies (see Implementation section) just by replacing the `Recoverer` and `RecoveryPoint` objects.
- Separates the object-independent part of the recovery policy from the object-specific part, such that it is possible to reuse the generic part of algorithms. Objects `Recoverer` and `RecoveryPoint` hold, respectively, the object-independent and object-specific parts of the algorithm.

This pattern also has the following disadvantage.

- There is an overhead when a straightforward use of the pattern is made. Objects of class `RecoveryPoint` may need to be created (when an invocation does not change the `Recoverer` object, it is not necessary to create a `RecoveryPoint` object) and deleted for each invocation, thus penalizing performance.

Implementation

The Customizable Object Recovery pattern may be implemented in several ways. Some issues and possibilities are discussed in the following points.

- *Definition of the object-independent part of policies.* Recovery policies can use two different generic algorithms: update-in-place, when the current `RecoverableObject` reflects the last changes, and deferred-update, when an invocation's updates do not occur on the current `RecoverableObject`. (a) Update-in-place policies make changes in the current `RecoverableObject`, such as interaction 7' in Figure 15-4. So, if it is necessary to recover, the changes must be undone. To implement an update-in-place policy the `Recoverer` object should return the current `RecoverableObject` at the end of the prepare phase. Afterwards, if a undo happens it is necessary to undo the changes on the current `RecoverableObject`. (b) Deferred-update policies do not change the current `RecoverableObject`, such as interaction 7'' in Figure 15-4. So, when the invocation commits, changes must be reflected on the current. To implement a deferred-update policy the `Recoverer` object should return a copy of the current `RecoverableObject` at the end of the prepare phase. Afterwards, if a redo happens, it is necessary to propagate the changes to the current `RecoverableObject`.

- *Definition of the object-specific part of policies.* This definition is supported by `RecoveryPoint` objects. There are two main solution groups, the copying state, when recovery is done using copies of an object's state, and compensating operations, when recovery is done using operations that know how to return to a previous state based on the current state. (a) Copy policies use copies of the object's state to redo and undo the effects of operations. Operation `prepare` of `RecoveryPoint` object copies the state of the current `RecoverableObject` (see interactions 5 and 6 in Figure 15-4). Operations `redo` and `undo` use the copied state to change the current `RecoverableObject`. (b) (Compensating policies use the current state instead of doing recovery based on data copies. In this policy it is not necessary to copy an object's data during the prepare phase. The `RecoveryPoint` object has operations that know how to redo and undo the effects of invocations, without using a previous object's state.

   Special care is necessary if a compensating policy is used with a deferred-update policy, because the `RecoveryPoint` object needs to return a `RecoverableObject`'s copy for the invocation to proceed, even if the copy is not used afterwards by the `RecoveryPoint` object.

- *Integration with object synchronization.* Object synchronization may need to recover an object's state due to synchronization conflicts. There are two generic kinds of synchronization policies: pessimistic, when the object is expected to have high contention, and optimistic, when the level of contention is supposed to be low. The integration of recovery and synchronization is not straightforward: some combinations of policies are not possible and others penalize performance. It has been proved that some operation compatibility relations require a particular kind of recovery policy [Weihl93a]. Common combinations are optimistic synchronization with deferred-update recovery policies, and pessimistic synchronization with update-in-place policies. The designer must be aware of both the allowed and the best combinations. The Customizable Object Synchronization pattern supports several object synchronization policies [Silva+96a].

- *Integration with user undo/redo models of interaction.* A single-user undo/redo model maintains an history of executed commands which is traversed forward and backward by the user doing, respectively, `redo` and `undo`. The undo (`redo`) of a command should be propagated to all the objects invoked during its execution. Since a command can be undone and redone several times, `RecoveryPoint` objects should not be discarded after the invocation has been done. To support user undo and redo, an update-in-place policy is used. In this case, the interface object must keep a list of `RecoveryPoint` objects.

SAMPLE CODE

This section describes a framework supporting several recovery policies, and the integration of recovery and synchronization in the context of the Cooperative Drawing Application.

Policies Implementation

A set of abstract classes is defined, as well as the classes' specializations for deferred-update synchronization, update-in-place synchronization, user undo and redo update-in-place, and copy policies. Due to the emphasis on reuse in this example, the implementation of compensating policies is not shown because they cannot be made object-independent.

Definition of Abstract Classes. Abstract classes define a framework which must be redefined according to the chosen policies. This framework forms a skeleton that enforces reusability. To improve reusability, classes are parameterized by ROBJECT.

Class Recoverer defines the interface of a recovery policy's object-independent part. The implementation of virtual methods whichObject, redo, and undo are policy dependent. Method prepare is implemented as a Template Method [Gamma+95].

```
template <class ROBJECT>
class Recoverer {
public:
  ROBJECT *prepare(RecoveryPoint<ROBJECT>*);
  virtual void redo(RecoveryPoint<ROBJECT>*) = 0;
  virtual void undo(RecoveryPoint<ROBJECT>*) = 0;
protected:
  virtual ROBJECT *whichObject(ROBJECT*) = 0;
private:
  ROBJECT *current_; // current object
};
```

The following template method sets the generic part of the policies while the specific part will be defined in subclasses.

```
ROBJECT *
Recoverer<ROBJECT>::prepare(RecoveryPoint<ROBJECT> *rp)
{
  ROBJECT *obj = rp->prepare(current_);
  // depending on the policy returns current or a copy
  return whichObject(obj);
}
```

Class `RecoveryPoint` defines the interface of the recovery policy's object-specific part as follows.

```
template <class ROBJECT>
class RecoveryPoint {
public:
  virtual ROBJECT *prepare(ROBJECT*) = 0;
  virtual ROBJECT *redo(ROBJECT*) = 0;
  virtual ROBJECT *undo(ROBJECT*) = 0;
};
```

Definition of an Update-in-Place Policy for Synchronization. Class `UpdatePlaceSyncRecoverer` is a subclass of `Recoverer` which implements this policy. Method `whichObject` returns the current object because the invocation is going to proceed on it. Method redo does not update `current_` because changes were done in the current object while method undo needs to change it.

```
ROBJECT *UpdatePlaceSyncRecoverer<ROBJECT>::
whichObject(ROBJECT *obj)
{
  return current_;
}
void UpdatePlaceSyncRecoverer<ROBJECT>::
redo(RecoveryPoint<ROBJECT> *rp)
{}
void UpdatePlaceSyncRecoverer<ROBJECT>::
undo(RecoveryPoint<ROBJECT> *rp)
{
  current_ = rp->undo(current_);
}
```

Definition of a Deferred-Update Policy for Synchronization. Class `DeferredUpdateSyncRecoverer` is a subclass of `Recoverer` which implements this policy. Method `whichObject` returns a copy of the current object because the invocation is going to proceed on it. Method redo changes the current object while method undo does not since the invocation was done on a copy.

```
ROBJECT *DeferredUpdateSyncRecoverer<ROBJECT>::
whichObject(ROBJECT *obj)
{
  return obj;
}
```

```
void DeferredUpdateSyncRecoverer<ROBJECT>::
redo(RecoveryPoint<ROBJECT> *rp)
{
  current_ = rp->redo(current_);
}
void DeferredUpdateSyncRecoverer<ROBJECT>::
undo(RecoveryPoint<ROBJECT> *rp)
{}
```

Definition of a Update-in-Place Policy for User Undo/Redo. Class `UpdatePlaceUndo-RedoRecoverer` is a subclass of `Recoverer` which implements this policy. A `RecoverableObject` can be undone and redone several times and so, `RecoveryPoint` objects should not be discarded after the invocation.

```
ROBJECT *UpdatePlaceUndoRedoRecoverer<ROBJECT>:
whichObject(ROBJECT *obj)
{
  return current_;
}
void UpdatePlaceUndoRedoRecoverer<ROBJECT>::
redo(RecoveryPoint<ROBJECT> *rp)
{
  current_ = rp->redo(current_);
}
void UpdatePlaceUndoRedoRecoverer<ROBJECT>::
undo(RecoveryPoint<ROBJECT> *rp)
{
  current_ = rp->undo(current_);
}
```

Definition of a Copy Policy. The implementation of an object-independent copy policy follows. The `RecoveryPoint` objects can be used with deferred-update and update-in-place recovery policies. This flexibility has costs for performance since copy objects can be unnecessarily created. The new instance variable `cpy_` holds an object's copy.

```
template <class ROBJECT>
class CopyRecoveryPoint : public RecoveryPoint<ROBJECT> {
public:
  ROBJECT *prepare(ROBJECT*);
  ROBJECT *redo(ROBJECT*);
  ROBJECT *undo(ROBJECT*);
private:
  ROBJECT *cpy_;
};
```

This policy can be reused by any type of object if a clone method is provided by the ROBJECT object. Note that in both methods, redo and undo, the instance variable cpy_ is updated to allow sequences of redo/undo.

```
ROBJECT *CopyRecoveryPoint<ROBJECT>::prepare(ROBJECT *cur)
{
  cpy_ = cur->clone();  // make a copy of current
  return cpy_;
}
ROBJECT *CopyRecoveryPoint<ROBJECT>::redo(ROBJECT *cur)
{
  ROBJECT *obj = cpy_;
  cpy_ = cur;
  return obj;
}
ROBJECT *CopyRecoveryPoint<ROBJECT>::undo(ROBJECT *cur)
{
  ROBJECT *obj = cpy_;
  cpy_ = cur;
  return obj;
}
```

Note that this is a very generic copy policy implementation. Other implementations, which are more object-specific, are possible.

Cooperative Drawing

In the Cooperative Drawing Application, invocations to shared rectangles need to be synchronized. The class RectShape represents a rectangle. It knows its coordinates, origin, and extent, and how to update them when the rectangle is moved. The Shape class is an abstract class from which the drawing classes are derived.

```
class RectShape : public Shape {
public:
  RectShape(const Point& ori, const Point& ext) {
    origin_ = ori; extent_ = ext;}

  void moveBy(Point delta) {
    origin_ += delta;}
private:
  Point origin_, extent_;
};
```

Class RectShapeInterface supports recovery of both pessimistic and optimistic synchronization policies. In the former case recoverer_ supports an update-in-place recovery policy, while in the latter it supports a deferred-update recovery policy. A RecMoveBy object is created and prepared if preControl returns CONTINUE. Operation preControl verifies whether there are concurrent conflicting invocations for the pessimistic policies. For optimistic policies, pre-Control always returns CONTINUE. The method execution continues on the rect object returned by operation prepare. Afterwards it is verified whether there were concurrent conflicting invocations (operation postControl). Operation postControl always returns CONTINUE in pessimistic policies.

```
void RectShapeInterface::moveBy(Point delta)
{
  RecMoveBy *recPoint;
  RectShape *rect;
  // precontrol
  if (preControl() == CONTINUE) {
    // create recovery point and prepare
    recPoint = new RecMoveBy(delta);
    rect = recoverer_->prepare(recPoint);
  } else return;

  // do invocation
  rect->moveBy(delta);

  // postcontrol
  if (postControl() == CONTINUE)
    recoverer_->redo(recPoint);
  else
    recoverer_->undo(recPoint);
  // recovery point is not needed anymore
  delete recPoint;
}
```

The class RecMoveBy is a RecoveryPoint subclass which can be implemented using the copy techniques presented in the previous section. Shown below is class CompensatingRecMoveBy which supports a compensating policy and is tuned for update-in-place policies for synchronization.

```
class CompensatingRecMoveBy : public RecoveryPoint {
public:
  RectShape *prepare(RectShape *cur) {
    return cur;}
  // update-in-place policies for
  // synchronization do not need to redo
  RectShape *redo(RectShape *cur) {
    return cur; }
```

```
    // undo corresponds to the compensating operation
    RectShape *undo(RectShape *cur) {
      cur->moveBy(-delta_);
      return cur; }
private:
  Point delta_; // invocation argument
};
```

Known Uses

The need for recovery is widely recognized in database and distributed systems. Most of the solutions to this problem restrict the number of policies supported and do not decouple recovery from other issues. Weihl describes two different recovery policies: update-in-place and deferred-update [Weihl93b].

Distributed systems, such as Argus [Liskov88], Arjuna [Shrivastava+91], and Hermes/ST [Fazzolare+93], use the recovery pattern encapsulated in the platform mechanisms. Argus uses a deferred-update policy; invocations are done on a version of the object which is discarded if the invocation is rolled back. Arjuna uses a copy policy: a class recoveryRecord is defined which contains the previous object's state to be used in case of roll back. In Hermes, only the persistent objects are recoverable, Hermes uses a copy policy that allows recovery with attribute granularity.

The architecture of the Mock's object-oriented model for distributed transaction processing provides recoverability for objects [Mock+92]. The recovery pattern is used in the context of distributed failure recovery of transactions.

The Customizable Object Recovery pattern is part of a framework supporting heterogeneous concurrency control policies to be used in distributed applications [Silva+96b]. It is implemented on top of the ACE environment [Schmidt94] and publicly available from *http://albertina.inesc.pt/~ars/dasco.html*.

Related Patterns

The Customizable Object Synchronization pattern abstracts several object synchronization policies [Silva+96a]. It decouples object synchronization from object concurrency and object functionality (sequential part). Some of the supported policies require object recovery. In the Implementation section we described the tradeoffs when integrating these two patterns.

The Memento pattern is used to externalize object state, without violating encapsulation, such that the object can be restored later [Gamma+95]. In the Customizable Object Recovery pattern RecoveryPoint objects contain, for copy policies, the RecoverableObject state. In this case the Memento pattern can be applied between the RecoverableObject and the RecoveryPoint where the former plays the role of Originator and the latter plays the role of Caretaker.

The Recoverable Distributor pattern, like the Customizable Object Recovery pattern, emphasizes the separation of concerns [Islam+96]. It decouples failure detection from recovery.

The Decorator pattern is used to add recovery responsibilities [Gamma+95]. The `RecoverableObject` corresponds to `ConcreteComponent`, while `RecoveryInterface` corresponds to `Decorator`. The `RecoverableObject` does not know anything about the `RecoveryInterface`.

The Strategy pattern is used between `RecoveryInterface` and `Recover`. It provides the configuration of `RecoveryInterface` with recovery policies [Gamma+95].

ACKNOWLEDGMENTS

We would like to thank our colleagues Pedro Sousa, David Matos, Francisco Rosa, and Teresa Gonçalves. We also thank our shepherd, Tom Jell, and the participants of the PLoP '96 writer's workshop on Concurrency and Operating Systems.

REFERENCES

[Booch94] G. Booch. *Object-Oriented Analysis and Design with Applications.* The Benjamin/ Cummings Publishing Company, 1994.

[Fazzolare+93] M. Fazzolare, B. G. Humm, and R. D. Ranson. "Concurrency Control for Distributed Nested Transactions in Hermes." International Conference for Concurrent and Distributed Systems, 1993.

[Gamma+95] E. Gamma, R. Helm, R. Johnson, and J. Vlissides. *Design Patterns: Elements of Reusable Design.* Reading, MA: Addison-Wesley, 1995.

[Islam+96] N. Islam and M. Devarakond. "An Essential Design Pattern for Fault-Tolerant Distributed State Sharing." *Communications of the ACM,* 39(10), October 1996, pp. 65–74.

[Liskov88] B. Liskov. "Distributed Programming in Argus." *Communications of the ACM,* 31(3): March 1988, pp. 300–312.

[Mock+92] M. Mock, R. Kroeger and V. Cahill. "Implementing Atomic Objects with the RelaX Transaction Facility." *Computing Systems* 5(3): Summer 1992, pp. 259–304.

[Schmidt94] D. C. Schmid. "The ADAPTIVE Communication Environment: An Object-Oriented Network Programming Toolkit for Developing Communication Software." In 11th and 12th Sun User Group Conferences, San Jose, CA and San Francisco, CA, December 1993 and June 1994.

[Shrivastava+91] S. K. Shrivastava, G. N. Dixon, and G. D. Parrington. "An Overview of the Arjuna Distributed Programming System." *IEEE Software*: 66–73, January 1991.

[Silva+96a] A. R. Silva, J. Pereira, and J. A. Marques. "Customizable Object Synchronization Pattern." Presented at EuroPLoP '96, July 1996.

[Silva+96b] A. R. Silva, J. Pereira, and J. A. Marques. "A Framework for Heterogeneous Concurrency Control Policies in Distributed Applications." In proceedings of the 8th International Workshop on Software Specification and Design, pp. 105–114, Schloss Velen, Germany: Los Alamitos, CA: IEEE Computer Society Press, March 1996.

[Weihl93a] W. Weihl. "The Impact of Recovery in Concurrency Control." *Journal of Computer and System Sciences*, 47(1): August 1993, pp. 157–184.

[Weihl93b] W. Weihl. "Transaction-Processing Techniques." In Sape Mullender, ed., *Distributed Systems—Second Edition*, Reading, MA: Addison-Wesley, 1993, pp. 329–352.

António Rito Silva can be reached at Rito.Silva@inesc.pt.
João Dias Pereira can be reached at Joao.Pereira@inria.fr.
José Alves Marques can be reached at jam@inesc.pt.

Chapter 16

Patterns for Logging Diagnostic Messages

Neil B. Harrison

Many software systems are transaction-oriented, that is, they take discrete, sometimes independent inputs, perform some operations, and generate some output. In business applications, programs deal with payroll or other personnel functions. Most database applications are query-response based. And in software development, compilers and other translators take input such as programs and produce output such as object code.

Every software system must deal with errors. These may come about from bugs in the software, but often arise simply from erroneous input. Most systems report errors to the user in some manner, and many provide additional diagnostic information to assist the user in tracking down the problem. In interactive systems, the system can give immediate feedback to the user that an input error has occurred. Ward Cunningham's Checks [Cunn95] pattern language is useful in this situation. However, if the input is batched, (for example, source code for a program is a batch of lines of code), the problem becomes one of producing diagnostic messages with sufficient context. Imagine trying to compile a program if the only message the compiler gives is "syntax error," with no line number!

A related issue is that although transactions themselves may be somewhat independent, processing a transaction may impact the processing of later transactions. At the very least, many programs keep track of the number of errors encountered and give up when a certain threshold is reached. In some systems, certain errors may happen repeatedly, such as when a system keeps trying to reestablish a connection to another machine. So the error message is given once, with periodic status messages (such as, "The above message repeated 10 times"). So it is necessary for many systems to remember information about errors after they happen.

Transaction-oriented systems lend themselves to common approaches to logging diagnostic messages embodied in three general software patterns. The first pattern, Diagnostic Logger, separates logging from the rest of the software and lays the groundwork for the other patterns. The second pattern, Diagnostic Context, provides association of diagnostics with the correct transactions. The third pattern, Typed Diagnostics, helps ensure uniformity of presentation for all diagnostics. It also allows the software to handle various diagnostics differently, depending on characteristics such as severity.

DIAGNOSTIC LOGGER

Each pattern builds on the previous pattern, so it is appropriate to begin with the Diagnostic Logger.

Problem

How do you report diagnostic information in a consistent manner?

Context

Software systems all need to provide feedback information to the user in case of errors or other difficulty. This pattern applies specifically to systems where users do not actively interact on a per-transaction basis, for example, batch mode processing, compiling, and other types of translation systems.

Forces

- Any part of a system might need to create a diagnostic message; therefore, any approach must be available to all parts of the system.
- Diagnostic messages are very important to the users; they should have a consistent look and feel.
- In most projects, error handling is largely ignored until coding is underway, and programmers realize that errors will happen. At this point, the programmers are most interested in simple, easy-to-use error reporting strategies. There is a strong temptation to throw something together with no regard to other programmers.
- The user may wish to specify the destination of diagnostic messages.
- The order of messages may be significant.
- Diagnostic messages almost always have specific information. For example, a compiler may report the line number and suspected offending token where a syntax error occurs.
- It may be important to retain information from one message to the next. For example, it is common to keep track of total errors and exit when a threshold is crossed.

Solution

Use a Diagnostic Logger object to handle all the details of diagnostics. Create it as a Singleton [Gamma+94], so that there is a single point for all messages to flow through.

The Diagnostic Logger has two types of functions. The first type is for control of logging in general, such as specifying the output destination, error thresholds, or debugging levels. These are used chiefly by some main controlling objects. The other type of functions provides the rest of the software with the ability to output the diagnostic messages. These message types may be as general as passing a message, but are usually broken down by type of message or event. In most cases, the Diagnostic Logger will provide an individual function for each type of message, such as errors and warnings.

In order to handle different methods of output, it may be desirable to derive different types of Diagnostic Loggers (see Figure 16-1). In such a case, the program specifies the destination of the output. The correct type of Diagnostic Logger is created either at that time or at the first time the instance() function is called. This is somewhat in the flavor of Gamma's Abstract Factory pattern. In this case, the message functions may be implemented using the Template Method pattern [Gamma+94].

Example

Simulation systems are often used for automated testing. A telephone simulator, for example, can instruct a telephone switching system to place a call and answer it, and can verify the connection. A person may run the simulator interactively, in which case the `WinDiagLogger` will be used. Often, though, the simulator is run unattended overnight, and messages are logged to a file via the `FileDiagLogger`.

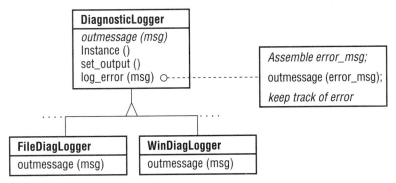

Figure 16-1 *Class diagram for Diagnostic Logger, showing two derived Diagnostic Loggers*

At startup, if a file is designated as the output destination, that information is remembered. When the `Instance()` function is first called, the correct type of `DiagnosticLogger` is created.

This is how the `DiagnosticLogger` class might be declared, and how the `Instance()` function might be written.

```
class DiagnosticLogger
{
public:
    virtual void outmessage (Message) = 0;

    // Set the output destination
    static void set_output (String f) { _fname = f; }

    // Access function for the Singleton instance
    static DiagnosticLogger* Instance ();

private:
    static DiagnosticLogger* _instance;
    static String _fname;
};


//  The Instance() function is an Abstract Factory

DiagnosticLogger*
DiagnosticLogger::Instance()
{
    if (_instance)
        return _instance;

    if (_fname)
    {
        _instance = new FileDiagLogger(_fname);

        // if creation fails, create a default DiagLogger,
        // in this case, WinDiagLogger (not shown)
        .
        .
        .

    }
    else
        _instance = new WinDiagLogger ();

    return _instance;
}
```

Resulting Context

The Diagnostic Logger pattern provides consistency in diagnostic messages, with the details of outputting the messages encapsulated and hidden from the rest of the program. Because it is a Singleton, it easily preserves the order of the messages. The messaging functions are readily accessible to all parts of the system, and are easy to use. In fact, the interface can be determined early in design, without worrying about details of format or the destination of messages. Developers may start out with rudimentary functionality in the Diagnostic Logger, such as dumping all messages to `stderr`.

On the other hand, Diagnostic Logger is slightly more complex to implement, and is slightly slower than simple writes to `stderr`, for example. But in all but the very simplest programs, it is expected that the advantages far outweigh the cost.

Rationale

This pattern began in a program which translated test cases to automatically executable test scripts. The program was later easily modified to generate a different test language, with the changes made inside the Diagnostic Logger. The Diagnostic Logger also sent diagnostic messages to a designated destination, while creating a different file for every test script it generated. This brings us to the next pattern, Diagnostic Context.

Variations

In client-server systems, a log server often handles the logging of diagnostic messages. In such cases, the Diagnostic Logger might be implemented as a Proxy [Gamma+94]. In distributed applications, Remote Proxy may be useful for implementing Diagnostic Loggers [Buschmann+96].

Related Patterns

Logging diagnostic messages is an activity that is particularly important in highly reliable systems. Diagnostic Loggers are compatible with the Fault-Tolerant Telecommunication System Patterns, particularly Five Minutes of No Escalation Messages, and Leaky Bucket Counters [Adams+96].

DIAGNOSTIC CONTEXTS

The Diagnostics Contexts pattern, as its name implies, provides a way for error messages to report not only the error itself, but also helpful contextual information.

Problem

If an error occurs in processing a set of discrete inputs, how do you associate error messages with the input that caused the error?

Context

The system is transaction-oriented; that is, it processes a set of discrete inputs. Examples include compilers, interpreters, database systems, or network servers.

You are using Diagnostic Logger to handle diagnostic messages.

Forces

- The inputs to the system are somewhat autonomous, and may even be entirely independent of each other. In addition, the input may be processed in batches, so it is often not obvious how the output corresponds to the input.
- However, the user wants to know which output was produced by which input. This is very important, and is absolutely critical with error or other diagnostic messages.
- A single input may produce multiple output messages.
- The results of the inputs are not necessarily independent, such as total error count. In some cases, such as compiling a program, the inputs are highly dependent on each other, but the diagnostic messages are linked to specific inputs.
- Internally, the place where an error occurs may be many function calls away from the information which identifies the input. For example, a syntax error of an input statement may be caught deep in the parser, far from the input line number.
- The information which identifies the input may be complex; for example, an input may be identified by the line number, file name, and directory name. It would be undesirable to pass such information through multiple functions in order to enable error reporting. Think what would happen if it becomes necessary to report machine name as well as the above information; many functions would have to change.

Solution

Use the Diagnostic Logger pattern, and augment it with Diagnostic Context objects. A Diagnostic Context is an object which exists for the life of processing a particular transaction, and provides unique identification of that transaction. Its birth marks the beginning of processing a transaction, and its death marks the end.

Obviously, the easiest approach to this is to take advantage of scoping to create and destroy Diagnostic Context objects. For example, when processing a set of lines

```
for (int i = 1; i < num_lines; i++)
{
    DiagContext      dc (i);
    // Process the input line, generating diagnostic messages as
    // appropriate

}   // The Diagnostic Context automatically gets destroyed.
```

The constructor for the Diagnostic Context registers with the Diagnostic Logger, and its destructor unregisters.

```
DiagContext::DiagContext (int line_no) :
                    _curr_line_no (line_no)
{
    DiagLogger::Instance()->sign_on (this);
}

DiagContext::~DiagContext ()
{
    DiagLogger::Instance ()->sign_off ();
}
```

Likewise, the `DiagLogger` ensures that there is only one transaction processed at a time.

```
void
DiagLogger::sign_on (DiagContext* dc)
{
    if (_curr_diag_context != NULL)
    {
        // Bad; take appropriate action
    }

    _curr_diag_context = dc;

    // Write a message indicating the start of a transaction
}

void
DiagLogger::sign_off ()
{
    _curr_diag_context = NULL;
}
```

With Diagnostic Context, the software still continues to log messages directly to the Logger. The Logger will associate the message with context information in the Diagnostic Context. Note that this presents a slight problem at startup; there may be errors to be logged before the first transaction is processed. One approach to this is until the first time a Diagnostic Context object registers with the Logger, the Logger simply outputs the messages, indicating that no context has been given because the program is in startup mode.

Example

The telephone simulator described earlier can process batches of test scripts. Not only is it necessary to associate output with the correct script, but it is often helpful to remember the state of the system under test (SUT) when a scripts starts. Therefore, at the start of each script, create a DiagnosticContext object, capturing the state of the SUT. Assume that there is a function which returns the current state of the SUT. Then the execution loop might look like this.

```
Script s;

while (s = get_next_script())
{
    DiagContext dc (s, get_sut_status());

    // execute the test script
    execute_script (s);
}
```

Resulting Context

The Logger can mark the start and end of transactions and provide context to messages. The context includes not only information that comes as part of the message (for example, immediate information), but also surrounding information, such as file name, line number, earlier state of the system, and so forth. New context objects can easily be added wherever needed.

Diagnostic Context objects provide an easy way to implement leaky bucket counters. Because the Logger hears about every transaction, it can count successful or unsuccessful processing of transactions. On the other hand, Diagnostic Contexts can handle errors on a per-transaction basis. For example, a Diagnostic Context may limit the number of errors from a single transaction, without aborting the entire session.

Note that Diagnostic Context objects incur a slight performance penalty through the creation and deletion of Diagnostic Context objects. This happens regardless of whether any messages are logged. As long as Diagnostic Context objects are not abused (for example, creating one for every character of input), the performance price is minimal.

Variations

It may be convenient to use a single Diagnostic Logger and Diagnostic Contexts to implement diagnostic message handling in a multithreaded environment. In such a case, the `DiagLogger` would keep track of a Diagnostic Context for each thread. Each Diagnostic Context would be created with some information which would uniquely identify its thread. This is similar to the registry of singletons discussed in the Singleton pattern description.

In other cases, it may be desirable to allow nested Diagnostic Contexts to provide layers of contextual information. The `DiagLogger` would manage the stack of Diagnostic Contexts. This makes adding messages and new context easy; simply create a new Diagnostic Transaction to capture the desired context.

Diagnostic Context may be implemented much like the Command Processor pattern [Sommerlad96]. The Diagnostic Context object is much like the Command object, with the Diagnostic Logger playing the role of the Command Processor. Of course, a Diagnostic Context object is not executed as Command objects are.

Rationale

The Diagnostic Context came about as a result of trying other, inferior, approaches to associating messages with the transactions from which they came. Originally, it was necessary to register explicitly at the beginning and end of processing each transaction. The Diagnostic Context is a more automatic and safer approach to this problem.

TYPED DIAGNOSTICS

Finally, the third of the hierarchy of patterns, Typed Diagnostics, differentiates the handling of different types of messages.

Problem

If you are logging many different messages (such as errors, warnings, or debugging messages), how do you ensure that these messages are handled consistently?

Context

The system uses the Diagnostic Logger to handle diagnostic messages. There are several different types of events which must be handled consistently, but with enough variation to allow the essential information to be trapped and passed on to the user. The system is a transaction-oriented system, and you are using the Diagnostic Context to associate messages with each other on a per-transaction basis.

Forces

- Once again, it is necessary to keep the details of handling messages out of the main program.
- For each event you want to log, you want to capture the important information of the moment. Depending on the nature of the event, what is important may vary.
- Handling diagnostic or debug messages can be troublesome. It is desirable to be able to simply call a diagnostic message handler member function of the Diagnostic Logger. Diagnostics, however, are usually turned off, although the user would still incur the cost of calling the message handler function. If character strings are created and passed as arguments to the function (which is likely), repeated calls to the function could create a noticeable performance impact.
- In some cases, it may be desirable to handle messages differently, depending on a later event. For example, an error report may include a record of previous events, but they would not normally be reported.

Solution

Create an inheritance hierarchy of Diagnostic Message Types. Each type encapsulates the characteristics of that category of diagnostics, and parameterizes the specific variations. In particular, details of diagnostic messages are embedded in the classes, so as not to incur overhead when creating the Diagnostic Message objects. In fact, the data in these classes should be kept pretty sparse to minimize the overhead of creation and destruction.

It is necessary to send Diagnostic Messages to the Logger, an activity that usually happens when the object is created. The standard interface to the Logger for messages becomes a simple function for all types of diagnostics.

```
// For an error
DiagnosticLogger::Instance()->message
        (new DiagMsg_Error(err_type, etc));

// For a debug message at debug level 2
DiagnosticLogger::Instance()->message
        (new DiagMsg_Debug (2, etc));
```

The Logger hands Diagnostic Messages to the Diagnostic Context, which then assumes the responsibility for managing them, including destruction of the Diagnostic Messages at the proper time.

Typed Diagnostic Messages combine with Diagnostic Contexts to handle conditional output of the messages. Message handling can be quite flexible. For example, debugging messages may or may not be output, depending on the current debugging level. On the other hand, context messages can be stored, and output in the event that an error message arrives.

Note that Typed Diagnostics are different from the previously discussed sub-classes of Diagnostic Logger. Diagnostic Logger subclasses designate approaches to the handling of all messages, such as output style or destination. Typed Diagnostics differentiate handling of different types of messages, such as error messages versus levels of debugging messages.

Example

The telephone simulator described earlier has two major types of errors. The most obvious errors are when the system under test does not do what is expected; these may indicate that the software being tested has an error. But the test script may have syntax errors, which should be handled differently from "real" errors. This can be done by having two `DiagMsg` types, `DiagMsg_ParseError` and `DiagMsg_RunError`. The parsing and execution functions create the type of Diagnostic Message that corresponds to the error encountered (see Figure 16-2).

Error handling and reporting is now more intelligent. If the `Diagnostic-Logger` keeps track of execution errors, it simply asks the `DiagMsg` to report the number of execution errors it represents. `DiagMsg_RunError` reports one, and `DiagMsg_ParseError` reports zero. The output of error messages can be similarly customized. The code for the Diagnostic Logger `log_err()` function is as follows.

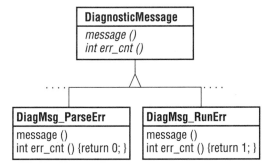

Figure 16-2 *Class diagram for Diagnostic Message, showing two derived Diagnostic Message classes*

```
void
DiagnosticLogger::log_error (DiagMsg* dm)
{
    // Assume that we keep track of total running errors
    _err_count += dm->err_cnt ();

    // Now output the message
    outmessage (dm->message ());
}
```

Resulting Context

With the application of Typed Diagnostic Messages, a program can output several different types of meaningful diagnostic messages, while still maintaining a consistent output style. It also retains the characteristics of Diagnostic Loggers, such as ease in changing output destination and adaptation to different output types.

Note that Typed Diagnostic Messages do incur a performance cost. Objects may be created and later destroyed, even though they do not create output. For example, debugging Typed Diagnostic Messages are created and destroyed, but only used when debugging is turned on. In addition, if they are passed to the Diagnostic Logger, they may implicitly invoke a copy constructor. Therefore, the classes should be designed so that creation and destruction are inexpensive. In practice, this has not been a problem. For message text, one might consider using a standard set of messages and message numbers. This can be useful in dealing with message sets in different languages. The user of Typed Diagnostic Messages may also wish to explore alternatives to passing them by value to the Diagnostic Logger.

Rationale

This pattern grew out of various attempts to create a way to handle different types of messages. In some cases the output was automatically processed, so the messages had to be consistent. This was coupled with a desire to produce different levels of debug messages, but to avoid excessive overhead if debugging was not enabled.

ACKNOWLEDGMENTS

The author wishes to thank Stephen Berczuk for his helpful comments, particularly for pointing out the benefits of nested Diagnostic Contexts.

REFERENCES

[Adams+96] M. Adams, et al. "Fault-Tolerant Telecommunication System Patterns," in J. M. Vlissides, J. O. Coplien, and N. L. Kerth (eds.), *Pattern Languages of Program Design 2*. Reading, MA: Addison-Wesley, 1996, pp. 549–573.

[Buschmann+96] F. Buschmann, et al. *Pattern-Oriented Software Architecture: A System of Patterns*. Chichester, England: John Wiley and Sons, 1996, pp. 263–276.

[Cunningham95] W. Cunningham. "The CHECKS Pattern Language of Information Integrity," J. O. Coplien and D. C. Schmidt (eds.), in *Pattern Languages of Program Design*. Reading, MA: Addison-Wesley, 1995, pp. 145–155.

[Gamma+94] E. Gamma, et al. *Design Patterns: Elements of Reusable Object-Oriented Software*. Reading, MA: Addison-Wesley, 1995.

[Sommerlad96] P. Sommerlad. "Command Processor," in J. M Vlissides, J. O. Coplien, and N. L. Kerth (eds.), *Pattern Languages of Program Design 2*. Reading, MA: Addison-Wesley, 1996, pp. 65–74.

Neil Harrison can be reached at nbharrison@lucent.com.

PART 5

Persistence Patterns

In this section we present two patterns for helping software engineers deal with the problems of persistence. *Persistence* refers to the ability of an object to outlive the application that creates it. Typically this means that the object must be written to long-term storage prior to the exit of its creating application. There are many schemes for achieving this, and none of them are trivial.

Chapter 17: Serializer, by Dirk Riehle, Wolf Siberski, Dirk Bäumer, Daniel Megert, and Heinz Züllighoven. The fact that this chapter has five authors is a clue to the complexity and popularity of the problem that they address. This chapter discusses the problems of converting a simple object or an object graph to a serial byte stream suitable for writing out to a file or for transmitting over a serial link. This kind of problem seems trivial at the outset, but then expands to become an engineering nightmare for those who have not properly thought it through. There are many twists and turns in the process of serializing an object, and this chapter does an admirable job of pointing them all out. If you are contemplating building such a serialization system, we strongly recommend that you read through this chapter very carefully.

Chapter 18: Accessing Relational Databases, by Wolfgang Keller and Jens Coldewey. Providing for the cooperation of an object-oriented application and a relational database is one of the more difficult problems facing software engineers. Several tools on the market claim to solve this problem. However, these tools do not—and cannot—address the prime issue: Object-oriented applications and relational databases are of a very different nature, and there is no mechanistic way to describe the mapping between them. The tools can help, but cannot completely solve the problem.

In this chapter, the authors describe the patterns addressing the forces that the engineers must resolve. It is, deservedly, one of the longer chapters in this book. Engineers who must deal with OO applications and relational databases would be well advised to study this chapter thoroughly.

Summary. Persistence is not a topic to be undertaken lightly, yet a very large number of applications must provide some form of persistence. Only two chapters in this book discuss persistence. Though the problem is widespread, general solutions remain elusive.

Chapter 17

Serializer

Dirk Riehle, Wolf Siberski, Dirk Bäumer, Daniel Megert, and Heinz Züllighoven

The Serializer pattern lets you efficiently stream objects into data structures of your choice as well as create objects from such data structures. The Serializer pattern can be used whenever objects are written to or read from flat files, relational database tables, network transport buffers, and so forth.

The Reader part of the pattern builds an object structure by reading a data structure from a backend. The Writer part of the pattern writes an existing object structure as a data structure to a backend. Both parts together constitute the Serializer pattern.

The pattern can be found in more or less pure versions in probably every framework that provides support for object streaming. The CORBA externalization service and the Java Serialization package are clean applications of the pattern. However, it develops its full potential only in the context of different streaming backends.

Intent

Read arbitrarily complex object structures from and write them to varying data structure-based backends. The Serializer pattern lets you efficiently store and retrieve objects from different backends, such as flat files, relational databases, and RPC buffers.

Also Known As

Atomizer, Streamer, Reader/Writer

Motivation

Suppose you are modeling a `Customer` class in the banking domain. The `Customer` class will have several attributes, for example, a name and a list of accounts. You will want to make Customer and Account objects persistent, for example, by storing them in a relational database. Sometimes you need to exchange customer data with other branch offices. This can be done by writing the objects to RPC buffers for transport via a network connection. Or, bank representatives visit the customer at home, using a notebook computer when doing so. They need access to the customer data. Therefore, the objects have to be saved to a file on the notebook. Thus, every major application needs to read objects from and write them to a varying number of backends with different representation formats.

Application classes should have no knowledge about the external representation format which is used to represent their instances. Otherwise, introducing a new representation format or changing an old one would require changing almost every class in the whole system. These classes should contain no representation-specific code for reading or writing their instances. It is much better to delegate the task of reading and writing to external and exchangeable classes which do the reading and writing, respectively.

To separate reponsibilities for reading and writing, we introduce a Reader/Writer class pair for each backend. These classes decouple the application classes from the backends. The Reader protocol is used for reading (activating) object structures, and the Writer protocol is used for writing (passivating) them. Different Reader/Writer pairs represent different external representation formats and interact with different reading and writing backends. Figure 17-1 shows an example of a Reader/Writer class hierarchy.

In turn, the Reader and Writer classes shouldn't know the concrete application classes, because they would have to be modified whenever an application class is added or changed. To achieve this, the application classes have to provide a generic access interface to their internal state.

Therefore, every application class provides an interface called Serializable. This interface consists of two methods, one for reading and one for writing the object. The readFrom method accepts a Reader object for reading, and the writeTo method accepts a Writer for writing. Subclasses of Serializable implement this

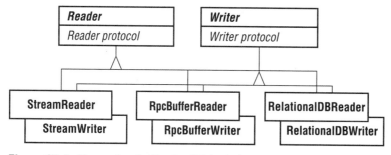

Figure 17-1 *Example of a Reader/Writer class hierarchy*

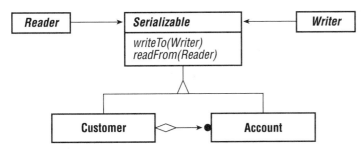

Figure 17-2 *The* Serializable *interface*

interface by accepting Reader/Writer objects and by reading from or writing their attributes to them. In Figure 17-2 the pattern is applied to the example.

The Reader and Writer protocols offer every Serializable object the possibility to read or write primitive value types, including object references. A Reader or a Writer can follow object references to traverse a whole object structure and to either create it or to write it to a specific backend.

Applying the Serializer pattern lets you traverse object structures on an attribute level, and while doing so convert the object structure into any required external representation format. Application objects are freed from having to care about how to read from or write to external media so that it becomes easy to introduce new or change old input and output formats and backends.

Applicability

Use the Serializer if you have to convert arbitrarily complex object structures into different data representation formats and back, and you don't want to put knowledge about the representation formats into the objects to be read or written.

Don't use the Serializer if the application objects have to provide backend-specific information to the format conversion algorithm.

The pattern can be used to store objects in any kind of data stream like ordinary files or debugging dumps; it is also useful for storing them in relational databases or data buffers that are used for transporting objects between processes. A Serializer can also be used as a Copier to copy an object structure; it is even useful for building an object browser like the Smalltalk Inspector, which displays objects at run time.

Structure

Figure 17-3 shows the structure diagram of the Serializer pattern.

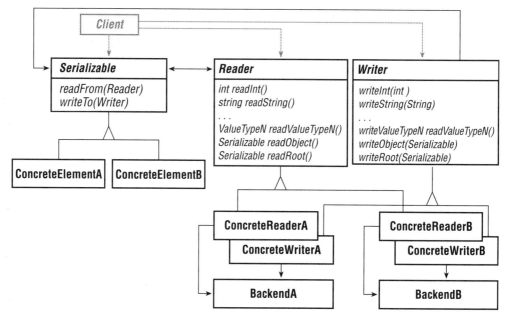

Figure 17-3 *Structure of the Serializer pattern*

Participants

- **Reader/Writer:**

  - The Reader/Writer pair declares a `Reader` protocol for reading objects and a `Writer` protocol for writing objects. These protocols consist of `read` and `write` operations respectively for every value type, including object references.
  - The protocol hides the Backend and external representation format from `Serializable` objects.

- **ConcreteReader/ConcreteWriter (`StreamReader/Writer`, `RpcBufferReader/Writer`):**

  - Concrete Reader/Writer pairs implement the `Reader` and `Writer` protocols for a particular `Backend` and external representation format.

- **Serializable:**

  - `Serializable` is an interface class which defines operations to accept a `Reader` for reading and a `Writer` for writing. These operations have to provide the attributes to the `Reader`/`Writer`.
  - The interface class also provides a `Create` operation which takes a class identification and creates an object of the denoted class.

- ConcreteElement (`Customer, Account`):

  - A concrete element implements the `Serializable` interface to read or write its attributes.

- Backend (`Stream, RpcBuffer`):

  - The Backend class represents a particular backend, such as a stream or a relational database frontend.
  - The Backend is used by the ConcreteReader/ConcreteWriter, which shields it from the application classes.
  - The backend does not have to be encapsulated in a class; its interface may also be procedural.

Collaborations

A `Reader`/`Writer` collaborates with the `Serializable` protocol class to read/write serializable objects. The `Reader`/`Writer` hands itself over to the serializable objects, while the serializable objects make use of its protocol to read/write their attributes. The reading and writing processes are nearly identical. They result in a recursive back and forth interplay between serializable objects and the `Reader`/`Writer`.

During the writing process, each object writes its attributes by calling the appropriate `write` method of the `Writer`. The `Writer` handles attributes that are object references according to some predefined specification (see discussion on streaming policies in the Implementation section). If the referenced objects are to be written, the `Writer` asks them to write themselves onto itself.

When reading an object, the `Reader` first creates a new instance of the appropriate class and then hands itself over to it. The new serializable object reads its attributes by calling the respective `read` methods for each attribute. During the reading process, the `Reader` creates all objects which are requested by already existing objects.

A ConcreteReader/ConcreteWriter reads from/writes to its backend using a backend-specific interface which need not be object-oriented.

Figure 17-4 is an interaction diagram for a sample collaboration. The client calls `writeRoot` with `aCustomer` which has the attributes `name` and `accounts`. The dotted lines indicate that `aConcreteWriter` remains active while calling `writeTo`. The diagram only shows the start of the write process.

Consequences

Take the following consequences into account when considering whether to apply the Serializer pattern.

- *Using the Serializer makes it easy to add new data representation formats for objects.* Object structures can be written to and read from new and unforeseen backends simply by introducing a new `Reader`/`Writer` pair. Often it suffices to

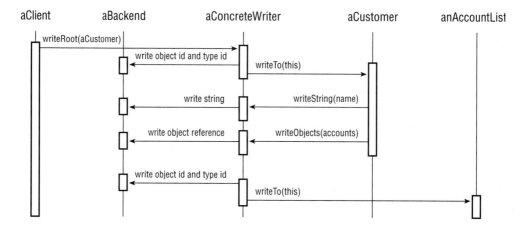

Figure 17-4 *Interaction diagram for a sample write process*

parameterize some standard `Reader/Writer` implementation with a storage backend, thereby easing the introduction of new data representation formats even more.

- *Using the Serializer takes knowledge about external data representation formats out of the objects to be streamed.* By using the `Reader/Writer` interface of simple `read` and `write` operations, the objects are effectively shielded from any data format of their external representation.
- *Using the Serializer pattern requires new classes to support the* **Serializable** *protocol.* Classes of streamable objects must implement the `Serializable` protocol. This requires reading and writing every relevant object attribute.
- *Using the Serializer pattern weakens encapsulation.* It is at the heart of the Serializer pattern to allow access to an object's internal state. Such access is provided through the `Serializable` protocol and should be used only for serialization purposes.
- *The set of value types supported by the* **Readers/Writers** *has to be considered carefully.* At first glance, one might consider supporting only object references and the programming language's built-in value types like `integer`, `float`, and the like. However, for some types it is appropriate to treat them like built-in value types (for example, `string` or `date` types) and to add special methods to the `Reader` and `Writer` interface to handle them. This may be the case with general as well as domain-specific value types.

Implementation

Consider the following issues when implementing the Serializer pattern.

- *Deciding between deep and nondeep streaming.* Deep streaming an object structure means streaming every referenced object. This is typically done when reading from a file or writing to it. With other kinds of backends (e.g., databases), deep streaming is unsuitable, so you will choose a different streaming policy—for example, a policy which streams only changed objects. Implementing nondeep streaming is more complex than implementing deep streaming. But deep streaming is potentially very costly since it might require transporting large amounts of data due to the highly interconnected nature of object structures.

- *Identifying objects.* Objects usually reference other objects. In a passive data format, these references must be represented by an unambiguous identification. Such an identification, an id, only has to be unambiguous within the type's name space, not necessarily for all types' name spaces, since the object's type is always stored together with its id. There are several possibilities to implement object-identification schemes. One is using a global counter. Many implementations use a global counter to create object ids. When an object is created it receives the counter value as an id with the counter being incremented. To avoid running out of ids eventually, most implementations we know of use eight-byte counters. Another is relying on externally generated ids. Very often, specific backends offer id generation mechanisms, for example, database systems. If possible, these facilities should be used.

- *Writing additional information.* The signatures of the `Reader`'s and `Writer`'s operations depend on the purposes for which you are using object streaming. The minimal information that must be written is the value to be streamed. But then reading depends on the sequence of the written attributes. Therefore, consider writing more information about the attributes.

  First, it is advantageous also to write the attribute name. This makes the read operations independent of the sequence of the written object attributes. Some backends need the attribute name to read and write the attributes correctly. For example, a relational database backend might have to interpret the data it receives in terms of the column names into which they are written. Then it is necessary to associate attribute names with the corresponding column names.

  Second, you can distinguish between transient and persistent data. You might be tempted to write out and read back only the primary attributes of the object and omit the functionally dependent ones, because they can be reconstructed from the primary ones. However, you end up focusing the application of this pattern on object streaming only, missing other possible uses like object browsers. Therefore, you might consider writing out all attributes and enhancing the (read and) write operations with a tag indicating whether an attribute is transient or persistent.

Finally, each object might write a version number identifying the version of its implementation. This provides some (though minimal) support for evolution. Conversion functions in the Reader or the streamed object's implementation itself might then provide the functionality for backward compatibility.

- *Providing an object manager.* When writing or reading, you need to keep track of objects that have already been read or written in order to avoid an endless loop when dealing with circular references. A possible solution is to introduce an object manager used for managing object tables that provide the needed information. The manager object can be asked whether an object of a certain id has already been read or written. It can also map object ids to object references.

  The object manager keeps track of objects on a global, system-wide level. It is to be distinguished from the object management facilities of a Serializer, which has to keep track of the objects read or written within a specific reading or writing process.

- *Implementing the reading and writing operations using a metaobject protocol.* If your runtime system provides a metaobject protocol which allows access to an object's attributes, it is possible to implement the read and write operations once, directly in Serializable. The disadvantage is that you usually can't mark attributes as transient or persistent anymore. An interesting exception is Java, which provides both field names and transient or persistent flags, so that the readFrom and writeTo operations can be written entirely on a metalevel.

- *Using a data buffer as a backend.* Sometimes you will want to decouple concrete services representing backends from the Serializer. You can do so by making the Serializer work on a generic data buffer instead of a specific backend. This allows for a generic implementation of large parts of the Serializer to simply stream the objects into the data buffer. The client can then provide specific backends with that buffer. Doing so, you effectively decouple the Serializer from a specific backend and allow its generic implementation. Furthermore, it becomes easy to define context boundaries of when a read or write begins and ends.

- *Providing additional initialization operations.* If some additional object initialization has to be carried out after reading an object (for example, initialization of nonpersistent attributes), consider providing an additional initialization operation. It is not advisable to do this while still reading the attributes, for the same reasons you separate initialization procedures from the basic object creation procedure. Objects at this early point of initialization may only be half-baked, and initializing functionally dependent attributes from a potentially inconsistent object state might cause unforeseen and unwanted side effects.

- *Folding the **read** and **write** method pairs into single methods.* It is possible to halve the coding effort for serializable classes by folding the Serializable protocol into a single operation, for example, attributes(). The Reader and

Writer protocol is also folded into one interface Serializer with the operations serializeInteger, serializeString, and so forth. The attributes() implementations call the serializewhatever methods with references to their attributes as parameters (instead of their actual values).

If the Serializer object is actually a concrete reader, its serialize methods will use the reference to replace the value of the referenced attribute. If the Serializer object is a writer, it will use the reference to retrieve and write the attribute. The client chooses whether to read or to write by giving the serializable object to the respective Serializer. This approach works particularly well in C++.

- *Creating objects during the read process.* During the read process you have to be able to create a new object, given its class id. For this task you should use a creational pattern, for example, a Factory Method. The simplest solution is to make Serializable provide a static function (in C++) or a class method (in Smalltalk) which receives the class name or class id and maps it to a class object or prototype using a dictionary or similar kind of mapping. A flexible pattern for this purpose is the Product Trader pattern [Bäumer+96].

- *Taking care of diamond inheritance structures.* When writing an object, care has to be taken that attributes are not written twice due to a diamond in the inheritance structure. Either the Writer must check that no attributes are written twice, or the object itself must flag the attributes as already written. The latter approach prevents redundant calls of a class's writeTo operation. The same applies to the reading process.

- *Aborting the reading or writing process.* If an unrecoverable failure occurs, the system should abort the reading or writing process and rollback all changes that have been carried out. Conceptually, the reading or writing of an object structure should be a transaction; that is, it provides its own execution context and only upon commit makes these changes visible to the environment. Implementing fail-safe object space transactions in a generic way is hard, though. Therefore, a specialized transaction manager for reading and writing should keep track of the objects and their embedding into the environment and be able to perform a rollback in case an exception occurs.

- *Treating class attributes separately.* Class attributes should be read only at program or image initialization time, and written only at program finalization time. Instead of reading or writing them in the readFrom and writeTo operations, their initialization and finalization should be handled separately.

The following sections have to be considered only when doing incomplete streaming:

- *Selecting a streaming policy.* Object structures can become arbitrarily deep; when doing nondeep streaming you must make a decision about the extent to which you want to stream object structures. We distinguish between the following streaming policies [Bischofberger+96]:

- *Shallow streaming.* An object is streamed only to the first level of attributes. No references within the object are followed. This solution should be applied if nothing can be said about streaming requirements except that it can be very costly to ask for more than a shallow object.

- *Fixed-level streaming.* Streaming is performed to a predefined depth. Starting with a root object, every reference is followed until a nesting count reaches a predefined value. This is a general solution applicable if deep streaming is too costly but there is no information about the object structure which would make it possible to specify a better strategy.

- *Partial streaming.* In this case, streaming is performed according to some predefined graph specification which defines which object references are to be followed and which are to be left dangling, for example, as proxies. This is the best solution since it lets developers map domain-specific requirements on streaming behavior. There is an interesting treatment of this called partial streaming "adaptive streaming," which unfortunately conflicts with the naming of our next policy [Lopes96].

- *Adaptive streaming.* Adaptive streaming is a specialization of partial streaming. Instead of deriving a streaming specification from the business requirements, adaptive streaming derives a streaming specification dynamically from actual client usage of an object structure. Starting out with shallow streaming, a streaming service starts to gather data about the frequency of streaming and dereferencing requests, and derives a dynamic partial streaming specification from this.

When writing an object structure, it makes sense only to write those objects which have actually changed since they were last read or written. This is particularly appropriate when writing to databases. You might have to provide "dirty flags" or some other technique to indicate that an object has changed.

- *Handling dangling references.* When partially reading an object structure, not all references will be resolved. The unresolved references are left dangling. There are two major ways of dealing with these dangling references: Proxies and replacing or modifying the reference interpretation mechanism of the runtime system. A proxy is used as a substitute for a real object which is not directly accessible for some reason [Gamma+95]. A dangling reference can be realized as a proxy. It can be an object of the correct type but without initialized attributes, or it can be an object of a special proxy type. Both variants must be capable of catching operation calls and dispatching them to some reading facility for the real object before executing the real operation.

In changing the reference interpretation mechanism, you might replace or modify the runtime system or the compiler to interpret references in an enhanced way. Such an enhanced interpretation might include checking a flag in the reference value which indicates whether the reference points to a valid main memory object or not. If not, the value could further be interpreted to provide a database id or the like for the real object in question. Such a modification is almost always system-dependent. It should be done only if proxies are considered unsuitable for reasons of performance.

Sample Code

We will now review the example from the Motivation section. First, we will describe the writing process, and then the reading process.

The general class `Serializable` offers an operation for accepting a `Reader` for reading, an operation for accepting a `Writer` for writing, and an operation for creating instances of its subclasses known only by the class name at runtime. The class interface looks like this

```
class Serializable
{
public:
    virtual void readFrom(Reader*) =0;
    virtual void writeTo(Writer*) const =0;
    static Serializable* newByName(char*);
};
```

Classes to be streamed via a `Reader` or `Writer` must inherit from `Serializable`, as discussed. This holds true for the `Customer` and `List<Account>` classes from the motivation section as well. Their interfaces might look like this

```
class Customer : public Serializable
{
public:
    virtual void readFrom(Reader*);
    virtual void writeTo(Writer*) const;
    ...
private:
        // attributes
    string name;
    List<Account*>* accounts;
};

class Account : public Serializable
{
    ... // like Customer
};
```

```
template<class T> List : public Serializable
{
public:
    virtual void readFrom(Reader*);
    virtual void writeTo(Writer*) const;
    ...
private:
        // implementation state
    long count;
    T* list; // C++ native array implementation
};
```

Both classes define an implementation state that must be considered for reading and writing. To do so, both classes overwrite the readFrom and writeTo operations. These operations make use of the Writer interface, which looks like

```
class Writer
{
public:
        // primitive "built-in" value types
    virtual void writeChar(const string& name, char value) =0;
    virtual void writeInt(const string& name, int value) =0;
    ...
        // non-primitive value types
    virtual void writeString(const string& name, const string& value) =0;
    ...
        // references to objects
    virtual void writeObject(const string& name, const Serializable*) =0;
    virtual void writeRoot(const Serializable*) =0;
    ...
};
```

This interface offers operations for writing all value types considered important, including all built-in value types like int and float, nonprimitive value types like string, and finally object references. The operation writeTo of class Customer and List might now be implemented in the following manner.

```
void Customer::writeTo(Writer* writer) const
{
        // simply write the two attributes
    writer->writeString("name", name);
    writer->writeObject("accounts", accounts);
}
```

```
template<class T> void List::writeTo(Writer* writer) const
{
        // first write the count attribute
    writer->writeLong("count", count);
        // then write the array as a succession of object references
    for(long i=0; i<count; i++) {
        write->writeObject("list[" + string(i) + "]", list[i]);
    }
}
```

The `Writer` can write all value types directly to a backend, using whatever physical representation seems suitable and fits the backend. Of interest, however, is the handling of object references. Writing them is simple (they just have to be converted into an id), but since they represent objects, the `Writer` must decide whether to write the full object and not just the reference and must keep track of which objects have already been streamed.

Let's pick a concrete example: An `ASCIIStreamWriter` uses the standard `iostream` classes as the output medium for the basic value type representations. In addition, it uses ASCII-based formatting to make the output both human- and machine-readable. Its interface looks like the `Writer` interface defined above; it only introduces some additional operations for receiving the input and output streams. We assume a deep streaming policy.

`ASCIIStreamWriter` uses an instance variable named `buffer` to hold the `ostream` instance to which the output data is written. Writing a primitive value like a `long` integer is simple.

```
void ASCIIStreamWriter::writeLong(const string& name, long value)
{
    buffer << "long " << name << " = " << value << endl;
}
```

Writing a general reference of type `Serializable` is slightly more complicated. First, the `Writer` writes the object id to the buffer. Then it has to check whether the referenced object is already written. If not, the `Writer` pushes it on a stack and writes it later. `wasHandled` is a list which collects all objects that have been written out and `toHandle` is the stack which receives all objects that must still be written. Both are attributes of the `Writer`.

```
void ASCIIStreamWriter::writeObject(const string& name, Object* object)
{
        // first write id for object reference
    buffer << typeid(object) << " " << name << " = ";
    buffer << object->objectId() << endl;
        // check whether object was already handled
    if (!wasHandled->contains(object))
        toHandle->push(object);
}
```

The writing process is started by a client with a call to `writeRoot`, with the root as parameter. Then `writeRoot` contains the main loop that continues until all referenced objects are written. During an iteration of the main loop, a single object's attributes are received by the `Writer` and written to the backend.

```
void ASCIIStreamWriter::writeRoot(Serializable* root)
{
    wasHandled->clear();
    toHandle->clear();

        // push first object to be written
    toHandle->push(root);

        // loop until all referenced objects are written
    while (!toHandle->isEmpty())
    {
            // pop this iteration's object
        Serializable* object = toHandle->pop();
            // write type id and object id
        buffer << typeid(object) << " ";
        buffer << object->objectId() << " = " << endl;
        buffer << "{" << endl;
            // note object as already handled
        wasHandled->append(object);
          // finally ask object to write its attributes into the Writer
        object->writeTo(this);
            // some more delimiters and pretty printing
        buffer << "}" << endl << endl;
    }
}
```

We have now seen all relevant aspects of the writing process. A client first instantiates or reuses an existing `Writer` and hands over the root object of the object structure to be written using `writeRoot`; `writeRoot` calls `writeTo` on this root object and waits to receive the object's attributes. Some of these attributes are primitive value types which can be written directly to the output buffer. Some of these attributes are references to other objects. After writing the id representing the referenced object, the `Writer` pushes the reference on a stack to write the object later.

The reading process is very similar to the writing process. All serializable classes implement the `readFrom` operation to read their attributes from a `Reader`. The classes `Customer` and `List` implement it like this.

```
void Customer::readFrom(Reader* reader)
{
    name = reader->readString("name");
    accounts = (List<Account*>*) reader->readObject("accounts");
}

template<class T> void List::readFrom(Reader* reader)
{
    count = reader->readLong("count");

    list = new T[count];
    for(long i=0; i<count; i++) {
       list[i] = (Account*) reader->readObject("list[" + string(i) + "]");
    }
}
```

The `Reader` protocol simply mirrors the `Writer` protocol. It consists of a long succession of read operations for all value types.

```
class Reader
{
public:
        // primitive "built-in" value types
    virtual char readChar() =0;
    virtual int readInt() =0;
    ...
        // non-primitive value types
    virtual string readString() =0;
    ...
        // references to objects
    virtual Object* readObject() =0;
    virtual Object* readRoot() =0;
    ...
}
```

While writing, a `Writer` can write attribute after attribute to the output buffer; a `Reader`, however, has to read all attributes in advance, because the object to be instantiated might ask for its attributes in a different order than that in which they were written. We could require serializable objects to always ask for their attributes in the same order in which they were written, but we prefer to avoid such ordering dependencies.

Attributes are maintained in a dictionary which maps the attribute names on pairs of strings representing the attribute's type and value. The `readChar` operation looks like this

```
char ASCIIStreamReader::readChar(const string& name)
{
    // retrieve attribute with key name, convert it to char and return it
    return attributes->at(name)->value().asChar();
}
```

First, the readObject operation checks whether the object indicated by the id already exists and, if not, creates it using the type id. All the relevant attribute information about the object, its values and types, is maintained in a dictionary named attributes, which is built in initAttributes. initAttributes is called by readRoot of ASCIIStreamReader before every call to readFrom.

```
Serializable* ASCIIStreamReader::readObject(const char* name)
{
    Serializable* object = null;
        // interpret value as long (representing ids)
    long id = attributes->at(name)->value().asLong();

        // check whether object was already instantiated
    if (!wasHandled->containsKey(id))
    {
        string type = attributes->at(key)->type();
            // create new object of given type to be returned
        object = Serializable::newByName(type);
            // note as already handled
        wasHandled->putAt(id, object);
    }
        // return old object
    else object = wasHandled->at(id);

    return object;
}
```

In analogy to writeRoot, readRoot implements the main reading loop. It is called by a client to initiate the reading process. The loop continues until the end of the buffer is reached. readRoot returns the first object which was read.

```
Serializable* ASCIIStreamReader::readRoot()
{
    Serializable* root = null;
    wasHandled->clear();
    toHandle->clear();

        // loop until entire stream is parsed
    while (!buffer.eof())
    {
```

```
        Serializable* object = null;
        char type[32], equal[4], bracket[4], tmp[4];
        unsigned long id;

            // read type id and object id
        buffer >> type >> id >> equal >> bracket;
            // was object already created (but not initialized)?
        if (!wasHandled->containsKey(id))
        {
                // create object using type information
            object = Serializable::newByName(type);
                // note as being created
            wasHandled->putAt(id, object);
                // the first object is the root object
            if (!root) root = object;
        }
            // get existing object
        else object = wasHandled->at(id);

            // read the object's attributes en block
        initAttributes(object->getAttributeCount());
            // tell object to retrieve its attributes
        object->readFrom(this);
        buffer >> bracket >> tmp;
    }

    return root;
}
```

The `initAttributes` operation simply reads a predefined number of values and puts them in the `attributes` dictionary.

```
void ASCIIStreamReader::initAttributes(int no)
{
    attributes->clear();

    for ( int i = 0; i < no; i++ ) {
        char type[32], name[32], equal[4], value[32];
            // read attribute type id, attribute name and value
        buffer >> type >> name >> equal >> value;
            // put type/value pair into attributes dictionary
        attributes->putAt(name, StringPair(type, value));
    }
}
```

Now we have all pieces at hand to understand the reading process. A main loop reads from a buffer until it reaches the end. This is identical to a deep streaming policy, assuming that the buffer contains a complete object graph. Thus `readRoot` creates the object to be read, then reads all its attributes using `initAttributes`, and finally calls `readFrom` on the serializable object. The object requests its attributes from the `Reader` which satisfies these requests by returning the values from the `attributes` dictionary. Attributes which are references are instantiated as shallow objects, that is, without initializing their attributes. Initialization is delayed until the object itself turns up in the stream.

Known Uses

Object streaming is supported by almost every mature (application) framework such as ET++, InterViews/Unidraw, and Smalltalk. Let's take a look at ET++'s implementation of object streaming [Weinand+94]. It is realized by an interplay between `Object` and `Stream` of which two subclasses, `IStream` and `OStream`, exist (for reading and writing respectively). The main difference between the ET++ and Serializer implementations is that ET++ handles only one output format for object streaming. That's why it doesn't bother to take this out of class `Object` as the Serializer pattern suggests. However, for metalevel access to an object's data members, a different operation called `AccessMembers` is defined. The object streaming functionality could have been based on a rewritten and enhanced `AccessMembers` operation.

Although strictly speaking the CORBA externalization service is only a specification, it uses the same interface and separation of responsibilities as the Serializer pattern [OMG96]. A stream service (either `Stream` or `StreamIO`) takes over the combined role of `Reader` and `Writer`, and a `Streamable` interface represents our protocol class `Serializable`. An object or a set of objects is streamed between a `begin_context` and an `end_context` call to `Stream`. All references within these bracketing calls are resolved without duplicating objects. When creating an object structure, the stream service uses the `readonly` attribute `Key` of every `Streamable` object. It serves as the specification to retrieve a new object from a Factory looked up via a `FactoryFinder`. CORBA distinguishes between `write_object` and `write_graph` operations: `write_object` only writes the referenced object, while `write_graph` writes out a full object graph specified via the CORBA relationship service.

Riggs et al. describe "Object Pickling in the Java System," which corresponds to the Serializer pattern [Riggs+96]. The interface `Serializable`, in contrast to our definition, has no operations but serves as an indicator of serializability to a `Reader/Writer` only. Concrete objects may implement operations `writeObject` and `readObject` if they wish to specialize the default implementation. The Serializer is separated into two distinct interfaces, a `Reader` interface (`ObjectInput`) and a `Writer` interface (`ObjectOutput`). Standard implementations for `ObjectInput` and `ObjectOutput` are the Java library classes `ObjectInputStream` and `ObjectOutputStream`. Writing an object always performs a deep streaming; only via specials is it possible to do a shallow streaming as required, for example, for remote procedure calls. Clients can put more than one object graph into an `ObjectOutputStream`; they indicate the end of a section by calling `flush()` on the `OutputStream`. Riggs et al. provide a metainformation-based implementation of the `readFrom` and `writeTo` operations. This works well, because the Java runtime metainformation not only allows access to an object's field but also provides information whether a field is to be considered as transient or persistent, and what the field's name is.

The Gebos series of banking projects developed at RWG in Stuttgart, Germany, uses the Serializer pattern to read and write arbitrary object structures from flat files and relational databases. Different formats for flat files like electronic logs, debugging dumps, etc., are supported [Bäumer+96].

The Geo project pursued at Ubilab uses the Serializer for network transport of objects, copying, object inspection, and file streaming. A number of different `Reader` and `Writer` classes implement the `Reader` and `Writer` interfaces.

The Beyond-Sniff project pursued at Ubilab is a distributed software development environment which uses the Serializer pattern to store and transfer arbitrarily large data structures, for example, for retrieval results from a symbol table to a client's programming environment instantiation [Mätzel+96].

Parrington uses the Serializer pattern in the context of the distributed programming system Arjuna to marshal and unmarshal the parameters of remote procedure calls [Parrington95].

Related Patterns

The `newByName` operation of the protocol class `Serializable` is best implemented using Product Trader [Bäumer+97]. Alternatively, it can be implemented using Factory Methods [Gamma+95]. The streaming policy used to decide whether to activate/passivate a certain object reference can be implemented as a Strategy [Gamma+95].

ACKNOWLEDGMENTS

Our shepherd, John Vlissides, provided valuable feedback that helped us improve the chapter significantly. We received very helpful comments from the members of the writers' workshop "Distribution" at PLoP '96. Ingrid Dörre and Frank Schneider shared their experience in implementing a Serializer subsystem with us and reviewed drafts of this chapter. Erich Gamma gave us important hints, especially on the type safety advantage of the `Reader`/`Writer` pair compared to a single class Serializer which contains both protocols.

REFERENCES

[Bäumer+96] D. Bäumer, R. Knoll, G. Gryczan, and H. Züllighoven. "Large Scale Object-Oriented Software-Development in a Banking Environment—An Experience Report." LNCS 1098, ECOOP '96, *Conference Proceedings*, pp. 73–91.

[Bäumer+97] D. Bäumer and D. Riehle. "Product Trader." Chapter 3, this volume.

[Gamma+95] E. Gamma, R. Helm, R. Johnson, and J. Vlissides. *Design Patterns: Elements of Reusable Design.* Reading, MA: Addison-Wesley, 1995.

[Lopes96] C. V. Lopes. "Adaptive Parameter Passing." LNCS 1049, ISOTAS '96, *Conference Proceedings.* Ed. K. Futatsugi and S. Matsuoka. Berlin, Heidelberg: Springer-Verlag, 1996, pp. 118–136.

[Mätzel+96] K. Mätzel and W. R. Bischofberger. "The Any Framework: A Pragmatic Approach to Flexibility." COOTS '96, *Conference Proceedings*, pp. 179–190.

[OMG96] Object Management Group, Inc. *CORBAservices: Common Object Services Specification, volume 1.* Revised edition March 31, 1995. Updated March 28, 1996.

[Parrington95] G. D. Parrington. "A Stub Generation System for C++." *Computing Systems* 8, 2 (Spring 1995), pp. 135–167.

[Riggs+96] R. Riggs, J. Waldo, A. Wolrath, and K. Bharat. "Pickling State in the Java System." COOTS-2, *Conference Proceedings*, pp. 241–250.

[Weinand+94] A. Weinand and E. Gamma. "ET++ — a Portable, Homogenous Class Library and Application Framework." *Computer Science Research at Ubilab.* Eds. W. R. Bischofberger and H. Frei. Konstanz: Universitätsverlag Konstanz, 1994, pp. 66–92.

Dirk Riehle welcomes e-mail at Dirk.Riehle@ubs.com **or** riehle@acm.org.
Wolf Siberski can be reached at Wolf_Siberski@rwg.e-mail.com.
Dirk Bäumer can be reached at Dirk_Baeumer@rwg.e-mail.com.
Daniel Megert can be reached at Daniel.Megert@ubs.com.
Heinz Züllighoven welcomes e-mail at Heinz.Zuellighoven@informatik.uni-hamburg.de.

Chapter 18

Accessing Relational Databases

Wolfgang Keller
and Jens Coldewey

This pattern language for relational database access layers helps you design database applications that reflect relational calculus at a business object level. Such applications are known as data-driven or representational [Martin95]. These systems need not be object-oriented; you may also use a 3GL. Hence the pattern language does not cover mapping, inheritance, and polymorphism.

This pattern language was developed during the ENTSTAND Project, sponsored by sd&m (Software Design & Management) and the German Ministry for Research and Technology.

Designing an application that uses a relational database means coping with an array of problems. How do you ensure adequate performance? How and where in your system should you code SQL statements? How do you deal with performance optimizations like denormalization of the data model that might cause a partial rewrite of your SQL code? What interface should an application kernel object use to access the data stores?

In a three-layer architecture, it is a proven technique to encapsulate aspects of database access in a database access layer [Denert91]. This chapter presents a framework and a set of patterns that help you design database access layers for relational databases.

RELATED WORK ON DATABASE ACCESS LAYERS

Representational systems are pretty common. They have a simple data model compared to full-blown object-oriented models. Though they may include thirty entities or more, you rarely find much inheritance or complex associations. Yet the application kernel encapsulates complex use-cases. It is a good idea to use relational calculus for modeling these systems.

Other persistence frameworks and pattern languages deal with full object persistence. These are Object to Relational Access Layers [Brown+96, Coldewey+96, Keller+96] using a relational database, and Object Access Layers using an object database [Coldewey97].

Figure 18-1 illustrates the relationship between the different access layers. Note that the framework presented in this chapter only covers the left-most column.

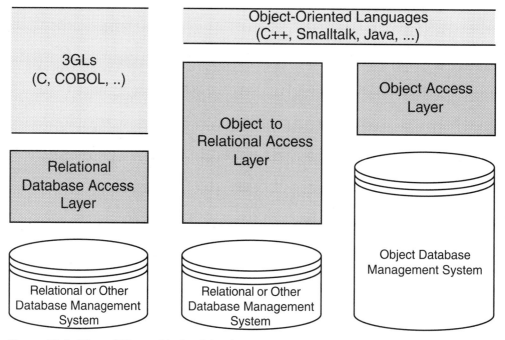

Figure 18-1 *Three different kinds of database access layers*

GENERAL FORCES

When designing a Relational Database Access Layer you will find a prevailing set of forces driving your design. Most of these are not specific to a single pattern of the language. Some of them are not even specific to our framework, for example, Separation of concerns versus cost. The general forces driving the design of the framework are

- *Separation of concerns versus cost.* Database programming is complex. So is application logic. Mixing them will yield more than just the sum of their complexities. The easiest way to reduce complexity is to separate application programming from database programming. Both parts will then be easier to implement and to test. On the other hand, the introduction of new layers of software increases the number of classes and adds to the design and implementation effort. The cost has to pay off with easier maintenance and performance tuning.
- *Performance.* During analysis you usually define the data model of the application in third normal form (3NF) [Dat94, chapter 10]. However, the entire system performs poorly if you also use 3NF as the physical table layout. Therefore, tuning is crucial to achieve acceptable performance. Because a database is several orders of magnitude slower than the main processor, tuning activities concentrate on database access. You iteratively change the physical parameters of the database engine as well as the table layout, or the API, to access the database.
- *Flexibility versus complexity.* As database tuning is crucial, you want to have an encapsulation of the database that allows frequent changes to the underlying data model while the application kernel remains untouched. Still, the more flexible a system is, the more complex and expensive it will be.
- *Ease-of-use versus power.* If you decide to encapsulate the database, the resulting interface should be easy to use. On the other hand, the complexity of a database interface stems from its power. Hence you have to design an interface that is easy to use but still powerful enough for your project.
- *Mass problems and cost of development.* Large databases may comprise hundreds of tables. This may require an automatic process to build the interface. Macros, generators, or templates reduce the effort. However, a generic interface takes more design effort to develop because it has to cover all possible cases.
- *Integration of legacy systems versus optimal design.* Business information systems are seldom developed from scratch. Instead, you have to connect to legacy systems, which you are not allowed to touch. Replacing the complete legacy code is usually not an option, as it would entail a risky and expensive "big bang" strategy. However, the structure of legacy data rarely fits your needs—if there is a structure at all. You may also have to bridge several generations of database technologies. To keep an application maintainable you have to encapsulate accesses to legacy data. This is a particularly strong force for reengineering projects.

RUNNING EXAMPLE

Throughout this chapter we use a running example to help explain the relationships between the logical data model, the physical representation of data in tables, and the application's views on the data.

Consider the excerpt from an order management system shown in the lower part of Figure 18-2. The logical data model contains the entities you need to process the invoice depicted in the upper left corner. The excerpt complies with 3NF. Suppose you have used this logical data model to define your physical database tables. The system will work correctly, but you will encounter poor performance.

In profiling the system you detect many superfluous database operations. You also find slow database operations caused by large joins or by moving large amounts of unnecessary data. To increase performance, you denormalize the physical data model. A statistical analysis of the database's contents yields the information that 90% of the Orders have no more than five OrderItems. Therefore, you decide to store the first five OrderItems in the Order table. To cover the remaining 10%, you create an OrderItemOverflow table as depicted at the upper right of Figure 18-2. Furthermore, you integrate the Article attributes ArtPrice and Art-Name into the Order table. The resulting database design allows 90% of the invoices

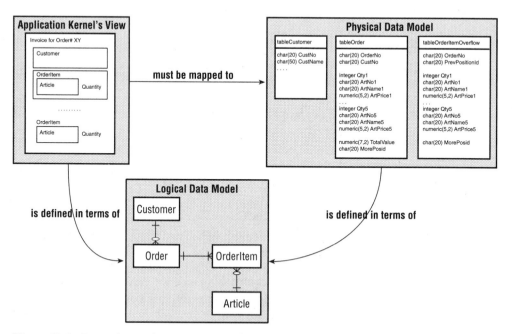

Figure 18-2 *Part of an order processing system*

to be read with two database accesses: one to the Order table and one to the Customer table. You have also eliminated all joins.

Now assume you have embedded SQL statements within the application kernel code. Adapting the code to the new table schemes means rewriting large portions of it. Furthermore, handling overflow tables makes the SQL code explode in size. Worst of all, you have to repeat this procedure for every improvement of the database structure.

The Relational Database Access Layers pattern language will help you avoid such problems.

PATTERN LANGUAGE MAP

The Relational Database Access Layer framework pattern defines roles and responsibilities for its components. It also describes three key abstractions: Hierarchical View, Physical View, and Query Broker (see Figure 18-3).

NOTATIONAL CONVENTIONS

We use OMT [Rumbaugh+91] for object diagrams. The notation for object interaction diagrams is taken from [Buschmann+96].

RELATIONAL DATABASE ACCESS LAYER PATTERN

Relational Database Access Layer describes the overall architecture proposed in this pattern language.

Context

You are writing a business information system like the preceding order processing system. The relational calculus is an appropriate representation of the domain logic. The resulting data model is simple and uses inheritance sparingly. The effort of mapping the relational model to an object-oriented representation is high compared to the gains.

Problem

How do you access the relational database?

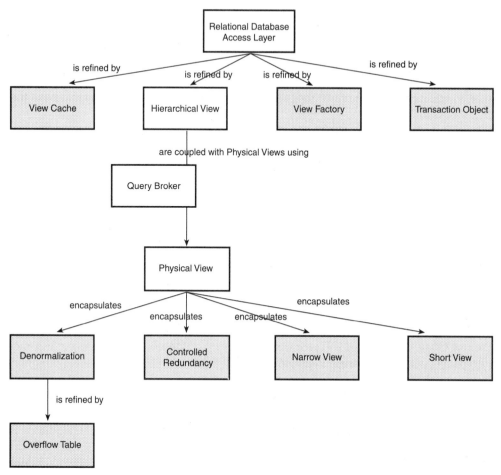

Figure 18-3 *A map of the pattern language. Unshaded boxes denote the key patterns presented in this chapter. Shaded boxes are contained only in the PLoP Proceedings [Keller+97].*

Forces

The general forces influencing the design of a Relational Database Access Layer were described earlier in detail. They are

- Separation of concerns versus cost of programming.
- Ease-of-use versus power of an interface.
- Performance of the resulting solution.
- Flexibility versus complexity.
- Possible integration of legacy systems versus optimal design for nonlegacy data.

Solution

Use a layered architecture consisting of two layers as depicted in Figure 18-4. The Logical Access Layer provides the interface to the stable application kernel, while the Physical Access Layer accesses the database system. The latter may adapt to changing performance needs. Use a Query Broker to decouple both layers.

Structure

Figure 18-5 shows the classes of the Relational Database Access Layer. The Logical Access Layer provides classes for caching and transaction management. The Physical Access Layer represents the interface to the database system. The latter splits into the physical views, representing data access, and the Database class, which encapsulates administrative calls. Hard-coded logic or—even better—a Query Broker mediates between the logical and the physical access layers.

Participants

HierarchicalView defines the abstract protocol for ConcreteHierarchicalViews. See also the Hierarchical View pattern. It offers a markModified() method to cause a database update when the current transaction commits. It also provides the requestDelete() method to generate a database delete at the end of a transaction. This method should not be confused with a destructor. While the destructor instantly eliminates the object from memory, requestDelete() sets a delete flag. At the end of a transaction, the ViewCache erases the object from the database (and from memory). To avoid dangling references, the requestDelete() method should be the only way to delete database records.

ConcreteHierarchicalView is a Hierarchical View on the logical data model. There are several ConcreteHierarchicalView classes, each of them tailored to

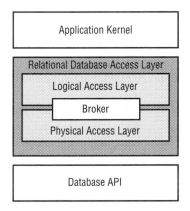

Figure 18-4 *The Relational Database Access Layers*

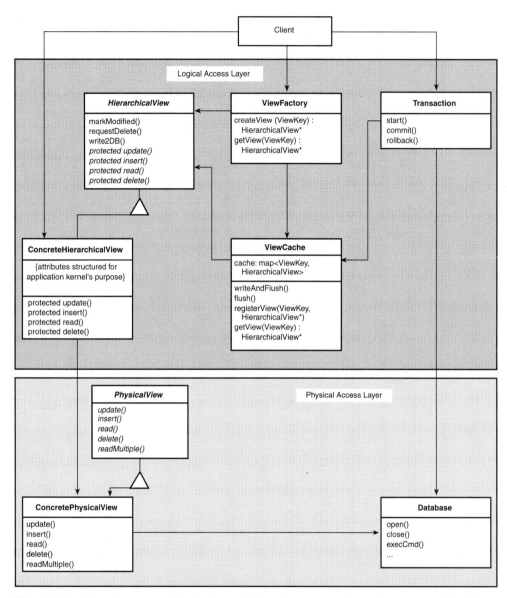

Figure 18-5 *The structure of the Relational Database Access Layer framework. The Client accesses only classes of the Logical Access Layer, which in turn use the Physical Access Layer to connect to the database. Classes and methods needed for the Query Broker pattern are not yet included.*

one or more use-cases of the application kernel. Members of ConcreteHierar-chicalViews are application data types, not raw database types.[1] It knows how to write and read itself to and from the database using ConcretePhysicalViews. The ConcreteHierarchicalView keeps track of its internal state and calls private update(), insert(), or delete() methods if it receives a write2DB() message from the ViewCache. You may use hard-coded calls to suitable ConcretePhysi-calViews or a QueryBroker.

PhysicalView defines a uniform protocol for ConcretePhysicalViews.

ConcretePhysicalView wraps one physical database table or a database view. If the database does not support direct update of views, the ConcretePhysical-View also issues appropriate write commands. It also bundles database access functions, encapsulates database behavior, and translates database error codes into application level errors.[2] In addition, it wraps database optimization if you use Denormalization, Controlled Redundancy, or Overflow Tables. In this case a ConcretePhysicalPhysical view may wrap more than one table. It may be generated from meta information, such as the table structure of the database.

Transaction offers an interface that allows start(), commit(), and rollback() of transactions. It is created at the beginning of every transaction. It is destroyed after a commit() or an abort(). This usage resembles the transaction object defined in [ODMG96, chapter 2.8].

ViewFactory delivers data identified by a key. Therefore it offers create-View() and getView() methods to create new Views and activate existing ones. These two methods are the only way for the Client to obtain a reference to a HierarchicalView. It uses a View Cache to avoid creating Views if they already exist in the context of the current transaction. It also allows predicates to identify ConcreteHierarchicalViews. An abstract key class ViewKey provides a standard interface for all keys. Transaction is a Singleton [Gamma+95].

ViewCache prevents data from being loaded twice. It is a keyed Container of Views forming the access layer's cache. It also offers the writeAndFlush method, which writes all modified Views to the database using their write2DB method. The Transaction object calls writeAndFlush when it commits. It calls the flush() method to clear the ViewCache when it aborts.

Database encapsulates the database management system. It provides methods for initiating database connections, issuing database commands, and receiving results.

---

[1] Application data types are often used instead of raw database data types at the application kernel level. They have additional methods to check their contents, reformat it, or format it for output [Denert91, chapter 5.2].
[2] Most database errors are not meaningful on application level. Therefore it is a good idea to translate them. Additionally you may have to translate the error mechanism when the database uses return codes to signal errors and your application uses exceptions [Renzel96].

Dynamic Behavior

To illustrate the dynamic behavior of the Framework we discuss two scenarios: Fetching a `ConcreteHierarchicalView` from the database (Figure 18-6) and managing a `Transaction` (Figure 18-7).

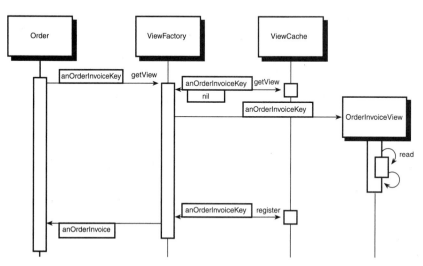

Figure 18-6 *Fetching an* `OrderInvoice` *from the database*

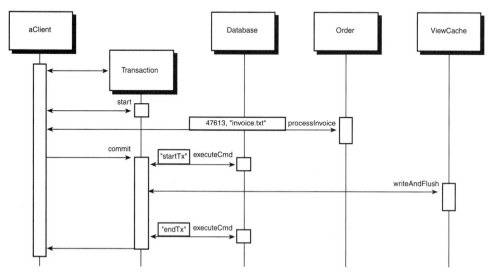

Figure 18-7 *Processing a transaction*

The following code, taken from Listing 18-2, initiates the first scenario.

```
OrderInvoiceView * pInvoice =
    (OrderInvoiceView *) ViewFactory::getView( anOrderInvoiceKey );
```

Presume the `OrderInvoiceView` identified by the `ViewKey` `anOrderInvoiceKey` has not yet been loaded. The `ViewFactory` first tries to ask the `ViewCache` for the `OrderInvoiceView`. As the `ViewCache` does not hold the required `OrderInvoice-View`, the `ViewFactory` creates a new `OrderInvoiceView`. The `OrderInvoiceView` loads itself with data from the database that match the given `ViewKey`. The `ViewFactory` will then register the freshly loaded `OrderInvoiceView` with the `ViewCache` and return it.

The second scenario demonstrates the lifecycle of a `Transaction` object created by a main program. The locking strategy used is optimistic. Consider the following piece of code.

```
try {
    Transaction trans;
    Trans.start();
        Order::processInvoice("47613","invoice.txt");
    trans.commit();
}
 catch (...) {
    // trans is automatically destroyed here, resulting in
    // an abort of the transaction
}
```

You might note that the call `Order::processInvoice("47613","invoice.txt")` is not exactly object-oriented. This call demonstrates the 3GL nature of our interface for representational applications. The code results in the interaction diagram shown in Figure 18-7.

Consequences

- *Separation of concerns.* The access layer forms a well-encapsulated subsystem for transactions, database access, and caching. The application kernel uses a logical interface and needs no knowledge about database access specifics.
- *Effort.* Implementing a Relational Database Access Layer framework requires from 0.5 to 35 person years, depending on its features. Using generators and hard-coded dependencies is cheaper than building maintenance tools and a Query Broker. Consider expected changes, time to market, and the lifetime of your software before you decide on a particular design.
- *Ease-of-use.* The access layer does not transform the relational model to an object-oriented view. Therefore, the application kernel has to cope with the relational view as presented in the Hierarchical View pattern. You should carefully

consider whether this data-driven approach matches the application logic or not. Check whether your project does better with an Object to Relational Access Layer. It is not a good idea to save the effort for a more complex access layer when the application kernel does the required mapping implicitly.

- *Inheritance and polymorphism.* The access layer contains no built-in precautions for handling inheritance or polymorphism. Check whether this suits your problem domain.
- *Flexibility.* The application code remains stable while the underlying physical database changes for tuning. If you use the Query Broker pattern, you may maintain and tune the database by adding new physical database access modules instead of modifying application kernel code.
- *Complexity.* The access layer contains mostly simple classes. The Query Broker is the most expensive item as it contains a complex tree matching algorithm. Omitting it results in a simple layer of adaptors but is less flexible.
- *Performance.* You pay a minor runtime penalty for the database access subsystems due to mapping and additional layers of software. The access layer compensates with easy tuning and caching. You invest in fast processor cycles and economize on slow I/O.
- *Reengineering of legacy data.* You may use the access layer to decouple the physical and the logical data models of existing applications. This is useful for reengineering legacy applications. First you insert a database access layer into the code, which is a single step with manageable risks. Then you start to rewrite the database and the application kernel in different projects. This is also feasible for a legacy database such as IMS/DB.

Implementation

- *Treatment of Mass Updates.* Mass updates are statements of the form `update .. where`, which manipulate a set of records with a single query. It is hard to integrate these statements with the View Cache. Handling mass updates using the View Cache means (1) perform a mass read into the `view-Cache`, (2) manipulate single records, and (3) write them back to the database one at a time. This solution is much slower than directly performing the task on the database using SQL statements.
- *Batches need special treatment.* There is a set of patterns dealing with batch database access just waiting to be mined.
- *Multiple Read Queries.* We have skipped multiple read queries. You can find further information in the Short View and Narrow View patterns.
- *Cursor Stability.* It is theoretically possible to submit mass read operations to a BFIM (before images) consistency check. This would provide level two transaction consistency (*cursor stability* [Gray+93]) instead of level one (*browse consistency*). Mass read operations are typically used to fill list boxes (see Short View). They have the form `select <fields> from ... where`. Checking them

for consistency at commit time would mean rereading all records read during the transaction and comparing them to their before images. If only a single record differs, you have to abort the transaction. This is not only a serious threat to performance—it also does not add any value to consistency. In most cases, records used to fill list boxes do not play any role that could compromise the consistency of a task. Hence it is usually sufficient to use browse consistency for data not involved in computations during the transaction.

- `ConcretePhysicalViews` *and dynamic SQL.* If the database system supports dynamic SQL without runtime penalty, you may skip the `ConcretePhysical-Views` and use the Query Broker pattern to generate the appropriate SQL statements. For static SQL, the `ConcretePhysicalViews` provide the queries.
- Database Connections should remain established as long as possible. Establishing a new connection for every transaction would result in poor performance.
- The use of database triggers and stored procedures containing business logic is strongly discouraged with this architecture. A View Cache will not be notified about autonomous changes in the database. Hence stored procedures may cause cache consistency problems. Similar problems arise with triggers. Since they work on the physical data model, it is hard to transform them to the logical level of the application kernel. However, you may use restricted stored procedures to implement Physical Views.

Variants

- *Omitting the* `ViewCache`. If you do not need long transactions, you may omit the `ViewCache`. This is a feasible approach for simple dialog systems supporting only the manipulation of a single record per transaction. However, you should use the `ViewCache` if the application kernel has a notion of transactions affecting more than one record.
- *Traditional transaction monitors.* A cache is the natural choice to implement user transactions on top of a transaction monitor such as IMS, CICS, or UTM. Transaction monitors start a new transaction for every step the dialog takes, while user transactions typically contain several dialog steps to complete. Using the `ViewCache` lets you collect all write activities to the database that occur during a user transaction. They are later executed in a single technical host transaction preserving transaction integrity over the multiple dialog steps of a transaction system.
- *Using nonrelational Databases.* The Physical Access Layer may also encapsulate nonrelational databases and file formats, such as IMS-DB, CODASYL, or VSAM. You may even adapt to several different database technologies, thus hiding access to legacy data.

Related Patterns

The pattern is an application of Layers [Buschmann+96, p. 31]. The View Factory is an application of the Abstract Constructor [Lange96].

Brown [Brown+96] and Coldeway [Coldewey+96] describe how to extend the pattern to offer an object-oriented view of a relational database to the application kernel. Brown and Whitenack [Brown+96] use a broker to decouple the layers, while we describe a hard-coded approach [Coldewey+96].

Known Uses

The VAA Data Manager specification uses this pattern, together with editors for metadata and complex mappings, for hierarchical database systems [VAA95]. The VAA Data Manager is derived from the Data Manager Architecture of Württembergische Versicherung [Württembergische96].

Denert sketches some basic ideas of the pattern language in [*Software-Engineering*, pp. 230–239]. Many projects at sd&m used the patterns in various variants including Thyssen [Zeh88], Deutsche Bahn [Bis96], and HYPO Bank [Keller+96].

HIERARCHICAL VIEW PATTERN

Hierarchical Views describe the interface the Relational Database Access Layer offers to the application kernel.

Example

Consider the detail of our order processing system shown in Figure 18-8. There may be use-cases involving invoices with the structure depicted on the right side. Note that this invoice has a hierarchical structure with two levels of indirection. The use-case may start with an order number and then navigate to the various items and their articles.

Context

You have decided to use the Relational Database Access Layer to decouple the physical database from the logical view the application kernel has upon its data.

Problem

What interface should the database access layer present to the application kernel?

Forces

Besides the general considerations listed in the introduction, you have to deal with the following set of forces.

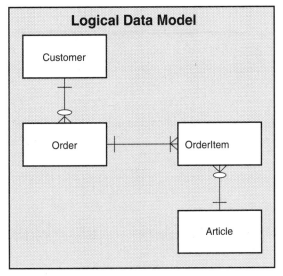
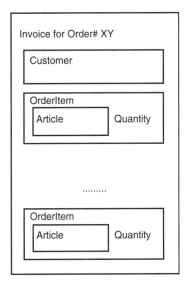

Figure 18-8 *A detail of our order processing system's logical data model. The left side shows the E/R diagram in third normal form, the right side the structure of an invoice composed of these entities.*

- *Complexity and power versus development cost.* The design of the interface has significant influence on its power and complexity and hence on the total development cost.
- *Complexity versus ease-of-use.* The more complex an interface for applications is, the harder it will be to use. If your goal is factoring out database concerns, you should try to hide as many of them as possible. This will result in a simple-to-use but less flexible interface.
- *Mass problems.* A large data model contains a hundred or more entities. Manually writing wrappers or embedded SQL code for hundreds of entities is a boring and expensive task. Boring tasks are error-prone. A generic solution enables you to use macro expansion, generators, or templates for database programming.

Solution

Express the interface in terms of the domain's problem space, that is, as a relational data model. Start at one point (or entity) of the data model and use foreign key relations to navigate to the other points of interest. Construct a directed acyclic graph (DAG) during navigation. Label every node with the entity, attributes of interest, and selection predicates. Label every edge with the foreign key you have used for navigation and its cardinality (one-to-one or one-to-many).

Structure

Figure 18-9 shows a graph on the right representing the invoice depicted on the left side. Figure 18-10 shows an object structure that implements this graph.

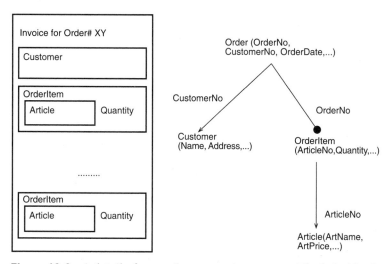

Figure 18-9   *A detail of our order processing system. The left side shows the invoice from Figure 18-5. The right side shows a DAG-like description of the data contained in the invoice. Every node or leaf of the DAG represents an entity of the logical data model.*

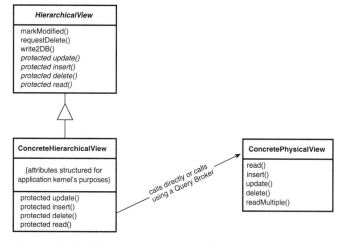

Figure 18-10   *Object structure of a Hierarchical view*

To transform this graph into a `ConcreteHierarchicalView`, make it the root of the DAG. Define a domain-level class for any one of the nodes. Use aggregation to implement *to one* relationship in the graph. Use containers to implement *to many* edges of the graph. A `ConcreteHierarchicalView` constructed this way fills its domain-level attributes from `ConcretePhysicalViews`. The suitable `ConcretePhysicalViews` may be found using hard-coded knowledge or the Query Broker pattern.

The database access layer should be able to treat all `ConcreteHierarchical-Views` uniformly. `HierarchicalView` defines their common interface to the other classes of the access layer.

Example Resolved

Listing 18-1 below shows the declarations for the invoice example. Listing 2 contains the code to process the invoice.

```
struct Customer {
    CustomerKeyType      iCustNumber;
    // other properties of the Customer in the logical data model
};
struct Article {
    ArticleNumberType    iArticleNumber;
    // Other properties
};
struct OrderItem {
    Article              iArticle;
    QuantityType         iQuantity;
};


class OrderInvoiceView : public HierarchicalView {
public:

    OrderInvoiceView(OrderKeyType anOrder);

    OrderKeyType                    iOrder;
    Customer                        iCustomer;
    Vector<OrderItem>               iItems;
                                    // Any other container will also do
    Money                           iSumOfInvoice; // computed attribute
protected:
    // protected methods you need to obtain data and write data
    // to PhysicalViews

    virtual void update ( void );
    virtual void insert ( void );
    virtual void remove ( void );
    virtual void read ( void );
};
```

Listing 18-1 *The declarations for the invoice example*

The code in Listing 18-2 is free of database aspects and follows the logical data model. The denormalized physical data model is invisible from the application code. There are only two lines that deal with persistence: The `ViewFactory::getView()` command gets data from the access layer. The `pInvoice->markModified()` method tags the `SumOfInvoice` to write itself back to the database.

```
Void Order::processInvoice (OrderKeyType anOrder) {
    // get the data from the database. We only specify the primary key
    // and leave the rest to the access layer
    OrderInvoiceView * pInvoice =
        (OrderInvoiceView *) ViewFactory::getView( anOrder);

    // process invoice items.
    ItemIterator itemIter = pInvoice->iItems.begin();
    for (; itemIter != iItems.end(); itemIter++) {
        pInvoice->iSumOfInvoice +=
            ( itemIter->iQuantity *
                itemIter->iArticle.iArticlePrice );
    }

    // the view has been changed, so mark it
    pInvoice->markModified();
}
```

Listing 18-2 *Implementation of* `processInvoice`*. The example demonstrates iteration through the items of an order, and sums up the prices of all items in the* `iSumOfInvoice` *property. Note that we traverse two levels of indirection in the logical data model. For reasons of simplicity we omitted the transaction brackets around* `Order::processInvoice` *as well as some obvious type definitions.*

Consequences

- *Inheritance and polymorphism.* The access layer does not support inheritance or polymorphism. There is no provision for one view inheriting from another. This is appropriate for most business information systems specified using data abstraction [Denert91].
- *Complexity of the interface.* The interface is minimal because it offers only the basic features the application kernel needs. However, you have to invest effort in generators or templates that allow dealing with the large number of `ConcreteHierarchicalViews` required. There may be a full payback due to cheaper tuning, but it may well take several maintenance cycles before you break even. Once you have finished the generators, defining new `ConcreteHierarchicalViews` is a matter of minutes.

- *Interface style.* An application using Hierarchical View follows a path in the logical data model starting from the root of the DAG. The logical data model determines the structure of the code using it. This is in contrast to an object/relational access layer, where the object model follows the internal structure of the domain.
- *Ease of use and requirements of the application kernel.* Hierarchical Views reflect only the domain logic while supporting exactly the navigation that the corresponding use-cases need. Calling the access layer is simple because the Hierarchical Views encapsulate database-specific functions.
- *Decoupling.* Hierarchical Views completely decouple the application kernel from the physical data model. This lets you tune the database any way you want without affecting the code of the application kernel. The resulting performance gain is much higher than the loss caused by the additional level of indirection introduced by the Hierarchical View.

Implementation

You may define the structure of the `ConcreteHierarchicalViews` using text files or a specialized tool [Württembergische96]. This allows automatic generation of the `ConcreteHierarchicalViews` for statically typed languages or even runtime definition for dynamically typed languages.

Variants

Many applications are a collection of mostly simple use-cases. They need views with only a single level of indirection (such as an entity and its dependent entity). In these cases, the `ConcretePhysicalViews` encapsulate the database access code and provide a sufficiently clean interface to the application, saving the Query Broker and the Hierarchical View. However, this variant is not suitable for complex use-cases that may affect a two-digit number of entities in a single use-case (for example, insurance applications).

A more complex variant allows retrieval of historic data. You need this variant if you are interested not only in the current state of a contract but in its state at a given time [Schlattmann96]. To navigate the data model, you have to enrich conditions and navigation edges with expressions for time-based navigation [Württembergische96]. Banking and insurance companies often need these features, as do audit applications.

Related Patterns

You may use a Query Broker to decouple Hierarchical Views from the underlying Physical Views. Use a View Cache to avoid multiple database accesses for the same physical data.

Known Uses

VAA, a standard architecture for German insurance companies, uses this pattern with time navigation [VAA95]. The corresponding Data Manager Component is currently under construction. Württembergische Versicherung is developing a Data Manager using Hierarchical View and a tool to define them [Württembergische96].

Many of sd&m's projects have used the simple variant (1:n views) of the Hierarchical View pattern. These projects use scripting languages to automatically generate views from view descriptions [Denert91].

PHYSICAL VIEW PATTERN

Physical View shows how to encapsulate a physical database so that it can be easily accessed and optimized without affecting higher layers of software.

Context

You have decided to build a Relational Database Access Layer. You use Hierarchical View as an interface to the application kernel, and you have chosen not to incorporate database access into the ConcreteViews.

Problem

How do you provide an easy-to-use interface to your physical database tables?

Forces

- *Simplicity versus performance.* To achieve good performance you have to optimize your physical table layout using Denormalization, Controlled Redundancy, or Overflow Tables. However, these techniques make database access complex. Overflow Tables, especially, result in intricate code. Despite these complex optimizations, you want to have an easy-to-use interface and maintainable classes.
- *Flexibility.* Most databases offer a choice of either static or dynamic SQL. Because the database precompiles and preoptimizes static SQL queries, it often reduces server load and yields better performance. Some database administrators allow only static SQL on their servers. The common reason for such a policy is database security, as most users do not use the built-in protection mechanisms of relational databases for cost reasons. On the other hand, dynamic SQL is more flexible, it adapts more easily to changes in the database scheme, and it is easier to use during development. To satisfy high-performance requirements, you may even want to use a low-level database API. Higher levels of the access layer should not be aware of these considerations.

Solution

Encapsulate every table and every view with a `ConcretePhysicalView` (Figure 18-11). Use these classes to encapsulate Overflow Tables and other database optimization techniques. To provide a uniform interface, derive `ConcretePhysicalViews` from `PhysicalViews`.

`ConcretePhysicalViews` use SQL statements to store their instance data. The main difference compared to `ConcreteHierarchicalViews` is that they shield a single physical table or view instead of multiple physical structures.

Structure

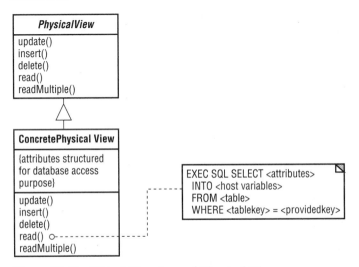

Figure 18-11 *Object Structure of Physical Views*

Example Resolved

Figure 18-12 shows the DAG-definitions of the two Physical Views needed for our invoice example. They correspond to the physical database structure modulo of the Overflow Table (see Figure 18-2). To simplify the `OrderPhysicalView`, it should grant update access only to the `Order` and `OrderItem` data, but not to the article information. There are other Physical Views for changing the `Article` table.

Consequences

- *Simplicity.* Physical Views hide the complexity of optimizations and database programming. Because they have no other responsibilities, they are easy to implement. Still, the extra layer adds additional classes. If you plan to omit the Query Broker for hard-coded connections to the `ConcreteHierarchical-`

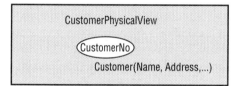

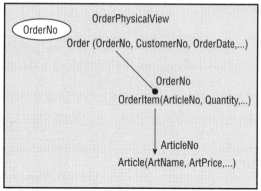

Figure 18-12 *DAG definitions for two* `ConcretePhysicalViews`. *Note that the* `Order-PhysicalView` *encapsulates the* `Order` *table with its overflow table* `OrderItemOverflow`, *while* `CustomerPhysicalView` *encapsulates the* `Customer` *table alone. See Figure 18-2 for the physical table structure.*

`Views`, you should consider carefully whether it is easier to add the layer or whether the `ConcreteHierarchicalViews` should do the database access themselves. The latter results in fewer classes but also less flexibility. Thus the layer of Hierarchical Views degenerates to a layer of Physical Views.

- *Flexibility.* Since Physical Views encapsulate database code, it is their choice what API they use to access the database. You may have separate sets of classes using different database APIs. If you want to experiment with different access techniques at runtime, you may even use a Bridge [Gamma+95] and switch access modes on the fly.
- *Performance.* Physical Views let you optimize the physical database structure without affecting upper layers. This simplifies tuning and results in better performance. The penalty of an additional level of indirection is negligible.
- *Mass problems.* It is easy to design a generator that builds first-cut versions of `ConcretePhysicalViews`. As long as you use no Overflow Tables, you just have to wrap the corresponding SQL statement. More sophisticated generators may also handle Overflow Tables.

Implementation

- *What to encapsulate?* Each `ConcretePhysicalView` should encapsulate a group of `read/write/update/delete` SQL statements on a physical table and its corresponding Overflow Table. Since Hierarchical Views refer to more than one `ConcretePhysicalView`, you also have the choice to either join two tables on the database using SQL or to join them in the access layer. A good point to start is to define a `ConcretePhysicalView` for every "root table" such as `Customer` and `Article`. Furthermore, build one `ConcretePhysical-View` for every compound entity for which you have defined database views, such as the `Order/OrderItem` relation. If you use a Query Broker, you may analyze its decisions to find further candidates.

- *Encapsulating read-only views.* To keep the Physical Views as simple as possible, you should consider which `ConcretePhysicalViews` have the right to update the data they have read. Physical Views represent database views, and most databases do not support writing to views. Hence if multiple tables are involved, a Physical View with read-only access is simpler than one with read-and-write access. A good idea is to start with exactly one Physical View having *write* access to a certain table.
- *Programming Tools.* `ConcretePhysicalViews` are generic. Use a generator or macro technique to implement them. You may also consider templates.
- *Use of stored procedures and other APIs.* Most databases offer stored procedures to do computation on the database server. Since Physical Views work directly on the database, you may implement them with stored procedures or any other API the database offers to access tuples. With this solution you may write tricky optimizations like Overflow Tables in database code instead of a host language plus embedded SQL. However, you put extra load on the database server, and you have to ensure that all applications comply with this architecture.

Variants

If you have a hard-coded connection between `ConcreteHierarchicalViews` and `ConcretePhysicalViews`, you may implement `ConcretePhysicalViews` as methods of the `ConcreteHierarchicalViews`. However, this solution is less flexible since you are not able to use the same `ConcretePhysicalView` twice.

You may also use Physical Views to encapsulate non-SQL databases and file systems such as ADABAS, IMS-DB, CODASYL, and VSAM. As mentioned, you may use this variant to build relational applications on top of legacy databases.

Related Patterns

For further discussion of database optimization, see [Keller+97]. The Overflow Table pattern describes in detail how to partially merge tables. Controlled Redundancy contains a discussion on when to grant write access. Narrow View gives hints on Physical Views to select data.

QUERY BROKER PATTERN

A Query Broker is an effective, though expensive, way to decouple Hierarchical Views and Physical Views in a database access layer.

Example

Consider the previous example of an invoice. The `OrderInvoiceView` models the logical data structure while the `OrderPhysicalView` and the `CustomerPhysicalView` model the corresponding physical tables.

Context

You have decided to use the Relational Database Access Layer. You use Hierarchical Views as an interface to the application kernel and Physical Views to encapsulate database access.

Problem

How do you connect the Hierarchical Views, which make the Logical Access Layer, and the Physical Views, which make the Physical Access Layer, for reading and writing?

Forces

- *Cost versus flexibility.*   The cheapest way to connect two layers is hard-coded coupling via function calls: A `ConcreteHierarchicalView` knows which `PhysicalViews` it has to call. You can generate the corresponding calls using compact table descriptions. This works fine as long as both layers are stable. However, if a layer is unstable, you should use some form of decoupling. In the access layer we have stable Hierarchical Views on top of an unstable Physical View layer. If the system is small enough, you may use a program generator to couple both layers. Still, this approach will produce extensive costs in terms of compilation and software distribution if the system lives for several years. Consider that you have to distribute megabytes of database access software to thousands of clients for every change in the physical database model.
- *Reusability.*   Though the Physical Views may change rapidly, they reflect the physical structure of the database. Therefore, it is likely that several applications use the same Physical Views but different Hierarchical Views. Writing a separate coupling mechanism for every application nullifies the gains you get from reusing the Physical Views.
- *Complexity.*   Since the hard-coded solution is not flexible enough, you need a more complex solution. However, extra complexity makes the system more expensive and, again, harder to maintain.

Solution

Use a Broker [Buschmann+96] to connect the layers. The Hierarchical Views form the client side of the Query Broker; the Physical Views constitute the server side. Describe services using directed acyclic graphs (DAG), and use a tree-matching algorithm to find best matches. Let the Query Broker assemble the Physical Views and deliver the result in a Query Result container.

Structure

A Broker is a standard technique for decoupling. Use the standard structure and adapt it to the Database Access Layer framework (see Figure 18-13). The most significant difference between QueryBroker and a standard Broker is that it usually takes more than one server to handle a request. The mapping to servers is not *one to one*, but *one to many*.

Brokers usually use symbolic names to identify services. As we have a 1:n relation between service requests and servers that fulfill them, this is not appropriate

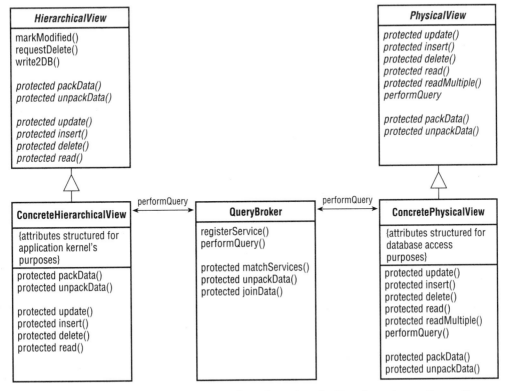

Figure 18-13 *The* QueryBroker *is a Broker adapted to the Database Access Layer Framework. The interfaces of* PhysicalViews *and* HierarchicalViews *have been expanded to adapt the framework to the* QueryBroker.

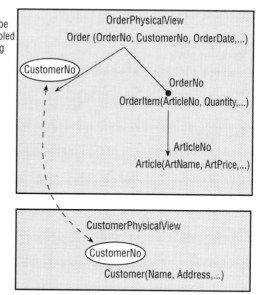

Figure 18-14 *Tree matching to resolve requests to the* QueryBroker. *The left side shows the* OrderInvoiceView *of our order processing system. The right side depicts the corresponding two Physical Views. If the* QueryBroker *gets the left presentation as a request, it figures out that the Physical Views on the right side are the best way to satisfy the request.*

here. Hence the QueryBroker uses semantic descriptions (DAGs) to describe requested views. Consider Figure 18-14: The left side shows the description of the request for the OrderInvoiceView. The right side depicts the corresponding services. To assemble the ConcretePhysicalViews, the QueryBroker matches the keys tagged with white ellipses.

Dynamic Behavior

In Figure 18-15, an application kernel object creates an OrderInvoiceView that processes a read() command. It issues a performQuery command to the Query-Broker. The QueryBroker matches a view description against available services via the matchServices() method. The QueryBroker forwards the request to two different ConcretePhysicalViews: the OrderPhysicalView and the Customer-PhysicalView. These two read() the data from the database and deliver the results, packing the data into result containers. The Broker has to merge both result containers using a joinData method to deliver one result to the Order-InvoiceView. The OrderInvoiceView unpacks the data into its instance variables.

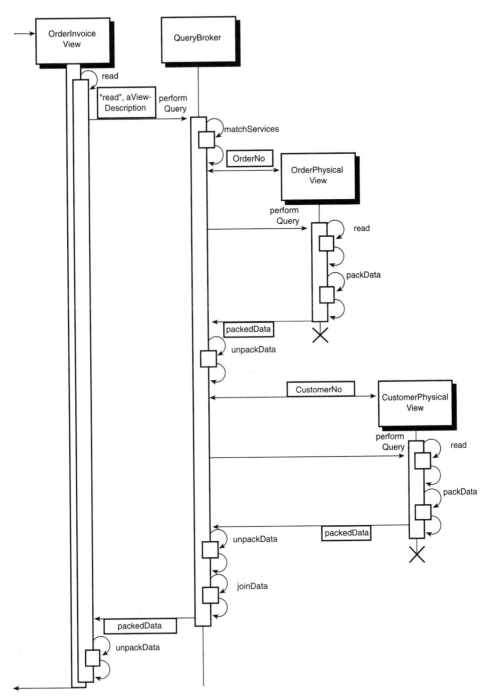

Figure 18-15 *Retrieving data using a* `QueryBroker`

Consequences

- *Flexibility.* The Query Broker decouples Hierarchical Views from Physical Views. New Physical Views may register and the associations to Hierarchical Views may change at runtime.
- *Complexity.* The tree-structured result containers, the request descriptions, and a tree-matching algorithm make the Query Broker complex to design. However, the Broker is well encapsulated, restricting complexity to a single subsystem.
- *Reusability.* Since the Query Broker is independent of the views it connects, you may implement it as part of a framework. This is even better than reusing only the Physical Views or generators.
- *Cost.* The complexity of the Query Broker makes it expensive to implement. A runtime dictionary increases the cost. Implemented in a reusable framework and used in more than one application, the Query Broker will pay off. Hard-coded coupling is cheaper to build but makes optimizations more expensive and causes nightmares when you think about software distribution among several thousand client sites.

Implementation

- *Server Registration.* All `ConcretePhysicalViews` have to register with the `QueryBroker` prior to the first database access. You have to take care of it during system initialization. You may use a runtime dictionary, some other form of registry, or language-specific initialization techniques.
- *Responsibility for Casting Data Types.* There are two choices for casting raw database types to application data types and vice versa. For example, you have to convert a `CHAR(20)` into an `OrderKeyType` and vice versa. You may assign the task of casting to the `ConcreteHierarchicalViews` as well as to the `ConcretePhysicalViews`. A runtime dictionary may support both alternatives if it contains the logical data model and the knowledge of which attributes to cast into which application data types.
- *Tree matching.* Matching the DAGs is similar to code generation in compilers, where you have to find good assembler code for a program. So you may use the corresponding algorithms [Aho+86, section 9.2]. The Broker may even find several query plans for a request, differing in speed. The matching algorithm has to deal with ambiguous derivations and has to find the fastest solution. You have similar problems in optimizing compilers which deal with ambiguous grammars for code generation purposes [Keller91].
- *Query descriptions and result containers.* You have to find a good representation for the DAGs used to describe queries. The Views should be able to specify their requests and services easily. On the other hand, the presentation should conform to the requirements of the matching algorithm. An easy-to-parse textual presentation is a good choice.

Variants

A further refined variant of a Query Broker allows a flexible development process. A Query Broker that can also generate on-the-fly dynamic SQL queries may be used to substitute the `ConcretePhysicalViews` during early development. This works fine for clean database models but becomes hard with Overflow Tables.

In a later phase of development, you add more and more `ConcretePhysicalViews` using static SQL. If even this proves to be too slow, the Physical View implementations can be made even faster using the tuple interface of the database. The Query Broker shields the application kernel from such tuning. It responds to requests with the fastest services it can find in its registry.

Related Patterns

Buschmann provides a comprehensive discussion of Brokers in general [Buschmann+96]. Brown and Whitenack describe a Broker on a per-class basis [Brown+96]. This is similar to the class mappers described by Roger Sessions in his book on CORBA Persistence Services (POS) [Sessions96]. Query Broker is a more general design.

Known Uses

The Query Broker pattern is a compilation of various best practices.

- The VAA data manager defines views in terms of the logical data model [VAA95]. It uses a generated hard-coded coupling of layers. Our experiences at HYPO-Bank taught us to use dynamic descriptions wherever possible [Keller+96, Coldewey+96]. Two projects at sd&m used other important parts of the approach.
- sd&m's LSM project used dynamic SQL, migrated to static SQL, and ended up with a tuple interface. The idea was born of bad experiences with a slow database server. The project makes extensive use of a runtime data dictionary and bridges dynamic queries and precompiled queries completely.
- The Fall/OK project for the German police uses tree matching. The software copes with queries by example on a large data model. The data model changes rapidly.
- CORBA Persistent Object Service also uses a Broker [Sessions96]. Application kernel objects write their instance data to streams, and a Broker (Persistent Object Manager) forwards the stream to some Persistent Object Service (database or other). Persistent Object Services may be arbitrary databases not known to the object. This is also a simple case of a one-to-one mapping between service requests and servers that fulfill them.

ACKNOWLEDGMENTS

We would like to thank Frank Buschmann, our PLoP shepherd, for his great advice and support. We are also obliged to the participants of the BOF workshop at EuroPLoP '96 and to the members of the PLoP '96 writers workshop.

Our colleagues Andreas Mieth, Uli Zeh, and Andreas Wittkowski and many others contributed their profound database knowledge during the review process. David Jenkins and Chad Smith helped improve the language. Wolfgang got many valuable insights from the VAA Data Manager Group and the VAA Architecture Board. Special thanks to Johannes Schlattmann (LVM Versicherungen), Hans Hoffmann and Gerhard Pallauro (both of Württembergische Versicherung), Volker Bohn, and Klaus-Walter Müller (Siemens Nixdorf Information Systems). Finally we thank Ernst Denert and sd&m for making this work possible, and the German Ministry for Research and Technology for funding our project under the contract name ENTSTAND.

REFERENCES

[Aho+86] A. V. Aho, R. Sethi, and J. D. Ullman. *Compilers: Principles, Techniques, and Tools.* Reading, MA: Addison-Wesley, 1986.

[Bis96] J. Bis. *TLR-WGLV - Entwicklerhandbuch Teil II, Systemkonstruktion.* Internal Technical Report, sd&m GmbH & Co. KG, 1996.

[Buschmann+96] F. Buschmann, R. Meunier, H. Rohnert, P. Sommerlad, and M. Stal. *Pattern-Oriented Software Architecture: A System of Patterns.* New York: John Wiley and Sons, 1996.

[Brown+96] K. Brown and B. G. Whitenack. *Crossing Chasms, A Pattern Language for Object-RDBMS Integration.* White Paper, Knowledge Systems Corp. 1995. A shortened version is contained in J. M. Vlissides, J. O. Coplien, and N. L. Kerth (eds.). *Pattern Languages of Program Design 2.* Reading, MA: Addison-Wesley, 1996.

[Coldewey+96] J. Coldewey and W. Keller. "Objektorientierte Datenintegration—ein Migrationsweg zur Objekttechnologie." *Objektspektrum* Juli/August 1996, pp. 20–28.

[Coldewey97] J. Coldewey. "An Access Layer for Object Databases." In A. Chaudri and M. Loomis (eds.), *Object Databases in Practice.* Prentice Hall, 1997 (in press).

[Date94] C. J. Date. *An Introduction to Database Systems, Sixth Edition.* Reading, MA: Addison-Wesley, 1994.

[Denert91] E. Denert. *Software-Engineering.* Springer Verlag, 1991.

[Gamma+95] E. Gamma, R. Helm, R. Johnson, and J. Vlissides. *Design Patterns: Elements of Reusable Object-Oriented Software.* Reading, MA: Addison-Wesley, 1995.

[Gray+93] J. Gray and A. Reuter. *Transaction Processing, Concepts and Techniques.* Morgan Kaufmann Publishers, 1993.

[Keller91] W. Keller. "Automated Generation of Code using Backtracking Parsers for Attribute Grammars." *ACM Sigplan Notices,* Vol. 26(2), 1991.

PART 6

User Interface Patterns

This part contains only one chapter, which is remarkable and puzzling. In a field that has brought us patterns such as Observer, Model-View-Controller, Taskmaster, and so forth, we would have expected this type of pattern to flourish. Aren't there any more user interface patterns to be found? Have we really exhausted this field? Perhaps this is an indication that this field needs more work, and many patterns are still waiting to be discovered.

Chapter 19: A Pattern Language for Developing Form Style Windows, by Mark Bradac and Becky Fletcher.   This chapter presents a set of interconnected patterns that helps to direct the detailed construction of a user interface based upon forms. The patterns in this chapter are compelling and common. The authors discuss how forms should be partitioned, organized, and interrelated. They describe how the coupling between *and* within forms can be minimized. They show how forms can be structured to be dynamically context-sensitive. All in all, this is a good set of guidelines for any engineer of graphical user interfaces to follow.

Chapter 19

A Pattern Language for Developing Form Style Windows

Mark Bradac and Becky Fletcher

A Graphical User Interface (GUI) consists of a window, or collection of windows, that contain interface widgets. The function of a widget is to enable the application user to view, create, update, delete, or invoke operations on application data. (Example widgets include input fields, lists, action buttons.) Often, a particular view of application data is referred to as a "form." A form serves to organize a collection of widgets to perform some sort of operation on data, for example, to collect, view, or edit. Typically, there is one window (or the appearance of a window) per form.

Nontrivial applications may employ many specialized forms to present different views of the same data to different users of the application. For example, one user may need to be able to create, update, and delete a customer billing record while another may be permitted only to view a subset of the captured information. As a consequence, the differences between various forms are often minor; for example, the widgets for viewing customer-sensitive information may be eliminated on all but a few user privileged forms.

The Developing Form Style Windows pattern language addresses how subforms can be employed to manage application form construction and reuse while minimizing the number of discrete windows that need to be built and maintained. Subforms can be implemented using a wide variety of application development tools/environments, such as subcanvases in VisualWorks, group panes in Visual Smalltalk, composite panes in ObjectShare's WindowBuilder, and visual parts in VisualAge [VisualWorks95; ObjectShare96; VisualAge95].

The language consists of five patterns and is depicted in the directed acyclic graph of Figure 19-1.

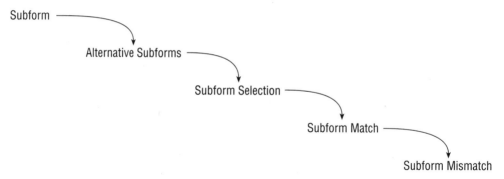

Figure 19-1 *Graph of the Developing Form Style Windows pattern language*

The Subform pattern is used to decompose a form into smaller sections and facilitates the reuse of a subform on multiple forms. Alternative Subforms allows for the dynamic selection of subforms at runtime. The Subform Selection pattern allows a form to select the appropriate subform and use it until it is no longer valid. Subform Match is used to facilitate subform selection, and Subform Mismatch is used to notify the parent form when it is no longer valid.

SUBFORM

Problem

How do you minimize development and maintenance effort when designing form style windows?

Context

A GUI-based application in which forms are used.

Forces

Forms decompose into categories of related data.

- Complex forms (that is, forms with many widgets) often have a significant amount of associated behavior that must be organized, designed, and maintained.
- Designing application forms is time-consuming, subjective, and iterative, requiring multiple prototype reviews with a number of prospective users.
- "People learn more easily by recognition than by recall" [Hobart95]. Therefore presenting a consistent data layout is essential for the user to understand and use an application interface.

• Designing each form from a basic set of widgets is redundant, error prone, and often leads to subtle differences between forms for the presentation of the same information.

Solution

Divide a form into a number of subforms that can be used to construct the window. These subforms should contain groups of widgets to control pieces of related data. Subform can be recursively applied by dividing a "parent" subform into a number of smaller "child" subforms.

Resulting Context

Instead of one form that needs to be customized, you have many smaller, simpler subforms that are easier to understand and maintain. You have also increased your chances of being able to reuse these subforms on future windows. Value-Models can be employed to provide a simple interface between a subform and the data domain [Woolf95]. Subforms can also be used dynamically to alter the appearance of a form at runtime (see Alternative Subforms).

Example

The sketch in Figure 19-2 illustrates the use of a parent Billing Subform composed of two widgets (a list and an action button) and two child subforms: Customer Subform and Address Subform. The Customer Subform contains the widgets that identify a customer by name and account number. The Address Subform contains widgets for a customer's address. Dividing the window into multiple subforms allows for the possible reuse of any of these subforms on other windows.

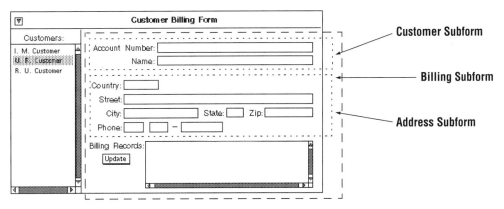

Figure 19-2 *The parent subform (Billing Subform) is composed of two child subforms (Customer Subform and Address Subform).*

ALTERNATIVE SUBFORMS

Problem

How do you design a window where different sets of widgets are needed based on the value of key application state data?

Context

A GUI-based application using Subforms where different sets of data will need to be gathered based on the user's answer to a key question.

Forces

- Providing the widgets for all possible variations on one form can make it appear cluttered and can be hard for users to comprehend.
- Creating multiple forms to handle variations in the data could result in a proliferation of forms that differ by a few widgets.
- Using class inheritance for window creation is straightforward, but it is unalterable at runtime and breaks encapsulation [Snyder86].
- Using composition supports the dynamic creation of forms at runtime but introduces more objects into the system [Gamma+95].

Solution

Compose a form using smaller subforms. Create one subform for each variation of the widgets that change, and alternately select the appropriate subform at runtime based on key application state data that resides in either the parent or child subform. Use Subform Selection to manage the selection of these subforms.

Resulting Context

The composed form will have the appearance of multiple forms without the cost of creating and maintaining separate static forms. The benefits of creating forms using composition outweighs the complexity of an inheritance hierarchy of alternative forms.

Example

The Alternative Subforms pattern is useful for varying the form based on data content. For example, as depicted in Figure 19-3, the Address Subform could be different for customers from different countries. Changing the country field could result in the selection of an entirely different address subform.

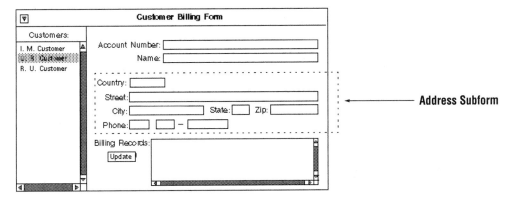

Figure 19-3 *The subform that is selected is based on key application state data. In this example, the country field is maintained by Address Subform.*

SUBFORM SELECTION

Problem

How do you choose from a collection of subforms that become active/inactive based on state data?

Context

A GUI-based application using Alternative Subforms where a change in subform state data results in a change in subform selection.

Forces

- Static assignment of subforms could result in a proliferation of dedicated, specialized, and, therefore, unreusable forms.
- Forms need to conform rapidly to data as it is entered or changed.
- Having the parent subform know about all of its child subforms and which ones should be active breaks encapsulation.
- Subforms are typically selected according to the value (or values) of key application state data.

Solution

Have the parent subform maintain a collection of all child subforms. When there is a change in key application state data, the parent polls each child subform using Subform Match. The most frequently used forms may be ordered at the front of the collection to facilitate rapid search.

Resulting Context

New child subforms can be added to this collection easily without breaking existing behavior. If the key application state data is owned/maintained by the child subform, then the child subform uses Subform Mismatch to notify the parent that it needs to start the polling process to find a new matching subform. During the polling process, the parent will again use Subform Match to find the new matching subform. If the key application state data is owned or maintained by the parent subform, then Subform Selection is used to find the matching subform.

Example

Figure 19-4 depicts an application where the window displays a customer billing form. In this example, the customer selected in the parent window is residential with a U.S. address. The window polls its collection of subforms (Residential Billing Subform and Corporate Billing Subform), and based on the key application state data (the list of customers), the Residential Billing Subform is found to be a match using Subform Match. The Residential Billing Subform, in turn, polls its collection of address subforms (U.S. Address Subform and Foreign Address Subform) to select the appropriate child address subform, that is, the U.S. Address Subform. In summary, the Residential Billing Subform was chosen based on the customer selection; U.S. Address Subform was chosen based on the type of address.

The following Smalltalk code creates the collection of application subforms and makes each subform invisible initially.

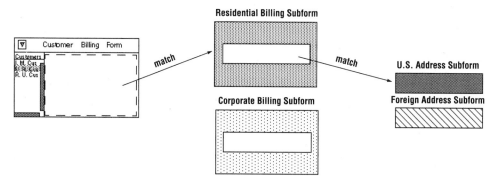

Figure 19-4 *The responsibility for searching through a collection of subforms is delegated to the parent subform. In this example, the Customer Billing Form has two subforms to choose from: the Residential Billing Subform and the Corporate Billing Subform. The Residential Billing Subform in turn has two address subforms to choose from: the U.S. Address Subform and the Foreign Address Subform.*

```
CustomerBillingForm>>initializeSubForms

    allSubforms := List new.
    allSubforms add: (ResidentialBillingSubform newForParent: self).
    allSubforms add: (CorporateBillingSubform newForParent: self).
    allSubforms do: [:each |  (self builder componentAt: each name)
        beInvisible].
    self subforms: allSubforms
```

The following Smalltalk code implements the polling behavior for parent subforms. First, the currently visible subform is made invisible. Then it searches through its collection of subforms looking to detect the matching subform. Finally, the subform is made visible by sending #beVisible to it.

```
CustomerBillingForm>>selectSubform

    (self builder componentAt: self currentSubcanvas name) beInvisible].
    newSubform := (self subforms detect: [:each | each match: self
        selectedCustomer]).
    (self builder componentAt: newSubform name) beVisible]
```

SUBFORM MATCH

Problem

How does the parent subform select the appropriate child subform based on state data located in the parent subform?

Context

A GUI-based application where Subform Selection is used.

Forces

- The number of subforms for a given application may be dynamic.
- Subforms which are composed of a dynamic number of child subforms will need to be selected at runtime.
- Centralized subform selection can be difficult to develop and maintain, particularly when there are numerous forms with complex selection criteria. Selection can also become complex due to the intricacies of application data and the relationship of application data to subform dependencies.
- Only one subform matches the selection criteria at any time.
- Centralized form selection is easier to understand but more difficult to maintain.
- Decentralized (distributed) form selection is more maintainable but more difficult to understand.

Solution

Every time there is a change in key application state data, poll the collection (cache) of subforms and let them identify themselves as a match for the state data. This is accomplished by associating a routine (method) with a subform that is able to test the key application state data for matching criteria.

Resulting Context

Selection is decentralized and distributed to the subforms that understand their state data requirements. Decentralizing simplifies and reduces the impact to the application for adding and updating subforms and associated child subforms. Having parent subforms hold onto their child subforms facilitates rapid search and further reduces complexity.

Subforms can be dynamically added or removed from the system without changing the selection criteria for existing (or remaining) subforms.

Example

Figure 19-5 depicts an application where the window displays a customer billing form. In this example, the customer selected in the parent window is residential with a U.S. address. The selected item in the customer list is the key application state data for selecting the Residential Billing Subform. Changing the country field would result in a different address subform being selected and displayed.

The following Smalltalk code implements the test and notify behavior of the `ResidentialBillingSubform`. The `#isResidential` message validates a match. If a match is detected, the state data (for example, `aCustomer`) is stored by invoking

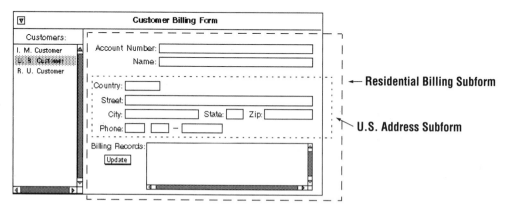

Figure 19-5 *The U.S. Address Subform determines if it matches based on key application state data contained in the country field.*

the `#setSubject:` message, and `#true` is returned to the parent. Otherwise `#false` is returned, indicating there is no match.

```
ResidentialBillingSubform>>match: aCustomer
    (aCustomer isResidential)
        ifTrue:
            [self setSubject: aCustomer.
             ^true]
        ifFalse: [^false]
```

Related Patterns

Subform Match is similar to State in that only one subform will match key application state data at any given time [Gamma+95, p. 62]. It is unlike State in that there is no implied state ordering.

SUBFORM MISMATCH

Problem

How does the parent subform determine when a child subform no longer applies based on a change of state data in the child subform?

Context

A GUI-based application where subforms are selected using Subform Match, and key application state data resides with the child subform.

Forces

- Key application state data for a child subform can change as data is entered or edited by the user.
- Polling the subforms for applicability wastes CPU resources and potentially allows ambiguous conditions to exist in the application for the duration of the polling interval.
- Centralized subform deselection can be difficult to develop and maintain, particularly when there are numerous forms with complex selection criteria. Selection can also become complex due to the intricacies of application data and the relationship of application data to subform dependencies.

Solution

Have the subform notify its parent when it no longer matches the selection criteria, that is, when there is a mismatch. This is easily accomplished by retesting matching criteria each time there is any change in key application state data maintained by the child subform.

Resulting Context

Deselection is decentralized and distributed to the subform that understands its state data requirements. Decentralizing simplifies and reduces the impact on the application for adding and updating subforms. Since parent subforms hold onto their child subforms, it facilitates rapid search and further reduces complexity.

Example

In this example, if the user changes the country for the selected customer to a foreign address, the child U.S. Address Subform sends #mismatch to the parent Residen-tialBillingSubform (see Figure 19-6). At this point, the ResidentialBillingSub-form polls for a matching address subform using Subform Selection.

The following Smalltalk code implements the test and notify behavior for the USAddressSubform. The #stateChange message tests for a match, and in the event of a mismatch, it notifies the parent form by sending a #mismatch message. The #mismatch message of ResidentialBillingSubform simply sends #selectsub-form to itself to select the appropriate subform.

```
USAddressSubform>>stateChange
    self countryIsUS
        ifFalse: [self parent mismatch]

ResidentialBillingSubform>>mismatch
    self selectSubform
```

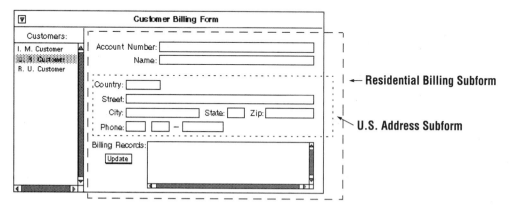

Figure 19-6 *The child U.S. Address Subform sends* #mismatch *to the parent Residential Billing Subform when the country field changes.*

SUMMARY

The Developing Form Style Windows pattern language presents a systematic approach to the construction and decomposition of application form style windows. Interface widgets are factored into a number of reusable components that are subsequently used to construct multiple application windows. Thus the pattern language facilitates reuse while minimizing the number of discrete components that need to be developed and maintained, making the application easier to understand and extend. The language adheres to the underlying premise that "many objects that do little are better than few objects that do too much" [Deugo+96].

ACKNOWLEDGMENTS

The authors would like to thank Bobby Woolf who gave us valuable insight into the content and organization of this pattern language. Additional thanks goes to all the members of the PLoP '96 Frameworks and Architectures workshop for their helpful feedback.

REFERENCES

[Deugo+96] D. Deugo and W. Beaton. "Managing Connection Complexity." In *The Smalltalk Report.* September 1996.

[Gamma+95] E. Gamma, R. Helm, R. Johnson, and J. Vlissides. *Design Patterns: Elements of Reusable Object-Oriented Software.* Reading, MA: Addison-Wesley, 1995.

[Hobart95] J. Hobart. "Principles of Good GUI Design." In *UNIX Review.* September 1995.

[ObjectShare96] *WindowBuilder Pro/V,* ObjectShare a division of ParcPlace-Digitalk, Inc. 1996.

[Snyder86] A. Synder. "Encapsulation and Inheritance in Object-Oriented Languages." In *Object-Oriented Programming Systems, Languages, and Applications Conference Proceedings.* Portland, OR: ACM Press, November 1986, pp. 38–45.

[VisualAge95] *VisualAge for Smalltalk—User's Reference*, Version 3.0. IBM, Inc., 1995.

[VisualWorks95] *VisualWorks Cookbook.* ParcPlace-Digitalk, Inc., 1995.

[Woolf95] B. Woolf. "Understanding and Using the ValueModel Framework in VisualWorks Smalltalk." In *Pattern Languages of Program Design,* James O. Coplien and Douglas C. Schmidt, eds. Reading, MA: Addison-Wesley, 1995.

Mark Bradac and Becky Fletcher can be reached at bradac@lucent.com **and** rlfletcher@lucent.com**, respectively.**

PART 7

Programming Patterns

The patterns in this book address many issues, both strategic and tactical. They range from the high-level architecture patterns in Part 3 to the low-level programming patterns of this section.

Programming patterns address daily programming matters. They tell you how to implement the many strategic and tactical decisions you make during system development. However, being of a low level nature does not mean that they are unimportant. Quite the opposite is true! Bugs that break systems occur at the programming level. There may be higher-level reasons why systems fail to meet their requirements, and these are usually much harder to solve than programming bugs; however, most system failures boil down to malfunctioning code. The unanticipated breakdowns and the all-too-familiar core dumps or protection violations are the result of erroneous programs.

Programming patterns are intended to prevent these kinds of problems. A programming pattern describes how to solve a specific programming problem, such that the problem is resolved properly within its context. The code becomes well focused and is usually easier to understand, to adapt, and to change.

Chapter 20: Double-Checked Locking, by Douglas C. Schmidt and Tim Harrison. Drawing on their experiences in designing and implementing concurrent systems, the authors demonstrate that the canonical implementation of the ubiquitous Singleton pattern [Gamma+95] can fail in subtle ways when applied in multithreaded environments. A Singleton is an object that exists only once; it is the sole instance of its class.

Doug and Tim show that in multithreaded systems, the access operation that retrieves the Singleton poses unanticipated problems. Usually, the Singleton access operation is implemented as a "lazy creation" operation, which means that the actual object creation is delayed until the object is first accessed. In multithreaded systems, however, this access must be made thread-safe. One way to accomplish this is to put a mutual-exclusion lock around the whole creation operation, turning it into a critical section. To avoid the performance degradation that would result from this excessive locking, the critical section should be guarded by checking whether the object had already been created. This must be done twice, once before acquiring the lock, and once after releasing the lock, to avoid subtle race conditions and to incur the cost of locking only when the Singleton is first created.

The motivation for documenting the Double-Checked Locking pattern is interesting. Doug and Tim explain how they discovered the pattern by tracking down a subtle bug in their multithreaded Singleton implementation. In fact, they explain the pattern by first giving an antipattern example (the faulty implementation they first chose). This mirrors the common sense we learn by reflecting on our failures. By documenting antipatterns, we can better understand the resulting patterns that resolve problems.

Chapter 21: External Polymorphism, by Chris Cleeland, Douglas C. Schmidt, and Tim Harrison. This paper presents a pattern that is structurally similar to the Adapter pattern [Gamma+95]. The pattern's purpose is to let clients utilize classes in a polymorphic manner, even though the classes may not be related by inheritance.

The pattern is C++-specific and makes extensive use of C++ language features like templates and stand-alone functions. This avoids much of the tedious programming effort required to implement general adapters. To work properly, the pattern expects that the classes to be adapted have interfaces that differ only in their syntax. Then it becomes possible to bridge between the externally imposed interface and the adapted classes using very simple implementations.

Summary. The second pattern in this part has brought attention to another interesting aspect of programming patterns: They may or may not be programming language–specific. The Double-Checked Locking pattern is clearly independent of a specific programming language, while the External Polymorphism pattern explicitly leverages C++-specific programming features.

There are at least three books which explore programming language–specific idioms and patterns, one for C++ [Coplien92], one for Smalltalk [Beck96], and one for Java [Lea96]. In the future, we can expect to see many more of them.

REFERENCES

[Beck96] K. Beck. *Smalltalk Best Practice Patterns.* Englewood Cliffs, NJ: Prentice Hall, 1996.

[Coplien92] J. O. Coplien. *Advanced C++ Programming Styles and Idioms.* Reading, MA: Addison-Wesley, 1992.

[Gamma+95] E. Gamma, R. Johnson, R. Helm, and J. Vlissides. *Design Patterns: Elements of Reusable Object-Oriented Software.* Reading, MA: Addison-Wesley, 1995.

[Lea96] Doug Lea. *Concurrent Programming in Java.* Reading, MA: Addison-Wesley, 1996.

Chapter 20

Double-Checked Locking

Douglas C. Schmidt and Tim Harrison

This chapter shows how the canonical implementation of the Singleton pattern does not work correctly in the presence of preemptive multitasking or true parallelism [Gamma+95]. To solve this problem, we present the Double-Checked Locking optimization pattern. This pattern is useful for reducing contention and synchronization overhead whenever critical sections of code should be executed just once. In addition, Double-Checked Locking illustrates how changes in underlying forces (that is, adding multithreading and parallelism to the common Singleton use-case) can impact the form and content of patterns used to develop concurrent software.

Intent

The Double-Checked Locking optimization pattern reduces contention and synchronization overhead whenever critical sections of code need to acquire locks just once, but must be thread-safe when they do acquire locks.

Also known as

Lock Hint [Birrell89]

Motivation

Developing correct and efficient concurrent applications is hard. Programmers must learn new mechanisms (such as multithreading and synchronization APIs) and techniques (such as concurrency control and deadlock avoidance algorithms). In addition, many familiar design patterns (such as Singleton or Iterator) that work well for sequential programs contain subtle assumptions that do not apply in the context of concurrency. To illustrate this, we will examine how the canonical implementation of the Singleton pattern behaves in multithreaded environments [Gamma+95].

The Canonical Singleton. The Singleton pattern ensures a class has only one instance and provides a global point of access to that instance. Dynamically allocating Singletons in C++ programs is common since the order of initialization of global static objects in C++ programs is not well defined and is therefore non-portable. Moreover, dynamic allocation avoids the cost of initializing a Singleton if it is never used [Gamma+95].

Defining a Singleton is straightforward.

```
class Singleton
{
public:
  static Singleton *instance (void)
  {
    if (instance_ == 0)
      // Critical section.
      instance_ = new Singleton;

    return instance_;
  }

  void method (void);
  // Other methods and members omitted.

private:
  static Singleton *instance_;
};
```

Application code uses the static `Singleton::instance` method to retrieve a reference to the `Singleton` before performing operations, as follows:

```
// ...
Singleton::instance()->method();
// ...
```

The Problem: Race Conditions. Unfortunately, the canonical implementation of the Singleton pattern shown above does not work in the presence of preemptive multitasking or true parallelism. For instance, if multiple threads executing on a parallel machine invoke `Singleton::instance` simultaneously before it is initialized, the `Singleton` constructor can be called multiple times because multiple threads will execute the `new Singleton` operation within the critical section shown above.

A *critical section* is a sequence of instructions that obeys the following invariant: While one thread/process is executing in the critical section, no other thread/process may be executing in the critical section [Tanenbaum 95]. In this example, the initialization of the `Singleton` is a critical section. Violating the properties of the critical section will, at best, cause a memory leak and, at worst, have disastrous consequences if initialization is not idempotent.[1]

Common Traps and Pitfalls. A common way to implement a critical section is to add a static `Mutex` to the class.[2] This `Mutex` ensures that the allocation and initialization of the `Singleton` occurs atomically.

```
class Singleton
{
public:
  static Singleton *instance (void)
  {
    // Constructor of guard acquires
    // lock_ automatically.
    Guard<Mutex> guard (lock_);

    // Only one thread in the
    // critical section at a time.

    if (instance_ == 0)
      instance_ = new Singleton;

    return instance_;
    // Destructor of guard releases
    // lock_ automatically.
  }

private:
  static Mutex lock_;
  static Singleton *instance_;
};
```

The `Guard` class employs a C++ idiom, as described by Stroustrup, that uses the constructor to acquire a resource automatically when an object of the class is created, and uses the destructor to release the resource automatically when it goes out of scope. Since `Guard` is parameterized by the type of lock (such as `Mutex`), this class can be used with a family of synchronization wrappers that conform to a uniform acquire/release interface. By using `Guard`, every access to `Singleton::instance` will automatically acquire and release the `lock_`.

Even though the critical section should be executed just once, every call to instance must acquire and release the `lock_`. Although this implementation is

---

[1] Object initialization is idempotent if an object can be reinitialized multiple times without ill effects.
[2] A mutex is a lock which can be acquired and released. If multiple threads attempt to acquire the lock simultaneously, only one thread will succeed; the others will block [Tanenbaum92].

now thread-safe, the overhead from the excessive locking may be unacceptable. One obvious (though incorrect) optimization is to place the `Guard` inside the conditional check of `instance_`:

```
static Singleton *instance (void)
{
  if (instance_ == 0) {
    Guard<Mutex> guard (lock_);

    // Only come here if instance_
    // hasn't been initialized yet.

    instance_ = new Singleton;
  }
  return instance_;
}
```

This reduces locking overhead it, but doesn't provide thread-safe initialization. There is still a race condition in multithreaded applications that can cause multiple initializations of `instance_`. For example, consider two threads that simultaneously check for `instance_ == 0`. Both will succeed, one will acquire the `lock_` via the `guard`, and the other will block. After the first thread initializes the `Singleton` and releases the `lock_`, the blocked thread will obtain the `lock_` and erroneously initialize the `Singleton` for a second time.

The Solution: The Double-Checked Locking Optimization. A better way to solve this problem is to use Double-Checked Locking, which is a pattern for optimizing away unnecessary locking. Ironically, the Double-Checked Locking solution is almost identical to the previous one. Unnecessary locking is avoided by wrapping the call to `new` with another conditional test.

```
class Singleton
{
public:
  static Singleton *instance (void)
  {
    // First check
    if (instance_ == 0)
    {
      // Ensure serialization (guard
      // constructor acquires lock_).
      Guard<Mutex> guard (lock_);

      // Double check.
      if (instance_ == 0)
        instance_ = new Singleton;
    }
```

```
    return instance_;
    // guard destructor releases lock_.
  }

private:
  static Mutex lock_;
  static Singleton *instance_;
};
```

The first thing that acquires the `lock_` will construct `Singleton` and assign the pointer to `instance_`. All threads that subsequently call `instance` will find `instance_ != 0` and skip the initialization step. The second check prevents a race condition if multiple threads try to initialize the `Singleton` simultaneously. This handles the case where multiple threads execute in parallel. In the code above, these threads will queue up at `lock_`. When the queued threads finally obtain the mutex `lock_`, they will find `instance_ != 0` and skip the initialization of `Singleton`.

The implementation of `Singleton::instance` above only incurs locking overhead for threads that are active inside of `instance` when the `Singleton` is first initialized. In subsequent calls to `Singleton::instance`, `singleton_` is not 0 and the `lock_` is not acquired or released.

By adding a `Mutex` and a second conditional check, the canonical Singleton implementation can be made thread-safe without incurring any locking overhead after initialization has occurred. It's instructive to note how the need for Double-Checked Locking emerged from a change in forces, that is, the addition of multi-threading and parallelism to Singleton. However, the optimization is also applicable for nonSingleton use-cases, as described below.

Applicability

Use the Double-Checked Locking pattern when an application has the following characteristics.

- The application has one or more critical sections of code that must execute sequentially;
- Multiple threads can potentially attempt to execute the critical section simultaneously;
- The critical section is executed just once;
- Acquiring a lock on every access to the critical section causes excessive overhead;
- It is possible to use a lightweight, yet reliable, conditional test in lieu of a lock.

Structure and Participants

The structure and participants of the Double-Checked Locking pattern is best shown with pseudocode. Figure 20-1 illustrates the following participants in the Double-Checked Locking pattern.

- *Just-Once-Critical-Section.* The critical section contains code that is executed just once. For instance, a Singleton is typically initialized only once. Thus, the call to new Singleton in the Motivation section is executed rarely, relative to the accesses to Singleton::instance.
- *Mutex.* A lock that serializes access to the critical section of code. Using the Singleton example from the Motivation section, the Mutex ensures that new Singleton only occurs once.
- *Flag.* A flag that indicates whether the Critical Section has been executed already. In the Singleton example, the instance_ pointer is used as the flag. If, in addition to signaling that the event occurred, the Flag is used for an application-specific reason (as in the Singleton example), it must be an atomic type that can be set without interruption. This issue is discussed in the Variations section.
- *Application Thread.* This is the thread that attempts to perform the Critical Section. It is implicit in the pseudocode in Figure 20-1.

```
if (Flag == FALSE)
    {
        Mutex.acquire ();
        if (Flag == FALSE)
            {
                critical section;
                Flag = TRUE;
            }
        Mutex.release ();
    }
```

Figure 20-1 *Structure and participants in the Double-Checked Locking pattern*

Collaborations

Figure 20-2 illustrates the interactions between the participants of the Double-Checked Locking pattern. The Application Thread first checks to see if the flag has been set as an optimization for the common case. If it has not been set, the mutex is acquired. While holding the lock, the Application Thread again checks that the flag is set, performs the Just-Once-Critical-Section, and sets the flag to true. Finally, the Application Thread releases the lock.

Consequences

There are several advantages of using the Double-Checked Locking pattern:

* *Minimized locking.* By performing two flag checks, the Double-Checked Locking pattern optimizes for the common case. Once the flag is set, the first check ensures that subsequent access requires no locking. The Performance section shows how this can affect application performance.

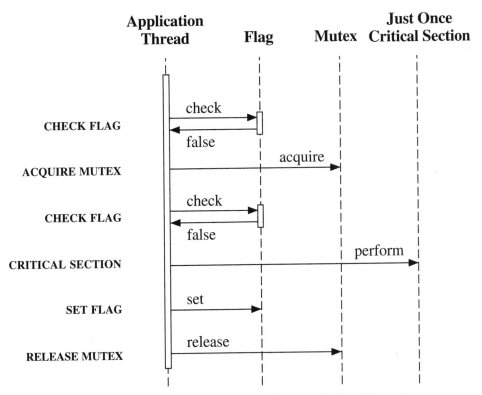

Figure 20-2 *Participant collaborations in the Double-Checked Locking pattern*

- **Prevents race conditions.** The second check of the flag ensures that the event is performed only once.

There is also a disadvantage to using the Double-Checked Locking pattern:

- **Potential for subtle portability bugs.** There is a subtle portability issue that can lead to pernicious bugs if the Double-Checked Locking pattern is used in software that is ported to hardware platforms that have nonatomic pointer or integral assignment semantics. For example, if an `instance_` pointer is used as the flag in the implementation of a `Singleton`, all the bits of the `Singleton::instance_` pointer must be both read and written in single operations. If the write to memory resulting from the call to `new` is not atomic, other threads may try to read an invalid pointer. This would likely result in an illegal memory access. Such a scenario is possible on systems where memory addresses straddle alignment boundaries, thereby requiring two fetches from memory for each access. In this case, it may be necessary to use a separate, word-aligned integral flag (assuming that the hardware supports atomic integral reads and writes), instead of using the `instance_` pointer.

Implementation and Sample Code

The ACE toolkit uses the Double-Checked Locking pattern in several library components [Schmidt94]. For instance, to reduce code duplication, ACE uses a reusable adapter `ACE_Singleton` to transform "normal" classes to Singleton-like behavior. The following code shows how the implementation of `ACE_Singleton` uses the Double-Checked Locking pattern.

```
// A Singleton Adapter: uses the Adapter
// pattern to turn ordinary classes into
// Singletons optimized with the
// Double-Checked Locking pattern.
template <class TYPE, class LOCK>
class ACE_Singleton
{
public:
  static TYPE *instance (void);

protected:
  static TYPE *instance_;
  static LOCK lock_;
};

template <class TYPE, class LOCK>
ACE_Singleton<TYPE, LOCK>
```

```
{
  // Perform the Double-Checked Locking to
  // ensure proper initialization.
  if (instance_ == 0) {
    ACE_Guard<LOCK> lock (lock_);
    if (instance_ == 0)
      instance_ = new TYPE;
  }
  return instance_;
}
```

ACE_Singleton is parameterized by TYPE and LOCK. Therefore, a class of the given TYPE is converted into a Singleton using a mutex of LOCK type.

One usage of ACE_Singleton is in the ACE Token_Manager. The Token_Manager performs deadlock detection for local or remote tokens (such as mutexes and readers/writers locks) in multithreaded applications. To minimize resource usage, the Token_Manager is created on-demand when first referenced through its instance method. To create a Singleton Token_Manager simply requires the following typedef.

```
typedef ACE_Singleton <ACE_Token_Manager,
                       ACE_Thread_Mutex>
        Token_Mgr;
```

The Token_Mgr Singleton is used to detect deadlock within local and remote token objects. Before a thread blocks waiting for a mutex, it first queries the Token_Mgr Singleton to test if blocking would result in a deadlock situation. For each token in the system, the Token_Mgr maintains a record listing the token's owning thread and all blocked threads waiting for the token. This data is sufficient to test for a deadlock situation. The use of the Token_Mgr Singleton is shown below.

```
// Acquire the mutex.
int Mutex_Token::acquire (void)
{
  // ...
  // If the token is already held, we must block.
  if (mutex_in_use ()) {
    // Use the Token_Mgr Singleton to check
    // for a deadlock situation *before* blocking.
    if (Token_Mgr::instance ()->testdeadlock ()) {
      errno = EDEADLK;
      return -1;
    }
```

```
    else
      // Sleep waiting for the lock...
  }
  // Acquire lock...
}
```

Note that the ACE_Singleton can be parameterized by the type of Mutex used to acquire and release the lock (for example, Singleton<ACE_Thread_Mutex>). This allows ACE_Singleton to be parameterized with an ACE_Null_Mutex for single-threaded platforms and a regular ACE_Thread_Mutex for multithreaded platforms.

Evaluation

The previous example highlights some advantages to the ACE_Singleton implementation.

- *Avoids implementation errors.* Reusing the thread-safe algorithm for Singletons in ACE_Singleton guarantees that the Double-Checked Locking pattern is applied.
- *Adapts non-Singletons.* Classes that were not originally implemented as Singletons can be adapted without altering code. This is especially useful when the source code is not accessible.

There is also a disadvantage with this implementation:

- *Intent violation.* Use of ACE_Singleton does not ensure that a class has only one instance. For example, there is nothing to prevent multiple Token_Managers from being created. When possible, it may be safer to modify the class implementation directly rather than using the ACE_Singleton adapter.

Performance Tests. To illustrate the potential performance gains of implementing the Double-Checked Locking pattern we've profiled the access to various implementations of Singleton. For these tests, we used the following implementations.

- *Mutex Singleton.* This implementation of Singleton acquired a mutex lock for every call to the instance accessor.
- *Double-Checked Singleton.* This implementation used the Double-Checked Locking pattern to eliminate unnecessary lock acquisition.
- *ACE Singleton.* This implementation of Singleton employs ACE_Singleton, which is a template that uses the Double-Checked Locking pattern, to test for any overhead associated with the additional abstraction.

Each of the tests used the following algorithm.

```
timer.start ();
for (i = 0; i < 100000000; i++)
  My_Singleton::instance ()->do_nothing ();
timer.stop ();
```

The code for all of these tests are available at `http://www.cs.wustl.edu/ schmidt/ACE_wrappers/performance-tests/Misc/test_singleton.cpp`. The table below shows results from an UltraSparc 2, with two 70 MHz processors, and 256 MB memory. The following are the optimized performance results.

Singleton Implementation	Mutex	Double-Checked	ACE
Real time (secs)	442.64	30.22	30.88
User time (secs)	441.47	30.12	30.86
System time (secs)	0	0	0
Time per call (usecs)	4.43	0.30	0.31

These results illustrate the performance impact of using the Double-Checked Locking pattern compared with the standard practice of acquiring and releasing a lock on every `instance` call. Both the `ACE_Singleton` and hand-coded implementations of the Double-Checked Locking pattern are more than 15 times faster than the standard mutex version. These tests were run with only a single thread to compute the baseline overhead. If multiple threads were contending for the lock, the performance of the mutex implementation would decrease even more.

Variations

A variation to the implementation of the Double-Checked Locking pattern may be required if the compiler optimizes the flag by caching it in some way (for instance, storing the flag in a register). In this case, cache coherency may become a problem if copies of the flag held in registers in multiple threads become inconsistent. In this case, one thread's setting of the value might not be reflected in other threads' copies. One solution may be to declare the flag as a `volatile` data member in the `Singleton`. This ensures that the compiler will not place it into a register.

Known Uses

- The Doubled-Checked Locking pattern is a special case of a very widely used pattern in the Sequent Dynix/PTX operating system.
- The Double-Checked Locking Pattern can be used to implement POSIX ONCE variables [IEEE96].
- Double-Checked Locking pattern is used extensively throughout the ACE object-oriented network programming toolkit [Schmidt94].
- Andrew Birrell describes the use of the Double-Checked Locking optimization in *An Introduction to Programming with Threads* [Birrell89]. Birrell refers to the first check of the flag as a lock "hint."

Related Patterns

The Double-Checked Locking pattern is a thread-safe variant of the First-Time-In idiom, which is often used in programming languages (like C) that lack constructors. The following code illustrates this pattern.

```
static const int STACK_SIZE = 1000;
static T *stack_;
static int top_;

void push (T *item)
{
  // First-time-in flag
  if (stack_ == 0) {
    stack_ =
      malloc (STACK_SIZE * sizeof *stack);
    assert (stack_ != 0);
    top_ = 0;
  }
  stack_[top_++] = item;
  // ...
}
```

The first time that push is called stack_ is 0, which triggers its initialization via malloc.

ACKNOWLEDGMENTS

Thanks to Jim Coplien, Ralph Johnson, Jaco van der Merwe, Duane Murphy, Paul McKenney, and Peter Sommerlad for their suggestions and comments on the Double-Checked Locking pattern.

REFERENCES

[Birrell89] A. D. Birrell. *An Introduction to Programming with Threads.* Technical report. Maynard, MA: Digital Equipment Corporation, 1989.

[Gamma+95] E. Gamma, R. Helm, R. Johnson, and J. Vlissides. *Design Patterns: Elements of Reusable Object-Oriented Software.* Reading, MA: Addison-Wesley, 1995.

[IEEE96] "Threads Extension for Portable Operating Systems." *(Draft 10). IEEE Journal,* February 1996.

[Schmidt94] D. C. Schmidt. "ACE: an Object-Oriented Framework for Developing Distributed Applications," in *Proceedings of the 6th USENIX C++ Technical Conference.* Cambridge, MA: USENIX Association, 1994.

[Stroustrup91] B. Stroustrup. *The C++ Programming Language, 2nd Edition.* Reading, MA: Addison-Wesley, 1991.

[Tanenbaum92] A. S. Tanenbaum. *Modern Operating Systems.* Englewood Cliffs, NJ: Prentice Hall, 1992.

[Tanenbaum95] A. S. Tanenbaum. *Distributed Operating Systems.* Englewood Cliffs, NJ: Prentice Hall, 1995.

Douglas C. Schmidt and Tim Harrison can be reached at schmidt@cs.wustl.edu **and** harrison@cs.wustl.edu**, respectively.**

Chapter 21

External Polymorphism

Chris Cleeland, Douglas C. Schmidt, and Tim Harrison

This chapter describes the External Polymorphism pattern, which allows classes that are not related by inheritance and/or have no virtual methods to be treated polymorphically. This pattern capitalizes on C++ language features and other core patterns (for example, Adapter and Decorator) to give the appearance of polymorphic behavior on otherwise unrelated classes. The pattern has been used in a range of C++ frameworks such as ACE and the OSE class libraries.

Intent

Allow C++ classes unrelated by inheritance and/or having no virtual methods to be treated polymorphically. These unrelated classes can be treated uniformly by application software.

Motivation

Working with C++ classes from different libraries and frameworks can be difficult. Often applications may wish to project common behavior on such classes, but they are restricted by the existing design of the classes. If the classes interfaces are the only aspects that require adaptation, a common solution is to apply an object structural pattern like Adapter or Decorator [Gamma+95]. However, when there are more complex requirements (such as the need to change both the interface and the implementation), classes that are otherwise unrelated may need to behave as if they shared a common ancestor.

For instance, consider the case where we are debugging an application composed of classes from various C++ libraries. It would be convenient to ask any instance to dump a humanly readable format of its state to a file or console display.

It would be even more convenient to gather all live objects into a collection, iterate over that collection, and ask each instance to dump itself.

Since these collections of objects are homogeneous, a common base class must exist to manipulate the collections polymorphically. Because the library classes are already designed, implemented, and in use, however, modifying the inheritance tree to introduce a common base class may not be an option (for example, we may not have access to the source). Moreover, classes in hybrid OO languages like C++ or Ada95 may be concrete data types [Stroustrup91], which require strict storage layouts that can be compromised by hidden pointers (such as a C++ virtual table pointer). Reimplementing concrete classes with a common polymorphic base class may not be feasible.

Therefore, projecting common behavior on unrelated classes requires the resolution of the following forces that constrain the solution.

- *Space efficiency.* The solution must not constrain the storage layout of existing objects. In particular, classes that have no virtual methods (that is, concrete data types) must not be forced to add a virtual table pointer.
- *Polymorphism.* All library objects must be accessed in a uniform, transparent manner. In particular, if new classes are included in the system, existing code should not change.

Consider the following example that uses classes from the ACE network programming framework [Schmidt92].

```
1. SOCK_Acceptor acceptor; // Global storage
2.
3. int main (void) {
4.    SOCK_Stream stream; // Automatic storage
5.    INET_Addr *addr =
6.      new INET_Addr // Dynamic storage.
7.    ...
```

The SOCK_Stream, SOCK_Acceptor, and INET_Addr classes are all concrete data types since they don't all inherit from a common ancestor or contain virtual functions. If during a debugging session an application wants to examine the state of all live ACE objects at line 7, we might get the following output.

```
Sock_Stream::this = 0x47c393ab, handle_ = {-1}
SOCK_Acceptor::this = 0x2c49a45b, handle_ = {-1}
INET_Addr::this = 0x3c48a432, port_ = {0}, addr_ = {0.0.0.0}
```

An effective way to add the capability to dump the state of these objects without modifying their binary layout is to use the External Polymorphism pattern. This pattern constructs a parallel, external inheritance hierarchy that projects polymorphic behavior onto a set of concrete classes that need not be related by inheritance.

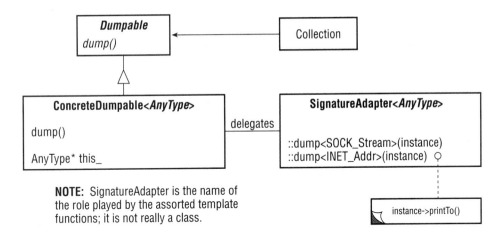

Figure 21-1 *Creating a Parallel Class hierarchy using External Polymorphism*

The following OMT diagram illustrates how the External Polymorphism pattern can be used to create the external, parallel hierarchy of classes.

As shown in Figure 21-1, we define an abstract class (`Dumpable`) having the desired `dump` interface. The parameterized class `ConcreteDumpable<>` inherits from `Dumpable` and contains a pointer to an instance of its parameter class, such as `SOCK_Stream`. In addition, `ConcreteDumpable<>` defines a body for `dump` that delegates to the `dump<>` template function (shown in the figure as the `Signature-Adapter<>` pseudo-class and parameterized over the concrete class). The dump template function calls the corresponding implementation method on the concrete class, for example, `SOCK_Stream::dump` or `INET_Addr::printTo`.

By using the External Polymorphism pattern, it is now possible to collect `Dumpable` instances and iterate over them, calling the `dump` method uniformly on each instance. Note that the original ACE concrete data types need not change.

Applicability

Use the External Polymorphism pattern when (a) your class libraries contain concrete data types, which cannot inherit from a common base class that contains virtual methods; and (b) the behavior of your class libraries or applications can be simplified significantly if you treat all objects polymorphically.

Do not use the External Polymorphism pattern when (a) your class libraries already contain abstract data types that inherit from common base classes and contain virtual methods; or (b) your programming language or programming environment allows methods to be added to classes dynamically.

Structure and Participants

Figure 21-2 depicts the general structure and participants of the External Polymorphism pattern.

- **Common (Dumpable):**
    - This abstract class forms the base of the external, parallel hierarchy of classes and defines the interface(s) whose behaviors will be projected polymorphically and used by clients.

- **ConcreteCommon<ConcreteType> (ConcreteDumpable):**
    - This parameterized subclass of Common implements the interface(s) defined in Common. A typical implementation will simply forward the call to the appropriate SignatureAdapter template function.

- **SignatureAdapter::request<ConcreteType> (::dump<>):**
    - This template function adapter forwards requests to the object. In some cases, this feature may not be needed, for example, where the signature of specificRequest is consistent. However, if specificRequest has different signatures within several Concrete classes, the SignatureAdapter can shield ConcreteCommon from these differences.

- **ConcreteType:**
    - The ConcreteType classes define specificRequest operations that perform the desired tasks. Although Concrete classes need not be related by inheritance, the External Polymorphism pattern makes it possible to treat all or some of their methods polymorphically.

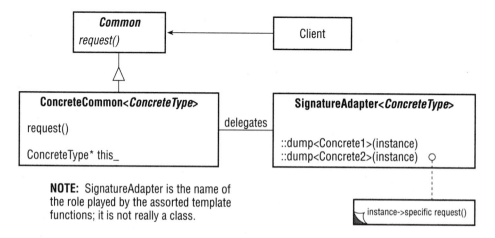

Figure 21-2 *Structure and participants of the External Polymorphism Pattern*

Collaborations

The External Polymorphism pattern is typically used by having an external client make requests through the polymorphic `Common*`. Figure 21-3 illustrates this collaboration.

Many examples of the External Polymorphism pattern maintain a collection of objects that the program iterates over, treating all collected objects uniformly. Although this is not strictly part of the pattern, it is a common-use case.

Consequences

The External Polymorphism pattern has the following benefits.

- *Transparency.* Classes that were not originally designed to work together can be extended transparently so they can be treated polymorphically. In particular, the object layout of existing classes need not change by adding virtual pointers.
- *Flexibility.* It's possible to polymorphically extend nonextensible data types (such as `int` or `double`) when the pattern is implemented in a language supporting parameterized types (for example, C++ or Ada95).
- *Nonintrusive.* Because the External Polymorphism pattern establishes itself on the fringes of existing classes, it's easy to use conditional compilation to remove all traces of this pattern from the source code. This feature is particularly useful for systems that use the External Polymorphism pattern solely for debugging.

However, this pattern also has the following drawbacks.

- *Instability.* The methods in the `Common` and `ConcreteCommon` must track changes to methods in the `Concrete` classes. This is most likely to happen when the optional signature adapter is not used and a method signature changes. However, instability can also occur when polymorphic methods are added to `Concrete`.

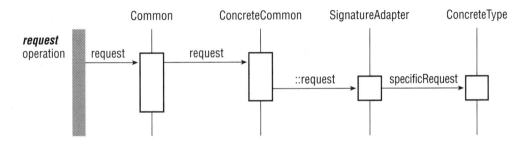

Figure 21-3 *Object interaction diagram of participants*

- *Inefficiency.* Extra overhead occurs due to multiple forwarding from virtual methods in the ConcreteCommon object to the corresponding methods in the Concrete object. Judicious use of inline (for example, within Signature-Adapter and Concrete) can reduce this overhead to a single virtual method dispatch.

There is another consideration when using this pattern:

- *Possibility of inconsistency.* Externally Polymorphic methods are not accessible through pointers to the concrete classes. For instance, using the example in the Motivation section, it's not possible to access dump through a pointer to SOCK_Stream. In addition, it's not possible to access other methods from the concrete class through a pointer to ConcreteCommon.

Implementation

This section describes the steps required to implement the External Polymorphism pattern by factoring behaviors into an abstract base class and implementing those behaviors in descendant concrete classes.

1. *Identify common polymorphic functionality and define it in an abstract base class.* Factor the desired shared behaviors into an abstract base class.[1] This class simply specifies an interface (that is, not an implementation) for the behaviors.

```
class Polymorphic_Object
{
public:
  virtual void operation1() = 0;
  virtual void operation2() = 0;
  ...
}
```

2. *(optional) Define a signature adapter for each behavior method.* The abstract base in Step #1 defines the signatures of the behaviors. The actual implementation of the behavior will differ (as one might expect) from concrete class to concrete class. Also, the names of interfaces to actual implementations may differ. For the latter case, access to the implementation of each shared behavior can be provided through a template wrapper function, such as

```
template <class T> void
operation1 (const T *t)
{
  t->operation_impl (...someargs...);
}
```

---

[1] In some cases it may be desirable to define more than one abstract class, grouping related behaviors by class.

This signature adapter provides a generic, default access point to an implementation named `operation_impl`. Likewise, the approach could be applied for `operation2`, and any other shared behaviors defined in the `Polymorphic_Object` class.

Names of class interfaces may differ, as well. In situations where `operation_impl` is not the correct interface name for some class `T`, a special-case access point can be provided. Consider a class `T1` implementing the required functionality through an interface named `some_impl`. The special-case access point would be defined as

```
void
operation1<T1> (const T1 *t)
{
  t->some_impl (...someargs...);
}
```

3. *Define a parameterized adapter, inheriting from the abstract base.*   Step #1 defines an abstract base class to aggregate desired polymorphic behaviors. As with language-based inheritance, concrete descendant classes implement custom behavior. In the External Polymorphism pattern, a concrete, parameterized adapter serves this purpose.

The parameterized adapter specifies an implementation for each interface defined in `Polymorphic_Object`. Each implementation calls the corresponding access point defined in Step #2, delegating to the access point the task of calling the actual implementation.

The adapter for `Polymorphic_Object` might be written as

```
template <class T>
class Polymorphic_Adapter : public Polymorphic_Object
{
public:
  Polymorphic_Adapter (T *t) : this_(t) { }

  virtual void operation1 (void) {
    // delegate!
    operation1<T> (this_);
  }

  virtual void operation2 (void) {
    // delegate!
    operation2<T> (this_);
  }

  ...
```

```
private:
  // Insure that this_ is always set.
  Polymorphic_Adapter();
  T *this_;
}
```

4. *Change application to reference through the abstract base.*   All facilities are now in place for the application to treat disparate classes as if they shared a common ancestor. This can be done by creating instances of `Polymorphic_Adapter` that are parameterized over different types `T` and managing those instances solely through a pointer to the abstract base, `Polymorphic_Object`.

It should be noted that this really is no different from managing concrete descendants in normal inheritance/polymorphism, except for the parameterization and additional layer of indirection provided by the signature adapter.

The following issues arise when implementing this pattern.

- *Arguments to* `specificRequest`.   Projecting polymorphic behavior usually requires changes to signatures of the various `specificRequests`. This can be complicated when some `specificRequests` require arguments, whereas others do not. Developers must decide whether to expose the additional arguments in the polymorphic interface or to shield clients from them.
- *Where does the code go?*   As mentioned in the Consequences section, the external class hierarchy must be maintained in parallel with the original classes. Thus, the source code for the parallel hierarchy must go somewhere. To maintain strict separation of concerns, this code should not go with the original code (if that code is available).
- *External Polymorphism is not an Adapter.*   The intent of the Adapter pattern is to convert an interface to something usable by a client. In contrast, the intent of the External Polymorphism pattern is to provide a new base class for existing interfaces. A serendipitous use of External Polymorphism would find all signatures for `specificRequest` identical across all disparate classes, and thus not require the use of `SignatureAdapter`. It is these situations where the fact that External Polymorphism is not an Adapter is most apparent.

Sample Code

As an example of implementation of the External Polymorphism pattern, recall the original scenario from the Motivation section. In this scenario, there are classes whose assistance is required to create a flexible debugging environment. The implementation shown below uses the External Polymorphism pattern to define a mechanism where all participating objects (a) can be collected in an in-memory object collection Singleton, and (b) can dump their state upon request.

The Dumpable class forms the base of the hierarchy and defines the desired polymorphic interface which, in this case, is for dumping:

```
class Dumpable
{
public:
  Dumpable (const void *);

  // This pure virtual method must be
  // implemented by a subclass.
  virtual void dump (void) const = 0;
};
```

ObjectCollection is the client, which is a simple collection that holds handles to objects. The class is based on the STL vector class [Musser+95].

```
class ObjectCollection : public vector<Dumpable*>
{
public:
  // Iterates through the entire set of
  // registered objects and dumps their state.
  void dump_objects (void);
};
```

The dump_objects method can be implemented as follows.

```
void
ObjectCollection::dump_objects (void)
{
  struct DumpObject
  {
    bool operator()(const Dumpable*& dp) { dp->dump(); }
  };

// Iterate over the entire collection from beginning to end and dump
// the state of each object.
  for_each(begin(), end(), DumpObject());
}
```

Now that the foundation has been provided, we can define ConcreteDumpable

```
template <class ConcreteType>
class ConcreteDumpable : public Dumpable
{
public:
  ConcreteDumpable (const ConcreteType* t);
  virtual void dump (void) const;    // Concrete dump method
```

```
private:
  const ConcreteType* realThis_;      // Pointer to actual object
};
```

The `ConcreteDumpable` methods are implemented as follows.

```
template <class ConcreteType>
ConcreteDumpable<ConcreteType>::ConcreteDumpable
(const ConcreteType* t)
  : realThis_ (t)
{
}


template <class ConcreteType> void
ConcreteDumpable<ConcreteType>::dump (void) const
{
  // Simply forward to the signature adapter
  ::dump<ConcreteType>(realThis_);
}
```

All that's left are the signature adapters. Suppose that `SOCK_Stream` and `SOCK_Acceptor` both have a `dump` method that outputs to `cerr`. `INET_Addr`, on the other hand, has a `printTo` method that takes the output `ostream` as the sole argument. To solve this problem, we can define the following two signature adapters.

1. A generic signature adapter that works with any concrete type that defines a `dump` method.

```
template <class ConcreteType> void
dump<ConcreteType>(const ConcreteType* t)
{
    t->dump();
}
```

2. A *specialized* signature adapter that is customized for `INET_Addr` (which does not support a `dump` method)

```
void
dump<INET_Addr>(const INET_Addr* t)
{
    t->printTo(cerr);
}
```

The `ObjectCollection` instance can be populated by instances of `Concrete-Dumpable<>` by making calls such as

```
...
ObjectCollection oc;
// Have instances of various SOCK_Stream, etc., types
...
oc.insert(oc.end(), aSockStream);
oc.insert(oc.end(), aSockAcceptor);
oc.insert(oc.end(), aInetAddr);
...
```

At some point during the lifetime of these objects in the process, we can query the state of those objects by simply calling

```
...
oc.dump_objects();
...
```

This call will dump the state of all objects that are live at this point during program execution.

Variations

If source code is available for concrete types, it is possible to enhance the previous example so that registration and deregistration with the `ObjectCollection` is handled by the constructor and destructor of each `ConcreteType` instance. This is particularly helpful in the use-case where External Polymorphism provides the ability to obtain debugging information on objects without adversely affecting the binary structure of the objects.

Thus, the `SOCK_Stream` constructor and destructor might look like

```
SOCK_Stream::SOCK_Stream()
{
  oc.insert(oc.end(), *this);
  // ...
}

SOCK_Stream::~SOCK_Stream()
{
  oc.erase(find(oc.begin(), oc.end(), *this));
  // ...
}
```

Naturally, this code is only illustrative and could benefit from enhancements (such as hiding the actual registration/deregistration code within macros or using a Singleton [Gamma+95] `ObjectCollection` in place of oc). However, with this code in place, `SOCK_Stream` instances can be created and destroyed while maintaining the integrity of `ObjectCollection`. This variation introduces a new liability to the pattern, however—transparency. In particular, the concrete class is not entirely shielded from change.

Known Uses

The External Polymorphism pattern has been used in the following systems.

- The ACE framework uses the pattern to register ACE objects in a Singleton in-memory object database. This database stores the state of all live ACE objects and can be used by a debugger to dump this state. Since many ACE classes are concrete data types, it is not possible to have them inherit from a common root base class containing virtual methods. Therefore, the External Polymorphism pattern provides an efficient and elegant solution.
- The *DV-Centro* C++ Framework for Visual Programming Language development from DV Corporation uses the External Polymorphism pattern to create a hierarchy of classes for otherwise unrelated internal system classes [Brown96].
- The Universal Streaming System from ObjectSpace's `Systems<Toolkit>` uses the External Polymorphism pattern to implement object persistence via streaming [Glass+96].
- A variation of this pattern was independently discovered and is in use at Morgan Stanley, Inc., in internal financial services projects [Shteynbuk96].
- This pattern has been used in custom commercial projects where code libraries from disparate sources were required to have a more common, polymorphic interface. The implementation of the pattern presented a united interface to classes from a locally developed library, the ACE library, and various other COTS libraries.
- The idea for the signature adapter came from usage in the OSE class library [Dumpleton96]. In OSE, template functions are used to define collating algorithms for ordered lists and so forth.

Related Patterns

The External Polymorphism pattern is similar to the Decorator and Adapter patterns [Gamma+95]. The Decorator pattern dynamically extends an object transparently without creating a variation of the original class. When a client uses a Decorated object it thinks it's operating on the actual object, when in fact it operates on the Decorator. The Adapter pattern converts the interface of a class into another interface expected by clients. Adapter lets classes work together that couldn't otherwise because of incompatible interfaces.

There are several differences between the Decorator and Adapter patterns and the External Polymorphism pattern. The Decorator pattern assumes that classes it adorns are already abstract (that is, they have virtual methods, which are overridden by the Decorator). In contrast, External Polymorphism adds polymorphism to concrete classes (classes *without* virtual methods). In addition, since the Decorator is derived from the class it adorns, it must define all the methods it inherits. In contrast, the `ConcreteCommon` class in the External Polymorphism pattern need only define the methods in the `Concrete` class it wants to treat polymorphically.

The External Polymorphism pattern is similar to the Adapter pattern. However, there are subtle but important differences.

- *Different intents.* An Adapter converts an interface to something directly usable by a client. In contrast, External Polymorphism has no intrinsic motivation to convert an interface, but rather to provide a new substrate that allows clients to access similar functionality in a uniform manner.
- *Layer vs. Peer.* The External Polymorphism pattern creates an entire class hierarchy outside the scope of the concrete classes. Adapter creates new layers within the existing hierarchy.
- *Extension vs. Conversion:* The External Polymorphism pattern extends existing interfaces so that similar functionality may be accessed polymorphically. Adapter creates a new interface.
- *Behavior versus Interface.* The External Polymorphism pattern concerns itself mainly with behavior, rather than the names associated with certain behaviors.

The External Polymorphism pattern is similar to the Polymorphic Actuator pattern documented and used internally at AG Communication Systems [Delano96].

ACKNOWLEDGMENTS

The authors would like to thank David Delano for his pre-PLoP shepherding, as well as all the participants (authors and nonauthors) at PLoP for their feedback.

Chris Cleeland extends his gratitude to his former employer, Envision, for generously supporting his collaboration on this paper.

REFERENCES

[Brown96] Personal correspondence between Paul C. Brown of DV Corporation and Chris Cleeland.

[Delano96] Personal correspondence between David Delano of AG Communication Systems, Inc., and Chris Cleeland.

[Dumpleton96] G. Dumpleton. *OSE C++ Class Library Reference Guide.* 1996. (unpublished). http://www.dscpl.com.au/ose-4.3/OTC_RankActions.html.

[Gamma+95] E. Gamma, R. Helm, R. Johnson, and J. Vlissides. *Design Patterns: Elements of Reusable Object-Oriented Software.* Reading, MA: Addison-Wesley, 1995.

[Glass+96] G. Glass and H. Alicia. "A Universal Streaming Service." *C++ Report*, **8**(8), September 1996.

[Musser+95] D. L. Musser and A. Saini. *STL Tutorial and Reference Guide: C++ Programming with the Standard Template Library.* Reading, MA: Addison-Wesley, 1995.

[Schmidt+92] D. C. Schmidt. "IPC-SAP: An Object-Oriented Interface to Interprocess Communication Services." *C++ Report,* **4**(9), November/December 1992.

[Shteynbuk96] Personal correspondence between Oleg Shteynbuk of Morgan Stanley and Chris Cleeland.

[Stoustrup91] B. Stroustrup. *The C++ Programming Language, 2nd Edition.* Reading, MA: Addison-Wesley, 1991.

The authors may be reached at cleeland@cs.wustl.edu, schmidt@cs.wustl.edu, harrison@cs.wustl.edu, **respectively.**

PART 8

Domain-Specific Patterns

Except for the user-interface patterns in Part 6, all patterns presented so far are of a technical nature. They address general problems like object creation, modeling, or context adaptation, or they address problems of technical domains, like real-time systems, distribution, or persistence. However, it is not by solving our own technical problems that we are able to develop software that users are willing to buy (and use!). Rather, this is accomplished by developing software that helps users solve their own problems. Most of us earn our paychecks by developing systems for use by people whose interest in computers is limited and defined by their business. Thus, we should start documenting the patterns that drive the design and architecture of successful business systems.

We believe that many interesting, challenging, and successful patterns will emerge from specific application domains. This part presents some fine examples of this kind, ranging from general business patterns as found in the banking or insurance domain to more specific patterns of transport and fire-alarm systems. These patterns only give a glimpse of what lies ahead in terms of business and domain-specific patterns, but they are a good beginning.

Chapter 22: Business Patterns of Association Objects, by Lorraine Boyd. In this paper, the author analyzes the use of association objects in large-scale business systems. This is part of a larger effort to document the patterns that the author's employer is using in the development of their systems. Association objects relate objects to each other. Frequently, such association objects describe a specific event in time. A specialization of this pattern is the Customer Contact pattern—a use of association objects that permeates modern information systems—and is therefore worthy of being documented as a pattern of its own. A customer contact object relates a customer object with a salesperson object and thus helps track customer contacts effectively. Finally, the author shows how association objects are used recursively to track order processing, which leads to the Three-Level Order pattern.

Chapter 23: A Pattern Language of Transport Systems (Point and Route), by Liping Zhao and Ted Foster.

The authors present two patterns that are used in the design and implementation of transport systems. These two patterns, Point and Route, are also part of a larger effort of devising a pattern language for the development of transport systems. Each pattern represents a key abstraction in the domain of transport systems, and each one is amazingly complex. Take, for example, the Point pattern; while the idea of modeling a confined location as a Point class may not seem surprising, the number of interpretation contexts for points is astonishingly rich. Thus, the Point class is adapted to different contexts by using PointRole objects. PointRole objects, in turn, are instances of concrete subclasses of a general PointRole class. This works much like the Extension Object pattern in Chapter 6, which lets you adapt components to new and unforeseen use contexts. The Route pattern repeatedly uses the Composite pattern [Gamma+95] to define the route between two points as a tree structure. It is a fine example of how a general pattern like Composite is used in a specific application domain to define domain-specific patterns. We expect to see many domain-specific patterns that are based on more general patterns, either as a specialization or a composition.

Chapter 24: The Points and Deviations Pattern Language of Fire Alarm Systems, by Peter Molin and Lennart Ohlsson.

In this paper the authors present a pattern language used for designing fire alarm systems. The language includes six closely interacting patterns that helped them design a successful framework for this domain. Being aware that a pattern language's power stems from being closely related to its application domain, they abstracted the domain's key concepts into patterns. Their pattern language therefore defines a kind of conceptual framework that users can instantiate and tailor to their needs.

Summary. The patterns in this part of the book can only provide a rough impression of what we hope to see in future books regarding patterns for specific domains. Today, we only know of two other fine examples: Martin Fowler's book on analysis patterns and David Hay's book on data model patterns [Fowler96, Hay96]. How many portfolio management systems are out there? How many business product patterns are waiting to get mined? We don't know, but we are sure that once these patterns are understood and documented, they will provide great leverage to their users.

REFERENCES

[Fowler96] M. Fowler. *Analysis Patterns*. Reading, MA: Addison-Wesley, 1996.

[Gamma+95] E. Gamma, R. Johnson, R. Helm, and J. Vlissides. *Design Patterns: Elements of Reusable Object-Oriented Software*. Reading, MA: Addison-Wesley, 1995.

[Hay96] D. Hay. *Data Model Patterns*. New York, NY: Dorset House, 1996.

Chapter 22

Business Patterns of Association Objects

Lorraine L. Boyd

There are two main types of persistent objects in large-scale business systems: static and association objects. Static objects represent tangible items that contain inherent identifying characteristics over their lifetime. Examples of static objects are product, customer, and employee. Association objects represent something that happens at a point in time, associating two other objects. The objects being associated may be either static objects or other association objects. Association objects have attributes inherent in the relationship, such as date, time, or cost, which change when a new association is formed. Examples of association objects are order, customer contact, and assignment.

This chapter discusses three patterns for associations and approaches for applying them to large-scale business systems during the analysis phase. What follows is a pattern language consisting of three association patterns that can aid in finding and defining business needs.

PATTERN LANGUAGE SUMMARY

"Find the nouns," the experienced OO designer tells the eager beginners as they start their first, large-scale OO business system development. "That's how to find objects."

Or, that's how to find the easy-to-find objects. Tangible nouns, like employee and product, are static objects, easy to identify, and are rarely missed during analysis. There are other objects, however, called association objects, which are more difficult to find because they are less tangible and are not as easily recognizable as nouns. Some associations, such as Order, have tangible representations. Other associations, such as Customer Contact, are more intangible.

First, this chapter takes up the Association Object pattern. This pattern is often used to represent assignments or schedules. The association object acts as a time-box and allows planned, historical, and current states to be captured in one object.

Then, a specific use of the association object, the customer contact, is discussed. This pattern provides for tracking historical customer contacts and projecting future contacts, a necessity as systems move from operational support to customer care.

Finally, the Association Object pattern is used to solve a recurring business problem—the need for a complex, yet flexible, order structure. With multiple recursive uses of the Association Object, the pattern captures multiple behaviors of order requests and order costs within the behavior of the order's rules.

ASSOCIATION OBJECT PATTERN

An Association Object represents something that happens at a specific point in time, associating two other objects.

Problem

In business systems, many of the necessary objects are easily identified because they represent tangible things in the real world. These are the static objects. In contrast, the associations between these objects have information and behavior of their own. How can the associations and movements between these static objects be identified?

Context

Many business systems focus on changes or movements of tangible items over time. Some examples are: scheduling systems, assignment systems, and inventory-tracking systems. The events in such systems cause associations between static objects to be created, modified, or destroyed. An association may change from describing future plans to describing a current state or history. The association may behave consistently whether future, current, or historic.

Consider the analysis phase in a system to assign rooms within a large facility. We need to assign rooms to departments. The computer system focuses on managing the change of assignments. When a room is assigned, does the user need to know the previous assignments? Are assignments planned, and how does a planned assignment become the current one? What changes about the room when it is assigned to a department? What changes about the department when it is assigned to a room? How often does an assignment happen? Understanding the assignment is key to developing a solid design.

Forces

- If we examine only the current state of an association, the relationship between two related objects is often simple. For example, today a room *has a* department. But when we add history or planning, the nature of that relationship changes. Over time, a room *has many* departments. All three states may have similar behavior and data which are of interest to the business.
- The current state, which is merely a *has a* relationship, may be all the business needs to know. Planning may be done very vaguely, and history may simply be reported.
- Integrating history, planning, and current state all in one approach will increase quantities of information stored and accessed. This may have a significant negative impact on performance.
- Separating history, planning, and current state associations may increase the amount of code needed and introduce artificial differences.

Solution

Define an Association Object, capturing the date and time of the association. Examine the lifecycle of the association. What changes during its lifecycle? What kinds of events trigger the changes? An association object is needed if the association has behavior of its own over time.

Determine attributes and responsibilities unique to the association. For example, costs for one object may be allocated among the set of associated objects. Determine if there is a performance impact by capturing details of each association, and whether different users of the association access it in the same way.

A key point is that association objects capture the changing states of associations, not just the changes in associations. That is, when a room is reassigned, the old association becomes a former one (that is, history) and the new one becomes current (it had been a future assignment). This allows the system to act as a time machine, because it can answer queries relative to any point in time, not just the current time. This integration of planning, current state, and history within a single object can eliminate the need for wholly separate systems.

In the class diagram shown in Figure 22-1, there can be many instances of the `Association` class for each unique combination of Static1 and Static2. When the Association `Begin_Date` and `End_Date` are both in the past, the Association represents history. When the *Association* `Begin_Date` is in the past, but the `End_Date` is in the future, the Association represents the current state. When the Association `Begin_Date` and `End_Date` are both in the future, the Association represents planning. Thus the Association integrates history, current state, and planning in one object. All three states share the same responsibilities and attributes.

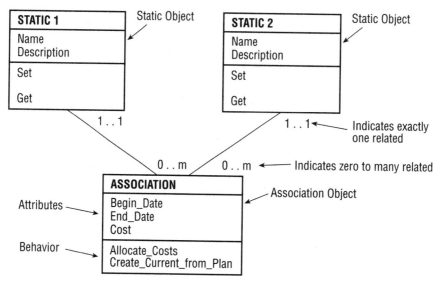

Figure 22-1 *Example of class diagram*

Example

Figure 22-2 illustrates a functional room assignment model. There can be many `Room_Dept_Assignment` instances for each combination of `Room` and `Department`. Historic assignment instances have both dates in the past; current ones have a `Begin_Date` in the past and an `End_Date` in the future, and planned ones have both dates in the future.

Analysis which verifies the need for this use of an association object includes

- The maintenance staff care about the current assignment. They use it to contact the owner before fixing the room. The accountants, however, care about the history of assignments. They use assignment history to calculate indirect costs.
- A new assignment is created whenever a room is reassigned, whether the assignment is planned for the future or effective immediately. The planned assignment becomes the current one. The current assignment becomes history.
- Costs for a room are allocated among its assigned departments according to a percentage. That is, a room may be used by several departments concurrently with each department charged a percentage of the room costs.

Known Uses

Peter Coad named this a Timed Association pattern and Martin Fowler describes these as objects representing, "actions which can be scheduled, resourced, peopled, started, and completed" in discussing planning. He also describes the associative

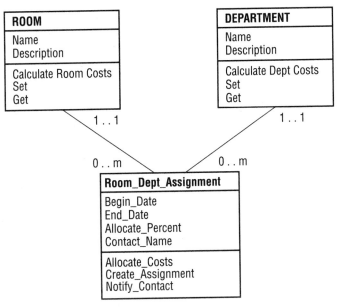

Figure 22-2 *Room assignment model*

type, when relationships themselves acquire attributes and behavior; and historic mapping, in which the objects capture history [Fowler97]. Each of these are examples of the Association Object pattern.

CUSTOMER CONTACT PATTERN

The Customer Contact pattern is a variation on the Association Object pattern. It represents an association between the business and the customer and is particularly important in systems that emphasize customer care.

Problem

Customer care is increasingly important in business. It is believed customers need to feel appreciated and looked after. How can we change the focus of a business system from information *about* the customer to information about past, current, and future *interactions with* the customer?

Context

In a day-to-day operational system, customers use the services of the business. Customers contact the business with questions and complaints; the business contacts customers to evaluate services or to encourage the use of services.

To provide optimal customer care, the business system must know the history of its customer contacts, be able to detect trends in these contacts, and then use these trends to drive responses to current questions and proactive contacts in the future.

Forces

- Customers are contacted by many different organizations within a business. The organizations may be competitive and protective of their individual information.
- Customers want to be treated the same way no matter which organization is contacting them.
- To track every customer contact in one class would create many similar instances. If these large volumes of data are stored in a single persistent data store, performance may be negatively impacted.
- Management wants to know about trends in customer queries. Thus, there is a need to store and examine large amounts of data to discern these trends.

Solution

Define a Customer Contact object. This object represents the association between the business and the customer. Define attributes such as the date and time of the contact, media used, and results.

Customer contacts can be both reactive and proactive. A reactive contact occurs when the customer contacts the business. A proactive contact occurs when the business contacts the customer. Proactive contacts can be based on time (for example, two months since last contact) or on changes in contact trends.

During analysis, determine how different organizations within the business contact the customer. Do they use similar media? Are they capturing similar information? Are they looking for similar trends? Is different automation required for different contact media? Should the system provide scripting for commonly asked questions?

Customer contact objects can be useful for scheduling proactive contacts, generating scripts, and discerning trends. Examine the volumes needed for trend analysis to determine if they are large enough to warrant separation from the operational volumes.

Most importantly, the process of defining the contact object can help change the focus of the system development effort from customer information to customer care. The Customer Contact association object looks like the diagram shown in Figure 22-3.

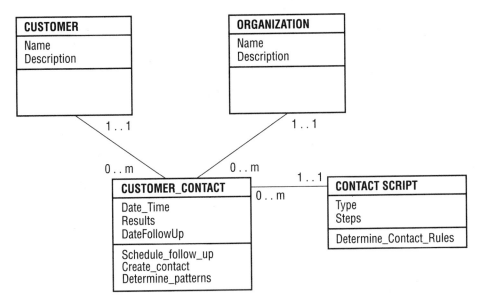

Figure 22-3 *Customer Contact pattern*

Related Patterns and Known Uses

The Customer Contact pattern is a variation of the Association Object pattern, as an association between the business and the customer. It is a business variation of Peter Coad's Event Logging pattern [Coad92]. The author has used it in help-desk management, telecommunications support, and work order customer services applications.

3-LEVEL ORDER PATTERN

A 3-Level Order is a series of association objects. The structure separates the order into three associated groups of responsibilities: rules, receivables, and costs.

Problem

Many business systems are driven by the concept of an order. An order needs to be simple to use while capturing complex and changing billing and costing requirements. During the analysis phase, how do you create a simple order structure which still allows maximum flexibility?

Context

An order can be thought of as a series of association objects. First, an order is an association which happens at a point in time between the business and the customer. Agreement rules are established. Then, products or services are requested at different times generating another association (between the order and the product) and a receivable. Finally, products or services are received or manufactured at different times, generating yet another association (between the order request and the product) and a cost.

The business needs systems to handle these complex changes over time. For example, within one order the business may need several different product requests at different points in time; or the business may fulfill the order with even different products at different points in time. Simple orders must be generated which request and fulfill one product all at once. However, even simple orders have separate behaviors for managing order rules, managing order receivables and managing order costs.

Forces

- Meeting the needs of some of the most high-value and profitable businesses often requires flexibility in the order structure. The high-value orders are often complex and require flexibility.
- The 80-20 rule usually applies. Eighty percent of the customers have simple orders and do not need complex support.
- Orders are viewed as a single piece of paper.
- Orders have different behaviors for different associations at different points in time.

Solution

Separate the order responsibilities into a 3-Level structure to provide the flexibility required for complex orders. The structure separates the order into three associated groups of responsibilities: rules, receivables, and costs. This 3-Level structure allows these three elements to have independent behavior and to happen at different points in time. For example, one order could request many different products at many projected times and different prices. The same order could later be fulfilled by substitute products at different times for different actual costs. Since the top tier contains the order rules, it provides consistency across this flexible billing and costing structure. At the same time, if a simple order is for a single product, the top tier would generate the lower tiers on creation while maintaining the separate responsibilities. The structure is shown in Figure 22-4.

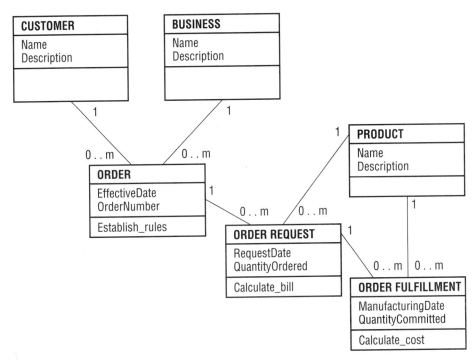

Figure 22-4 *The 3-Level Order pattern*

The structure shown in Figure 22-4 can be described more specifically as seen in Table 22-1.

Examples

There are many examples of orders in business systems, ranging from purchase orders for goods the business has available to sell to work orders for services the business will perform if requested.

The purchase order example (see Figure 22-5) is nearly identical to the generic solution. Here, one `Purchase_Order` may have many `Order_Line_Items`, both historic and current, for different products at different times. Each `Order_Line_Item` instance would be for one particular `Product` instance, with the `Quantity_Ordered` indicating how many of that `Product` have been requested. The `Order_Shipment` captures data about when products are shipped, with the dates and quantities shipped (and even a different `Product` instance if a substitute `Product` is used, differing from the `Order_Line_Item`). Thus, `Purchase_Order` is responsible for enforcing rules, `Order_Line_Item` is responsible for calculating suggested price and total bill, and `Order_Shipment` is responsible for calculating actual cost.

Table 22-1 *Order Level Description*

Level	Description
First tier: Order	• An association between the business and the customer • Establishes rules for allowed products and services • Captures past orders as history • May want to project future orders for planning • Can generate one subordinate Order Request for simple single-product orders
Second tier: Order Request	• An association between Order and the requested product or service, following rules established in the Order • Establishes billing requirements for the product and contains all billing responsibilities • Allows multiple requests: for different products, different receivables, at different times, within one Order • Can generate one subordinate Order Fulfillment if there is no delay or difference between request and fulfillment
Third tier: Order Fulfillment	• An association between Order Request and the product or service actually delivered • Establishes costs for each delivery and contains all costing responsibilities • Captures the history of multiple cost items • Cost items may have many uses in the business and different uses may require different cost calculations • Allows multiple fulfillments: for different products, at different costs, at different times within one Order Request

A more complex example is a service or work order (see Figure 22-6). In this example, the Work_Order is a request for services or work to be done. Employees

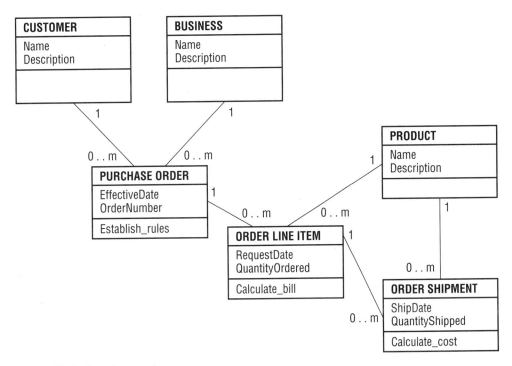

Figure 22-5 *Purchase order*

fulfill the request by expending time and doing the work. There is no tangible `Product` object, but there is a multilayered Order association with rules, receivables or billing, and costing responsibilities.

In this example, a `Work_Order` is for work to be done in one or many rooms. The `Order_Request` is by room, and provides the dates the work is requested and the types of workers anticipated. If one `Work_Order` is for work in multiple rooms, possibly at different times, then multiple bills may be needed. Separating the `Work_Order_Task`, through the Order Request pattern, allows work to be requested in different rooms and even billed at different times within one order. Once work starts, the time to complete the work (and the work itself) may differ from the original request. Separating the `Work_Assignment`, through the Order Fulfillment pattern, allows actual time to be captured and costs to be calculated separately from the requested service.

The three objects can be described as indicated in Table 22-2.

Table 22-2 *Work-Order Level Description*

Class	Description	Responsibilities
Work_Order	Agreement with the customer that work will be done.	• Determines allowed pricing policy • Generates a default Task for simple work orders
Work_Order_Task	An association defining work to be done in different rooms at a point in time. Complex orders will have different tasks in different rooms at different times.	• Calculates bill • Schedules work in different rooms • Estimates work
Work_Assignment	An association defining planned or completed work by an employee on a specific Work Order Task. Used to cost employee's time.	• Calculates labor cost per work order • Calculates payroll costs per employee • Generates actual assignments from planned assignments

Known Uses

Examples of 2-Level Orders (Order and Order Line Item) are common throughout the industry. For example, Martin Fowler uses the 2-Level Order and Order Line Item example in his discussion on object destruction. Such a 2-Level structure would apply to the simple case where orders are placed but never fulfilled. When the business fulfills the Orders, there are additional responsibilities of tracking actual costs which require the third level of this structure. The author has used the 3-Level Order structure in manufacturing ordering systems, telecommunications ordering systems, work order systems, and purchasing systems.

CONCLUSION

The Association Object patterns can be powerful drivers for business systems. By their very nature, they integrate history, current state, and planning. They provide a means for tracking the movement of items, interactions between objects, and events which change over time. Thus, they can be used in the design of scheduling systems with the Association Object pattern, in customer-care systems with

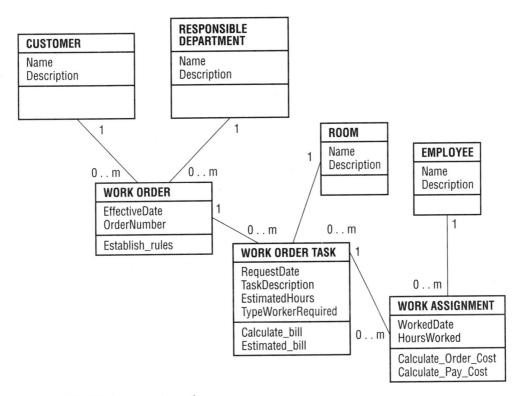

Figure 22-6 *Work or service order*

the Customer Contact pattern, and in many different types of ordering systems with the 3-Level Order pattern.

ACKNOWLEDGMENTS

Thanks to all the people who have helped shape this pattern language. Special thanks to Gerard Meszaros, who shepherded this chapter from a rough idea to its final form; to Jean Schab, who told me I had to make time to do it; and to Frank Armour, who first did a double-take and asked me to repeat what I meant by association objects.

REFERENCES

[Beck96] K. Beck. "Patterns 101." *Object Magazine.* 5(8):25–30, 63, 1996.

[Coad92] P. Coad. "Object-Oriented Patterns." *Communications of the ACM.* September 1992, vol 35, No. 9.

[Fowler97] M. Fowler. *Analysis Patterns of Reusable Object Models.* Reading, MA: Addison Wesley, 1997.

[Gamma95] E. Gamma, R. Helm, R. Johnson , and J. Vlissides. *Design Patterns: Elements of Reusable Object-Oriented Software.* Reading, MA: Addison-Wesley, 1995.

[Johnson95] R. Johnson. "Patterns and Frameworks." *Report on Object Analysis and Design.* 1(6):46–68, 1995.

[Vlissides96] J. Vlissides, J. Coplien, N. Kerth (eds.). *Pattern Languages of Programming Design 2.* Reading, MA: Addison-Wesley, 1996.

Lorraine L. Boyd welcomes correspondence at lorrie_boyd@mail.amsinc.com.

Chapter 23

A Pattern Language of Transport Systems (Point and Route)

Liping Zhao and Ted Foster

A point in a transport network plays many roles. The Point pattern provides a flexible structure that decouples a point's role from the point itself and supports multiple concurrent roles. Points (or the links between points) are used to define routes. A route is a path through an ordered sequence of points (or links) in a transport network. It may build upon different layers of components. The Route pattern provides a consistent tree structure for layering and ordering the route components. Route can cope with many variations in defining routes and allows clients to treat all objects used for route definition uniformly. Point and Route are patterns in PLOTS, a pattern language for building transport systems. This chapter shows how Point and Route provide a design solution for describing the spatial structure of a transport network, and how they interact with other patterns in PLOTS.

THE PUBLIC TRANSPORT DOMAIN

Passengers need to travel throughout their area at various times and this translates into a demand for services. Transport companies assess this demand for passenger trips and provide services to meet it. The main process that supports these services is the production of operational timetables, vehicle schedules, driver schedules, and rosters. The construction of timetables is the first step in this planning process as it sets the level of service to be provided, that is, when and where vehicle journeys are to be made. From the passengers' viewpoint, timetables show the times at which vehicles arrive at some or all of the stops on a route. Vehicle scheduling allocates vehicles to cover these journeys. Driver scheduling assigns the work in a vehicle schedule to drivers to form driver shifts or duties, and rostering combines driver shifts with rest days to form work plans for drivers. This planning phase is followed by the actual operation and monitoring of the service on a particular day.

These planning and operating processes, from timetabling through actual operations, are constrained by many complex and interdependent factors, such as network structures, perceived demand for services, vehicle availability, driver availability, labor costs, and union rules. These constraints and rules vary considerably from one transport company to another, particularly across national boundaries. Over the past 30 years, computer systems have been developed to assist these processes [Zhao93]. However, it has often proved difficult to adapt these systems to the needs of different transport operators and integrate them with other transport applications. This problem has been exacerbated by the rapidly changing requirements of urban transport and the emergence of new real-time scheduling applications made possible by advances in automatic vehicle monitoring systems. As a result, transport companies have been looking for new methods for integrating their applications [Foster91a, Foster91b, Zhao93, Zhao+94, CEN95a, Foster+96]. A general framework that can be customized for specific transport problems is urgently needed. PLOTS has been set up in response to this need.

PLOTS AND ITS PATTERN FORM

PLOTS is a pattern language for building transport systems. The PLOTS language consists of a collection of TOPS (transport object patterns) which collaborate with each other to solve transport problems [Foster+96]. "It is through pattern languages that patterns achieve their fullest power" [Coplien96].

The PLOTS language focuses on pattern interactions, as none of the individual patterns in this system are isolated. Each pattern depends on the smaller patterns it contains, on the patterns it interacts with, and on the larger patterns it is contained within [Alexander79].

Some of the TOPS build upon other patterns [Coad92; Gamma+95]. While TOPS are found in the transport domain, they can be generalized and applied to other areas as well. We leave you, the reader, to generalize our patterns for your own use.

TOPS are not simply mined from existing transport systems. Instead, they have been carefully constructed through our understanding of the strengths and weaknesses within these systems and our many years of experience of working on transport problems. We see patterns not only as recurring solutions to problems, but also as evolving solutions to recurring and evolving problems. The quality of patterns captured only from recurring and evolving solutions is limited by the quality of those solutions.

We document our patterns using our own hybrid pattern form, which has been adapted from the Gang of Four [Gamma+95] and Coplien [Coplien96] forms. We have also studied other pattern forms, but were satisfied with the detailed design and implementation information in the Gang of Four form and the explicit treatment of problem-solution pairs and their context in Coplien's form. Two of our main goals in deriving this pattern form have been

- To support the primary focus on pattern interactions in PLOTS. There are two levels of collaborations in PLOTS. At the lower level, objects collaborate with each other to form patterns; at the higher level, patterns collaborate to form PLOTS.
- To use patterns for discussion with domain experts as well as software designers. From the domain experts' viewpoint, patterns state problems and their solutions and the reasons why problems are solved this way; from the software designers' viewpoint, patterns provide a detailed and seamless specification of software components, from design to implementation.

In this chapter, we present two TOPS, that is, Point and Route patterns. Point represents the most basic component in a transport network and is used to construct Route.

POINT PATTERN

The following sections present the Point pattern.

Intent

The Point pattern provides a flexible structure that decouples a point's role from the point itself and supports multiple concurrent roles played by the point in a transport network.

Also Known As

Node

Problem

How do we represent points in a transport network? A point is a node on the graph of a transport network. It is the smallest component in the transport network and may play multiple concurrent roles. For example, a point could be

- A network point, or
- A route definition point, or

- A junction point, or
- A journey definition point, or
- A garage, or
- A reserve point, or
- A stop point, or any other role.

In the past we used a class hierarchy to represent these roles. Figure 23-1 illustrates this representation. It shows that even with just seven different roles, we soon reached five levels of inheritance. In a full description of a transport network, a point would play many more roles than these.

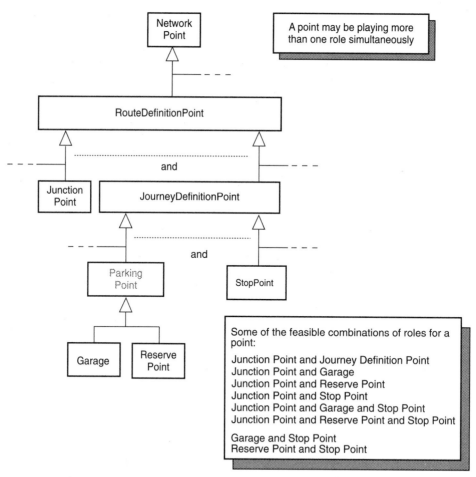

Figure 23-1 *A class hierarchy for point roles*

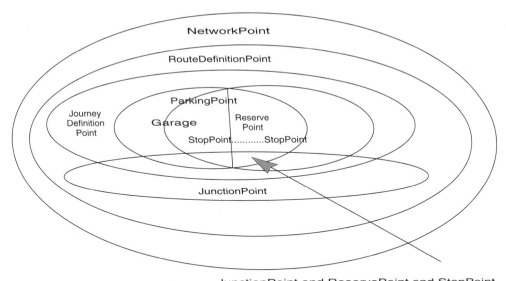

Figure 23-2 *Venn diagram showing multiple overlapping point roles*

In Figure 23-1, we may have (1) a `RouteDefinitionPoint` that is neither a `JunctionPoint` nor a `JourneyDefinitionPoint`, and (2) a `JourneyDefinition-Point` that is neither a `StopPoint` nor a `ParkingPoint`. Figure 23-2 shows multiple overlapping point roles in a Venn diagram.

When one considers the myriad of things that can happen at a point, the classification hierarchy gets very complicated indeed. There is also a lot of implementation inheritance taking place in this structure. Such an inheritance monster is impossible to maintain and hard to reuse.

Structure

Point is shown in Figure 23-3. We represent a `Point` object as an aggregation of one or more `PointRole` objects [Coad92]. All the roles that a point plays will be defined as specializations of the abstract class `PointRole`. A `Point` will hold references to all instances of its concrete `PointRole` classes. A point will delegate to these concrete `PointRole` objects.

A point's role in the network is changeable and not a property of the `Point` itself. Anything that is changeable, or is not a direct component of an object, should always suggest an indirect composition. A `Point` should have a relationship with a separate class from which each specific role is derived. In this way, the various behavioral traits supplied by each of the roles can be accessed through a `Point` by delegation.

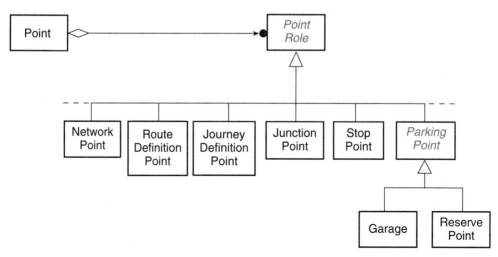

Figure 23-3 *Point*

Participants

- **Point:**

  - defines the `Point` interface to clients.
  - holds references to all the instances of its concrete `PointRoles`.
  - delegates the request from clients to specific `PointRoles`.

- **PointRole:**

  - defines an interface for encapsulating the behavior associated with a particular `PointRole`.

- **ConcretePointRoles (NetworkPoint, RouteDefinitionPoint, JunctionPoint):**

  - each `PointRole` implements a behavior delegated by `Point`.
  - can be in different subsystems (see Figure 23-4).

Pattern Interactions

Point interacts with the following patterns.

Role or State. Point builds upon Role [Coad92] or State [Gamma+95]. Point extends Role/State to support the multiplicity of roles and has its own intent in transport networks. The Role/State pattern is in our opinion particularly suitable for modeling independent objects like point. Objects that are defined upon other objects (like route, section, and link) imply a layered tree structure and cannot simply be modeled as roles. We have defined a pattern for cascades of roles.

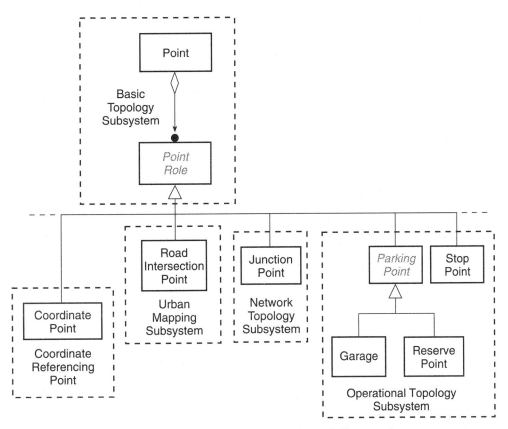

Figure 23-4 *The concrete roles played by points can be in different subsystems.*

Route. A route is a path through an ordered sequence of points in a transport network. A route can also be constructed using `RouteComponents` (that is, basic links between its points) that are clients of `Point` (see Figure 23-5).

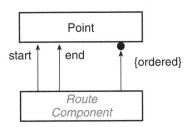

Figure 23-5 *Pattern interaction:* `RouteComponent` *as a client of* `Point`

Context

Use Point to structure the roles played by a point in a transport network. This pattern has the following features.

- It can cope with the addition of new roles as they are required without disruption to the existing specification.
- It reifies variant behavior of a point and allows a change of point roles at run time.

Forces and Design Rationale

The proliferation of `PointRoles` within our system does involve some overhead. We must always question whether the increased flexibility provided by Point justifies the departure from other ways of representing roles such as using attributes, which are familiar and therefore more readily accepted by traditional data modelers.

As in many aspects of design, we believe that the answer to this question is not a matter of opting for one particular method of representation, rather it requires a balancing act between different methods. In cases where the roles do not have any influence on the behavior of the software system, then attributes will suffice, public transport operators often want only a description of the roles their transport objects play for presentation purposes.

The big payoff from reifying roles comes when different behaviors occur in different roles. As soon as this occurs in the software development process, it is advisable to create a new concrete subclass of `PointRole` and abandon the use of attributes.

Point copes with the numerous concurrent roles played by a point or node in a transport network and allows roles to be changed much more easily than would be the case with multiple inheritance. It overcomes the restriction imposed by many object-oriented languages where an object can belong to only one class which cannot be changed. The point object appears to belong to many classes which can be changed even at runtime.

Similar Patterns and Applications

Point is a domain-specific application of Role [Coad92] or State [Gamma+95] that has been used in many different applications. Odell used a mechanism like the State pattern, which he called object slicing, for multiple dynamic classification of objects [Martin+92, pp. 407–410]. This was incorporated in the Ptech CASE tool which we used in our first object model of this domain. The movement of a vehicle through its various states during daily operations can be represented this way.

ROUTE PATTERN

The Route pattern is presented below.

Intent

The Route pattern provides a consistent tree structure for layering and ordering the components that define a route in a transport network. It can cope with many variations in defining routes and allows clients to treat all objects used for route definition uniformly.

Also Known As

RouteVariant

Problem

How do we represent routes in a transport network? A route is a path through an ordered sequence of points (or links between those points). Four closely related routes belonging to a single service line are shown in Figure 23-6.

A-C-D-E-F	B-C-D-E-F
A-C-D-E-G-H	B-C-D-E-G-H

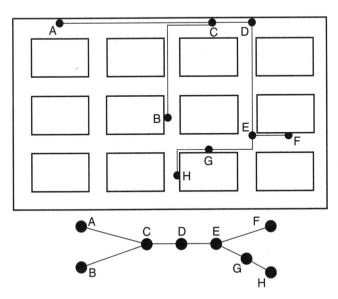

Figure 23-6 *Routes through* StopPoints

In this example, all these points are `StopPoints` (for example, bus stops) where passengers can either board or alight from a vehicle. The links between adjacent `StopPoints` have the role of `InterStopLinks`.

`Points` are the most basic components of a route. Particular roles can be assigned or removed from a `Point` and yet it is still the same point. This is not the same for links. The roles played by a link are determined by the roles of its begin and end points. Points are components of a link, so changing the role of the point at the beginning or end of a link changes its role. This is one of the reasons why some transport operators prefer to define routes in terms of points rather than links. However, others do have link-based definitions, which we think need to be considered as well as point-based definitions.

Some transport operators introduce even higher-level concepts than links between `StopPoints` to describe a route. For example, the concept of a section for the path between two `JunctionPoints`, or between a `JunctionPoint` and a `TerminalPoint` is introduced. In Figure 23-7, there are five sections (AC, BC, CE, EF, and EH) between terminal points (A, B, F, and H) and junction points (C and E). In other words, the idea of layering is introduced. The sections are made up of links.

If a section is defined using only links that are wholly contained within it (that is, no link stretches across its ends), then a route can be defined as a 2-tier structure made up of sections and links as shown in Figure 23-8. This representation is accepted by some companies, but not others. Some companies (or different departments within the same company) may want to view a route as having sections but not links, or links but not sections. Or, they may want to consider links at a finer granularity (that is, consider points hitherto ignored) and create a further layer of sublinks. General acceptance of one particular representation is very hard to achieve.

In Figures 23-6 and 23-7, links and sections are defined solely in terms of `Stop-Points` and `InterstopLinks`. This may be sufficient for some applications, such as off-line vehicle scheduling, but not for others, such as automatic vehicle monitoring and real-time control. For those who want to plot routes on street maps, points corresponding to the ends of roads (role: `RoadIntersectionPoints`) have to be introduced.

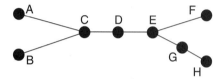

Figure 23-7 *Sections defined using* `StopPoints`

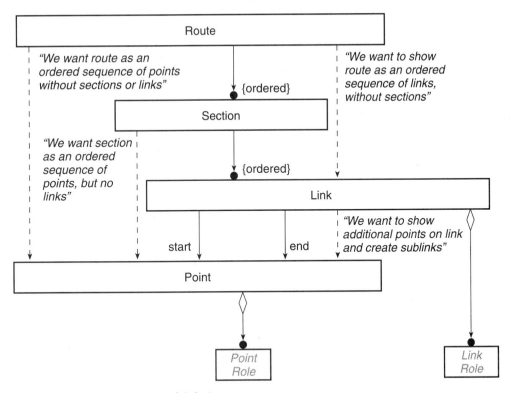

Figure 23-8 *Different ways of defining a route*

As new points or point roles are introduced to support further applications, new links and sections can be defined. For example, in Figure 23-9, a new point X (not a `StopPoint`) has been introduced where links AC and BC physically meet. Three new links are created (AX, BX, and XC). Since X is not a `StopPoint`, none of these new links play the role of `InterStopLinks`. A new link role is required.

Our definition of a section may also need to be revised. If we define a `JunctionPoint` role as the point where two links (role: `InterStopLinks`) meet, then points C and E (see Figure 23-6) are candidates for this role. This produces five sections (AC, BC, CE, EF, and EH in Figure 23-7).

If, however, we define a `JunctionPoint` role for a point that is not a `StopPoint` (such as X in Figure 23-9), then this also produces five sections (AX, BX, XE, EF, and EH in Figure 23-10), but three of them differ from those in the example shown in Figure 23-6.

Precise definition of these `RouteComponents` is essential. In addition, the rules for layering them must be clearly specified. Perfect tree structures are recommended for this layering. In other words, every higher-level link must only be expressed in terms of the links at the next level down in the hierarchy. In a layered

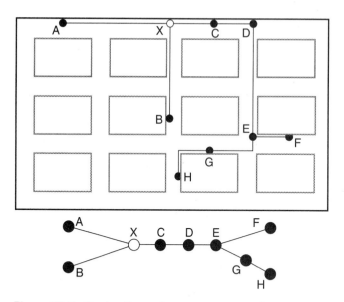

Figure 23-9 *Routes through* StopPoints *and one* NonstopPoint

structure made up of sections, links, and sublinks, we have to enforce these two rules: a sublink cannot stretch across the ends of a link, and a link cannot stretch across the ends of a section.

If we want to work with sections like XE in Figure 23-9, we have to accept that some links (role: InterstopLink), cannot be components of this section, such as AC and BC. Both of these links stretch across the end of section XE. We would have to work with more than one tree structure to layer these InterstopLinks.

If we use the definition of section inherent in Figure 23-9, and consider other points within links (such as W in AX, Y in DE, and Z in GH), then we are in effect introducing a 3-tier layering made up of sections, links, and sublinks (see Figure 23-11).

In our first transport object model (TOM) for the scheduling domain [Foster+94, Zhao+94], we defined any point used for route definition as a RouteDefinition-Point. This has become one of the roles in our Point pattern. All other points in

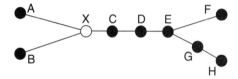

Figure 23-10 *Sections defined using a point other than a* StopPoint

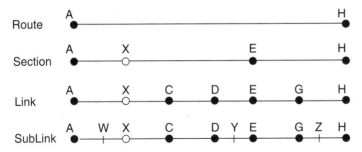

Figure 23-11 *A layered structure for a route*

Figure 23-11 could play the role of `RouteDefinitionPoint` as well as their own more specific roles.

We want to create a perfect tree structure within which the links traversed by a journey can always be expressed in terms of the links and sublinks used for defining routes. To meet this requirement, some `RouteDefinitionPoints` also play a `JourneyDefinitionPoint` role. All `JourneyDefinitionPoints` must also play the `RouteDefinitionPoint` role. Nearly all the `JourneyDefinitionPoints` play the role of `StopPoints`, but this is not mandatory.

Other route structures and hierarchies may be more suitable for applications focusing on different point roles. How can we cope with the variety of route structures which are produced when one selectively considers different point roles and their layering?

Structure

Route is presented in Figure 23-12. A `Route` is composed of `RouteComponents` (sections, `Links`, or `SubLinks`), `SectionComponents` (`Links` or `SubLinks`) and `Link-Components` (`SubLinks`). At each level, an abstract component class provides an interface to a leaf or composite class. The composite classes are ordered aggregates of their parent component class. In the special case where a composite class is instantiated with no children, the composite class is in fact behaving as a leaf class.

A component in a particular layer does not have to be instantiated. For example, a `Route` can be expressed as an ordered sequence of the following components.

1. `SubLinks` only
2. `SubLinks` and `Links`
3. `SubLinks` and `Sections`
4. `Links` only
5. `Links` and `Sections`
6. `Sections` only
7. `SubLinks`, `Links`, and `Sections`

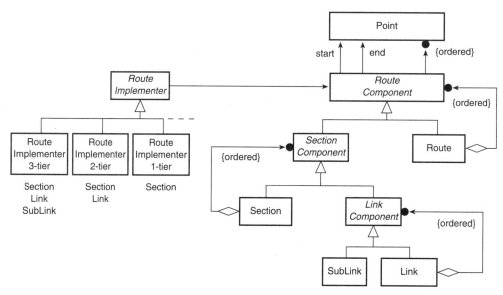

Figure 23-12 *Route*

At every level, a component can be expressed as an ordered sequence of Points rather than an ordered sequence of lower-level components.

The rules and algorithms for implementing a particular route representation are contained in the concrete subclasses of the abstract class RouteImplementer. The implementation can be varied simply by delegating to a different Route-Implementer. This can even be done at runtime.

Example

To illustrate the Route pattern in Figure 23-12, we use the route structure in Figure 23-11 as an example. The three layers of route AH (A-W-X-C-D-Y-E-G-Z-H) are as follows.

1. Route which is an ordered sequence of Sections (for example, AH —> AX, XE, and EH) or SectionComponents.
2. Section which is an ordered sequence of Links (for example, XE —> XC, CD, and DE) or LinkComponents.
3. Link which is an ordered sequence of SubLinks (for example, DE —> DY and YE).

The option to express each lower-level component (that is, Sections, Links, and SubLinks) in terms of Points is inherited from the parent class RouteComponent.

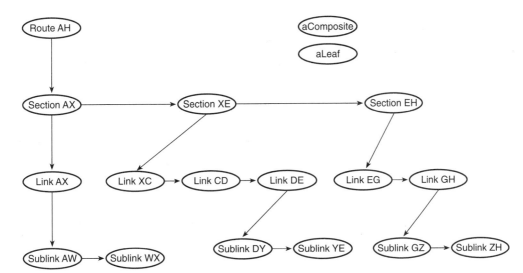

Figure 23-13 *Typical 3-tier route structure*

A typical route structure involving SubLinks (such as route AH) is shown in Figure 23-13. RouteImplementer3-tier would be responsible for constructing this Route structure.

Other route structures at a higher level of abstraction (that is, not down to the SubLink level) would be the responsibility of other concrete subclasses of Route-Implementer. Route would hold a reference to the appropriate concrete Route-Implementer object, which could be changed even at run time. For example, RouteImplementer2-tier would represent AH as shown in Figure 23-14.

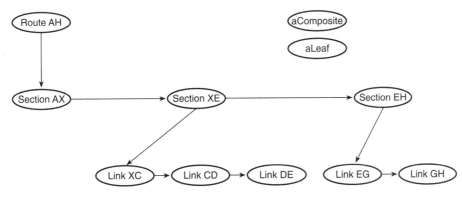

Figure 23-14 *Typical 2-tier route structure*

Participants

The responsibilities of the participating objects are assigned as follows.

Components (`RouteComponent`, `SectionComponent`, `LinkComponent`).

- **`RouteComponent`:**
  - – declares the interface for route itself and `SectionComponent` objects.
  - – implements default behavior for the interface common to these `RouteComponent` objects as appropriate.
  - – declares an interface for managing the ordered sequence of these `RouteComponent` objects.

- **`SectionComponent`:**
  - – declares the interface for section itself and `LinkComponent` objects.
  - – implements default behavior for the interface common to these `SectionComponent` objects as appropriate.
  - – declares an interface for managing the ordered sequence of these `SectionComponent` objects.

- **`LinkComponent`:**
  - – declares the interface for `Link` itself and `SubLink` objects.
  - – implements default behavior for the interface common to these `LinkComponent` objects as appropriate.
  - – declares an interface for managing the ordered sequence of these `LinkComponent` objects.

Note that the relationship between the abstract component class (for example, `RouteComponent`) and its concrete subtypes (`Route` and `SectionComponent`) is one of interface rather than class inheritance. Both `Route` itself and `SectionComponents` share a common interface defined by the `RouteComponent` class.

Leaf (`Route`, `Section`, `Link`, or `SubLink`):

- – defines behavior for these leaf objects.

Note that `Route`, `Section`, and `Link` would be composite objects if defined with one or more children.

Composite (`Route`, `Section`, `Link`)

- **`Route`:**
  - – defines behavior for `Routes` with zero or more `RouteComponent` objects.
  - – stores an ordered sequence of `RouteComponent` objects.
  - – implements operations for managing this ordered sequence of `RouteComponent` objects.

- **Section:**

  - defines behavior for sections with zero or more `SectionComponent` objects.
  - stores an ordered sequence of `SectionComponent` objects.
  - implements operations for managing this ordered sequence of `SectionComponent` objects.

- **Link:**

  - defines behavior for `Links` with zero or more `SubLinks`.
  - stores an ordered sequence of `SubLinks`.
  - implements operations for managing this ordered sequence of `SubLinks`.

Note that instantiating `Route`, `Section`, and `Link` without any children turns them into leaf objects; the client can view them without further subdivision.

- **Client (`RouteImplementer`):**

  - manipulates `Sections`, `Links`, and `SubLinks` through a `RouteComponent` interface.
  - each concrete `RouteImplementer` is responsible for the structuring of the `RouteComponents`.

Pattern Interactions

Route interacts with the Point and Composite patterns.

Point. Point is used to build `RouteComponent` (see Figure 23-5). Every `RouteComponent` starts and ends at a point and can be expressed as an ordered sequence of two or more `Points`.

Composite. The underlying pattern of Route is Composite [Gamma+95]. Composite is a very powerful and generic construct for Route, which has two particularly elegant features. First, it can represent layered tree structures consistently. Most of many variations in representing routes that we have encountered are covered by Composite. For example, if we have a consistent 3-tier structure and then have to extend the system to cover a rogue sublink, one that is not a subdivision of one of the existing links, then this can be introduced as shown in Figure 23-15 without disrupting the existing structure. Identifying such inconsistencies may prompt a redefinition of requirements. However, we often have to live with these inconsistencies because of the need to provide continuing support for legacy systems and find other means of integrating the applications concerned. Composite helps us to deal with these mismatches.

A second feature is that it can express the cascade of roles in a clear order. The Role pattern is particularly suitable for modeling independent objects like point. Objects that are defined upon other objects like `Route`, `Section`, and `Link` imply a

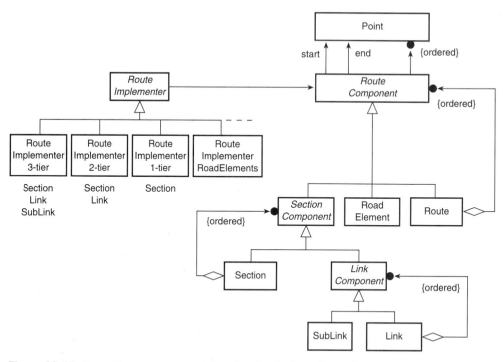

Figure 23-15 *Inserting a component that breaks the layering rules*

layered tree structure and cannot simply be modeled as roles. Composite has been used to cope with the cascade of roles in Route.

Composite has also been used to build our Duty pattern and a generic layered tree pattern that we are calling Cascade. The Cascade pattern considers this hierarchical layering of Composite patterns stripped of its transport domain specific content.

Context

Use Route to order and layer the components that define a path through a road network. Sections, Links, and SubLinks are in a part-whole relationship with Route and rely for their definition on the roles of the Points they pass through.

Clients of a Route can ignore the difference between compositions of objects and individual objects. Clients will treat all objects used for route definition uniformly.

Forces and Design Rationale

All RouteComponents, even the Route itself, are in effect basic links playing particular roles determined by the roles of their begin and end points. The sections,

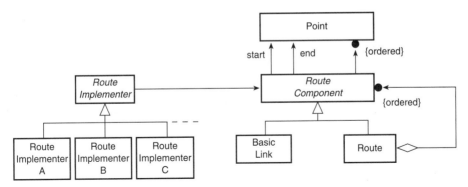

Figure 23-16 *Using basic links*

links, and sublinks described in this chapter differ only in that they have been assigned to a particular layer in a perfectly layered tree structure. Many other basic link roles can be defined which do not fit neatly into this tree structure.

An alternative to the explicit layering of links would be to work only with basic links (see Figure 23-16). The rules for implementing many different tree structures made up of basic links would also be encapsulated within appropriate concrete `RouteImplementers`. This solution is a special case of the Cascade pattern (that is, the one-tier case). This solution may be preferred when there is no real-world need to describe basic links in terms of their position within one particular tree structure and/or where the behavior and rules to be assigned to a `RouteComponent` in each layer do not differ significantly.

Some of the responsibility for implementing and maintaining the internal structure of the cascade of composites can be assigned to concrete subclasses of the `Route`, `Section`, and `Link` classes rather than `RouteImplementer`. For example, in our Duty pattern (Figure 23-17), we have applied the Gang of Four composition-compositor solution [Gamma+95, pp. 41–42] to `Duty`, `DutyPart`, `Stretch`, and `Spell` which are also cascaded like `Route`. The algorithms and rules for composing `Dutys`, `DutyParts`, `Stretches`, and `Spells` are complex, and vary with the type of `DutyComponent` being constructed, which makes them particularly suitable for this treatment.

Should points themselves be layered? For example, a point playing the role of a station may be viewed as several lower-level points playing the role of a platform. For many applications, points indeed must be layered. The representation of a transport network also has to cover some of the spaces or areas bounded by links between points. These areas also need layering. For example, the area covered by a station may be viewed as several lower-level parking bays. Cascade can also be used for this purpose. Many examples of transport-user requirements for layering can be found in the EU Geographic Data File (GDF) standard [CEN95b]. The basic patterns in the GDF standard are expressed as entity-relationship models.

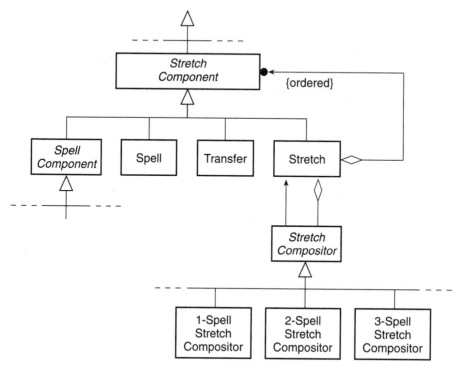

Figure 23-17 *Using Composite-Compositor*

Route considers the requirements of those transport operators and designers who use link- or edge-based algorithms as well as point- or node-based algorithms; the representation is not hard-coded into a route object; and responsibility for managing the structure is delegated to concrete route implementers and/or compositor objects. Different types of RouteComponents, defined by the roles of the points making up these components, can be layered into one or more perfect tree structures. The Route pattern helps to structure the complex movements of vehicles, drivers, and passengers within a transport network.

Similar Patterns and Applications

The Route pattern is a domain-specific application of a Cascade of Composite patterns for layering RouteComponents playing multiple concurrent roles [Gamma+95]. The same cascading of roles is also suitable for representing other transport domain objects (such as journeys and duties). Other patterns interact with this cascade of composites. For example, the Gang of Four Composite-Compositor solution has been applied to each of the layers of our Duty pattern. Riehle proposes an

Observer pattern within his larger Bureaucracy pattern to perform a similar function [Riehle96]. The application of these patterns help to bring order and comprehensibility to complex dynamic systems such as the operation of a transport system.

ACKNOWLEDGMENTS

We wish to thank our EuroPLoP '96 and PLoP '96 Shepherd, Bob Hanmer, for his encouragement in writing up our transport domain patterns, for his continuing enthusiasm, and for providing many invaluable comments on our pattern papers. We would also like to thank colleagues in various Science and Engineering Research Council (UK) and European Union (EU) funded projects (especially within Cassiope and Titan), with whom we have discussed the problems of modeling public transport operations.

REFERENCES

[Alexander79] C. Alexander. *The Timeless Way of Building.* New York: Oxford University Press, 1979.

[CEN95a] CEN. "Reference Data Model for Public Transport." *Drive II Programme: Eurobus Project and Harpist Task Force.* TC278/WC3 Draft V4.1 prENVxxxx.1. European Prestandard, 1995.

[CEN95b] CEN. "Geographic Data Files." *TC278/WG7.2. V3.0. European Standard,* 1995.

[Coad92] P. Coad. "Object-Oriented Patterns." *Communications of the ACM,* 35(9): 152–159, 1992.

[Coplien96] J. O. Coplien. *Software Patterns.* New York: SIGS Publications, 1996.

[Foster91a] E. Foster. "Demonstration of the Cassiope Data Model Expanded for Scheduling and its Implementation as a Relational Database." Drive I Programme: Cassiope Project (V1019). Deliverable 10.2., 1991.

[Foster91b] E. Foster. "The Cassiope Project." *Proceedings of the International Workshop on Data Management for Public Transport,* East Germany, 1991.

[Foster+94] E. Foster, A. J. Barnard, and L. Zhao. "PoeT: Object-Engineering in Public Transport. An Object Model for Timetabling and Vehicle Scheduling." Report, University of Leeds, School of Computer Studies, 1994.

[Foster+96] E. Foster and L. Zhao. "Modeling Transport Objects with Patterns." *Proceedings of EuroPLoP '96,* 1996. To appear in *Journal of Object-Oriented Programming* in 1997; also appears in July/August issue of *Object Expert,* 1997.

[Gamma+95] E. Gamma, R. Helm, R. Johnson, and J. Vlissides. *Design Patterns: Elements of Reusable Object-Oriented Software.* Reading, MA: Addison-Wesley, 1995.

[Martin+92] J. Martin and J. J. Odell. *Object-Oriented Analysis & Design.* Sydney: Prentice-Hall, 1992.

[Riehle96] D. Riehle. "Bureaucracy." Chapter 11, this volume.

[Zhao93] L. Zhao. *A Knowledge Based Driver Duty Estimator.* Ph.D. Thesis. Leeds University, 1993.

[Zhao+94] L. Zhao and E. Foster. "ROO: Rules and Object-Orientation." In C. Mingins and B. Meyer (eds.), *Technology of Object-Oriented Language and Systems:* TOOLS 15, pp. 31–44. Sydney: Prentice-Hall, 1994.

Liping Zhao can be reached at liping@cs.rmit.edu.au.
Ted Foster can be reached at ted@class-sc.demon.co.uk.

Chapter 24

The Points and Deviations Pattern Language of Fire Alarm Systems

Peter Molin and Lennart Ohlsson

The pattern language in this chapter documents the architecture of an object-oriented framework for a family of fire alarm systems. Important patterns in the pattern language are the *Point* pattern, covering the abstraction of sensors and actuators, and the *Deviation* pattern, dealing with alarms, faults, and other abnormal conditions.

The evolution of this and many other real-time embedded systems began by transforming a hardware-only implementation of some functionality to a micro-controller-based software solution. The high degree of flexibility of the software solution typically led to a continuous growth in functional capability, and what was once a small and conceptually simple device soon became a large and complex system.

Most design efforts in the early stages of this evolution are focused on performance optimization and optimal utilization of limited memory. While these issues are still important as the system grows, the design focus must now shift to the problem of managing complexity. Reliability, maintainability, and portability are all affected by architectural choices.

This chapter derives from a major architectural redesign effort undertaken by the Swedish security company, TeleLarm AB, on a family of fire alarm system products, which have over the years followed the typical path of evolution described above. The project was initiated in 1992 in an attempt to take advantage of the potential benefits offered by object-oriented technology. The concrete goal of the project was to develop an object-oriented framework that was to be used for all fire alarm system products, ranging from small home and office systems to large complex systems intended for industrial multibuilding plants. The first product based on the framework was completed during 1994, and since then approximately 500 systems per year have been delivered. Not a single fault has been detected after beta-testing, and the software has proved easy to modify. For example, adaptations for different national standards have been made unexpectedly fast. In all, the project is thus far considered highly successful.

After the project was finished we needed to better express the rationale for the design. This need was dictated by curiosity, and the conviction that an explicitly expressed rationale helps protect against entropic forces during maintenance and will increase the expected lifetime of the architecture. Somewhat unexpectedly, it turned out to be very difficult to express why the framework was designed as it was. We found that we had more difficulties and disagreements when trying to explain design decisions than we had had when we made them. It appeared that many decisions had been based on unconscious knowledge, but a knowledge which was nevertheless somehow shared. This is somehow reminiscent of the notion of a "Quality Without a Name" [Alexander+77], and we therefore made an attempt to use patterns as a tool to better understand our design rationale and make it more concrete and explicit. The result was the pattern language for fire alarm systems presented in this chapter. It is written in the same spirit as Kent Beck's and Ralph Johnson's "Patterns Generate Architectures"; it should be possible to use the patterns as a set of axioms from which the architecture can be logically derived [Beck+94]. This goal may not necessarily be achievable, but it is nevertheless important to strive for. The pattern language contains the six patterns in Figure 24-1.

These patterns capture the key architectural principles of the framework. The language is specific to the domain of alarm systems, and each pattern is also cast in this narrow domain. Each individual pattern can be seen as an illustration of a design pattern of broader applicability.

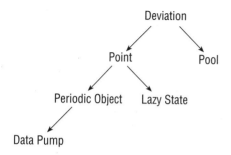

Figure 24-1 *Patterns in the pattern language*

SYSTEM OVERVIEW

A fire alarm system can be described by the actual physical entities and how they are interconnected as in Figure 24-2.

Another way of viewing the system is based on its interfaces to the environment. Such an abstract system contains a number of output devices which are dependent on input devices as is shown in Figure 24-3.

DEVIATION PATTERN

The Deviation pattern provides a compact representation of the state of the system.

Context

The purpose of a fire alarm system is to survey a plant, a building, or some smaller unit like an office or an apartment. The system makes use of a number of sensors distributed across the area being surveyed. Each sensor is connected to one of several control units. The control units, each of which is an autonomous computing node, are all connected to a common communication network and they normally operate as a single integrated system. A fire alarm system does not

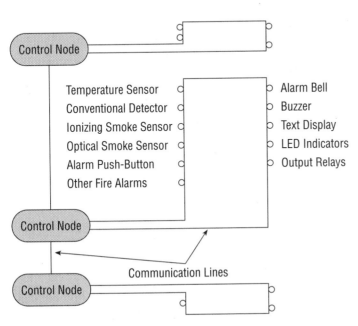

Figure 24-2 *Overview of a fire alarm system*

Figure 24-3 *Abstract view of a fire alarm system*

do very much most of the time. The key function of the system is to detect when something out of the ordinary occurs, such as a fire or an indication thereof, and generate an alarm. When this happens, the fire alarm system takes appropriate action such as alerting people in the building through alarm bells and text displays, invoking extinguisher systems, and calling the fire brigade automatically.

The system can handle several alarms simultaneously. Information about each alarm, such as time, location of detection or informative texts, can be presented to fire brigade staff and other users. What action should be taken when an alarm is generated and how the alarm should be presented are, to a large degree, determined by national and international product standards, for example, the European Standard concerning Fire Alarm Systems [CEN96]. Other actions, such as the closing of fireproof doors, the automatic initiation of fire extinguishers, or sending text information to displays, are determined by the system configuration for the particular installation.

Although fire indications in the environment are the main thing to be detected by the system, it also monitors itself continuously for abnormal internal conditions. Such conditions may be faults, for example, some communication channel is broken or a backup battery is failing. There is another category of less critical abnormal conditions (disturbances such as temporarily disabled sensors or dirty sensors). When faults and disturbances are detected, they cause action to be taken in a manner similar to that of fire alarms.

Problem

How do you implement the dependencies and information flow between alarm detection and actuators, user interfaces, and other outputs?

Forces

The logical behavior of the system is completely independent of its distributed nature; an actuator may depend on some particular input regardless of whether it is connected to the same control unit or some other control unit in the system. Furthermore, the number of inputs to the system can be considerable, and the number of control units can also be large.

If every control unit were to store the current status of every input sensor, it would place heavy demands on the memory capacity of each control unit. An alternative would be for each control unit to have only a proxy for remote inputs. Each proxy would consist of a system-wide reference, and any requests would be forwarded to the control unit where the input actually exists. However, even storing as little as one reference per input in each control unit requires a great deal of memory space.

On the other hand, the ratio of alarms, faults, and disturbances to the total number of inputs is very low. Most of the sensors are in a normal state most of the time. All inputs need not therefore be *known* at each control unit since an *unknown* input can be assumed to be in a normal state. Only information about deviations from the normal state must therefore be globally accessible from each control unit.

Solution

Represent each detected deviation from the normal state as a `Deviation` object. Use `Deviation` subclasses, such as `Alarm`, `Fault`, and `Disturbance` to represent different kinds of deviations. Let deviations be the unit of distribution in the system in the sense that all deviations are replicated to all control units (see Figure 24-4). Since the set of deviations defines the complete system state, this is immediately available on all nodes.

Related Patterns

Point defines entities responsible for creating and deleting `Deviations`, and Pool provides access to all `Deviation` instances.

POINT PATTERN

The Point pattern separates the behavior logic from variations in input and output devices.

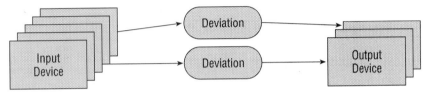

Figure 24-4 *System view based on Deviations*

Context

To survey the building, the system makes use of a number of sensors distributed to various places. When an abnormal measurement value is recorded, a fire is considered detected in that sensor and an `Alarm` deviation should be created. Similarly, when the sensor detects that the fire condition is no longer present, the `Alarm` should be removed. This routine should also be followed when a `Fault` and other kinds of `Deviations` are detected.

A great variety of input sensors can be used with the system. Fire is not a phenomenon that can be directly identified. Sensors must instead measure secondary effects such as temperature or smoke intensity and detect specified patterns of variation. In conventional detectors this analysis is rather primitive and performed by the hardware, whereas modern sensors use more elaborate software algorithms in the control unit. Each of the secondary effects can in turn be measured. For example, smoke intensity can be measured either by ionizing or by optical methods. The situation is similar, although there are not quite so many variations, for actuators and other outputs such as alarm bells, alarm transmitters, buzzers, light emitting diodes (LED), or text displays.

Another degree of variation among sensors and actuators is the means by which they are connected to the system. Some are connected directly to the control units and can be accessed immediately. Others are attached to a device that is connected to a communication loop and is accessed via different communication protocols and/or dedicated device controllers. Sometimes one device contains only one sensor; in other cases, a single device contains a number of sensors or actuators, which may be of different types.

Problem

How can the logical behavior of the system be separated from the variation among input sensors and output actuators?

Forces

Product standards and system configuration determine how actuators should be activated when fire is detected. In either case, this behavior is independent of the type of sensor, its detection algorithms, access protocols, and physical packaging. It is therefore important to have a standardized interface which separates the logical behavior from the device variations.

One possibility would be to have an abstract base class which defines this standard interface and uses subclasses to implement the variations among devices. But a sensor is often the source of two kinds of `Deviation`, both `Alarms` and `Faults`. Furthermore, a device may contain more than one sensor or actuator. Using inheritance only would thus not prevent the variations in packaging from affecting the interface.

Solution

Define the interface between the part of the system representing the logical behavior and the part implementing different kinds of devices as a set of Points, either InputPoints or OutputPoints. A Point has a binary state, either active or inactive, without references to implementation details of how this state is represented or maintained.

Use the Bridge pattern [Gamma+95] to connect Points to separate Device objects that implement actual I/O-behavior of the Points. Devices encapsulate access protocols and other details of how they perform actual I/O from the Points, as well as whether they are polled or interrupt driven. Let the number and kind of Points connected to the same Device be determined by the characteristics of the physical devices (see Figure 24-5).

Related Patterns

Periodic Object gives Points and Devices the opportunity to operate as concurrently active entities, and Data Pump enables them to be synchronized efficiently. Lazy State provides Points with a compact implementation of state-dependent behavior.

POOL PATTERN

When Deviation is used to represent the system state, there is a need for a uniform way of accessing all instances regardless of their distribution on different nodes.

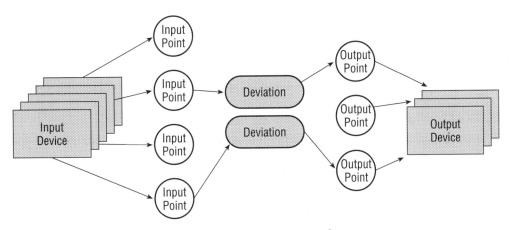

Figure 24-5 *System view based on* Points, Devices, *and* Deviations

Context

Although outputs and actuators can be programmed to depend on particular inputs, it is more common that they depend on aggregate conditions. The most important condition of this kind is, of course, whether there are any alarms in the system. There are, however, other conditions, such as certain indicators that may show if there are any disabled sensors in the system or if there are any faults present. These dependencies can be expressed in subsets of the current deviations which fulfill certain criteria.

Another situation where there is a similar need is presentation of the system status to human operators. An operator can ask the system to list all active alarms, all faults that are not acknowledged, or all dirty sensors that need to be replaced. In this scenario, the user sees the system as a database to which selection queries can be directed.

Problem

How do you provide a standardized interface for accessing the set of all instances of a class, such as retrieving the subset which fulfills certain criteria?

Forces

In an application that uses a relational database this is a trivial problem. Although it is meaningful to speak about "the set of all instances" in an object-oriented context, there is no explicit support for this notion in a language such as C++. Furthermore, in a distributed system it is not only the set of all instances in one address space which is of interest, but the set of all instances on all nodes in the whole system. Selection, iteration, and other operations should be made on this complete set and the mechanism should be independent of the location of instances.

Solution

For the relevant classes, collect all instances in Pools (see Figure 24-6). A Pool is a virtual container that contains all instances of the class in the whole system. There is a copy of each Pool on each node in the system. The instances that belong to the same node are actually contained in the Pool, whereas instances belonging to other nodes may be accessed by strategies such as duplication in all Pools, remote iteration, or by using the Proxy pattern [Gamma+95]. Different strategies involve different tradeoffs regarding fault tolerance, memory consumption, or response time. The strategy can be chosen differently for different Pools. Alarms, for example, must be quickly available and should be duplicated in all nodes since a fire may damage the network. Rarely performed device monitoring involves a much larger number of instances, but makes lower demands on response times and availability and can therefore be implemented by remote iteration techniques.

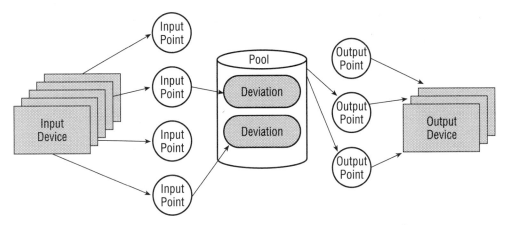

Figure 24-6 *System view based on* Points, Deviations, Devices, *and* Pools

LAZY STATE PATTERN

Most Points have state-dependent behavior. The Lazy State pattern implements objects whose state-dependent methods are rarely executed.

Context

The behavior of Points may be affected by user commands. A user can disable one or more InputPoints which will thereafter not generate alarms. Another example is test mode commands that put a set of InputPoints into a specific mode where an alarm condition results in only partial output behavior. For each behavior-changing command there is an inverse command that should make the Points return to normal behavior, for example, for each disable command there is a corresponding reenable command.

Problem

How should you implement the state dependent behavior of Points?

Forces

A natural approach would be to implement this behavior by using the State pattern [Gamma+95]. The behavior in each state would be represented by a subclass of an abstract PointState class. However, in many cases different commands have a similar effect on the Point. One example is OutputPoints, which can be disabled either by a specific command for an individual OutputPoint or by a command for all OutputPoints of a particular category, such as all alarm bells. Each of these similar commands has its own inverse, so if a Point is disabled both individually and because it is an alarm bell, it returns to normal behavior only after both inverse commands have been applied. The commands require, therefore, partial command history to be stored, which in a pure state machine would require additional states for this purpose. This state transition logic increases significantly the complexity of the state machine as compared with having states that implement variations in behavior only.

Moreover, each of the various commands would require a separate operation on the Point class, for example, disableIndividually() and disableAsAlarm-Bell(). New commands can easily be imagined, perhaps disabling physical locations like rooms instead of a number of sensors corresponding to that room. Such changes are much more frequent than changes in basic alarm detection behavior and would soon pollute the Point interface with command dependencies.

However, the normal operation of Points, sensor evaluation, is not affected by commands. The state-dependent behavior occurs only after an alarm condition has been detected. This occurs very rarely and the performance is thus less critical. This can seem counter-intuitive as one might think that alarms must be handled as fast as possible. However, sensors are evaluated sequentially in a round-robin way, and the worst-case response time thus depends mainly on the sensor evaluation capacity.

Solution

Apply the State pattern [Gamma+95] on Points but replace the member variable, state, by a member function state(). Current state is thus not stored explicitly but computed each time state-dependent behavior is invoked. Implement the state() function on Points by examining the Pool of Disablements. A Point is, for example, in a disabled state if there is a Disablement in the Pool that affects this Point. Different kinds of disablement are represented by different subclasses to Disablement. The execution of a disable command consists of storing a corresponding Disablement in the Pool (see Figure 24-7). The execution of a reenable command locates the corresponding Disablement and removes it from the Pool.

PERIODIC OBJECT PATTERN

The Periodic Object pattern separates task logic from scheduling strategy.

Context

Most input devices to a fire alarm system are sensors. These sensors are sampled periodically and evaluated. At the same time other monitoring tasks need to be performed periodically. The application shows a large degree of inherent concurrency where, at least conceptually, a large number of sensors and several subsystems should be checked in parallel, and, in some respects, independently of

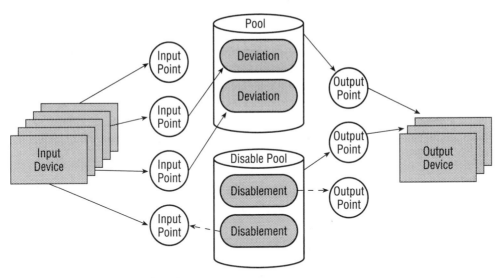

Figure 24-7 *System view based on* Points, Devices, Deviations, Disablements, *and* Pools

each other. Traditionally, the scheduling alternatives are a cyclic scheduler, a non-preemptive thread scheduler, or a preemptive thread scheduler.

The framework is supposed to be used for both small and large systems with different amounts of memory: the chosen solution must therefore be efficient with respect to memory usage.

Another important requirement of a fire alarm system is, in addition to reliability, demonstrability. Demonstrability makes it possible to convince the developing organization, the customer, or in some cases a third-party software assessment organization, that requirements can and will be met with sufficient confidence.

Problem

How can inherent concurrency be preserved, and requirements on performance, demonstrability, and memory efficiency be met while still separating scheduling strategies from task behavior?

Forces

The simplest possible solution is the cyclic scheduler. The cyclic scheduler makes it relatively easy to predict performance and no racing conditions will occur. The solution has the disadvantage that there is no distinct division between the task logic and the scheduling algorithm. The scheduling algorithm is dependent on the deadline requirements and the CPU requirement of each task, but not on what the task actually does.

In a multithreaded system this separation of concerns is very clear. On the other hand, the thread solution may present well-known synchronization problems, as well as racing problems. Another problem with such concurrent systems is that they require a kernel and a stack for each thread, resulting in a large overhead in memory usage.

A nonpreemptive solution provides high demonstrability and no racing condition problems. The solution requires, however, that tasks and algorithms are sliced into suitable parts reflecting response-time requirements. Slicing implies additional work and may decrease the understandability of the code.

Solution

Represent each periodic task as a `PeriodicObject`. The abstract class defines a pure virtual function `Tick`. Different tasks are implemented as subclasses that define the `Tick` operation as appropriate. Define scheduling classes that iterate over a collection of `PeriodicObjects` according to different scheduling strategies. These schedulers can range in complexity from simple cyclic schedulers, to various priority schedulers, to advanced schedulers that dynamically choose other schedulers as collaborators. With the abstract coupling to the `PeriodicObject` interface, there is a clear separation of concern between task logic and scheduling strategy, and these can easily be changed independently.

By applying the Composite pattern [Gamma+95] and having schedulers inherit from `PeriodicObject`, the scheduling can be further modularized by building a hierarchy of schedulers.

The `PeriodicObject` does not need a stack of its own and the schedulers require less memory than a full-blown real-time kernel, so less memory is needed. On the other hand, the `PeriodicObject` must rely on its own internal state as it will always resume execution from the `Tick` function. As a consequence, all functions called from the `Tick` function must be nonblocking. The Periodic Object pattern requires all potentially blocking scenarios to be transformed to equivalent nonblocking scenarios.

Related patterns

Data Pump describes how `PeriodicObjects` can be combined with `Points` and `Devices`.

DATA PUMP PATTERN

The Data Pump pattern describes how to combine `PeriodicObjects` with `Points` and `Devices` in an efficient manner.

Context

A fire alarm system spends the majority of its CPU cycles on periodically evaluating sample values from sensors. `Devices` communicate with the physical devices using some relatively slow shared communication channel.

The sample evaluation involves `Points` and `Devices`. The `Points` are responsible for the actual evaluation of the sample. `Devices` are responsible for interpreting device data according to type and distributing the data to corresponding `Points`.

Problem

Which of the components involved in sensor evaluation should be designated as `PeriodicObjects`?

Forces

To improve the portability of the scheduler and the scheduler algorithms, we prefer to schedule high-level components as opposed to low-level components. Since lower-level devices are more likely to change between different instantiations, the scheduler should not be dependent on them.

The capacity of the system can be measured by the number of sensors it can evaluate per time unit. Evaluation of a sensor value is, therefore, the performance-critical operation which most needs to be tightly optimized. High performance also requires the slow communication channel to be used efficiently.

Blocking situations where a `PeriodicObject` must wait for data should be avoided, both for reasons of efficiency and because `PeriodicObjects` do not support such cases. Moreover, potential synchronization problems require additional use of memory for buffers.

Solution

Designate the `Devices` as `PeriodicObjects`. Let them pump or push data to the `Points` whenever new data are available. Since control flow follows data flow, and since `Points` are made passive and reactive, there is no need for buffers and synchronization between `Points` and `Devices`. Let the `Devices` be responsible for keeping the slow communication channel working at the highest possible rate (see Figure 24-8). Portability is assured by allowing scheduling to be based on the general base class `Device`, not on specific device objects.

CONCLUDING REMARKS

The basic architecture in the fire alarm system can be seen as an example of the Half-Sync/Half-Async pattern [Schmidt+96]. The framework described by the pattern language in this chapter covers only the synchronous part. During the

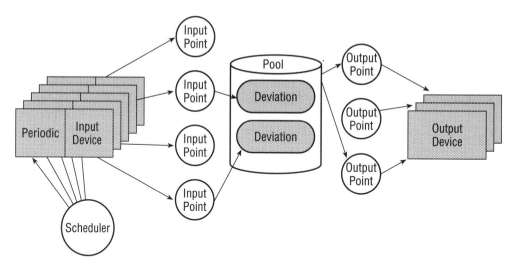

Figure 24-8 *System view based on* `Points`, `Devices`, `Deviations`, `Pools`, `Periodic-Objects` *using the Data Pump pattern*

writing of this pattern language, a pattern similar to our Pool pattern has been presented by Peter Sommerlad. His Manager pattern collects all instances of a class, but does not include all instances in a distributed system [Sommerlad96].

External circumstances determined that we first designed the system and then carried out pattern mining. Would we do differently a second time? Although the design was heavily scrutinized during pattern mining, we found no major flaws. So design quality could probably not be improved much. On the contrary, it could suffer from parallelization. Design is hard and requires many rapid iterations. If each iteration had had to include the even harder task of making all decisions explicit, the iterations would not have been as rapid, nor would there have been time to carry out as many of them. On the other hand, pattern exercise during design might have eliminated the need for some of the iterations and provided time for making others. We therefore suggest a moderate dose of pattern exercise during design in the relaxed form of documenting problem-solution pairs.

Another reflection on this pattern work is concerned with the level of generality best for a pattern language. Our pattern language is specific to fire alarm systems, but most of its patterns are not that specific. They could probably be rewritten for a wider range of systems: for other kinds of alarm systems, for various detection systems, and at least some of the patterns could be used for distributed measurement and control systems. Although the main purpose of pattern mining was not to reach a wide audience, the writing of this chapter rendered a slightly different perspective. Given that you want to make the mined knowledge as widely accessible as possible, what is the optimal level of generality? Stating the patterns in the most general terms makes them more directly applicable to many situations. The drawback is that something that is generally expressed is harder to understand at the level where the reader can actually apply it. In many cases, a more specific story can be a better carrier of general knowledge; analogy can be more powerful than specialization. There is no conclusive answer to this question, no definitive criteria that can be applied, but we think it is better to err on the side of specificity, rather than be too quick to "go meta."

ACKNOWLEDGMENTS

We would like to thank Östen Lundgren and Björn Svensson at TeleLarm for their support in the framework project, and Rutger Pålsson and Magnus Håkansson for their design contributions. We also thank all the participants of the writer's workshop at PLoP '96 and our colleague Jan Bosch for many valuable suggestions for improvement.

REFERENCES

[Alexander+77] C. Alexander, S. Ishikawa, M. Silverstein, M. Jacobsen, I. Fiksdahl-King, and V. Angel. *A Pattern Language*. Oxford University Press, 1977.

[Beck+94] K. Beck and R. Johnson. "Patterns Generate Architectures." Proceedings of the 8th European Conference on Object-Oriented Programming. Bologna, Italy, 1994, pp. 139–149.

[CEN96] European Committee for Standardization (CEN). "Fire Detection and Fire Alarm Systems part II—Control and Indicating Equipment." Final Draft prEN54-2, TC72 N752, 1996.

[Gamma+95] E. Gamma, R. Helm, R. Johnson, and J. Vlissides. *Design Patterns: Elements of Reusable Object-Oriented Software*. Reading MA: Addison-Wesley, 1995.

[Schmidt+96] D. C. Schmidt and C. D. Cranor. "Half-Sync/Half-Async: An Architectural Pattern for Efficient and Well-Structured Concurrent I/O." In J. Vlissides, J. O. Coplien, and N. Kerth (eds.), *Pattern Languages of Program Design 2*. Reading, MA: Addison-Wesley, 1996, pp. 437–459.

[Sommerlad96] P. Sommerlad. "Manager." This volume, Chapter 3.

Peter Molin and Lennart Ohlsson can be reached at Peter.Molin@ide.hk-r.se **and** Lennart.Ohlsson@ide.hk-r.se**, respectively.**

PART 9

Process Patterns

At the first two PLoP conferences, patterns and pattern languages on process and organization played an important role. This reflects the fact that problems in software design and programming are not the only problems faced by software engineers. We also need to set up the right organization and project structures for software development projects, and must organize the software development process itself—all adjusted to the needs of the people who build the system and the system under development.

Thus, it is no surprise that even more process organizational patterns were presented at PLoP '96 and EuroPLoP '96. They cover a wide range of aspects.

Chapter 25: The Selfish Class, by Brian Foote and Joseph Yoder. This chapter addresses the issue of how to build code that can be used in many different applications—code that is attractive for programmers, code that "lives" and can evolve.

The main pattern, Selfish Class, discusses what it actually means to build code that is used and reused. Six other patterns help to complete Selfish Class. Works Out of the Box addresses how to build software artifacts that exhibit useful behavior with minimal arguments and configuration. Low Surface-to-Volume describes how to develop artifacts that are easy to understand. Gentle Learning Curve admonishes designers to build artifacts that reveal their complexity and power gradually. Programming-by-Difference shows how code can evolve without jeopardizing its identity. First One's Free and Winning Team contrast two strategies an artifact may employ to solve the problem of finding an audience.

The Selfish Class is especially interesting, because it focuses on code aspects only, ignoring organizations, processes, methods, and personnel. The authors express it best: "The Selfish Class takes a code's-eye view of software reuse and evolution."

Chapter 26: Patterns for Evolving Frameworks, by Don Roberts and Ralph Johnson.

This chapter presents a pattern language that deals with how to build frameworks that really pay off. It covers how to start building a framework, what kind of framework suits one best, how to support building frameworks with existing artifacts, how to design such artifacts, and how to support the development process with appropriate tools.

In total there are nine patterns. The authors emphasize that these patterns describe a common path that frameworks take, but that it is not necessary to follow the path to its end to have a viable framework. In fact, the chapter covers the process space of building frameworks, with several possible paths inside.

Chapter 27: Patterns for Designing in Teams, by Charles Weir.

While most existing works on software design assume a single designer, in reality most systems are designed by a team. This creates a host of new challenges: how to deal with competing design proposals from different team members, how several team members can contribute to a single design how the team can review a design, and how to keep the design documentation up-to-date.

This chapter describes a system of five very coherent patterns which address these issues. Though the patterns do not build on each other to create a complete language, they do complement each other. If you run into one of the problems, it is likely that you will face some of the others as well.

Chapter 28: Patterns for System Testing, by David DeLano and Linda Rising.

This chapter presents patterns that deal with testing, an aspect of software development that, though important, is often neglected. According to the authors, system testing is currently more an art than a science, even when considering current testing procedures and methodologies.

In total there are twenty patterns covering four areas: testing organization, testing efficiency, testing strategy, and problem resolution. The patterns address important technical aspects of testing, but also stress its human side. For example, these patterns look at the amount of work you can assign to a tester and how testers and designers can cooperate effectively.

As a pattern language, this chapter is not yet complete. Not all aspects and problems in testing are covered, yet the chapter addresses many important problems that arise when testing a system. While not all may apply to you, the authors describe particular parts of the whole problem space, and the possible paths through it.

Summary   Interestingly, three of four chapters in this section, and most works on organizational and process aspects presented at PLoP '94 and PLoP '95, are pattern languages. However, this should be no surprise. While design patterns address technical problems that can be discussed well in isolation, most problems in organizing the software development process are closely coupled. None of the problems appear in isolation, and if you solve one problem is a specific way, you may encounter another problem.

Another important observation is that most organization and process pattern languages do not just address technical aspects. They also cover—very explicitly—the human aspects of software development. Examples are the patterns for system testing in this book, and Jim Coplien's Generative Development Process Pattern Language in [PLoPD1]. The process pattern languages you find in the PLoPD series take into account the simple fact that software systems are built by humans. Moreover, systems will continue to be built by humans—independent of any attempts of automating software development.

REFERENCES

[PloPD1] J. O. Coplien and D. C. Schmidt (eds.). *Pattern Languages of Program Design.* Reading, MA: Addison-Wesley, 1995.

Chapter 25

The Selfish Class

Brian Foote and Joseph Yoder

I want to claim almost *limitless power* for slightly inaccurate self-replicating entities, once they arise anywhere in the universe. This is because they become the basis for Darwinian selection, which, given enough generations, cumulatively builds systems of great complexity.

—*The Selfish Gene* [Dawkins, 1989]

This chapter takes a code's-eye view of software reuse and evolution. A code-level artifact must be able to attract programmers in order to survive and flourish. The paper addresses the question of what an object might do to encourage programmers to (re-)use it, as opposed to using some other object, or building new ones. The Selfish Class pattern examines how the sociobiological notion that evolving artifacts tend to behave in the interests of their own survival applies to evolving code. The radical shift in perspective that Dawkins proposed was that from the standpoint of a gene, the organism itself was just a convenient vehicle the gene employed to propagate itself. Our perspective is that programmers stand in just this sort of relationship to evolving code artifacts. The remaining six patterns examine specific strategies that code artifacts can employ to attract programmers.

Programs, and the artifacts from which they are built, have lifecycles that evolve within and beyond the applications that spawn them [Foote and Opdyke 1994]. Software is seldom built from the ground up anymore. Instead, programmers redeploy a variety of artifacts as they confront changing requirements. Among these are function libraries, template applications, legacy code, and object-oriented abstract classes, frameworks, and components. Each step of the way, programmers make choices among existing artifacts to determine which, if any, of them to use or reuse. There is something distinctly Darwinian about this process. The patterns presented herein take a code's-eye view of software evolution. They examine ideas drawn from evolutionary biology, to see whether they might inform our notions of how software evolves.

During the 1970s, sociobiologists proposed that evolution could be best understood by focusing not on species, or even organisms, but on genes themselves as the basis for evolutionary selection. A particularly accessible treatment of these ideas was given by Richard Dawkins in *The Selfish Gene* [Dawkins 1989].

Dawkins suggested that any evolving system must be built around replicators. A replicator is an entity which is capable, via some process or mechanism, of creating exact (or nearly exact) copies of itself, in the presence of a suitable medium, appropriate resources, and so forth. The best known replicators are of course based on the DNA molecule, and are the basis for all life as we know it.

Dawkins goes on to observe that replicators need not be based on DNA. They need not even be biological entities. Dawkins coined the term *meme* to refer to a replicator which, in effect, is an idea, propagated through a culture from mind to mind. While a successful gene might take many generations to predominate its gene pool, a promising meme can penetrate the meme pool at T1[1] speed. It took nature four billion years to build a brain that could serve as a host to the array of memes that constitute human culture. It has taken only thousands of years for the meme pool to attain the richness and variety we see everywhere around us.

No matter what the nature of the replicator, its survival depends on three factors: its longevity, its fecundity, and its fidelity. In order to replicate, a replicator must survive long enough to make copies of itself. A replicator's fecundity is a measure of how prolific it is. Finally, a replicator's fidelity is the degree to which the copies it spawns retain a resemblance to the original replicator. Obviously, a replicator which is not around long enough to make copies of itself will not contribute to posterity. All other things being equal, a replicator should strive to leave as many copies of itself as it can. However, as the copies become less and less faithful, the replicator's aim of preserving itself is undermined. If a replicator becomes extinct as a species evolves and adapts, it might be good for the species, but it is bad for the replicator.

Therein lies the central thesis of the *Selfish Gene*, that replicators, will, over the course of any sustained processes of differential selection, come to behave as if their only interest is their own survival, to the exclusion of any other consideration. In particular, phenomena such as altruism or other behavior that would appear to be exhibited for the good of a clan or species, can be explained solely in terms of replicators looking out for number one.

The seven patterns in this chapter are, first, the Selfish Class and then the six additional patterns that help complete the Selfish Class.

- Works Out of the Box
- Low Surface-to-Volume Ratio

---

[1] T1 speed is 1,544,000 bits/s.

- Gentle Learning Curve
- Programing-by-Difference
- First One's Free
- Winning Team

THE SELFISH CLASS

Also Known As

Software Darwinism
Plumage

Context

We can think of software in terms of a pool of potentially reusable artifacts. In order for these artifacts to flourish, programmers must find them appealing. That is, programmers must elect to use these artifacts in lieu of other artifacts, and in lieu of writing new ones. A successful artifact may find its code copied into (replicated), or better yet, called from, an increasingly large number of programs.

What is the analogue to gene or meme in this tale? Is it the patterns that reside in the minds of software architects, which are expressed in individual artifacts as patterns like aisle and buttress are expressed in individual cathedrals? Or is it more appropriate to construe the artifacts themselves as the durable, evolving repositories of architectural insight? Our own belief tends towards this latter belief, that is, that *artifacts* embody *architecture*.

Problem

Software artifacts that cannot attract programmers are not reused, and fade into oblivion.

Forces

Decisions regarding what objects to reuse, or whether to reuse any code at all, are subject to a host of forces. One of these forces is the Availability of existing, potentially reusable code. Cost can be thought of as one dimension of Availability, since high cost has the effect of making an artifact less available, whereas low (or nonexistent) cost increases availability. Reusable artifacts that are already part of a system are highly available, as are artifacts that are standard parts of programming environments. The enormous body of code that is available on the Internet makes it imperative that programmers scour the net to see what is available before building an artifact themselves. The marketplace itself is also becoming a more important source of reusable artifacts.

A primary consideration is the Utility of an artifact, or whether it in fact does what you want. The fundamental appeal of reuse is simply this: if there is something out there that already does what I need, then I'm done. A widely available artifact which solves a pervasive problem will become quite popular indeed.

A related force is the Suitability of an artifact to the task at hand. An artifact might be unsuitable to a particular task, even if it does what is needed if, for example, it was written for a different operating system or tied to an incompatible GUI.

A particularly powerful force in the realm of reuse is Comprehensibility. If an artifact is easy to understand, programmers are more likely to use it than if it is inscrutable. Code that is easy to read is easier to modify. Comprehensibility is determined by the quality of the code itself, as well as any available examples and documentation. There may be differences among programmers in the perceived comprehensibility of a particular artifact based upon their backgrounds and experience. There are a variety of forces that drive programmers to rewrite artifacts that already exist. Vanity and perversities in the reward structure for reuse are certainly among them. However, artifacts that are too hard to understand remain one of the greatest obstacles to more widespread software reuse.

Another force is the Reliability, or robustness of the artifact. Code that is buggy, and hence is a source of aggravation for programmers who try to use it will (all other things being equal) be driven from the code pool. Interestingly, an artifact can protect itself by exhibiting incorrect behavior only in rare or unpredictable circumstances. These might be thought of as *nonfatal mutations*. A related force might be called Fragility. Fragile code is code which operates correctly out-of-the-box, but which breaks as soon as someone tries to change it.

Solution

Therefore, design artifacts that programmers will want to reuse. Strive to make them widely available. Make sure they reliably solve a useful problem in a direct and comprehensible fashion.

Software artifacts that appeal to programmers will flourish. Those that do not will not. How might a potentially reusable artifact flourish? It can be an integral part of the code for a successful application. The success of such an application will guarantee that this code will remain a focus of programmer attention. However, the mere fact that thousands or millions of copies of an artifact are present in the object code of applications in the field does not help to propagate the code. Only its reincorporation into subsequent versions of the applications in which it resides, or its incorporation into new applications, allows it to reproduce.

In any system subject to such selection pressures, the artifacts which, for whatever reason, prove most effective at surviving these pressures will come, over time, to predominate. This is, after all, Darwinism in a nutshell. It follows then, that for a software artifact to win at this game, it must appeal to programmers. If it is able to do so, it will prosper. If not, it shall not. We think this perspective is unique, in that rather than focusing on programmers or the software development process, it focuses on the code itself. This approach might be thought of as software sociobiology, since it takes the attitude that systems, users, and programmers exist merely as vehicles to abet the evolution of code. By analogy with the selfish gene, one might ponder the notion of the selfish class.

Species are subject, it is said to the law of the jungle. The jungle that anoints the winners and losers in the software domain is the marketplace. An inferior artifact may flourish if it is hosted by an application, that, for whatever reason, succeeds in the marketplace, which in turn makes the source code for the application containing the artifact the subject of additional development efforts. Life in the jungle can be merciless. For example, there is little to prevent a mass extinction of Macintosh software should the marketplace pull its platform out from under these applications.

Related Patterns

We present six additional patterns that help to complete the Selfish Class. A software artifact that Works Out of the Box is immediately able to exhibit useful behavior with minimal arguments or configuration. Enough defaults are provided to get the user up and running without needing to know anything about the system. An artifact that presents a Low Surface-to-Volume Ratio is easier to understand, and provides greater leverage than an artifact that presents a broader cross-section. Gentle Learning Curve admonishes designers to build artifacts that reveal their complexity and power gradually. Programming-By-Difference shows how code can evolve without jeopardizing its identity. First One's Free and Winning Team contrast two strategies an artifact may employ to solve the problem of finding a broad audience.

WORKS OUT OF THE BOX

Also Known As

Batteries Included
Working Example
Good First Impression

Problem

If it is too much trouble to reuse an artifact, programmers may not bother.

Context

There was a time when a programmer's reuse options were limited to a handful of standard library routines. Today, programmers are faced with a rich but daunt-

ing range of potential reuse opportunities. Simply evaluating the relative merits of each possibility can be an overwhelming task. Designers find that they don't have the time to carefully study each new, potentially useful artifact they come across. Instead, they often just try them out, and see what they can do.

Forces

Designers are more likely to reuse an object if it is easy to try it out and see how it works. A good initial impression can motivate the designer to spend the additional time to develop a detailed sense of an object's reuse potential. When the designer can actually see that an object works, he or she develops the confidence that a more detailed exploration will be time well spent. Conversely, if an artifact, such as a class, framework, component, or application, can't be made to work at all, or requires elaborate preparation in order to work, the designer may become discouraged, and look to other options.

Solution

Therefore, design objects so that they will exhibit reasonable behavior with default arguments. Provide everything a programmer needs to try out these objects. Make it as easy as possible for designers to see a working example.

Reuse is an act of Trust. The designer must be confident not only that an object will merely conform to its public interface, but that the semantics associated with this interface are consistent with his or her needs. In other words, the designer must be able to understand how the object works.

Of course, other factors, such as an artifact's Heritage influence whether programmers will trust it as well. A programmer may (or may not) regard code written by Microsoft, for example, as being more reliable, dependable, or polished than that from a less well-known supplier.

When a designer first encounters a class or framework, he or she may not have the time to develop a full comprehension of the power and possibilities implicit in these public interfaces. Hence, designers of such objects should strive to identify a minimal subset of this interface necessary to get a working version of their objects on-the-air.

Classes should be equipped with constructors that supply reasonable working defaults for as many parameters as possible. Arcane, inscrutable mandatory parameters can be as annoying to a test driver as finding the brakes and clutch reversed. A successful test drive may encourage a longer look under the hood.

Abstract classes and frameworks should be bundled with at least one fully functional set of working, concrete subclasses or components (in other words, a working example). Such example objects, classes, and frameworks should come with fully functional, working test programs, and these programs should be accompanied by sample input and output objects or files, where relevant. It's almost always not enough to merely document an artifact's interface. Providing working examples of how interfaces are actually used helps to resolve ambiguity and uncertainty and fosters confidence. Instructions that describe how to run these examples should be included too. These minimal working examples are particularly important when the user is called upon to master complex interfaces. Users should not be left frustrated on Christmas Day because the batteries were *not* included.

One way to learn how a new artifact works is to methodically study its code and documentation. Another is to dive in cold and experiment with the artifact, and thereby get a sense of what it can do. Initial success with such experiments will give programmers the confidence they need to delve more deeply into these objects. Working examples can serve as test beds for exploratory experimentation. Such exploration can permit programmers to incrementally learn how to use an artifact, while keeping the growing example working. Programmers can progress from tinkering with this working example to verifying that they can rebuild it correctly, to a point where they feel that their command of the interface objects they are using is sufficient to justify embedding these objects in their own applications. At the beginning of this process, when every aspect of such a program will be new and probably opaque to the programmer, it is particularly important that getting an artifact to work be as painless as possible.

Programs should exhibit reasonable behavior in the absence of arguments or preexisting data. Designers should strive to ensure that users' first encounters with their creations do not require elaborate preparation.

You should strive to make installation effortless and minimize user configurations. A user will never be so ignorant of the ramifications of configuration decisions as the first time he confronts a new application. Hence, programs delivered in source form should build in responses. Installation programs should provide a default configuration button and allow customization later on.

A design, and the objects that embody it, survive and evolve only if they are used. To be reused, they must attract programmers. To do this, they must make a good first impression. Like a peacock's feathers, an initial, painless presentation of impressive functionality can enhance an object's appeal. Objects which do this can flourish, and others, even if they are technically superior, may not.

Table 25-1 gives several examples of things that work out-of-the-box and things that don't.

Table 25-1 *Artifacts that Encourage or Discourage Adoption*

Works Out of the Box	Does Not Work Out of the Box
Frameworks that subsume the event loop.	Window systems that require elaborate event handling and detailed interaction with arcane APIs to get a single simple window on the air.
`Window new open.`	Objects that can only be built using complex constructors, requiring many unfamiliar arguments.
Objects that are self-contained.	Objects that are loosely coupled to others, that must themselves be prepared in ways that are not carefully explained.
`make all.`	
Supplying working grammars with `lex/yacc/flex/bison`.	

Consequences

One consequence of this pattern is that some abstract classes, like `Window`, will not be pure abstract classes. Instead, they can beget instances that exhibit simple default behavior. C++-style pure abstract classes usually define interfaces. Abstract classes that work out-of-the-box will provide default behavior as well. It is, of course, possible to partition these functions between two classes: a superclass that defines an interface, and a subclass that provides the default behavior.

Related Patterns

Two patterns that might be gleaned from Works Out of the Box and presented as distinct patterns: Default Arguments and Working Examples.

LOW SURFACE-TO-VOLUME RATIO

Also Known As

High Volume-to-Surface Ratio
Simple Interface

Context

Objects that allow a user to control a large volume of complex machinery with a small, simple interface are more likely to flourish than those that don't. See the

A sphere has the lowest surface-to-volume ratio of any three-dimensional object.

Selfish Class. An object with a simple interface relative to its internal complexity may be more likely to Work Out of the Box.

Problem

Objects with complex interfaces that conceal few of their internals are hard to understand and reuse.

Forces

Objects that marshal the resources to perform complex tasks in response to simple external protocols provide the programmer with a high degree of leverage and power. To be effective though, it must be easy to understand how these objects work. The interfaces must be easy to comprehend. This comprehension must be based on the clarity of the interface, and its accompanying documentation and examples, and should not depend on a thorough understanding of the object's internals.

Several forces can conspire to prevent the emergence of these self-contained artifacts. Complex legacy objects may be fragile and difficult to comprehend. The lack of domain experience that inevitably accompanies the start of a project can lead to expedient, first-pass prototype code that properly defers structural improvement in the name of getting the system on the air. And of course, some problems are just inherently complicated and demand that complex artifacts be produced in their image.

Solution

Therefore, Design objects with low surface-to-volume ratios, that is, objects with small external interfaces, or surface areas, that encapsulate a large volume of internal complexity.

In other words, programmers are attracted to good abstractions, with clear separations between the public interfaces and the system's internals. A good abstraction becomes an element of the vocabulary of a domain-specific language. These abstractions must be well encapsulated in order to make them easy to use in multiple contexts. Encapsulation is not enough. An artifact may be self-contained, but still expose all its internals to the public. Such an artifact will, of course, have a surface-to-volume ratio of one. Abstraction is not enough. An artifact might present a tidy interface to the world, but draw in with it a tangled, gangling collection of global variables and resources.

If programmers need a thorough understanding of an object's internal workings in order to use it, it is likely the programmers will find it easier to write their own code. When it comes to being certain about how an object works, there is simply no substitute for having written it yourself. If an artifact encapsulates too little functionality, programmers may again find it preferable to write the code themselves. For example, no collection classes were supplied with C++ until the recent development of the Standard Template Library, so C++ programmers have historically written their own collection classes. It was not the case that no collection code existed. Instead, libraries like the NIH package were not universally available, and were not suitable for a number of platforms [Gorlen86]. However, an overriding factor was that, in the simple cases, programmers could be certain of the architecture of their own abstractions if they built their own. Since the simple cases are by far the most common ones, it can be some time before these home-brewed artifacts evolve into mature, reusable artifacts.

This was not the case with Smalltalk-80 [Goldberg+83]. Smalltalk's Collection classes provide a convenient, comprehensible, and powerful vocabulary for manipulating aggregates that most programmers have come to regard as an integral part of the language.

An artifact with a low surface-to-volume ratio presents a compact vocabulary, with a small number of powerful nouns and verbs. The verbs are the artifact's operations and the nouns are its arguments. To keep the surface area low, the designer must strive to find a concise set of nouns and verbs that can be expressively combined. For instance, lengthy parameter lists can be consolidated into parameter objects [Johnson+88]. These objects, in turn, can be constructed with default fields that spare the user the burden of making decisions about them one at a time.

When mature frameworks and components are available, much of a programmer's time will be spent gluing these elements together. A good fit between the operations and arguments of different elements means less glue is needed to get them to work together. One the other hand, if getting elements to work together requires cumbersome argument packing and unpacking, and awkward protocol translation, programmers may become discouraged, and turn elsewhere.

Another technique that can be used to minimize the effective surface area of an object is to provide simple template methods that call other methods to fill in the details [Gamma+95]. These methods, in turn, can be defined by subclasses of an original class, thereby permitting customization and tailoring.

Ironically, comprehensibility can work against an artifact's preservation, by causing it to mutate more rapidly than artifacts that are harder to understand. Such objects may proliferate, but quickly become unrecognizable. This is often the fate of simple template applications and boilerplate code. An object with a clear interface and hard to understand internals may remain relatively intact. This is a good example of the phenomenon Dawkins called selfishness, whereby the needs of the individual object seem at odds with those of the system as a whole.

Indeed, it's fair to ask what role this phenomenon plays in the proliferation of mediocre code. Will highly comprehensible code, by virtue of being easy to modify, inevitably be supplanted by increasingly less elegant code until some equilibrium is achieved between comprehensibility and fragility? Perhaps simple on the outside/fragile on the inside can be an effective survival strategy for evolving artifacts.

Of course, from the perspective of someone on the outside looking in, allowing good code to evolve into bad code is obviously a bad thing. We don't advocate making good code bad. Instead, we hope that by making programmers aware of how mediocre code might protect itself, we will encourage them to counteract this tendency by refactoring their code so that it is both general and readable.

Related Patterns

A system in the early, Prototype Phase of its evolution is often haphazardly organized [Foote+94]. Such systems may be thought of as white boxes, because so many internal details are left exposed. As systems are redeployed, during the Exploratory Phase, encapsulation often erodes even further, as first-pass guesses as to what needs to be hidden are proven wrong by experience. It is only as an artifact matures, after being reused in a variety of contexts, that the interfaces that have really proven valuable can be discerned. It is for this reason that a Consolidation Phase emphasizing refactoring, late in the lifecycle, is so valuable. During this phase good abstractions emerge and white-box, inheritance-based artifacts give way to black-box components. [Roberts+96] present these notions as the White-Box Framework and Black-Box Framework patterns.

Hence, a high surface-to-volume ratio may be a sign of immaturity or of evolutionary flux. A high surface-to-volume ratio might also be a sign that an object needs to be factored into several distinct objects. In other words, there may be distinct objects trapped inside, crying to get out.

The Gentle Learning Curve pattern states, in essence, that an object should strive to give the appearance to new users of having a lower surface area than it really does. The full interface is gradually exposed as the users learn their way around the object.

GENTLE LEARNING CURVE

Also Known As

Gradual Disclosure
Incremental Revelation
Fold-Out Interfaces

Problem

Complex interfaces can overwhelm beginning users.

Forces

In order to be flexible and adaptable, artifacts may provide a variety of customizable and tailorable interfaces. The variety and complexity of these interfaces can be confusing and intimidating to users who are unfamiliar with an artifact. These users are precisely the ones an artifact must attract if it is to broaden its mind-share. Artifacts that exhibit high utility without imposing an up-front learning burden on the programmer have an advantage over those that do not.

An important force here is time. Given unlimited time, programmers might elect to learn a complex but powerful artifact as an investment in their skills. However, it is far more likely that such programmers, faced with the overwhelming array of choices that the marketplace now, will opt for the easier to *Comprehend* artifact every time.

Solution

Therefore, design artifacts that allow users to start with a simple subset of their capabilities, and permit them to gradually master more complex capabilities as they go along.

An artifact should require the mastery of a simple, minimal set of capabilities at first. One way to do this is to provide defaults. Default constructors and arguments not only allow an artifact to work out of the box, they also provide direct, simple templates and examples that show how an artifact can be used to perform likely tasks. A Gentle Learning Curve provides many of the same benefits that Works Out of the Box does early on, while rewarding more advanced programmers with more intricate and powerful capabilities later on.

One way to do this is to use what might be called a fold-out interface. The name was inspired by the PKZIP help system, which displays a list of rudimentary switches when the user asks for help, and reveals more complex options incrementally in the manner of a programmer's fold-out reference card. The simple options are those which provide more or less out-of-the-box functionality while providing the appearance of a low surface to volume ratio. Then as the user becomes more proficient and comfortable, ways to get to additional features of the interface are exposed

As users become more sophisticated, they can gradually delve more deeply into more powerful and exotic aspects of artifacts' capabilities. For instance, UNIX and DOS commands are usually designed to perform common useful tasks with no arguments at all. In other cases, the no-argument form provides a simple help message. More complicated forms can be learned as the user gains confidence with these commands. Manuals and online documentation can then provide examples of a command's more powerful but arcane variants.

VisualWorks provides a couple of good working examples of Gentle Learning Curve. One example can be seen in the `ApplicationModel` class. A method called Open is provided for opening an applications on a default canvas. As the users become more proficient, they can develop different canvases and use the open-`Interface:` method to dynamically choose which canvas to open. Users can also add new widgets, enable/disable widgets, and so forth by using the `postBuild:` and `postOpen:` methods.

Also, when new developers learn Smalltalk, they are taught the basics of the collection hierarchy by learning simple methods such as `do:` and `add:`. After becoming comfortable with using the basics of collections, developers are pointed to more advanced methods such as `collect:`, `select:`, `inject:into:`, and `contains:` for doing the same work they had been doing with the basic methods.

An artifact which presents a Gentle Learning Curve can appeal to programmers because it places a minimal burden on prospective users at precisely the time they are choosing from among alternatives. There are, of course, artifacts that require programmers to immerse themselves in all their details before they can be used. In other words, they present steep learning curves. Usually these artifacts are essentially in monopoly positions. Programmers must learn them, because there are no simpler alternatives. When this is the case, programmers will dutifully, but reluctantly, bite the bullet and master these artifacts.

PROGRAMMING-BY-DIFFERENCE

Also Known As

Wrap It, Don't Bag It

> The true value of object-oriented techniques as opposed to conventional programming techniques is not that they can do things conventional techniques can't, but that they can often extend behavior by adding new code in cases where conventional techniques would require editing existing code instead. Objects are good because they allow new concepts to be added to a system without modifying previously existing code. Methods are good because they permit adding functionality to a system without modifying previous existing code. Classes are good because they enable using the behavior of one object as part of the behavior of another without modifying previously existing code.
>
> —*The Treaty of Orlando* [Stein et al., 1988]

Problem

You want to adapt an artifact to address new requirements while maintaining the artifact's integrity.

Forces

There is a tension between the forces of change and the forces that encourage stability. One force that leads to wrapping is a lack of availability. If the code for an artifact is unavailable, it may be difficult (to say the least) to change it. For example, the artifact may reside in a legacy system and provide a service which the developer is compelled to use. One can use these existing services by writing wrappers around these services. Even in those instances where rewriting the code might be a better long-term strategy, expediency might dictate that simple wrappers be used with legacy code to get something running quickly.

More commonly, artifacts are available, but may be fragile, or difficult to comprehend. Under these circumstances, changes to them might undermine not just the new application, but existing code that shares the artifact. Isolating changes in an entourage of distinct subclasses or components that leaves the original artifact untouched avoids these pitfalls. This strategy is often the ideal way to balance new requirements against a reluctance to jeopardize existing, working artifacts.

Solution

Therefore, use translators, subclasses, and/or wrappers to supply new states or behavior while leaving the original artifact intact.

A translator is an adapter that takes results from existing artifacts and converts them to some other format that may be more usable by other artifacts. A translator can take existing output, say from a legacy system, do some work on it, and put it in some new artifact, say a relational database, which is more easily accessible. Sometimes this is done by using the Interpreter pattern [Gamma+95].

Subclassing preserves the behavior of the original code while making it easy to extend and/or specialize. Ralph Johnson calls this style of programming Programming-by-Difference [Johnson+88]. Composition allows one to use two or more existing artifacts to get the desired results. Of course, these approaches can be mixed.

There is one quality of reusable artifacts that does not have a direct analog in biology. That is, when a reusable artifact is shared and called, rather than copied. Every program that refers to it immediately benefits from any changes made to the artifact. One might say there is a Super-Lamarkian character to this kind of sharing, in that descendants can benefit immediately and retroactively from changes made to their parents.[2]

Related Patterns

The Adapter, Composite, Decorator, Facade, and Interpreter patterns all provide ways by which an existing artifact might be wrapped to provide extended functionality [Gamma +95].

Approaches like this one that preserve the integrity of existing artifacts are particularly valuable during the Prototype and Expansionary Phases of the lifecycle, since they allow objects to be redeployed in new contexts without the potential disruption to existing applications that might ensue if they were subject to invasive modification.

---

[2] Lamarkism is the belief that characteristics acquired during an organism's lifetime can be inherited by that organism's offspring.

An artifact with a Low Surface-to-Volume Ratio will be easier to wrap than one with a more complex external interface. An artifact that is widely available, and that Works Out of the Box, is more likely to be incorporated in new work than one that is less accommodating.

FIRST ONE'S FREE

Also Known As

Netscape Now
Doom
Copyleft
Freeware/Shareware

This pattern helps to solve the problem presented in Selfish Class by encouraging wide dissemination of an artifact.

Problem

In order to survive, an artifact must become widely available.

Forces

No matter how good an artifact is, it will have no chance of proliferating if other programmers never see it. To survive an artifact must gain a wide audience. One of the forces that may limit an artifact's availability is its cost. A countervailing force is bankruptcy. With this strategy, there is always the risk of giving away the store.

Solution

Therefore, give the artifact away.

One scheme that artifacts use to gain wide dissemination is the First One's Free strategy. Urban legend has it that drug peddlers give away introductory samples of their otherwise expensive wares as a way of recruiting new addicts. Once a potential customer is addicted, this 100% discount no longer applies.

All other things being equal, an artifact which is less expensive and easier to acquire will proliferate faster and farther than one that is not. When cost drops to next to nothing, its usual effect on an artifact's availability is minimized. In the software world, these discounts often reach 100% and beyond, as in the case of promotions like those of America Online or Compuserve, that include postage and floppy disks. If only a small number of customers become dependent on a steady diet of services from these suppliers, this strategy can prove profitable in the long run.

The World Wide Web browser wars provide a striking example of this dissemination strategy in action. To gain market share, Netscape and Microsoft simply give away their Navigator and Explorer products.

The Free Software Foundation's GNU project has long given away dozens of complex applications, complete with source code. Their novel *copyleft* license requires that new applications derived from their code be distributed under the same terms as the original source code. The focus on source code distinguishes this approach from the Freeware/Shareware and First One's Free variants.

WINNING TEAM

Also Known As

Piggybacking
Remora[3] Strategy
Whatever for Windows
Hitch Your Wagon to a Star

Problem

In order to survive, an artifact must become widely available.

Forces

No matter how good an artifact is, it will have no chance of proliferating if other programmers never see it. In order to survive, an artifact must gain a wide audience. One way an artifact can become widely available is to hitch a ride on a popular platform. The way for an artifact to win big is to have its code universally included with every copy of a system that ships. This strategy's drawback is that the artifact loses its autonomy. Its fate becomes tied to that of its platform.

Solution

Therefore, strive to become bundled with a popular platform.

Interestingly, every commercially successful object-oriented framework has been distributed with full source code. In the case of the GUI frameworks such as Model-View-Controller (MVC), MacApp, Object Windows Library (OWL), and Microsoft Foundation Classes (MFC), the framework, with its source and documentation, is bundled with the development tools for a particular language/platform pair.

---

[3] The remora is a parasitic marine fish of the family *Echeneidae*.

It's interesting that giving away the store in this fashion doesn't seem to under-mine the product. The phenomenon seems to work something like this: give away a thousand lines of code and ruin your business, give away a million lines of code and ruin the other guy's business. While it may be possible to steal key ideas from a small body of code, actually copying a million-line product without being obvi-ous is more difficult. More importantly, few organizations are willing to assume the comprehension burden and maintenance responsibility for a large body of someone else's code.

A drawback to this strategy is the possibility of mass extinction. If the platform itself loses favor, all the artifacts that depend on it, regardless of their individual strengths or weaknesses, will perish as well.

The Java programming language has employed both the First One's Free and Winning Team strategies [Gosling+96]. The runtime environment necessary to support Java applets hitches a ride inside the popular World Wide Web browsers, which in turn are given away. Hence, Java gleans the benefits of both, without incurring the risk associated with tying itself to a specific platform.

CONCLUSION

Software that does not evolve will die [Foote+95]. Of course, an anonymous chunk of code trapped in a successful application may persist inside it for decades, dutifully doing whatever it is that it does. However, if an application is so inscrutable and fragile that programmers never dare touch it, our chunk of code is as sterile as a mule, and will never have the opportunity to propagate. Artifacts flourish only by attracting programmers. This, in turn, ultimately leads to specialization. One of the major benefits of reuse is that responsibility for the maintenance, improvement, and evolution of a widely reused artifact that retains its distinctive identity can remain in one place.

We think an interesting and unexpected result of our code's eye perspective on reuse is that phenomena like selfishness, which have been observed by zoologists in their own studies of evolution, may arise as software evolves as well. Software, it would seem, plays by the same rules as everyone else when it comes to evolu-tion. Of course, just as biology is not necessarily destiny, we need not give in to entropic evolutionary tendencies in our code. Judicious refactoring, good docu-mentation, and an eye for architectural integrity can overcome the tendency of our artifacts to just look out for themselves.

Programmers with a commitment to reuse, while focusing on the problems at hand, keep one eye toward the future and the potential for the artifacts they are building to find a wider audience within or beyond the application they currently inhabit. Such programmers are not content that their craftsmanship be seen only by God, like the medieval artisans who carved gargoyles that could be viewed only from lofty perches and would never be seen by mere mortals.

ACKNOWLEDGMENTS

We are grateful to the members of the University of Illinois Patterns Group: Jeff Barcalow, John Brant, Ian Chai, Charles Herring, Ralph Johnson, Mark Kendrat, Donald Roberts, and Dmitry Zelenko. They soldiered through a particularly rough earlier draft of this paper and provided a variety of commentary and advice, a good deal of which was genuinely useful.

We would also like to thank Desmond D'Souza who shepherded our next draft.

We are grateful as well to Doug Lea, who provided detailed and provocative comments on a later version of this chapter.

We'd like to gratefully acknowledge the assistance of Tom Lee and Vic Alcott of General Electric, who helped us obtain permission to use the vintage air conditioner advertisement depicted in the "Works Out of the Box" pattern.

Finally, we'd like to express our gratitude to the PLoP '96 writers workshop participants who, with their candid and constructive criticism, helped us shape and polish the current incarnations of these patterns.

REFERENCES

[Alexander79] Christopher Alexander. *The Timeless Way of Building.* Oxford: Oxford University Press, 1979.

[Alexander+77] C. Alexander, S. Ishikawa, and M. Silverstein. *A Pattern Language.* Oxford: Oxford University Press, 1977.

[Dawkins89] Richard Dawkins. *The Selfish Gene.* Oxford: Oxford University Press, 1989.

[Foote+94] B. Foote and W. F. Opdyke. "Life-cycle and Refactoring Patterns that Support Evolution and Reuse," in *Pattern Languages of Program Design.* J. O. Coplien and D. C. Schmidt (eds). Reading, MA: Addison-Wesley, 1995.

[Foote+95] B. Foote and J. Yoder. "Architecture, Evolution, and Metamorphosis," in *Pattern Languages of Program Design 2.* In J. Vlissides, J. O. Coplien, and N. L. Kerth. (eds). Reading, MA: Addison-Wesley, 1996.

[Gamma+95] E. Gamma, R. Helm, R. Johnson, and J. Vlissides. *Design Patterns: Elements of Reusable Object-Oriented Software.* Reading, MA: Addison-Wesley, 1995.

[Goldberg+83] A. Goldberg and D. Robson. *Smalltalk-80: The Language and Its Implementation.* Reading, MA: Addison-Wesley, 1983.

[Gorlen86] K. Gorlen. *Object-Oriented Program Support (OOPS) Reference Manual.* National Institutes of Health, May 1986.

[Gosling+96] J. Gosling, B. Joy, and G. Steele. *The Java™ Language Specification.* Reading, MA: Addison-Wesley, 1983.

[Johnson+88] R. E. Johnson and B. Foote. "Designing Reusable Classes." *Journal of Object-Oriented Programming* 1:2, June/July 1988, pp. 22–35.

[Roberts+96] D. Roberts and R. Johnson. "Patterns for Evolving Frameworks." This volume, Chapter 26.

[Stein+88] L. A. Stein, H. Lieberman, and D. Ungar. "A Shared View of Sharing: The Treaty of Orlando" in *Object-Oriented Concepts, Databases, and Applications,* W. Kim and F. H. Lochovsky (eds.). New York: ACM Press, 1989.

Brian Foote and Joseph Yoder can be reached at foote@cs.uiuc.edu **and** yoder@cs.uiuc.edu, **respectively.**

Chapter 26

Patterns for Evolving Frameworks

Don Roberts and Ralph Johnson

Frameworks are reusable designs of all or part of a software system described by a set of abstract classes and the way instances of those classes collaborate. A good framework can reduce the cost of developing an application by an order of magnitude because it lets you reuse both design and code. They do not require new technology, because they can be implemented with existing object-oriented programming languages.

Developing a good framework, unfortunately, is expensive. It must be simple enough to be learned, yet must provide enough features that it can be used quickly and enough hooks for features that are likely to change. Frameworks, which must embody a theory of the problem domain, are always the result of domain analysis, whether explicit and formal or hidden and informal.

Therefore, frameworks should be developed only when many applications are going to be developed within a specific problem domain, which allows the time savings of reuse to recoup the time invested to develop them.

The patterns in this chapter form a pattern language, a set of patterns that are used together to solve a problem. In general, you start at the beginning of a pattern language and work to the end. However, many of these patterns are applied repeatedly, so you will be working with many of them at once.

Figure 26-1 shows how the patterns are related to each other in a sort of time-line. Some patterns never overlap. Others usually do. When two patterns have the same time-span, it means that sometimes one goes first, sometimes the other. The Rationale and Implementation sections of the pattern descriptions discuss some of the complexities that cannot be illustrated by a diagram like Figure 26-1.

Evolving Frameworks describes a common path that frameworks take, but it is not necessary to follow the path to the end to have a viable framework. In fact, most frameworks stop evolving before they reach the end. In some cases, this is because the frameworks die; they are not used so they do not continue to change

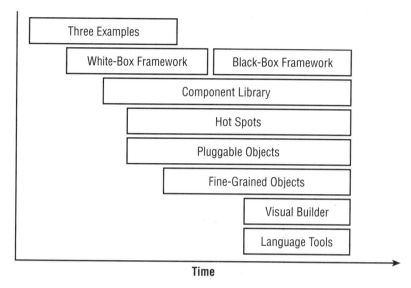

Figure 26-1 *Relationship between patterns in the Evolving Frameworks pattern language*

or evolve. In other cases, it is better for the frameworks to stay more White-Box [Johnson+88]. The forces for the various patterns should describe why.

THREE EXAMPLES

You have decided to develop a framework for a particular problem domain.

Problem

How do you start designing a framework?

Forces

- People develop abstractions by generalizing from concrete examples. Every attempt to determine the correct abstractions on paper without actually developing a running system is doomed to failure. No one is that smart. A framework is a reusable design, so you develop it by looking at the things it is supposed to be a design of. The more examples you look at, the more general your framework will be.
- Designing applications is hard. You can't have too many examples or you'll never get your framework done.

- Having a framework makes it easier to develop applications, even when the framework is only marginally useful. Once you get the first version of the framework, it will be easier to develop more examples.
- Projects that take a long time to deliver anything tend to get canceled. There is usually a window of market opportunity that must be met. If the project doesn't start producing or saving money, the organization will run into cash-flow problems. Political fortunes within a company rise and fall, and a system must be built before its champions move on to other interests or other companies.

Solution

Develop three applications that you believe that the framework should help you build. These applications should pay for their own development.

Rationale

Developing reusable frameworks cannot occur by simply sitting down and thinking about the problem domain. No one has the insight to come up with the proper abstractions. Domain experts don't understand how to codify the abstractions they have in their heads, and programmers don't understand the domain well enough to derive the abstractions. In fact, there are often abstractions that do not become apparent until a framework has been reused. Quite often these hidden abstractions have no physical analogs (for example, Strategy objects).

While initial designs may be acceptable for single applications, the ability to generalize to many applications can only come by actually building them and determining which abstractions are being reused. Generalizing from a single application rarely happens. It is easier to generalize from two applications, but it is still difficult. The general rule is: build an application, build a second application that is slightly different from the first, and, finally, build a third application that is even more different for the first two. Provided that all of the applications fall within the problem domain, common abstractions will become apparent.

Your framework, however, won't be done after three applications. You can expect it to continue to evolve. However, it should be useful and you can use it to gather more examples. Just don't acquire too many users initially—the framework *will* change.

Implementation

There are several approaches to developing these applications.

In the first approach, you simply build three applications in succession, making sure that both code and people are carried over from one project to the next. This allows the team to begin reusing design insight immediately at the possible expense of narrowness.

In the second approach, the applications are developed in parallel by separate teams. This approach allows for diversity and different points of view at the expense of the time it takes to unify these applications in the future. To reduce this integration time, it is best to have a reuse team, separate from the application teams, whose responsibility it is to identify and extract reusable components from the developing applications.

A third approach is that you have a series of applications built without trying to reuse any code, and then suddenly realize you need to build a framework. Since you've already developed your three applications, you can often do a good job at the framework the first time. This is not a counterexample; it's just a different approach in which you built your examples before you decided to start the framework.

A fourth approach is to prototype several applications without building industrial-strength versions of any of them. You'll probably have to refactor the framework when you use it, but you'll be a lot closer than you would be after one application. An advantage of this approach is that you can sell your customer the rights to use the framework from the beginning, and not have to sell ownership of it. Even though you'll change the framework because of what you learn with the application, you'll still retain ownership. The main disadvantage is that you have to do some work up front.

When you build a series of applications, it is often difficult to get the right to use code written for one to build the next. Note that no special object-oriented design techniques are needed when you are building these applications. Just use standard techniques and try to keep your system flexible and extensible.

Examples

The Runtime System Expert framework was initially developed by developing runtime systems for various platforms. The first platform was Tektronix Smalltalk. The second was ParcPlace Smalltalk [Durham+96]. Bill Reynen created a C frontend for the RTL system which required a C runtime system (which was quite trivial). We don't know what original examples the designers of MVC had in mind, but we do know that the way the application has used MVC affected how it evolved into the framework currently implemented in VisualWorks 2.5.

Related Patterns

This is a special example of the Rule of Three [Tracz88]. The initial versions of the framework will probably be White-Box Frameworks.

WHITE-BOX FRAMEWORK

You have started to build your second application.

Problem

Some frameworks rely heavily on inheritance, others on polymorphic composition. Which should you use?

Forces

- Inheritance results in strong coupling between components, but it lets you modify the components that you are reusing, so you can change things that the original designer never imagined you would change.
- Making a new class involves programming.
- Polymorphic composition requires knowing what is going to change.
- Composition is a powerful reuse technique, but it is difficult to understand by examining static program text.
- Compositions can be changed at runtime.
- Inheritance is static and cannot easily be changed at runtime.

Solution

Use inheritance. Build a white-box framework by generalizing from the classes in the individual applications [Johnson+88]. Use patterns like Template Method and Factory Method to increase the amount of reusable code in the superclasses from which you are inheriting [Gamma+95]. Don't worry if the applications don't share any concrete classes, although they probably will.

Rationale

Inheritance is the most expedient way of allowing users to change code in an object-oriented environment. This allows you to create new classes by simply inheriting most of the desired behavior from an existing class and overriding only the methods that are different in the subclass. At this point, you should not be worrying about the semantics of inheritance, just the ability to reuse existing code. Once you have built a working framework, you can start using it. This will show you what is likely to change and what is not. Later, immutable code can be encapsulated and parameterized by converting the framework into a Black-Box framework. However, at this point in the lifecycle, you probably do not have enough information to make an informed decision as to which parts of the framework will consistently change across applications and which parts will remain constant.

Implementation

While developing the subsequent applications, whenever you find that you need a class that is similar to a class that you developed in a prior application, create a subclass and override the methods that are different. This is known as programming-by-difference [Johnson+88]. After you've made a couple of subclasses, you will recognize which parts you are consistently overriding and which parts are relatively stable. At that point, you will be able to create an abstract class to contain the common portions.

Also, while overriding methods, you will probably discover that certain methods are almost the same in all of the subclasses. Again, you should factor out the parts that change into a new method. By doing this, the original methods will all become identical and can be moved into the abstract class.

Examples

The Model-View-Controller framework for graphical user interfaces was originally a white-box framework. New View and Controller classes were created by making subclasses of the View and Controller classes, respectively. For example, to create a scrolling view, a programmer would have to create a new subclass of ScrollController to handle the scrolling behavior for the view.

Related Patterns

As you develop additional applications, you should begin to build a component library. Black-Box Framework addresses the same problem, but in a different context.

COMPONENT LIBRARY

You are developing the second and subsequent examples based on the White-Box Framework.

Problem

Similar objects must be implemented for each problem the framework solves. How do you avoid writing similar objects for each instantiation of the framework?

Forces

- Bare-bones frameworks require a lot of effort to use. Things that work out of the box are much easier to use [Foote+96]. A framework with a good library of concrete components will be easier to use than one with a small library.
- Up front, it is difficult to tell which components users of the framework will need. Some components are problem-specific, while others occur in most solutions.

Solution

Start with a simple library of the obvious objects and add additional objects as you need them.

Rationale

As you add objects to the library, some will be problem-specific and never get reused. These will eventually be removed from the library. However, these objects will provide valuable insight into the type of code that users of the framework must write. Others will be common across most or all solutions. From these, you will be able to derive the major abstractions within the problem domain that should be represented as objects in the framework.

Implementation

These objects are the concrete subclasses of the abstract classes that make up the framework. The framework consists of the classes, typically abstract, that are reused across all applications that use it. The component library consists of the classes, typically concrete, that are reused in some applications, but not necessarily every one. The component library can be created by accumulating all of the concrete classes created for the various applications derived from the framework. In the long run, a class should only be included in the component library if it was used by several applications, but in the beginning, you should put all of them in. If a component gets used a lot, it should remain in the library. If it never gets reused, it gets thrown out. Many components will get refactored into smaller sub-components by later patterns and disappear that way.

Examples

The first step in creating a component library for MVC, which took place in the early 1980s, was the creation of pluggable views. Pluggable views provided a way to adapt a controller and view-pair to the interface of a particular model. For example, `SelectionInListView` was a pluggable view that provided a list view that could be adapted to any model that contained a list. Despite this step, MVC as a whole was still fairly white-box, since you had to make a new subclass to do anything other than adapt the view to a particular model.

Related Patterns

As components get added to the library, you will begin to see recurring code that sets of components share. You should look for Hot Spots in your framework where the code seems to change from application to application.

HOT SPOTS

You are adding components to your Component Library.

Problem

As you develop applications based on your framework, you will see similar code being written over and over again. Wolfgang Pree calls these locations "hot spots" in the framework [Pree94]. How do you eliminate this common code?

Forces

- If changeable code is scattered across an application, it is difficult to track down and change.
- If changeable code is located in a common location, program flow can be obfuscated since calls are always being made to the object that contains the changeable code.

Solution

Separate code that changes from code that remains stable. Ideally, the varying code should be encapsulated within objects whenever possible, since objects are easier to reuse than individual methods. With the code encapsulated, variation is achieved by composing the desired objects rather than creating subclasses and writing methods.

Rationale

If the framework is being reused extensively (as it should be), certain pieces will vary often. By gathering the code that varies into a single location (object) it will both simplify the reuse process and show users where the designers expect the framework to change. Good names for these objects will make the control flow less important to understanding the framework [Beck96].

Implementation

Many of the Gang-of-Four design patterns encapsulate various types of changes. Table 26-1 shows possible design patterns to use when different portions of the framework change from application to application [Gamma+95].

Examples

Objectworks 4.0 began the extensive use of wrappers, which is an example of the Decorator pattern. The code to add features to views was stored in the wrappers. This was in response to framework users who had to write similar code each time they wanted to add a particular function to a view or controller. In the new ver-

Table 26-1 *Design Pattern Recommendations for Framework Variations*

What Varies	Design Pattern
Algorithms	Strategy, Visitor
Actions	Command
Implementations	Bridge
Response to change	Observer
Interactions between objects	Mediator
Object being created	Factory Method, Abstract Factory, Prototype
Structure being created	Builder
Traversal algorithm	Iterator
Object interfaces	Adapter
Object behavior	Decorator, State

sion of the framework, window features are added by adding the appropriate wrapper for each desired behavior. For example, to create a view with a menu bar and scrolling behavior, the programmer simply adds a `ScrollWrapper` and a `MenuBarWrapper` to his view.

Related Patterns

To encapsulate the Hot Spots, you will often have to create finer-grained objects. Often these fine-grained objects will cause your framework to become more Black-Box.

PLUGGABLE OBJECTS

You are adding components to your Component Library.

Problem

Most of the subclasses that you write differ in trivial ways (for example, only one method is overridden). How, then, do you avoid having to create trivial subclasses each time you want to use the framework?

Forces

- New classes, no matter how trivial, increase the complexity of the system.
- Complex sets of parameters make parameterized classes more difficult to understand and use.

Solution

Design adaptable subclasses that can be parameterized with messages to send, indexes to access, blocks to evaluate, or whatever else distinguishes one trivial subclass from another.

Rationale

If the difference between subclasses is trivial, creating a new subclass just to encapsulate the small change is overkill. Adding parameters to the instance creation protocol provides for reuse of the original class without resorting to programming.

Implementation

Determine what changes in each of the subclasses that you have been required to write. If the difference is simply in some constant, symbol, or class reference, create an instance variable to contain the reference and pass it into the object in the instance creation method. If the variation is in a small piece of code, pass a block representing the code to the instance creation method and, again, store it in an instance variable. If you are in an environment that does not support blocks, such as C++, use the available facilities for anonymous functions, such as function pointers.

Examples

Early versions of the Model-View-Controller framework included the notion of pluggable views. These were standardized view classes (such as `Selection-InListView`) that could be opened on any model provided the appropriate messages to retrieve the information from the model were passed as parameters when the view was created. In more recent versions of the framework, the pluggable views have been mostly supplanted by `PluggableAdaptors` that allow the standard `value` and `value:` messages that `Models` must understand to be translated into arbitrary pieces of code stored in blocks. This essentially allows `Views` to be plugged into any object regardless of what set of messages it understands.

Related Patterns

Creating pluggable objects is one way to encapsulate the Hot Spots in your framework. The parameters can be automatically supplied by a Visual Builder.

FINE-GRAINED OBJECTS

You are refactoring your Component Library to make it more reusable.

Problem

How far should you go in dividing objects into smaller objects?

Forces

- The more objects there are in the system, the more difficult it is to understand.
- Applications can be created by simply choosing the objects that implement the functionality desired within an application. No programming is required.

Solution

Continue breaking objects into finer and finer granularities until it doesn't make sense to do so any further. That is, dividing the object further would result in objects that have no individual meaning in the problem domain.

Rationale

Since frameworks will ultimately be used by domain experts (nonprogrammers), you will be providing tools to create the compositions automatically. Therefore, it is more important to avoid programming. The tools can be designed to manage the proliferation of objects.

Implementation

Anywhere in your component library that you find classes that encapsulate multiple behaviors that could possibly vary independently, create multiple classes to encapsulate each behavior. Wherever the original class was used, replace it with a composition that recreates the desired behavior. This will reduce code duplication, as well as reduce the need to create new subclasses for each new application.

Examples

Beginning with Objectworks 4.0, the Model-View-Controller became more fine-grained. This was accomplished by using new objects that represented finer-grained concepts than the original `Model`, `View`, and `Controller` classes. A couple of examples of these objects were `Wrappers`, which allowed a unit of functionality to be added to any view, and `ValueHolders`, which allowed views to depend on only a portion of a model rather than the entire model [Woolf94]. With this version, to make a view scrollable the programmer needed only to apply a `Scroll-Wrapper` to his view.

Related Patterns

As objects become more fine-grained, the framework will become more Black-Box.

BLACK-BOX FRAMEWORK

You are developing Pluggable Objects by encapsulating Hot Spots and making Fine-Grained Objects.

Problem

Some frameworks rely heavily on inheritance, others on polymorphic composition. Which should you use?

Forces

- Inheritance results in strong coupling between components, but lets you modify the components you are reusing, so you can change things that the original designer never imagined you would change.
- Making a new class involves programming.
- Polymorphic composition requires knowing what is going to change.
- Composition is a powerful reuse technique, but it is difficult to understand by examining static program text.
- Compositions can be changed at runtime.
- Inheritance is static and cannot easily be changed at runtime.

Solution

Use inheritance to organize your component library and composition to combine the components into applications. Essentially, inheritance will provide a taxonomy of parts to ease browsing and composition will allow maximum flexibility in application development. When it isn't clear which is the better technique for a given component, favor composition.

Rationale

A Black-Box Framework is one where you can reuse components by plugging them together and not worry about how they accomplish their individual tasks [Johnson+88]. In contrast, White-Box Frameworks require an understanding of how the classes work so that correct subclasses can be developed.

People like to organize things into hierarchies. These hierarchies allow us to classify things and quickly see how various classifications are related. By using inheritance, which represents an is-a relationship, to organize our component library, we can rapidly see how the myriad of components in the library are related to each other. By using composition to create applications, we both avoid programming and allow the compositions to vary at runtime.

Implementation

Convert inheritance relationships to component relationships. Pull out common code in unrelated (by inheritance) classes and encapsulate it in new components. Many of the previous patterns provide the techniques for locating and creating new component classes.

Examples

VisualWorks is MVC turned into a Black-Box Framework. Now, rather than creating various subclasses of `View` or even reusing various subclasses of `View`, we take a generic `View` and add wrappers to it corresponding to the various behaviors that we require. In the same way, rather than creating a complex model class and ensuring that dependencies get updated correctly, we simply compose a bunch of `ValueHolders` to hold the values in our model and let them worry about updating their dependents.

Another example of this is Alan Durham's Runtime System Expert for the Typed Smalltalk Compiler [Durham+96].

Related Patterns

By organizing the component library in the manner, we support the creation of a visual builder that allows the library to be browsed and compositions to be created graphically.

VISUAL BUILDER

You have a Black-Box Framework and can now make an application entirely by connecting objects of existing classes. The behavior of your application is then determined entirely by how these objects are interconnected. A single application consists of two parts. The first part is the script that connects the objects of the framework and then turns them on. The second part is the behavior of the individual objects. The framework provides most of the second part, but the application programmer must still provide the first part.

Problem

The connection script is usually very similar from application to application with only the specific objects being different. How do you simplify the creation of these scripts?

Forces

- The compositions that represent applications of the framework are convoluted and difficult to understand and generate.
- Tool building is expensive.
- Domain experts are rarely programmers.

Solution

Make a graphical program that lets you specify the objects that will be in your application and how they are interconnected. It should generate the code for an application from its specifications.

Rationale

Since the code is basically just a script, the tool can generate it automatically. The tool will also make the framework more user-friendly by providing a graphical interface that should draw on the standard notations present in the problem domain. At this point, domain experts can create applications by simply manipulating images on the screen. Only in rare cases should new classes have to be added to the framework.

Implementation

Sometimes you can specify the components and relationships in an application entirely with dialog boxes and browsers, but usually you need to draw graphs to represent the complex relationships present in more complicated domains. In this case, you should use a framework for graphical editors like HotDraw [Johnson92].

Examples

In Visualworks 1.0, ParcPlace provided an interface builder to allow users to "paint" the GUI on a canvas. The builder takes the graphical description of the GUI and creates the application from it. It does this by creating an `Application-Model` with `ValueHolders` of the appropriate type for each control. It creates composite `View` objects that make up the main `View` and adds `Wrappers` to create the appropriate functionality for each widget. All of this information is stored in a `windowSpec`, which is a declarative description of the entire GUI. At runtime, the `windowSpec` is fed to a `UIBuilder` that interprets it, creates the objects it describes, and composes them to create the final user-interface. `UIBuilder` is implemented as an Interpreter [Gamma+95].

Related Patterns

Congratulations. You have just developed a visual programming language. Note that this implies that you will need language tools, just as in any other language.

LANGUAGE TOOLS

You have just created a Visual Builder.

Problem

The Visual Builder creates complex composite objects. How do you easily inspect and debug these compositions?

Forces

- Existing tools are usually inadequate for dealing with the specialized composition relationships present in the framework.
- Building good tools is an expensive task that can be viewed as overhead.

Solution

Create specialized inspecting and debugging tools.

Rationale

Since the system you have created is essentially a graphical, domain-specific, programming language, it will require language tools to help debug and understand it. The tools that came with the language in which you built your framework will probably not be as good as they should be, because your framework will be filled with little objects that all look alike—and half of them will be completely uninteresting to someone who just wants to build an application.

Implementation

Find the portions of your framework that are difficult to inspect and debug. These can usually be found where objects are being composed extensively using things such as wrappers and strategies. Create specialized tools to navigate and inspect the compositions. These tools should allow the user to `elide` portions of the composition that are not interesting.

Examples

Visualworks doesn't have this yet, but it is the next logical step in its evolution. Many long-time MVC programmers have complained that the current framework is difficult to use since the views contain too many wrappers. The real problem is that there are no inspectors or debuggers specifically designed for handling these compositions. If such tools existed, debugging or inspecting a view should be no more difficult than inspecting any other object in the system.

ACKNOWLEDGMENTS

We would like to thank Ward Cunningham for his shepherding and valuable insight that is reflected in the final version of this chapter. We would also like to thank the UIUC patterns group members for their scathing reviews that helped us discover some of the weaknesses in our presentation.

REFERENCES

[Beck96] K. Beck. *Smalltalk Best Practice Patterns—Volume 1: Coding.* Prentice-Hall, 1996.

[Durham+96] A. Durham and R. Johnson. A Framework for Run-time Systems and its Visual Programming Language. In *Proceedings of OOPSLA '96, Object-Oriented Programming Systems, Languages, and Applications.* San Jose, CA, October 1996.

[Foote+95] B. Foote and W. Opdyke. "Life Cycle and Refactoring Patterns that Support Evolution and Reuse." *Pattern Languages of Program Design.* J. O. Coplien and D. C. Schmidt (eds.). Reading, MA: Addison-Wesley, 1995.

[Foote+96] B. Foote and J. Yoder. "The Selfish Class." This volume, Chapter 25.

[Gamma+95] E. Gamma, R. Helm, R. Johnson, and J. Vlissides. *Design Patterns: Elements of Object-Oriented Software.* Reading, MA: Addison-Wesley, 1995.

[Johnson+88] R. Johnson and B. Foote. "Designing Reusable Classes." *Journal of Object-Oriented Programming,* 1(2):22–35, June/July 1988.

[Pree94] W. Pree. *Design Patterns for Object-Oriented Software Development.* Reading, MA: Addison-Wesley, 1994.

[Tracz88] W. Tracz. RMISE Workshop on Software Reuse Meeting Summary. In *Software Reuse: Emerging Technology,* pages 41–53. Los Alamitos, CA: IEEE Computer Society Press, 1988.

[Woolf94] B. Woolf. Understanding and Using ValueModels. (URL: *http://www.ksccary.com/valujrnl.htm.*) 1994.

The authors can be reached at droberts@cs.uiuc.edu **and** johnson@cs.uiuc.edu**, respectively.**

Chapter 27

Patterns for Designing in Teams

Charles Weir

This chapter discusses some techniques to use teams effectively in software design. Few sources appear to cover this subject. Most books on software design or methods appear to assume a single designer, possibly kept from wilder excesses by a system of reviews. However, software development is almost invariably a team process. How then can we leverage the individual strengths of each development team member to get a better result than one single designer could achieve alone?

The purpose of design is to agree on what will be built. Designs must be written down to achieve agreement, or, in the words of A. Goldberg, "If it's not written down, it doesn't exist." So in practice, the design will exist as a set of written documents. According to the needs of the design process, these may be anything from a collection of sketches to an encyclopedic set of formal specifications. It is difficult but vital to produce such documents as a team, because the design process reflects much of the creative manpower expended in the project.

Five patterns describe some of the most effective techniques for this purpose.

- *Multiple Competing Designs.* This pattern uses designers working independently to generate a variety of design ideas.
- *Decision Document.* This uses a document and a facilitator to compare and contrast two different designs.
- *Creator-Reviewer.* This pattern uses different skills available to provide effective feedback to designers.
- *Ad-Hoc Corrections.* This uses a corrections copy of a design document to coordinate design changes by different members of the implementation team.

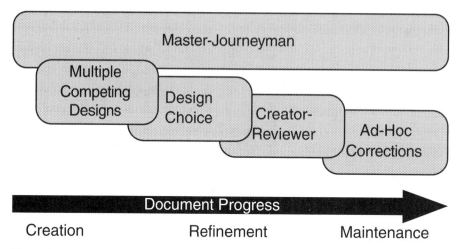

Figure 27-1 *Pattern interactions*

- *Master-Journeyman.* This pattern divides a large development effort into manageable components to allow many design teams to work in parallel.

To provide an idea of how the patterns interrelate, Figure 27-1 shows how the patterns might apply within the lifetime of a design. These patterns derive from the author's experience as an OO design consultant working with a variety of team projects in banking, telecommunications, and industry. Many of the examples of use come from this experience. The set of patterns is by no means complete; there are other related patterns [Cockburn95] and relationships to patterns in project management [Coplien94, Harrison95].

Each description contains a role diagram showing the roles involved and their interactions. An individual may change roles or undertake more than one role. The patterns use the word *designer* to mean anyone sufficiently skilled to carry out the job of design alone. Some sources use the term architect with the same meaning [Coplien94]. Of course in practice designers may receive assistance from mentors or others in the team. The role descriptions ignore this additional complexity. Also outside the scope of these patterns is the effect of dysfunctional teams. We assume the team members to be cooperative, intelligent, and constructive in their working relationships.

MULTIPLE COMPETING DESIGNS PATTERN

In this pattern, several designers generate a variety of design ideas, the best of which are then incorporated into a single design.

Problem

A team can think itself into a cul-de-sac. A single person or coherent team can easily get stuck on a single design solution and fail to see alternatives that may be more appropriate to the particular situation. Once the team has reached one conclusion, the combined effects of ego and inertia make it very difficult to consider any other possibilities.

Solution

Working individually or in pairs, several designers produce a different design for the same item. The design should be sufficiently detailed to establish the major issues and major choices for the design, but not have every aspect completed. A reasonable maximum amount of time for working on the design might be a day; a minimum might be half an hour. It's a good idea, though, to allow a longer elapsed time to allow ideas to mature.

The entire team of designers then evaluates each design in a series of reviews. It is vital that the reviews are constructive; there is a moderator to ensure this. In particular the review should establish for each design

- A list of significant strengths
- A set of circumstances which would favor that design over any of the others
- A list of the specification questions raised by this design that the team may need to resolve for the project as a whole.

Finally, a lead designer combines the strengths of each design into a single design using the information extracted from the reviews.

Roles Involved

This pattern requires at least two people capable of completing the design as it stands. Since it requires all the designers to participate in a meeting, a reasonable maximum would be six designers working in pairs. One of the design team members occupies the role of lead designer (see Figure 27-2). In addition, the pattern needs an independent moderator.

Forces

It is vital to the success of this approach that the lead designer responsibly avoids undue bias or ego in the choice of design ideas. Also, the demands of the designer roles mean that this approach is best suited to experienced teams with a number of experienced designers.

It is possible to try having a single team produce multiple designs as a group. In practice, this does not work as well as we would hope. There are two psychological traits we all share that mitigate against its success. The first is the desire for closure, to see a single completed design rather than work in hand. The second is

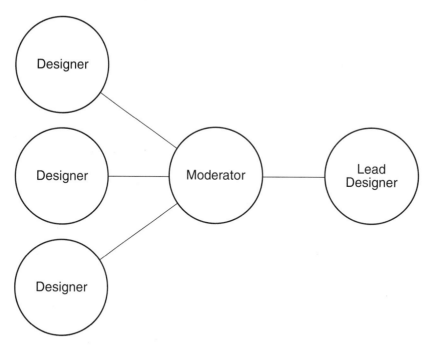

Figure 27-2 *Roles in the Multiple Competing Design pattern*

the natural avoidance of cognitive dissonance, of holding conflicting ideas at the same time. The *Psychology of Computer Programming* discusses this issue in more detail [Weinberg71].

There are costs associated with this pattern, too. There is the time taken to generate the alternative designs, to briefly document and to discuss them. In addition, there is the danger that if the synthesis process is not handled tactfully, individual designers may resent the rejection of their designs. Such dissension may cause problems later in the project.

In practice, however, the creation of multiple designs is common in projects. Individual developers and factions will create their own best designs whether or not there is a convention encouraging it. It is important that this diversity be seen as a positive feature, so that the differences generate a better finished solution.

Example

Figure 27-3 shows extracts from two designs for the OMT object diagram of part of a sales administration system. A constructive evaluation of the first design might find it the best solution when the system needs to know which salesperson is responsible for each client, rather than who made a specific visit.

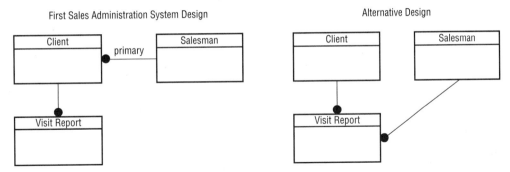

Figure 27-3 *Sales administration system design and an alternative system design*

Similarly the alternative design might be appropriate when the system needs to know which sales representative made each specific visit. Thus, unless other information is available to make the decision, the comparison reveals a question to ask about the specification—which of the two is appropriate—or is a combination of both necessary?

Known Uses

The situation covered by this pattern, of having competing design solutions proposed by different team members, happens very often during the design process of any significant project. I have had considerable success in several recent projects in following this pattern and treating this situation as positive, rather than as a situation to be overcome.

Related Patterns

The Decision Document pattern provides a good format and procedure for choosing the best elements from the competing designs. The Creator-Reviewer pattern is appropriate to take the results of the lead designer's work. Since all of the team members are now familiar with the problem, they are in a good position to review the design actually produced.

DECISION DOCUMENT PATTERN

This pattern uses a facilitator and text document to choose between or extract the strengths of different designs or design approaches.

Problem

It is difficult to make an objective choice between design options. It would be nice to think that software designers are cool rational professionals, who make each separate design choice using a rational process to make the best choice from all of the available options. Sadly, this is seldom the reality. Instead, teams typically make design choices somewhat arbitrarily.

Sometimes the design choices take place as a battle between competing designs; the option chosen is that proposed by the most powerful member or the best debater on the team. Other times, the team may accept one particularly good design and take in all of its design choices as a single decision. Frequently this loses sight of the many other secondary choices present in other design options.

Solution

The team meets with a facilitator and produces a single working text, a *decision document*, comparing and contrasting the two approaches. This is a short document, perhaps a couple of sides of paper. Its purpose is to provide a firm basis for a decision between the options. It therefore highlights the strengths and weaknesses of each option and analyzes what set of requirements and priorities would favor one over the other.

This decision may be a clear synthesis between the two options ("combine this aspect of option A with that of option B"). Or it may be a set of tests and evaluation procedures to make the choice ("do A if the performance text is adequate for our needs"). Or else it may be a balanced decision for the project architect or sponsors ("A will give better reliability in the future for a higher cost. Do we want to pay for it?").

Roles Involved

There are two major roles: designers represent each competing design option, and the facilitator acts as an impartial moderator of the discussion (Figure 27-4).

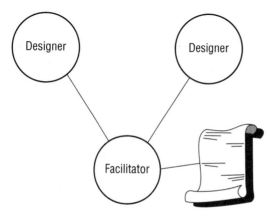

Figure 27-4 *Roles in the Decision Document pattern*

The responsibilities of the designers are

- To explain their options effectively.
- To participate in coming up with options and conclusions.

The responsibilities of the facilitator are

- To create and write the decision document. This will initially be where all those involved with the meeting can see it.
- To encourage the participants to identify and analyze each area of dissent and divergence between the options. They will aim to create a set of underlying assumptions or requirements for each option.
- To defuse antagonism and destructive discussion between the participants.

The format of the decision document may vary. We recommend a format with the headings shown below.

Options.   A brief description of each option, with a sketch diagram.

Forces.   A list of considerations that may affect the choice between options.

Conclusions.   Either a straightforward conclusion ("therefore we shall do X") or a statement in objective terms of how the decision will be made ("if the performance of approach Y is adequate in a prototype, we shall do Y, otherwise X").

Forces

This approach requires a mediator who doesn't champion one approach or the other, and who has the respect of the designers involved. If no such mediator is available, it's possible for one of the designers to assume this role, but then it is difficult for the process to be unbiased. This decision process clearly requires a significant time input from the participants. For simple decisions it may simply be too expensive to put into practice.

Another problem may be an inconclusive decision; it may turn out that the team cannot find an objective basis to use. Even in this case, the process usually adds understanding to the decision process. The participants may see the analysis process as threatening; there is the possibility that their designs will not be chosen. It is vital that the facilitator emphasize the positive aspects of getting the best aspects from every design.

It is usually best if the first version of the decision document is handwritten and available where all the participants can see it. If there are several participants, it may be best to use wall posters rather than a small sheet of paper.

The resulting document becomes part of the project documentation. As requirements and the project implementation change, some of the project constraints and other constants may change. The decision documents can help future designers understand which of the early design decisions later became invalid; the designers may even choose to reimplement if necessary.

Example

Take as an example the two design options for the sales administration system in the Multiple Competing Designs pattern. The design team would generate a short decision document as follows.

- The problem description section would contain diagrams much like those shown in Figure 27-3.
- The forces section might include brief comments on such aspects as the design, performance considerations, space considerations, the implementation of persistence and distribution for each option.
- Assuming that none of these are significant in this particular project, the conclusions section might then read: "Do we need to know which salesperson is responsible for each client? If so, select option one; otherwise select the alternative option."

Known Uses

As a software design consultant, I frequently find myself in the position of adjudicator between two or more design options. I have used this approach in a variety of different projects. Paul Fertig has used a similar but more formal approach in work for IBM.

Related Patterns

This pattern is particularly useful to get the best from the competing approaches in the Multiple Competing Designs pattern.

CREATOR-REVIEWER PATTERN

This uses the experience and critical faculties of team members who need not be experienced designers to add value to the work of a single designer or design team.

Problem

People make mistakes. It is notoriously difficult to see problems and errors in your own work. There is much research work available on the reasons behind this; all suggest that any realistic solution must involve other people [Weinberg71]. Thus if we have one or two designers producing a design alone, there is a strong likelihood of undetected errors.

Solution

The designer produces a draft or a complete design. Each of one or more reviewers receives a copy and provides constructive feedback. There are many possibilities for ways to do reviews, but two are particularly effective.

Meeting Review. The reviewers meet to walk through the document section by section. A review leader moderates the process; a recorder keeps track of the comments agreed upon.

Distribution Review. The document circulates to each reviewer, along with a form to receive comments. Sometimes this can occur electronically, using a mechanism such as Lotus Notes.

It is important that the reviewers concentrate on constructive feedback for the document. In a meeting review, it is the task of the review leader to ensure this.

There are significant benefits to doing reviews in this way. In particular, it improves communication between team members and those whose skills are less suited to design, but who can make a significant contribution to the design process.

Roles Involved

The pattern in Figure 27-5 requires a single designer or design team and a number of reviewers who need not be skilled at design.

The review leader has the role of ensuring the effectiveness of the review. In a meeting review the leader acts as moderator; in a distribution review the leader must ensure that each reviewer contributes within a reasonable time limit. In a meeting review, it is important that there is also a recorder who notes down each

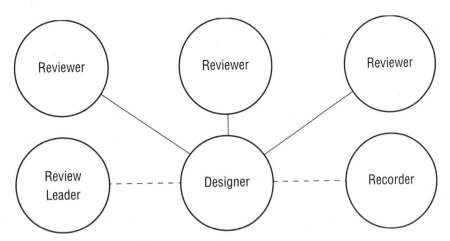

Figure 27-5 *Roles in the Creator-Reviewer pattern*

defect discovered. Fagin's inspection process is a particularly effective format for reviews [Gilb88].

It is best if the reviewers are as varied as possible in skills, knowledge, and personality. Particularly good candidates for reviewers are

- Someone with detailed knowledge of the application domain.
- A finisher—typically someone who likes to get paperwork correct [Belbin81].
- Another designer who has not been involved with this design.

Forces

There are significant costs associated with reviews. First, they are expensive in time and effort. Also, programmers often find them less fun than normal programming or writing, so they may be demotivating to the team.

Accordingly, we must be careful to keep reviews short and effective, and to limit them to the documents that really require them. For many documents we can achieve much of the same effect with less formality by asking a single colleague for comments.

There are many variations to the review procedures. In some, the designer may not be allowed to speak at all during the review. See [Gilb88] for other possibilities.

Known Uses

Code reviews are used widely within the software industry, particularly on safety-critical applications. There is a large body of research justifying their effectiveness.

Related Patterns

A related pattern is Coplien's pattern 16, Review the Architecture [Coplien94]. The emphasis of that pattern is on team communication, another valuable consequence.

MASTER-JOURNEYMAN PATTERN

Problem

We need to partition the design work for a large system. It is essential that there is a single architect or at most a small team to provide the design integrity for the entire system [Cook+95]. Yet in a large development project, it is unlikely to be possible for this core architecture team to do all of the design work.

Solution

A master design team provides an overview of the system architecture and divides the system into components, each of which can be a separate autonomous development. Journeyman architects then take on the design of each separate component, each being the chief designers of their own component of the system.

The master design team must identify and specify the items shared by all of the components. Typically these will be

Core Architecture. This might include the physical system description, a description of the components and their interactions, examples of interactions between them, and a description of the changes anticipated by the architecture.

Architectural Vision. This is the most difficult area to define, and one of the most important to specify. Some examples of this policy are design patterns for all the subprojects to share, and a set of priorities for handling design tradeoffs: size vs. speed, for example.

Interfaces. This might include a description of the types of transaction across each interface and an outline of the specifications. The details of the specifications will typically be left to the designers responsible for each component.

Specification Control. The master team must vet any significant changes to the specifications, to ensure that the overall system architecture remains consistent with the requirements.

In addition, in a development where the components are within the same item of software, the master design team must typically specify or commission software policies common to the whole development. These might include

- Error handling policy
- Coding guidelines
- Testing strategy
- Use of third-party libraries
- Multithreading strategy

Journeymen propose; masters dispose. The journeyman designers are encouraged to propose policies and changes that affect other parts of the system than their own. However, the master designer retains the decision of whether and how these become part of the master plan.

Roles Involved

There are two significant roles in the pattern in Figure 27-6: master designer and journeyman designer. Each may in practice be a team of up to three people.

Forces

A key success factor of this approach is the cleanness of the division into different autonomous developments. A design requiring too much coordination between

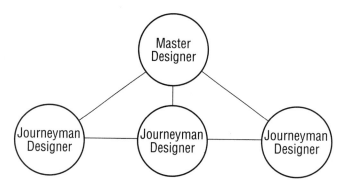

Figure 27-6 *Roles in the Master-Journeyman pattern*

any two journeyman teams will lead to conflict or misunderstandings. The division is difficult to get right the first time, so we must be prepared to change it as required. One effective approach is to divide the system into domains and to specify the domain interfaces only [Cook+95, chapter 11].

To be workable, this design requires at least one separate component for each journeyman designer. It may be effective, however, to have one designer take on responsibility for more than one component.

Example

A large financial information company had a project for a new telecommunications system comprising separate developments at more than ten sites worldwide. The whole software design took several hundred work years to develop. A core architecture team of two people defined the protocols and architectural vision of the system.

Then, as the project got under way and the developments started around the world, core team members traveled between the sites ensuring the coordination of the developments involved. They provided a set of master design documents that they modified as required (see the Ad-Hoc Corrections pattern).

The initial project was a success. Over the next five years, as changes occurred in the system, there has continued to be a single team coordinating the design, and the system has kept its integrity.

Known Uses

The name of this pattern comes from an arrangement common to many medieval crafts. A master craftsman would define and take responsibility for an entire piece of work; many journeyman craftsmen would work on separate pieces, coordinated by the master. Most large software projects use this approach.

Related Patterns

Coplien's pattern 13: Architecture Controls Product [Coplien94] is related.

AD-HOC CORRECTIONS PATTERN

Problem

Design documents are seldom up to date. New developers coming to a project often have to depend on verbal descriptions of the changes since the original design, or to find out for themselves by reading the code. Developers already on the project find the same problem when they need to find out about unfamiliar parts of the system. The failure to update documents costs time and reduces the architectural cohesion of the system.

Solution

The team needs to keep available a master hard copy of the design that is accessible to the entire team. Anyone who needs to deviate from the design must write a correction in the margin, delete sections that are now inappropriate, or write in a short description of the nature of the change.

Ultimately one team member needs to take responsibility for updating machine-readable copies of the design to correspond to the corrections. This may be the designer. Alternatively the update may be a learning task for a new team member.

Roles Involved

There may be one or more designers and developers working on a single design (see Figure 27-7). Any individual may be in a position to identify and make corrections to the design.

Forces

It may be tempting to keep the document and its annotations online (and be able to have version control and remote access). However this approach is often less than satisfactory for two reasons.

It is key to the pattern that the corrections be added as annotations, not as changes to the original document. Ownership of the document remains with the author. In many documentation systems, support for such annotations is distinctly limited. It is particularly difficult to annotate diagrams effectively. Similarly, there are technical issues of ownership, locking, and version control.

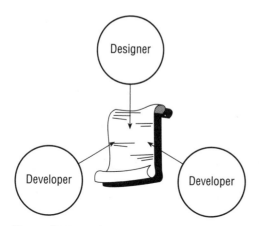

Figure 27-7 *Roles in the Ad-Hoc Corrections pattern*

With the paper approach, amendments are being inserted only on a copy of the master document. Psychologically they are easier to add, since they can be discarded later without affecting the master document. However, with good tool support, both these problems would be surmountable.

Known Uses

The telecommunications system described in the previous pattern (Master-Journeyman pattern) was coordinated using some twenty large paper documents describing the protocols and interactions of the components. Each of these was modified in pencil as changes occurred. They were updated formally in due course.

Related Patterns

This pattern is particularly suitable for the master documents for a project produced by a master design team (Master-Journeyman pattern), since these are often subject to change from a variety of forces. It should be used after the initial reviews of the documents concerned (Creator-Reviewer pattern).

ACKNOWLEDGMENTS

I would like to thank Gary Birch for reviewing the initial versions of this chapter, and all of the team at EuroPLoP '96 for their inspiration and comments.

REFERENCES

[Belbin81] R. M. Belbin. *Management Teams.* Butterworth-Heinemann, 1981.

[Cockburn95] A. Cockburn. *"Prioritizing Forces in Software Design."* J. M. Vlissides, J. O. Coplien, and N. L. Kerth (eds.). *Pattern Languages of Program Design 2,* Reading, MA: Addison-Wesley, 1995.

[Cook+95] S. Cook and J. Daniels. *Designing Object Systems: Object-Oriented Modeling with Syntropy.* Prentice Hall, 1994.

[Coplien94] J. O. Coplein. "A Generative Development-Process Pattern Language." In J. O. Coplien and D. E. Schmidt (eds.). *Pattern Languages of Program Design,* Reading, MA: Addison-Wesley, 1994.

[Gilb88] T. Gilb. *Principles of Software Engineering Management.* Reading, MA: Addison-Wesley, 1988.

[Goldberg+95] A. Goldberg and K. Rubin. *Succeeding with Objects: Decision Frameworks for Project Management,* Reading, MA: Addison-Wesley, 1995.

[Harrison95] N. B. Harrison. "Organizational Patterns for Teams." In J. M. Vlissides, J. O. Coplien, and N. L. Kerth (eds.). *Pattern Languages of Program Design 2.* Reading, MA: Addison Wesley, 1995.

[Weinberg71] G. Weinberg. *The Psychology of Computer Programming.* Van Nostrand Reinhold, 1971.

Charles Weir can be reached at charles.weir@iee.org.uk.

Chapter 28

Patterns for System Testing

David E. DeLano and Linda Rising

Testing of systems is presently more of an art than a science, even considering current procedures and methodologies that support a more rigorous approach to testing. This becomes even more apparent during the testing of large embedded systems that have evolved over time. To deliver the best possible product, the role of a System Tester has become vital in the lifecycle of product development. This pattern language has been derived from the experience of veteran System Testers to help System Testers evaluate the readiness of a product for shipping to the customer. Though these patterns have been derived from experience during the system test phase of the product lifecycle, many of the patterns are orthogonal to all testing phases. In addition to System Testers, these patterns may be useful to Designers and Project Managers.

These patterns have been categorized according to their usefulness in the system testing process: The Test Organization, Testing Efficiency, Testing Strategy, and Problem Resolution. This is not a complete pattern language (see Figure 28-1).

COMMON CONTEXT

As a pattern language, these patterns share a common context. Each of the patterns may add to this context or slightly modify it, but it is this common context that helps focus these patterns into a pattern language. Thus, the context for an individual pattern in this chapter will be given only when it modifies the common context.

A system is under development into which new features are being introduced. The system may be new development work, or may be an existing working system. There are a limited number of customers for the system and the features are being developed at the request of these customers. The customers then sell the features to the end users. New features integrate well into the system, but intro-

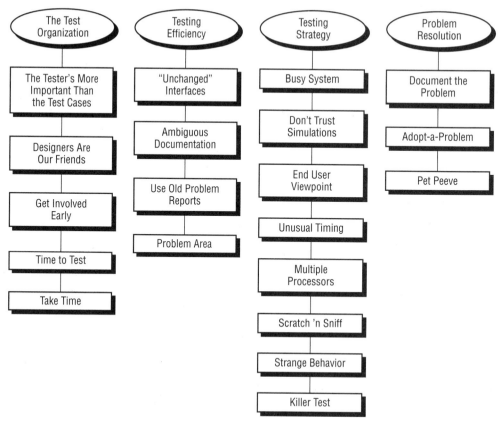

Figure 28-1 *System Test pattern categories*

ducing new features runs the risk of breaking old features. These features are implemented in the system by Designers in a design group. The Designers are responsible for everything from analysis, design, and implementation, through unit testing and integration testing.

The features of the system are designed in parallel. As code becomes available, incremental loads of the system are released for testing. Each of these loads may include a combination of complete or partial features. This process compresses the development schedule, but it also results in the introduction of problem resolution and features in parallel. Problems resolved in one load need to be resolved in any feature development that is in progress.

The system, in this case, is a large embedded system. It consists of multiple processor units and each processor is controlled by a multiprocessing operating system. Events in the system are thus nondeterministic. Any feature of the system can have an interaction with any other feature in the system. Most of these patterns apply to the testing of any multiprocessing, nondeterministic system. The set of all tests needed to completely verify such a system is infinitely large. The set of regression tests to reasonably test the system grows with every release, so that executing all of the tests would require more than the development schedule allows for a new feature release.

The features are being tested in parallel with the design effort by an independent group known as *System Test* whose members are known as *System Testers*. The testing done by this group is largely "black box" in nature. There is a reliable process in place for testing the system, from unit testing to system testing. The System Test group is responsible for regression testing the system, the conformance of new features to the specification, the equivalence of the system to prior releases, and the evaluation of the release of the system according to criteria set by the customer. These criteria are consistent with every release. System testing concentrates on the functionality of the system and ensures that the system continues to operate in a consistent manner. To accomplish this, the testing often takes the form of stressing or breaking the system.

These patterns do not represent the process of system testing any more than the GOF book represents object-oriented design [Gamma+95]. The System Testers understand the system testing process. Instead, the patterns are a means of sharing some of the secrets of experienced system testers. Following these patterns will help minimize stress and maximize the enjoyment of system testing.

COMMON FORCES

Just as these patterns share a common context, they also share common forces. The individual patterns may place more emphasis on specific forces, ignore some forces, or add forces that are not important to the pattern language as a whole. Like context, forces for an individual pattern will only be given where they are emphasized, modified, or added.

Most of the forces for these patterns are elements of risk management. The patterns evaluate these risks to find an acceptable, intelligent balance among cost, time, content, and quality. The common forces are as follows.

- The scheduled interval for testing is short.
- Compressing the development schedule risks introducing problems.
- Compressing the test interval risks not finding all critical problems.
- Not all problems can be found.
- A release with some noncritical problems is acceptable.
- Specifications are often unclear or ambiguous.
- Problems should be found and corrected as early as possible.
- Reporting problems is often negatively viewed.
- Testing resources, such as prototype systems or person-hours, are at a premium.
- Software load stability is critical to progress.

- The content of a given software load is uncertain.
- Designers traditionally have a higher value within the organization.
- System testers traditionally have a low status within the organization.
- Designers are preoccupied with new development.
- System testers must have a global view of the system.
- Designers are primarily concerned with their own area of development.
- System testers represent the customer and end user point of view.
- End users don't always use features as specified by the customer.

THE TEST ORGANIZATION

The following patterns focus on the relationship of the System Testers to the rest of the organization. They are less technical in nature and are closely related to the patterns of James Coplien [Coplien95], Neil Harrison [Harrison96], Alistair Cockburn [Cockburn96], and Don Olson [Olson95].

The Tester's More Important Than the Test Cases

Problem

How should work be assigned to Testers to achieve maximum testing efficiency?

Forces

- Testers do not all have the same capabilities.
- Everybody needs to develop new capabilities.
- Creative testers are effective testers.
- Familiarity breeds contempt.

Solution

Assign tasks to System Testers based on their experience and talent. No matter how effective the test cases are, the testing results are highly dependent on the Tester. Davis states, "People are the key to success." [Davis95].

Resulting Context

Testers will be more effective if their skills are used appropriately. The resulting test activity will be more efficient and the Testers will be more productive.

Repeated applications of this pattern can result in burnout of the Tester or the development of irreplaceable expertise. Testers who become too familiar with an area often overlook problems by making invalid assumptions. Career development gets overlooked when existing skills are always used and no new skills are acquired. It is sometimes better to give assignments a half step beyond capabilities.

Rationale

The Tester is the most important element in the testing equation. The same test case will not necessarily produce the same result in the hands of different Testers. Testers look at a list of errors differently. Some Testers know how to break the system versus getting a correct result. Some Testers are good at finding problems. Some Testers are good at working with Designers. Matching the skills of the Testers with the appropriate tasks will produce more effective testing.

DeMarco and Lister documented a wide variance in performance between the worst and best performers for a given task [DeMarco+87]. To be successful, the best performers should be assigned to the appropriate tasks and all Testers should be given assignments that best fit their skills.

Designers Are Our Friends

Problem

How can System Test work effectively with the Designers?

Solution

Build rapport with Designers. Approach Designers with the attitude that the system has a problem that both of you need to work on together to resolve. This gives the Designer and the System Tester a common goal. Always Document the Problem.

Resulting Context

The System Tester/Designer relationship becomes one of cooperation in an attempt to resolve a problem. Designers are less likely to become defensive and run and hide when a System Tester approaches.

Rationale

We are all employees of the same company and should work with each other to solve problems. Designers and System Testers are partners. Building good relationships with Designers gets things done faster. Personalizing problems makes Designers defensive. We can learn from each other and benefit both.

Related Patterns

All members of a team should remain open to the contributions of other members. Don't Flip the Bozo Bit and close off the relationship, regardless of past history [McCarthy95, Rising96].

Design by Team stresses the importance of working together to develop and design software [Harrison96]. This notion can be extended to include the Designer/System Tester relationship.

Get Involved Early

Problem

How can System Test maximize the support from the Designers?

Forces

- During early development phases, System Testers have test plans to write.
- Impacts of social relationships aren't considered critical by the project.

Solution

Establish a good working relationship with the Designers early in the project. Don't wait until you need to interact with a Designer. By that time it is too late. Trust must be built over time.

One way to accomplish this is to learn the system and the features at the same time the Designer is learning them. Attend reviews of the requirements and design documentation. Invite the Designer to test plan reviews.

Resulting Context

When a good working relationship is built over time, it is easier to resolve problems when they are discovered. Be sure that the relationship with the Designer does not affect your judgment as an effective System Tester. There can be a tendency to avoid areas of conflict when friends are involved, to look the other way when problems are found in a certain area where the Designer is a close friend. It is also dangerous to have too much information about an area. This can lead to testing that depends on this knowledge instead of an objective black-box view.

Rationale

We are all more willing to work with people we know. Waiting until the heat of battle to get to know the people who can help you resolve problems leads to delays in solutions. If a trusting relationship has already been established, the problem-solving process is smoother.

Related Patterns

Get Involved Early is important in establishing that Designers Are Our Friends.

Time to Test

Alias

Test When There's Something to Test

Problem

When is it appropriate to start testing?

Context

The system can be broken into areas, such as features or functional areas that are minimally dependent on each other. Once an area is released for system testing, it would not be impacted in future software loads. Remember that Designers Are Our Friends.

Forces

- Designers don't want testing to start until everything is perfect.
- Testers want to start testing early.
- Testing an incomplete system may require retesting on later software loads.

Solution

Start testing when an area of functionality is available for testing, but not before. An agreement should be reached with the Designers that the area is ready for testing (see Designers Are Our Friends). Track areas that aren't yet ready for testing so you don't waste time in those areas.

Resulting Context

More interval is available for testing if testing begins on early increments of the software loads. This also exposes the load to more testing, which will uncover more problems. More problems will be discovered earlier, when there is time to correct them.

By starting early, there is a risk that regression testing of the area will be required. Use an End User Viewpoint for this testing. Additionally, if testing is started too early, untested fixes start finding their way into the load.

Rationale

System testing should not start until all the software is finished. However, waiting until everything is complete leaves no time for doing all the system testing. System Test is often pushed to start testing as early as possible. However, starting to test the system too early is a waste of time. It is possible, however, to test parts of the system that are ready earlier than others.

Related Patterns

You must Take Time in determining whether an area is ready for testing.

Take Time

Problem

How much time should Designers be given to finish work that is behind schedule?

Context

Testing for an area is scheduled to start, design is not complete. Remember that Designers Are Our Friends.

Forces

- Designers always want more time.
- More effort up front usually produces a better product in the end.

Solution

Give Designers the time they request, within reason. It is Time to Test other areas in the interim.

Resulting Context

System testing will take less time if the design quality is better.

Rationale

Higher-quality systems take less time to test than poorer-quality systems. By giving Designers time they truly need, there will be a significant payback in the end in avoiding the effort to test and fix all the problems in a poor quality system. Increasing planned development time by 15% cuts the number of defects in half [Remer96]. All the forces of Take Time and Time to Test must be carefully weighed before deciding which pattern to follow.

TESTING EFFICIENCY

As stated in the context, it is not possible to completely test a system. The following patterns steer the Tester toward areas that are more likely to contain errors. Test plan development and testing can concentrate on these areas to find more problems earlier in the project.

"Unchanged" Interfaces

Problem

How should testing of third-party interface functionality developed outside the organization be scheduled?

Context

Interfaces developed outside the organization are used in the system, in whole or in part, without changes to those interfaces. An interface might be a GUI, a library, a hardware component, or any other third-party product. The initial assumption is that if third-party interface functionality is to be supported in the new system, and if the same interface has been used in other systems and has not changed, then no testing or very limited testing is required.

Forces

- Time can be saved by no or limited testing of unchanged third-party interface functionality.
- There is limited knowledge or training on third-party software.
- The project assumes that unchanged code will function as expected in the new product.

Solution

The System Tester must not fall into the trap of assuming that unchanged interfaces will function correctly in the new system. The System Tester must pay particular attention to any interface ported from outside the company that is not assigned for inclusion in the feature list of the new system. Since no one else is directly impacted by this change, the System Tester needs to be proactive in scheduling this testing.

Testing the correct operation of the interface on the new system should begin as soon as that interface is chosen for the new system. This will verify the functionality of that interface. Once the ported interface is operational in the new system, testing should begin immediately to ensure that the functionality is the same and that it does not affect the rest of the system. This can be done while the Designers are working on the new features for the system.

Resulting Context

System Test will find problems with ported interfaces early in the project's life-cycle and limit the impact of any problems on the system release. This will allow focused effort on fixing the problems while there is still time to change how the system functions, what is included in the system, or when a system is ready to be released. Less overall effort and stress will be expended during system development, time will be saved, and the system will be released as planned.

Rationale

No matter how established a product is or how well written a chunk of code is, if it is not an in-house product there will always be problems with porting that functionality into a new system. If testing of the functionality is not immediately begun, problems will invariably be found at the worst possible time—right before release of the system.

Any product brought in from outside the organization will not meet the quality, functionality, or customer expectations of the organization. Thus, changes will have to be made.

Ambiguous Documentation

Problem

How can possible problem areas of the system be pinpointed so that the most problems can be found in the least amount of time?

Context

Feature design documentation and/or user documentation is available. This can be the requirements from which the feature is developed, documentation developed by the Designer, or documentation developed for the customer.

Forces

• Some areas of a system are more likely to have problems than others.

Solution

Study the documentation available on the system. Look for areas that seem ambiguous or ill-defined. Write test plans that cover these areas more thoroughly and concentrate testing in these areas (see End User Viewpoint). If Designers can tell you all about a feature, it probably works. It's what they can't tell you that needs attention during testing.

Call these areas to the attention of the Designers so that problems in these areas can be resolved prior to system testing. These areas should still be tested more thoroughly than areas that are well documented and well understood.

Resulting Context

Problems are likely to be found and corrected earlier.

Rationale

If there's more than one interpretation of the documentation, Designers will write more than one code interpretation. This must be uncovered during system test if it is not detected earlier. If you Get Involved Early, there is a better chance of getting documentation fixed early, and getting the implementation correct. If problems still exist, finding them early makes it more likely that they will be fixed. Good specs help everyone!

Related Patterns

Reviewing documentation reinforces that Designers Are Our Friends.

Use Old Problem Reports

Problem

What areas of the system should be targeted for testing so that the most problems can be found in the least amount of time?

Context

Testing of existing features is being considered. Problem reports from previous releases are available.

Solution

Examine problem reports from previous releases to help select test cases. Since it would be inefficient to retest for all old problems, look at problems reported after the last valid snapshot of the system. Categorize problem reports to see if a trend is determined that could be used for additional testing.

Resulting Context

Problems that still exist will be found and corrected.

Rationale

Since a problem report represents something that escaped detection in a previous release, this could be a good indicator of a problem in the current load. Problem reports tend to point to areas where problems always occur. Problem reports often represent a symptom that is difficult to connect with an underlying problem.

Additionally, fixes of a previous release are often done in parallel with new development on the current releases. These fixes don't always find their way into the current load.

Problem Area

Problem

What areas of the system should receive concentrated testing, regardless of the features being implemented?

Context

Historical data is available for the system under test.

Solution

Keep a list of persistent problem areas and test cases to verify them, not just for resolution of the current problems, but also for use in subsequent testing. Test these areas thoroughly, even if there are no new features going into them. Retest regularly using these test cases, even one last time before the release goes out the door. These areas can be identified by considering the experience of the System Testers; Use Old Problem Reports; Ambiguous Documentation; and areas that Designers tend to avoid from one release to the next.

Resulting Context

By testing problem areas early in the schedule, more time is available to correct any problems found.

Rationale

Areas of the system that historically have problems don't magically become error-free overnight. Some problems occur in every incremental release of the system. Some areas have problems in every release. These problems and problem areas should be tracked so that they can be systematically retested on every release of the system.

TESTING STRATEGY

Once a testing strategy has been set into place and testing has commenced, the following patterns help find problems that might not be found until it is too late to correct them. They also ensure that the delivered product will be acceptable to the customer.

Busy System

Problem

Under what conditions should system tests be executed to find the most problems?

Context

Simulators exist that provide a reasonable amount of activity on the system.

Solution

Test in an environment that simulates a busy system. The level of activity need not stress the system, but should approach a level that the system regularly experiences.

Resulting Context

Tests that work fine under normal conditions often fail in an unacceptable manner when the system is busy.

Rationale

It is redundant to run a feature test case that has already passed during the system testing phase. However, these cases will often fail under a busy system. A telephony system can be busied using a Traffic Load Simulator that simulates phone calls into the system. By running feature tests with a moderate amount of traffic on the system, problems are found that don't appear when the system is idle.

Related Patterns

Don't Trust Simulations

Don't Trust Simulations

Problem

How should the test environment be configured when using test simulations?

Context

Simulations of system use are available, including simulators of real uses of the system.

Forces

- Simulators are often a more accessible testing environment.
- Some testing cannot be accomplished without using simulations.
- It's impossible to have a real-world environment for all testing.

Solution

Test in an environment as close to the real world as possible.

Resulting Context

Systems that handle simulations, which tend to give predictable input to the system, often fail in the real world of unpredictable behaviors. By supplementing the simulation with real world testing, such situations are minimized.

Rationale

There is a proper use for simulations, but they are not substitutes for real-world testing. While a large portion of the testing can be done using simulations, testing of the system is not complete without providing real-world scenarios in the testing process. A simulator can run a test case successfully one hundred times, but the test case may fail when run by a human because of unpredictable behaviors that are introduced.

Related Patterns

Follow End User Viewpoint to accomplish real-world testing.

End User Viewpoint

Problem

How do you test the new features in a system without repeating testing that has already been completed?

Forces

- Duplicate testing takes more time in the schedule.
- There is a perception that code not changed since feature testing doesn't need system testing.
- Because of feature interactions, changes to one feature can break another.

Solution

Test outside the normal scope of the features. Take the End User Viewpoint. Don't system test with the same tests used for feature testing. Use the customer documentation. Test feature interactions.

Resulting Context

By testing from an End User Viewpoint, flaws in the system, as the end user will use it, can be discovered and corrected before the system is shipped. These tests expand the scope of previous testing and are not redundant.

Rationale

End users don't use systems as they are designed. Designers develop features, but the system is sold to provide services to the end user. It is these services that the end user sees, not the features that are developed by the Designers.

Unusual Timing

Problem

What additional testing should be done that may not be covered by the test plans for an area?

Solution

Test unusual timing. Run tests more quickly or slowly than expected. Abort tests in the middle of execution. Real end users will have an End User Viewpoint.

Resulting Context

Errors caused by unusual timings are detected and corrected.

Rationale

Things that work properly under normal timing conditions may break under unusual timing conditions. Testing for unusual timing scenarios is often difficult to set up and run. Test cases that are difficult to run are the ones that probably most need to be run.

Multiple Processors

Problem

What strategy should be followed when System Testing a system comprised of multiple processors?

Solution

Test across multiple processors.

Resulting Context

Problems that occur in one processor will probably occur in other processors. Tests that pass on one processor may fail on another.

Rationale

When a problem is found in one processor, that feature will usually have problems running on other processors. A dirty feature is a dirty feature. A feature may be designed for a single processor, assuming that it will then work for all processors.

Scratch 'n Sniff

Alias

Problem Cluster

Problem

Once testing is started, what is a good strategy for determining what to test next?

Context

A problem has already been found in an area.

Solution

Test areas where problems have already been found.

Resulting Context

Problematic areas will be targeted sooner and problems resolved earlier.

Rationale

Problems tend to be found in clusters. A problem found in an area is a good indicator of other problems in the same area. Scratch 'n Sniff—if it smells bad, it probably is.

Software bugs are like roaches: Find one and you'll find a lot of them. They also evolve quickly.

Testing can be organized so that a first pass is taken that tests the breadth of the system. Half of the problems found will be in 15% of the modules [Davis95]. Deeper testing of the problem areas will likely find more problems.

Related Patterns

Use Old Problem Reports for areas that may need more testing.

Strange Behavior

Problem

What should be done when a feature is working, but not as expected?

Context

The System Tester has participated in the system testing of previous releases of the product and is familiar with feature behavior.

Solution

Take any unusual behavior as an indication of a possible problem and follow up. This should be done even if the problem is not related to the test being executed. Look for features that behave differently. Be wary when familiar tests produce results that, while acceptable, are not what was expected.

Resulting Context

A problem won't be missed because it doesn't produce feature behavior that is not significantly different from the expected outcome.

Rationale

Changes to the way a feature works, even though it may still work correctly, often indicate that the feature may have broken. If the change is deliberate, all System Testers should be notified.

Killer Test

Problem

How can the quality of a system under development be determined?

Context

Development is drawing to a close. The system is stable. The features are stable and all parties involved, especially management, are interested in how close the system is to being ready for release.

Solution

Develop a favorite Killer Test (usually a set of test cases) that can be run at any time, a test that always seems to find problems. This test should provide good system coverage and should be expected to fail, in some manner, most of the time. You can borrow a Killer Test, but it is better if the test is based on your own experience, as the effectiveness of the test depends on the individual's skill and knowledge of the system.

Killer Test is only used toward the end of a release, and is above and beyond a common regression test. It tends to be free-wheeling in nature and typically hard to document. The success of this type of testing is directly related to the individual running the test, because The Tester's More Important Than The Test Cases. Don't wait until the very end of the release or there won't be time to correct the problems found.

Resulting Context

The results of the tests are a good gauge of the stability of the system. By finding and fixing the uncovered problems, the system becomes incrementally more stable.

Rationale

A test that usually fails and can be run in a reasonably short time gives a good measure of how the system is stabilizing. Additionally, since problems are likely to be found, this type of testing is highly efficient.

PROBLEM RESOLUTION

The following patterns aid in communication and resolution of problems.

Document the Problem
Problem

How should problems found in testing be communicated?

Context

A problem-tracking system is available for problem documentation.

Forces

- Testers want to be sure that problems are fixed.
- Designers have good intentions but don't always get problems resolved.
- Problem-tracking systems are often cumbersome.
- Problem-tracking systems make problem areas very visible.
- People inherently avoid documentation.
- Problem reports are often used as indicators of Designer's competence.
- Problem reports are often used as an indicator of project status.

Solution

Write a problem report. Don't argue with a Designer. Don't accept a well-intentioned promise that may or may not get results. Don't informally document the problem. The project should not keep a private list of problems.

Testers should not be penalized for documenting problems. Designers should not be punished when problems are documented against them.

Do your homework before reporting problems to Designers. Be sure you can explain what happened. Designers always want to see a system debug output.

Resulting Context

Problems documented in a problem-tracking system are more likely to be resolved in a timely manner.

Rationale

Use all the tools that are available, even if they are cumbersome. By thoroughly and officially documenting a problem, information does not get lost and a timely resolution is more likely.

Documenting problems is always an area that a project wants to cut back. Cutting back causes many more problems than it seems to solve. In the end, it always takes longer to determine what the problems are than to resolve them.

Related Patterns

Remember, Designers Are Our Friends and System Testers should Get Involved Early.

Adopt-a-Problem

Problem

How can nagging problems be resolved efficiently so that productive testing can continue?

Context

A problem has been uncovered in the system that has no clear-cut solution. Resolving the problem will most likely take a great deal of effort, or worse, it might not get resolved. This pattern should be followed in the context of Designers Are Our Friends.

Forces

- Some problems are difficult to reproduce.
- Ambiguous problems result in ambiguous fixes.
- Designers don't have time to track down problems they may not be able to resolve.

Solution

Adopt-a-Problem. Treat it as if it were your child. If you uncover a difficult problem, stick with it until it is resolved. Document the Problem. Retest the problem periodically to gather more data on it. Become the responsible Designer for the problem.

Resulting Context

Following the progress of the solution for a problem shows the Designer that you are concerned about getting the problem resolved. Taking an active role in resolving the problem can prevent the problem from bouncing among Designers. Periodically retesting the problem leads to a better understanding of the problem and more symptomatic data. As a result, the probability that the Designer can solve the problem and provide a solution in a timely manner is increased.

Once the problem is resolved, retest for it periodically to ensure that it stays fixed. If the problem reappears consistently, it may be a Problem Area.

Rationale

Designers have a multitude of things to do. They tend to work first on things that are known, concrete, and easy. Because of this, trying to resolve a difficult problem often gets pushed to a lower priority. By adopting the problem, there are in effect two people working on the problem. As the System Tester, you can continue to test and debug the problem to gain more information on it, whether it is information that the Designer requests or information that appears to be different from previously collected data. The attention you give to the problem also communicates to the Designer that you think it is important to get the problem resolved and are willing to help in facilitating the problem resolution. This second point is important because you should not come across as a nagging irritant that won't go away, but as a willing participant in the resolution process. Be sure the problem doesn't become a Pet Peeve.

Pet Peeve

Problem

The validity of a problem has been debated to the point of holding up progress. What should be done to resolve the debate?

Context

This problem should be applied in the context of Adopt-a-Problem and Document the Problem.

Solution

When you Adopt-a-Problem, be sure that the problem doesn't become an annoying thorn in the Designer's side. Don't carry concern for an unresolved problem to extremes, especially when you have no supporting documentation. Keep discussions at a professional level.

When the status of the problem becomes a detriment to progress, the System Tester should bring in a third party, such as a requirements group, to help resolve the impasse. At this point, stop following the status of the problem and start testing other areas. Don't involve the third party too early in the process.

Resulting Context

Problems are resolved and not forgotten, but no one goes overboard in focusing on one problem to the detriment of the rest of the system.

Rationale

When deciding to Adopt-a-Problem, a System Tester can become so focused on a particular problem that it becomes a Pet Peeve. Carried to an extreme, this can destroy a good working relationship between the System Tester and the Designer. Problems in the system should not be taken personally by the System Tester [Davis95].

KNOWN USES

The individuals involved in the mining of these patterns have many years of experience in System Testing on the GTD-5 and other projects at AG Communication Systems. The GTD-5 is a central office telephone switch that has gone through many major releases over the past 16 years. Other projects have benefited from this experience and validate the existence of these patterns. Some releases of the GTD-5 and other projects have suffered the consequences of not applying one or more of these patterns. Many of these patterns have been observed and used by individuals while employed at other companies involved in the development of real-time embedded systems. More information on AG Communication Systems and its product line can be found at (URL) `http://www.agcs.com`.

ACKNOWLEDGMENTS

These system test patterns were mined in a patterns mining workshop held on May 10, 1996. The patterns were captured by David DeLano and Linda Rising with Greg Stymfal serving as facilitator for the group. The workshop was attended by the following AGCS System Testers: Dave Bassett, Arvind Bhuskute, Bob Bianca, Ray Fu, Hubert Fulkerson, Eric Johnstone, Rich Lamarco, Krishna Naidu, Ed Nuerenberg, and Lori Ryan. Many of these System Testers, as well as the following, have participated in reviews of the patterns: John Balzer, Terry Bartlett, Ernie Englehart, Carl Gilmour, Neil Khemlani, Jim Kurth, Bob Nations, John Ng, Jim Peterson, Mike Sapcoe, Bill Stapleton, Frank Villars, and Weldon Wong. Thanks to Dave Strand for suggesting the name *Scratch 'n Sniff*.

"Unchanged" Interfaces has been adapted from a pattern written by Mike Sapcoe during an earlier Patterns Writing course held by David DeLano and Linda Rising.

We are grateful for the time and effort given by Ralph Johnson, Neil Harrison, and Brian Marick in shepherding these patterns. We would also like to thank the participants of the PLoP '96 writers workshop for their many valuable comments.

REFERENCES

[Cockburn96] A. Cockburn. "A Medical Catalog of Project Management Patterns." Submitted for PLoP '96. (URL: `http://members.aol.com/acockburn/papers/plop96.htm`), 1996.

[Coplien95] J. O. Coplien. "A Generative Development—Process Pattern Language." In J. O. Coplien and D. C. Schmidt (eds.), *Pattern Languages of Program Design*. Reading, MA: Addison-Wesley, 1995, pp. 183–237. (URL: `http://www.bell-labs.com/user/cope/Patterns/Process/index.html`), 1996.

[Davis95] A. M. Davis. *201 Principles of Software Development*. New York, NY: McGraw-Hill, 1995.

[DeMarco+87] T. DeMarco and T. Lister. *Peopleware: Productive Projects and Teams.* New York: Dorset House, 1987, pp. 45–47.

[Gamma+95] E. Gamma, R. Helm, R. Johnson, and J. Vlissides. *Design Patterns: Elements of Reusable Object-Oriented Software.* Reading, MA: Addison-Wesley, 1995.

[Harrison96] N. B. Harrison. "Organizational Patterns for Teams." In J. M. Vlissides, J. O. Coplien, and N. L. Kerth (eds.), *Pattern Languages of Program Design 2.* Reading, MA: Addison-Wesley, 1996, pp. 345–352.

[McCarthy96] J. McCarthy. "#4: Don't Flip the Bozo Bit." In J. McCarthy, *Dynamics of Software Development.* Redmond, WA: Microsoft Press, 1995, pp. 23, 30–32.

[Olson95] D. Olson. "Don Olson's Patterns on the Wiki Wiki Web." Portland, OR: Portland Patterns Repository (URL: `http://c2.com/cgi/wiki?search=DonOlson`), 1995.

[Remer96] D. Remer. "Cost and Schedule Estimation for Software Development Projects." UCLA, 1996, pp. SW 11-8, Guideline #35.

[Rising96] L. Rising. "Don't Flip the Bozo Bit." Phoenix, AZ: AG Communication Systems Patterns Home Page (URL: `http://www.agcs.com/patterns/BozoBit.html`), 1996.

David DeLano and Linda Rising can be reached at delanod@agcs.com **and** risingl@agcs.com, **respectively.**

PART 10

Patterns on Patterns

While the previous parts of this book comprise concrete patterns and pattern languages for specific domains and aspects of software development, this part includes patterns about patterns. Initially, this may seem esoteric—a playing ground for intellectual games for a few patterns enthusiasts. However, a closer look reveals that there are valid considerations involved with successfully propagating and applying patterns. For example, composing patterns into large structures in a meaningful way requires some experience in using patterns. However, general guidelines for applying patterns are typically not part of the scope of those patterns. Therefore, capturing such guidelines in pattern form seems to be a good idea.

Chapter 29: A Pattern Language for Pattern Writing by Gerard Meszaros and Jim Doble. This chapter addresses an aspect beyond the mere use of patterns; it discusses the problem of *writing* patterns. In order to use a pattern successfully, its readers need to understand the problem, the context in which the problem arises, and the solution that the pattern provides. They also need to know how to implement the solution, and the implications involved with that implementation. Without an appropriate pattern description, however, this is hard to achieve. It is not just the technical content that determines a pattern paper's value—the presentation quality has an important impact. A paper that describes a pattern is a piece of literature. Of course, the content must be sound, but it must also be presented clearly and understandably. It must convey the essence of the pattern quickly and in a way that everybody can understand. And in every paragraph, it must keep the reader interested and motivated to read more. To achieve this, we need an appropriate structural pattern form and, most important, an attractive writing style.

But are software engineers skilled enough to produce high-quality pattern descriptions? Do we need poets to write good pattern papers? Is there any way to enable us to write good patterns without going through a long education in the art of writing?

Clearly, without practice no one can write a good paper. But with some guidance, engineers can get on the right track. One form for such guidance is a pattern language! A pattern language for writing patterns would address appropriate pattern structure, how to include examples, and how to write in a style that informs and entertains readers at the same time. If such a pattern language were available, our lives as pattern writers would be much easier.

The authors realized this and wrote a whole pattern language on writing patterns. This pattern language emerged from their own experience, and also from the experience of other patterns writers worldwide. The authors held long discussions at previous PLoP conferences and collected what they learned in this chapter. The chapter serves both as a pattern-writing tutorial for novices and as a reference manual for experienced pattern writers. It is a nice example of the power that patterns have to enable us to explore new domains.

Chapter 29

A Pattern Language for Pattern Writing

Gerard Meszaros and Jim Doble

As the patterns community has accumulated experience in writing and reviewing patterns and pattern languages, we have begun to develop insight into pattern-writing techniques and approaches that have been observed to be particularly effective at addressing certain recurring problems. This pattern language attempts to capture some of these best practices of pattern writing, both by describing them in pattern form and by demonstrating them in action. As such, this pattern language is its own Running Example.

The use of patterns to communicate wisdom and insight in computer/software systems design is a relatively new idea. As such, techniques and approaches for writing patterns and pattern languages are continually being improved, as creative individuals try new ways to organize and communicate their thoughts. Although there is no single right way to write patterns, this pattern language describes and demonstrates a collection of writing practices which have been observed to be particularly effective. The language is targeted at both novice and experienced pattern writers. Novices may choose to treat these patterns as suggestions to be tried and to be adopted where they help, and experts can use these patterns as a form of checklist, helping them keep in mind some of the issues and forces in effective pattern writing.

Unlike a prescriptive pattern language, which describes the steps or recipes for solving some problem, this pattern language describes the desired result. The pattern author is free to employ different techniques to achieve these results. This approach should allow this pattern language to be employed in whole or in part as the reader sees fit.

HISTORY OF THIS PATTERN LANGUAGE

Most of the patterns in this language started out as observations about things which worked well in a particular pattern or language being reviewed in a PLoP '95 writers workshop. As PLoP '95 progressed, these observations led to hypotheses that certain of these techniques and approaches would be particularly effective at addressing recurring pattern-writing problems. These hypotheses were tested in subsequent pattern reviews; if the hypotheses were shown to be true more often than not, we started referring to them by evocative names. (In the beginning, the names were all we had to communicate them, so they had to be evocative to be effective.) Comparing notes based on our respective review groups' experiences, we began to observe that the kinds of practices that were being applauded were very much the same despite the independence of our review groups. It was quickly recognized that these techniques and approaches could themselves be expressed in the form of a pattern language.[1]

While we did not keep detailed statistics, we only present patterns here which emerged from this broad consensus. In the months which followed PLoP '95, many of these patterns were made available to practitioners conducting pattern writing courses, and feedback to the authors indicates that they have been very helpful. In addition, these patterns were reviewed extensively at PLoP '96 and became part of the working vocabulary of several review groups.

PATTERN LANGUAGE SUMMARY

The patterns in this language are grouped into five sections.

- A. Context-Setting Patterns introduces the concept of a pattern (a Solution to a Problem in a Context) and a pattern language (collections of patterns that are related to each other by virtue of solving the same problems or parts of a solution to a larger, partitioned problem) so that they may be used throughout this pattern language.
- B. Pattern Structuring Patterns contains patterns describing the desired content and structure of individual patterns, whether free-standing or part of a larger pattern language.
- C. Pattern Naming and Referencing Patterns contains patterns that describe techniques for naming your pattern(s) and for including references to other patterns within your pattern(s).

---

[1] Clearly the result of overexposure to pattern languages. After two intensive days of reviewing pattern languages, just about any collection of scatterbrained ideas begins to look like a candidate for a pattern language.

- D. Patterns for Making Patterns Understandable contains patterns that capture techniques for making your patterns and pattern languages easier to read, understand, and apply.
- E. Pattern Language Structuring Patterns contains patterns that describe the desired content and structure of pattern languages.

Each section starts with a brief summary which introduces the patterns described in the section. The patterns in the entire collection are depicted graphically in Figure 29-1 and summarized at the end of this chapter in the appendix in Tables 29-1 to 29-4.

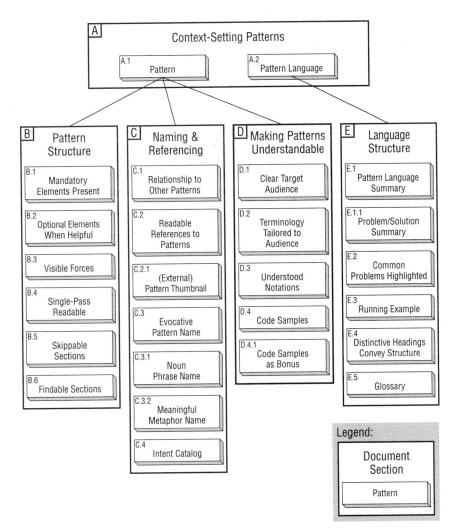

Figure 29-1 *Pattern language structure*

HOW TO USE THESE PATTERNS

Readers searching for a solution to a particular pattern writing problem should refer to the Problem/Solution Summary tables to see if any of the problems resemble the ones they are trying to solve. Since each pattern has been written with skippable sections; readers could flip through the language looking at the Name, Problem, and Solution sections. Once they have determined that a pattern is of interest, they can look at the Context and Forces sections for guidance on determining whether it is applicable to their situation. Finally, they can look at the Rationale, Resulting Context, Related Patterns, and Examples sections to further appreciate the nuances of the pattern.

CONVENTIONS

Throughout this pattern language, pattern names are capitalized (initial caps).

A. CONTEXT-SETTING PATTERNS

It is not the primary purpose of this pattern language to define the concept of a pattern or a pattern language. However, since the patterns in this language are applied within the context of writing patterns or pattern languages, we must include some sort of working definition. In keeping with the spirit of the patterns movement, we do this in the pattern form.

A.1 Pattern Pattern

Here we present the Pattern pattern.

Context

You are an experienced practitioner in your field. You have noticed that you keep using a certain solution to a commonly occurring problem. You would like to share your experience with others.

Problem

How do you share a recurring solution to a problem with others so that it may be reused?

Forces

• Keeping the solution to yourself doesn't require any effort.

- Sharing the solution verbally helps a few others but won't make a big impact in your field.
- Writing down your understanding of the solution is hard work and requires much reflection on how you solve the problem.
- Transforming your specific solution into a more widely applicable solution is difficult.
- People are unlikely to use a solution if you don't explain the reasons for using it.
- Writing down the solution may compromise your competitive advantage (either personal or corporate).

Solution

Write down the solution using the pattern form. Capture both the problem and the solution, as well as the reasons why the solution is applicable. Apply Mandatory Elements Present to ensure that the necessary information is communicated clearly. Include Optional Elements When Helpful to capture any additional useful information. Distribute the resulting pattern to the largest audience you feel it could help that does not compromise your competitive advantage. Often, this means publishing your patterns exclusively within your company via intranets or company journals.

A.2 Pattern Language Pattern

Context

You are trying to use the "pattern form" to describe a procedure with many steps or a complex solution to a complex problem. Some of the steps may only apply in particular circumstances. There may be alternate solutions to parts of the problem depending on the circumstances. A single pattern is insufficient to deal with the complexity at hand.

Problem

How do you describe the solution such that it is easy to digest and easy to use parts of the solution in different circumstances?

Forces

- A single large solution may be too specific to the circumstance and impossible to reuse in other circumstances.
- A complex solution may be hard to describe in a single pattern. A divide-and-conquer approach may be necessary to make the solution tractable.
- Factoring the solution into a set of reusable steps can be very difficult. Once factored, the resulting pieces may depend on one another to make any sense.

- Other pattern languages may want to refer to parts of the solution; they require some sort of handle for each of the parts to be referenced.

Solution

Factor the overall problem and its complex solution or procedure into a number of related problems with their respective solutions. Capture each problem/solution pair as a pattern within a larger pattern language. Each pattern should solve a specific problem within the shared context of the language. Strive to ensure that each pattern could conceivably be used alone or with a limited number of patterns from the language.

To give the pattern language an identity of its own, give it an Evocative Name by which it can be known and referenced. Describe the overall problem and how the patterns work together to solve it in a Pattern Language Summary. Relate the patterns to each other using Readable References to Patterns within the pattern description, especially in the Context and Related Patterns elements.

Example

This pattern language is itself an example of tackling the complex problem of writing patterns and pattern languages. It presents the solution as a number of patterns, each of which describe the solution to a specific smaller problem.

B. PATTERN STRUCTURE PATTERNS

A pattern is just a description of a solution to a problem found to occur in a specific context. But many other types of writing would claim to satisfy this definition. What sets patterns apart is their ability to explain the rationale for using the solution (the why) in addition to describing the solution (the how). A key contributor to this characteristic is the structure of the pattern form.

The patterns in this section describe the structure of an individual pattern, whether free-standing or part of a larger pattern language. Patterns are easier to understand and apply when all Mandatory Elements (are) Present regardless of the pattern style chosen. Optional Elements When Helpful gives pattern writers considerable flexibility in what additional information they present and how they structure it to maximize the readers' understanding. While structuring your pattern, strive to make it Single-Pass Readable to minimize the frustration of the pattern reader. Some techniques for achieving this include having Visible Forces so they can easily be picked out, and Skippable Sections that can be bypassed to speed up the first reading.

B.1 Mandatory Elements Present Pattern

Aliases

All Elements Present

Problem

How do you make sure that all necessary information is covered in a pattern?

Context

You are writing a pattern, either as a stand-alone or as part of a pattern language.

Forces

- Not all patterns require the same kinds of information to be effectively communicated. Capturing all elements regardless of need only clutters many patterns.
- For a pattern to be truly useful, it must have a minimum set of essential information. These information elements are required to allow patterns to be found when required and to be applied when applicable.
- If the necessary elements are missing, it becomes much harder to determine whether the pattern solves the reader's problem in an acceptable way.
- There is no single correct style or template for patterns; trying to impose one could stifle creativity and get in the way of effective communication.
- Readers expect certain information to be present in a pattern. This is what differentiates a pattern from a mere problem/solution description.

Solution

Include the following mandatory elements in the pattern. The exact names of these elements vary from one pattern style to another and the exact order in which they appear in is not as crucial as ensuring that they are all present. They are presented here in an order chosen to facilitate understanding of their relationships. The nature of the relationships between the elements is illustrated in Figure 29-2.

Pattern Name.   A name by which this problem/solution pairing can be referenced.

Context.   The circumstances in which the problem is being solved imposes constraints on the solution. The context is often described via a situation rather than stated explicitly. Sometimes, the context is described in terms of the patterns that have already been applied. The relative importance of the forces (those that need to be optimized at the expense of others) is determined by the context.

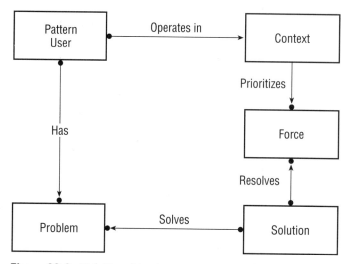

Figure 29-2 *Relationships between pattern elements*

Problem. The specific problem that needs to be solved. Use Context-Free Problem[2] to ensure that the problem is kept separate from the constraints on the solution.

Forces. The often contradictory considerations that must be taken into account when choosing a solution to a problem. The relative importance of the forces (those that need to be optimized at the expense of others) is implied by the context.

Solution. The proposed solution to the problem. Note that many problems may have more than one solution, and the appropriateness of a solution to a problem is affected by the context in which the problem occurs. Each solution takes certain forces into account. It resolves some forces at the expense of others. It may even totally ignore some forces. The most appropriate solution to a problem is the one that best resolves the highest priority forces as determined by the particular context. Use Solution Clearly Related to Forces[3] to ensure that the reader understands why this solution was chosen.

---

[2] "Context-Free Problem" (not published). The problem statement should be independent of the context. This allows other patterns to be written that solve the same problem in different circumstances. In [Roberts+96], the same problem appears twice, with two different contexts and two different solutions.
[3] "Solution Clearly Related to Forces" (not published). The solution section of a pattern should clearly describe how the solution optimizes the forces that the context implies should be given the highest priority. This ensures that the reader can understand how the forces influenced the selection of this solution.

Rationale

A pattern goes beyond a mere description of the solution by providing a window on the thought processes behind choosing the solution. The mandatory pattern elements described here are essential to communication of this information. In the many patterns that have been written since *The Timeless Way of Building* [Alexander79] and *A Pattern Language* [Alexander77] were first published, these mandatory elements have been found to be the minimum information required to effectively communicate a pattern.

Examples

All the patterns in this language have Mandatory Elements Present. This ensures that potential users of these patterns understand why and when to apply them. The elements are highlighted through the use of headings. Most of these patterns start with the Problem statement followed by the Context, while others start with the Context. This was done to illustrate both styles. Berczuk consistently places the Context before the Problem section [Berczuk96].

In some pattern styles, the pattern elements have different names or are organized differently. See Coplien for a more complete list of pattern styles and their features [Coplien96].

Christopher Alexander and his associates used this basic structure in *A Pattern Language*. The mandatory elements are separated typographically, with the solution paragraph(s) being introduced with a "therefore."

In *Design Patterns*, the Problem and Context sections are replaced with an Intent and an Applicability section, respectively, which are augmented by a more concrete example of the problem in the Motivation section [Gamma+95]. The Solution section is replaced by four sections: Structure, Participants, Collaborations, and Implementation.

B.2   Optional Elements When Helpful Pattern

Problem

How do you communicate essential information that does not fit well into the mandatory elements?

Context

You are writing a pattern and have applied Mandatory Elements Present.

Forces

- All patterns do not require the same kinds of information to be effectively communicated.
- Capturing all elements regardless of need only clutters many patterns.

Solution

The following sections may be included if they make the pattern easier to understand or provide better linkage between the pattern in question and related patterns.

Indications.   The symptoms that might indicate that the problem exists.

Resulting Context.   The context that we find ourselves in after the pattern has been applied. It can include one or more new problems to solve. This sets us up for applying more patterns, possibly the next pattern(s) in a language.

Related Patterns.   Other patterns that may be of interest to the reader. The kinds of patterns include:

- Other solutions to the same problem
- More general or (possibly domain) specific variations of the pattern
- Patterns that solve some of the problems in the resulting context (set up by this pattern)

Examples.   Concrete examples that illustrate the application of the pattern.

Code Samples.   Sample code showing how to implement the pattern.

Rationale.   An explanation of why this solution is most appropriate for the stated problem within this context.

Aliases.   Other names by which this pattern might be known.

Acknowledgments.   You should acknowledge anyone who contributed significantly to the development of the pattern (or language) or the techniques described in it. If your pattern has been through a shepherding process or writers workshop, significant contributors (such as the shepherd) are candidates for acknowledgments.

Examples

In *Design Patterns,* the Resulting Context is known as Consequences and Code Samples is called Sample Code. Examples is called Known Uses and is augmented by a more concrete representation of the problem in the Motivation section.

Cockburn introduced the idea of an Indications element, there called Symptoms [Cockburn96].

B.3   Visible Forces Pattern

Problem

A pattern presents a solution to a problem within a context. How do you ensure that the reader understands the choice of solution?

Context

You are writing a pattern or pattern language that is intended to convey one of potentially several solutions to a problem. You have applied Mandatory Elements Present; you are now writing the Forces section.

Forces

- There are many different styles of patterns, some more structured than others.
- People like to have convenient handles for concepts such as the forces which affect the choice of solution.
- Prose pattern descriptions can be very pleasing to read but may be hard to use as a reference because the forces are buried in the prose.
- Having a separate Forces heading makes the forces very easy to find but may make the pattern less pleasing to read.
- Too much structure can impinge on the literary quality of a pattern.

Solution

Regardless of the style chosen for the pattern description, ensure that the forces are highly visible. This can be done by defining a meaningful "name" for each force and visually setting if off from text by making them minor headings, or by highlighting them using fonts, underlining, or other typographic techniques.

Examples

This pattern language uses a bulleted list within a Forces heading to make the forces visible.

Foote highlights the forces within the prose of the pattern description [Foote96a].

B.4   Single-Pass Readable Pattern

Problem

A person in search of a solution may need to look at many potential solutions. How do you help the reader understand your pattern in the least amount of time, in order to facilitate this search?

Context

You are writing a pattern with Mandatory Elements Present.

Forces

- People frequently have only limited time to read a pattern.
- People get frustrated and give up when the effort is too great.
- A pattern that must be read several times before being understood is more likely to be misunderstood.
- A simple message is more likely to be understood correctly.

Solution

Single-Pass Readable is easier said than done, and probably merits a pattern language on its own. However, here are a variety of techniques which can be helpful to achieve single-pass readability.

- Use Evocative Pattern Names or Pattern Thumbnails in cases where some understanding of a forward referenced pattern is necessary for the reader to keep reading.[4]
- Help the reader locate key information by using Findable Sections and Visible Forces to highlight the tradeoffs involved.
- Use Skippable Sections (such as Code Samples as Bonus) to highlight information which can be skipped on first reading.
- In a pattern language, provide a clear, concise Pattern Language Summary outlining the structure of the pattern language, then remind the readers where they are within the structure as they go along, using (Distinctive) Headings to Convey Structure.
- If you need to introduce and/or define a number of concepts or terms in the introductory sections of your pattern, try to pare down your list by selecting only the most essential concepts and terms, and write your pattern using this reduced list. Remember that normal adults are able to keep seven (plus or minus two) items of information within their short-term memory [Miller56]. If you introduce more information than your reader can remember, he or she will need to keep referring back to the beginning, which defeats single-pass readability.
- Provide a Glossary so that readers don't have to search around for definitions of terms that they can't remember. This isn't Single-Pass Readable per se, but it is preferable to the alternative.

---

[4] A brief footnote summarizing the main idea of a pattern. Just like this one.

Rationale

In order to help the readers get what they need from your patterns in the minimum amount of time, you need to help them to read only the sections they need, only once. Skippable Sections and Findable Sections will help readers to find the sections they need. The techniques described above help the reader avoid going back (or forward) to read sections more than once.

Related Patterns

- Pattern Language Summary introduces the larger problem being solved and how the solution has been factored into a number of patterns.
- (Distinctive) Headings Convey Structure helps the readers understand the structure of the pattern language by reminding them where they are in the pattern language.
- Skippable Sections and Findable Sections help the users quickly find only the sections they need to understand the essence of the pattern solution.
- Evocative Pattern Names and Pattern Thumbnails reduce the need to follow pattern references before proceeding.
- Glossary defines the terminology in one place so the reader doesn't have to scan the pattern (language) looking for it.

B.5   Skippable Sections Pattern

Context

You are writing a pattern that is part of a collection intended to be used as a reference. You have applied Mandatory Elements Present and Optional Elements When Helpful. You are striving to make the pattern easily understood and Single-Pass Readable.

Problem

How do you make it easy for the reader to get the essence of a pattern while still providing enough information to apply it?

Forces

- The information required to determine whether a pattern is applicable may be a small subset of the information required to actually apply the pattern.
- People require different amounts of information to understand and apply a pattern.
- People sometimes have only limited time to invest in reading a pattern.

- A long-winded pattern description may cause a reader to skip the pattern entirely because the expected return does not justify the investment.
- Separating information into sections may make a pattern more bulky.

Solution

Clearly identify the Problem, Context, and Solution parts so that the readers can quickly determine whether this pattern applies to them. Put more detailed information (such as forces or code samples) in clearly identified sections that may be skipped if a person doesn't want all the detail.

Rationale

When readers are trying to become familiar with a set of patterns, they often want to cut to the chase quickly. Too much information gets in the way. Much of the information in a pattern is only required once you have narrowed down the list, or have decided to use the pattern. This pattern makes it easier to get the essence of a pattern without becoming bogged down in detail, thus allowing the reader to assimilate more patterns in a shorter period of time.

Resulting Context

Unless the Skippable Sections are at the end, the reader may need to scan for the beginning of the next section of interest. Use Findable Sections to make this easier.

Related Patterns

The pattern Code Samples as Bonus describes a special case of a Skippable Section. Optional Elements When Helpful describes when to include a section while Skippable Sections focuses on helping the reader read a pattern efficiently.

Examples

The Alexandrian pattern style uses fonts and ***-delimited paragraphs to allow the reader to pick out the problem and solution sections. More structured styles (such as used in this pattern language) use headings to separate the different sections. The introduction of this pattern language tells the reader which pattern elements they should concentrate on for a quick read.

In *Design Patterns*, the Applicability section allows the rest of the pattern to be skipped when searching for a pattern to solve a particular problem.

B.6 Findable Sections Pattern

Context

You are writing a pattern that is part of a collection intended to be used as a reference. You have applied Mandatory Elements Present, Optional Elements When Helpful, and Skippable Sections. You are striving to make the pattern easily understood and Single-Pass Readable, and usable as reference material.

Problem

How do you make it easy to find key elements of the pattern, most notably the Problem, Context, Forces, and Solutions elements?

Forces

- The information required to determine whether a pattern is applicable may be a small subset of the information required to actually apply the pattern.
- People require different amounts of information to understand and apply a pattern.
- People sometimes have only a limited time to invest in reading a pattern.
- A long-winded pattern description may cause a reader to skip the pattern entirely because the expected return does not justify the investment.
- If a section is skipped, it may be hard to determine where to resume reading.

Solution

For your pattern style, determine which sections a reader may be specifically looking for when using the material as reference. Clearly identify the beginnings of each of these sections so that the reader may find them easily. This can be done typographically (using fonts, underlining), by using headings, or by graphics (using diagrams, *'s and so forth between sections).

The start of a pattern is a special case of a Findable Section. Techniques to help find the reader find the start of patterns include starting all patterns on a new page, shaded headers, and evocative illustrations at the start of patterns.

Rationale

A section is only truly skippable if the next section of interest is easily found without reading or skimming the section to be skipped. The more visible the section demarcations, the easier it is to skip directly to them.

Related Patterns

Skippable Sections focuses on helping the reader read a pattern efficiently while this pattern improves the usability of the pattern as reference material.

Examples

The Alexandrian pattern style uses fonts and *** delimited paragraphs to allow the reader to pick out the problem and solution sections. More structured styles (such as used in this pattern language) use headings to separate the different sections. In some pattern languages, it is often possible to find key elements by merely lifting one's finger and flipping the page. This is because all patterns start on a new page and each pattern element starts at roughly the same point on the page.

Foote makes effective use of a combination of shaded headers and evocative illustrations to make the start of individual patterns easy to find [Foote96b]. He also achieves a similar effect using evocative illustrations alone [Foote96a].

C. PATTERN NAMING AND REFERENCING PATTERNS

Few patterns live in isolation. Typically, they introduce new, hopefully smaller and more tractable problems which will lead you to other patterns. Or, there may be other patterns that solve the same problem. The patterns in this section all deal with how to describe these Relationships to Other Patterns in a pleasing and efficient manner. Many elements of a pattern may need to refer to other patterns. Including Readable References to Patterns within the prose makes these references informative without being intrusive. Naming your patterns with Evocative Pattern Names makes it easier to refer to them and reduces the need for the reader to follow the references every time you include a pattern name. Two especially useful patterns for creating Evocative Pattern Names are Noun Phrase Name which names the pattern after the resulting solution, and Meaningful Metaphor Name, which names the pattern after some commonly understood metaphor. When the reader may need more information about the pattern than just the name, include a Pattern Thumbnail. A pattern's Intent Catalog is a good source for Pattern Thumbnails.

C.1 Relationship to Other Patterns Pattern

Context

You are writing the Related Patterns element of a pattern with Mandatory Elements Present.

Problem

How do you make a pattern part of a larger group of patterns?

Forces

- Few patterns are truly isolated; they usually lead to other patterns, or they solve problems set up by other patterns.
- Patterns are more useful if their relationships to other patterns are documented.
- Determining and describing related patterns can be hard work.
- Too many references to patterns may distract the reader from the solution you are trying to describe.
- It may be hard to find all the related patterns.

Solution

One of the key advantages of a pattern language over a stand-alone pattern is its ability to guide the reader to the solution of a complex problem by leading them from one pattern to another. Stand-alone patterns have to work harder to establish their relationships.

These relationships can take many forms. The pattern being written may

- *Lead to* other patterns, often within a pattern language, by creating a problem which a subsequent pattern solves. The problem introduced (and possibly the pattern to solve it) should be described in the Resulting Context or Solution section.
- The pattern may be *set up* by other patterns which introduce the problem this pattern solves. Capture the preceding patterns in the Context section.
- The pattern may *specialize* a more general version of a pattern to make it more easily applied within a specific problem domain, or
- It may *generalize* one or more domain-specific patterns to allow more general applicability. Capture these in the Related Pattern sections.
- The pattern may have *alternative* patterns which solve the same problem in different ways. Capture these in the Related Pattern sections.

The pattern description should point out similarities or differences from other patterns which might seem, on the surface, to be the same. Capture these in the Related Pattern sections.

A pattern addressing a problem in one domain may be complemented by a pattern in an orthogonal domain. While thinking or writing about a pattern, read other pattern languages and identify relationships to other patterns. Refer to related patterns as appropriate throughout the pattern, most notably in the Context, Solution, Resulting Context, and Related Patterns sections. Use Readable References to Patterns to cite the related patterns. Where necessary, include a Pattern Thumbnail so that your reader doesn't have to look up the pattern to understand how it is related.

To make your pattern(s) easier to refer to from other patterns, give your patterns Evocative Pattern Names and summarize their intent(s) in an Intent Catalog or Problem/Solution Summary.

Rationale

Understanding the relationships between a pattern and other patterns makes a pattern more understandable and useful since alternative solutions can be assessed and follow-on patterns can be found and applied.

Example

Berczuk does a particularly good job of relating technical patterns to organization patterns [Berczuk96].

C.2   Readable References to Patterns Pattern

Context

You are writing a pattern structured according to Mandatory Elements Present. You need to refer to other patterns in one or more of the elements.

Problem

How do you refer to other patterns within the description of your pattern?

Forces

- A pattern may be described much more concisely if it can delegate much of its solution to other patterns.
- Citations to other patterns could disrupt the reader's train of thought or cause them to lose their context.
- The reader may want to read the pattern being referred to and will require more information than just the name.

Solution

When referring to patterns within the body of your pattern, weave the pattern names into the narrative. Augment the pattern name with a pattern reference which can be used to look it up. Set off the pattern name from the surrounding text by highlighting it typographically.

Where the patterns have Noun Phrase Names, you should be able to use the pattern name directly in the sentence (as we have done in this sentence.) In most cases, Meaningful Metaphor Names can be treated in the same way. Verb Phrase

Names[5] are somewhat more difficult to weave into the narrative because they are typically imperative or prescriptive in nature; it may be harder to use them to describe the result.

To make it easier for the reader to find the description of the pattern, it is desirable to include a reference to the pattern description. This could take the form of a traditional literary reference of the form pattern-name[reference-name], or you can use an External Pattern Thumbnail.

Rationale

Weaving the pattern names into the text makes the pattern easier and more pleasurable to read while the reference satisfies those readers who want to find the original.

Related Patterns

External Pattern Thumbnails can be used to refer to patterns that must be understood to get the essence of the current pattern.

Example

In this pattern language, we have used a special character style for pattern names to distinguish them from the surrounding text. Because most of the pattern referenced have Noun Phrase Names, we have been able to weave the pattern names into the text. The names have been augmented with a footnote or an internal pattern reference number. We have included an External Pattern Thumbnail for any patterns that are not included within the language.

C.2.1   (External) Pattern Thumbnail Pattern

Context

You are writing a pattern that makes reference to related patterns that appear later or are not included within the pattern or pattern language you are writing. A basic understanding of these patterns may be necessary for the reader to fully understand your pattern.

---

[5] "Verb Phrase Name" (not published). Name the Pattern after the process used to create the solution. Example: Verb Phrase Name is itself a Noun Phrase Name. To recast this as a Verb Phrase Name, you could try: Name the Pattern After the Process Used to Create the Solution.

Problem

How do you refer to other patterns in a concise but meaningful manner with minimum interruption of the reader's flow, so that the understanding of your pattern is maximized?

Forces

- Referencing external patterns is an effective way to build upon, or relate your work to existing patterns and pattern languages.
- Including the complete description of related external patterns within your pattern will make it too large, and will distract the reader from what you are trying to communicate.
- A basic understanding of related external patterns may be necessary for the reader to fully understand your pattern.
- Some readers will be familiar with the referenced external patterns, while others will not.
- The most concise way to refer to an existing pattern is to provide sufficient information for the reader to obtain the complete description of the referenced pattern, typically using an author/year tag and a References section.
- Readers may not have the time (or energy) to obtain and read the complete description of the referenced pattern prior to finishing reading and understanding your pattern. Even if readers do this, they will be significantly distracted from your pattern.

Solution

Include the Evocative Name of the external pattern within the text. The first time the external pattern is referenced, provide both an author/year tag and a footnote with a brief (one or two sentences) thumbnail description of the essence of the external pattern. The thumbnail should provide just enough information about the external pattern to maximize understandability of your pattern.

As an alternative to using footnotes, you can include the thumbnail and reference in the body of your text (in parentheses).

Rationale

Readers who are familiar with the external referenced pattern should not be distracted by the thumbnail footnote. Other readers will be able to continue reading and understanding your pattern after they have read the thumbnail. Readers who want to understand the referenced pattern in detail should be able to obtain its complete description using the information in the References section.

Related Patterns

Evocative Pattern Name helps reduce the need for Pattern Thumbnails.

Examples

Several of the patterns in this language include External Pattern Thumbnails. For example, Evocative Pattern Name contains a thumbnail reference to Buffalo Mountain.

Episodes includes a table of External Pattern Thumbnails as an appendix to help the reader understand the essential aspects of yet unpublished patterns [Cunningham96].

C.3   Evocative Pattern Name Pattern[6]

Aliases

Understandable Pattern Name, Solution Revealing Pattern Name

Context

You are writing a pattern (or pattern language) that may need to be referenced by other patterns or pattern languages.

Problem

How do you name a pattern so that it is easy to remember and refer to?

Forces

- Patterns may vary based on differences in problem, context, forces, solutions, or any combination of these. Each combination may require a distinct pattern name.
- People should be able to use patterns as a vocabulary, that is, the identity of the pattern becomes a *word* in a person's design vocabulary.
- A name short enough to use as a noun in a sentence may not convey enough meaning to be understandable out of context.
- The most memorable patterns are those whose names conjure up a clear image of the solution.
- Cute but obtuse pattern names may be meaningful to the writer but few readers will understand what they mean later.

---

[6] Evocative: *adj.* Tending or having the power to evoke. Evoke: *n.* To call to mind or memory. (*American Heritage Dictionary*) Not the same as *provocative.*

Solution

Choose a pattern name that is likely to conjure up images which convey the essence of the pattern solution to the target audience. Imagine using the name in conversations or referring to it from other patterns. Test the name by having people unfamiliar with the pattern description guess at what the pattern might be about based on its name.

Rationale

As patterns are used to construct systems or to express how they are related to one another, the name is used without the accompanying description. A name chosen using this pattern is more likely to be understood, which makes it more likely to become part of the vocabulary of the readers.

Related Patterns

Intent Revealing Method Selector describes the solution to the problem of naming methods in Smalltalk programming [Beck96]. By capturing the intent in the method name, readers of the program should not have to refer to the method description every time they see the name.

Two patterns for creating Evocative Pattern Names are: Noun Phrase Name and Meaningful Metaphor Name. Buffalo Mountain[7] is an example of a cute but obtuse name for a pattern. Many people may remember it, but few can recall what it describes.

This pattern can also be applied to pattern languages since they, too, require names which are memorable and easy to refer to.

Examples

All the patterns in this language have Evocative Pattern Names.

Many of the patterns in well-known pattern books, such as *Design Patterns,* use names designed to invoke images of the solution: Bridge, Adapter, Proxy, Decorator, to name a few.

---

[7] Buffalo Mountain describes how to optimize communication within an organization [Coplien94]. "The Pattern's name comes from the similarity between the visual graph (when the communications between roles in a project are plotted in a scatter gram) and the characteristic shape of a mountain in Colorado, and from analogies that can be made about the forces contributing to each."

C.3.1   Noun Phrase Name Pattern

Aliases

Solution Phrase Name

Context

You are writing a pattern (or pattern language) that may need to be referred to by other patterns or pattern languages. You have created a pattern that you are attempting to name by applying Evocative Pattern Name.

Problem

How do you name a pattern so that it is easy to remember and refer to?

Forces

- Names that describe the problem are not unique since there may be several solutions to the problem. Suppose you were directed to "Apply the Implementing State Machine pattern." If there were several patterns which solved this problem, which solution does this name refer to?
- Names containing verbs or prepositions are difficult to use in conversation. Note the tension in this conversation: "What's that?" "Oh, it's an Object from a State."
- Names that describe the process of creating the solution are hard to use in a sentence describing the solution. It forces you to use a phrase like: "In this design, we have an example of Create Objects for States."
- Describing the result of applying a pattern helps the reader visualize the result but it does not help convey the problem being solved. "What's that?" "Oh, that's a State Object."
- Since an important purpose of patterns is to foster communication by creating a shared vocabulary, pattern names should be easy to say.

Solution

Name the pattern after the result it creates. This allows the name to be used easily in conversation. In a pattern language, use a Problem/Solution Summary to help the reader find the right solution.

When referring to a pattern with a Noun Phrase Name where an understanding of the problem is important, include the problem in the referring phrase as in: "In this design, we used a Proxy to allow an object to be referred to remotely."

Rationale

One of the most compelling aspects of a pattern is the way it transforms a situation, resolving some forces and giving rise to others. This is what makes patterns more than just design rules or a style guide.

Focusing on the thing created by a pattern for naming leads to noun phrases. Naming the pattern above after the object it creates results in the name "State Object."

Example

The name of this pattern, Noun Phrase Name, is itself an example of a Noun Phrase Name.

Related Patterns

This pattern is a way to create an Evocative Pattern Name.

Another way to create an Evocative Pattern Name is to use Meaningful Metaphor Name. A Meaningful Metaphor Name may itself be a Noun Phrase Name.

C.3.2   Meaningful Metaphor Name Pattern

Context

You are writing a pattern (or pattern language) that may need to be referred to by other patterns or pattern languages. You have created a pattern that you are attempting to name by applying an Evocative Pattern Name.

Problem

How do you give your pattern a useful and memorable name?

Forces

- Metaphors are a good source of short Noun Phrase Names.
- People often find it easier to understand new concepts if they can be related to other concepts with which they are already familiar.
- If you try to explain new concepts in terms of unfamiliar concepts, the reader will be baffled. Rocket science metaphors are typically understood only by rocket scientists. *Star Trek* metaphors ("Darmok and Jalad at Tenagra"[8]) are best understood by Trekkers. Hockey metaphors are understood best by Canadians.
- If the link between the metaphor and your pattern is clear, readers will be able to transfer their knowledge of the metaphor into the context of your pattern, helping to clarify and facilitate their understanding of your pattern.

---

[8] In the *The Next Generation* episode, "Darmok," the *Enterprise* crew encounters the Tamarians, whose language is based entirely on metaphors such as "Darmok and Jalad at Tenagra," taken from their own mythology [Okuda94]. Picard and the crew are initially frustrated in their attempts to understand the Tamarians because they are unfamiliar with Tamarian mythology. Note that this is an example within an example. Quite appropriate for a paper on metapatterns, *n'est-ce pas?*

- If the link between the metaphor and your pattern is unclear, the reader will be baffled. "I understand rocket science, but what does that have to do with your pattern?"

Solution

Find a meaningful metaphor for the pattern, and name the pattern accordingly. Some people are better with metaphors than others, so if a good metaphor doesn't jump out at you, go back to Noun Phrase Name. Ideally a metaphor will be familiar and easily understood by the average reader. If you have to explain the metaphor, it is not familiar enough. Clearly identify how the problem and solution relate to the metaphor, so that the reader is able to link his or her understanding of the metaphor concepts with your pattern.

Rationale

A metaphor effectively creates an association between your pattern and a set of parallel concepts with which the reader is familiar (we hope). Naming your pattern according to the metaphor you use to explain it helps the reader remember both your pattern and the metaphor. Clearly linking metaphor concepts with pattern concepts will help readers transfer their knowledge of the metaphor into the context of your pattern, helping to clarify and facilitate their understanding of your pattern

Examples

The Visitor pattern from *Design Patterns,* is an example of a Meaningful Metaphor Name.

The Shopper pattern is another example of a Meaningful Metaphor Name [Doble96]. This design pattern describes how a Shopper object visits a number of objects to fill its Shopping Bag with items specified in a Shopping list. The name evokes an image of a person wandering from store to store trying to gather all the items on their shopping list.

Related Patterns

This pattern is a specialization of Evocative Pattern Name.

Noun Phrase Name is an alternative way to create an Evocative Pattern Name, though many Meaningful Metaphor Names are also Noun Phrase Names.

Buffalo Mountain is an example of a metaphor name that is not clearly explained as part of the pattern description, thus it has meaning only for the author and those with whom it has been shared verbally.

This pattern is itself an example of Duplicate Problem Description[9] since it has the same problem statement as Noun Phrase Name.

C.4 Intent Catalog Pattern

Context

You are writing a pattern to which you would like other pattern writers to refer.

Problem

How do you make it easy for other pattern writers to reference your pattern in a meaningful way?

Forces

- Coming up with concise summaries of problems and/or solutions is hard work; not everyone can do a good job of it.
- People will not provide references if it is too much effort.
- People who don't understand your pattern completely may make up inappropriate summaries of it.
- Patterns get too big if everything must be included.
- Patterns are hard to understand if relevant information is not included or referenced.

Solution

Provide a catalog of pattern intents that can be used as Pattern Thumbnails when other patterns need to refer to this pattern. The intents in the catalog should provide a one or two sentence thumbnail of what this pattern does. Where the pattern can be used to achieve more than one intent, each intent should be in the catalog.

Resulting Context

You may have more text to maintain as you evolve your pattern (language).

Rationale

A good way to encourage something to happen is to make it the path of least resistance. Providing the intent catalog makes cross referencing less work than duplicating the information.

---

[9] "Duplicate Problem Description" (not published). Solves the problem of having several patterns which describe alternate solutions to the same problem using the brute force method of cloning the problem description into each pattern which provides a solution. As an example, Meaningful Metaphor Name and Noun Phrase Name solve the same problem and share a Duplicate Problem Description.

Related Patterns

The result of this pattern may be used as an External Pattern Thumbnail in a pattern which needs to refer to this pattern. In a pattern language, the Intent Catalog may be incorporated into a single Problem/Solution Summary. The main difference between the two concepts is that an Intent Catalog provides a list of possible uses for a single pattern while a Problem/Solution Summary lists the problem solved by each pattern in a language.

Examples

In this pattern language, the Intent Catalogs of all the patterns have been collected into a Problem/Solution Summary table as part of the Pattern Language Summary.

D. PATTERNS FOR MAKING PATTERNS UNDERSTANDABLE

A pattern is only as useful as it is perceived by its users. Pattern writers can put a lot of effort into describing their patterns but all this effort is for naught if the reader cannot understand it or gives up out of frustration. A key contributor is the quality of the writing, a factor into which we will not delve here. There are other factors—some more specific to patterns, others somewhat general. The patterns described here are included because the reviewers felt they made a significant difference in how easily a pattern or pattern language was understood.

The patterns in this section apply to all elements of a pattern or pattern language. They all strive to help pattern writers communicate their thoughts to pattern readers in the most effective manner possible. A key step is the identification of a *Clear Target Audience*. This helps the writer choose Terminology Tailored to Audience as well as commonly Understood Notations for diagrams and illustrations. If the audience includes programmers, it is appropriate to include Code Samples, while Code Samples as Bonus ensures that the reader isn't obligated to read them to understand the pattern.

D.1 Clear Target Audience Pattern

Aliases

Target Audience, Identified Audience

Problem

Many people may read a particular pattern. How do you ensure that a pattern is easily understood by its intended audience?

Context

You are writing a pattern or pattern language.

Forces

- A pattern can be different things to different people.
- You can't satisfy all the people all of the time.
- Different people use different terminology.
- People with different backgrounds require different amounts of detail.

Solution

Clearly identify a primary target audience to whom you would like to communicate the solution. Keep this audience in mind while writing the pattern. Test the pattern with representative members of the target audience.

It may even be useful to explicitly describe the target audience in the pattern (language) introduction. This helps set the expectations of the readers by telling them up front that they are (or are not) the intended audience. It also helps people determine which meaning of an ambiguous term you intended.

Rationale

A Clear Target Audience focuses the pattern by providing criteria for including some information in the pattern and omitting other information.

Related Patterns

Once you have identified the target audience, choose Terminology Tailored to Audience to maximize the bandwidth of communication to them.

Example

This pattern language identifies its target audience in the first paragraph of the Introduction.

D.2 Terminology Tailored to Audience Pattern

Problem

How do you maximize the likelihood of the intended reader understanding your pattern?

Context

You are writing a pattern or pattern language and have identified a Clear Target Audience.

Forces

- Concepts can be described using a variety of language styles and terminology.
- Translating abstract concepts into concepts within a specific domain may be difficult for some people. The more concrete the terminology, the more likely it is to be understood by people familiar with the terminology.
- The goal of a pattern is to be useful to the reader. If the reader doesn't understand the terminology, the pattern will not be as useful.
- Expanding all acronyms and technical terms makes a pattern description more wordy.
- Using terms without defining them can lead to misunderstandings, that is, false agreement.
- Using too much audience-specific jargon may limit the potential audience.

Solution

Use terminology that is tailored to the audience. Use only those terms with which the typical member of the audience could reasonably be expected to be comfortable. Test the terminology with representative members of the target audience. As part of the introduction be sure to inform the reader of the default terminology source.

To ensure that you do not limit the audience unnecessarily, use the simplest language which effectively communicates the concepts. Include a Glossary of terms that may be unfamiliar. Introduce new terms in footnotes as they are encountered (or refer the reader to the Glossary).

Resulting Context

The pattern or pattern language may not be as understandable to those readers outside the Target Audience if the terminology is too specialized.

Rationale

A pattern that can be understood by the target audience is more likely to be useful.

Example

This pattern language uses terminology specific to the patterns community. It does not explain terms such as Forces and Context because the Target Audience is already familiar with them and would be put off by detailed explanations.

D.3   Understood Notations Pattern

Context

You are writing a pattern and are trying to communicate concepts that are most appropriately communicated using diagrams or illustrations. You have identified a Clear Target Audience.

Problem

How do you ensure that the diagrams are easily understood by your entire target audience?

Forces

- Diagrams and illustrations are often more effective than prose when it comes to communicating concepts, especially those related to software design. A picture is worth a thousand words.
- For any given concept (such as object model relationships) there may be a variety of diagramming notations and styles that can be used (such as Booch, OMT).
- Readers are not necessarily familiar with all such notations and styles. If the readers are not familiar with the notation you have used, they may be unable to understand your pattern. A picture you can't understand is worth a thousand words you can't understand.
- Readers are diverse. If you leave room for interpretation, different readers may interpret your diagram in different ways.
- Providing a detailed description of diagramming notations to your pattern will make it too large, and will distract the reader from what you are trying to communicate.
- An expressive but obscure notation is less effective at communicating with most audiences than a less expressive but better-known notation.

Solution

Use diagramming notations that are likely to be familiar to the target audience. Such notations should be widely used and easily understood (for example, message sequence charts). If you are using a standard notation, always provide a reference to the standard. If not, or if there is any likelihood that potential readers are not familiar with the notation you are using, provide a clear, concise explanation of the notation when you first use it, or refer the reader to a more detailed explanation in an appendix.

Rationale

The more widely used your notation, the more likely that readers will be able to understand your diagrams without the need for bulky and distracting explanations. Brief explanations of less common notations will help readers who are unfamiliar with them understand your diagrams, hopefully without creating too much of a distraction from the essence of your pattern. References for standard notations provide a means for curious readers to learn more.

Related Patterns

If the explanation is included within the pattern or pattern language, ensure that it is a Skippable Section.

D.4 Code Samples Pattern

Aliases

Code Examples

Context

You are describing a solution to a software architecture or design problem. You have identified a Clear Target Audience that includes significant numbers of software designers and programmers.

Problem

How can you make a software pattern sufficiently clear and unambiguous to facilitate straightforward implementation?

Forces

- Software-related concepts are often complex and difficult to explain.
- Informal descriptive text is often unclear and ambiguous.
- Programming languages are designed to convey software concepts in a formal, precise, and unambiguous manner.
- Many software workers are experienced and adept at reverse engineering concepts from software samples, and in fact prefer to learn ideas by looking at code.
- Many software patterns can be implemented in many different ways.
- Too much code interrupts the pattern's flow and may make it unmanageably large.

Solution

Provide one or more implementation code samples, written in a prevalent programming language, to illustrate the pattern concepts. Use a programming language likely to be understood by the Target Audience. Choose an implementation approach that clearly demonstrates the essence of the pattern in a straightforward manner while minimizing unnecessary or distracting detail. Ensure that the code samples are well-commented and that all assumptions and design decisions are stated. Differentiate between aspects of the example that are essential to the pattern versus aspects that are arbitrary. Ensure that your code samples are ready to run, that is, they are free from syntax errors and are complete. Syntax errors in code samples can be as distracting to people as they are to compilers.

Rationale

Well-commented example code is formal, precise, and unambiguous, and can be readily understood by many experienced software workers. Code examples provide concept reinforcement, providing a means for the reader to verify that they have understood the essential concepts of the pattern.

Example

All of the patterns in *Design Patterns* include Code Samples [Gamma+95].

Related Patterns

Code Samples as Bonus ensures that the pattern can be understood without the Code Samples and can help reduce disruption of flow.

D.4.1 Code Samples as Bonus Pattern

Aliases

Code Examples as Bonus

Problem

How can you ensure that the essence of your software pattern can be understood by your entire target audience, regardless of their familiarity with specific programming languages?

Context

You are describing a software architecture or design pattern and are including Code Samples.

Forces

- Well-commented example code is formal, precise, and unambiguous, and can be readily understood by many experienced software workers.
- There is no universally understood programming language. Code Samples will be understood only by those readers who are familiar with the language you use.

Solution

Ensure that the pattern can stand on its own, that it is, able to communicate its essential concepts even if the code examples were deleted. Code Samples should be treated as an optional bonus, providing concept reinforcement and implementation guidance for those readers who are familiar with the language of the examples. Ensure that Code Samples embedded within the text can easily be skipped, or that they are in a separate Skippable Section.

Descriptions of essential algorithms and key object relationships and interactions should be provided using notations other than implementation code. Suitable notations include: pseudocode, flowcharts, object modeling notations, event traces, and object interaction diagrams. Whatever notations you choose, ensure they are Understood Notations; don't invent your own or use little known notations unless absolutely necessary.

Rationale

The purpose of a pattern is to communicate to as wide an audience as possible. If the pattern cannot be fully understood without reading the code examples, then readers who are not familiar with the example language will not be able to understand the pattern.

Code Example

```
Reader >> understandsSmalltalk
        "Answers True if the reader understands Smalltalk,
        otherwise signals an exception"

        self understands: #Smalltalk
                ifTrue: [^True]
                ifFalse: [self doesNotUnderstand].
```

E. PATTERN LANGUAGE STRUCTURING PATTERNS

This section contains patterns that solve problems unique to pattern languages. They deal primarily with how to assemble a number of related patterns into a cohesive pattern language that is more than the sum of its parts. The language should be introduced using a Pattern Language Summary that introduces the overall problem and the patterns that will be used to solve it. The Problem/ Solution Summary is a key part of this introduction because it allows individual patterns in the pattern language to be picked out when the document is used as a reference manual. Larger pattern languages often have a nontrivial structure that can be better communicated using (Distinctive) Headings (that) Convey Structure. They also often contain alternative, possibly mutually exclusive, solutions to the same problem; these can be pointed out by ensuring that Common Problems (are) Highlighted.

A good way to tie together the patterns in a pattern language is through the use of a Running Example that illustrates the application of the patterns to an example of the larger problem. To improve understanding, any nonstandard terminology should be expanded in a Glossary.

E.1 Pattern Language Summary Pattern

Problem

How do you give the reader an overview of a set of patterns?

Context

You are writing a pattern language describing the solution for a complex problem.

Forces

- A pattern language should be more than just the sum of its parts.
- The connections between patterns (how they relate to one another) are not always obvious.
- Interpattern relationships are sometimes difficult to understand solely from the perspective of the patterns involved in the relationships.
- Describing the relationships between many patterns in one place takes extra effort and increases the bulk of the language.

Solution

Identify the set of patterns as a pattern language and write a summary which introduces the larger problem and the patterns which contribute to solving it.

This summary explains why the patterns belong together, the common threads found in more than one pattern, and how the patterns can be used together to do something useful. It can also be used to introduce the Running Example. By describing the overall context, it may significantly reduce the need to provide duplicate, detailed contexts within each pattern, although this could make the individual patterns less usable outside the context of the language.

In larger pattern languages, it is useful to provide a Problem/Solution Summary to help the readers find the pattern(s) which solve their specific problems.

Rationale

A Pattern Language Summary provides the big picture while the related patterns section of each pattern provide the detailed linkages. The Pattern Language Summary may be the only place one can talk about the pattern language as a whole.

In the PLoP '96 review sessions in which the authors participated, the reviewers consistently preferred languages that introduced the patterns in a Pattern Language Summary over those that launched right into describing the patterns.

E.1.1   Problem/Solution Summary Pattern

Context

You are writing the Pattern Language Summary of a pattern language that includes patterns which may be useful individually as well as within the flow of the language. Many of the patterns have Noun Phrase Names based on the solution.

Problem

How do you make it easy for a reader to pick out useful patterns that solve their problem?

Forces

- The problems and solutions in a pattern language may be spread across many pages of text. It could be very time consuming to read the whole language in search of a particular (yet to be identified) pattern.
- A person using a pattern language may not need to use all the patterns in the language (and certainly not all at once).
- Summarizing patterns in the introduction takes extra effort and increases the size of the pattern language.

Solution

Provide a table in the Pattern Language Summary that summarizes all of the patterns, including a brief description of each pattern's problem and the corresponding solution. You can do this by collecting the Intent Catalogs for all the patterns in the language into a single convenient table as part of the Pattern Language Summary or in an Appendix or References section.

Rationale

This additional information helps readers of the pattern language quickly zero in on the pattern(s) that may solve their specific problem.

Example

This pattern language uses a Problem/Solution Summary to give the reader an early indication of the structure of the language.

E.2   Common Problems Highlighted Pattern

Context

You are writing a pattern language that provides several patterns that solve the same problem.

Problem

How do you make readers aware that they should choose one of the alternative solutions?

Forces

- A pattern is normally considered to be a problem-solution pair. Most pattern forms currently in use do not lend themselves to sharing a problem section among several competing patterns without taking some liberties with the form.
- Repeating the problem in each pattern that provides a solution may confuse readers by giving them a sense of *deja vu* without explaining the cause for it. They may not realize that there are several solutions to choose from and may expend considerable energy trying to figure out how to apply all the solutions simultaneously.
- Having the problem repeated in each pattern that provides a solution increases the effort required to maintain each pattern.
- The problem section is not the only part of the pattern that would have to be duplicated. All patterns which solve the same problem should include the same set of forces, while the context determines their relative priority.

Solution

When several patterns solve the same problem, make this obvious by pointing out to the reader that there are several solutions to this problem. You can capture the common problem and forces in one place using Separate Problem Description[10] or Referenced Problem Description.[11] If you choose to repeat the problem description as described in Duplicate Problem Description you should notify the reader that you have done so.

Related Patterns

Separate Problem Description solves the problem by factoring out the common solution into a separate pattern.

Duplicate Problem Description solves the problem using the brute force method of cloning the problem description into each pattern which provides a solution.

Referenced Problem Description solves the problem by including the problem description in one pattern and referring to it from each other pattern that provides an alternate solution.

Rationale

It is very easy for readers to become confused if several patterns have similar or identical problem descriptions unless it is pointed out to them that these patterns provide alternative solutions.

Example

Common Problems Highlighted is itself an example of Separate Problem Description since it exists primarily to point the reader to the alternative solutions. This is easily recognized by the fact that the solution section merely refers the reader to a number of other patterns; it acts like a traffic cop.

E.3   Running Example Pattern

Problem

How can you make it easier for the reader to put a pattern language into practice?

---

[10] "Separate Problem Description" (not published). Solves the problem of having several patterns which describe alternate solutions to the same problem by factoring out the common problem into a separate pattern.

[11] "Referenced Problem Description" (not published). Solves the problem of having several patterns which describe alternate solutions to the same problem by including the problem description in one pattern and referring to it from each other pattern that provides an alternate solution.

Context

You are writing a pattern language that provides step-by-step instructions on how to do or implement something.

Forces

- The pattern should be clear and complete so that the reader can use it with minimum effort or chance of mistake.
- The pattern should be as concise as possible without being too terse for most people to understand.
- Many people find abstract descriptions very hard to understand.
- Examples are very useful but must not take a lot of effort or prior knowledge to understand.
- Any one example may not be ideal for explaining a specific pattern.
- When a language contains a significant number of patterns, each pattern must necessarily be more concise than a free-standing pattern if only for reasons of overall pattern language size.

Solution

Try to use a single example in all patterns in the language. Explain it once, possibly in the language introduction. Use it to illustrate how each pattern in the language contributes to the solution. Use additional examples where the Running Example does not illustrate the pattern effectively.

Rationale

A single Running Example gives the reader more insight into applying the whole pattern language than a bunch of individual examples. In effect, it is a case study. The reader does not need to invest time and effort into understanding the example for each pattern; they pay this cost only once, when the example is introduced.

While this rationale has been expressed in terms of pattern languages, the same arguments are applicable to the use of a running example within stand-alone patterns.

Example

This pattern language attempts to be a Running Example of all the patterns it contains. The authors have also tried to identify one or two examples of each pattern from published pattern works to augment the Running Example.

E.4 (Distinctive) Headings Convey Structure Pattern

Problem

How do you help readers understand how the individual patterns they are reading fits within the overall structure of the language?

Context

You are writing a pattern language that has a nontrivial structure. You are applying Visible Language Structure[12] because you recognize that it is important for readers to be able to understand how the individual patterns they are reading fit within the overall structure of the language. You are attempting to make the resulting language Single-Pass Readable.

Forces

- In pattern languages with complex structure, readers may find it easier to appreciate the individual patterns if they understand how they fit within the structure of the language.
- When reading through a complex pattern language for the first time, it is easy to lose track of where you are within the structure of the language.
- A lengthy "you are here" section for each pattern is repetitive, adds unnecessary bulk to the language, and may distract the reader from the patterns themselves.
- An introductory section, at the beginning of the pattern language, can be an effective means to communicate the overall structure of the language.
- A language takes longer to read (and is not Single-Pass Readable) if the readers need to constantly refer back to the introductory section to figure out where they are.

Solution

Make individual pattern headings visibly different from all other document section headings. Prefix pattern headings with hierarchical section numbers, where the section numbering hierarchy parallels the language structure.

Rationale

The reader can easily recognize pattern sections and can tell at a glance how the given pattern fits within the language structure. Section numbers are concise, and do not distract the reader from the patterns themselves. Major changes in section

---

[12] "Visible Language Structure" (not published). Ensure that the structure of your language is visible so that readers can keep track of where they are in the language.

numbers can signal the reader that he or she has come to a new section of the pattern language.

Example

In this pattern language, we have organized the patterns into five major categories lettered A through E. Individual patterns within a category are designated using a combination of a letter and a number (for example, A.1, A.2). Patterns which are clearly subservient to another pattern have been numbered by adding a third digit to the pattern number of the higher-level pattern. For example, Code Samples (D.2) is a pattern within the Maximizing Understanding category (Section D). Code Samples as Bonus (D.2.1) is an extension of Code Samples, hence the subordinate numbering. Similarly, Evocative Pattern Name (C.3) is supported by Noun Phrase Name (C.3.1) and Meaningful Metaphor Name C.3.2); all fit within the Pattern Naming and Referencing category (Section C). A version of the pattern language using this heading structure can also be found on the Web at http://st-www.cs.uiuc.edu/users/patterns/Writing/pattern_index.html.

In *Episodes,* the patterns are divided into three sections, Product, Development, and Programming [Cunningham96]. The patterns in each section are numbered accordingly.

Related Patterns

Section-Name Running Footers/Headers is another pattern which can be used to achieve Visible Language Structure.

Page Numbered Pattern References make it easier for a reader to flip to the page describing a specific, referenced pattern.

E.5   Glossary Pattern

Problem

How do you clarify unfamiliar terminology in a pattern language without interrupting the flow of the pattern?

Context

You are writing a pattern language that involves terminology that may not be familiar to the Target Audience.

Forces

- Patterns may need to use terminology that is unfamiliar to readers.
- Patterns should be concise. Defining all terms within the pattern description may make it hard to follow for those familiar with the terminology.

- Expanding the terminology elsewhere may require the reader to flip pages often.
- Putting all the definitions in one place makes it easier to find them.

Solution

Provide a glossary of terms as part of the pattern language. The glossary gathers terms that are used in multiple patterns within the language with definitions of the terms. If you feel that it is essential to have the definition handy, you may include a short definition of the term in a footnote as well.

Rationale

A glossary collects terminology from multiple patterns in one place, thereby making the patterns more concise. The definitions make the patterns understandable by people unfamiliar with the terminology. Glossaries are a proven technique used in many written publications to achieve the same purpose.

CONCLUDING REMARKS

This pattern language is by no means complete. As long as the art of pattern writing continues to evolve and mature, this language will need to evolve with it. There are many areas that this language has not even attempted to cover. It does not prescribe a process for creating a pattern or pattern language. A number of such patterns come to mind, patterns such as Record the Solution, Determine the Problem, Find the Forces, and Separate the Problem from the Context.

Except for the section on pattern Naming and Referencing, this language has deliberately tried to avoid any questions of style. Style is a very personal thing and it is too early in the life-cycle of the pattern to prescribe a specific style. Each style of pattern writing probably warrants its own pattern language.

The authors hope that you find this language useful in your pattern and pattern language writing endeavors and that you will share your favorite pattern writing patterns with the patterns community. Please forward any comments to the authors via e-mail.

ACKNOWLEDGMENTS

The authors would like to thank all the participants of PLoP '95 for their contributions. Special thanks go to Linda Rising and Brandon Goldfedder who provided feedback on early versions of the language as well as many words of encouragement, and to John Vlissides whose shepherding of this language helped us get it into the form you see now. Special thanks to the UIUC Patterns Reading Group who reviewed this language in great detail.

REFERENCES

[Alexander+77] C. Alexander, S. Ishikawa, and M. Silverstein. *A Pattern Language.* New York: Oxford University Press, 1977.

[Alexander79] C. Alexander. *The Timeless Way of Building.* New York: Oxford University Press, 1979.

[Beck96] K. Beck. *Smalltalk Best Practice Patterns.* Prentice-Hall, 1996.

[Berczuk96] Steven P. Berczuk. "A Pattern Language for Ground Processing of Science Satellite Telemetry" in J. M. Vlissides, J. O. Coplien, N. L. Kerth (eds.), *Pattern Languages of Program Design 2.* Reading, MA: Addison-Wesley, 1996, pp. 193–206.

[Cockburn96] A. Cockburn. "A Medical Catalog of Project Management Patterns." PLoP '96 Proceedings.

[Coplien94] J. Coplien. "A Generative Development-Process Pattern Language," in J. O. Coplien and D. C. Schmidt, *Pattern Languages of Program Design.* Reading, MA: Addison-Wesley, 1995, pp. 183–237.

[Coplien+95] *Pattern Languages of Program Design.* Reading, MA: Addison-Wesley, 1995.

[Coplien96] J. Coplien. "A White Paper on Patterns." *SIGS Books,* 1996.

[Cunningham96] W. Cunningham. "Episodes: A Pattern Language of Competitive Development" in J. M. Vlissides, J. O. Coplien, N. L. Kerth (eds.), *Pattern Languages of Program Design 2.* Reading, MA: Addison-Wesley, 1996, pp. 371–388.

[Doble96] J. Doble. "Shopper" in J. M. Vlissides, J. O. Coplien, N. L. Kerth (eds.), *Pattern Languages of Program Design 2.* Reading, MA: Addison-Wesley, 1996, pp. 143–154.

[Foote+96a] B. Foote and J. Yoder. "The Selfish Class," Chapter 25, this volume.

[Foote+96b] B. Foote and J. Yoder. "Attracting Reuse." PLoP '96 Proceedings.

[Gamma+95] E. Gamma, R. Helm, R. Johnson, and J. Vlissides. *Design Patterns: Elements of Reusable Object-Oriented Software.* Reading, MA: Addison-Wesley, 1995.

[Meszaros+96] G. Meszaros and J. Doble. "A Pattern Language for Pattern Writing." PLoP '96 Proceedings.

[Miller56] G. A. Miller. "The Magical Number Seven, Plus or Minus Two: Some Limits on our Capacity for Processing Information." *Psychology Review,* 63, 81–97.

[Okuda+94] M. Okuda, D. Okuda, and D. Mirek. *The Star Trek Encyclopedia.* Pocket Books, 1994.

[Vlissides+96] *Pattern Languages of Program Design.* Reading, MA: Addison-Wesley, 1996.

[Roberts+96] D. Roberts and R. Johnson. "Patterns for Evolving Frameworks," Chapter 26, this volume.

APPENDIX: PROBLEM/SOLUTION SUMMARIES

The following tables summarize the patterns in this pattern language for reference purposes.

Table 29-1 *Pattern Structure Patterns*

Problem	Solution	Pattern Name
How do you make sure that all necessary information is covered in a pattern?	Include the following elements: Pattern Name, Problem, Context, Forces, and Solution.	B.1 Mandatory Elements Present
How do you communicate essential information that does not fit well into the Mandatory Elements?	Include the following sections when they help convey the information: Resulting Context, Related Patterns, Examples, Code Samples, Rationale, and Aliases.	B.2 Optional Elements When Helpful
How do you ensure that the reader understands the choice of solution?	Regardless of the style chosen for the pattern description, ensure that the forces are highly visible.	B.3 Visible Forces
How do you make it easy to get the essence of a pattern solution quickly?	Write the pattern so that it is not necessary to read the later parts in order to understand the earlier parts.	B.4 Single-Pass Readable
How do you minimize the amount of reading required to get the essence of a pattern?	Clearly identify the Problem, Context, and Solution parts so that the readers can quickly determine whether this pattern applies to them.	B.5 Skippable Sections

Table 29-2 *Pattern Naming and Referencing Patterns*

Problem	Solution	Pattern Name
How do you refer to other patterns within the description of your pattern?	When referring to patterns within the body of your pattern, weave the pattern names into the narrative.	C.2 Readable References to Patterns
How do you name a pattern so that it is easily remembered and referred to?	Choose a pattern name that conjures up images which convey the essence of the pattern solution.	C.3 Evocative Pattern Name
How do you give a pattern a useful and memorable name?	Name the pattern after the result it creates.	C.3.1 Noun Phrase Name
How do you give a pattern a memorable name?	Find a meaningful metaphor and name the pattern after it.	C.3.2 Meaningful Metaphor Name
How do you make a pattern part of a larger group of patterns?	Read other pattern languages and describe the relationships to other patterns.	C.1 Relationship to Other Patterns
How do you refer to external patterns in a concise but meaningful manner, so that the understanding of your pattern is not compromised?	Include the Evocative Pattern Name, an author/year tag, and a footnote with a brief summary of the pattern.	C.2.1 External Pattern Thumbnails

Table 29-3 *Patterns for Making Patterns Understandable*

Problem	Solution	Pattern Name
How can you make a software pattern sufficiently clear and unambiguous to facilitate straightforward implementation?	Provide one or more implementation code examples, written in a prevalent programming language, to illustrate the pattern concepts.	D.4 Code Samples
How can you ensure that the essence of your software pattern can be understood by your entire target audience, regardless of their familiarity with specific programming languages?	Ensure that the pattern can stand on its own, able to communicate its essential concepts even if the code examples were deleted.	D.4.1 Code Samples as Bonus
How do you ensure that diagrams are easily understood by your entire target audience?	Use diagramming notations that are likely to be familiar to the target audience.	D.3 Understood Notations
How do you ensure that a pattern is easily understood by its intended audience?	Identify a clear target audience and keep this audience in mind while writing the pattern.	D.1 Clear Target Audience
How do you maximize the likelihood of the intended reader understanding your pattern?	Use only those terms with which the typical member of the audience can reasonably be expected to be comfortable.	D.2 Terminology Tailored to Audience

Table 29-4 *Language Structure Patterns*

Problem	Solution	Pattern Name
How do you give the reader an overview of a set of patterns?	Summarize the pattern language in the Introduction.	E.1 Pattern Language Summary
How do you make it easy for readers to pick out useful patterns that solve their problems?	Provide a table that summarizes all of the patterns, including a brief description of each pattern's problem and the corresponding solution.	E.1.1 Problem/ Solution Summary
How do you make readers aware that they should choose one of the alternative solutions?	When several patterns solve the same problem, make this obvious by pointing out to the reader that there are several solutions to this problem.	E.2 Common Problems Highlighted
How do you help readers understand how the individual patterns they are reading fit within the overall structure of the language?	Prefix pattern headings with hierarchical section numbers, where the section numbering hierarchy parallels the language structure.	E.4 (Distinctive) Headings Convey Structure
How can you make it easier for the reader to put a pattern language into practice?	Try to use a single example in all patterns in the language.	E.3 Running Example
How do you clarify unfamiliar terminology in a pattern language without interrupting the flow of the pattern?	Provide a Glossary of all terms that may be unfamiliar to the audience.	E.5 Glossary

Gerard Meszaros may be reached at gerard@osgcorp.com.
Jim Doble may be reached at jdoble@inmind.com.

About the Authors

Bruce Anderson is a Senior Architect in the IBM European Object Technology Practice. He has been instrumental in raising the profile of work at the architecture and pattern level. He has published many papers on object technology and architecture and is well-known in the international object technology community.

Dirk Bäumer is interested in object-oriented frameworks, software architecture, and distributed systems.

Lorraine L. Boyd has over 20 years' experience in designing, developing, implementing, and architecting large-scale business systems. Recently, she was the system architect for a facility management system involving space allocation, work assignment, work-order tracking, personnel management, and financial accounting. This system contains over 2,000 objects and interacts with a relational database of more than 450 tables. She is currently providing object analysis support to the development and implementation of a variety of systems in industries ranging from telecommunications to maintenance management.

Mark Bradac manages an I/O driver and advanced processes development group at Lucent Technologies. He was the principle inventor and architect of HSI Designer, an application development environment that captures hardware/software interface specifications and derives several outputs for downstream development processes such as documentation, header files, source code, and hardware synthesis data for subsequent VHDL generation. Mark has worked for nearly 20 years in various aspects of hardware/software architecture, design, code, and test for synchronous and asynchronous communication peripherals and disk file subsystems.

Frank Buschmann is software engineer at Siemens Corporate Technology in Munich, Germany. His research interests include object technology, application frameworks, and specifically, patterns. Frank has been involved in several concrete industrial software development projects. At Siemens Corporate Technology, he is responsible for the research activities in patterns. Frank is co-author of

Pattern-Oriented Software Architecture: A System of Patterns, recently published by John Wiley and Sons.

Chris Cleeland recently joined the Distributed Object Computing Laboratory at Washington University as a research associate performing research in real-time CORBA. Previously, Chris consulted to Motorola Satellite Communications Division, where he was the primary contractor for the Iridium Global Satellite System, through the consulting firm of Envision, headquartered in St. Louis. The majority of his work has focused on designing and implementing communication infrastructure components used in the financial, communications, and medical industries. He has been an active user of and contributor to publicly available C++ frameworks, such as the Adaptive Communication Environment (ACE) and the OSE Class Toolkit, and has used primarily the C++ language for more than 5 years.

Jens Coldewey studied computer science at Technical University at Munich, concentrating on network management and compiler techniques. After graduating in 1991, he started working at sd&m, where he helped design the company's first access layer between an object-oriented application and relational databases. He subsequently worked in several other object-oriented projects as designer, consultant, and project manager.

Fernando Das Neves has studied computer science for the last 5 years at the Universidad Nacional de La Plata in Argentina. He has been working on hypermedia, GIS, and OOP at LIFIA, a university laboratory started in 1988 by Dr. Gustavo Rossi. While searching for a way to share objects among cooperative applications with limited requirements, he discovered the Bodyguard Pattern. With Alejandra Garrido, he was able to complete the design of a hypermedia application. After finishing his degree of Licenciado in computer science in Argentina, he began graduate studies at Virginia Tech in August 1997.

David DeLano is a member of the Technical Resource Center at AG Communication Systems. He has a B.S. in computer science and a B.A. in mathematics from the University of Kansas. He has developed, tested, and managed software in the embedded telecommunications industry since 1980, and his work has focused on object technology since 1989. His current activities focus on increasing the productivity of software developers using object technologies.

Jim Doble has worked as a software developer, manager, and architect in the telecommunications industry for more than 15 years. He is currently employed as chief software architect for Allen Telecom Systems in Forest, Virginia. His primary focus is the application of advanced software tools and techniques in the development of sophisticated telecommunications products. Jim received a B.Sc. in electrical engineering from Queen's University, Kingston, Ontario, in 1982, and a M. Eng. in systems and computer engineering from Carleton University, Ottawa, Ontario, in 1988.

Paul Dyson is currently finishing a Ph.D. at the University of Essex, where he also lectures in software engineering. Paul's research interests are in the software architecture field, particularly frameworks and patterns, and their effective use in industrial projects.

Becky Fletcher is currently the lead engineer of the HSI Designer project at Lucent Technologies. This project is an application development environment that captures hardware/software interface specifications and derives several outputs for downstream development processes such as documentation, header files, source code, and hardware synthesis data for subsequent VHDL generation. Becky has worked for 11 years in various aspects of hardware/software feature development and coordination, in such areas as call processing and hardware diagnostics.

Brian Foote is a researcher in Ralph Johnson's design patterns group at the University of Illinois. He has more than 20 years of professional programming, consulting, teaching, and research experience, and has been working with objects since 1984. His research interests include object-oriented frameworks and languages, reflection, software reuse, software evolution, software architecture, and patterns. Brian was the general chair of the PLoP '96 conference, held in Monticello, Illinois, in September 1996.

Ted Foster established Class Software Construction Ltd., UK, in 1994 to pursue his special interest in object technology and modeling, which began while researching object engineering in public transport and cassiope data modeling at the University of Leeds in 1989–1994. He is currently working with a consortium of public transport operators, consultants, and academics on a European Union project on data and object modeling, a continuation of work initiated in 1989. This work involves the identification and definition of patterns inherent in many software solutions to problems in transport scheduling found in European systems. He worked closely with Liping Zhao to formulate a pattern language of transport systems made up of interacting transport object patterns. He has also worked as a systems analyst and operational researcher in industry, and as a research and intelligence officer in local government. He has an M.A. in social administration and a B.Sc. in psychology, despite having worked mainly on computing and information systems.

Erich Gamma has been discovering and working with design patterns for the past eight years. He currently works for Object Technology International and is the technical director of the Software Technology Center in Zurich, Switzerland. In his previous positions, he has applied patterns as a consultant at IFA in Zurich and as an engineer at Taligent.

Alejandra Garrido is a computer analyst who has been working at LIFIA (Research and Teaching in Advanced Computer Science Laboratory), a part of the Computer Science Department at Universidad Nacional de La Plata, Argentina, since July 1993. Her areas of research interest are object-oriented frameworks and patterns, hypermedia, and object-oriented programming in Smalltalk. She has been researching the use of OO-Navigator as a framework for extending object-oriented applications with hypermedia functionality as her thesis to complete the degree of Licenciado in computer science. She began graduate studies at the University of Illinois at Urbana-Champaign in the fall of 1997.

Neil B. Harrison has been working at Lucent Technologies since 1984. He has worked in telephony software development, design and development of testing and simulation tools, and software process and organization issues. His work in software organizations drew him to patterns in 1994. Together with Jim Coplien, also of Lucent, he published articles on patterns of productive software organizations in *The Bell Labs Technical Journal* and *The Annals of Software Engineering*. His patterns of design teams appear in the PLoPD2 book. He also has an article on patterns pending publication in *Best Practices: A Patterns Handbook*. Within Lucent, he is active as a teacher and advocate of patterns, software quality assurance tools and techniques, organizational issues in software, and domain engineering. He is the program chair of the ChiliPLoP conference, to be held March 1998.

Tim Harrison is a research associate in the Department of Computer Science at Washington University, St. Louis, where he does research on strategies and tools for concurrent and distributed object-oriented programming. He has consulted for Motorola, Kodak, Siemens, and McDonnell Douglas to build concurrent networking software for communications systems and medical imaging systems on Windows NT and UNIX platforms using CORBA and C++.

Ralph Johnson is the coordinator of senior projects for the Department of Computer Science at the University of Illinois at Urbana-Champaign. He is one of the authors of *Design Patterns* and was the conference chair of the first conference on pattern languages of programs. He has taught courses on object-oriented design and Smalltalk for 12 years, and has taught courses on how to develop frameworks for 6 years. He has worked on frameworks for operating systems, code generators, music synthesis, network software, drawing editors, and telecommunication billing.

After a business apprenticeship with Siemens, *Wolfgang Keller* studied computer science and business administration at Technical University Munich (TUM). Following a short period as a teaching assistant at the institute Allgemeine und Industrielle Betriebswitschaftslehre (chair, Professor R. Reichwald), he joined software design & management (sd&m) in 1991. He worked as a software developer, consultant, and project leader in various object-oriented projects. Until early 1997 he led the project ARCUS, documenting patterns for business information system. He is now managing the base of reusable object-oriented components at EA Generali Insurances in Vienna, Austria.

Right Reverend C. Marin III is a well-known right-wing pragmatist and software reactionary. He is dedicated to the battle against analytic overemphasis. Two years ago, he earned the coveted Rambo-Coder award from the L. E. Ott Foundation of Holistic and Overanalytic Studies. More recently he was added to the extremely prestigious 'netscum' list. Marin is in the process of finishing up the much awaited book, *Pragmatism: The Final Solution* to be published by C. J. and Associates in 1999.

José Alves Marques is a full professor at Instituto Superior Técnico, Technical University of Lisbon (IST/UTL), and head of software research groups at INESC. He received a B.S. in computer science from New University of Lisbon and a Ph.D. in computer science from Institut Nationale Polytechnique of Grenoble in 1980. He has published numerous articles and papers in the areas of distributed systems and platforms.

Robert C. Martin, a software engineer since 1969, is the president of Object Mentor Inc., a firm that offers training, mentoring, and software development services to businesses around the world. He is author of the bestselling *Designing Object-Oriented C++ Applications Using the Booch Method*, published in 1995 by Prentice Hall. He is also editor-in-chief of *The C++ Report*, and one of the editors and authors of this book.

Daniel Megert works in the information technology department of the corporate customer business of Union Bank of Switzerland.

Gerard Meszaros is an object technology consultant specializing in system architecture, development processes, and patterns. He is currently chief architect at Object Systems Group, an OO consulting company specializing in managed transitions to object technology. He received a B.Sc. (with honors) in computer science from the University of Manitoba in 1981. Since then, he has been involved in a number of large-scale projects in a variety of roles. These include software design, development management, project management, architecture, and process improvement in both "doer" and "mentor" capacities. He has worked on projects involving telecommunications, real-time reactive systems, system performance and overload controls, in-memory databases, distributed objects, and telecommunication protocols. Gerard's involvement in patterns predates the publication of the first book on software design patterns. He is a member of the Hillside Group, which organized the first conferences on pattern languages of program design. His contributions to previous volumes of the PLoPD book series include the pattern Half-Object Plus Protocol and a pattern language on increasing the capacity of reactive systems. Gerard organizes an annual workshop on patterns in software architecture at OOPSLA, the premiere object technology conference. He has been invited to speak at several conferences on the topics of patterns and software architecture.

Peter Molin received both an M.S. in physical engineering from Lunds Institute of Technology, Sweden, and a diploma of mathematical engineering from the Swiss Federal Institute of Technology in Lausanne, Switzerland in 1981. His industrial experience comprises Ada compiler development, specifically for embedded systems, and surveillance system development. Since 1994, he has worked at the University of Karlkrona/Ronneby, Sweden, as a teacher and researcher. His current interests are software architecture in general, but specifically the design of flexible and reliable software for embedded systems.

Since completing a Ph.D. in chemical engineering in 1989, *Martin E. Nordberg III* has gradually shifted from computational fluid dynamics and process modeling to C++ and visual object-oriented programming. His early study in numerical analysis and modeling was followed by work to combine real-time instrument control, signal processing, and data analysis. These have since given way to an entrepreneurial interest in visual programming and the automation of software patterns and idioms. Martin is founder of Quintessoft Engineering, Inc., and is primary developer of Code Navigator for C++, a C++ CASE tool that emphasizes visual editing, language- and model-specific version control, and dynamic code patterns.

Lennart Ohlsson received a Techn. Lic. degree in computer engineering from Lund University, Sweden, in 1984, where he then held a position as assistant professor. He has been an independent software engineering consultant since 1989, specializing in software design and architectural development. He has served as an external research advisor to the University of Karlskrona/Ronneby in the area of object-oriented frameworks and has also participated in several European collaborative research projects.

João Dias Pereira is a teaching assistant at Instituto Superior Técnico, Technical University of Lisbon (IST/UTL), and researcher in the software engineering group at INESC. He received a B.S in electrical engineering in 1990, and an M.S. in computer science in 1995, both from IST. Currently he is at INRIA, in France, working toward his Ph.D. At INRIA, he is involved in the RODIN project. His research interests include active database rules, design patterns, concurrency control, and object-orientation.

Irfan Pyarali is currently completing his M.S. in computer science at Washington University in St. Louis. His research focuses on the development of high-performance, real-time, distributed object computing systems. Currently, he is designing and implementing a real-time Object Request Broker (ORB). His recent projects have involved designing high-performance Web servers and asynchronous I/O frameworks on Windows NT.

Dirk Riehle works at Ubilab, the information technology laboratory of Union Bank of Switzerland. He is interested in object-oriented software engineering, frameworks, and software architecture models as well as their application to the design and implementation of distributed systems. Currently, the primary focus of his work is metalevel architectures for distributed systems, which he views as the next step beyond today's service architectures. He is one of the editors as well as an author of this book. He takes some pride in counterbalancing the Right Reverend C. Marin III, the fourth (virtual) editor of this book, during his infrequent appearances. If he isn't working, he is probably reading, swimming, or hiking.

Linda Rising is a member of the Technical Resource Center at AG Communication Systems. She has a Ph.D. from Arizona State University in object-based design metrics. Her background includes university teaching experience as well as work in industry in telecommunications, avionics, and strategic weapons systems. She has been working with object technologies since 1983. Her many publications include "A Training Experience with Patterns" in the October '96 issue of *Communications of the ACM*, "Patterns: Spreading the Word" in the December '96 issue of *Object* magazine, and "The Road, Christopher Alexander, and Good Software Design" in the March '97 issue of *Object* magazine. She is currently writing a book on patterns experiences within her company.

Don Roberts is the only person in his family with no musical talent, but he has made up for it with an interest in math and computers. He discovered computers at the age of 12, but unknowingly suffered Smalltalk-deprivation for the next 9 years. He worked on the Typed Smalltalk compiler and the Refactoring Browser; has consulted for Lucent Technologies, Sprint, and Hewitt Associates; and teaches Smalltalk courses. His interests include software evolution, frameworks, patterns, and most things involving Smalltalk. He is a Hertz Fellow and hopes someday to hike the Appalachian Trail from Georgia to Maine. Don is the General Conference Chair for the PLoP '97 Conference.

Douglas C. Schmidt is a faculty member of the Computer Science and Radiology departments at Washington University in St. Louis, Missouri. His research focuses on design patterns, and implementation and experimental analysis of object-oriented techniques that facilitate the development of high-performance, real-time, distributed object computing systems on parallel processing platforms running over high-speed ATM networks. Dr. Schmidt is the chief architect and implementer of the ACE concurrent network programming framework, which is a widely-used OO framework that implements design patterns for high-performance communication systems and Object Request Brokers. ACE has been used in many large-scale distributed telecommunications switch monitoring systems, medical imaging systems, and real-time avionics systems at companies such as Ericsson, Siemens, Motorola, Kodak, and McDonnell Douglas. Dr. Schmidt co-edited the first PLoPD book with Jim Coplien and was the program chair for the 1996 PLoP conference in Allerton Park. He has served as the editor-in-chief of *The C++ Report* and currently edits the Patterns++ section in that magazine. He received B.S. and M.A. degrees in sociology from the College of William and Mary in Williamsburg, Virginia, and an M.S. and a Ph.D. in computer science from the University of California, Irvine (UCI) in 1984, 1986, 1990, and 1994, respectively.

Bran Selic is the Vice President of Advanced Technology at ObjecTime Limited. He has been developing software and managing software projects in various industrial settings since 1974. His experience ranges from real-time software (telecommunications, aerospace, and robotics) to traditional business-oriented IT applications. He is the principal author of the book *Real-Time Object-Oriented Modeling* (co-authored with Garth Gullekson and Paul Ward). At present, he is working on defining a next-generation specification language to characterize the architectures of distributed heterogeneous software systems. Mr. Selic graduated from the University of Belgrade with a B.Sc. in electronics and an M.Sc. in system theory.

Wolf Siberski is an in-house project consultant and member of the systems architecture group at the RWG GmbH. He studied computer science at the University of Hamburg.

António Rito Silva is a teaching assistant at Instituto Superior Técnico, Technical University of Lisbon (IST/UTL), and researcher of the software engineering group at INESC. He received a B.S. in applied mathematics/computer science in 1987 from University of Lisbon and a M.S. in applied mathematics/computer science in 1991 from Technical University of Lisbon. As part of his Ph.D. work, he is developing the DASCo (Development of Distributed Applications with Separation of Concerns) approach, based on design patterns, pattern languages and object-oriented frameworks. His research interests include design patterns and pattern languages for distribution and concurrency, software architectures, object-oriented analysis and design patterns for organizational computing.

Peter Sommerlad is the head of object technology at IFA Informatik in Zurich, Switzerland. In the past 7 years at Siemens Corporate R&D (Munich), he participated in several projects related to and using object technology and frameworks. He is one of the authors of the book *Pattern-Oriented Software Architecture: A System of Patterns*, published in 1996 by Wiley and Sons. He uses his expertise in C++, object technology, and patterns to train and consult.

Eugene Wallingford is an assistant professor in the Department of Computer Science at the University of Northern Iowa. He received his Ph.D. in 1992 from Michigan State University, where his work focused on the development of a functional model of legal arguments to support content-based retrieval in case-based reasoning. His current research interests include knowledge-based systems and object-oriented software development. Eugene's involvement with patterns began while teaching introductory computer science, where he began to organize his course around a small catalog of programming idioms. From there, he began to explore the role of patterns in other undergraduate courses as well as in the KBS software that he studies and writes.

Charles Weir is a consultant software architect based in England. He has more than 12 years' experience of working on software development projects and has been using object-oriented techniques for more than 7 years. His consulting work builds on several years' experience as a senior consultant with Object Designers Ltd. He has provided on-site mentoring to many companies in several European countries. He specializes in working with individual developers and teams to facilitate the introduction of object-oriented skills and techniques. Charles' interest in patterns comes from recognizing their value as a format for describing and learning many aspects of software engineering. He has presented courses using patterns for design and implementation techniques, and workshops using patterns to describe implementation, team behavior, and architectural design.

Bobby Woolf is a senior member of technical staff at Knowledge Systems Corp., a Smalltalk consulting company in Cary, North Carolina. He specializes in mentoring clients in VisualWorks Smalltalk, ENVY/Developer, and design patterns. He has published in all three PLoP books, as well as publishing several articles in *The Smalltalk Report*. He has presented tutorials at OOPSLA, Smalltalk Solutions, the ParcPlace-Digitalk International Users' Conference, and Software Development East. He is co-author of the forthcoming book, *The Design Patterns Smalltalk Companion*, published by Addison-Wesley.

Joseph Yoder graduated with high distinction and honors from the University of Iowa in computer science and mathematics. Since then, he has completed a Master of C.S. degree in the study of problems of the computer-based documenting of medical records at the University of Illinois. This research primarily focused on the development of a computer-based system for collecting physical exam findings. The design of this system employs an object-oriented approach through the direct manipulation of graphical objects, integrated with hypertext approaches and semantic networking, to build a system that is more natural to the user. Joseph has been involved with many facets of software development since 1985 and is currently a Smalltalk consultant while working on his Ph.D. with Professor Ralph Johnson at the University of Illinois at Urbana-Champaign. Over the last two years, Joseph has been working on developing a black-box framework for a business-modeling project. The system has been built, installed, and tested at Caterpillar. This current work has focused on using, finding, and describing patterns to develop frameworks and to implement domain-specific visual languages for use with business modeling. He believes there are general principles that can be applied to the development of black-box frameworks, especially when a domain-specific language is involved.

Liping Zhao is a lecturer at the Department of Computer Science, RMIT, Australia. Her research interests include object technology, software patterns and pattern languages, software architectures, transport object modeling, problem solving, and transport scheduling. She is currently working with Ted Foster to formulate a pattern language of transport systems. Over the past 10 years, she has worked on many research projects, including object-oriented database modeling, transport object modeling, driver duty estimation, and rules and object-orientation. She has B.Sc., M.Phil., and Ph.D. degrees in computer science.

Heinz Züllighoven is a professor of computer science at University of Hamburg.

Index

H

habituation
  as systems design principle, [Gabriel96], 144
Half-Sync/Half-Async pattern
  Points and Deviations relationship, 443
Harrison, Neil B.
  (patterns for logging diagnostic messages), 277
Harrison, Tim
  (Asynchronous Completion Token), 245
  (Double-Checked Locking), 363
  (External Polymorphism), 377
has-a relationship
  has-many relationship vs., as Association Object force, 397
help desk
  as Customer Contact application, 401
heritage
  impact on reuse, (Works Out of the Box), 457
Hermes/ST
  (Customizable Object Recovery), 274
hidden semantics
  as Extension Object drawback, 84
Hierarchical View pattern
  benefits, 330
  as component of Relational Database Access Layer pattern language, 326
  (map diagram), 318
  forces, 327
  Hierarchical View, 326
  sample code, 329
hierarchy
  self-contained, as Bureaucracy motivation, 164
  self-contained, containing state and behavior, as Bureaucracy motivation, 167
High Volume-to-Surface Ratio pattern
  as alternate name for Low Surface-to-Volume Ratio, 459
history
  tracking, as Association Object motivation, 396
Hitch Your Wagon to a Star pattern
  as alternate name for Winning Team pattern, 467

Hot Spots pattern
  as component of Evolving Frameworks pattern language, 478
  implementation strategies, 478
HotDraw
  (Bureaucracy), 177
HTML parsing, 225

I

idempotent
  object initialization, requirements for, 365
implementation strategies
  Component Library, 477
  Fine-Grained Objects, 481
  Hot Spots, 478
  Pluggable Objects, 480
  The Selfish Class, 468
  Three Examples, 473
  White-Box Framework, 475
Implicit Invocation pattern
  as an alternate name for Sponsor-Selector, 67
inconsistency
  as potential drawback of External Polymorphism, 382
Incremental Revelation pattern
  as alternate name for Gentle Learning Curve, 462
inefficiency
  as drawback of External Polymorphism, 382
inexperience
  as Low Surface-to-Volume Ratio force, 460
information systems
  library, (Manager), 19
inheritance
  benefits and drawbacks
    (Black-Box Framework), 482
    (White-Box Framework), 475
  not required, as Hierarchical View benefit, 330
  polymorphic composition vs.
    as Black-Box Framework force, 482
    as White-Box Framework force, 474
initialization
  communications services, decoupling from processing, 191
inspector
  object, as Language Tools motivation, 485